DICTIONARY

OF

EUROPEAN HISTORY

MIDCENTURY REFERENCE LIBRARY

DAGOBERT D. RUNES, Ph.D., *General Editor*

Available

Dictionary of Ancient History
Dictionary of the Arts
Dictionary of European History
Dictionary of Foreign Words
and Phrases
Dictionary of Linguistics
Dictionary of Mysticism
Dictionary of Mythology
Dictionary of Philosophy
Dictionary of Psychoanalysis
Dictionary of Science and Technology
Dictionary of Sociology
Dictionary of Word Origins
Dictionary of World Literature
Encyclopedia of Aberrations
Encyclopedia of the Arts
Encyclopedia of Atomic Energy
Encyclopedia of Criminology

Encyclopedia of Literature
Encyclopedia of Psychology
Encyclopedia of Religion
Encyclopedia of Substitutes and
Synthetics
Encyclopedia of Vocational
Guidance
Illustrated Technical Dictionary
Labor Dictionary
Liberal Arts Dictionary
Military and Naval Dictionary
New Dictionary of American History
New Dictionary of Psychology
Protestant Dictionary
Slavonic Encyclopedia
Theatre Dictionary
Tobacco Dictionary

Forthcoming

Beethoven Encyclopedia
Dictionary of American Folklore
Dictionary of American Grammar
and Usage
Dictionary of American Literature
Dictionary of American Maxims
Dictionary of American Proverbs
Dictionary of American Superstitions
Dictionary of American Synonyms
Dictionary of Anthropology
Dictionary of Arts and Crafts
Dictionary of Asiatic History
Dictionary of Astronomy
Dictionary of Child Guidance
Dictionary of Christian Antiquity
Dictionary of Discoveries and
Inventions
Dictionary of Etiquette
Dictionary of Forgotten Words
Dictionary of French Literature
Dictionary of Geography

Dictionary of Geriatrics
Dictionary of German Literature
Dictionary of Hebrew Literature
Dictionary of Judaism
Dictionary of Last Words
Dictionary of Latin Literature
Dictionary of Mathematics
Dictionary of Mechanics
Dictionary of Mental Hygiene
Dictionary of New Words
Dictionary of Physical Education
Dictionary of Russian Literature
Dictionary of Science
Dictionary of Social Science
Dictionary of Spanish Literature
Dictionary of the American Language
Encyclopedia of American Philosophy
Encyclopedia of Morals
Encyclopedia of Pastoral Psychology
Personnel Dictionary
Teachers' Dictionary
Writers' Dictionary

PHILOSOPHICAL LIBRARY
Publishers

15 East 40th Street   New York 16, N. Y.

DICTIONARY

OF

EUROPEAN HISTORY

COMPILED BY WILLIAM S. ROEDER

WITH AN INTRODUCTION BY HARRY ELMER BARNES

PHILOSOPHICAL LIBRARY

NEW YORK

Printed in the United States of America

FOREWORD

by HARRY ELMER BARNES

Conceptions of history have been varied and numerous, although the divergencies of emphasis have usually been supplementary rather than contradictory.

In a review of James Harvey Robinson's *The Human Comedy*, which I had the honor to arrange and edit, the eminent historical scholar, Lynn Thorndike, thus specified some of these diverse notions of what really constitutes history: "For some, history is literature; for others, facts; for some, delving into archives; for others, interpretation of the sources; for some, an art; for others, a science; for some, drudgery; for others, a romance; for some, an explanation of the present; for others, a revelation and realization of the past. For James Harvey Robinson, it was a religion, the religion, his religion; a gospel to preach in classes and out of classes, an evangel to save society, an elixir to transmute the dross of past trivial records into the gold of final philosophy. . . . He had the faith that would not only move mountains but would also move muttonheads."

While my personal historical philosophy coincides with that of my respected mentor, Professor Robinson, I would not exclude the validity of other and supplementary conceptions of the scope and purpose of history and historical writing.

History is regarded by many as the most futile and irrelevant of the social sciences. Indeed, not a few deny that it is a social science at all and proclaim that it is a branch of romantic literature, with its raw materials chiefly battles, dynastic successions, political campaigns, diplomatic intrigues, and the feats of heroic figures in the political and military realms.

Yet it is surely possible for history to be of great practical and constructive service in the social thinking and planning of our time. Once we come to regard history as the record of the progress of human knowledge, the genesis and alterations of world outlook, and the growth and mutations of institutions, it can present to the social scientist and philosopher a large body of cogent and useful information which will produce a more intelligent orientation toward the past, present and future of human society. Nothing has proved more obstructive to social sanity than persistent misconceptions of the human past.

The up-to-date historian maintains that the primary purpose of history is to give the present generation such a complete and reliable picture of the past that we shall be able to comprehend how the present social order and convictions have developed. Only in this way can we attain any sound appreciation of what is really essential and progressive in our civilization and what is only a mischievous encumbrance which has come down to us from earlier times. To impel the historian to carry on his work no other motive is needed than the zeal to know with all possible accuracy the whole story of the human past. Enthusiasm concerning the achievements of particular nations or statesmen should be subordinate to the vital necessity of learning just what has happened in the past and, if possible, why events took place as they did. Truth must in all cases be preferred to either personal gratification or patriotic enthusiasm.

If, as many believe with ever greater conviction, the "race between education and catastrophe" is more acute and undecided than ever before, it is the duty of the historian to do all in his power to battle against that portion of "catastrophe" which arises from those misconceptions of the past that frustrate more intelligent planning for a better human future. A main way in which history can contribute to assuring a more satisfactory future state of mankind is to expose clearly those elements in our civilization which are obstructive and useless antiquities and to emphasize those forces and factors in our culture which are most likely to free the mind for the task of creating greater happiness, security and progress for the human race. History, intelligently written and studied, can free us from the paralyzing influence of the "Dead Hand," as Herbert Spencer once aptly described the archaic customs and superstitions of the past. We can now boldly plan our own future. The sciences of life, man and society enable us, if we so desire, to create a human utopia on this earth. Where we go from here need no longer be a myth, legend or maze. It is, rather, a specific challenge to human imagination and social engineering. It is, moreover, a challenge which cannot safely be ignored. If we drift without informed and intelligent planning, then indeed the human future may well be a tragic voyage on an uncharted sea.

The most striking aspect of our culture at the mid-century is the fact that we have an impressive, varied and up-to-the-minute scientific and mechanical equipment but seek to control and manage this material culture through ideas and institutions which date from somewhere between the Stone Age and the late eighteenth century. This ever-widening gulf between our material culture and our institutions—what social scientists call *cultural lag*—is not only the great problem of our era but, in its incidental effects, produces or intensifies all the lesser social problems of the age, such as poverty, crime, mental disease, and the like. Unless this gulf is bridged by competent social planning and world peace is assured, there is little hope ahead for humanity. History may, as we have suggested, clear away some of the obstacles to this process of bridging the gulf.

Three of the leading obstacles to a dynamic approach to the future are: (1) the notion that the supreme wisdom of mankind was achieved in the past; (2) that we can find lessons in the past which can directly guide the planning of today; and (3) that the very idea of planning for a better future is fruitless and unsound because we cannot change human nature. History can readily refute all of these menacing beliefs and assertions.

The obvious error of identifying supreme goodness and wisdom with past knowledge and experience was pointed out centuries ago by Francis Bacon, even without our present knowledge of psychology and cultural history. Bacon emphasized the obvious fact that, under normal conditions, each generation is wiser than its predecessor. Any generation not only possesses all preceding knowledge but also that added in its own time. History teaches us that the further we press back into the past the nearer we get to savagery, ignorance and paralyzing superstitions rather than to primordial and unique human wisdom. The revolutionary changes in knowledge and culture produced by the scientific and industrial revolutions of the last two centuries have so altered our perspectives and increased our knowledge and experience that the wisest individuals in earlier centuries could have had little valid information to be brought to bear upon the world scene today.

These facts expose the fallacy of the contention that we should look back to the past to find complete guidance for the present. The vast cultural changes of the past two hundred years have brought it about that the life of our era is so different from that of any previous age that no precise analogies can be drawn between the distant past and the present. For example, the political life of ancient Athens or Rome offers little more relevant basis for guiding the government of Greater New York today than does the construction and operation of a Phoenician galley for taking the *Queen Elizabeth* or the *United States* over the waters of the Atlantic Ocean.

The assertion that we cannot achieve a happier future because of the inability to change human nature is equally fallacious. In the first place, there is no proof that human nature is incompatible with or opposed to social change for the better. Even more important is the fact that anthropology and cultural history have shown that human nature has not actually changed for at least thirty thousand years. Yet, in this time man has passed from the fist-hatchet to the hydrogen bomb, from cave dwellings to the penthouse apartments of the Waldorf Towers, and from small tribal groups to great national states and empires and incipient experiments with world government. If all this has taken place without any change in human nature, then surely we can adapt our institutions to our present technology without any basic change in human nature.

The supreme fact which we may gain from an intelligent study of history is that the twentieth century is a novel era. It represents the fourth outstanding transitional epoch in human experience—the fourth great world-revolution. It may be roughly compared with the passage from preliterate culture to orderly civil society at the dawn of history, the breakup of pagan society with the fall of the Western Roman Empire, or the disintegration of the medieval order following 1500. Our institutions are today in a condition of crisis and flux comparable to the situation of such medieval institutions as feudalism, the manor, the guilds and scholasticism in the days of Columbus, Martin Luther and Henry VIII. Our age is more critical than any earlier transitional period because ahead of us lies either utopia or the destruction of civilization by an uncontrolled technology gone wild in destruction through atomic warfare.

While the general history of ideas and culture is most relevant for social guidance, history without specific factual basis is bound to be vague and unreliable. Even the greatest scholars daily require handy books of reference. Only a Macaulay can retain in his mind at any time all the detailed data and biographical facts of the human past. Professor Robinson, a great medievalist, tells the story how he and Professor Breasted, our greatest orientalist, were writing a textbook. But at a given moment neither of them could recall the precise date of Mohammed's Hegira (622)—one of the outstanding events in both medieval and oriental history. It is on occasions like this that a book like Mr. William S. Roeder's *Dictionary of European History* becomes indispensable. It provides concise and reliable information concerning most of the events and prominent personalities from 500 A.D. to the present. While it deals primarily with the data of European history, there are references to the more important happenings and figures in the history of the colonies, of the Western Hemisphere and the Near and Far East.

The *Dictionary* has been designed especially to help understand the situation in contemporary Europe. Hence, special emphasis is placed upon the events and personalities connected with what are the major powers of our day. This emphasis emerges in both a numerical and a quantitative sense. There are proportionately more references dealing with the history of the chief states of our time, and each of these references is longer and more detailed than in the case of the events and personages of the minor powers. Although the *Dictionary* gives more attention to the data of political history than to those of social, economic and cultural history, the latter broader phases of history are not neglected. Likewise, the political figures of the past are given precedence over those famed in other realms of human endeavor.

Historical writers, teachers of history, and students in various courses in European history will find Mr. Roeder's compilation a work of great convenience in their activities.

DICTIONARY

OF

EUROPEAN HISTORY

A

Abbot. The head of a monastery.

Abdication of Napoleon. April 11, 1814. After the allied armies entered Paris on March 31, Napoleon was forced to abdicate (at Fontainebleau) in favor of his son (April 6). The allies refused to accept this abdication and compelled him to abdicate unconditionally (April 11). The allies granted him the Island of Elba as a sovereign principality with an annual income of 2 million francs, to be paid by France. His wife, Marie Louise, received the Duchies of Parma, Piacenza, and Guastalla. Both Napoleon and Marie Louise retained their imperial titles. Napoleon arrived on Elba on May 4.

Abdul Hamid II. 1842-1918. Sultan of Turkey (1876-1909). His long reign was marked by many events of importance. Losing a war to Russia (1877-78), he lost most of his possessions in Europe by the Treaty of San Stefano (1878) (q.v.). He carried out severe Armenian massacres (1895-6). His misgovernment led to much revolutionary activity (1896-1908). Finally the Young Turks forced him to abdicate (1909).

Abelard, Peter. 1079-1142. French philosopher and theologian. Born in Nantes. Master of a school of philosophy (1091-1113). Student under Anselm of Laon (1113-17). Teacher of philosophy (1117-21). Secretly married Héloïse, thus incurring the anger of her uncle Fulbert, whose hired bravos mutilated him so that he was incapable of ecclesiastical preferment. He withdrew to a monastery. His nominalistic teachings were declared heretical (1121). He wandered from monastery to monastery and was declared a heretic (1140). He died while on the way to Rome to defend himself. His body was given to Héloïse, who was then the prioress of the convent of the Paraclete at Nogent-sur-Seine. She buried it in the oratory there. Later, she was interred beside him. The ashes of both were brought to Paris (1800) and interred in one sepulchre at Père la Chaise (1817).

Academy of Science, Russian. Founded in 1726 according to plans drawn up by Peter the Great before his death in 1725. The interest of the Academy was in mathematics and science. The Academy fostered a geographical survey of Siberia and supported the Siberian expedition of 1733-43. By spreading technical information it encouraged inventions.

Act of Settlement (1701). To assure a Protestant successor to William III, the

English Parliament passed the Act of Settlement, fixing the succession upon Anne, the daughter of James II, and upon her death upon Sophia, Electress of Hanover, and her descendants. Sophia was the granddaughter of James I and the nearest Protestant representative of the English royal house. Also included in the Act were provisions that the king of England must be a member of the Church of England and that judges shall hold office during good behavior and shall be removed only by parliamentary action.

Act of Supremacy, British. An act of Parliament (Nov. 2, 1534), by which the king and his successors were named Protector and only Supreme Head of the Church and Clergy of England. This is the beginning of the English Reformation.

Action Libérale. French political party organized by Count de Mun (1841-1914) for the purpose of reconciling Catholicism with Republicanism. While it stood for the repeal of anti-clerical legislation, it supported the Republic and the social program of Pope Leo XIII. It demanded: proportional representation, professional representation, and public financial support for Catholic and other private schools.

Addison, Joseph. 1672-1719. English essayist, poet, and statesman best known for *The Spectator Papers* which he wrote with Steele (q.v.) and others.

Adrian IV (name Nicholas Breakspear). ?-1159. Pope (1154-59). The only Englishman ever to become pope. He entered into a spirited conflict with Frederick Barbarossa over papal supremacy. This conflict ultimately played a major part in the downfall of the Hohenstaufen dynasty. Adrian gave Henry II of England permission to invade Ireland (1154).

Adrian VI (name, Adrïaan Boyers). 1459-1523. Pope (1522-23). Born in Utrecht; became Vice Chancellor of the University of Louvain and tutor of Archduke Charles (later Charles V); grand inquisitor (1516) and regent of Spain (1520); created cardinal (1517); as pope, failed in efforts to reform the church and to oppose the advance of the Turks.

Adrianople, Treaty of. (1829). See Russo-Turkish War; also Nicholas I.

Afrika Korps. See Rommel, Erwin.

Agadir Incident. 1911. One of the Moroccan crises that featured the "cold war" which preceded World War I. The German government dispatched a warship to the Moroccan port, Agadir, ostensibly to safeguard German mining interests. At the same time Germany hinted that the warship would be withdrawn as soon as the French army evacuated Fez. England supported France. Not wishing to start a war at this time, Germany backed down and agreed to a French protectorate over Morocco if the French maintained an "open door" in Morocco and ceded two strips of the French Congo.

Age of Reason (called by some Enlightenment or Aufklärung). The climate of thought of most of the advanced thinkers and writers of the 18th century, particularly in France. They examined social institutions by asking of each, "Is it reasonable?" or "Is it rational?" Voltaire ridiculed the Church for being irrational. Montesquieu claimed that divine-right monarchy was unreasonable. Rousseau claimed that class inequalities were unreasonable.

Agincourt, Battle of. See Henry V.

Agricultural Revolution. This was a movement which began in 18th century

England to improve the yield of the soil and the quality of livestock by applying the principles of science to agriculture. Its leaders were Jethro Tull, Lord Townshend, Robert Bakewell, and Arthur Young (q.v.).

Aix-la-Chapelle, Peace of. Oct. 18, 1748. This agreement ended the War of the Austrian Succession (q.v.). It contained the following provisions: (1) Mutual restorations of all conquests. (2) The Asiento (q.v.) was to be renewed for four years. (3) The Protestant succession of England was again guaranteed; France promised to exclude the English Pretender and his family from its national domain. (4) Emperor Francis was acknowledged by France and the Pragmatic Sanction (q.v.) was renewed. (5) Silesia was to remain in the hands of the King of Prussia. (6) Don Philip, the second son of Philip V of Spain and Elizabeth Farnese, secured the Duchies of Parma, Piacenza, and Guastalla, while his brother Charles retained Naples and Sicily. Thus the dynastic aspirations of their mother were realized.

Aix-la-Chapelle, Treaty of. May 2, 1668. A treaty between France and the Triple Alliance (England, Sweden, Holland) and Spain, ending the War of Devolution. France restored the Franche-Comté to Spain and received 12 fortified towns along the borders of the Spanish Netherlands, among which were Lille, Tournay, and Oudenarde.

Alberoni, Giulio. 1664-1752. Italian statesman in the Spanish service, cardinal of the Roman Catholic Church. As a representative of the Duke of Parma at the court of Philip V of Spain, Alberoni gained great influence and became prime minister. He arranged the marriage of the king to Elizabeth Farnese. His aim was to strengthen Spain by diminishing the influence of Austria in Italy. His actions led to the creation of the Quadruple

Alliance (Britain, Netherlands, France, and Austria) against Spain. Spain had to yield and to dismiss Alberoni, who now entered the service of the Church. Even though his foreign policy did not succeed, Alberoni was able to revive the economic life of Spain from the doldrums into which it had fallen.

Albert I. 1875-1934. King of the Belgians (1909-34). He became a heroic world figure when the Germans invaded his country in 1914. He led his people in futile but heroic resistance. He spent the entire war at the head of his army. He did much to improve the social conditions in Belgium and the Belgian Congo. He was killed in a rock-climbing accident in the Ardennes Mountains. He was succeeded by his son Leopold III.

Albert, Archduke of Austria. 1559-1621. Governor of Spanish Netherlands (1599-1621). Married the Infanta Isabella, daughter of Philip II of Spain. Made truce with the Netherlands (1609). Great patron of the Arts and the University of Louvain.

Albert (Prince Albert). 1819-61. Husband and royal consort of Queen Victoria of Britain. See Victoria.

Albert II (Albrecht). 1397-1439. King of Germany and first Holy Roman Emperor of the house of Hapsburg (1438-39). This man is called the second founder of the Hapsburg dynasty, for he not only reacquired for the Hapsburgs the crown which was lost at the death of Albert I (1308), but also united those dominions which composed the Austrian monarchy down until 1919. He held sway over Austria proper, Styria, Carniola, Tyrol, Bohemia, and Hungary. With one exception (Charles VII of Bavaria, 1742-45) all Holy Roman Emperors were Hapsburgs from Albert II on until the Empire was abolished in 1806.

Alberti, Leon Battista. 1404-72. Italian Renaissance painter, architect, writer, and organist. Born in Florence. He designed the church of San Francesco in Rimini and the Palazzo Rucellai in Florence. He is credited with being the first to investigate scientifically the laws of perspective.

Albertus Magnus (Count von Bollstädt. *Called* Albert the Great or the Universal Doctor). d. 1280. German scholastic, theologian, scientist, and writer. Dominican. Taught at Paris (1245) and at Cologne (1248-54), where Thomas Aquinas was his pupil. Bishop of Regensburg (1260-62). He retired and devoted the remainder of his life to scientific experimentation and in the preparation of a commentary on Aristotle. His extensive knowledge gave him the reputation of being a magician. Author of *Summa de Creaturis.* Beatified (1622). Canonized (1932).

Albigensians. A heretical sect which lived in southern France in the 12th and 13th centuries. They were named after the town of Albi, although their greatest concentration was in and around Toulouse. It is very difficult to know what their exact beliefs were, since all of our sources of information come from their enemies. They were anti-sacerdotal and much opposed to the Roman Church, and raised continued opposition to the corruption of the clergy. Among them there were a few ascetics, called Cathari or *perfecti.* The mass of believers (*credentes*) were uninitiated in Catharist doctrine. At all events they were free from all moral prohibitions and religious obligations on condition that they received the "baptism of the Spirit" some time before death or even *in extremis.* The Church tried to overcome the Albigensians by persuasion. Failing in that, a crusade was launched against them (1209). They were destroyed with great severity. Thus was lost the brilliant Provençal civilization.

Albuquerque, Alfonso de. 1453-1515. Viceroy of Portuguese Indies and founder of Portuguese empire in the East. Captured Goa (1510) and made it chief Portuguese center in the East. Secured control of Malabar Coast, Ceylon, Malacca, and Ormuz.

Alcabala. A ten per cent sales tax levied by the Spanish government on all business transactions in Spain and the colonies from the time of Philip II (1556-98) to Philip V (1700-1746). This tax contributed greatly to the economic decline of Spain, since it stifled trade and commerce.

Alcuin. 735-804. English scholar who aided Charlemagne in the revival of learning at the court of the Franks (781). He headed Charlemagne's famous Palace School (q.v.).

Alemanni. A Germanic tribe which settled along the Rhine in the 5th century where Alsace and Baden are now located. By 536 they were completely conquered by the Franks. High German dialects in SW Germany are Alemannic. In French, *Allemands* signifies all Germans.

Alembert. See D'Alembert.

Alexander I. 1777-1825. Czar of Russia 1801-1825, succeeding Paul I. One of the greatest political minds of the time.

Foreign policies: From 1801 to 1815 Alexander's chief concern was the struggle with Napoleon. This required a series of alliances, sometimes with Austria, sometimes with Prussia, broken by periods of friendship with France, the most important of which followed the failure of the first coalition against Napoleon and the Peace of Tilsit in 1807 (q.v.). The struggle was decided by a gigantic duel between Napoleon and Alexander in 1812 and was concluded by the organization of an all-European coalition against Napoleon, which led to his downfall. In opposition to Napoleon's principle of civil equality, Alexander brought forward the idea of a liberal federation of national states, which culminated in the Holy Alliance (1815). Although this alliance was later corrupted by Metternich into an instrument of reaction, it was originally a liberal organization.

Alexander attempted, without much success, to promote a federation of South Slavs. As the result of the Russo-Swedish War (1808-1809), Russia annexed Finland. By the Treaty of Vienna (1815), Russia acquired most of the Grand Duchy of Warsaw, which was organized as the autonomous Kingdom of Poland in permanent union with the Russian Empire with Alexander as sovereign.

In the Far East Russia encouraged the development of the Russian-American Company in Alaska and even in northern California.

Domestic policies: Under the leadership of Speransky and later Novosiltsev, an attempt was made to promote a constitutional reorganization of the state. Following 1815, the policies of Alexander proved unpopular with many of the younger army officers and led to the formation of secret societies. The Southern Society, headed by Colonel Pestel, drew up a future constitution for a centralized democratic republic. Pestel was a disciple of the French Jacobins and a forerunner of Lenin. The Northern Society, headed by Colonel Muraviev, drew up a future constitution which resembled the constitution of the United States.

Alexander I. 1888-1934. King of Yugoslavia (1921-1934). Commander-in-chief of the Serbian armies (1914-19). Prince regent of Serbia (1914-21) for his father, Peter I. He became king of the new kingdom of Yugoslavia in 1921. Because of disturbed conditions (1928) following the assassination of Stefan Radic (q.v.), he dismissed parliament and abolished the constitution. He did much to secure friendly relations with neighboring coun-

tries. He was assassinated in Marseilles, along with Foreign Minister Jean Louis Barthou of France, by a Macedonian terrorist. He was succeeded by his son, Peter II (1923-). During Peter's minority, the country was ruled by a regency, headed by Prince Paul (1934-1941), Peter's uncle. Peter deposed the regent (March, 1941), but left Yugoslavia (April, 1941) after the German invasion. He has since been in exile, being prevented from resuming his throne by the Tito (q.v.) government.

Alexander II. 1818-1881. Czar of Russia (1855-1881). Succeeded Nicholas I. Called "Czar Liberator," since during his reign a number of important reforms, notably the freeing of the serfs, took place.

Domestic policies: Serfdom was abolished Mar. 3, 1861 (see Russian serfdom). The Zemstvo Law of 1864 created local self-government without regard to class (q.v.). The judicial reform of 1864, promoted by S. I. Zarudny, improved court procedure, introduced the jury system, and organized lawyers into a formal bar. The universal military service law of 1874 affected equally all classes of the Russian people.

Despite these reforms, the revolutionary movement became quite strong, particularly among the Raznochisti (q.v.). Under the leadership of Herzen, Bakunin, Lavrov, and Chernoshevsky, a secret society, *Land and Liberty*, was organized. Although the uprising in Poland temporarily quieted the revolutionary movement, it flared up again and led to the formation in 1879 in Lipetsk in Central Russia of an Executive Committee, pledged to kill the czar. Alexander was assassinated in St. Petersburg on Mar. 13, 1881 as he was about to implement a moderate constitution drawn up by Louis Melikov, the Minister of the Interior.

Foreign affairs: Under Prince Bariatinsky the Caucasus were subdued. Between 1865-1876 Russia advanced in Kokand, Bokhara, and Khiva. In 1867 Alaska was sold to the United States for $7,200,000. Following the Franco-Prussian war (1870) Russia strengthened its position by placing a fleet in the Black Sea, thus abrogating a clause of the Treaty of Paris (1856), and by joining (1872) the Three Emperors' League (Germany, Austria, Russia) (q.v.). Russia fought and defeated Turkey in 1877-78 and at San Stefano forced Turkey to form a kingdom of Bulgaria, recognize the independence of Serbia, Montenegro, and Romania, and cede to Russia southern Bessarabia, Batum, and Kars. In 1878 the Congress of Berlin modified the terms of San Stefano by reducing the size of Bulgaria, returning Macedonia to Turkey, and placing Bosnia and Herzegovina "temporarily" under the protection of Austria.

Alexander III. 1845-1894. (Czar of Russia 1881-1894.) Profoundly affected by the assassination of his father, Alexander II, Alexander III instituted a policy of repression which was directed by Constantine Pobêdonostsev (1827-1907). Local self-government was curtailed, censorship was tightened, education was controlled, suspected people were placed under police surveillance. Russification was instituted, particularly in Poland and the Baltic Provinces; strict measures were taken against religious dissenters, especially the Jews; peasant landowning increased; head tax was abolished; the first labor laws were passed. Count Witte (1849-1915), a brilliant statesman, reorganized finances. Following the defeat at the Congress of Berlin, Russia strove for allies to counteract the worsening relations with Great Britain. Accordingly, in 1881 it again joined the Three Emperors' League. But Austria broke with Russia in 1887 and Germany and Russia drifted apart in 1890. When a financial rapprochement with France was reached in 1890, an Entente with France was signed August 22, 1891.

Alexander VI (*name* **Rodrigo Lanzol y Borgia**). 1431-1503. Pope (1492-1503). He had many mistresses. One, Vannozza Cattanei, bore him Cesare Borgia and Lucrezia Borgia. He was elected to the papacy through bribery. The foreign relations of his time were strongly affected by the growing influence of France in Italy, culminating in the invasion of Charles VIII in 1494. Alexander prevented Charles from seizing Church property in Rome. He divided the New World between Spain and Portugal. He executed Savonarola (1498). He instituted the censorship of books. He patronized artists, especially Michelangelo, Raphael, and Bramante.

Alexander, Harold Rupert Leofric George, Viscount Alexander of Tunis. 1891-. British field marshal. He has had a long military career, highlighted by service during the First World War and in the Northwest Province of India (1935). In the Second World War he commanded the retreats at Dunkirk (1940) and in Burma (1942) before, as commander of the Middle East, he directed the conquest of North Africa. He then commanded the conquest of Sicily and the bitter fighting in Italy. Made field marshal (1944) and Allied Commander-in-chief of the Mediterranean. In 1945 he was made Governor-General of Canada and (1946) he was created viscount.

Alexius I Comnenus. 1048-1118. Byzantine emperor (1081-1118). One of the ablest of the Byzantine emperors. He defended his kingdom against the Scythians, Turks, and Normans. His domains were invaded by the Crusaders in the First Crusade (1096-99).

Alfonso X, *called* **Alfonso el Sabio (the Learned).** 1226-1284. King of Castile and Leon (1252-1284); candidate for office of Holy Roman Emperor (1257) but not elected; engaged in wars with the Moors; promulgated code of laws, *Las Siete Partidas,* the basis of Spanish law; patron of learning; poet.

Alfonso XII. 1857-1885. King of Spain (1875-1885). Proclaimed king by army at end of a civil war; temporarily suppressed Carlist opposition (1876) (q.v.); summoned a Cortes which made a new constitution (1876) under the influence of Prime Minister Cánovas del Castillo.

Alfonso XIII. 1886-1941. King of Spain (1886-1931); first under the regency of his mother (1886-1902); during regency, Spain lost Philippine Islands and last possessions in New World; his reign was marked by rioting in Madrid and Barcelona over trouble in Morocco, by Spanish neutrality in World War I, and by defeat in Morocco by Abd-el-Krim; appointed Primo de Rivera dictator (1923-25); National Assembly opened (1927); this period marked by riots, strikes, etc.; martial law proclaimed (1930); forced to abdicate (1931).

Alfred (*called* The Great). 849-901. King of the West Saxons (871-901). Fought against the Danes. Reorganized civil government. Captured London. Patronized learning. Caused many books to be translated into Anglo-Saxon. Under his auspices, the *Anglo-Saxon Chronicle* was begun.

Algeçiras Conference. 1906. A conference to decide the fate of Morocco. On March 31, 1905, the Kaiser of Germany landed at Tangier, Morocco, and delivered a speech which was a threat to the French influence. France could do nothing to counteract this threat, since its ally, Russia, was being defeated badly by the Japanese. France agreed to dismiss Foreign Minister Delcassé, who had strengthened French interests in Morocco, and agreed to submit the Moroccan question to an international conference. This

congress, which met in Algeçiras, Spain, guaranteed the territorial integrity of Morocco, the sovereignty of the sultan, and an "open door" for foreign investors and merchants. This whole affair was staged by Germany to try to break up the Triple Entente.

Alliance between Germany and Austria-Hungary. 1879. At the Congress of Berlin (q.v.) (1878), the relations between Russia and Germany worsened. Although Bismarck said that Germany was strictly neutral in this conference and that he was an "honest broker," he agreed that Russia's share of spoils in the Balkans should be reduced while Austria-Hungary was given control of Bosnia and Herzegovina. To guard against the effects of Russian hostility, Bismarck concluded a secret defensive alliance with Austria-Hungary. This treaty was not made public until 1888. It paved the way for the foundation of the Triple Alliance (q.v.) (1882).

Allied Control Committee. June 5, 1945. This Committee, which included General Eisenhower, Field Marshal Montgomery, and Marshal Zhukov, assumed full control throughout German territory following the surrender of Germany at the end of World War II. German territory, as it was on Dec. 31, 1937, was divided into Soviet, French, British, and American zones of occupation.

Allied High Commission. 1949. A three-man body consisting of high commissioners appointed by the United States, France, and Great Britain to supervise the German Federal Republic. The powers of this commission were defined in the Occupation Statute (see German Federal Republic). It has the authority to veto the laws of the Republic and to exercise plenary powers over foreign policy, reparations, decartelization, security, and control of the Ruhr.

Allies, The. The name given to the 23 countries which opposed the Central Powers during World War I.

Country	Date of Entrance into the War
Serbia	July, 1914
Russia	August, 1914
France	August, 1914
Belgium	August, 1914
England	August, 1914
Montenegro	August, 1914
Japan	August, 1914
Italy	May, 1915
San Marino	June, 1915
Portugal	March, 1916
Romania	August, 1916
Greece	November, 1916
United States	April, 1917
Panama	April, 1917
Cuba	April, 1917
Siam	July, 1917
Liberia	August, 1917
China	August, 1917
Brazil	October, 1917
Guatemala	April, 1918
Nicaragua	May, 1918
Haiti	July, 1918
Honduras	July, 1918

Almagest. In the 2nd century, a resident of Alexandria, Claudius Ptolemy, published his *Syntaxis* (System). It described a system of astronomy and geometry based on the theory that the sun, planets, and stars revolve about the earth. This book, presently known as the great system or construction (He Megiste Syntaxis), was translated in the 9th century by Arabs under the title of *Al Magisthi.* This was called by medieval Europeans *Almagest.* It was the standard frame of reference in the science of astronomy until the appearance of the Copernican system.

Almohades, The. 1147-1269. A Berber dynasty in Moorish Spain. During their reign, Moorish Spain was gradually conquered by the Christians until by 1248 only the kingdom of Granada remained in Moorish hands.

Almoravids. 1056-1147. A Berber dynasty in Moorish Spain.

Alva, Fernando Alvarez de Toledo, Duke of. 1508-1583. Spanish general. Commander under Charles V (1535-56). Sent by Philip II to suppress revolt in the Netherlands (1567). Set up Council of Blood (1567-73) (q.v.). Acted with extreme cruelty. Executed Counts Egmont and Horn and many others. Defeated William of Orange. Led expedition that conquered Portugal (1580-81).

Amiens, Treaty of. March 27, 1802. Between England and France. England surrendered to France and its allies all colonial conquests except Trinidad, which was ceded by Spain, and Ceylon, which was ceded by the Batavian Republic (Holland). Malta was restored to the Order of the Knights of Malta.

Anabaptists. From the earliest times there were Christians who believed that baptism had no value unless the candidate made a profession of faith. Hence, adult baptism was necessary; infant baptism had no efficacy. If one were baptized during infancy, one must be baptized again during adult life. (Hence the name: *ana,* meaning *again.*) A sect of Anabaptists arose in Zürich in 1523 among the followers of Zwingli. In 1525 they took an active part in the Peasants' War. In 1534 they attracted much attention when they got possession of Münster in Westphalia, Germany, and tried to set up a primitive Christian community in which all property was held in common. Anabaptists were thus regarded as dangerous radicals, especially since some of them attempted to establish group marriage. Persecuted everywhere, the sect survived, and is today regarded as a respectable member of the international religious community.

Anarchism. William Godwin (1756-1836) (q.v.) has always been acclaimed as the father of philosophical Anarchism. However, Pierre Joseph Proudhon (1809-65) (q.v.) was much more influential in starting the movement. In his *System of Economic Contradictions or the Philosophy of Poverty* (1846) he laid down four principles: (1) Private property is theft. It and capital are secured by exploiting the labor of other men. Every man should have the right to use property and to enjoy the full product of his own labor. (2) There should be "no more (political) parties, no more authority, absolute liberty of man and citizen." (3) Voluntary contracts between free individuals should be substituted for a regime of obligatory laws. (4) Man can achieve a state of perfectibility by education. When that day arrives, society would be intelligently transformed of its own volition.

In general, Anarchists have accepted the first three principles, but have rejected the fourth. Under the leadership of Mikhail Bakunin (1814-76) (q.v.), Anarchists began to follow "direct action" in order to overthrow the existing State to make way for the perfect society of the future.

Andersen, Hans Christian. 1805-75. Danish story-teller. Born in Odense in Fünen. He is famous for his fairy tales, including *The Ugly Duckling, The Red Shoes, The Tin Soldier, The Emperor's New Clothes.*

Andrusovo, Treaty of. Jan. 20, 1667. Concluding a 13-year war between Poland and Russia, which was disastrous for Poland. Poland was forced to cede to Russia the eastern Ukraine and Smolensk.

Angelico, Fra. 1387-1455. Florentine painter. A Dominican monk, he painted the walls of the cells and the common rooms of the monastery of San Marco in Florence.

Angevin Empire. The holdings of the Angevins, kings of England and feudal lords of regions in France. The empire reached its height during the 12th century, when Henry II was king of England. Through inheritance, conquest, and marriage with Eleanor of Aquitaine, Henry possessed the following: England, part of Ireland (Munster, Leinster, and part of Ulster), Normandy, Brittany, Maine, Anjou, Touraine, Poitou, Marché, Auvergne, Aquitaine, Gascony, and part of Languedoc. The English retained part of France until the end of the Hundred Years' War, when their holdings were reduced to the single city of Calais.

Anglo-French Agreement. 1904. By this agreement, France allowed England to become the virtual protector of Egypt. In return, England gave France undisputed right to Morocco.

Anne. 1665-1714. Queen of Great Britain and Ireland (1702-1714). She was the second daughter of James II and Anne Hyde. Educated in the Protestant faith, she succeeded William III. As queen she was much influenced by Sarah Jennings, the wife of John Churchill, the duke of Marlborough. The War of the Spanish Succession raged throughout most of her reign. The most important public event of her reign was the Act of Union with Scotland (1707).

Anschluss (Union between Austria and Germany). March 12-13, 1938. Schuschnigg, chancellor of Austria, called for a referendum to reaffirm the independence of his country to be held March 13. On March 11, Germany submitted an ultimatum demanding the postponement of the plebiscite and the resignation of Schuschnigg. Unable to resist, Schuschnigg resigned in favor of Seyss-Inquart, who immediately appealed to Germany for help to restore order. On March 12, German troops invaded Austria. On March 13, Seyss-Inquart proclaimed the union with Germany. On April 10, a plebiscite revealed a vote of 99.75% in favor of union with Germany.

Anselm, Saint. 1033-1109. Archbishop of Canterbury. Born near Aosta in Piedmont. Went to school at the famous abbey of Bec in Normandy. When Lanfranc, the abbot, became Archbishop of Canterbury, Anselm became head of the abbey and made it the most famous school of the 11th century. Succeeded Lanfranc as Archbishop of Canterbury. Became embroiled with William the Rufus and was exiled. Returned under Henry I. Wrote numerous philosophical works and *Meditations* and *Letters*. Canonized in 1494.

Anti-Clericalism. A 19th Century European point of view which opposed the Syllabus of Errors, the Encyclical of 1864, and the doctrine of Papal Infallibility. Anti-clericals maintained that these statements of policy constituted an attack by the Catholic Church on liberty and nationalism. Catholics were also accused of being unprogressive, inimical to reason, and bent on keeping people in ignorance.

Anti-Comintern Pact. Nov. 17, 1936. An agreement between Germany and the Japanese against communism and the Third International. Italy and Spain signed this agreement at later dates, as did Hungary, Romania, Bulgaria, Slovakia, Croatia, Denmark, Finland, and the Japanese puppet governments of Manchukuo and Nanking.

Anti-Corn Law League. See Corn Laws, Repeal of.

Anti-Semitism, Nazi. From the first, anti-Semitism was one of the most popular catchwords of the Nazi program. Within a short time after Hitler became Chancellor of Germany (Jan. 30, 1933), an active campaign against Jews was be-

gun. A national boycott of all Jewish businesses and professions (April 1, 1933) was followed by a long series of outrages. By the end of 1938 there were virtually no practising Jewish doctors, nurses, dentists, professors, teachers, judges, lawyers, and so on. Many thousands of these had been placed in concentration camps. Jewish children could not number more than 1½% of the total of any school. After 1938, Jews were barred from all schools. Eventually Jews were barred from the stage, the motion pictures, musical performances, and journalism. The Nuremberg Laws (Sept. 15, 1935) deprived Jews of citizenship (a Jew was defined as one who had one or more Jewish grandparents). All intermarriage with Jews was forbidden. Any Jew who did not have a name officially listed as Jewish was required to add "Israel" or "Sarah" to his or her name. After the annexation of Austria, the same measures were extended to the new state. Following the assassination of a German diplomat by a Jew in Paris (Nov. 1938), a new wave of terror broke out in Germany. The government levied a fine of one billion marks on the Jewish community.

Antonescu, Ion. 1882-1946. Romanian general. As head of the fascist pro-German Iron Guard he forced Carol II to abdicate in 1940. Antonescu was the pro-German dictator of Romania (1940-44). He was executed in 1946.

Antwerp, Truce of. Aug. 9, 1609. The United Provinces of the Netherlands gained their independence, liberty to carry on Indian trade, and the right to prevent the Catholic religion in their dominions. The truce was to last for 12 years.

Apprentices, Statute of. 1663-1813. An English law which stated that all able-bodied men, with certain exceptions, were liable to serve as agricultural laborers. The act also was aimed to prevent vagrancy and migration of laborers. By this act, the term of apprenticeship was set at seven years.

Aquinas, Saint Thomas. d. 1274. Italian scholastic, often called "The Angelic Doctor." Born in the family castle of Roccasecca, near Aquino. Educated at Monte Cassino and the University of Naples. He became a Dominican (1243). Studied under Albertus Magnus (1248-52). Lived in the monastery of St. Jacques, Paris (1252-61). Lived in Italy after 1261. Canonized (1323). Declared the patron of Catholic schools (1880). He is known as the systematizer of Catholic theology and for a philosophical system called Thomism. Thomism is an application of the philosophy of Aristotle to the doctrines of religion. It holds to divine predestination and grace. It denies the immaculate conception of the Virgin Mary. It magnifies the power of the sacraments. Aquinas is the author of *Summa Theologiae*.

Ariosto, Lodovico. 1474-1533. Italian poet. Born in Reggio Emilia. His best-known work is the epic poem *Orlando Furioso*.

Arkwright, Sir Richard. 1732-1792. English inventor and manufacturer; invented the water frame (1769); is often called the "First Modern Capitalist."

Armada, The Spanish. A great fleet assembled by Philip II of Spain in 1588 to capture England. The original sailing was postponed when in April 1587 Drake sailed into the harbor of Cadiz, plundered the town, and destroyed much shipping. He then sailed into Lisbon Bay and wrought much damage. Finally, off Cape St. Vincent he intercepted a squadron of transports from the Mediterranean. In May 1588, the Armada was ready to set sail, but a storm postponed its departure until July 12. The English fleet, commanded by Lord Howard of Effingham, engaged the Armada in the Channel and caused much damage. A great storm dispersed the Armada, wrecking many of the ships.

Armistice, The. Nov. 11, 1918. This agreement between the Allies and Germany ended the fighting in World War I. It was signed at 11:00 A.M. in a railroad car in the forest of Compiègne. Within 14 days the Germans were to evacuate France, Belgium, Alsace-Lorraine, and Luxemburg; within a month, all territory west of the Rhine. Allied troops were to occupy the evacuated portion of Germany as well as the Rhine bridgeheads at Cologne, Coblenz, and Mainz to the depth of 30 kilometers east of the Rhine. The treaties of Brest-Litovsk and Bucharest were to be renounced (q.v.), and all German troops withdrawn from Russia, Romania, Turkey, and Austria-Hungary. A specified number of warships and all submarines were to be surrendered. Within two weeks the Allies were to receive 5,000 locomotives, 150,000 railway cars, and 5,000 motor trucks. All Allied prisoners of war were to be repatriated at once. The blockade of Germany was to remain in force. Large quantities of arms and artillery were to be surrendered.

Armistice between Austria-Hungary and the Allies. Nov. 3, 1918. By this agreement, Austria-Hungary withdrew from World War I. All Austro-Hungarian armies were to be demobilized. Half of the equipment was to be surrendered. Disputed territory was to be evacuated. Allied forces were to occupy strategic points.

Arndt, Ernst Moritz. 1769-1860. German nationalistic poet and historian. His verse had a nationalistic and martial character. It strongly influenced Germans in their struggle against Napoleon. His book, *Geist der Zeit,* was so bitter against Napoleon that Arndt was forced to go into exile into Sweden and Russia to escape Napoleon's wrath.

Arnold of Brescia. 1100?-1155. Italian political reformer. A student of Abelard. He opposed the corruption of the clergy. He led a popular revolt against the bishop of Brescia. He was condemned (with Abelard) by the Council of Sens (1143). He fled to Switzerland, but was called to Rome (1145). He forced Pope Eugene III into exile and set up a government modeled after the ancient Roman republic. Pope Adrian IV placed him under interdict (1155). He was betrayed and executed by Frederick I (1155).

Arnold, Matthew. 1822-88. English poet and critic. *Culture and Anarchy, Literature and Dogma, Essays on Criticism,* and *Civilization in the United States* are examples of his critical work. *Dover Beach, Sohrab and Rustum,* and *Tristram and Iseult* are representative poems.

Arnulf. 850?-899. Natural son of Carloman of Bavaria. He deposed Charles III. Elected king of Germany and Holy Roman Emperor (887-899). He won a great victory over the Northmen at Louvain (891). He invaded Italy and stormed Rome (894-5). He captured Rome and was crowned emperor there (896). He then was stricken with paralysis and returned home. He was the last Carolingian to be crowned emperor.

Asiento. An agreement between England and Spain which was part of the Peace of Utrecht at the end of the War of the Spanish Succession (1713). Through this agreement, England broke the Spanish monopoly in the colonial trade of the New World. The English were given a thirty-year monopoly of importing Negro slaves to Spanish America. English merchants had the right to send one ship a year to trade in Spanish-American ports.

Asquith, Herbert Henry. First Earl of Oxford and Asquith. 1852-1928. English statesman. Liberal M.P. (1886-1918; 1920-24). Home secretary (1892-95). Chancellor of the exchequer (1905-08). Prime minister (1908-16). During his term as prime minister, the Liberal Party enjoyed some dramatic triumphs. The social-insurance program was instituted and the power of the House of Lords was broken. The First World War led to Asquith's downfall.

Assembly of Notables. 1787. An assembly of 145 of the chief nobles, bishops, and magistrates, which was called by Louis XVI of France to recommend financial reforms. The interest-bearing debt of France amounted to (1786) 600 million dollars. The government of France was running into debt at the rate of 25 million dollars a year. The notables recommended abolishing compulsory labor on roads, establishment of provincial assemblies, and the dismissal of the finance minister, Calonne. The question of taxation they referred to the Estates-General.

Assignats. 1789-97. Literally, first mortgage. The assignats were paper money issued during the French Revolution (q.v.) by the National Assembly (Dec. 1789). They were originally short-term notes bearing five per cent interest issued pending the sale of confiscated Church and royal land. In April, 1790, they were made legal tender. Subsequent issues bore no interest. The assignats became so inflated due to over-issue that their value fell to less than the cost of printing them. They were finally voided May 21, 1797.

Assize of Arms. 1181. By this decree, Henry II of England required that every free subject should arm himself according to the value of his property, and hold himself in readiness for war. A man's ability to arm himself was determined by the sworn testimony of his neighbors.

Associations Act, French. 1901. By this law, all voluntary societies—except those contrary to law, monastic congregations, or the Catholic Church—were recognized as legal upon declaration to the administrative authorities. It was further provided that no religious order should exist in France unless it had received governmental authorization and no member of an unauthorized order should be permitted to teach in any school in France. The law was so rigidly enforced, especially with respect to teaching and business associations, that within two years hundreds of monks and nuns were driven out of France and ten thousand church schools were closed.

Atlantic Charter, The. Aug. 14, 1941. A joint declaration by President Roosevelt and Prime Minister Churchill. The Charter asserted that the signatory nations wished no aggrandizement, no increase of territory which was against the wishes of the people directly concerned. They respected the right of people to choose their own form of government. They favored equality of economic opportunity for all nations. They hoped to promote fair labor standards, freedom from want and fear, freedom of the seas, and disarmament of aggressor nations. This pact was endorsed (Sept. 24) by 15 governments (9 in exile): Australia, Belgium, Canada, Czechoslovakia, the Free French, Great Britain, Greece, Luxemburg, the Netherlands, New Zealand, Norway, Poland, Russia, Union of South Africa, and Yugoslavia. Eventually all the United Nations signed the Atlantic Charter.

Attlee, Clement Richard. 1883-. British statesman. After being admitted to the bar (1905), he became a social worker and a lecturer in the London School of Economics prior to World War I, in which he gained the rank of major. He entered Parliament in 1922 and held posts in the Labor cabinets in 1924 and 1929. In 1935 he succeeded George Lansbury as party leader. In Churchill's war-time coalition cabinet he was lord of the privy seal (1940-42), deputy prime minister (1942-45), dominions secretary (1942-43), and lord president of the council (1943-45). He was prime minister in the Labor government from 1945 to 1951.

Augsburg, Diet of. 1530. An imperial diet presided over by Charles V. Here the Protestants presented the *Augsburg Confession,* prepared by Philip Melanchthon. It was designed to set up the principal tenets of Protestantism, but to be as little obnoxious to Catholics as possible. From Strassburg, where the teachings of Zwingli had made considerable progress, there came the *Confession of Four Cities.* This document resembled the Augsburg Confession in most details. The Diet commanded abolition of all innovations and strict adherence to the Edict of Worms (q.v.), the decree that proclaimed Luther to be a heretic. The result was to divide the German people into two definite parties.

Augsburg Interim. See Schmalkaldic War.

Augsburg, Religious Peace of. 1555. An agreement between the Emperor and the Protestant princes of Germany which ended the religious wars of the 1540's and 50's. This agreement applied only to Catholics and Lutherans. It was decided that any state of the Empire might allow Catholic and Lutheran worship, or permit one and exclude the other. An individual was supposed to practice the religion which his state government prescribed. This was the doctrine of *cuius regio eius religio* (of whom the region of him the religion). The treaty ended religious wars in Germany in the 16th century. However, religious wars broke out again with great violence during the first half of the 17th century.

Augustine, Saint. d. 604. "Apostle of the English." In 596 he was sent with forty monks as missionaries to the English by Pope Gregory I. Baptized Ethelbert, King of Kent (597). Consecrated Archbishop (601). Founded the monastery of Christ Church, Canterbury.

Augustus II (*called* **the Strong**). 1670-1733. Elector of Saxony (1694-1733). King of Poland (1697-1704, 1709-33). He made an alliance with Peter the Great of Russia (1701). As a result of this alliance, he entered the Great Northern War (q.v.). He was defeated by the Swedes and forced to give the crown of Poland (1704-09) to Stanislaus Leszczynski. He was restored to the throne of Poland after the battle of Poltava (q.v.) (1709).

Aulic Council (Hofrath). Created in 1502 by Emperor Maximilian I, it was the emperor's privy council. Later it became the Austrian Council of State.

Ausgleich (Compromise). 1867. Following the defeat of Austria in the Austro-Prussian War (1867), the Hapsburg dominions were divided into two parts—Austria and Hungary. Each managed its own internal affairs by means of separate parliaments. They had a common sovereign, a common army, and common foreign relations. There was also a dual parliament composed of 60 members chosen by the parliament of Austria and 60 chosen by the parliament of Hungary which sat alternately at Vienna and Budapest to coordinate common defense.

Austen, Jane. 1775-1817. English novelist. She wrote at a time when women rarely wrote for publication. The daughter of a country clergyman, her novels contain a vivid picture of English domestic life. *Pride and Prejudice, Sense and Sensibility,* and *Mansfield Park* are representative works.

Austerlitz, Battle of. Dec. 2, 1805. This was one of Napoleon's greatest victories. Here he defeated the combined Austrian and Russian armies. After this battle the Austrians hastily agreed to an armistice. The Russians retreated.

Australian Ballot, Adoption of in England. 1872. The Australian, or secret, ballot was adopted in England by the Ballot Act of 1872. Gladstone sponsored the measure.

Austrasia. Medieval kingdom of the Franks. It comprised in area parts of eastern France, western Germany, and the Netherlands. Its capital was Metz.

Austria-Hungary, Origin of. Austria was created by Charlemagne as an eastern march (Ostmark) for defense against the Avars. The Avars were one of three groups of Asiatic nomads who invaded central Europe. The first group was the Huns, who invaded Europe in the 4th and 5th centuries. The Avars appeared in the 8th century. The Magyars, or Hungarians, invaded Europe in the 9th century, destroyed the great Moravian kingdom, and conquered Transylvania. Their westward advance was halted at the battle of Augsburg (955). Under the Babenburg dynasty (976-1246), Vienna became a cultural center. Hungary, under its two great rulers—Geza (972-997) and Stephen (997-1038)—was Christianized and developed into a strong kingdom. It annexed Croatia in 1102. During the 13th century, Hungary declined because of feudal wars and the Mongol invasions.

In 1273, Rudolf of Hapsburg became Holy Roman Emperor. He strengthened his dynastic hold on central Europe by making his three sons rulers of Austria, Styria, and Carinthia respectively.

Frederick III (Hapsburg) (1440-93) created the Austrian Empire by initiating a series of favorable marriages. He married his son Maximilian I (1493-1519) to Mary of Burgundy (heiress of Burgundy and the Netherlands). Their son married the heiress of Aragon and Castile, and thus brought the vast Spanish possessions in the New World under Hapsburg control. Maximilian concluded an agreement with Ladislas II, of the Lithuanian-Polish house of Jagiello and King of Bohemia (1471-1516) and of Hungary (1490-1516), by which Maximilian or his heirs would inherit the thrones of Bohemia and Hungary should the family of Ladislas become extinct. Ladislas' only son, Louis II, King of Bohemia and Hungary (1516-1526), was killed in the battle of Mohacs against the Turks. Maximilian's younger son Ferdinand I, who inherited the Austrian lands upon the death of his father (1519) and became Holy Roman Emperor after Charles V (1556), married Louis' sister Anne and was chosen King of Bohemia and of Hungary in 1526.

As the result of victory at Mohacs, the Turks occupied most of Hungary. For nearly two hundred years, the Turks continued their attacks upon Austria. In 1529 and 1683 they besieged Vienna. Following their repulse at Vienna in 1683, the Turks went on the defensive. In 1687, at the second battle of Mohacs, the Austrians defeated the Turks. The Hapsburgs were then elected hereditary rulers of Hungary. The treaty of Carlowitz (1699) gave Austria legal possession of Hungary, Transylvania, Croatia, and Slavonia. War with the Turks finally ended in 1791.

Austrian Constitution. 1861. Following defeat in the Austro-Sardinian War (1859), Austria granted additional powers of local self-government to the provincial diets and restored Hungarian political institutions to the status quo ante 1849. In 1861, a formal constitution provided for a united parliament of the whole empire, elected by the provincial diets, to meet in Vienna to perform functions of taxation and legislation.

Austrian Netherlands. Name for modern Belgium. Passed from control of the

Spanish at Treaty of Utrecht (April, 1713). By this treaty, the provinces of Artois, Flanders, and Hainault were ceded to France. Belgium remained under Austrian control until conquered by the French (1792).

Austrian Succession, War of. 1740-48. Emperor Charles VI, the last male of the Hapsburg line, died in October, 1740. Before his death, he had called his nobles together and had them swear to support his daughter, Maria Theresa (the so-called Pragmatic Sanction) (q.v.). Believing that Maria Theresa would not get complete support from her people and being anxious to secure additional territory, Frederick II (the Great) of Prussia now made war on Austria. He was joined by France, Spain, Bavaria, and Saxony. England and Holland were the principal allies of Austria. Although Maria Theresa's power tottered perilously at one time, she was able to regroup her forces and allies and to emerge from the war with virtually all of her territory intact and with her husband accepted as Emperor. Her only major loss was Silesia, which was lost to Prussia. The war ended with the Treaty of Aix-la-Chapelle (Oct. 18, 1748) (q.v.).

Austro-Prussian War. Also known as the "Seven Weeks' War" (1866). To achieve the unification of Germany, Bismarck realized that Austria would have to be expelled from the Germanic Confederation. By skillful diplomacy, he induced Austria to attack Prussia over the fate of Schleswig and Holstein (see Danish War). Before the outbreak of war, Bismarck had isolated Austria as follows: (1) he was assured of England's neutrality because of trade considerations and because England wished to build up a strong rival to France; (2) he had secured the gratitude of the Czar by assisting him to quell the revolt in Warsaw in 1863; (3) he had secured (at Biarritz) from Napoleon III the promise of neutrality; (4) he had made an alliance with Italy. The war ended with surprising abruptness with the single battle of Sadowa (Königgrätz) on July 3, 1866. By the Treaty of Prague (Aug. 23, 1866) Austria lost no territory, except Venetia to Italy and her claims to Holstein to Prussia, and was forced to pay only a small indemnity. However, Austria had to consent to the dissolution of the Germanic Confederation and to Prussia's position as leader of the Germans.

Because they sided with Austria against her, Prussia annexed the north German states of Hanover, Hesse-Cassel, Nassau, and the free city of Frankfurt-on-Main. She also annexed Schleswig and Holstein.

Austro-Sardinian War (1859). By clever diplomacy, Cavour (q.v.) incited Austria to declare war on Sardinia. According to the Plombières agreement, Napoleon III of France then intervened on behalf of Sardinia. After defeating the Austrians at Magenta, the allies entered Milan. Shortly after occurred the bloody battle of Solferino. Though the Austrians were defeated, they fell back on their strong fortresses in the Quadrilateral. Fearing more bloodshed, Napoleon concluded an armistice with Francis Joseph of Austria at Villafranca (1859). According to this agreement, Sardinia was to receive Lombardy, but Venetia was to remain under Austria. The pope was to be made president of an Italian confederation. The terms of the truce were ratified by the Treaty of Zürich (Nov. 1859).

Auto-da-fé. 15th-18th century. Literally, an act of faith. The public judicial announcement, with its execution, of the sentence of the Inquisition (q.v.), together with attendant ceremonies. Most of these celebrations took place in Spain and Portugal and their colonies. The first recorded auto-da-fé was held by Torquemada (q.v.) in Seville in 1481.

Averroës (Ibn Ruschd). 1126-1198. Spanish-Arabian philosopher and physician. Born Cordova. Wrote many treatises on jurisprudence, astronomy, grammar, and medicine. His most important works were commentaries on Plato and Aristotle.

Axis, Berlin-Rome. Oct. 25, 1936. A pact between Germany and Italy which marked the division of Europe into contending groups. The Axis was solidified by an Italo-German treaty of alliance (May 22, 1939). This alliance was later extended (Sept. 27, 1940) to include Japan. (See Anti-Comintern Pact.) Later, Hungary, Romania, Bulgaria, Slovakia, and Croatia all adhered to this alliance.

Axis Satellite Nations, Fate of. On Dec. 12, 1946 the Council of Foreign Ministers (q.v.), meeting in New York, completed peace treaties with Italy, Hungary, Bulgaria, Romania, and Finland. On June 5, 1947, the United States Senate ratified all of them except the treaty with Finland (the United States never declared war on Finland).

Italy lost small border regions to France and Yugoslavia, and Trieste (which became a Free Territory under supervision of the Security Council of the UN). To Greece, Italy ceded the Dodecanese Islands. The future of Italy's African colonies was to be decided later. (Italy retains a trusteeship over Somaliland. Eritrea has become independent and is incorporated into Ethiopia. Libya has become an independent kingdom.) Italy was to pay reparations to the extent of 360 million dollars to Greece, Ethiopia, Albania, and the USSR. Severe restrictions were placed on future military strength.

Hungary ceded some territory to Czechoslovakia and the eastern half of Transylvania to Romania. Reparations of 300 million dollars were to be paid to the USSR, Czechoslovakia, and Yugoslavia.

Romania lost Bessarabia and Bukowina

to the USSR and paid Russia 300 million dollars in reparations.

Bulgaria lost no territory, but was forced to pay reparations to Greece and Yugoslavia.

Finland lost the province of Petsamo to Russia and paid to Russia 300 million dollars.

Azaña, Manuel. 1880-1940. Spanish statesman. He was a lawyer, author, and teacher in Madrid University. War minister (1931), prime minister (1931-33), president (1936-39). He was a leader of the Republican Left. In Feb. 1939, he fled to France, where he lived until his death.

B

Baboeuf, François Emile (*pseudonym* Gracchus). 1760-97. French agitator. Journalist during the French Revolution, advocating communistic theories. Involved in a conspiracy to overthrow the Directory (1797) and reestablish the Constitution of 1793.

Babylonian Captivity. 1309-1377. Clement V (pope 1305-14) was a Frenchman. He was a good friend of Philip the Fair, King of France. At Philip's request, which he feared to refuse, he removed the papal residence from Rome to Avignon (1309). Clement VI (pope 1342-52), also a Frenchman, purchased Avignon for the papacy (1348). The last pope to reside in Avignon was Gregory XI (pope 1370-78). This period of residence in Avignon is called the Babylonian Captivity. It weakened the power of the papacy, since the doctrine of papal supremacy was founded upon the fact that St. Peter had been the first bishop of Rome.

Bach, Johann Sebastian. 1685-1750. German organist, composer, and master of counterpoint. Born at Eisenach. Violinist in the royal chapel orchestra in Weimar (1703). Organist at Arnstadt (1703). Organist in Mülhausen (1707). Court organist, Weimar (1708). Court concertmeister, Weimar (1714-17). Court Kapellmeister, Köthen (1717-23). Cantor in the Thomasschule and director of university music in Leipzig (from 1723). He composed many works for the church. *Vocal:* about 200 church cantatas, a mass, oratorios, magnificats, etc. *Instrumental:* preludes, fugues, toccatas, fantasias, etc. Also *The Well-Tempered Clavier* and the *Art of Fugue.* In addition he composed much music for various instruments. Four of his sons and one grandson were outstanding musicians.

Wilhelm Friedmann (1710-84), the "Halle Bach," was organist at Dresden (1733-47) and at Halle (1747-64). He composed music for organ and clavier.

Karl Philipp Emanuel (1714-88), the "Berlin or Hamburg Bach," was a composer who pioneered the sonata form. He was chamber musician to Frederick the Great (1740) in Berlin and director of church music in Hamburg (from 1767).

Johann Christoph Friedrich (1732-95), the "Bückeburg Bach," was Kapellmeister in Bückeburg (1756) and a composer of sonatas, oratorios, motets, etc.

Johann Christian (1735-82), the "Milan, or London Bach," was cathedral organist in Milan (1760) and music master for Queen Charlotte Sophia in London (1762). He composed operas, oratorios, arias, etc.

Wilhelm Friedrich Ernest (1759-1845), son of J. C. F. Bach, was an organist, pianist, and composer. Kapellmeister in Berlin (1789).

Bacon, Francis (Lord Verulam and Viscount St. Albans). 1561-1626. English philosopher, statesman, and scientist. He sought to win the favor of Queen Elizabeth by attaching himself to her various favorites. But his efforts met with only moderate success. Upon the accession of James I, Bacon's rise was rapid. He became attorney-general (1613), privy-councillor (1616), lord keeper (1617), and lord chancellor (1618). His fall from favor in 1621 was equally rapid, when it was proven that he had accepted bribes from suitors in his court. He was fined heavily, imprisoned, and banished from parliament and the court. He was soon released from prison and was pardoned. But he never returned to parliament and the court. He wrote his famous scientific treatise, *"Novum Organum,"* in 1620. Other notable writings are *"Essays," "New Atlantis,"* and *"History of Henry VII."* Bacon's contribution to philosophy and science was his formulation and introduction of the inductive method.

Bacon, Roger. 1214-1294. A monkish philosopher who was born of a well-to-do family at Ilchester, England; studied at Oxford and Paris; joined the Franciscan Order upon his return to Oxford; physics seems to have been his chief interest. He invented the magnifying glass; wrote about optics; prepared a rectified calendar; and understood the nature of gunpowder; his greatest work is called *Opus Magnus.*

Bagdolio, Pietro. 1871-. Italian field marshal. After serving in the First World War, he was governor of Libya (1929-33). He finished the conquest of Ethiopia (1936). He was made duke of Addis Ababa, viceroy of Ethiopia, and chief of staff of the Italian army (to 1940). After the fall of Mussolini (1943), he was made premier and negotiated an armistice with the United Nations. He resigned (1944) because of much opposition.

Baillie. Royal officer of medieval France whose duty it was to administer matters for the king within his district (bailiwick). He was required to hold court once a month, to collect all the money possible for the king, and to deliver the money in Paris.

Bajazet. Name of two rulers of the Ottoman Turks:
Bajazet I (called **Yilderin, lightning).** 1347-1403. Sultan (1389-1403). He overran the countries of southeast Europe. At Nicopolis (Bulgaria) he defeated an allied Christian army composed of French, Poles, and Hungarians. He might have captured Constantinople had his eastern flank not been threatened by the Mongols. He was defeated by the Mongols at Ankara (1402) and taken prisoner.
Bajazet II. 1447-1513. Sultan (1481-1512). He strengthened the Turkish power in Europe by wars against Poland, Hungary, and Venice. Engaged in a long struggle with Persia. Abdicated (1512) in favor of his son Selim.

Bakewell, Robert. 1725-95. English stockbreeder. Up to his time, sheep had been reared for wool and cattle for milk and draught purposes. He determined to breed fat types that would yield more mutton and beef. His efforts were most successful.

Bakunin, Mikhail Aleksandrovich. 1814-76. Russian anarchist. Born in Tuer. Educated in St. Petersburg military school. Served in the Imperial Guard. Traveled in western Europe (1841-47). Refused to return to Russia and lost his property there. Expelled from Paris (1847). Active in European revolutionary movements (1848-49). Exiled to Siberia (1855). Escaped (1861). The leading anarchist of Europe (1861-72). Principal tenets: atheism, destruction of the state, ultraindividualistic rights. He is the founder of Nihilism (q.v.) in Russia.

Baldwin, Stanley. First Earl Baldwin of Bewdley. 1867-1947. British statesman. Active head of iron and steel firm (1892-1916). He entered Parliament in 1908. He was prime minister in Conservative governments in 1923 and 1924-29 and (1935-37) in the National government.

Baliol, John. 1249-1315. On the death of the Scotch queen, the Maid of Norway (1290), he became a claimant for the crown of Scotland. Supported by Edward I of England, he was crowned king (1292). In 1295, he concluded an alliance with France, then at war with England, and was defeated and imprisoned. In 1302 he was permitted to retire to his estates in Normandy.

Balkan Pact. Feb. 9, 1934. A treaty between Turkey, Greece, Romania, and Yugoslavia. It created an alliance like the Little Entente (q.v.). It was designed to protect the Balkans from the aggression of other countries. Its weakness was the absence of Bulgaria.

"Balkanizing." Dividing up a geographical region into a number of small countries as was done in the Balkan Peninsula in the late 19th and early 20th centuries. Since the problems that follow division are usually more acute than the ones that precede division, "balkanizing" is a term of reproach, rather than of approbation.

Balkan Wars. 1912, 1913. The Balkan League (formed in 1912) encouraged the Albanians to revolt against the Turks. Montenegro, Serbia, Greece, and Bulgaria then joined in the war. The League was victorious and at London (May 30, 1913) secured all of Turkey's European possessions except that portion east of a line drawn from Enos on the Aegean Sea to Midia on the Black Sea. Greece secured Crete. In the quarrel over the division of the former Turkish possessions, the members of the League attacked Bul-

garia (1913), which was defeated. In the Treaty of Bucharest (Aug. 10, 1913), Bulgaria was forced to surrender western Macedonia and to give some territory to Romania. The important port of Salonika went to Greece. At the behest of the Great Powers, the Kingdom of Albania was created. Greece occupied all the Aegean Islands except the 12 Sporades held by Italy. In these wars, Greece increased its territory 68%; Bulgaria, 29%; Serbia, 82%; and Montenegro, 62%.

Ball, John. d. 1381. A priest who was one of the leaders in Wat Tyler's rebellion (q.v.).

Baltic States, Soviet annexation of. Sept.-Oct. 1939. On Sept. 29, 1939, the day after Germany and Russia partitioned Poland, the USSR signed a pact of mutual assistance with Estonia. Within two weeks the USSR signed similar agreements with Latvia and Lithuania. All three pacts contained promises that the USSR would not interfere with the liberty of the Baltic States. On June 14, 1940, the USSR presented an ultimatum to Lithuania, which charged that Lithuania had violated the pact. On June 16, 1940, similar ultimatums were sent to Estonia and Latvia. Each document demanded the right to have Red troops enter the Baltic States. Thus the Baltic States were occupied by the USSR. Following occupation, the constitutional governments of the Baltic States resigned and were replaced by Russian puppets. After plebiscites, all three countries became republics in the Soviet Union.

Balzac, Honoré de. 1799-1859. French novelist. He is one of France's greatest novelists and the founder of the realistic school. He wrote a series of novels providing a many-sided picture of contemporary French life under the general title of *La Comédie Humaine.* His aim was to present a complete picture of modern civilization. In his attempt to carry out this impossible design, he produced what is almost a literature in itself. His industry was phenomenal. He wrote 85 novels in 20 years, and he was a fastidious writer. A "definitive edition" of his works was published in 24 volumes in 1869-75.

Bank of England, Foundation of. 1694. The bank was created through the activities of Charles Montagu. It had authority to engage in private banking, to borrow and lend upon security, to deal in bullion and bills of exchange, and to issue notes. The last function was made a monopoly in 1697.

Bank of France, Founding of the. Feb. 13, 1800. One of the most acute problems which Bonaparte inherited from the Directory was the chaotic state of French finances. By strict economy and a new, sound method of tax collection, he balanced the budget. After this he was able to establish the Bank of France, an institution which had the sole privilege of issuing notes and regulating public credit. The Bank remained a privately-owned institution until 1934, when it was nationalized.

Bank for International Settlement. An international bank chartered in Switzerland in 1930 according to the proposals of the Young Plan (q.v.). The bank was founded to assist the transfer of international funds (see European Payments Union), to act as trustee for German reparations (see Reparations), and to foster the cooperation of central banks.

Barbon, Nicholas. 1640-98. An English economist who anticipated Adam Smith and the Physiocrats in advocating free trade.

Barebones Parliament. See Nominated Parliament.

Barneveldt, Jan van Olden. 1547-1619. Dutch statesman; champion of Dutch independence; grand pensionary of the Province of Holland (1586); negotiated a treaty with Spain (1609); illegally arrested (1618); condemned as traitor and executed (1619).

Barras, Vicomte Paul François Jean Nicolas de. 1755-1829. French politician. Member of the National Convention. He took an active part in the overthrow of Robespierre (1794). As commander-in-chief, he appointed Bonaparte to defend the Convention (whence the famous "whiff of grapeshot" episode). Member and dominant force in the Directory (q.v.). He secured the appointment of Bonaparte to command the French Army in Italy. He arranged the marriage of Bonaparte to Josephine de Beauharnais. He was banished from Paris (1799-1815) for intriguing for a Bourbon restoration.

Barricades, Day of. See War of the Three Henrys.

Batavian Republic. 1795-1806. When Holland was conquered by the French Revolutionary armies, it was organized as the Batavian Republic. In 1806, Napoleon made it into the Kingdom of Holland for his brother, Louis Bonaparte.

Bathory, Stephen. 1533-1586. Prince of Transylvania (1571-76) and king of Poland (1575-86). A famous soldier, he was elected king of Poland by the nobility. In a war with Russia (1579-82), he gained victory over Ivan the Terrible.

"Battle of Wheat." An attempt by the Fascist government of Italy to increase domestic production of wheat. Prizes for wheat production were contributed by the government, which also encouraged the formation of farm-cooperatives. An educational campaign to improve farm methods was inaugurated. Attempts were made to induce Italians to eat less spaghetti and macaroni. Later the campaign became known as the "Battle of Agriculture" and efforts were made to increase the yield of rice, oats, and corn, as well as wheat.

Batu. Mongolian prince; grandson of Genghis Khan. In 1237 he invaded Russia, capturing Kiev in 1240, defeating combined German and Polish armies, defeating and subjugating Hungary and Bulgaria. He thus brought under Mongolian sway the south Russian steppes, the northern Russian forests, and the lower Danube.

Bazaine, Achille. 1811-88. Marshal of France. Born in Versailles. Served in the Crimean War (1854-56). In command of French troops in Mexico (1863). A leading French commander in the Franco-Prussian War (1870-71). Defeated at Gravelotte (1870). Besieged in Metz. Surrendered the fortress (Oct. 27, 1870). Court-martialed (1873). Sentenced to death. Sentence commuted to 20 years' imprisonment. Escaped (1874) and fled to Spain, where he lived in exile.

Beauharnais. Name of a French noble family of Orléans. Prominent members include:

Alexandre, Vicomte de Beauharnais (1760-94), army officer. Born in Martinique. He served under Rochambeau in the American Revolution. Member of the Estates-General (1789). Commander of the Army of the Rhine (1793). Blamed for the surrender of Mainz (1793). Guillotined (1794).

Josephine Beauharnais (1763-1814), wife of Alexandre. Born in Martinique (Marie Josephine Rose Tascher de la Pagerie). She married Napoleon Bonaparte (1796). Empress of France (1804). Divorced by Napoleon (1809).

Eugène de Beauharnais (1781-1824), son of Alexandre and Josephine. Served under Napoleon in Egypt (1798-99).

Viceroy of Italy (1805). Married (1806) Princess Amalie Auguste of Bavaria. Adopted by Napoleon and made heir-apparent to the crown of Italy (1806). Commanded an army corps in the Russian campaign (1812). He retired to Bavaria (1814) and became in 1817 the duke of Leuchtenberg and prince of Eichstätt.

Hortense Beauharnais (1783-1837), daughter of Alexandre and Josephine. Married (1802) Louis Bonaparte, King of Holland. One of her sons became Emperor Napoleon III.

Bebel, August. 1840-1913. German Social Democratic leader and writer. He joined the German labor movement (1861). Was converted to Marxism by William Liebknecht (1867). Cofounder of the German Social Democratic Labor Party (1869). Member of the Reichstag (1871-81; 1883-1913). Editor of *Vorwärts*. He wrote *Der Deutsche Bauenkrieg* (1876).

Becket, Thomas à. 1118-1170. Trained as a youth in knightly exercises, he later studied canonical jurisprudence in Church schools and was given several important positions by the Church. In 1155, one year after Henry II became king, he was appointed chancellor of England. He lived in sumptuous style, and fought like a knight in military campaigns. In 1162, he was made Archbishop of Canterbury. He resigned his office as chancellor and lived as a rigid ascetic. He figured as a champion of the rights of the Church against aggressions of the king and nobles. He was forced by the king to submit to the Constitution of Clarendon (q.v.). When Henry tried to confiscate his goods, Becket escaped to France to appeal to the pope. After spending several years abroad, Becket returned to England in 1170. Fresh quarrels between him and Henry now broke out. At last, Henry exclaimed: "Of the cowards that eat my bread, is there none will rid me of this turbulent priest?" Four knights —Fitzurse, Tracy, Brito, and Morville— overheard these words and slew Becket before the altar of St. Benedict in Canterbury Cathedral. Two years afterwards, Becket was canonized.

Bede, the Venerable. 673-735. "The father of English History." For many years head of the monastery of Jarrow on the Tyne, he compiled the *Ecclesiastical History of the English Nation,* extending from 55 B.C. to 731 A.D.

"Beer-Hall Putsch." Nov. 8-11, 1923. An unsuccessful *coup* against the government organized by Ludendorff and Hitler. It took place in Munich. One reason for its failure was that it ran counter to the schemes of a second group of conspirators. Hitler was sentenced to five years in prison for his part in the Putsch. While in prison he wrote *Mein Kampf.* He was released after serving less than one year.

Beethoven, Ludwig van. 1770-1827. German composer of Flemish descent. He was born in Bonn, where his father was a tenor singer in the Elector of Cologne's band. His father was his first teacher. In 1783 Ludwig joined the band as an accompanist. In 1784 he was made second organist. He afterwards played viola in the band. In 1792 the Elector sent him to Vienna to study under Haydn and Albrechtsberger. He remained in Vienna or in the country nearby for most of the remainder of his life. He never received an official appointment. From 1798 he was afflicted by defective hearing. He became totally deaf in 1819. His last years were saddened because of family troubles, his deafness, and his extreme hypochondria. His instrumental compositions include 9 symphonies, numerous sonatas for piano solo or piano and other instruments, 5 concertos for piano and orchestra, a violin concerto in D, 21 sets of variations for piano solo, string quartets, etc., music to *Prometheus* and to *Egmont.* His vocal compositions include one oratorio (The Mount of Olives), one opera (Fidelio), 2 masses, cantatas, canons, songs, etc.

"Beggars." A term coined on April 8, 1566 to describe those people of the Netherlands who opposed the policies of Philip II. Later, the name was employed to describe all Hollanders who fought against the Spanish in the War of Liberation.

"Beggars of the Sea." Dutch seamen who fought against the Spanish during the War of Liberation (1568-76).

Belgium, Independence of. 1839. The union of Belgium with Holland following the Congress of Vienna (1815) was not a happy one. The Dutch were traditionally hostile to France, mostly Protestant, and almost wholly engaged in agriculture and commerce. The Belgians were sympathetic to France, overwhelmingly Roman Catholic, and industrial. When King William I of Holland alienated the Belgians by imposing the Dutch language on them, hampering their schools, and taxing their factories, the Belgians revolted. At London (1831) an independent state of Belgium was proclaimed. It was to be a constitutional monarchy, headed by Leopold of Saxe-Coburg. However, the French had to invade Belgium and capture Antwerp and the English navy had to blockade Dutch ports before the Dutch evacuated Belgium. In 1839, a treaty, signed by Great Britain, France, Russia, Austria, and Prussia, guaranteed the independence and neutrality of Belgium. In the same year, the Dutch finally acknowledged the sovereignty of Belgium.

Belisarius. 505?-565. General of the Eastern Roman Empire. Born in Illyria. He served with great distinction under Emperor Justinian. He saved Justinian by suppressing the Nika riots (532).

Conquered the Vandal kingdom in Africa (534), Sicily (535), and southern Italy (536-37). He occupied Rome (536) and Ravenna (540). In his later years he fell into disfavor and was blinded by Justinian's orders.

Bell, Gertrude Margaret Lowthian. 1868-1926. British archaeologist and agent. Educated at Oxford. She traveled much in the Middle East and did intelligence work for her government during World War I. She helped form the postwar administration of Iraq and Transjordan. Author of *The Palace* and *Mosque of Ukhaidir.*

Bellini. Name of a family of celebrated Venetian artists. The father, Jacopo Bellini (1400-70), brought to Venice the skill of Florentine painting. His eldest son, Gentile Bellini (1429-1507), was a distinguished portrait painter. With his brother, he decorated some of the famous buildings in Venice. His more famous brother, Giovanni Bellini (1430-1516), was influenced by the style and technique of his brother-in-law, Andrea Mantegna. Giovanni is admired for his beautiful airy backgrounds (they contain the germ of landscape painting) and his rich tone and poetic feeling.

Benedict, St. 480-543. Founder of western monasticism. Born in Spoleto. As a boy of 14 he withdrew from the world to a grotto near Subiaco for religious exercises. The fame of his piety caused him to be chosen abbot of a monastery at Vicovaro. Finding discipline there poor, he left and established a monastery at Monte Cassino. Here he promulgated his famous *Rule,* which has become the model for all subsequent monastic orders.

Benedictus Levita, Capitulary of. 847. A famous forgery by a deacon of Mainz. These documents were alleged to have been written by Pippin, Charlemagne, and Ludwig the Pious. The purport of them was that clergy, because of their spiritual office, were superior to secular officials and, therefore, could not be tried by the ordinary laws of the land.

Benelux. 1947. A tripartite customs union formed by Belgium, the Netherlands, and Luxemburg.

Benes, Eduard. 1884-1948. Czechoslovak statesman. Born in Kozlany. A professor of sociology in the University of Prague, he became an exile during World War I. He worked with Masaryk for Czechoslovak independence. He was foreign minister (1918-33) and premier as well (1921-22). He was president (1935-38). He resigned the presidency in 1938 and went into exile. In 1939 he became president-in-exile, living first in France and later in England. In 1945 he returned to Czechoslovakia and was re-elected president in 1946. After the communist *coup* of 1948 he was president in name only. He resigned, to die a few months later.

Bentham, Jeremy. 1748-1832. English jurist and philosopher. One of the chief exponents of utilitarianism. Called to the bar (1772). He made recommendations for improvement in the mode of criminal punishment (1778). He wrote *Defense of Usury* (1787), a treatise on economics in which he followed the lead of Adam Smith. In 1789 he published *Introduction to the Principles of Morals and Legislation* in which he expounded his basic ethical doctrine that morality of action is determined by utility; the object of all conduct and legislation is "the greatest happiness of the greatest number"—the key phrase of Benthamism.

Berchtold, Count Leopold von. 1863-1942. Austrian statesman. Ambassador to St. Petersburg (1907-11). Foreign minister (1912-15). He prepared the ultimatum to Serbia (1914), which precipitated World War I. He is one of the leaders who must assume grave responsibility for beginning the war.

Bering Expedition. Sent out by Peter the Great of Russia in 1724-30 to see whether Asia and America were joined, not realizing that the problem had been solved by Dezhnev in 1648. Interest aroused in Russia by the Bering Expedition led to the sending out of the Great Northern Expedition of 1733-1743 which was one of the most remarkable scientific expeditions in history.

Berlin, Congress of. 1878. The treaty of San Stefano at the conclusion of the Russo-Turkish War (1877-78) aroused the anger of Great Britain and Austria-Hungary, as it made Russia the dominant power in the Near East. The Austro-Hungarians claimed that the treaty was a revision of the treaty of Paris (1856) and could not be valid without the consent of the nations which had sworn to uphold the treaty (Great Britain, Germany, Austria-Hungary, France, Italy, Russia, and Turkey). The Congress of Berlin was called under the leadership of Germany. (In this connection Bismarck referred to himself as the "honest broker." Since Germany had nothing to lose in the conference, he assumed a neutral attitude.) Disraeli gave the conference a dramatic air, since he threatened to walk out several times, and his departure would have been tantamount to a declaration of war against Russia. The accomplishments of the Congress were incorporated into the Treaty of Berlin (July 13, 1878): 1. Russia acquired part of Bessarabia. Romania was compensated for the loss of this region by being allotted the barren Dobruja. Russia also retained Ardahan, Kars, and Batoum, and some Armenian districts. 2. Austria-Hungary was given the right to occupy and administer the Turkish provinces of Bosnia and Herzegovina and to keep garrisons and maintain roads

in the adjacent Turkish sanjak of Novi-Bazar.
3. Great Britain secured the promise that Russia would not seek additional territory in Asia Minor; that the Sultan would treat his Christian subjects with justice. As surety for these pledges, Britain was allowed to hold and administer Cyprus.
4. Bulgaria was granted autonomy.
5. The independence of Romania, Serbia, and Montenegro was recognized.
6. Greece secured territory in Thessaly.

The Russians believed that Bismarck had not remained neutral as he professed, but had supported the claims of Austria-Hungary at the expense of Russia. From this time forward, relations between Germany and Russia worsened.

Berlin Decree. Nov. 21, 1806. Napoleon proclaimed a blockade of England and the closing of the continent to English goods. Thus he began the Continental System (q.v.).

Berlioz, Hector. 1803-69. French composer. A pioneer of modern orchestration. His compositions include *Damnation of Faust, Harold in Italy, The Trojans,* and *Symphonie Fantastique.*

Bernadotte, Jean Baptiste Jules. 1763-1844. Son of a lawyer, he was born in Pau. He became a general in the French Revolutionary armies and served with great distinction under Napoleon. He achieved great fame for his administration of Hanover and Bavaria. One of the 18 imperial marshals of France. He was elected (1810) as the heir to the throne of Sweden. King of Sweden (1818-44) under the name of Charles XIV John. Founder of the present royal family of Sweden. One of his famous descendants was Count Folke Bernadotte (1895-1948), the nephew of Gustave V of Sweden. He acted as mediator in both World Wars. He was appointed by the UN to mediate between Israelis and Arabs in Palestine. He produced a partition plan, but was assassinated by Jewish terrorists on Sept. 17, 1948.

Bernard of Clairvaux, Saint. 1091-1153. French ecclesiastic. Founder and first abbot of the Cistercian monastery of Clairvaux. He exerted much influence at the papal court. He opposed the teachings of Abelard. He was responsible for starting the Second Crusade (1147).

Bernhardi, Friedrich von. 1849-1930. German general and author. Born in St. Petersburg. Although he held numerous high commands, he is best known as the author of *Germany and the Next War* (1911), a work which helped to prepare German thinking for World War I.

Berruguéte, Alonso. 1486-1561. Spanish sculptor and painter; pupil of Michelangelo; court sculptor, painter, and chamberlain to Charles V.

Bessarabia, Annexation of by the USSR. June, 27, 1940. On June 26, 1940, the USSR informed Romania that "justice" demanded the return to Russia of Bessarabia, a region which Romania annexed from Russia in 1919. In addition, northern Bukowina was also to be ceded because of the "community of historic interest" between that region and Russia. King Carol II appealed to Berlin and Rome for advice. He was evidently told to accede to the demand. On the next day Russian troops occupied both regions. They have since become the Moldavian Republic, one of the 16 republics in the USSR.

Bessemer, Sir Henry. 1813-98. English inventor. He obtained patents (1855 ff.) for the manufacture of steel by a method which is since called the Bessemer process. His steel works at Sheffield specialized in making arms and steel rails.

Bethlen, Istvan (Stephen), Count. 1874-1951. Hungarian statesman. Born in

Transylvania. He was the leader of the "White" (counter-revolutionary) movement in the days immediately following World War I. He was premier from 1921-31, and greatly promoted the economic reconstruction of Hungary. He retired from politics in 1939.

Bethmann-Hollweg, Theobald von. 1856-1921. German statesman. Chancellor of the German Empire (1909-17). He advocated greater autonomy for Alsace-Lorraine and other reforms. He referred to Belgian neutrality treaty as a "scrap of paper." Forced out of office by Hindenburg and Ludendorff (1917).

Bevan, Aneurin. 1897-. British Labor politician. A coal miner and trade union leader, he became minister of health in 1945 and administered the program of socialized medicine instituted by the Labor government.

Bevin, Ernest. 1881-1951. British Labor leader and statesman. After working as a longshoreman, he became a trade union organizer. He unified 32 separate unions into the Transport and General Workers' Union (1922). In the Churchill war coalition cabinet (1940-45) he held the post of Minister of Labor and National Service. In the Attlee government he was Foreign Secretary (1945-51). A cardinal principle of his was opposition to the Soviet Union.

Bianchi and Neri (Whites and Blacks). Two factions of medieval Florence which supported the great families of Cerchi and Donati. Violent feuds took place between these factions.

Bill of Rights, English. 1689. The convention which acknowledged William and Mary to be joint sovereigns of England met for a second session Oct. 19, 1689. Its chief work was to turn the Declaration of Rights into a Bill. This Bill of Rights is one of the cornerstones of

English liberties (along with the Magna Carta and the Petition of Rights). It states:

(1) Suspending courts is illegal.

(2) Levying money without the consent of Parliament is illegal.

(3) Subjects may petition the king: prosecutions for such petitioning are illegal.

(4) The king may not obtain a private army.

(5) Election of members of Parliament should be free.

(6) There should be freedom of debate in Parliament.

(7) There should not be excessive bail, fines, or cruel or unusual punishments.

(8) Parliament should meet frequently.

(9) A sovereign professing the "popish" religion should not reign in England.

Bishop's War. In August, 1640, Charles I invaded Scotland to enforce his religious regulations. His army was defeated. The Scots crossed the border, and occupied Durham and Northumberland. They refused to withdraw unless they were paid an indemnity. Lacking funds for this purpose, Charles was forced to convene a Parliament for the first time since 1629. (Except for the "Short Parliament" of April 13–May 5, 1640.) This was the famous Long Parliament.

Bismarck, Prince Otto Eduard Leopold von. 1815-98. Prussian statesman and first chancellor of the German Empire. Born in Schönhausen. He studied law at Göttingen and Berlin (1832-35). In the Prussian civil service (1836-39). Prussian ambassador to the Germanic Diet at Frankfurt (1851-58) where he strongly opposed the influence of Austria in German affairs. Ambassador to Russia (1859) and to France (1862). President of the Prussian cabinet and foreign minister (1862). In this office he enunciated his famous "blood and iron" policy. He successfully directed wars against Denmark (1864), Austria (1866), and France (1870-71). Created prince (1871). Suc-

cessfully united the German states into an empire (1871). Engaged in an unsuccessful struggle with the Catholics (1872 ff.) (see Kulturkampf). Instituted comprehensive social insurance, protective tariff, and a colonial agency. Resigned (1890) when he disagreed with Kaiser Wilhelm II. Made duke of Lauenburg (1890).

Bizet, Georges. 1838-75. French operatic composer. He entered the Paris Conservatory at the age of nine. He took the *Prix de Rome* in 1857. Although he enjoyed some success during his lifetime, he matured late and died at a relatively young age. His one real masterpiece is the opera *Carmen,* which today enjoys great favor among opera-goers.

Black-and-Tans. English "Auxiliaries" sent over to reinforce the Irish police in the troubled times following the end of World War I. They were so called because their uniform consisted of a khaki outfit with black bands on hat and arm.

Black Death. (1348-1349). A plague of Asiatic origin which first appeared in England in 1348. It killed 1/3 of the inhabitants. Laborers became so scarce that the system of farming had to be changed. Great landlords ceased to farm their estates with the aid of stewards. Instead, they leased the land to tenant cultivators or turned their fields into sheep pastures.

Black Prince. See Edward (the Black Prince).

Blackstone, Sir William. 1723-80. English jurist. He was so unsuccessful in legal practice that he took up teaching law instead. He inaugurated English law courses in several British universities. He published (1765-69) his lectures under the title *Commentaries on the Law of England.* This book has had a great influence upon the practice of law in England and the United States. In later life, Blackstone entered Parliament (1768-70) and became a judge (1770-80).

Blanc, Louis. 1811-82. French socialist leader, often regarded as the father of state socialism. Born in Madrid, Spain. Journalist. He gained prominence through his *Organization du Travail* (1840) in which he contended that the state should create "social workshops." These were to be independent shops in which the workers were to choose the managers and divide the profits. He took an active part in the Revolution of 1848. He became a member of the provisional government and forced the government to set up "National workshops." Following the failure of his plan and the "Terrible June Days" (q.v.) (1848), he took refuge in England. Author of *Histoire de la Révolution Française* (1847-60) and numerous other writings. His brother, Auguste, (1813-82) was an art critic.

Blanche of Castile. 1187?-1252. Daughter of Alfonso IX, King of Castile. Married (1200) Louis, son of Philip II of France. Queen of France during the reign of Louis VIII (1223-26). She was regent during the minority of her son Louis IX (1226-36) and again when he was absent from France on a crusade (1248-52). As regent she proved to be possessed of great courage and cleverness, deep political insight, and remarkable executive ability. Although possessing a strong will and great energy, she was very feminine in appearance and exploited her womanly qualities to the utmost.

"Blank check." On July 5 and 6, 1914, Germany promised to support Austria-Hungary without qualifications in its quarrel with Serbia over the assassination of Archduke Francis Ferdinand. This act provided the impetus which induced Austria-Hungary to issue the ultimatum which began World War I.

Blasco-Ibañez, Vincente. 1867-1928. Spanish novelist. Author of *Blood and Sand, The Four Horsemen of the Apocalypse, Mare Nostrum,* etc.

Blenheim, Battle of. Aug. 13, 1704. Here the English under Marlborough and the Imperial forces under Prince Eugene decisively defeated the French, thus saving the Holy Roman Empire and bringing Bavaria under Imperial authority.

"Blood and Iron." A famous remark by von Bismarck. He said: "Not by speeches and resolutions of majorities are the great questions of the time decided—that was the mistake of 1848 and 1849—but by blood and iron." Because of this remark, and because during his career he adhered to this principle, he is known as the "Iron Chancellor."

"Blood Purge," Nazi. June 30, 1934. Early in 1934 there was serious unrest in the Nazi ranks. Many of the SA (storm troops) had once been communists and resented the fact that the socialistic planks in the Nazi program had not been carried out. Brown Shirt leader, Röhm, also wanted a large number of the SA to be incorporated into the regular army. This Hitler and the generals opposed. The malcontents plotted to overthrow the government. The plot was discovered and its leaders were "purged," that is, assassinated. The purge was carried out by the SS (Elite Guards). It is not known how many people perished. Among the prominent persons who were killed were Röhm, former chancellor von Schleicher and his wife, the leader of Catholic Action, and three of von Papen's assistants. Soon after the purge the size of the SA was drastically reduced, and the members were largely disarmed.

"Bloody Assize." Following the defeat of the attempt of the Duke of Monmouth to overthrow James II, Judge Jeffreys conducted the notorious "Bloody Assize" in the autumn of 1685 in which more than 300 were hanged, drawn and quartered, and 800 more were transported.

Blum, Léon. 1872-1950. French statesman and writer. He entered politics during the Dreyfus Affair. In 1936, he effected a coalition of Radical Socialists, Socialists, and Communists called the Popular Front (q.v.). The Popular Front enacted a kind of New Deal program, proposed nationalizing major industries, and reorganized the Bank of France. Defeated in 1937, Blum served as vice premier (1937-38). He was arrested (1940) by the Vichy government and imprisoned in Austria. After negotiating a credit arrangement with the United States (1946), he again served as premier for two months (1946-47). Author of *Marriage* and *For All Mankind.*

Boccaccio, Giovanni. 1313-1375. Italian writer. Born in Paris. He went to Naples (1323); to Florence (1340). Celebrated writer whose fame rests on the classic *Decamerone* (published in 1353). His writings have influenced many other authors and have furnished plots for Shakespeare, Chaucer, Lessing, Molière, and Keats.

Boerhaave, Herman. 1668-1738. Dutch physician. Professor of medicine and botany (1709) and of chemistry (1718) at Leyden. The most celebrated physician of the 18th century. His great fame rests upon *Institutiones Medicae* (1708) and *Aphorismi de Cognoscendis et Curandis Morbis* (1709). These works were translated into all European languages and into Arabic. He subjected organic matter to chemical processes, and thus founded organic chemistry.

Boethius, Anicius Manlius Severinus. 480?-?524. Roman philosopher. Friend of Theodoric, the Ostrogothic ruler of Rome (500 ff.), who first made him consul (510) and finally executed him for

conspiracy (524). His greatest work is *The Consolation of Philosophy*, written while he awaited his fate in prison in Pavia.

Boileau-Despréaux, Nicolas. 1636-1711. French critic and poet. Born in Paris. Studied law. Author of *Satires* (1666), several volumes of *Epîtres*, and *L'Art Poétique* (1674). His works, especially the last, established the principles upon which classic French literature is grounded.

Bolshevism. A form of revolutionary socialism developed in Russia and based upon the teachings of Karl Marx (q.v.). Today it is generally known as communism. The major point of Bolshevism is the dictatorship of the proletariat for the purpose of creating a communistic society. The term came into being in 1903 at the meeting of the Social Democratic party when Lenin's theory of revolution clashed with that of Martov. Lenin's supporters, who outnumbered the others, were called *Bolsheviki* (majority); the opponents were called *Mensheviki* (minority). Some of the tenets of Bolshevism are belief in an armed revolution of the proletariat; complete abandonment of the bourgeois liberals; hostility to religion; complete nationalization of means of production; and belief in world revolution.

Bonaparte. A Corsican family of Italian origin. The name originally was Buonaparte, but was changed to Bonaparte in 1796 by Napoleon, the most famous member of the family. Napoleon's parents were Carlo Buonaparte (1746-85), a lawyer, and Marie Letizia Ramolino (1750-1836). Of their 13 children, 8 survived.

(1) Joseph (1768-1844). Member of the Council of Five Hundred (1798). He signed the treaties of Luneville and Amiens and assisted in the negotiations which led to the Concordat (1801). King of Naples (1806-08). King of Spain

(1808-13). He resided in Bordentown, N. J. (1815-32) under the name of Comte de Survilliers. He returned to Europe and died in Florence. His wife, Julia Clary (1777-1845), was the daughter of a wealthy merchant of Marseilles and sister-in-law of Bernadotte, King of Sweden.
(2) Napoleon (1769-1821): see Napoleon I.
(3) Maria Anna Elisa (1777-1820). Married (1797) Felice Pasquale Bacciocchi. She was made by Napoleon princess of Lucca and Piombino (1805), and grandduchess of Tuscany (1809).
(4) Lucien (1775-1840). As president of the Council of Five Hundred (1799) he assisted Napoleon in overthrowing the Directory and setting up the Consulate. Ambassador to Madrid (1800). On condition that he would divorce his second wife, he was offered the crowns of Italy and Spain. He refused, and lived quietly on his estate of Canino in the States of the Church. He was created Prince of Canino by the Pope. He retained his Republican views, and having denounced the arrogance of his brother, he was "advised" to emigrate to America. He was captured by the British and interned at Ludlow until 1814. Later, he lived in and near Rome, devoting his time to science and art. Of his eleven children, the following are noteworthy:
(a) Charles Lucien Jules Laurent (1803-57). Naturalist. Resident of Philadelphia (1822-28). Author of *American Ornithology, or History of Birds Inhabiting the United States not Given by Wilson.*
(b) Louis Lucien (1813-91). Philologist. Investigator of the Basque language.
(5) Louis (1778-1846). Married (1802) Hortense de Beauharnais. King of Holland (1806-10). Abdicated when he opposed the Continental System as being injurious to Holland. He took the title of Comte de St. Leu. His third son, Charles Louis Napoleon, became Emperor Napoleon III.
(6) Maria Paulina (Carlotta) (1780-

1825). Married (1797) General Charles Victor Emmanuel Leclerc. After his death, she married (1803) Prince Camillo Borghese and became duchess of Guastalla.
(7) Maria Annunciata (Caroline) (1782-1839). Married Marshal Joachim Murat and became queen of Naples (1808). After 1815 she was known as Countess Lipona.
(8) Jerome (1784-1860). He took refuge from the British in the United States. There he married (1803) Elizabeth Patterson (1785-1879) of Baltimore. The marriage was annulled by the French Council of State (1805). He returned to France and married Catherine of Württemberg. He was made King of Westphalia (1807-13). After the abdication of Napoleon he settled in Florence. He returned to France (1848) and was created Marshal of France (1850). His son, Napoleon Joseph Charles Paul (1822-91), known as Plon-Plon, married Princess Clotilde, daughter of Victor Emmanuel II of Sardinia. He and his descendants are the Bonaparte pretenders to the throne of France.

Boniface VIII (name Benedetto Caetani). 1235?-1303. Pope (1294-1303). He tried to dominate the affairs of Europe as had Innocent III one hundred years earlier. In 1296 he promulgated the bull *Clericis laicos* against Philip IV of France, forbidding collection of taxes on church property without the consent of the papacy. In 1302 in the bull *Unam Sanctam* he asserted the temporal as well as the spiritual supremacy of the pope. As the result of his quarrel with Philip he was taken prisoner by Philip's Italian aides and died within a month.

Boniface, Saint (name Winfrid). 680?-755. English Benedictine missionary. Called "Apostle to the Germans." He was sent by Gregory II to Germany. He preached in Bavaria, Thuringia, Friesland, and Hesse. Bishop (723).

Archbishop (732). He was entrusted with the reformation of the Frankish church (741). Archbishop of Mainz (748). He was killed by a mob at Dokkum in West Friesland.

Bonn Protocol. Nov. 1949. At the Potsdam Conference (July-Aug. 1945) it was decided that German reparations were to be collected from current assets in the form of factories, machinery, locomotives, and similar capital goods. The bulk of the reparations was to go to the Soviet Union, although 18 other countries, including France, Czechoslovakia, Norway, Albania, India, and Holland, were to have a share. This program was to have been completed by June, 1948, but was extended to July, 1950. As time progressed, it became clear that if many factories in the Western zone of Germany were dismantled, severe shortages would result, which would have to be made up by American aid. Accordingly, the Bonn Protocol was signed between West Germany and the Western Allies under which the dismantling program was halted and plants already dismantled, but not removed from Germany, would remain in the country. Under the original program, 1977 plants were scheduled for dismantling. Actually, only 754 plants were dismantled.

Book of Common Prayer. See Cranmer.

Borgia, Cesare. 1475-1507. Son of Rodrigo Borgia (Pope Alexander VI) and brother of Lucrezia Borgia. He was created archbishop of Valencia (1492) and cardinal (1493). He relinquished the cardinal's office (1498). He became the duke of Valentinois (1499). Duke of Romagna (1501). He captured Piombino, Urbino, etc., in central Italy. He acted with extreme treachery and cruelty. When opposed by Pope Julius II, he fled to Naples and was captured by Gonzalo de Córdoba (1504). He was sent to Spain and imprisoned (1504-06). He escaped and was killed during the siege of the castle at Viàna. His character is portrayed by Machiavelli in *The Prince*.

Borgia, Lucrezia. 1480-1519. Duchess of Ferrara. Daughter of Rodrigo Borgia (Pope Alexander VI) and sister of Cesare Borgia. Married three times for political reasons. (1) To Giovanni Sforza (1493). Marriage annulled (1497). (2) To the nephew of the king of Naples, Alfonso of Aragon (1498), who was murdered (1500) by order of Cesare Borgia. (3) To Alfonso of Este, son and heir of the duke of Ferrara (1501). At Ferrara she maintained a brilliant court, which was frequented by artists, poets, and scholars. Recent historical research has cleared her name of many of the crimes formerly attributed to her.

Boris III. 1894-1943. King of Bulgaria (1918-1943).

Borromeo, Saint Carlo. 1538-84. Italian ecclesiastical reformer. Cardinal and archbishop of Milan (1560). He improved the discipline of the clergy, founded schools, hospitals, and libraries. He founded the order of the Oblates of St. Ambrose (1578).

Boscan Almogaver, Juan. 1493-1542. Spanish poet. He is credited with establishing the Italian school of poetry in Spain.

Bosnia-Herzegovina. Two Turkish provinces in the Balkans which were awarded to Austria-Hungary by the Congress of Berlin (1878). Austria-Hungary was given the right to occupy and administer them. At the time of the Young Turk Revolution, Emperor Francis Joseph announced that his country would annex the provinces (Oct. 7, 1908). This move was very unpopular among Slavic nationalists. It was at Sarajevo, Bosnia, that the Austrian Archduke was assassinated by a

Slav (June 28, 1914), the act which began World War I.

Bossuet, Jacques Bénigne. 1627-1704. French Roman Catholic prelate. Born in Dijon. Tutor to the dauphin (1670-81). Bishop of Meaux (1681). Renowned pulpit orator. He was a great moralist and stylist. In his *Politique Tirée de l'Écriture Sainte* (1709) he upheld the theory of the divine right of kings. His arguments in support of this theory were later much used to defend the institution.

Boswell, James. 1740-95. Scottish lawyer. Because of his intimacy with Dr. Samuel Johnson, he was able to write the *Life of Samuel Johnson* (1791), a masterpiece of biography.

Bosworth, Battle of. See Richard III.

Botticelli, Sandro (Alessandro Filipepi). 1447-1510. Florentine Renaissance painter. Son of a tanner, he early gave promise of genius for painting and was sent to the school of Fra Lippo Lippi. Among his famous works are: *Birth of Venus, Primavera, Coronation of the Virgin, Madonna and Child, Assumption of the Virgin, Mars and Venus,* etc. He was much impressed with the preaching of Savonarola. In his later years he occupied himself with Dante's works and produced 84 pen and silver-point drawings illustrating the *Divine Comedy.*

Boulanger Episode. After the formation of the Third Republic, Monarchism remained strong in the French army. A general, Georges Boulanger (1837-91), utilized this sentiment to attempt to overthrow the Republic. Posing first as a Republican, he became minister of war in 1886. He used this post to utter jingoist proclamations for a "war of revenge" against Germany. Forced out of the cabinet (1887), he gathered a large following of Monarchists and Imperialists. When President Grevy's son-in-law was found guilty of selling decorations of the Legion of Honor, Boulanger's followers seized the occasion to denounce the Republic as corrupt. Dismissed from the army, Boulanger was elected a deputy (1889). Being merely a talker and boaster with no real plans, Boulanger lacked the courage to attempt a *coup d'état.* When he was to be prosecuted for conspiracy, he fled to Belgium and committed suicide. This episode strengthened the Republic.

Bourbon. A French royal family, named for a castle in central France. Its remote ancestor (9th century) was Baron Aimar. The Bourbon family supplied kings for France, Spain, and Naples.

France	Ruled
Henry IV	1589-1610
Louis XIII	1610-1643
Louis XIV	1643-1715
Louis XV	1715-1774
Louis XVI	1774-1792
Louis XVII	(never reigned)
Louis XVIII	1814-1824
Charles X	1824-1830
Louis Philippe*	1830-1848

*Louis Philippe was a member of the Orleans branch of the family.

Spain: Philip V, the first Bourbon king of Spain (1700-24, 24-46), was the great-grandson of Philip IV (1621-65), who had married Elizabeth, daughter of Henry IV of France. The Bourbon kings of Spain after Philip V were:

	Ruled
Louis	1724
(ruled only a few months)	
Ferdinand VI	1746-1759
Charles III	1759-1788
Charles IV	1788-1808
Ferdinand VII	1808, 1814-33
Isabella II	1833-1868
Alfonso XII	1874-1885
Alfonso XIII	1886-1931

Naples: Charles IV, the founder of the Neapolitan Bourbon family, was the third son of Philip V of Spain. He was made king of Naples and Sicily (1735). He resigned the throne (1759) to become Charles III of Spain. He was succeeded by his son Ferdinand, who as Ferdinand IV was dethroned by Napoleon (1805). He was restored as Ferdinand I, King of the Two Sicilies (1815-25). He was succeeded by Francis I, Ferdinand II, and Francis II. The kingdom of Francis II became part of Italy in 1860.

Bourbon, Charles, The Constable of. 1490-1527. Of the younger branch of the Bourbon family. Created Constable of France for bravery at the battle of Marignano (1515). He quarreled with Francis I and made an alliance with Emperor Charles V and Henry VIII of England. He helped the imperial army drive the French out of Italy. He took part in the defeat of the French at Pavia (1525). Charles V made him Duke of Milan (1526). He led an army of Spanish and German mercenaries in the attack on Rome (1527), which resulted in the complete sack of the city. During this attack, he received a mortal wound, said to have been inflicted by Benvenuto Cellini.

Bouvines, Battle of. 1214. Frederick II (q.v.) formed an alliance with Philip II of France and the German princes of the Rhine valley. In 1212, Frederick set out to take Germany away from Emperor Otto IV. Otto called for help, and was reinforced by John of England, the count of Flanders, the duke of Brabant, and many nobles of north France. Philip II won a complete victory over Otto at Bouvines. Otto was compelled to yield to Frederick, who was crowned Holy Roman Emperor at Aachen in 1215.

Boyar. A member of a Russian aristocratic order next below that of the ruling princes. The order was abolished by Peter the Great (1689-1725). Also, one of the privileged classes in Romania.

Boyle, Robert. 1627-91. He was one of the founders of the English Royal Society and the "father of modern chemistry." He established the relationship between pressure and volume of gases known as Boyle's Law.

Boyne, Battle of the. July 1, 1690. After he was deposed from the throne of England, James II attempted to regain his throne with the support of the Irish. At the Battle of the Boyne, the English forces, led by William of Orange, scattered the Irish in utmost confusion. James hurried away from the battlefield to seek asylum in France. This victory is celebrated annually by Orangemen as having secured Protestantism as the state religion of Great Britain.

Brahe, Tycho. 1546-1601. Danish astronomer. Established an observatory on the island of Hven (1576). He went to Bohemia under the patronage of Rudolf II (1599). His assistant was Kepler (1600). He rejected the Copernican theory. He held that five planets revolve around the sun, which in turn revolve around the earth. He discovered a new star—Tycho's star—in Cassiopeia (1572) and variations of the moon. His work included the most accurate astronomical computations made down to his time.

Brahms, Johannes. 1838-97. German composer. His works (some 120 in number) are marked by high regard for pure musical form. He has had few rivals as a song writer. His works include four symphonies, numerous instrumental pieces and concertos, and five major vocal works, of which the *German Requiem* is an example.

Bramante, Donato. 1444-1514. Italian architect. Born near Urbino. Resided in Milan (1472-99). He went to Rome

(1499) where he was employed by Popes Alexander VI and Julius II. He was the first architect to begin work on St. Peter's. Upon his death, the work was assigned to others who radically altered his plans.

Bratianu. Name of a family of Romanian statesmen. Demeter (1818-92) and his brother Ion (1821-91) were the first to engage in politics. Ion's son Ion (1866-1927) was the war-time premier who in 1916 allied Romania with the Allies. Vintila (1876-1930), brother of Ion, was premier from 1927 to 1928.

Breda, Peace of. July 21, 1667. A pact between England, the Netherlands, France, and Denmark ending the Second Dutch War (q.v.). From France England received Antigua, Montserrat, and St. Kitts. France received Acadia. England and the Netherlands adopted the *status quo* of May 21, 1667. Thus England retained New Amsterdam and the Netherlands retained Surinam.

Brest-Litovsk, Treaty of. March 3, 1918. Between Russia and Germany following the Bolshevik Revolution. Eastern Poland, Ukraine, Lithuania, Estonia, and Latvia were ceded to the Germans. In the south, part of Transcaucasia was ceded to Turkey. Thus, Russia lost 26% of its population; 27% of its arable land; 32% of average crops; 26% of its railroads; 33% of its factories; 73% of its iron industries; 75% of its coal fields. Germany was forced to renounce this treaty by the Treaty of Versailles (1919).

Bretigny, Peace of. Between France and England. 1360. Edward III of England renounced his rights to the throne of France. In return, he received all of ancient Aquitaine and Calais. The French renounced their alliance with the Scots; the English, their alliance with the Flemings.

Brian Boru. 926-1014. King of Ireland (1002-14); slain while defeating the Danes at the battle of Clontarf, near Dublin.

Briand, Aristide. 1862-1932. French statesman. Born in Nantes. Deputy (1902-19). Founded Socialist newspaper L'Humanité (1904) with Jaurès. Prime minister (1909-11). Head of coalition government (1915-17). Prime minister (1921-22). French representative at the Washington Conference (1922). Minister of foreign affairs (1925-32). Awarded Nobel Peace Prize (1926) with Gustav Stresemann. With Kellogg, developed the Briand-Kellogg Peace Pact (1927-28) (also known as the Paris Peace Pact).

Bright, John. 1811-89. English orator and statesman. Son of a Quaker cotton-mill owner of Rochdale. He worked with Richard Cobden to secure the repeal of the Corn Laws (q.v.) (1838-46). Supported the North in the United States Civil War. He was a great admirer of Lincoln. President of the Board of Trade under Gladstone (1868-70).

Brindley, James. 1716-72. A humbly-born English engineer. Up till the last he remained illiterate. His problems were solved without writing or drawing. He is remembered as a great canal-builder, constructing 365 miles of canals in all. His most famous canal connects Worsley and Manchester. It was built for the Duke of Bridgewater (1772).

Brissot, Jacques Pierre. 1754-93. French revolutionary. One of the mob that stormed the Bastille (July 14, 1789). Member of the Legislative Assembly (1791-2). A moderate member of the National Convention. Prominent in the Girondist Party. Guillotined in Paris (Oct. 31, 1793).

British Commonwealth of Nations. See Imperial Conference, 1926.

British East India Company. This Company was granted a royal charter in 1600. At first it established trading centers in Madras, Bombay, and Calcutta. It developed forts and trading stations, and had its own army and merchant marine. In 1616 it extended its operations to include trade with Persia. This action was resented by the Portuguese. But the British defeated the Portuguese at Jash (1616) and later at Hormunz (1622) and consolidated their position in Persia. Through gifts and medical services, the Company secured exemption from customs duties in peninsular India (1715). The Company opened trading centers in Burma (1619) and Afghanistan (1803). In 1867 the rule of the Company was ended.

British Union of Fascists. This black-shirted group was organized by Sir Oswald Mosley in 1932. It advocated greater development of the home market, the establishment of a national council of industry, and a social and moral rejuvenation. After 1934, the British Fascists had numerous clashes with the police. In 1937 the Public Order Act, aimed at the Mosley group, forbade the wearing of political uniforms and the formation of semi-military organizations. Mosley was imprisoned during the war and his organization disbanded.

Browning, Elizabeth Barrett. 1806-1861. English poetess, wife of Robert Browning. Among her many works are *Sonnets from the Portuguese, The Cry of the Children,* and *Aurora Leigh.*

Browning, Robert. 1812-89. English poet. A poet of great power and originality. Among his many poems are *Pippa Passes, The Ring and the Book, The Lost Leader, Childe Roland, My Last Duchess.*

Brownists. See Non-conformists.

Bruce, Robert. 1274-1329. Hero of the Scottish War of Independence. His memorable action is the Battle of Bannockburn (June 24, 1314) in which he led the Scotch army that routed the English army under Edward II. By the Treaty of Northampton (1328), England recognized the independence of Scotland and Bruce's right to the throne.

Brunelleschi, Filippo. 1377-1446. Florentine architect. By training a master goldsmith, he first took up sculpturing and then architecture. He journeyed to Rome and devoted much time to studying the ruins of the ancient Roman buildings. Upon his return to Florence, he was commissioned to design and build a dome for the cathedral. Measured diametrically, it is the largest in the world. It served as a model for the dome of St. Peter's. He designed the Florentine churches of Spirito Santo and San Lorenzo and the Pitti Palace.

Bruno, Giordano. 1548?-1600. Italian philosopher. Forced to leave the Dominican order (1576), he traveled widely, lecturing, teaching, and writing. He championed the Copernican theory. He declared that the universe stretched to infinity and was of everlasting duration. Within this universe was one vast all-pervading spirit that entered into all things alike. He denied transubstantiation and the immaculate conception of the Virgin. He was arrested by the Inquisition (1592) as a heretic and burned at the stake (1600).

Brunswick, Proclamation (or Manifesto) of the Duke of. July 25, 1792. War broke out between Revolutionary France and Austria and Prussia in 1792. The commander of the invading army, the duke of Brunswick, issued a proclamation declaring that it was the intention of the invading army to restore the royal family of France to its "legitimate authority." If the slightest harm befell any member of the royal family, the Austrian and Prussian troops would inflict an "ever-memorable vengeance" upon the city of Paris. This manifesto sealed the fate of the French monarchy. The French reply to the manifesto was the insurrection of August 9-10, 1792 in which the king was deposed and made a prisoner.

Brussels Pact. In March, 1948, the Benelux countries, France, and Great Britain formed a defensive alliance called Western Union, under whose terms an attack on any one was to be considered an attack on all. To defend the Union, a comprehensive military organization, called Uniforce, was set up at Fontainebleau. This Union has been incorporated into NATO.

Buckingham, George Villiers, Duke of. 1592-1628. A favorite of James I. Although he led an immoral life, James heaped favors upon him until he became the wealthiest noble in England. Entrusted with arranging a marriage between the Spanish Infanta and Prince Charles, he bungled affairs so badly that England and Spain went to war. Impeached by Commons for mismanaging the expedition against Cadiz, he was rescued by James. He had a notorious affair with the Queen of France. He was assassinated by a subaltern.

Buffon, Count Georges Louis Leclerc de. 1707-88. French naturalist. Director of the Jardin du Roi (now Jardin des Plantes) and of the royal museum (1739). He is the author (with others) of the *Histoire Naturelle* (44 volumes; published between 1749 and 1789). It was the most important contribution to natural history since Aristotle.

Bulgaria, Origin of. Bulgaria has passed through five stages: (1) It was part of the Roman provinces of Moesia and Thrace; (2) It was fought for by the Byzantine Empire and the barbarians, who invaded it from the north. (3) It was a national Bulgarian Empire. (4) It was a Turkish province. (5) It became an independent country. In Roman times, Bulgaria was occupied by people of Thraco-Illyrian descent. These folk were driven out or absorbed by the Slavs, who arrived between the 2nd and 6th centuries. The Slavs, in turn, were subjugated by the Bulgars, a people of Finno-Tatar origin. The Bulgarians accepted Christianity during the reign of Czar Boris I (852-888). At the same time they adopted the Cyrillic alphabet. Under Simeon (893-927), the Bulgarians reached the zenith of their power. Between 971 and 1014 Bulgaria was reconquered by the Byzantine Empire and reincorporated into it. In 1186 the Bulgarians reestablished their independence and retained it until they were conquered by the Turks (1396). In the period 1396-1878, Bulgaria was a Turkish province. At the Congress of Berlin (q.v.) (1878), part of Bulgaria was granted autonomy under the protection of Turkey. But East Rumelia remained a province of Turkey. In 1908, at the time of the "Young Turk" revolution (q.v.), Bulgaria declared its independence.

Bülow, Prince Bernhard von. 1849-1929. German statesman and diplomat. Born in Holstein. Served (1876-88) in the German embassies in Rome, Vienna, Athens, Paris, and St. Petersburg. Minister at Bucharest (1888-93). Ambassador at Rome (1893-97). Foreign secretary (1897-1900). Imperial chancellor (1900-09). He attempted to effect a foreign policy of friendly relations with England, but failed. He was forced to resign over the budget. As ambassador to Rome, he failed to keep Italy from entering the war on the side of the Allies.

Bundesrat. Bundesrat is a term used in Germany and Switzerland to describe a federal council. In Germany, the Germanic Confederation, the North German

Confederation, and the Empire each had a Bundesrat, as does the present Bonn government. The Bundesrat of the Empire was composed of 61 members distributed among the 26 states of the empire, according to their population. Each delegation was chosen by its own state and was required to vote as a unit according to instructions given by the state. The Bundesrat normally initiated laws and had to pass on constitutional amendments. The constitution could not be amended, and taxes and the army could not be decreased if 14 adverse votes were cast. Prussia, which had 17 votes and also controlled 3 for Alsace-Lorraine, could control the Bundesrat.

Bunyan, John. 1628-88. A lay Nonconformist British preacher who, when in jail, wrote the immortal *Pilgrim's Progress* (1678), one of the world's great allegories.

Burghley, William Cecil, Lord. 1520-1598. A brilliant scholar at Cambridge, he became an even more brilliant student of law; became secretary of state (1550); conformed to Catholicism during Mary's reign; made chief secretary of state when Elizabeth became queen; his policy at home and abroad was at once shrewd and cautious, liberal and comprehensive; was made Baron Burghley (1571) and lord high treasurer (1572), an office which he held until his death.

Burgundians. A Teutonic tribe which had been given lands on the upper Rhine by the Romans. They moved south and established a kingdom along the Rhone between the Franks and the Ostrogoths. Their kingdom lasted about 100 years until they were conquered (534) by the Franks.

Burgundy. During the period of the Germanic invasions, Burgundians settled in the upper Rhone valley. During the early Middle Ages, two kingdoms of Bur-

gundy arose and disappeared. Most of their territories became fiefs of the Holy Roman Empire. The French Burgundian country became a feudal dependency of the king of France. In the 14th century, when the ducal line became extinct, Burgundy fell to the king of France. But in 1363, King John made one of his sons duke of Burgundy.

During the Hundred Years' War, Burgundy increased in power by siding now with the English, now with the French. By the Treaty of Arras (1453) the duke of Burgundy received numerous cities and districts as reward for siding with the French. Burgundy now reached nearly to Paris. By marriage with the heiress of the count of Flanders, Burgundy acquired Flemish Netherlands. Charles the Bold, Duke of Burgundy (1467-77), was thus one of the richest and most powerful rulers of Europe. Being ambitious, he warred with the French and nearly conquered them. But after he was defeated by the Swiss at Granson (1476), his power waned rapidly. In the following year he was killed at Nancy. Within two years the French overran the duchy of Burgundy and annexed it to France.

Burke, Edmund. 1729-97. British statesman and orator. Among his writings are *On the Present State of the Nation* (1769), *American Taxation* (1774), *Conciliation with America* (1775), and *Reflections on the French Revolution* (1790). He took an active part in the investigation of the East India Co. and the impeachment of Warren Hastings (1794) (q.v.) and supported Wilberforce in advocating the abolition of the slave trade (1788-89). His political knowledge and force of character gave him a foremost place among his contemporaries. Although he championed many reform causes, he believed that the current social, political, and cultural institutions represented the best thought and experience of the ages. Hence, he became the leading European conservative. His influence as such was great, particularly in his own country.

Burney, Fanny (originally Frances). 1752-1840. English novelist. Married General d'Arblay, a French refugee. She wrote *Evelina, Cecilia, Camilla,* and *The Wanderer.*

Burns, Robert. 1759-96. Scotch poet. Burns is so much the greatest of Scotch poets that no other comes within reckoning. He is a lyric poet of unsurpassed energy. He is also an excellent satirist and descriptive poet. He wrote such beloved poems as *The Cotter's Saturday Night, To a Mouse, Tam o' Shanter.* He wrote many songs, including *Flow Gently, Sweet Afton; Auld Lang Syne;* and *John Anderson.*

Burschenschaften. 1815-1935. Student organizations in German universities, founded at Jena in 1815 to stimulate patriotism. The nationalistic ideals of Friedrich Jahn (q.v.) became the creed of the Burschenschaften. After the murder of Kotzebue (q.v.), the Burschen-schaften were dissolved by the Carlsbad Decrees (q.v.). The ban against them was lifted in 1849. They resumed as social organizations until they were dissolved by the Nazis in 1935.

Bute, Earl of (John Stuart). 1713-92. Scottish favorite of George III. British prime minister (1762) after the ejection of Pitt the Elder. He aroused popular hostility because of the Treaty of Paris (1763) (q.v.) and resigned (1763). He was forced to retire from the court (1765).

Byron, George Gordon, 6th Lord Byron of Rochdale. 1788-1824. English poet. He led an exciting and controversial life in England and the continent. Many of his long poems are autobiographical. Among his famous poems are *Childe Harold, Don Juan, The Prisoner of Chillon, The Giaour, The Bride of Abydos.*

Byzantine. Of or pertaining to, or characteristic of Constantinople or the Byzantine Empire (395-1453) whose capital city was Constantinople.

C

Cabal, The. 1667-73. This term in reality was borrowed from the Hebrew word *cabala*, which means "secret." The word was suggested from the initial letters of the Privy Council of Charles II of England—Clifford, Ashley, Buckingham, Arlington, and Lauderdale. This group assumed an important executive function after the fall of Chancellor Clarendon, and thus became the forerunner of the British Cabinet.

Cabot (or Cabotto), Giovanni. ?-1557. A Genoese pilot, who was naturalized at Venice in 1476, settled in Bristol in 1490. In 1497 he was commissioned by Henry VII to undertake a westward voyage of exploration. On June 24 he sighted Cape Breton Island and Nova Scotia. On the strength of this voyage, England later claimed possession of land in America.

Cabral, Pedro Alvarez. 1460-1526. Portuguese navigator. On a voyage from Portugal to the Orient, he took a westward course and was blown onto the coast of Brazil (April 22, 1500). He took possession of it in the name of Portugal.

Cade, Jack. d. 1450. Leader of the insurrection of 1450. Irish by birth, he led an adventurous career until he settled down in Kent as a physician and married a magistrate's daughter. Assuming the name of Mortimer and title of "Captain of Kent," he marched on London at the head of 40,000 malcontents. He seized and held London for two days, when his insurgents were dispersed. He was killed (July 13) in Sussex.

Cahiers. Lists of grievances and suggestions for their alleviation that were drafted in various parts of France prior to the calling of the Estates-General in 1789. They were not revolutionary documents. With great uniformity they expressed loyalty to the king. However, all of them reflected the idea which philosophy had made popular—namely, that reason demanded fundamental, thorough reforms in government and society. Because of the nature of the cahiers, we might say that the French Revolution had been accomplished in men's minds before it actually took place.

Cairo Declaration. Dec. 1, 1943. F. D. Roosevelt, Churchill, and Chiang Kai-Shek announced that it was the intention of the United Nations to limit Japan, after defeat, to the four main islands.

Calderón de la Barca, Pedro. 1600-81. Spanish poet and dramatist. He entered the Spanish army. Created knight of the Order of Santiago (1637). He entered the Order of St. Francis (1650). Later, he became a superior in the Brotherhood of San Pedro. Author of 120 comedies and many religious mysteries, called *autos*, including *El Médico de Su Honra, El Alcalde de Zalamea.*

Calendar, French Revolutionary. To do away with all remembrance of historic Christianity, the French National Convention adopted a new calendar. September 22, 1792 was the first day of the year I. The year was divided into twelve months, each containing 3 weeks of 10 days (*décades*), every 10th day (*décadi*) being a day of rest. The five or six days left over at the end of the year were national holidays (*sans-culottides*). The months were named from the seasonal weather of the month or from the usual agricultural occupation of the month (*Brumaire*, fog; *Ventôse*, wind; *Floréal*, blossom; *Prairial*, pasture, etc.). The calendar was discontinued Dec. 31, 1805.

Caliph. Successor to Mohammed. The first was Abu Bakr. He was succeeded by Omar, Othman, and Ali. After Ali's death, there was a division among Mohammedans; hence, there were often several rival caliphs until the Ottoman sultans assumed the title. From that time until 1924, when the position was abolished, the sultan of Turkey was also Caliph. The last sultan, Mohammed VI (1861-1926), was deposed in 1922. His cousin held the caliphate for the next two years, when the position was abolished.

Calonne, Charles Alexandre de. 1734-1802. French finance minister under Louis XVI (1783-86). Born in Douai. Finding financial affairs in chaos when he became minister, he began a policy of spending and new loans which completed the bankruptcy of France. He opened the Assembly of Notables (1778). Lived in England (1787-1802). He was permitted by Napoleon to return to France (1802). He died one month later.

Calvin, John. 1509-64. A reformer who was born at Noyon, Picardy, where his father Gerard Caulvin, or Cauvin, was an official. Educated to be an ecclesiastic, he issued his great work, *Institutes of Christian Religion,* in 1536. Persuaded by Farel to settle in Geneva, he instituted there a theocracy. Through Beza he influenced the great struggle between the Guises and Huguenots in France. He rendered a double service to Protestantism: he systematized its doctrine; and he organized its ecclesiastical discipline.

Cambacérès, Duke of. Jean Jacques Regis. 1753-1824. French jurist and statesman. Born in Montpellier. He was a member of the National Convention (1792), president of the Committee of Public Safety (1794) and the Council of Five Hundred (1796). He became minister of justice and Second Consul in 1799. He was largely responsible for drawing up the Code Napoleon. He was created duke of Parma in 1808.

Cambridge Platonists. See Latitudinarians.

Camelot du roi. French rightist party which in the 1920's and 30's advocated a monarchical revival and clericalism.

Camoëns, Luiz Vaz de. 1524-1580. Portuguese poet. Became a soldier (1550). Fought in India (1553-69). Led an adventurous life there. Returned to Lisbon (1570). Secured the patronage of King Sebastian. Author of *The Lusiads* (1556 ff.), epic poems dealing with the chief episodes of Portuguese history. Portugal's greatest poet.

Camperdown, Battle of. Oct. 11, 1792. At the instigation of the French, a Dutch fleet was assembled off the Texel to invade England. It was defeated and destroyed by the English fleet under Admiral Duncan at Camperdown.

Canning, George. 1770-1827. British statesman. Born in London. Educated at

Oxford where he was a Jacobin. M.P. (1793). Undersecretary of foreign affairs under Pitt (1796-99). Foreign secretary (1807-10). He succeeded Castlereagh as foreign secretary and leader of the House of Commons (1822), and was the real director of the government. He became prime minister and chancellor of the exchequer (1827). He acknowledged the independence of the Spanish colonies in the Western Hemisphere. He fostered liberalism and nationalism in Europe. He repudiated the membership of Great Britain in the Quadruple Alliance.

Canossa. 1077. Henry IV, the Holy Roman Emperor, engaged in a controversy with Pope Gregory VII over the question of lay investiture. Henry defied the pope; whereupon Gregory excommunicated Henry and absolved all his subjects from obedience. Fearing the loss of his throne, Henry hastened to Italy and met the pope at the Castle of Canossa in Tuscany. Dressed as a penitent, Henry had to wait outside this castle three days before he was admitted. On the fourth day he was admitted and absolved; but he was forced to accept many hard conditions. Henry was deeply humiliated. But Gregory had overshot the mark. Public opinion was against him. From this time on, Henry's power increased while Gregory's diminished.

Canute II (Cnut). 994?-1035. King of England (1016-1035) and of Denmark (1018-35). He defeated Edmund Ironside and thoroughly conquered all of England. An able, just, and popular ruler. He strongly supported the Church.

Cape St. Vincent, Battle of. Feb. 14, 1797. The French were bent on invading England. A Spanish fleet was to join the French at Brest and, together with a Dutch fleet off the Texel, the combined forces were to attack England. Sir John Jervis defeated the Spaniards off Cape St. Vincent and forestalled the invasion.

Capetian dynasty. A family of kings that ruled France from 987 to 1328. Its founder was Hugh Capet. It was of greatest importance to the history of France that in this line there was always a male heir, generally of mature years, able to take up and carry out the policies of his predecessors. Hence there were no disputed successions or disastrous regencies. The Capetian kings were as follows:

	Born	Ruled
Hugh Capet	c. 940	987-996
Robert II the Pious	c. 970	996-1031
Henry I	1008	1031-1060
Philip I	1052	1060-1108
Louis VI the Fat	1081	1108-1137
Louis VII the Young	c. 1121	1137-1180
Philip II Augustus	1165	1180-1223
Louis VIII the Lion	1187	1223-1226
Louis IX (St. Louis)	1214	1226-1270
Philip III the Bold	1245	1270-1285
Philip IV the Fair	1268	1285-1314
Louis X the Quarreler	1289	1314-1316
John I	1316	1316-1316
Philip V the Tall	1294	1316-1322
Charles IV the Fair	1294	1322-1328

Capitano del Popolo. See Italian cities.

Capitation (Poll tax). A direct tax in France during the days of the Old Regime. It was a head tax which varied according to whichever of the 22 classes the individual rated. Thus, maid-servants paid 3 livres and 12 sous annually (about 72 cents).

Capitulary of Charlemagne. 780. A document issued by Charlemagne to arrange all affairs of the church and government in the land newly acquired from the Saxons. The churches were to be places of asylum. Any injury done to a Church or slight put upon it was punishable by death. To offer human sacrifices, to refuse to be baptized, to burn instead of bury the dead, to disregard the rules of the church in regard to fasting, all were offenses punishable by death. Sunday must be observed. The churches were endowed with large tracts of land and the payment of the tithe was enforced.

Caporetto Campaign. Oct. 24-Dec. 26, 1917. German-Austrian troops attacked the Italians during a heavy fog. The Italian troops broke at once. Within three days they were completely demoralized. They fell back on the Piave River, where, with French and British support, they made an effective stand. The troops of the Central Powers, outrunning their supplies, were forced to slow down. Italian General Cadorna was replaced by General Diaz, who established a strong defensive position. The Italians lost 300,000 prisoners and even more than that number of deserters.

Caprivi, Georg Leo von. 1831-1899. Chancellor of Germany (1890-94), succeeding Bismarck. He secured the Island of Helgoland from Britain (1890) and valuable concessions in Africa. He made reciprocal tariff treaties with Austria-Hungary, Russia, Romania, and Italy whereby duties on imported grain were lowered in return for favorable treatment of German exports. As these measures enraged conservatives, who were agrarians, the emperor was forced to dismiss Caprivi.

Carbonari (**Charcoal-Burners.**) An Italian secret society for revolutionary propaganda which existed during the first half of the 19th century.

Carlist Wars. A series of attempts to seize the throne of Spain.
(1) Carlos, 1st (1788-1855). Second son of Charles IV of Spain. When his brother, Ferdinand, the king, abrogated the Salic Law, he revolted and started the Carlist Wars (1833-39). He was defeated and fled to France. He was called Charles V by his followers.
(2) Carlos, 2nd (1818-1861). Continued the unsuccessful attempts to seize the throne of Spain. Known as Charles VI by his supporters.
(3) Carlos, 3rd (1848-1909). Entered Spain and waged an unsuccessful civil war (1873-76).

Carlota (*in full* **Maria Charlotte Amélie Augustine Victoire Clémentine Léopoldine**). 1840-1927. Empress of Mexico (1864-67). Only daughter of Leopold I of Belgium. Wife of Maximilian (q.v.). Sent by her husband to Europe to secure help from Napoleon III and the pope against Mexican republicans. Upon realizing that her mission was a failure, she became hopelessly insane. Confined in a castle near Brussels (1879-1927).

Carlowitz, Treaty of (1699). A crushing loss for the Turks as the result of the Holy War (1684-99). Turkey ceded to the Emperor of Austria all of Hungary, except the province of Temesvar, all of Transylvania, most of Slavonia, and part of Croatia. Venice gained certain islands of Greece, some cities along the Dalmatian coast, and all of the Morea. Poland regained the districts of Kamenik, Podolia, and western Ukraine. In a subsequent treaty with the Russians (1702) the Turks surrendered Azov and a region around it.

Carlsbad Decrees. Sept. 1819. The German Federal Diet issued these decrees to stamp out liberalism. The decrees contained measures to control university professors and students, muzzled the press, and repudiated republicanism. A central committee was set up at Mainz to investigate revolutionary plots.

Carnot, Lazare Nicolas Marguerite. 1753-1823. French statesman. "Organizer of Victory." Member of the Legislative Assembly (1791). Member of the National Convention (1792). Member of the Committee of Public Safety (1793). He organized the first of the "citizen armies" (1793-95). Member of the Directory (1795-97) and twice its president. He fled to Switzerland (1797), but returned later to be minister of war (1800-01) and a member of the Tribunate (1802-07). He was minister of the interior during the Hundred Days (1815). Exiled by Louis XVIII, he lived in Warsaw and Magdeburg. Author of a book on mathematics and military strategy, which was accepted as standard by most European armies.

Carol I. 1839-1914. King of Romania (1881-1914). A member of the House of Hohenzollern, he was made Prince of Romania in 1866 and king in 1881.

Carol II. 1893-1953. King of Romania (1930-40). When crown prince he formed a liaison with Magda Lupescu. For this he was forced to renounce his rights to the throne and go into exile (1925). When his father, Ferdinand (q.v.), died in 1927, his son, Michael, became king. Carol returned to Romania (1930) and had himself declared king. His reign was stormy. He was deposed (1940) by Antonescu (q.v.) and the Iron Guard. He lived in exile thereafter.

Caroline of Anspach. 1683-1737. Queen of Great Britain and Ireland and wife of George II. She gathered a distinguished circle including Pope, Gay, Chesterfield, and Lord Hervey. At her insistence, Walpole was kept in power as prime minister. She exerted an excellent influence upon her husband.

Caroline of Brunswick. 1768-1821. Queen of Great Britain and Ireland. Wife of George IV. Forced to marry him while he was Prince of Wales (1795). Abandoned by her husband (1796), she traveled on the continent until the death of George III (1820). Her husband excluded her from Westminster Hall on coronation day (1821). When he tried to divorce her for adultery, she won the case and the sympathy of the public. The trial cost the king whatever patriotic devotion he might have been able to inspire.

Carolingian Dynasty. 751-987. This dynasty was named after Charlemagne. Due to the family tradition of dividing the dominions among surviving sons, the empire was badly broken up by the end of the 10th century when the dynasty came to an end. By this time, France had become a separate country. The other parts of Charlemagne's empire were much less stable and had achieved no definite nationality. The following are the various Carolingian rulers:

	Born	Ruled
Pippin the Short	c. 714	751-768
Charlemagne	742	768-814
Ludwig the Pious	778	814-840
Charles the Bald	823	840-877
Ludwig II the Stammerer	846	877-879
Louis III	c. 863	879-882
Carloman	?	879-884
Charles II the Fat	839	884-887
Odo, Count of Paris	?	888-898
Charles III the Simple	879	893-923
Robert I	865	922-923
Rudolf, Duke of Burgundy	?	926-936
Louis IV d'Outremer	c. 921	936-954
Lothair	941	954-986
Louis V the Sluggard	c. 966	986-987

Carpaccio, Vittore. 1455-1522. Venetian painter. His most characteristic work consists of nine subjects from the life of St. Ursula. Other subjects are *Presentation in the Temple* and *Virgin and Child*.

Cartel. A voluntary association of private entrepreneurs, sometimes encouraged by the government, which coordinates marketing techniques and often exerts a monopolistic influence on world markets. The term is often applied in Europe to describe industrial firms which operate in domestic as well as foreign markets. Cartels may be organized to fix prices, limit production, divide marketing territory, or pool profits.

Cartwright, Edmund. 1743-1823. English clergyman and inventor. He invented the power loom (1785).

Casa de Contratacíon (House of Commerce). A business organization which was set up (1503) by the government of Spain to regulate Spanish trade, particularly colonial trade.

Casablanca Conference. Jan. 14-24, 1943. President F. D. Roosevelt and Prime Minister Churchill conferred on war-time strategy in this Moroccan city. They announced (Jan. 27) that they had worked out plans for an Allied offensive in 1943 and that they expected to secure the "unconditional surrender" of the Axis powers.

Casimir III (called the Great). 1309-70. King of Poland (1333-70). He concluded the war with the Teutonic Knights which had been going on for a number of years prior to his elevation to the throne. He seized Galicia (1340). He codified the laws of Great and Little Poland (1347), befriended the peasants (hence he was called the "Peasants' King"), laid the foundations for the University of Cracow. He was the last of the Piast dynasty. He was followed (1386) by the Jagellon dynasty (q.v.).

Cassiodorus, Flavius Magnus Aurelius. Roman statesman and writer. Government official under Theodoric. Retired (c. 540) to devote himself to study and writing. Though his *History of the Goths* has been lost, we learn much from his existing writings about the Goths.

Castlereagh, Viscount, Robert Stewart, 2nd Marquis of Londonderry. 1769-1822. English statesman. Educated at Cambridge. Viscount Castlereagh (1795). Marquis of Londonderry (1816). Chief secretary of Ireland (1799-1801). War secretary under Pitt the Younger (1805-06) and later (1807-09). He was responsible for the Peninsular Campaign (1808-14) and for naming Wellington commander. Foreign secretary and leader of House of Commons (1812-22). He planned much of the strategy which led to the defeat of Napoleon. He took a prominent part in the Congress of Vienna (1814-15). He was blamed for the Six Acts (q.v.) (1819) and the impairment of civil liberties. He opposed Metternich's policy of intervention in the Spanish revolution of 1820.

Cateau-Cambrésis, Treaty of. 1559. A treaty at the end of a war between the French, under Henry II, and the Spaniards, under Philip II. England joined in the war on the side of the Spaniards. (Mary, queen of England, was the wife of Philip II.) The English lost Calais, their last foothold on the continent, during this war. France regained the territory which the Spaniards had taken and kept Calais, Toul, Metz, and Verdun. The French restored Savoy to its duke, and thus gave up any further attempt to conquer Italian lands.

Cathari. See Albigensians.

Catherine of Aragon. 1485-1536. Daughter of Ferdinand and Isabella and first wife of Henry VIII of England. She was married to Arthur, Prince of Wales, eldest son of Henry VII (Nov. 14, 1501). Arthur was barely 16 and sickly. He died April 2, 1502. On June 25, 1502, she was betrothed to her brother-in-law Henry, a boy of eleven. She married him in June, 1509, seven weeks after he became king. Between 1510 and 1518 she bore him five children, of whom only Princess Mary survived infancy. Until 1527, Henry treated Catherine with respect. Then, expressing doubts about the legality of his marriage, he sought a divorce. He secured a divorce in May, 1533. Catherine remained in England until her death, leading an austere, religious life.

Catherine II (the Great). 1729-96. Czarina of Russia (1762-96). A German princess of Anhalt-Zerbst, she became ruler of Russia when officers deposed her husband, Czar Peter III, because of his pro-Prussian attitude in the Seven Years' War (q.v.). In foreign policy, Catherine abandoned the Far East to the individual initiative of fur traders. In the Middle East, she tried to maintain peace among Turkish peoples by supporting the Mohammedan faith. In the West, prior to 1780 Catherine fostered a northern alliance among Russia, England, Prussia, and Sweden. Following the Act of Armed Neutrality of 1780 which favored the American Revolutionists against the English, Catherine drew close to Austria, thus leading to the three partitions of Poland (1772, 1793, 1795) from which Russia secured Polotsk, Vitebsk, Mogilev, Minsk, Podolia, Mazowia, and Warsaw. In a series of wars with Turkey, Russia secured a firm grip on the northern shores of the Black Sea.

Catholic Emancipation Act. April 13, 1829. Under the sponsorship of Sir Robert Peel, Roman Catholics were admitted to all offices in Great Britain except those of Guardian or Justice of the United Kingdom, Lord Lieutenant or Lord Deputy of Ireland, Lord High Chancellor, Lord Keeper of the Great Seal, and all those of ecclesiastical or collegiate establishment. Catholic rejoicing over this victory was soon moderated by the disenfranchisement of 200,000 "forty-shilling freeholders" in Ireland.

Catholic League. 1609. The Catholic League was founded in south Germany to offset the Protestant Union. Its leader was Bavaria, whose ruler, Maximilian, played a large part in the early phases of the Thirty Years' War. The pope was a member of the League. Spain made a treaty of alliance with it. The army of the League, commanded by Tilly, played a big part in the early phases of the Thirty Years' War.

Cato Street Conspiracy. 1820. A handful of violent London radicals formed a plot to murder the whole Tory cabinet. The plot was discovered and five of the conspirators were hanged.

Cavaignac. French family including:
Jean Baptiste (1762-1829), lawyer and revolutionist. Member of the National Convention (1792); member of the Council of Five Hundred. His son
Louis Eugène (1802-1857) was an army commander. As minister of war (1848) he suppressed an uprising in Paris. He was the chief of the executive body of the Provisional Government (June-Dec. 1848), and an unsuccessful candidate for president of France (Dec. 1848).

Cavalier Parliament. 1661-79. This Parliament was elected following the restoration of the Stuart kings of England in 1660. It had a longer continuous existence than any other in English history.

Cavour, Conte Camillo Benso di. 1810-61. Italian statesman. Born in Turin. Educated for a military career. He greatly improved his estates at Leri. Founded, with Count Balbo, *Il Risorgimento* (1847), an organ of Italian nationalism. As prime minister of the Kingdom of Sardinia, he engineered the unification of Italy. He is often called "The Head" of Italian unification.

Caxton, William. 1422-91. The first English printer.

Cellini, Benvenuto. 1500-1571. Italian goldsmith and sculptor. Born in Florence. Pupil of Michelangelo, Bandinelli, and Marconi. He was banished from Florence (1523) as the result of a duel. He went to Rome, where he was the protege of Pope Clement VII. He went to France

(1540) in the service of Francis I. He returned to Florence (1545) as the protege of Cosimo d' Medici. His works include *Nymph of Fontainebleau, Crucifixion, Perseus with the Head of Medusa,* gold saltcellar of Francis I, many decorative works in gold, medallions, etc. His *Autobiography* presents an invaluable picture of Renaissance Italy, and is also a classic of Italian literature.

Center Party, German. The Center Party was composed of Roman Catholics. Recruited from the Rhenish province of Prussia, which distrusted the conservative ruling majority, and from Bavaria, Baden, Hesse, and Württemberg, which were jealous of their local privileges, the Center Party was essentially a states'-rights party. After the outbreak of the *Kulturkampf* (q.v.) (1872), the Center Party became a permanent and important political organization.

Central Powers, The. Four countries, headed by Germany, which fought against 23 Allied countries during World War I.

Country	Date of Entrance into War
Austria-Hungary	July, 1914
Germany	August, 1914
Turkey	October, 1914
Bulgaria	October, 1915

Cervantes, Miguel de. 1547-1616. Spanish novelist. He served as a soldier. Wounded at Lepanto. Captured by Algerian pirates. Held for ransom in Algeria for five years. He held several government positions. His masterpiece is *Don Quixote,* a novel burlesquing the chivalric romances of the day.

Cézanne, Paul. 1838-1906. French painter. An outstanding innovator in modern painting and leader of the post-impressionist school.

Chamberlain, Sir Austen. 1863-1937. British statesman. Son of Joseph Cham-

berlain and half-brother of Neville Chamberlain. Unionist M.P. (1892). Civil lord of the admiralty (1895-1900). Chancellor of the exchequer (1903-06). Secretary of state for India (1915-17). Chancellor of exchequer (1919-21). Conservative leader in Commons and lord of privy seal (1921-23). Foreign secretary (1924-29). Awarded Nobel peace prize jointly with Charles G. Dawes (1925). Attended all meetings of the Council and Assembly of the League of Nations. Supported the Kellogg-Briand Peace Pact (1928).

Chamberlain, Houston Stewart. 1855-1927. Author. Born in Southsea, England. He resided in Dresden (1885-89), Vienna (1889-1908), and Bayreuth (1908-27). He became a naturalized German citizen (1916) and married (1908), as his second wife, Eva Wagner, the daughter of Richard Wagner. His writings encouraged German nationalism. Many of his theories later became the basic tenets of Nazi Germany.

Chamberlain, Joseph. 1836-1914. British statesman. Born in London. He expanded his father's screw-manufacturing business in Birmingham (1854-74) and retired with a fortune. As mayor of Birmingham (1873-76) he greatly improved the housing, sanitation, etc. of the city. M.P. (1876) as Bright's colleague. Liberal. Member of Gladstone's second cabinet. Opposed Irish Land Bill and Home-Rule Bill (1886) and resigned. Organized Liberal Unionists (q.v.). Formed coalition with the Conservatives (1895) and became colonial secretary in Salisbury's cabinet (1895). Aimed at imperial federation. Strove for imperial tariff preference. Withdrew from public life (1906). He was largely instrumental in founding Birmingham University (1900). Father of Austen and Neville Chamberlain (q.v.).

Chamberlain, Neville. 1869-1940. British statesman. Son (by second marriage) of Joseph Chamberlain. Lord Mayor of Birmingham (1915-16), Chancellor of Exchequer (1923-4; 1931-37), Minister of Health (1924-29), Prime Minister (1937-40). For the sake of peace, while his country was unprepared, he adopted a policy of appeasement. Criticism of the Munich Settlement (q.v.) and his conduct of the war forced his resignation a few months before his death.

Chambre Ardente. 1574. The Catholic party in France wished to set up the Inquisition in their country. However, the parlement of Paris, the supreme court of the land, opposed the move. A special tribunal of the parlement, called the Grande Chambre, was set up to try heretics. So vigorously did this tribunal act that it soon acquired the name of Chambre Ardente.

Chancellor, Richard. ?-1556. English seaman. On a voyage to discover a northeast passage to India, Chancellor entered the White Sea and traveled thence to the court of Ivan the Terrible in Moscow. This voyage pioneered trade between England and Russia.

Charlemagne. 742-814. King of the Franks (768-814) and emperor of the West (800-814). He subjugated the Saxons (785). Destroyed the kingdom of Lombardy and crowned king of Lombards (773). Established boundaries, or marks, for his kingdom. Crowned Carolus Augustus (Christmas Day, 800) by Pope Leo III. Strengthened Christianity. Founded schools (see Palace school). Patron of literature, art, and science. Buried at Aachen.

Charles Martel. 689?-741. Ruler of Austrasia (715-741) (q.v.). Overcame the Neustrians (q.v.) and made himself mayor of the palace (716-717). Defeated the Moors at Tours, near Poitiers (732), thus overthrowing the Moslem menace to

France. Grandfather of Charlemagne (q.v.).

Charles the Bald. 823-877. Son of Ludwig I. Born in Frankfurt. King of France (840-77) as Charles I. Holy Roman Emperor (875-77). He became king of France by Treaty of Verdun (843) (q.v.). During his reign France was ravaged by Normans. Bordeaux, Rouen, Orléans, and part of Paris were sacked by them.

Charles the Bold (last duke of Burgundy). 1433-1477. A bitter enemy of Louis XI of France, he spent most of his reign (1467-77) in continuous war with France. He conquered Lorraine (1475). His death ended Burgundian resistance to France. His daughter Mary married Maximilian Hapsburg and became the grandmother of Emperor Charles V.

Charles of Anjou. 1226-1285. Son of Louis VIII of France. King of the Two Sicilies (1266-85). He became one of the most powerful rulers in Europe. His harsh rule led to a revolt called the Sicilian Vespers (q.v.) (1282). He was driven from Sicily by the Spaniards (1284).

Charles I. 1600-49. King of Great Britain and Ireland (1625-49). Second son of James I, he became heir to the throne when his older brother, Prince Henry, died in 1616. As king he was readily influenced by his ministers, Buckingham, Laud, and Strafford. He tried to rule without Parliament, raising necessary funds meanwhile by forced loans, tonnage, poundage, ship money, etc., which aroused a great deal of opposition. When he tried to impose the system of bishops upon the Scotch Church, war between England and the Scotch Covenanters broke out. Compelled to summon Parliament to secure funds, Charles now became involved in a bitter struggle with that body which resulted in the Civil War (1642-46). During this war, Charles and his party (Cavaliers) were defeated.

Charles surrendered to the Scotch, who turned him over to Parliament. Parliament tried Charles before a court of 59 judges. They found him guilty of tyranny and of being an enemy of the country. He was condemned to death and beheaded.

Charles II. 1630-85. King of England (1660-85). Often called "The Merry Monarch." Son of Charles I, he passed the period of the Commonwealth in exile. After the fall of the Protectorate, he negotiated with General Monck to return to England and issued the Declaration of Breda (1660), promising amnesty and liberty of conscience. His reign was marked by the great plague (1665) and fire of London (1666). Struggle between king and Parliament led to the creation of the forerunner of the cabinet system and the Whig Party (q.v.). He was the patron of the theatre and encouraged science. He died without legitimate offspring and was succeeded by his brother James II.

Charles III (the Simple). 879-929. King of France (898-923). He ceded Normandy to Rollo (911).

Charles IV (the Fair). 1294-1328. King of France (1322-28). Son of Philip IV. Last of the Capetian kings of France. He endeavored to strengthen the royal power by increasing taxes, exacting fines, and debasing the currency. Upon his death, the nearest male relative was Philip of Valois, who became king (1328-50). However, Edward III of England claimed the throne (q.v.), since he was a nephew (through his mother) of Charles IV. However, in 1330 he renounced his claim.

Charles V (the Wise). 1337-80. King of France (1364-80). He became regent when his father was captured at the battle of Poitiers (1356). He put down the Jacquerie, or peasants' revolt (1358).

Concluded the Treaty of Brétigny with the English (1360) (q.v.). As king, he regained most of the territory held by the English (1369-75). His rule was generally wise. He was a patron of the arts and literature and collected a large library in the Louvre.

Charles VI (the Well-Beloved). 1368-1422. King of France (1380-1422). He ruled well until he became afflicted with mental disorders (1392). There then began a struggle for the regency between the houses of Orléans and Burgundy. Each appealed to the English for help at various times. The Hundred Years' War resumed and the French were defeated at Agincourt (1415). Peace followed the Treaty of Troyes (1420) (q.v.).

Charles VII. 1403-61. King of France (1422-61). At the outset of his reign, all of northern France and much of southwest France was in the hands of the English. Through the help of Joan of Arc he captured Orléans (1429) and was crowned at Reims (1429). He made peace with Burgundy (1435) and entered Paris (1436). He recovered all parts of his country from the English except Calais (1437-53). During the latter part of his reign he promulgated many reforms, including a permanent tax. He was the first to create a standing army for France.

Charles VIII. 1470-98. King of France (1483-98). He was eager to revive the rule of the house of Anjou in Naples. Hence, he made concessions to the English and the Emperor, neglected France, and made common cause with the Sforzas in Milan. He entered Naples in great pomp (1495) but was driven out in the same year by the troops of the Holy League commanded by Gonzalo de Córdoba.

Charles IX. 1550-1574. Second son of Henry II and Catherine de Médicis. King of France (1560-74). He was under the domination of his mother throughout his reign. While king, France was in the throes of a fierce religious civil war. The Massacre of St. Bartholomew's Day (1572) occurred during this conflict.

Charles X. 1757-1836. King of France (1824-30). Grandson of Louis XV. Brother of Louis XVI and Louis XVIII. Born at Versailles. Count of Artois. During the Revolution and the Napoleonic period he lived in England and Scotland. After the restoration (1814), he became the leader of the Ultra-Royalists. As king he tried to restore absolute monarchy. After the enactment of the July Ordinances (1830) (q.v.), he was overthrown by the revolution of July 27-29. He abdicated (Aug. 2) and fled to England. He lived the remainder of his days in Scotland and Prague.

Charles IV (also called Charles of Luxemburg). 1316-78. Son of John of Luxemburg, the king of Bohemia. He was the King of Germany and Bohemia and Holy Roman Emperor (1347-78). He was more interested in the arts and learning than in government administration. He was instrumental in founding the University of Prague (1348). He issued the Golden Bull (q.v.) (1356), which established the method of electing the emperor.

Charles V. 1500-58. Holy Roman Emperor (1519-56) and king of Spain as Charles I (1516-56). Son of Philip of Burgundy (Philip I of Spain) and grandson of Emperor Maximilian I and Ferdinand and Isabella. He inherited the county of Burgundy and Netherlands (1506). Crowned emperor (1520). Married Isabella of Portugal (1525).

Attitude toward the Reformation: He was tolerant in Germany for political reasons, but persecuted heretics in Spain. He summoned the Diet of Worms (q.v.) (1521) to deal with Martin Luther and

presided in person. The Diet of Augsburg (1530) failed to settle the religious controversy. The Council of Trent (1545-63) failed to unite Catholics and Protestants. He won the Schmalkaldic Wars (1546-47) against the Protestants and made the Peace of Augsburg (1555) with them.

Wars with France: He defeated Francis I at Pavia (1525), made him prisoner and forced him to sign the Treaty of Madrid (q.v.). The wars terminated with the Treaty of Crépy (1544), favorable to the Empire.

Activities in Italy and other countries: He took Rome and made the Pope prisoner (1527). His troops sacked the city (the so-called "German Fury"). He was crowned king of Lombardy (1530). Successful against the Turks under Suleiman (1532). Conquered the pirates of Tunis (1535).

As ruler of Spain: He extended New World possessions through the conquests of Mexico by Cortes (1519-21) and of Peru by Pizarro (1531-35).

Closing years: He relinquished the kingdom of Naples (1554) and Netherlands (1555) to his son Philip. He resigned control of Spain and the Indies to his son Philip II (1556) and the imperial crown to his brother Ferdinand I (1556). He retired to the monastery of Yuste in western Spain (1557).

Charles Albert (Carlo Alberto). 1798-1849. King of Sardinia (1831-1849). Born at Turin. He attempted to introduce order into his kingdom. He reorganized the finances, granted a constitution, and created an army. He was an outstanding Liberal and a leader in the movement for the unification of Italy. He was defeated by the Austrians at Custozza (1848) and Novara (1849). He resigned in favor of his son Victor Emmanuel II.

Charles II. 1661-1700. King of Spain (1665-1700). Son of Philip IV. During his reign, Spain was in a weak, demoralized condition. He joined the Grand Alliance in its war against Louis XIV, which ended in the Peace of Ryswick (q.v.). Having no offspring, he was prevailed upon to select Philip of Anjou, grandson of Louis XIV, as his successor. His death was the signal for the beginning of the War of the Spanish Succession (q.v.).

Charles III. 1716-88. King of Spain (1759-88). Son of Philip V and Elizabeth Farnese. Upon becoming king of Spain, he gave up his previous position as king of Two Sicilies to his son Ferdinand. Charles has been classified as an enlightened despot. He gave considerable impetus to administrative and economic reform.

Charles IV. 1748-1819. King of Spain (1788-1808). A well-intentioned but weak ruler. His ministers tried to shut out the influence of the French Revolution. He soon came under the dominance of Manuel Godoy, the Prince of Peace (q.v.). He made war against France and Portugal. By the Second Treaty of San Ildefonso (Jan. 20, 1801) he ceded Louisiana to France. He entered the War of the Third Coalition on the side of France. The Franco-Spanish fleet was defeated in this war at Trafalgar (Oct. 21, 1805). He abdicated (1808). He died in Rome.

Charles X Gustavus (1622-1660). King of Sweden (1654-60). He fought in the Thirty Years' War (1642-48). He became king when his cousin Christina abdicated (1654). He invaded and overran Poland (1655-56). He made war against Denmark (1657-58) and won back south Sweden (Scania).

Charles XI. 1655-97. King of Sweden (1660-97). Son of Charles X Gustavus. He was defeated by a coalition of the Holy Roman Empire, Denmark, and Holland (1675-76), but was more successful during the latter part of the war (1676-79) and won good terms at the Treaty of Nijmwegen. He began a reorganization

of his country (1680) and forced the great estates of the nobles to revert to the crown. He was granted (1682) virtually absolute power. He improved the armed forces and economic conditions of his country.

Charles XII (*called* the Alexander of the North; *also* the Madman of the North). 1682-1718. King of Sweden (1697-1718). Confronted by an alliance of Poland, Denmark, and Russia (1699), he invaded Denmark and forced the peace of Travendal (1700). Then he attacked the Russians and won a great victory at Narva (1700). He defeated the Saxons and Poles (1702) and deposed Augustus II in favor of Stanislaus Leszczynski (1704). He again invaded Russia (1707-08) and defeated Peter the Great. However, he penetrated too deeply into Russia with a small army and was defeated at Poltava (1709). He became a fugitive with Mazepa (q.v.), leader of the Don Cossacks. He fled to Turkish territory and persuaded the Turks to attack Russia (1711-12). He was captured and held prisoner (1712-14). He escaped to Sweden and found his country in a deplorable state. He raised another army, held the Russians at bay, and then invaded Norway. He was killed by a cannon ball at the siege of Fredrikshald.

Charles XIV John. 1763-1844. King of Sweden (1818-44). See Bernadotte.

Chartist Movement of England. 1838-48. This was a movement among English workmen to secure political democracy as a step towards economic relief. The movement took its name from the *People's Charter*, a document which contained the following points: (1) universal manhood suffrage; (2) secret ballot; (3) annual Parliaments; (4) payment of members of Parliament; (5) removal of property qualifications for members of Parliament; (6) equal electoral districts. In 1839, a National Convention, or

"Workingmen's Parliament," met in London to present a petition to Parliament for universal suffrage. This petition was refused, as was a similar petition in 1842. Hard times in 1847 led to a renewed effort to get Parliament to accept the Charter. A third petition, said to contain 5 million names, was carried to London early in 1848. The Duke of Wellington was called from retirement to deal with the anticipated riot. When the fateful day, April 10, 1848, arrived, there was a heavy shower of rain, and the demonstration was called off. The petition was soon found to contain less than 2 million names and many forgeries. This exposure caused a complete failure of Chartism as a movement.

Chateaubriand, Vicomte François René de. 1768-1848. French writer and statesman. Born in Saint-Malô, Brittany. In his earlier days he served in the army and held several posts under Napoleon. After the execution of the duke of Enghien (q.v.) (1804), he went into exile and traveled in the Holy Land, Greece, and northern Africa. Under the Bourbons he was created a peer (1815), and was ambassador to Britain (1822) and foreign minister (1823-24). Among his writings are: *Essai Historique, Politique 'et Moral sur les Révolutions Anciennes et Modernes* (1797); *Atala* (1801); *Génie du Christianisme* (1802); *René* (1802). *René* and *Atala* are said to mark the beginnings of the romantic movement in French literature.

Chaucer, Geoffrey. 1345-1400. Author of the *Canterbury Tales* and other poems. In order of time, he is the first great poet of the English race. In order of merit, he stands among the first. In the Middle Ages in England, he stands supreme.

Cheka (Extraordinary Commission for the Suppression of Counter-Revolution). Created on Dec. 20, 1917, by the Russian Soviets to suppress counter-revolution. It was often called "The Red Terror."

Chekhov, Anton. 1860-1904. Russian playwright and story writer. He originally studied medicine, but took to literature and won his way to the front rank. His short stories of Russian life show great psychological penetration. *Uncle Vanya, The Seagull, The Three Sisters,* and *The Cherry Orchard* are some of his memorable works.

Cherasco, Treaty of. 1631. A treaty ending a war between Spain and France over Italian possessions. France renounced all conquests in Italy. By a secret treaty with Victor Amadeus, Duke of Savoy, Pignerol was surrendered to France.

Chetniks. Yugoslav guerillas who, under the leadership of General Mikhailovitch, carried on a continuously successful warfare against the Nazi conquerors of their country.

Children Act, English. 1908. The Education Act of 1908 provided free meals for the children of the poor. The Children Act of the same year contained many provisions designed to protect children. Protection of infant children, correction of juvenile delinquency, treatment of children in industrial schools, prevention of burns, prohibition of juvenile smoking are some of these provisions.

Chioggia, War of. 1378-81. Between Venice and Genoa. Cause of the war: John V Palaeologus, Byzantine Emperor, granted to Venice the Island of Tenedos, the key to the Dardanelles. Luciano Doria, the Genoese admiral, defeated the Venetians at Pola, seized Chioggia, a strategic point near Venice, and blockaded the city. The Venetian fleet blockaded the channel leading to Chioggia and starved out the Genoese, forcing their surrender. From this blow Genoa never recovered. From this time on, Venice dominated the Levantine trade.

Chivalry. A code of conduct which grew out of the customs and ideas of the knights of the Middle Ages. The Church participated in establishing this code. Chivalry required specified conduct towards other men and particular duties towards women. However, the code of chivalry governed the conduct of knights towards others of knightly class only. It did not apply to the conduct of knights toward the lower classes.

Choiseul, Duke Étienne François de (*in early life* Count of Stainville). 1719-85. French statesman. A distinguished soldier in the War of the Austrian Succession (1740-48). Ambassador to Rome (1754-57) and to Vienna (1757-58). Minister of foreign affairs (1758-61), of war and marine (1758-63), of war and foreign affairs (1766-70). He directed French policy during the Seven Years' War (1758-63). A leader in European diplomacy (1764-70). He was dismissed through the influence of Madame du Barry (1770).

Chopin, Frédéric. 1810-49. Polish composer. He lived in exile most of his life in France. He was a noted piano virtuoso and one of the world's greatest composers of piano music.

Christian III. 1503-59. King of Denmark and Norway (1534-59). Called "Father of the People." An ardent Lutheran, he introduced the Reformation (1536) into his country. The Danish Diet abolished the Roman Catholic religion in the country and seized Church property for the crown.

Christian IV. 1557-1648. King of Denmark and Norway (1588-1648). He strengthened the influence of Denmark along the Baltic coast. Founded Christiana in Norway (1624). He joined the Protestant cause in the Thirty Years' War, but was decisively defeated at Lutter (1626). Later he was attacked and defeated by Sweden. He was forced to yield power to his nobles.

Christian Socialism. This movement arose during the latter part of the 19th century from the growing sense of social responsibility. Many people began to accept the idea that it is society's duty to *prevent* poverty rather than to *relieve* it. Many clergymen felt that the capitalistic system was unChristian, since it imposed poverty on the masses while the rich capitalists lived in luxury. When Pope Leo XIII issued his famous Encyclical, *Rerum novarum*, in 1891 (q.v.), many European Catholics adopted Christian Socialism. Following this lead, the Catholic Center Party of Germany (q.v.) and the Catholic Party in Belgium, although strongly opposed to Marxism, began to support the Socialist parties to obtain social reform. In England there was a similar movement. Many distinguished persons, such as J. F. D. Maurice (1805-72) and Charles Kingsley (1819-75), belonged to the movement. British Christian Socialists advocated a return to those principles which had guided the Christian communities in the 1st century.

Christina. 1626-1689. Queen of Sweden (1632-54). Daughter of Gustavus Adolphus. She ruled under a regency, headed by Axel Oxenstierna, until she became of age (1644). She found affairs in Sweden to her disliking and abdicated (1654). She embraced Roman Catholicism (1655). She lived first in Paris and later in Rome. In her later years she maintained a salon for men of letters and science.

Church, Feudalization of. To secure protection during the turbulent times of the 10th century, the Church was frequently forced to enter the feudal system to secure protection. Churches and monasteries often became vassals to feudal lords. Church lands belonged to the Church and could not be alienated. As late as the 11th century, clergymen frequently married. Their children, thus, could inherit the Church property. One of the purposes of advocating celibacy for clergymen was to prevent Church lands from passing through inheritance into the hands of laymen. Some bishops and abbots became feudal lords and administered many fiefs.

Churchill, Sir Winston Leonard Spencer. 1874-. English statesman, soldier, and author. Educated at Harrow and Sandhurst, he first saw active military service for the Spanish in Cuba in 1895. Thereafter, he served in the Northwest Frontier of India, the Sudan, and the Boer War. He was elected to Parliament as a Conservative in 1900. In 1906 he became a Liberal and was secretary for colonies in the Campbell-Bannerman cabinet (1905-08). President of the Board of Trade (1908-10); home secretary (1910-11), first lord of the admiralty (1911-15). He was discredited by the failure of the Gallipoli Campaign which he sponsored and was forced to resign. He returned to the cabinet as minister of munitions (1917) and secretary of state for war and for air (1918-21). Again as a Conservative, he served as colonial secretary (1921) and chancellor of the exchequer (1924-29). He held no cabinet positions for the next 10 years. In 1939 he was made first lord of the admiralty. In May, 1940, when Chamberlain was forced to resign, Churchill became prime minister. He was Britain's great war prime minister. He, together with Roosevelt and Stalin, were three of the most powerful figures in the world. In 1945, just after victory in Europe, his party was defeated at the polls, and Churchill had to resign. He and his party were returned to power in 1951.

Churchill is a prolific writer of books. Among his works are *Marlborough, World Crisis, The Gathering Storm, Their Finest Hour,* and *The Grand Alliance.* He received the Nobel Prize for literature in 1953.

Ciano, Count Galeazzo. 1903-44. Italian Fascist leader. Mussolini's son-in-law. Minister of propaganda (1935); minister of foreign affairs (1936-43). He supported his father-in-law's expansionist and foreign policy. As the war went against Italy, he wavered. In 1943 he voted to discontinue the Fascist regime. He was later captured by the Germans in north Italy, tried by the new Fascist government, and executed by a firing squad.

Cid, The (*Spanish***, el Cid Campeador —the lord champion) (***Real name*** Rodrigo *or* Ruy Diaz).** 1040-1099. Spanish soldier, originally in the service of Sancho II of Castile. Exiled, he returned to Castilian service, only to be exiled a second time. He entered service with the Moors and became governor of Valencia. Cruel, selfish, and proud, he has become a legendary hero of Spain.

Cinque Ports. Originally five port towns in Sussex and Kent (Hastings, Romney, Hythe, Dover, and Sandwich) to which Rye and Winchelsea were subsequently added. Before England had a permanent navy, it was the duty of the Cinque Ports to furnish ships and men to repel invasions. The Warden of the Cinque Ports was one of the most responsible men in the country. Since 1688 the importance of the Cinque Ports has declined, and the position of Warden is now only an honor.

Ciompi (wool-carders). In medieval Florence, the ciompi did not belong to guilds. In 1378 they staged a revolution to secure political power. They were successful, only to lose out completely by the counter-revolution of 1382.

Cisalpine Republic. When the French Revolutionary armies expelled the Austrians from the Po Valley of Italy, they reorganized the region as the Cisalpine Republic (July 9, 1797).

Cities, Medieval. The cities of Europe, which had flourished in the days of the Roman Empire, went into complete eclipse during the 4th and 5th centuries because of the Barbarian invasions and the subsequent decline of commerce. During the 8th and 9th centuries, cities began to grow up around castles or monasteries, where people gathered for protection from violence. These cities were under the rule of some noble, who collected taxes, appointed officials, kept order, and punished offenders.

Starting with the 12th century, many cities, particularly in southern France, began to revolt against their overlords. City folk had become accustomed to work together through their guild organizations. The guild merchants, particularly, were anxious to throw off feudal restrictions, which hampered trade and commerce. Many cities secured their freedom by force; others, by purchase. Upon securing freedom, they set up communes to govern themselves. Some cities never secured freedom, but were called *villes de bourgeoisie*. These were subject to a king or lord, but had virtual autonomy. Paris and Orléans are examples. Nobles frequently established new cities, known as *villes neuves*. To induce people to settle in these new cities, the lords offered special privileges. Some cities thus became places of safety (*salvites*), because they could offer the right of asylum to all criminals except thieves or murderers. Serfs who resided in a place of safety for a year and a day were declared free men.

Officials of a commune were chosen by the commune itself. Generally the method of election was very complex. Officials were called consuls, mayor, jurati, aldermen, échevins, or podestà. They exercised legislative and executive power. They controlled city finances. Since they were not directly responsible to the citizens of the cities, officials often were guilty of financial fraud. Cities often became bankrupt. Bad administration of finances also resulted in riots in which various factions fought one another over real or fancied cases of maladministration. Rioting and insolvency led to the destruction of the communes. As the kings of various countries pursued a policy of gathering power into their hands, they interfered more and more in the affairs of the cities. By 1400 virtually all communes had disappeared.

Civil Constitution for Clergy. 1790-1801. A measure adopted by the National Assembly during the French Revolution (q.v.) to control the Church. Believing that the chief business of the Church was to teach those practical moral virtues that would make good citizens, the Assembly proceeded to make the Church a national institution. All Church divisions were to coincide in area with civil political divisions. Bishops and parish priests were no longer to be appointed; they were to be elected by *all* the citizens who had the right to vote for civil officials. Clergymen were to be paid a salary by the government. The pope was to have no more authority over the Church in France, although he was still permitted to define its doctrines. Clergymen were to take an oath to support the Constitution. Those that refused (the great majority) were known as Non-Juring Clergy. The Constitution remained in effect until the Concordat (q.v.).

Civil list. A grant of money which the English Parliament pays to the king to maintain the royal household.

Civil War, English. 1642-46. On January 3, 1642, Charles I ordered his Attorney-General to arrest five members of Parliament, including Pym and Hampden. The next day he entered Commons with soldiers to effect the arrest. Warned in advance, the members had fled. This incident precipitated the Civil War, since if the king could thus enter the House of Commons, there was little hope of safeguarding civil liberties through parliamentary procedure. Five days later, Charles withdrew from London with his family and never returned, except as a prisoner.

The war was a struggle between Parliament (Roundheads) and the supporters of King Charles I (Cavaliers). The aim of the parliamentary leaders was so to restrict the powers of the king that the people might be secure in their religious and political liberties. When the victorious Parliament leaders came to realize that King Charles would not submit to any considerable loss of his power, and that he was conspiring to recover such power as he had already lost, they felt constrained to execute the king.

The nobles, gentry, small freeholders of western England, the universities, the established Church, and the great Catholic families were Cavaliers. The trading classes of the towns and most Non-Conformists (q.v.) were staunch Roundheads. In general, the laboring classes were indifferent and fought only when their homes were in danger. The north, west, and extreme southwest, regions that were predominantly agricultural, pastoral, and backward, supported the king.

The war was waged with extreme bitterness. After losing the Battle of Naseby (June 14, 1645), King Charles became a fugitive. He tried unsuccessfully to raise supporters in both Scotland and Ireland. He gave himself up to the Scots on May 5, 1646. In January, 1647, the Scots delivered the king to Parliament. Parliament tried Charles for treason, found him guilty, and beheaded him (1649).

Clarendon. See Hyde, Edward.

Clarendon Code. See Conventicle Act and Five Mile Act.

Clarendon, The Constitutions of. 1164. Henry II of England assembled a Great Council at Clarendon to settle all questions at issue between the king and the clergy. The assembly fixed the relations between the royal and ecclesiastical courts, making the latter inferior to the former. In effect, the king was made head of the English Church, and the Church was made subordinate to the law of the land.

Clemenceau, Georges. 1841-1929. French statesman. "The Tiger." War correspondent with the United States army in the Civil War (1865). Member of the Chamber of Deputies (1876-93). Senator (from 1902). Premier (1906-09). Again premier (1917-1920) when he led France through a critical period of World War I. He represented France at the Versailles Peace Conference (1919). He retired to private life in 1920.

Clericalism. Clericalism is a term applied by 19th century Europeans to all those who supported the Syllabus of Errors, the Encyclical of 1864 (q.v.), and the Doctrine of Papal Infallibility of 1870. Opponents called the supporters of clericalism unpatriotic and undemocratic.

Clericis Laicos. 1296. A bull issued by Pope Boniface VIII. It forbade, on pain of excommunication, all laymen to collect taxes on Church lands, and all clergymen to pay them. Although this bull was addressed to all Christendom, it was aimed specifically at Philip IV of France.

Clermont, Council of. 1095. A Council called by Pope Urban II. After various matters were considered, the Pope preached (Nov. 26) to a vast multitude in the open air. He called for a crusade. After picturing the wretched condition of the Holy Land, how its shrines were polluted, and after stressing the danger which threatened Europe if the Mohammedans were allowed to retain possession of Asia Minor, he called upon all present to give up their private warfare and recover the holy places from the Mohammedans. The appeal fell on willing ears. Within a short time the great crusading movement (1096-1270) was begun.

Clovis I (*German,* Chlodwig; *English,* Louis). 466?-511. King of the Salian Franks and one of the earliest rulers of the Merovingian dynasty (481-511). He married Clotilda, a Christianized Burgundian princess, who converted him to Christianity (496). He defeated the Gallo-Roman colony at a battle near Soissons (486). Defeated the Alemanni (496). Established his court at Paris (507). Defeated the West Goths (507). He tried to unite all Frankish people into one kingdom, but divided his realm among his four sons just before his death.

Cluniac reforms. A movement to reform monastic life which originated in the monastery of Cluny, situated in the hills to the west of Mâcon, France. This monastery was founded in 910. Under the direction of a series of capable abbots, Cluny achieved a wide reputation for piety. Monks from Cluny were asked to reside in other monasteries to introduce and administer the Cluniac reforms. Such monasteries were called a "congregation." The abbot of Cluny, who was at the head of the congregation, thus had great power. The Cluniac reforms were taken up by Gregory VII and thus made the program of the papacy. The monastic rule was made more rigorous and secular clergy were required to model their lives after it. Thus the whole clergy were purged of many of their corrupt and immoral practices.

Coalition, First against France. 1793-97. This was a union of England, Russia, Sardinia, Spain, Naples, Prussia, Austria, and Portugal against France. Prussia made peace with France April 5, 1795, and Spain followed suit July 22, 1795. Holland was conquered by the French. Austria made peace with France at Campo Formio (q.v.) (Oct. 17, 1797). England supported its allies with subsidies. Its fleet played a big role with victories at Cape St. Vincent (Feb. 14, 1797) (q.v.) and Camperdown (Oct. 11, 1797) (q.v.).

Coalition, Second against the French. 1799-1801. This was a union between England, Russia, Austria, Portugal, Naples, and Turkey against the French. During the winter of 1799, Russia withdrew. After the defeats by the French at Marengo (June 13, 1800) and Hohenlinden (Dec. 3, 1800), the Austrians made peace at Luneville (Feb. 9, 1801) (q.v.). Thus the coalition broke up. On March 25, 1802, the English and French signed the Treaty of Amiens. England gave back to France all conquered territory except Trinidad and Ceylon, which had been captured from France's allies Spain and Holland. The Cape of Good Hope, taken from the Dutch, was to be a free port. Egypt was returned to Turkey. Malta was restored to the Knights of St. John.

Coalition, Third against Napoleon. 1805. This was a union of Great Britain, Russia, and Austria against Napoleon. When Napoleon was foiled in his attempt to invade England by Nelson's great victory at Trafalgar (Oct. 21, 1805) (q.v.), he marched his "Army of England" across the Rhine and entered Vienna (Nov. 13, 1805). At Austerlitz (Dec. 2, 1805) he gained a decisive victory over the Austrians and Russians and forced Austria to withdraw from the war (Treaty of Pressburg, Dec. 26, 1805). Thus the coalition was broken up.

Cobbet, William (*pseudonym* Peter Porcupine). 1763-1835. English political journalist and essayist. During service in the British army (1783-91), he taught himself grammar and composition. He sailed to Philadelphia (1792) to avoid prosecution for writing a pamphlet attacking the army. Returned to England (1800) and edited (from 1802) a weekly, *Political Register*, which at first was Tory and later radical. Farmed in Hampshire (1804-17). Took up the cause of dispossessed rural laborers. Imprisoned in Newgate (1810-12). Had to flee to Long Island (1817-19). Developed a successful seed farm in Kensington. M.P. (1832). Author of *A Grammar of the English Language* (1818), *Advice to Young Men* (1830) and about 50 prose works.

Cobden, Richard. 1804-65. English statesman. Advocate of free trade. Son of a Sussex farmer. As a partner in a calico-printing factory, he gained an independent fortune. He studied the economic and financial systems of the United States, the Near East, and Germany. With Bright he organized the Anti-Corn Law League (1838-46) (q.v.). He succeeded in forcing a repeal of the Corn Laws (1846). He organized a series of international congresses to promote world peace (1848-51). In 1859-60 he persuaded Napoleon III of France to adopt partial free trade and negotiated with him the "Cobden Treaty" for reciprocal trade between England and France. He favored the North in the United States Civil War. With Bright he led the Manchester school of economics. He believed in a minimum of government at home and a minimum of intervention abroad.

Code Napoléon. It had long been the dream of the French liberals to reduce the complicated laws of the land into a simple, uniform code, so that everyone who could read might know what was legal or illegal. The National Convention had begun to formulate a legal code; but it remained for Napoleon to complete the task. The draftsmen of this code of laws were the most competent jurists of the day, with Bonaparte himself for their president. The aim of these lawmakers was to be clear and practical. The Civil Code appeared on March 21, 1804. It was followed by a Code of Civil Procedure, a Code of Criminal Procedure, a Penal Code, and a Commercial Code. These laws commended themselves not only to France but also to a greater part of continental Europe. They preserved the most important social gains of the Revolution, such as civil equality, religious toleration, equality of inheritance, emancipation of serfs, freedom of land, legal arrest, and trial by jury. On the debit side, the codes contained many harsh punishments and relegated women to an inferior position.

Code of Czar Alexis Michaelovitch. A code of law drawn up in 1648-49 in Russia, based on Lithuanian and Byzantine law. It was the basis of Russian law until it was superseded by the code of 1832.

Codex of Justinian. Justinian, the Eastern Roman emperor (527-65), ordered all the laws of the empire to be codified. A commission, headed by Tribonian, codified all existing laws. The commission made many changes in the text of the laws in order to reduce them to harmony. A collection of laws, called *Pandects*, contained a summary of opinions, explanations, and decisions of famous judges, as well as the text of the laws themselves. For the use of law students, a treatise on the general principles of Roman law was prepared, which was called the *Institutes*. Justinian himself kept a record of all laws which were enacted during his reign and published them under the title of *Novellae*. Although this code of laws was essentially pagan, it was adopted by many of the countries of Europe.

Coeur, Jacques. 1400?-1456. Merchant and financier of Bourges. He financed Charles VII, who later imprisoned him for conspiracy.

Coke, Sir Edward. 1552-1634. English jurist. He held many high offices, including chief-justice of the King's bench. He was the prosecutor against Essex, Raleigh, and the Gunpowder conspirators (q.v.). He resisted the royal prerogative against judges. He took an active part in writing the Petition of Rights (q.v.) (1628). His four *Institutes* and his Law Reports are famous in legal literature.

Colbert, Jean Baptiste. 1619-83. French statesman. Born in Reims. Secretary in the war office (1639). Entered the employ of Mazarin (1651). Made controller of finance by Louis XIV (1665). He revised the financial system of France to enforce honesty in the collection of taxes. He greatly increased the state revenues. He developed French industry. As minister of marine (1669) he created the French navy and merchant marine. He encouraged colonial expansion and foreign trade. He devised a system of protective tariffs to encourage French industry. He is often called the "father of mercantilism." He acquired a great private fortune and patronized arts and letters.

Cold War, The. The rivalry between the United States and the Soviet Union since 1945. Every device short of actual military conflict has been used by both sides. Propaganda, blockade and airlift, economic pressure, aid to other countries, threats and promises have been some of the weapons used by both sides.

Coleridge, Samuel. 1772-1834. English poet and critic. He was associated with Wordsworth in producing the *Lyrical Ballads*. He is the author of *The Rime of the Ancient Mariner, Kubla Khan, Table Talk, Confessions of an Inquiring Spirit*, etc.

Colet, John. 1466-1519. An outstanding scholar at Oxford, he later became Dean of St. Paul's. Applying himself to study for the purpose of understanding the Bible better, he devoted his whole force toward raising the standards of scholarship. He was unsparing in his denuncia-

tion of the worldliness of the church and the clergy.

Colonna. A noble Roman family which originated in the 12th century. It held great estates in the Campagna. It was frequently engaged in feuds with the Orsini and Caetani families. It generally sided with the Ghibelline (q.v.) faction against the pope. It furnished one pope (Martin V), 30 cardinals, and many distinguished generals and senators.

Columba, Saint (*Irish* Colum). 521-97. Irish missionary; called "Apostle of Caledonia." With 12 disciples he founded (563) a monastery on Iona and converted the northern Picts to Christianity. He was largely independent of papal supervision.

Columbus, Christopher. 1446-1506. Discoverer of America. Born at or near Genoa. Settled in Lisbon. Believing the theory that the earth is round, he tried to influence the King of Portugal to equip an expedition to sail west to the Orient. Failing in this, he went to Spain (1484) and finally secured financial backing from Ferdinand and Isabella (Apr. 17, 1492). He fitted out three vessels, Santa Maria (which he commanded, with Juan de la Cosa as pilot), Niña (Vincente Pinzón, captain), and Pinta (Martín Pinzón, captain). He sailed from Palos (Aug. 3, 1492) and sighted land (Oct. 12, 1492), Watling Island, one of the Bahama group. He sailed around Cuba and Haiti and returned to Palos (Mar. 15, 1493). He sailed on a second voyage (Sept. 25, 1493) with 17 ships and 5,000 men. He discovered Dominica and Jamaica. Made a settlement, Isabella, on Haiti (Dec. 1493), the first European town in the New World. He returned to Spain (March, 1496). Left Spain on a third voyage (May 30, 1498). Discovered Trinidad and the mouth of the Orinoco River. Complaints of trouble in the new colonies brought an official investigator,

Francisco de Bobadilla (Aug. 24, 1500). Columbus and his brothers were arrested and sent to Spain in chains. Released in Spain, he was unable to have his honors restored. He departed on a fourth voyage (March, 1502). He discovered Honduras and sailed down to the Isthmus of Panama. He returned to Spain (Nov. 7, 1504). He failed to gain restitution of his honors. He died in poverty at Valladolid (May 20, 1506). He believed to his death that he had discovered the coast of Asia.

Cominform (Communist Information Bureau). An organization which has replaced the Comintern (q.v.), which was abandoned in May, 1943. The Comintern was revived in this new form, following a secret meeting in Poland in 1947. The Cominform was created ostensibly to issue information and to direct propaganda activities. Actually, it coordinates the political, economic, cultural, and military affairs in Communist Europe. Its influence is manifest in Italy, France, and even the United States. Its headquarters were located originally in Belgrade. After the defection of Tito, the Cominform headquarters were moved to Bucharest.

Comintern. See Internationals, First, Second, and Third.

Commercial Revolution. 16th century. Following the discovery of the New World by Columbus (q.v.) and a way of sailing to India *via* the Cape of Good Hope by Vasco da Gama (q.v.), the commercial importance of the Italian cities in the Mediterranean Sea declined while the commercial power of Spain, Portugal, France, Holland, and England increased. The shift of trade from the Mediterranean to the Atlantic seacoast is known as the Commercial Revolution.

Commission on Human Rights. In 1946, ECOSOC (q.v.) established a Commission on Human Rights, which

prepared a Universal Declaration of Human Rights that was accepted by the General Assembly of the United Nations on Dec. 10, 1948. The Declaration contains 30 articles which deal with individual and personal rights; rights of relationship; economic, social, and cultural rights. It also sets forth conditions under which human rights can be attained.

Committee of General Security. See Reign of Terror.

Committee of Public Safety. 1793-95. Created by the National Convention of France in the spring of 1793, this committee of 9 (later 12) members was given supreme executive authority in France. This body, which included from time to time such men as Robespierre, St. Just, and Carnot, acted in secret. It issued directives to the ministers of state, appointed local officials, and administered the entire country. It conducted foreign affairs, supervised the army, and rallied all classes of people to support the regime.

Committee on Economic Cooperation. See Marshall Plan.

Common law. A system of law based on custom, usage, and court decision. Starting from the inquest, a device of the Frankish emperors who sent around officials to gather information on the sworn testimony of the communities they visited, the system was developed on French soil and brought to England by William the Conqueror. Henry II so simplified and unified divergent practices that common law became firmly implanted in England.

Commonwealth and Protectorate, English. 1649-60. This was an era of English history between the execution of Charles I and the accession to the throne of Charles II. During this period, the House of Lords, the office of king, and the established Church were abolished. England was proclaimed a commonwealth, the first national republic in the history of the world. The dominant figure during this period was Oliver Cromwell, the Lord Protector.

Commune del Popolo. See Italian cities.

Commune of Paris. March-May, 1871. Before the treaty with the Germans was ratified to end the Franco-Prussian War, a "Commune" was formed by the workmen of Paris to look after their interests. During the siege of Paris a "central committee" had been formed by the workmen to look after their interests. It was joined by a similar "central committee" of Republican guardsmen to form a "Joint Committee." This body established itself in the city hall and was the real government of Paris from March to May, 1871. It was not a homogeneous body. Half were Republicans; one-fourth, Marxian Socialists; one-fourth, Anarchists. When the commune revolted against the National Assembly and declared Paris free and sovereign and that the French state should be a loose federation of communes, the army of the National Assembly attacked Paris and defeated the "Communards." The fighting lasted from April 1 to May 28, 1871. At least 15,000 "Communards" were killed and 125,000 deported to New Caledonia.

Communist Manifesto. Published by Marx and Engels in 1848, it is the "birth-cry of modern Socialism." According to the Manifesto, the contemporary conflict between capitalists and wage-earners is but a phase of the age-old economic struggle between social classes. Proletarians were urged to organize into a class party, to gain political power, and to abolish middle-class property ownership. As transitional measures, proletarians were to demand the following: (1) Confiscation of land rent; (2) high direct taxes; (3) abolition of inheritance; (4) confiscation of the property of emigrants; (5) centralization of credit by a national bank; (6) public ownership of all means of transportation; (7) national factories and national cultivation of land; (8) compulsory labor for all; (9) abolition of distinction between town and country by a redistribution of population; (10) free public education for all children.

Communist Party of the USSR. The only party permitted in the USSR. It operates through "cells" which are located in every activity where decisions are made. Its activities are controlled through a Central Committee, which, in turn, is dominated by the Politburo. Membership in the party is severely limited. Each applicant must pass a rigorous trial period and must justify his membership periodically. He must at all times conform to the "party line."

Compactata. See Utraquists.

Compte Rendu. 1781. "Account Rendered of the Financial Condition." This was the first accounting of the condition of the royal treasury to be published in France. It was prepared by Necker, who was the finance minister for Louis XVI (1776-81). For the first time it was possible for the public to read how much money was secured from various sources and for what the money was spent.

Compurgation. A legal form much used in medieval German courts. The accused was allowed to clear himself by *compurgation,* that is, by taking a solemn oath that he was innocent and by presenting a definite number of associates to swear that his oath was pure. Great stress was laid upon the form of the oath. Upon the slightest verbal slip, the defense collapsed. Much depended upon the rank of the one who took the oath. An oath of a nobleman normally counterbalanced the oaths of six ordinary freemen.

Comuneros, Uprising of. 1520-21. A group of Spanish cities (led by Toledo and the Toledan, Juan de Padilla) took issue with the king and the aristocracy. They were defeated at Villalar (Apr. 23, 1521). The leaders were executed and the authority of the king was reestablished.

Concert of Europe. See Quadruple Alliance.

Conciliar Movement. 15th century. An attempt to make the power of the pope subordinate to Church councils. Ever since the early days of Christianity, great councils had assembled on important occasions. At the time of the Great Schism (q.v.), a Church council, the Council of Constance (q.v.), claimed to be superior to the pope. Such a claim involved not only a temporary means of healing the Great Schism, but a profound alteration in the Church's historic constitution. This movement continued sporadically for the next four centuries until the Vatican Council (1869-70) (q.v.) ended it by enunciating the doctrine of papal infallibility.

Concordat between France and the Papacy. 1801. By this agreement it was determined that French archbishops and bishops should be appointed by the French government, but confirmed by the Pope. The clergy were to be paid by the government. The Pope agreed to accept as valid the titles of those who had bought former church property confiscated by the revolutionary government. Pius VII (elected 1800) was given the possession of the Papal States, but without Ferrara, Bologna, and Romagna. This concordat lasted until 1905.

Concordat of Worms. 1122. The 11th century witnessed a classic struggle between the Emperors and the Popes over the right of selecting bishops and investing them with authority. The question

had two angles: (1) Who was the head of the Church, the Emperor or the Pope? (2) Since bishops were feudal lords as well as ecclesiastics, to whom did they owe allegiance? After much controversy, the Concordat of Worms finally settled the issue with a compromise. The Pope was given the right to invest the clergy with spiritual authority, which was symbolized with a ring and the staff. The Pope had the right of appointing bishops and abbots, who were to be canonically elected in the presence of the Emperor or his representative. Contested elections were to be decided by the Emperor. The Emperor was given the right to invest clergymen with their lands and all their civil and judicial functions. The symbol of this was the sceptre. In Germany the oath of allegiance to the Emperor was to be taken before investiture; in other lands, within six months after investiture. The Pope really got the better of the compromise. German clergy, who up to this time were one of the greatest supports of the Emperor, were now alienated. An independent German clergy from this time on was almost impossible.

Condé, Prince de. Louis II de Bourbon, Duke of Enghien. "The Great Condé." 1621-86. French soldier. He won the battle of Rocroi (1643) (q.v.) against the Spanish. Commanded the French armies (with Turenne) in the Thirty Years' War (1643-46). Given the duty of putting down the Fronde, he later quarreled with Mazarin and fought on the side of the Fronde. Defeated at the Dunes (1658). Pardoned (1659). Again commanded the French armies (1673-75). Friend of Molière, Racine, Boileau, and Bossuet.

Condorcet, Marquis de (Marie Jean Antoine Nicholas de Caritat). 1743-94. French philosopher, mathematician, and revolutionary. Member of the Legislative Assembly (1791) and president of it (1792). Member of the National Convention (1792). Author of a plan for public education, which was later put into effect by Napoleon. Member of the Girondist Party. Arrested with the other Girondist leaders, he died in prison (March 28, 1794).

Condottieri. Mercenary soldiers employed by medieval Italian city-states. The reason for the use of mercenaries was two-fold: (1) Most Italian people were employed in business or the arts and did not care to take up arms as a profession; (2) the city tyrants preferred a standing army dependent on themselves to a militia of free bourgeoisie. An Englishman, John Hawkwood, employed by Pope Gregory XI against Florence in 1375, made the institution popular. Eventually, successful condottieri became city tyrants (Sforza in Milan, etc.).

Confederation of the Rhine. Formed by Napoleon on July 12, 1806. The Holy Roman Empire was abolished. Napoleon was to be the protector of this confederation. The initial members were the Prince Primate (of Mainz); the Kings of Bavaria and Württemberg; the Grand Dukes of Baden, Hesse, Berg, Darmstadt; the Duke of Nassau, etc. Later, all German princes joined the confederation except those of Austria, Prussia, Brunswick, and the Elector of Hesse.

Confirmation of Charters. (Confirmatio cartarum). 1297. In this document the barons of England forced Edward I to promise not to levy any new or extraordinary taxes without the consent of Parliament.

Congo Free State, Establishment of. May 2, 1885. This great African empire was built up by Leopold II of Belgium as a personal enterprise. As a result of scandals and an investigation, it was ceded by the king to the Belgian nation (1905) and became the Belgian Congo.

Congregationalists. See Non-Conformists.

Congress of Oppressed Austrian Nationalities. Apr. 10, 1918. Czech, Yugoslav, Polish, and Romanian representatives met in Rome and declared the right of self-determination. They denounced the Hapsburg government for its opposition to the free development of nations. They called upon all fellow nationals to fight against Austria-Hungary. Following this declaration, the independence of Czechoslovakia was recognized by Italy and France on June 30, by Great Britain on Aug. 13, and by the United States on Sept. 3.

Conrad II (called the Salian). 990?-1039. Holy Roman Emperor (1024-39). Founder of the Franconian or Salian dynasty. Put down a formidable revolt in Swabia (1025-30). Added Burgundy to the Empire (1033).

Conrad III. 1093-1152. King of Germany (1138-52). He founded the Hohenstaufen dynasty of the Holy Roman Emperors, but was never crowned himself. In company with Louis VII of France, he led the Second Crusade (1147-49). He began a struggle with Henry, Duke of Saxony and Bavaria, which developed into a long struggle between the Guelfs and the Ghibellines (q.v.).

Conrad IV. 1228-1254. King of Germany and Sicily (1250-54). Last of the Hohenstaufen dynasty to rule as emperor. His death was followed by the Great Interregnum (1254-73) (q.v.).

Conservative Party, The British. Following the enactment of the Reform Bill of 1832, many English Tories rallied around the new standard of "Conservatism," which was erected by Sir Robert Peel. Peel accepted the principles of the Reform Bill, but wished in the future to proceed in a conservative manner. This party has remained a dominant force in England ever since.

Consolidation Act, English. 1878. By this law, measures regulating hours of employment, employment of children, etc., were gathered together and codified. The various regulations so consolidated stretch all the way back to the Act of 1819, which specified that children under 9 years of age should not be compelled to work more than 12 hours a day in the cotton mills. In 1901, the Consolidation Act was again revised. In it the minimum age for child-workers was raised to 12 years. The law contained elaborate provisions governing plant sanitation and inspection.

Constance, Council of. 1414. A great Church Council which was called to deal with the problems connected with the Great Schism (q.v.) (1378-1417). This council was a revival of the conciliar idea which had figured so prominently in the early days of the Church. The Council of Constance deposed three rival popes and chose Martin V to be the sole pontiff. It also tried John Hus for heresy and had him burned at the stake (1415).

Constance, Treaty of. 1183. See Lombard League.

Constantinople, Capture of by the Turks. May 29, 1453. The Turks under Mohammed II closed in on Constantinople in the spring of 1453. Catalans, Venetians, and Genoese sent assistance to Constantinople because they enjoyed valuable trading privileges there. Actually, they offered most of the resistance to the Turks. Towards the end of May the walls were breached and the city was taken by assault. Thus the Byzantine Empire came to an end.

Constitutional Laws of 1875, French. By these laws, passed in February and July, 1875, the National Assembly practically recognized the Third Republic and created an instrument of government which served as its constitution. There were to be a Chamber of Deputies, elected by universal manhood suffrage, and a Senate, elected indirectly. Laws were to be administered by a cabinet which was responsible to both houses of Parliament. The head of state was to be a president, chosen for a term of seven years by the joint action of the Chamber and the Senate.

Constitution of the Year III. Aug. 22, 1795. This constitution was prepared by the National Convention. It reflected the bourgeois influences that had come to dominate that body. Law-making was intrusted to a bicameral legislative body, chosen by indirect election. A Council of Five Hundred had the duty of proposing laws. A Council of Ancients (250 in number) had the functions of examining and enacting laws. A Board of Directors, or Directory, was to enforce laws and appoint the ministers of state, who would be responsible to the Directory. This Board of Directors was composed of five members, elected by the legislature. One member was to retire each year and be replaced by a newly chosen member.

Constitution of the Year VIII. Dec. 24, 1799. This constitution authorized the Consulate in France. It was ratified by a vote of 3 million ayes to 1500 noes. While preserving the appearance of a republic, it set up the dictatorship of Bonaparte. Below the three consuls were the following institutions:

Senate (80), appointed for life from lists of names sent in by departments, legislative bodies, and higher officials.

Tribunate (100), which debated government matters, but did not vote upon them.

Legislative Chamber (300), which accepted or rejected government measures without debate.

Council of State, appointed by the First Consul.

The people of France voted for the notables of the communes, who then elected 1/10 of their own number as notables of departments, of whom 1/10 became the notables of France. From this final group were selected, by the Senate, the members of the legislative bodies.

Consulate. 1799-1804. A form of government inaugurated in France following the coup d'état by Bonaparte. Bonaparte was to be first consul for ten years (in 1802 he was made first consul for life) and was assisted by two other consuls—Cambacérès and Lebrun. During the period of the Consulate, France enjoyed a short period of peace, during which numerous public works and administrative reforms were either accomplished or initiated. The Consulate ended when Bonaparte crowned himself emperor (see Constitution of the Year VIII).

Containment. A series of steps, military and otherwise, which were designed (since 1947) to check Russian expansion. The United States has been the prime mover in developing this policy and has financed the major part of it.

Continental System. 1806-1814. This was an attempt by Napoleon to force England to submission by an economic blockade. On Nov. 21, 1806, Napoleon issued the Berlin Decree in which he proclaimed a blockade of the British Isles; prohibited all commerce between them and France and states dependent on her; and announced the confiscation of British goods in the harbors of these countries. In Dec. 1807, Napoleon's Milan Decree imposed other restrictive measures. By the end of 1808, every country of Europe except Sweden and Turkey was brought under the System. This blockade was never enforced strictly. There was widespread smuggling. Napoleon was forced to issue licenses authorizing exceptions in special cases. Nevertheless, the blockade caused serious hardships and contributed to Napoleon's unpopularity.

Contractual Agreement. 1952. Since there are deep differences between the Western Powers and the USSR, it has been impossible to conclude a treaty of peace with Germany. In June, 1952, a so-called Contractual Agreement was drawn up between France, the United States, Great Britain, and the Bonn government to end the war between them and to give West Germany virtual sovereign powers. The United States Senate and Great Britain have ratified this agreement.

Conventicle Act. 1664. An English law aimed against religious Non-Conformists (q.v.). Five or more persons, exclusive of members of a family, were forbidden to hold religious worship unless Established Church forms were used. This act bore down heavily upon the Quakers.

Cooper, Anthony Ashley. See Shaftesbury.

Copernicus, Nicolaus (*Latinized form of* Niklas Koppernigk). 1473-1543. Polish astronomer. Born in Thorn. Educated in Cracow and Bologna. Canon of the cathedral at Franenburg (1497). Lectured on astronomy in Rome (1500). Doctor of canon law (Ferrara, 1503). Medical student in Padua (to 1506). Physician to his uncle and patron, the Bishop of Ermeland (to 1512). Occupied in his duties at Franenburg thereafter. Completed his great work, *De Revolutionibus Orbium Coelestium,* in 1530. The printing of it was delayed (1543) until Copernicus was on his deathbed. He is regarded as the founder of the theory that the earth rotates daily on its axis and that the planets revolve around the sun.

Corday, Charlotte (*full name* Marie Anne Charlotte Corday d'Armont). 1768-93. She believed in the principles of the French Revolution, but was horrified at the bloodshed during the Reign of

Terror. She gained entrance to the home of Marat, a leader of the Terrorist faction, and stabbed him to death with a butcher knife while he was in his bath (July 13, 1793). She was guillotined July 17, 1793.

Cordelier Club. A radical club organized in Paris during the early days of the Revolution (1790). It took its name from a confiscated monastery building where the club meetings were normally held. It was organized as a "society of the friends of the rights of man and of the citizen." It was very radical from the beginning and numbered among its members most of the foremost revolutionaries of Paris.

Cordon Sanitaire. A French policy of the 1920's and 30's to contain Communist Russia. This was done by strengthening the Baltic States, Poland, and Romania.

Corn Laws, British, Repeal of. The British Corn (grain) Laws forbade the importation of foreign wheat unless the average price of wheat in the United Kingdom was 70 *s.* per quarter. If wheat were scarce or sold for over 70 *s.*, foreign wheat was admitted under a heavy duty, which became lower as the price of wheat rose. Landowners defended the Corn Laws because high prices for wheat meant high rents. They also argued that England ought to raise its own breadstuff, something which it had not done since 1820. The new industrialist class wanted to have the Corn Laws repealed, so as to reduce the price of bread; thus, they could pay their workers lower wages. Along with the repeal of the Corn Laws, the industrialists urged abolition of import duties, such as tariffs on raw wool and raw silk. In 1838, Richard Cobden and John Bright founded the Anti-Corn Law League, which conducted one of the best organized propaganda campaigns of modern times. Bad harvests in 1845 and the Irish Potato Famine aided the opponents of the Corn Laws.

Under the sponsorship of the Conservative Prime Minister, Sir Robert Peel, a law was passed (1846) specifying that all duties on grain were to be abolished within three years. In the same year, duties on foreign manufactured goods were greatly reduced and were finally abolished (1850). Sir Robert Peel was forced by his party to resign because he had defied his party by advocating repeal of the Corn Laws. Cobden received £80,000 in gifts from his grateful admirers for the part he had played in securing the repeal of this legislation.

Corneille, Pierre. 1606-1684. French playwright. Born in Rouen. He studied law and was admitted to the bar (1624), but turned his attention to the stage. He is regarded as the creator of French tragedy and one of France's greatest tragic poets. Author of *Médée* (1635), *Le Cid* (1636), *Oedipe* (1659), etc.

Corot, Jean. 1796-1875. French artist. Primarily a landscape painter. His main sketching ground was at Barbizon, in the Forest of Fontainebleau. He is generally considered the greatest of the Barbizon school of landscape painters. Among his masterpieces are *Danse de Nymphes, Orphée, Macbeth.*

Corporate State, Italian. Before 1914 there developed in Italy the doctrine of syndicalism, which advocated the abolition of political government in favor of government by economic groups. Under the leadership of Edmondo Rossini, the syndicalists united with the Fascists in the struggle against communism. Since by 1926 the syndicalists numbered 2½ million, Mussolini determined to control them. By the Law of 1926, 13 confederated Fascist syndicates (6 of employers, 6 of employees, and 1 of intellectuals) were given legal status. The syndicates acquired the sole right to prepare collective contracts. Strikes and lockouts were forbidden. Sixteen labor courts, from which there was no appeal, were set up. In 1928 a law was passed which made Italy the first Western state to have a national legislature representing economic groups. Membership in the Chamber of Deputies was fixed at 400. The 13 syndicates nominated 800 candidates for this body and the charitable and cultural institutions selected 200 more. From this list of 1,000 names, the Fascist Grand Council chose 400 nominees. Voters were required to vote "Yes" or "No" for the entire 400. In 1934 the Italian Government created 22 new corporations, each of which represented the state, capital, and labor. Three functions were assigned to the corporations: to advise the government; settle labor disputes; and regulate production, distribution, and prices. After several years of further study, the Fascist Grand Council recommended (1938) that the Chamber of Deputies be replaced by a Chamber of Fasces and Corporations. This house was composed of 700, representing the state, the Fascist Party, and the 22 corporations. All were to be appointed by the Head of State (Mussolini). This body first met in March, 1939. Thus national elections were abolished.

Corpus Juris Civilis. See Codex of Justinian.

Cort, Henry. 1740-1800. An English navy agent. He invented (1784) the process of "puddling," by which wrought iron could be made efficiently. He became a great ironmaster.

Cortes. The parliament of Spain, first summoned in Castile about 1250. It was a consulting body with no legislative power. After the defeat of the popular body (las comunidades) (q.v.) by Charles V, the commons and the Cortes of Spain lost all power.

Cortés, Hernán. 1485-1547. Spanish conqueror of Mexico. Born at Medellín. He sailed to Santo Domingo (1504).

Given command of an expedition against the mainland (1518-19), he founded Veracruz and entered Mexico City (Nov. 8, 1519). Driven out, he reentered the city in triumph (Aug. 1521). Made governor (1523). Deposed (1526). Called back to Spain (1528). Granted honors and made Marquis of the Valley of Oaxaca. Returned to Mexico (1530). Died on an estate in Seville.

Corvée. A labor-tax during the days of the Old Regime in France. Peasants were required to labor on the roads as part of their tax to the state. This road-making sometimes consumed several weeks each year.

Cossacks. Independent frontiersmen who in the 15th and 16th centuries broke away from Tartar rule, forming two independent communities: the Host of the Don and the Zaporog ("beyond the cataracts," i.e., those of the Dnieper River) Host. They were democratic bodies who elected their leaders—called Ataman by the Don Cossacks and the Hetman by the Zaporog Cossacks. There were no class differences, and no private property in land. All land belonged to the Hosts. In the 17th century, the Cossacks gradually lost independence. In 1614 the Host of the Don became the vassal of Moscow.

Council of Blood (*also known as* **the Council of Troubles**). 1567-73. A tribunal set up by the Duke of Alva to stamp out opposition in the Netherlands.

Council of Foreign Ministers. 1945. Although the Potsdam Conference (q.v.) came to a general agreement regarding the fate of Germany, there were still many unsolved specific problems regarding Germany and its satellites. It was agreed that a Council of Foreign Ministers, composed of representatives of the United States, the USSR, Great Britain, China, and France, should work on these problems. The Council met in London

(Sept. 11-Oct. 2, 1945) without success. The second meeting (Dec. 1945) in Moscow was barren of accomplishment. In Nov.-Dec. 1946, a meeting in New York produced treaties for Italy, Finland, Hungary, Romania, and Bulgaria (see Axis Satellites, Fate of). No progress was made on treaties with Japan, Austria, and Germany. In Sept. 1950, the representatives of the United States, Great Britain, and France prepared a treaty for Germany. The USSR has not accepted that treaty, nor the agreement between Japan and the United Nations. No Austrian treaty has been prepared.

Council of Pavia. 1018. At this Council Pope Benedict VIII (1012-24) issued an order forbidding clergymen to marry. The reason for this prohibition was not so much religious as financial and political. If clergymen married, there was danger that their children would inherit church lands, thus diminishing the income of the church.

Counter-Reformation, Catholic. To counteract the initial success of the Reformation, the Roman Catholic Church launched a strong campaign to purge itself of its abuses and to recapture lost territory. The Council of Trent (1545-63) (q.v.) accomplished the first aim. The Society of Jesus, the Holy Inquisition, the Index, and the creation of ghettos for Jews were designed to accomplish the second purpose. So successful was the Counter-Reformation that large areas of central Europe and southern Germany, which had become Protestant, were regained by the Church.

Covenanters. A Scotch faction which supported the National Covenant, which was signed in February, 1638. The signers pledged themselves on oath to defend the Crown and true religion. These two contradictory principles of devotion to Presbyterianism and of loyalty to the king played a curious part in 17th century struggles. Frequently, the Scots made war upon the king; but only, they insisted, in defense of their religion.

Coverdale, Miles. 1488-1568. An English ecclesiastic who in 1539 brought out the "Great Bible," which was presented to Henry VIII by Thomas Cromwell.

Cranmer, Thomas. 1489-1556. English reformer; Archbishop of Canterbury. He gained favor with Henry VIII by declaring his marriage with Catherine of Aragon null and void. He played a major part in Henry's ecclesiastical revolution. Repudiated the doctrine of transubstantiation. Converted the Mass into Communion. Wrote the Thirty-Nine Articles of Religion (q.v.) and the Book of Common Prayer (q.v.). On the accession of Queen Mary, a Roman Catholic, he was condemned as a heretic and burned at the stake.

Crécy, Battle of. Aug. 26, 1346. A decisive battle in the Hundred Years' War between England and France. It was an overwhelming victory for the English. The ultimate consequences of this battle were momentous. The foundations of medieval society were shaken, since the flower of French knighthood were defeated by English archers.

Crédit Foncier (Land Bank). This institution was created in France by Napoleon III (1852). (Afterwards it was absorbed into the Bank of France.) It offered long-term loans with low rates of interest upon mortgages secured by land. Many nobles used this bank to purchase land to enlarge their estates. This privilege predisposed them favorably toward Napoleon.

Crédit Mobilier (Commercial Bank). This was a joint-stock company which was formed in France by Napoleon III (1852). People invested money in it by buying shares, which paid annual dividends. It was designed to loan large sums of money, at low interest, for the promotion of industrial enterprises and public works. It supplied much of the money for building French railroads and telegraph lines, for establishing transatlantic steamship lines, for rebuilding Paris. For some years, the institution prospered and investors received 35% annual interest. When the company failed, many former supporters of the emperor turned against him.

Crimean War. 1854-56. Quarrels at the holy places in Palestine between the monks of the Roman Catholic Church and the Greek Orthodox monks were used by Czar Nicholas I of Russia as a pretext for claiming a protectorate over all Christians in the Ottoman Empire and by Napoleon III as the occasion for reasserting the ancient protective principles of France in the Near East. Russia hoped to exploit this situation so as to extend its influence over Turkish territory. This Great Britain would not tolerate without going to war. War between Turkey and Russia began in 1853. In 1854, France and Great Britain joined Turkey, as did Sardinia in 1855. Most of the fighting occurred in the Crimea. The war ended with the Congress of Paris (q.v.).

Criminal code of England, Revision of. In 1821, the criminal code of England was revised to make it more humanitarian in spirit. In about 100 cases (such as shoplifting, picking pockets, poaching) the death penalty was abolished and replaced by fining and/or imprisonment.

Cripps, Sir Stafford. 1889-1952. British statesman. Brilliant lawyer. Knighted in 1930. A left-wing Labor leader, he was solicitor general (1930-31), but was expelled from the party for being too pro-Communist. When Churchill became prime minister (1940), he made Cripps ambassador to the USSR (1940) and

later (1942) lord of the privy seal. In 1942 Cripps was sent to India with a plan for self-government, which India rejected. Upon his return to England he was placed in charge of aircraft production (to 1945). In the Labor Ministry, Cripps (now reinstated in the party) was first (1945) president of the Board of Trade and later (1947) Chancellor of the Exchequer. He was virtually in charge of all of Britain's economy. He carried through the Labor Party's schemes for nationalization of certain industries. He also inaugurated the "austerity" program of food rationing.

Crispi, Francesco. 1819-1901. Italian politician. Prime minister (1887-1891; 1893-1896). He advocated militarism for his country. He renewed the Triple Alliance, seized Eritrea and Somaliland.

Croix de Feu. A French fascist association of war veterans during the 1930's. It was led by Colonel François de la Rocque.

Crompton, Samuel. 1753-1827. English inventor of the spinning mule (1779), a machine which combines the principles of the spinning jenny and the water frame. All modern spinning machines make use of the basic principle invented by Crompton.

Cromwell, Oliver. 1599-1658. A cousin of John Hampden, he espoused the Puritan cause with vigor. At the outset of the Civil War (q.v.) (1642), he organized a troop of cavalry, the famous Ironsides. He played a decisive role in bringing victory to the Parliament or Roundhead faction. In the years following the Civil War, he united the kingdoms of England, Scotland, and Ireland. He was installed as "Lord Protector." He ruled the country by martial law. His vigorous conduct of foreign affairs greatly strengthened England's international position.

Cromwell, Thomas. Earl of Essex. 1485-1540. English statesman, who was the son of a brewer of Putney. He became an assistant of Wolsey (q.v.). After the fall of Wolsey, he became privy councilor (1531), master of jewels (1532), chancellor of the exchequer (1533), king's secretary (1534), lord privy seal (1536), Baron Cromwell (1536), lord great chamberlain (1539), Earl of Essex (1540). He carried into effect the Act of Supremacy (q.v.) and suppression of monasteries and confiscation of their property (1536-39). He strove to Protestantize England, chiefly to increase the absolute power of Henry VIII. Because he arranged Henry's marriage with Anne of Cleves, he fell from favor. He was accused of treason and beheaded. He died in the Catholic faith.

Cromwellian Settlement. 1652. After the execution of Charles I, the Irish, led by Ormonde, rose in rebellion. Cromwell put down the uprising mercilessly. A settlement was devised by Parliament whereby the Catholic religion was suppressed and Celtic owners of land were dispossessed in Leinster, Munster, and Ulster, receiving nominal compensation in the wild areas of Connaught.

Crusades, The. Military expeditions from Europe for the purpose of recovering the Holy Land from the Mohammedans. The crusading movement was launched by Pope Urban II in his sermon at Clermont on Nov. 26, 1095. The movement continued sporadically until 1270. During this time there were several outstanding crusades.

1. The First Crusade was made up mostly of men from France and Normandy. There was no single leader. This fact hampered the Crusaders, but was offset by a worse lack of unity among the Turks. Robert of Normandy, Godfrey of Boulogne, Godfrey's brothers Eustace and Baldwin, Raymond of Toulouse, and Boemund of Otranto were some of the outstanding personalities. Alexius Comnenus, the Byzantine Emperor, played a prominent part in the events. Nicaea was captured in 1097 and secured by Alexius. Baldwin seized Edessa (1098) and made himself ruler of it. Antioch fell in 1098 and was awarded to Boemund. Jerusalem was captured on July 15, 1099. After the city had been sacked and the Mohammedan population massacred, Godfrey of Boulogne was made Protector of the Holy Sepulchre.

2. The stronghold city of Edessa was captured by the Turks in 1144. Immediately, Christian Europe became alarmed. Bernard of Clairvaux persuaded the French king Louis VII and the Holy Roman Emperor Conrad III to lead a crusade (1147). Conrad's army was routed in Asia Minor. The French fought unsuccessfully and abandoned the expedition in 1149. The only success of this crusade occurred in Portugal. In 1147 an army of English and Flemish landed in Oporto to help its bishop against the Mohammedans in Lisbon. They captured Lisbon and turned it over to king Alphonso, who made it his capital and principal city.

3. A Turkish leader, Saladin, unified all the Mohammedans in Asia Minor and captured Jerusalem (Sep. 19, 1187). A call now went out to Europe to launch another crusade. Frederick Barbarossa of Germany, Philip II of France, and Richard I of England each led contingents. The German army started out overland in the spring of 1188. On June 9, 1190, Frederick Barbarossa was drowned while trying to cross a stream in Asia Minor. His army scattered, some returning to Europe, some being killed by the Turks. The English and French armies journeyed to the Holy Land by water. There were continual quarrels between Richard and Philip. After the capture of Acre, Philip abandoned the crusade, leaving Richard in charge. Richard proved to be a poor leader. At length he made a wretched peace with Saladin, by the terms of which

Christians were granted permission to enter Jerusalem as unarmed pilgrims during the next three years. Saladin retained all of his lands, his Christian slaves, and the true cross, which he had captured at the battle of the Horns of Hattin (1187). Richard sailed for home (Sept. 1192), but was made a prisoner near Vienna and delivered up to Emperor Henry VI.

4. Pope Innocent III organized a crusade against Egypt. Venetians were hired to transport the soldiers. The date of departure was 1202. The Doge of Venice, Dandolo, urged the Crusaders first to attack Zara, a city on the Adriatic which belonged to the Byzantine Emperor, because it was a haven for pirates. They captured Zara (1202) and then sailed against Constantinople, which they took April 12, 1204. The city was sacked. A "Latin Kingdom" was created (1204-1261). The Venetians took the occasion of this crusade to seize many of the Aegean Islands.

5. The "Children's Crusade" took place in 1212. Two boys—Stephen of Cloyes and Nicholas, a German—went about preaching that children could secure the Holy Land through a miracle. Many thousands of children followed these leaders. Many died on the way, some were sold into slavery, only a few returned to their homes.

6. Frederick II launched a crusade in 1228. Although he did not fight one battle, he secured great concessions from the Turks (1229). Jerusalem, except for the Mosque of Omar, was surrendered to him, as well as several cities and strongholds. All Christian slaves were released. Frederick promised to protect the sultan against his enemies. Frederick entered Jerusalem and crowned himself King of Jerusalem. Nazareth, Bethlehem, and several other holy places were recovered at the same time. The Turks recaptured Jerusalem in 1244.

7. Louis IX conducted two unsuccessful crusades against Egypt (1248-54; 1270). He died during the second crusade.

The crusading movement ceased because people of Europe had infidels to fight that were nearer home. The holy places of Europe came to be venerated as much as their originals in the Holy Land. The sale of indulgences removed the need to travel to Asia Minor to win religious peace.

The Crusades failed to accomplish what they were organized to do because the crusaders lacked good leaders. There were too many quarrels among the crusaders and with the Byzantine Emperors. It was too difficult to colonize so large a territory as Asia Minor and absorb the Mohammedan population.

The crusades led to a decline of feudalism. The barons sold their rights to raise funds to go on the crusades and neglected their fiefs by long periods of absence. On the other hand, the association of so many knights in these expeditions stimulated the social side of feudalism and developed greatly the usages of feudalism, such as tournaments, heraldic devices, and coats of arms.

Commerce was stimulated. The crusaders learned the use of many unfamiliar commodities while in Asia Minor and wished to import them into Europe. Windmills were introduced into Europe from Asia Minor by crusaders. Sugar, cotton, rice, indigo, the mulberry-tree, figs, citron, watermelon, muskmelon, apricot, plum, artichoke, the mule, the donkey, and the Arabian horse all were introduced into Europe by returning crusaders. Knowledge of medicine, chemistry, mathematics, and astronomy was secured by Europeans from the Arabs.

Cuius regio eius religio. See Religious Peace of Augsburg.

Culloden, Battle of. See Rising of 1745.

Curia Regis. See Magnum Concilium.

Curie, Pierre. 1859-1906. French chemist. With his wife, Marie Sklodowska Curie (1867-1934, born in Warsaw), he discovered and isolated the element radium. The Curies made important discoveries in the field of radioactivity.

Curzon, George Nathaniel, first Marquess Curzon of Kedleston. 1859-1925. British statesman. Undersecretary of state for India (1891-92), undersecretary of foreign affairs (1895-98). As Viceroy of India (1899-1905) he strengthened the northwest border defenses and promoted higher education. Lord of the privy seal (1915-16), foreign secretary (1919-24). He presided over the Lausanne Conference (1922-23) and paved the way for the Dawes Plan. During the Paris Peace Conference (1919) he prepared what is since known as the Curzon Line to divide Polish and Russian territory.

Curzon Line. 1919. A line for the eastern boundary of Poland which was suggested at the Versailles Conference (q.v.) by Lord Curzon (q.v.). It ran somewhat east of north, from a point on the Carpathians slightly west of where they are intersected by the 23° meridian to a point on the East Prussian frontier northwest of Suwalki. The present boundary between Poland and the USSR follows this line fairly closely.

Custozza, Battle of. See Revolutions of 1848.

Czechoslovakia, Annihilation of. March 10-16, 1939. After the Munich Agreement (q.v.), a quarrel arose between Prague and Mgr. Tiso, the premier of Slovakia. This dispute was inspired by the Germans to give them the excuse to interfere further in Czech affairs. The latter appealed to Hitler for help. Hitler's answer was to declare (March 15) Bohemia and Moravia a German protectorate. It was promptly occupied by German troops and von Neurath was made "protector." On March 16, Tiso put Slovakia under German protection.

D

Dail Eireann. The parliament of Ireland.

Daladier, Édouard. 1884-. French politician. After World War I he was a frequent member of various cabinets. Premier (1933, 1933-34, 1938-40). He was premier during the Stavinsky riots (1934). As premier of France he signed the Munich Agreement (1938) (q.v.). Arrested by Vichy (1940), he was interned in Austria until 1945. He re-entered politics in 1946. He is a Radical Socialist.

D'Alembert, Jean Le Rond. 1717?-1783. French mathematician and philosopher. Born in Paris. Author of scientific and philosophical treatises. Associate of Diderot in editing the *Encyclopedia*.

Dalton, John. 1766-1844. English chemist. He developed an atomic theory which elevated chemistry to a science. He conducted researches on the expansion of gases which are caused by heat, on carbonic acid, and the force of steam.

Danegeld. 991-1163. A tax levied on land to provide a fund to repel the Danish invasions of Saxon England. It was continued a long time after the danger was past, and for many years was the only tax that was levied.

Danelaw. Following the Peace of Wedmore (878), Alfred of England and Guthrun the Dane divided the country between them. The Danelaw, north of the Thames-Lea line, went to Guthrun; south, together with London, went to Alfred.

Danish War. 1864. In the peninsula between the Elbe River and Denmark were three duchies: Schleswig, Holstein, and Lauenburg. Though peopled largely by Germans, they were joined in personal union under the King of Denmark. Since 1815, Holstein had been a member of the Germanic Confederation. In 1863 the new Danish king, Christian IX, announced that he was going to annex these duchies. Austria and Prussia thereupon invaded Denmark and forced the Danes (at Vienna—Oct. 1864) to renounce all rights in the duchies in favor of the Emperor of Austria and the King of Prussia. A quarrel between Austria and Prussia over the disposition of the spoils precipitated the Austro-Prussian War (q.v.).

D'Annunzio, Gabriele. 1863-1938. Italian poet, novelist, dramatist, journalist, airman. Born in Pescara. Author of *Il Piacere, L'Innocente, Trionfo della Morte, Il Fuoco, La Citta Morte, La Gioconda,*

Le Martyre de St. Sebastian. Grace and affectation characterized his style. He advocated war against Austria, served, and was wounded (1916). In 1919, he organized a black-shirted group of *Arditi* and captured Fiume. He was a staunch supporter of Mussolini.

Dante, Alighieri. 1265-1321. Italian poet. Born in Florence. He is said to have studied at the Universities of Bologna, Padua, Paris, and possibly Oxford. An active supporter of the Guelf faction and the Bianchi (White) Party of Florence (q.v.), he entered political life (1295). After holding several important political and diplomatic positions, he was banished and never again resided in Florence. He is known especially for the *Divine Comedy* (begun 1307), a philosophical-political poem, comprising 100 cantos. *La Vita Nuova* is a collection of 31 love poems, mostly sonnets. These works were written in Italian and have had great influence upon shaping Italian into a literary language. He also wrote several works in Latin, notably *De Vulgare Eloquenta,* a defense of the vernacular.

Danton, Georges Jacques. 1759-94. French revolutionary leader. Lawyer. A founder of the Cordelier Club (1790). He advocated extreme direct action. Fled to England (1791) but returned and led the riots against the Tuileries (Aug. 10, 1792) which resulted in the suspension of the king. In the face of public dangers (Aug. 10-21, 1792), he urged action and rallied the people. Member of the National Convention (1793). Member of the Committee of Public Safety (Apr.-Sept. 1793). He approved of the expulsion and death of the Girondists (May-Oct. 1793). He was arrested as being too moderate and guillotined (April 5, 1794).

Danzig. Free city and district on the Baltic Sea, formerly part of the German Empire and one of its principal ports. Danzig was nominally under the control of the League of Nations, by which a High Commissioner was appointed to govern the city. With the rise of the Nazis in Germany, agitation developed to have Danzig reincorporated in the Reich. On Aug. 29, 1939, Hitler called upon Poland to sign away all of its rights to Danzig (Danzig's foreign interests were entrusted to Poland, with whom it had a customs union). On Sept. 1, 1939, Germany invaded Poland and the Second World War began. At the end of the war, Danzig was incorporated into Poland.

Darby, Abraham. 1677-1717. An English ironmaster of Coalbrookdale who first used coke in smelting iron ore. His grandson, Abraham (1750-91), made iron rails and built the first iron bridge over the Severn River.

Darlan, Jean Louis Xavier François. 1881-1942. French admiral. Commander of the French navy during World War II. On the fall of France in 1940 he supported collaboration with the Germans and became a high official in the Vichy government. Being present in North Africa at the time of the Anglo-American invasion, he issued an order to all French troops to surrender. For this act he became an object of hatred to both French factions. He was assassinated several days later.

Darwin, Charles Robert. 1809-1882. English naturalist. Born at Shrewsbury. Educated for the ministry at Edinburgh and Cambridge. Darwin came under the influence of Sedgwick, a geologist, and Henslow, a botanist. He sailed as a naturalist on the *Beagle* on a surveying expedition to the southern islands, the South American coast, and Australia (Dec. 1831-Oct. 1839). Published *Zoology of the Voyage of the Beagle* (1840). Secretary of the Geological Society (1838-41). Encouraged by Sir Charles Lyell, he wrote out (1856) the results of his theory of evolution by natural selection. He received from Alfred Russel Wallace (June, 1858) a manuscript presenting an identical theory of natural selection. He published Wallace's paper along with his own theory. Among his books are *On the Origin of Species by Means of Natural Selection* (1859), *The Variation of Animals and Plants under Domestication* (1868), and the *Descent of Man* (1871).

Daumier, Honoré. 1808-79. French painter. A caricaturist whose works criticize and satirize the French society of his day.

Davenant, Sir William. 1606-68. English poet and playwright. He was the first officially designated poet laureate.

Davy, Sir Humphrey. 1778-1829. English chemist. He made many discoveries about the nature and properties of hydrogen, nitrogen, and other gases. He first prepared potassium (1807), sodium (1807), and calcium (1808). He demonstrated that chlorine is an element and that diamond is carbon. He invented the miner's safety lamp (1815).

Dawes Plan. 1924-29. A plan for payment of German reparations (q.v.), worked out by an Allied commission headed by Charles G. Dawes. It contained the following features:

(1) Evacuation of the Ruhr.

(2) A new issue of money to replace the inflated marks.

(3) Reparation payments should be one billion gold marks for the first year and should rise gradually to two-and-one-half billion gold marks a year.

(4) A foreign loan of 800 million gold marks should be floated.

(5) Reparations should be paid out of taxes imposed on railways, alcohol, tobacco, beer, sugar, and customs.

(6) An Agent-General should be in charge of the execution of the plan.

D-Day. June 6, 1944. On this day the troops of the United Nations, commanded by General Eisenhower, established beachheads on the Cherbourg Peninsula. Thus was opened a new, western front in the general attack upon German-held territory.

Deák, Francis. 1803-1876. Hungarian lawyer and statesman. He became the acknowledged leader of the conservative faction of Hungary (c. 1861) and secured the formation of the Dual Monarchy, Austria-Hungary.

Debussy, Claude. 1862-1918. French composer. He is regarded as a leader of the modern school of French music. He produced nocturnes and other orchestral works, piano compositions, and songs. His *Prélude à l'Après-Midi d'un Faune* and his opera *Pelléas et Mélisande* have brought him fame.

Decartelization Program. It was originally intended to break up the huge German cartels, not only because they had supported Hitler's plans for world conquest, but also because they represented a gigantic concentration of power which could not be tolerated in a truly democratic society. The Allied Military Government in 1945 set up a Decartelization Branch to wipe out German cartels. The plan had the strong support of the United States, France, and Russia. Only the British held out for a milder procedure, which would involve careful consideration of the merits of each case. In 1946, the United States came over to the British point of view, influenced by the cold war. Steps were taken to dismember I. G. Farben (the great German chemical cartel); also action was taken against cartels which controlled locomotives, electrical equipment, roller-bearings, linoleum, and Diesel engines. By 1950 the decartelization program had collapsed. In the Soviet zone, huge cartels have been formed under Soviet sponsorship. The stock of giant companies producing all kinds of products is controlled by a master cartel called "Soviet Industries."

Decembrists. At the death of Czar Alexander I (Dec. 1, 1825), his brother Constantine was to succeed to the throne of Russia, but refused. The crown was given to Nicholas, a younger brother who was unpopular because of his conservative policies and his Prussian wife. On Dec. 26, 1825, when Nicholas took the oath of office, a revolt broke out to displace Nicholas with Constantine and a constitution. The revolt was quickly quelled. The revolters have since been known in Russian history as Decembrists.

Declaration of Indulgence. 1672-73. Charles II of England suspended all penal laws pertaining to Non-Conformists. All Protestant sects now were granted permission to worship in public, while Roman Catholics were allowed only private worship. The Declaration was really designed to aid Roman Catholics to whom Charles was partial.

Declaration of the Rights of Man. Oct. 2, 1789. A statement of basic philosophy issued by the National Assembly during the French Revolution (q.v.). It affirmed the principles of religious toleration, freedom of speech, and freedom of press. It proclaimed that ownership of property is a basic human right. Law is the expression of the public will and must be the same for all. Men are born free and remain equal in rights. Human rights are liberty, property, security, and the privilege of resisting oppression. Anyone accused of a crime or arrested should have a legal trial and should be punished, if guilty, according to the law.

Defenestration of Prague. May 23, 1618. Having conspired together to preserve their political and religious independence, a group of Bohemian noblemen invaded the room in the palace in Prague where some of the Emperor's envoys were stopping and threw them into the moat 60 feet below. The envoys were only slightly injured since they landed in an immense pile of dung. This incident led to war between the Bohemian Protestants and the Emperor. The conflict expanded into the great Thirty Years' War (q.v.).

Defoe, Daniel. 1659?-1731. English journalist and novelist. Frequently employed by the government as a writer. Among his works are: *Shortest Way with Dissenters* (1702), *Moll Flanders* (1721), *Robinson Crusoe* (1719).

De Gaulle, Charles. 1890-. French soldier and politician. He served with distinction in the First World War. In 1921 he served in Poland under Weygand. In 1934 he wrote *The Army of the Future*, in which he foresaw the mobile war of the future. Made brigadier general (1940), he was undersecretary of war in the Reynaud cabinet. At the time of the German-French armistice, he flew to London, where he organized the Free French Forces. He proclaimed a provisional government for France in June, 1944. He returned to Paris (Aug. 26, 1944). His government was not recognized by the Allies until Oct. 1944. He was elected provisional president of the new French republic (Nov. 1945) but resigned (Jan. 1946) when the left-wing parties ceased to support him. Always believing that he had a personal mission to "save" his country, he returned to politics in 1947 as the head of the "Reunion of the French People." Although his party scored successes in the local elections of 1947 and 1948, his strength became less with the passing of time.

Deism. Deism is a school of thought which rejects supernaturalism in religion and clings to natural religion. Its earliest exponent was Lord Herbert of Cherbury (1583-1648) who maintained that religion should meet these tests: (1) Belief in the existence of God; (2) encouragement of the worship of God; (3) promotion of better living as the chief end of worship; (4) better living must be preceded by the repentance of sins; (5) belief in a world to come, in which man will be dealt with in accordance with his daily life on earth. Conyers Middleton (1683-1750), Thomas Woolston (1669-1731), and David Hume (1711-1776) were prominent deists. Alexander Pope's *Universal Prayer* (1737) and Thomas Paine's *The Age of Reason* (1796) were outstanding deistic works.

Delcassé, Théophile. 1852-1923. French statesman. Minister of colonies (1893-95). Minister of foreign affairs (1898-1905). During his ministry he negotiated with Britain the Fashoda settlement and the Anglo-French Entente (1904). He was forced out of office (1905) as a result of the dispute with Germany over Morocco.

Departments of France. These are administrative units into which France was divided early in the Revolution to obliterate the old provincialism. Under the Consulate (q.v.), local government was placed completely in the hands of the First Consul. He had the power to appoint all prefects (heads of the departments) and sub-prefects (heads of the smaller arrondissements). These administrators were responsible solely to the first consul. This system is still in force in France.

Depretis, Agostino. 1813-1887. Italian statesman. Prime minister (1876-1887). A Leftist leader, he favored Neapolitans and Sicilians at the expense of north Italians. Greatly increased the suffrage (1882). Maintained a large army and navy. Completed the railway system. Formed the Triple Alliance with Germany and Austria-Hungary (1882). Initiated colonialism by seizing Massawa in Africa (1885).

Descartes, René. 1596-1650. French philosopher and mathematician. Born in La Haye, in Touraine. Resident in Holland (1629-49). He is famous for his treatise *Discours de la Méthode* (1637), with its supporting essays *La Dioptrique, Les Météores, La Géometrie*. It was in mathematics that he achieved his most lasting results, especially in equations. He first introduced exponents, and was practically the founder of analytical geometry. His style of writing has had a lasting effect upon French scientific and philosophical literature. His influence upon philosophy was great. Many call him the "father of modern philosophy." His direct followers, known as Cartesians, have devoted themselves chiefly to the problem of the relation of the soul and body, of mind and matter.

Desirée, Bernardine Eugénie. 1777-1860. Queen of Sweden (1818-44). Born in Marseilles, where her father, François Clary, was a rich merchant. Her sister Julia married Joseph Bonaparte. Desirée married General Jean Baptiste Bernadotte (1798) who became King Charles XIV John of Sweden. She visited Sweden (1810-11) after her husband was chosen as heir to the throne, but did not live there until after 1823.

Desmoulins, Camille (Lucie Simplice Camille Benoit Desmoulins). 1760-94. French journalist and revolutionary leader. Called *Procureur de la lanterne* from his pamphlet against aristocrats *Le Discours de la Lanterne aux Parisiens.* He studied law, became a lawyer (1785-88), but did not succeed. Upon the dismissal of Necker (July 11, 1789), he became excited and began haranguing crowds of people. His speeches precipitated the attack on the Bastille (July 14, 1789). He won the friendship of Mirabeau. He published *La Tribune des Patriots,* the organ of the radical Cordeliers Club. Later he joined forces with Danton. He was arrested by order of Robespierre and guillotined with Danton (April 5, 1794).

Destroyers-for-bases deal. Sept. 2, 1940. An exchange between Great Britain and the United States, consummated through an exchange of letters between Ambassador Lord Lothian and Secretary of State Hull. The United States acquired the right to lease naval and air bases in Newfoundland, Bermuda, the Bahamas, Jamaica, St. Lucia, Trinidad, Antigua, and British Guiana. The right to bases in Newfoundland and Bermuda were gifts. The right to the others was secured in exchange for 50 over-age destroyers. The leases were for 99 years, free of rent.

De Valera, Eamon. 1882-. Irish patriot and statesman. Born in New York City of Spanish and Irish parentage, he took an active part in the Easter Rebellion of 1916. He was imprisoned several times for his activities. He led the Sinn Fein (1917-26) and then the Free State Opposition (Fianna Fail). He was president of the executive council (1932-37) and, under the new constitution, prime minister (1937-48). During World War II he maintained strict neutrality.

Devereux. The name of an English family bearing the title of Earl of Essex, among whom were:

Robert (1566-1601), favorite of Elizabeth I. After a career as a soldier, he was made earl marshal of England (1597). He was later (1599) made lieutenant and governor general of Ireland. He was defeated by the Earl of Tyrone. When he left his post to try to vindicate himself, he was arrested. He joined a conspiracy against the queen. The plot failed, and Essex was executed. He was a patron of literature and an author of sonnets.

Robert (1591-1646), 3rd earl of Essex and son of Elizabeth's favorite. He was one of the prominent English nobles who fought on the side of Parliament during the Civil War (1642-46).

Devolution, War of. 1667-68. After the death of his father-in-law, Philip IV of Spain, Louis XIV claimed certain Spanish possessions in Belgian provinces (Flanders, Brabant, etc.) on the ground that, being the personal estates of the Spanish royal family, their inheritance ought to be governed by the law of devolution. This was a principle of law which declared that in the event of the dissolution of a marriage by death, the survivor was entitled only to the use of the property, the ownership being vested in the children. Daughters of a first marriage, thus, inherited before the sons of a second marriage. Louis XIV's wife had renounced all claims to Spanish property upon her marriage. Louis was to have been paid a dowry of 500,000 crowns in lieu of this renunciation. As the dowry had never been paid, he claimed that the renunciation was invalid. After the French had overrun part of Flanders and Hainault, Jan de Witt of Holland and Sir William Temple of England concluded a Triple Alliance of Holland, England, and Sweden against France. This move induced Louis to conclude the war with the Treaty of Aix-la-Chapelle (q.v.) (1668).

De Witt, Jan. 1625-72. Dutch statesman. Grand pensionary of Holland (1653-72). He concluded peace with England (1654). Restored national finances and strengthened Dutch commercial supremacy in the East. Secured passage of the Perpetual Edict against the House of Orange (1667). Forced to resign when Louis XIV invaded the United Provinces (1672) and the Dutch called William III to leadership. He was killed by an angry mob along with his brother Cornelius (1623-72), who was a famous sailor.

Dias, Bartolomeu. 1450-1500. Portuguese navigator. He discovered the Cape of Good Hope (1488). Thus he paved the way for Vasco da Gama's pioneer voyage from Europe to India.

Dickens, Charles. 1812-70. English novelist. His novels provide us with a picture of English life of the 19th century. Dickens discusses many of the social questions of the day in his books. *David Copperfield, Oliver Twist, Bleak House, Nicholas Nickleby* are representative of this type of novel. *Martin Chuzzlewit* is a story about the United States, written after his first visit there. *A Tale of Two Cities* is a story of the French Revolution.

Diderot, Denis. 1713-84. French author and editor. His great work was the production of the *Encyclopedia*. He labored (with D'Alembert) twenty years on this task (1751-72). He was aided by Voltaire, Montesquieu, Rousseau, Buffon, and others.

Diet, Imperial. A deliberative body of the Holy Roman Empire that was summoned from time to time to consider matters of imperial concern. The term was derived from the Latin *dies* (day). It was composed of three colleges or groups: (1) The electors, except the king of Bohemia. (2) The lesser princes—spiritual and lay—but not the knights of the empire. (3) Representatives of the imperial cities. The diet deliberated matters that concerned the empire, pronounced a ban on those who did not obey, and, with the approval of the emperor, levied taxes and passed laws for the empire.

Directory. 1795-99. The second phase of the First French Republic. It was inaugurated by the Constitution of the Year III (q.v.). The period got its name from the Board of Directors, a committee of five, which was the executive authority of France. It was a period of reaction against some of the extreme measures of the Reign of Terror. There was much luxurious and ostentatious living. There was widespread public graft. Napoleon overthrew the Directory by his coup d'état and replaced it with the Consulate.

Disraeli, Benjamin. 1st Earl of Beaconsfield. 1804-81. British statesman and author. Born in London. M.P. (1837-80). Championed protection (1845-50). Chancellor of exchequer (1852, 1855-59, 1866-69). Leader of Commons for the Conservative Party (1858-59). He carried the Reform Bill of 1867. Succeeded Lord Derby as prime minister (1868), but resigned after the general election (1868). Prime minister (1874-80). He bought Suez Canal shares for the English government (1875). Had Queen Victoria assume the title of Empress of India (1876). Created earl (1876). English representative at the Congress of Berlin (1878) (q.v.), where he played a major part. Author of *Vivian Grey* (1826), *The Young Duke* (1831), *Henrietta Temple* (1837), *Coningsby* (1844), etc.

Dissenters. See Non-Conformists.

Dollfuss, Engelbert. 1892-1934. Austrian statesman. Born in Texing, Lower Austria. He became the leader of the Austrian Christian Socialist Party, and (1932) chancellor. In 1933 he suspended parliamentary government, drove the Socialists into revolt and crushed them. Dollfuss was now given authority to remodel the state. He now became embroiled in a conflict with the Nazis and was murdered by them (July 25, 1934).

Domesday Book. 1085. This was a record prepared for William the Conqueror by a royal commission to estimate the resources of England for the purpose of taxation.

Donatello (Donato di Betto Bardi). 1386-1466. Italian Renaissance sculptor. He was among the first Renaissance artists who made a complete study of the nude. Among his statues are: *David, St. George, The Boy Jesus,* and the equestrian statue of Gattamelata.

Donation of Constantine. One of the famous forgeries of the Middle Ages. Its author is unknown, but it must have been made at Rome and by one acquainted with the Papal court. It first made its appearance about 780. It related the story that when the Emperor Constantine was smitten with leprosy, he appealed to Sylvester, the Bishop of Rome, for help. Sylvester baptized him and cured him of the disease. Out of gratitude, Constantine withdrew from Rome and took up residence in Constantinople, giving Italy and the West to the Bishop of Rome. The pope was to inhabit the Lateran Palace, to wear the diadem, the collar, the purple cloak, to carry the sceptre, and to be attended by a body of chamberlains. His clergy were to ride white horses and receive the honors and immunities of the senate and patricians.

Donation of Pippin. 756. Pope Stephen III (752-757) had performed a great service for Pippin the Short, the ruler of the Franks. He had sanctioned Pippin's seizure of the throne and had had Pippin anointed king. He visited Pippin for two years and gave his personal attention to many problems, such as marriage laws, baptism, and the control of the clergy. He reanointed Pippin with his own hands. Accordingly, when the Lombards in Italy threatened to conquer Rome, Stephen called upon Pippin for help. Pippin invaded Italy twice and thoroughly subdued the Lombards. Having no desire to hold lands in Italy himself, Pippin gave the pope possession of all the lands in Italy which he had conquered—the Exarchate of Ravenna, the Pentapolis, and the duchy of Rome. Thus the pope became a temporal sovereign.

Donne, John. 1571-1631. English poet. For many years he was one of the foremost preachers in England and was dean of St. Paul's (1621-31). Among his poetical works are *Of the Progress of the Soul, Divine Poems,* and *Epithalamium.*

Dopolavoro (After Work). An Italian Fascist organization founded in 1925 to provide workers and their families with physical and cultural facilities. The society promoted hygiene, education, and art. A membership card entitled the holder to reduced admission fees to theatres, concerts, etc. In 1939 there were over 3 million members.

Doria, Andrea. 1468?-1560. Genoese admiral and statesman. Captain-general of galleys (1513 ff.). As high admiral of the Levant, he commanded the French fleet against Charles V (1524-28). He transferred his allegiance from France to Charles V (1528). He took Genoa and set up an aristocratic form of government there (1528). He defeated the Turks at Patras (1532). Conquered Tunis (1535) for Charles V. As a reward he was given the principality of Melfi.

Dostoevski, Fedor. 1821-81. Russian novelist. Author of *Crime and Punishment, The Idiot, The Brothers Karamazov.* He was the creator and supreme master of the psychological novel. He was recognized in Russia as a great writer during his lifetime. Elsewhere an appreciation of his excellence has developed more slowly.

Dover, Secret Treaty of. May 22, 1670. Charles II of England and Louis XIV of France signed the following secret agreement: In return for a sum of money, Charles agreed to join Louis in war against the Dutch. Also, at some fitting time in the future, Charles was to declare himself a Roman Catholic. If his subjects resisted, Louis was to send troops to assist him.

Drake, Sir Francis. 1540-96. The greatest of Elizabethan seamen, one of the so-called "Sea-Dogs." After many successful attacks on Spanish shipping, on Dec. 13, 1577 he sailed from Plymouth with five small ships on a memorable expedition. He entered the Pacific around Cape Horn in 1578, his squadron then being reduced to three ships. When one of these foundered and the other returned to England, Drake pressed on in the Golden Hind, captured rich prizes in Valparaiso, touched the Golden Gate, struck out across the Pacific, and returned home via the Cape of Good Hope Sept. 26, 1580. He was knighted (1581). He raided Cartagena, destroyed a Spanish fleet in the harbor of Cadiz, and played a large part in the defeat of the Armada. In 1595 with Hawkins he sailed against the Spanish Main. Ill-fortune followed this voyage. Hawkins died off Puerto Rico, and Drake died of dysentery off Porto Bello (Jan. 28, 1596).

Drang nach Osten (Pressure towards the East). A German policy announced by Emperor William II. It pointed to German interests in the Balkans and the Near Eastern countries. This policy had, as one of its consequences, the effect of driving Britain into an alliance with France and Russia.

Dreikaiserbund (Three-Emperor League). 1872-90. In Sept. 1872, Emperor William I of Germany, Emperor-King Francis Joseph of Austria-Hungary, and Czar Alexander II of Russia met in Berlin and formed an informal defensive alliance. Though there was no formal treaty, there were frequent conferences between the members of the League. Following the Congress of Berlin (q.v.) (1878), Russia was inclined to withdraw from the League, because she thought that Germany had been too partial to the claims of Austria-Hungary at the expense of Russia during the Congress. Russia was on the verge of coming to an understanding with France, when Czar Alexander II was murdered (1881). His successor, Alexander III, was too conservative to join with republican France. Thus, Russia remained in the League until Bismarck was dismissed as chancellor of Germany (1890). Czar Alexander III did not like Kaiser William II personally. Bismarck's successor, Caprivi, did not wish to continue the League. Accordingly, the agreement upon which the League rested was not renewed in 1890.

Dreyfus Affair. Anti-Semitism characterized the politics of France in the latter part of the 19th century, as well as the politics of Germany and Austria-Hungary. A certain Édouard Drumont published an anti-Semitic newspaper, *La Libre Parole,* which attacked Jewish capitalists, blamed anti-clerical legislation on the Jews, and deprecated the influence of Jews on the army. The Panama Canal scandals of 1894 added to the flood of anti-Semitism, for several Jewish bankers were implicated. Then it was charged that a Captain Alfred Dreyfus (1859-1935), a member of the general staff who was a Jew and a republican, had sold military secrets to the Germans. He was courtmartialed, convicted, and sentenced to life imprisonment on Devil's Island off the coast of French Guiana.

In 1897, Colonel Picquart, the new head of the intelligence bureau of the French army, became convinced that Dreyfus was innocent and that the real culprit was Major Esterhazy, an avowed monarchist. But the "honor" of the French army required its chiefs to abide by the original verdict. Thus, the army committed itself to anti-Semitism. Esterhazy was acquitted and Picquart disgraced (1898). Then the novelist Émile Zola published a scathing denunciation of all who had taken a decisive part in the case. Zola was convicted of libel. But his open letter crystallized public opinion into camps—Dreyfusards and Anti-Dreyfusards. In the former were republicans and socialists; in the latter, monarchists, clericals, army officers, anti-Semites, and many workingmen.

In 1898, Esterhazy fled from France. In 1899, Dreyfus was retried at Rennes. He was again found guilty, but with the recommendation of Presidential clemency. President Loubert pardoned him. In 1906 the Supreme Court annulled the Rennes verdict and restored Dreyfus to the army.

This case discredited anti-Semitism. It crushed monarchism. It welded all republicans and socialists into a bloc which lasted for many years. It led to numerous anti-clerical laws.

Drogheda, Statute of. See Poynings' Law.

Dryden, John. 1631-1700. English poet and dramatist. Among his works are *The Hind and the Panther* and *Absalom and Achitophel.*

Dual Alliance between France and Russia. 1891-95. During the 1890's Pan-Slavism became quite popular in Russia. The Czars desired to purge their country of all Teutonic influences. At the same time, Russia and France came close together because French bankers began to finance Russian industrial expansion. The French fleet visited Kronstadt in 1891. The Russian fleet returned the visit at Toulon in 1893. Diplomatic protocol for an alliance between the two countries was signed in 1891. A military convention between them was agreed upon in 1894. In 1895 the French premier spoke openly of an alliance existing between France and Russia.

Du Barry, Comtesse (Marie Jean Beçu). 1746-93. Mistress of Louis XV of France. She became mistress of the king in 1768 and until his death (1774) she controlled the king and court. She was a patron of men of arts and letters. She caused the dismissal of Choiseul

(1770) (q.v.). She was arrested by Robespierre, tried by the Revolutionary Tribunal, and guillotined (Dec. 7, 1793).

Dubrovnik, Republic of. See Serbia, Origin of.

Dudley, Robert, Earl of Leicester. See Elizabeth I.

Dukhobors. A Russian religious sect which seeks "Spiritual Christianity." It was begun in the 1750's. Dukhobors believed in equality of all men before God and therefore they rejected all authority, including that of the government. They were frequently persecuted. Some of their number migrated to British Columbia, Canada.

Dumas, Alexandre. 1803-70. French novelist. A prolific writer of romantic stories, among which are *The Three Musketeers, The Man in the Iron Mask, The Count of Monte Cristo.* His natural son, Alexandre (1824-95) (Dumas fils) was a novelist and playwright. Among his works are *La Dame aux Camélias (Camille)* and *Henry of Navarre.*

Dumbarton Oaks Conference. Aug.-Oct. 1944. This conference drew up the preliminary blueprint for the United Nations Charter. Although the proposals prepared at Dumbarton Oaks were later changed in various important respects, they became the basis of the UN Charter which was eventually drafted at San Francisco.

Dumouriez, Charles François. 1739-1823. French general. Under Louis XVI he was commandant of Cherbourg (1778-88) and major general (1788). At the outbreak of the Revolution, he joined the Jacobin Club. Minister of foreign affairs (1792). He checked the advance of the Austrians at Valmy (Sept. 1792) and defeated them at Jemappes (Nov. 1792). When he was defeated at

Neerwinden (1793), he was denounced by the National Convention. He deserted to the Austrians and wandered through Europe. He was in exile in England (1804-23).

Dunbar, Battle of. Sept. 3, 1650. After the execution of Charles I, Scotland remained loyal to the Stuarts. Cromwell invaded Scotland and defeated the Scotch army and the future Charles II at Dunbar. After another defeat at Worcester (Sept. 3, 1651), Charles II went into exile in France.

Dürer, Albrecht. 1471-1528. German painter and engraver. Born in Nuremberg. Court painter for emperors Maximilian I and Charles V. He is regarded as the inventor of etching. He is famous as an engraver and woodcut artist.

Dutch War for Independence. 1568-1648. The Netherlands had long enjoyed important privileges. Calvinism had become the religion of the northern provinces, but the southern provinces remained Catholic. When Philip II (q.v.) became king of Spain (1556), he also became ruler of the Netherlands (he inherited this region from his great-grandmother, Mary of Burgundy—q.v.). His tax policy, the heavy garrison of Spanish troops, and the dread of the introduction of the Inquisition (q.v.) (during the rule of the regent, Margaret of Parma—q.v.—, the natural sister of Philip II, and her adviser, Bishop Granvelle—q.v.—) led to the formation of a league of nobles for mutual protection. Three hundred nobles presented a petition for the redress of current grievances and for assurance of future security. In connection with this petition, the term "Beggars" (q.v.) was first used. A revolt against the Spanish rule developed among the lower classes. Prominent nobles, like Count Egmont (q.v.) and William of Orange (q.v.), who opposed these popular demonstra-

tions, soon lost control of the movement.

Now (1567) Philip sent to the Netherlands the Duke of Alva (q.v.) with 20,000 troops. He immediately indicated that he was going to pursue a severe policy of repression against all who resisted royal authority. William of Orange and many thousands of Netherlanders left their native land. Margaret of Parma resigned in protest. Nevertheless, Alva held his notorious Council of Blood (q.v.). Egmont and Horn (q.v.) were executed. War now broke out between the Netherlanders and the Spaniards. William of Orange and his brother Louis invaded the country to help the rebels. With the capture of Brill by the "Water Beggars" (1572) (q.v.) the insurrection spread far and wide. In 1573 Alva was recalled. The sack of Antwerp (1576) (see Spanish Fury) led to the Pacification of Ghent (1576) (q.v.) in which all the provinces united to repel the Spaniards. The new governor, Don Juan of Austria (q.v.), could not quiet the country. He died in 1578 and was succeeded by Alexander Farnese (q.v.), a shrewd statesman and the foremost soldier of the time. He subdued the southern provinces and restored their ancient political liberties. The seven northern provinces formed (1579) the Union of Utrecht (q.v.). In 1581 they proclaimed independence from Spain. After the murder of William of Orange (the Silent) (1584), his son Maurice continued the struggle until (1609) the Republic of the United Provinces (Netherlands) and Spain concluded a 12-year truce. In 1648 the Treaty of Westphalia (q.v.) recognized the independence of the Republic of the United Provinces.

Dutch War, First. 1652-54. This was a conflict between Holland and England over commercial rivalry in the Far East and fishing rights in the Channel. The peace treaty was favorable to the English. It marked the beginning of the decline of Dutch sea power.

Dutch War, Second. 1665-1667. This conflict between the Netherlands and England was caused by the desire of each to protect its own shipping and to inflict as much damage as possible upon the shipping of the enemy. The English defeated the Dutch fleet off Lowestoft (June 3, 1665). France entered the war as an opponent of England (Jan. 1666). In June, 1667, the English navy was all but driven from the sea by the Dutch. This marks the low point in England's career as a naval power. The war ended with the Peace of Breda (q.v.) (July 27, 1667).

Dutch War. 1672-78. Louis XIV secured the dissolution of the Triple Alliance (England, Sweden, Holland) which had fought him in the War of Devolution (1667-68) (q.v.). He secured the alliance of England by means of the Secret Treaty of Dover (1670) (q.v.). He made an alliance with Sweden (1672). He also made treaties with Cologne and Münster. About 20,000 Germans fought for Louis during the Dutch War. A great French army swept over the Netherlands and would have captured Amsterdam had the Dutch not cut the dikes. The Dutch fleet under de Ruyter defeated the English. The emperor and several princes came to the assistance of the Netherlands. After an exhausting war, the French were checked. This struggle, which ended with the Treaty of Nijmegen (q.v.), marked the beginning of the decline of French power.

Dvorak, Anton. 1841-1904. Czech composer. Director of the Conservatory of Prague. He composed operas, orchestral works (symphonies, overtures, rhapsodies, scherzos), and choral works. His piano music includes the well-known *Humoresque.*

E

Easter Rebellion. 1916. An uprising in Ireland aimed at expelling the British and setting up an Irish Republic. The rebels were radicals who had left the Irish Nationalist Party to form an Irish Republican Brotherhood. Most of the "Brothers" were also members of the Sinn Fein (q.v.). Germany had promised aid by land, sea, and air, but could not help because of the British blockade. The British put down the rebellion within a week, shot a number of leaders, and placed Ireland under martial law. Several thousand were arrested and many were deported to Britain.

Ebert, Friedrich. 1871-1925. First president of the Weimar Republic of Germany (elected 1919). A saddler by trade, he became a Social Democratic journalist and a member of the Reichstag (1912). He became chairman of the Social Democratic Party in 1913. He was a leader of the Revolution of 1918.

Eckhart, Johannes. 1260?-1327. German Dominican mystic and preacher. He advocated a sort of pantheistic system of philosophy which was a mixture of scholasticism, Neoplatonism, and Arabic concepts.

Economic and Social Council of the UN (ECOSOC). ECOSOC is composed of 18 members elected by the General Assembly for 3-year terms. Six members are replaced each year. Decisions are made by majority vote of the members present, each member having one vote. ECOSOC works through specialized committees. It recommends action to various nations, and cannot compel any nation to carry out its recommendations.

Among the commissions which work for ECOSOC are the following:

Commission on Human Rights (q.v.)
Population Commission
Statistical Commission
Commission on Narcotic Drugs
Commission on the Status of Women
Economic and Employment Commission
Economic Commission for Latin America
Economic Commission for Asia and the Far East
Economic Commission for Europe

Certain specialized agencies are autonomous bodies. Their work is coordinated by ECOSOC (See ILO, International Bank for Reconstruction and Development, IMF, UNESCO, WHO, FAO).

Economic Cooperation Administration. See Marshall Plan.

Eden, Robert Anthony. 1897-. British statesman. After service in the first World War, he entered politics (1923) as a

Conservative. He devoted himself to foreign affairs, particularly to matters pertaining to the League of Nations. He became Foreign Secretary in 1935, but resigned in 1938 because of the appeasement policy of the government. Dominion Secretary (1939), War Secretary (1940), Foreign Secretary (1940-45; 52-).

Edict of Nantes. 1598. The most important contribution towards religious toleration in Europe down to that time. Issued by Henry IV, it granted Huguenots in France freedom of worship in a great many places. They were granted admission to all hospitals, schools, and colleges. They could found their own schools and publish books. They were not debarred from holding public office by religious oaths. On the other hand, they were forced to disband their political organization and pay tithes for the support of the Catholic Church.

Edict of Nantes, Revocation of. 1685. Louis XIV of France was persuaded that destruction of heresy in France would be an act very pleasing to God. He began his campaign against heretics by excluding Huguenots from public offices, forbidding them to become doctors or lawyers or to engage in printing or selling books. Huguenots who refused to turn Catholic were required to take soldiers into their homes and give them food and lodging (*dragonnades*). In 1685, Louis revoked the Edict of Nantes (q.v.). It is estimated that because of the revocation, which deprived Huguenots of religious freedom, 400,000 Huguenots emigrated from France. They migrated to Holland, Prussia, Switzerland, England, and America, taking with them their industrial skill. The consequent blow to French industry and wealth was heavy.

Edict of Restitution. March 29, 1629. After the defeat of the Protestant forces in the Thirty Years' War (q.v.) Emperor Ferdinand II issued this decree.

All ecclesiastical estates which had been confiscated since the Convention of Passau were to be restored. This ruling affected two archbishoprics and 12 bishoprics, besides 120 monasteries and other religious foundations. Only adherents of the Augsburg Confession were to have free exercise of religion. All other sects were to be broken up. Wallenstein mercilessly enforced the Edict.

Education Act, English. 1870. Before 1870, half of the children of England received no schooling. Maintenance of schools was left to the Church of England and voluntary societies. The Act of 1870 provided that while "voluntary" or church schools giving religious instruction should receive financial aid from the government, there should be created non-denominational "Board Schools" in which no denominational religious teaching was permitted. These Board Schools were to be supported partly by parents' fees, partly by local taxes, and partly by government subsidy.

Edward (the Confessor). 1002?-1066. Last of the Anglo-Saxon kings of England (1043-66). Royal in bearing, affable, and gentle, he was utterly lacking in decision. His personal reputation for holiness was so high that he was called "The Confessor" and canonized within 100 years of his death. Having passed most of his early life in Normandy, he brought over to England a number of Norman advisers. He enfranchised the Cinque Ports (q.v.), remitted the Danegeld, favored monasticism, and was the first English king to employ the royal touch for alleged cure of the scrofulous taint. Queen Anne (1702-14) was the last to try this "royal cure."

Edward I (*called* Longshanks). 1239-1307. King of England (1272-1307). He received from his father Gascony, Ireland, and Wales, and learned the arts of warfare in administering these possessions. He married Eleanor of Castile, who became perhaps the most popular queen of England. At the Parliament of Oxford (1258) (q.v.) he sided with his father against the barons, but thereafter sided with de Montfort. At the battle of Lewes (1254) his rashness paved the way for the defeat of the royal army and the capture of the king and himself. While being held hostage for his father, he escaped and, joining forces with Gloucester, defeated and killed de Montfort at Evesham (1265). In 1270 he joined the last Crusade. On his return, he heard of his father's death. He did not return to England to be crowned until 1274. Edward pursued a wise domestic policy, particularly in legal and money matters. By the Statute of Wales (1284), he ended trouble between England and Wales. In 1290 he expelled all Jews from England for practicing usury. The death of the Scottish queen, the Maid of Norway (1290), who was betrothed to one of Edward's sons, opened a chance for intervention in Scotch affairs. Edward decided in favor of John Baliol against Robert Bruce. In 1295, Edward called together the "Model Parliament." In 1295, he invaded Scotland, accepted Baliol's surrender of the crown, and returned to Berwick with the coronation stone. In 1297, Sir William Wallace began guerilla warfare in Scotland with marked success. He was defeated by internal jealousies (1298), and executed (1305). However, Bruce continued warfare against the English.

Edward II. 1284-1327. King of England (1307-27). His reign was filled with troubles and defeats in Scotland and France. Edward was ultimately defeated by a party headed by his estranged queen, Isabella, and a disaffected noble, Mortimer. He was taken captive and murdered.

Edward III. 1312-77. King of England (1327-77). During his minority the country was governed by his mother,

Isabella, and Mortimer. In 1328, Edward married Phillipa of Hainault. Two years later he executed Mortimer and banished his mother. He invaded Scotland on the death of Bruce to assist Edward Baliol. In 1333 the Scots were defeated, whereupon Baliol did homage to Edward. Charles IV of France died without heir. Edward claimed the crown, as his mother, Isabella, was the sister of Charles. The claim was groundless, since, by Salic Law, no woman could inherit the throne of France. Nevertheless, Edward invaded France and, with the aid of his son, the Black Prince, inflicted a crushing defeat on the French at Crecy (Aug. 24, 1346) in the Hundred Years' War (q.v.). In 1349, the Black Death carried off one-third of the population of England and permanently changed the relationship between laborer and master. In 1356, the Black Prince again crushed the French at Poitiers and captured King John. During the last years of Edward's reign, affairs at home were chaotic. Finances were in ruin. The king quarreled with Parliament. The king's third son, John of Gaunt, was the real ruler of the country.

Edward (the Black Prince). 1330-76. Eldest son of Edward III of England. A great warrior, he distinguished himself at Crecy and Poitiers. In 1361, he married his cousin, Joan, the "Fair Maid of Kent" (1328-85), who bore him two sons, one of whom became Richard II. A great soldier, he failed as a civil administrator.

Edward IV. 1442-83. King of England (1461-70 and 1471-83). Leader of the Yorkist faction of England after the defeat and death of his father at Wakefield (Dec. 30, 1460) (during the War of the Roses, q.v.). After several defeats, he entered London and was crowned king (March 29, 1461). He was handsome and popular, but alienated Warwick (q.v.) by his marriage (1464) to Elizabeth Woodville, a daughter of Warwick's enemies. In 1470, Warwick landed in England, forced Edward into exile, and restored Henry VI to the throne. Edward returned to England, and at the battle of Barnet (Apr. 14, 1471), defeated and killed Warwick. Edward again became king. His later years were marred by debauchery and by popular discontent caused by his execution of the Duke of Clarence and his support of Burgundy against France.

Edward VI. 1537-53. King of England (1547-53). Son of Henry VIII and Jane Seymour, his reign was influenced by his protectors, the Duke of Somerset and later (1552) John Dudley, the Duke of Northumberland. Aiming to secure the succession for his family, Dudley married his son Guilford to Lady Jane Grey and induced Edward to name Lady Jane as his successor. During Edward's reign, the Reformation in England made much progress.

Edward VII. 1841-1910. King of Great Britain and Ireland (1901-10). Eldest son of Queen Victoria. He sustained the position of constitutional monarch as established by his mother. Promoted friendly relations by visits to European capitals. He prepared the way for the creation of the Entente Cordiale (q.v.) (1904) and the Triple Entente (q.v.) (1907). He visited Berlin (1909) to foster Anglo-German relations. He so typified the period that it has been called after him— "The Edwardian Age."

Edward VIII. 1894-. Eldest son of George V, he served in both the navy and army during World War I. As Prince of Wales he traveled much, and was known as the "foremost salesman of the British Empire." He succeeded his father Jan. 20, 1936, but abdicated the following Dec. 11 on account of general disapprobation of his proposed marriage to a divorced American. He was given the title of Duke of Windsor and the marriage took place June 3, 1937. He was governor of the Bahamas (1940-45). Returned to private life, living most of the time in America and France.

Egmont, Count Lamoral. 1522-68. Flemish general and statesman. He made a brilliant record as a soldier, particularly in victories over the French at St. Quentin and Gravelines. He joined William the Silent in opposition to the policies of the Duke of Alva. Arrested and condemned to death by the Council of Blood. Executed with Count Horn. Their deaths led to the revolt of the Netherlands. Egmont's tragic fate is the theme of Goethe's drama *Egmont* (1788).

Einhard. 770?-840. Secretary and biographer of Charlemagne. Minister of public works under Charlemagne. After 820 he was abbot of various monasteries.

Einstein, Albert. 1879-. Mathematical physicist and astronomer. Born at Ulm, he has been a professor in Zürich, Prague, Berlin, Leyden, and Princeton. He formulated a theory of relativity. His researches on the mathematical relationship between mass and energy made the atomic bomb possible.

El Greco. 1547-1614. Spanish name for Domenico Theotocopuli. Celebrated painter. Born in Crete. He went to Venice, where he studied under Tintoretto and Titian. He stayed briefly in Rome. He then settled in Toledo, where he did all of his celebrated painting. His masterpiece is *Burial of Count Orgaz.*

El Siglo de Oro (the Golden Age). The great period of Spanish literature. It began during the reign of Ferdinand and Isabella. It is characterized by Don Jorge Manrique (1440-78) who wrote *Las Coplas;* the romance, *Amadis of Gaul; La Celestina,* written by Fernando de Rojas (1475-1536). Also the first Castilian grammar, written by Antonio de Nebrija, and the polyglot Bible of Cardinal Ximenes.

Eleanor of Aquitaine. 1122-1204. Wife of Louis VII of France (1137). Divorced by him (1152), she married the future Henry II of England in the same year. Mother of Richard and John, kings of England. Through her marriage, her estates in France became the possessions of the kings of England. Thus, England became embroiled in French problems (see Angevin Empire).

Elite Guards (Schutzstaffeln; SS). An organization of especially picked Nazis who were assigned to act as bodyguards for the Nazi leaders and to carry out very difficult missions. They wore a black blouse decorated with a white skull.

Elizabeth I. 1533-1603. Queen of England (1558-1603). Only child of Henry VIII and Anne Boleyn. Studied under exponents of the New Learning and the Reformation. Succeeded Mary to the throne (1558). She issued a proclamation that the English litany should be read in the churches (1559). She helped Protestants in their struggles in France, Holland, and Scotland. She promulgated the Thirty-Nine Articles (q.v.) (1563). When she found her rival, Mary Queen of Scots, in her power after the defeat at Langside (1568), she imprisoned her in Carlisle, thus giving rise to plots to liberate her. Being convinced by her advisers that Mary alive threatened her security, Elizabeth signed Mary's death warrant (1587). This act led to the attempted invasion of England by the Spaniards (1588). But the invading fleet was destroyed by the English and a great storm. Her early favorite, Robert Dudley, Earl of Leicester, died in 1588. Another favorite, Robert Devereux, Earl of Essex, was made governor-general of Ireland to quell the revolt of the Earl of Tyrone. Essex failed in his mission and attempted to revolt against the queen. Accordingly, he was executed (1601).

From her father she inherited physical strength, resolution, energy, a fiery temper, and a tendency to cruelty. From her mother she inherited such physical attractions as she possessed. She was cruel, capricious, insincere, at once unpleasantly masculine and weakly feminine. But she was highly popular with her subjects. She has given her name to the great literary Renaissance which occurred in England during her reign.

Elizabeth II. 1926-. Queen of Great Britain and head of the British Commonwealth of Nations (1952-). She succeeded her father, George VI, in February, 1952. In 1947 she married Philip Mountbatten, the Duke of Edinburgh.

Elizabethan Age. 1558-1603. During the 16th century, English life experienced a tremendous expansion. The Elizabethan Age, so called from the fact that Elizabeth I was queen from 1558 to 1603, was characterized by a thirst for knowledge of the Latin and Greek classics, an appetite for adventure and discovery, a love of beauty, and a longing for unlimited self-expression. England had become a power of first rank, and her people had increased in numbers and become prosperous. Commerce grew, as did the navy. Agriculture was stimulated. As wealth increased, so did luxury and display.

More noteworthy even than changes in material conditions were the advances in intellectual and literary life. This English Renaissance began with Spenser (q.v.) and Marlowe (q.v.), and reached its height in the plays of Shakespeare (q.v.). Elizabethan literature, like the deeds of Elizabethan seamen, stands as an expression of national confidence and enthusiasm.

Emigration, Italian. The heavy taxation which the Italian government imposed in the latter part of the 19th century and the first decade of the 20th century caused heavy emigration. While about half of the emigrants returned after earning money abroad, by 1910 Italy had permanently lost 5½ million citizens who settled in the United States, Argentina, Uruguay, and Brazil. About 80% of this number were peasants, most of whom came from southern Italy. Although there was considerable emigration from Italy to southern France in the early 1920's, the Fascist government discouraged the practice. By 1930, emigration had virtually ceased.

Emigrés. Fugitives from the French Revolution. They were mainly nobles and clergymen. They gathered in some force in foreign cities, particularly at Coblenz on the Rhine. Headed by the count of Artois, the brother of Louis XVI (later Charles X), they maintained a continual agitation against the new regime by means of newspapers, pamphlets, and intrigues.

Ems Telegram. See Franco-Prussian War.

Enclosures. During the Middle Ages, agriculture in England was worked by a kind of cooperative system. Much of the land was common land which was planted according to a three-field system —one division growing barley, one oats, one lying fallow. In addition, there was common grazing ground. Beginning in the 14th century, some lords began enclosing common land with fences, the better to herd livestock. In the 18th century, enclosing reached its peak. From 1760 to 1800 much common land was enclosed by acts of Parliament to allow arable farming to be done more effectively. Many of these Acts of Enclosure severely hurt the small farmers of the country.

Encyclopédie. This famous Encyclopedia was prepared (1750-80) by French phi-

losophers under the editorship of Diderot (q.v.). With the aid of D'Alembert (q.v.), Quesnay (q.v.), Montesquieu (q.v.), Voltaire (q.v.), Rousseau (q.v.), Turgot (q.v.), and other distinguished authorities, Diderot produced the first volume in 1751. Jesuit influence caused the permit for the *Encyclopédie* to be withdrawn. D'Alembert and Voltaire now withdrew from the project. Diderot persisted, protected by Mme. de Pompadour (q.v.), Choiseul (q.v.), and others. In 1772, twenty-eight volumes were completed and published clandestinely. In 1776-7, a supplement of five volumes was published. In 1780, there appeared a two-volume index. The *Encyclopédie* differed from similar previous works in that it gave voice to the philosophy of scientific determinism, derived from Bacon, Descartes, Locke, and Newton. Through its stress upon the abuses of existing institutions, it was a major factor in causing the French Revolution.

Engels, Friedrich. 1820-95. German socialist. Collaborated with Karl Marx on the *Communist Manifesto* (1848). For a number of years he supported Marx while the latter was writing *Das Kapital.* He was a manufacturer in Manchester, England (1850-69). He lived in London (1870-95).

Enghien, Duke of. A title borne by the oldest son of the prince of Condé. Louis Antoine Henri de Bourbon-Condé (1772-1804), the only son of the last Condé prince, held a command in the army of emigrés (1792) during the French Revolution. While living in Ettenheim, Baden, he was falsely accused of plotting against France. He was secretly seized (1804) by orders of Napoleon, condemned by a military court, and shot. This act caused European nobles to hate Napoleon bitterly.

Enlightened despots. Frederick the Great of Prussia, Catherine the Great of

Russia, Charles III of Spain, and Joseph II of Austria are known as enlightened despots since each aimed at absolute power, which they would use for the good of their people. The idea originated with Voltaire. The monarch would be the patriarch of his people, exercising his judgment in caring for them and chastising them.

Entente Cordiale. 1904. An agreement between France and Great Britain which put an end to colonial rivalry and laid the foundation of the so-called Triple Entente (q.v.). Although it was not a formal alliance, since it contained no specific promises of military and naval support, it cleared the air and permitted England and France to conduct their foreign affairs in harmony. The formation of the Entente was largely the work of Théophile Delcassé and King Edward VII.

Erasmus, Desiderius (Gerrit Gerritszoon). 1446-1536. Outstanding humanist. Born in Rotterdam. Rebelling from the bleak and narrow monastic training of his youth, he became a wandering scholar. He turned into the most learned man of his time. He labored for the reformation of society—religious, moral, and intellectual. While he was a welcome visitor in many European countries, he spent a majority of his adult years in England. His *Praise of Folly* (1511) is a famous satire in which he criticized the men and the tendencies of his age. His edition of the *New Testament* in Greek helped pave the way for the Reformation. His life presents a curious combination of boldness of speech and timidity of action.

Erfurt Program. See Revisionists, Socialist.

Erfurt Union. 1849-1850. During the Revolution of 1848 (q.v.), the Frankfurt Parliament elected King Frederick William IV of Prussia as Emperor of Germany. Frederick William refused the honor. Hoping to unite Germany according to his own ideas and with the consent of his fellow princes, he drew up a plan for a large confederation of Middle European countries with a population of 60 million and with great economic possibilities. This great empire was to be divided into an *inner confederation* (roughly, Germany of 1914) under the leadership of Prussia and the Hapsburg Monarchy. A draft of a constitution for the inner confederation was prepared in May, 1849. On Oct. 19, 1849, a national assembly met at Erfurt. It was attended by representatives from Prussia and the petty German states. Hanover, Saxony, Württemberg, and Bavaria refused to join. To counteract the Erfurt Union, Schwarzenberg (q.v.) revived the old Diet of the German Confederation (May 16, 1850). Both Prussia and Austria now mobilized for war. Russia sided with Austria. Frederick William decided to beat a retreat. At a conference in Olmütz (Nov. 29, 1850) the Prussian delegates abandoned the Erfurt Union completely. This act is called by Prussian historians the "Humiliation of Olmütz."

Estates-General, Convocation of the. Aug. 1788. The Parlement of Paris refused to register any further loans or taxes. Encouraged by popular approval, it drew up a declaration of rights, asserting that subsidies could be granted only by the Estates-General. Louis XVI now ordered the Parlement abolished. This led to much popular excitement. The soldiers refused to arrest the judges of the Parlement. Although the Estates-General had not convened for 175 years, Louis XVI now decided to convene the body, and sent summons for them to meet in May, 1789. The convocation of the Estates-General resulted in the end of absolute monarchy in France.

Estates-General of France, Origin of. 1302. Philip IV called together a meeting of the Estates-General to gain support in his quarrel with the pope. When the summons was issued, he invited each city of France to send two or three representatives to attend the meeting. A similar body was assembled in 1308 to hear charges against the Knights Templars. In 1314, when war with Flanders broke out and the royal treasury was empty, the Estates-General was convoked to raise funds. While it is true that the Third Estate (commoners) attended these meetings in the person of chosen representatives, it did virtually nothing and remained a nonentity until the days of the French Revolution. It had no such history and development as had the English House of Commons.

Este. A distinguished Italian princely family which goes back to Alberto Azzo (997-1097), who was invested by Emperor Henry IV with Este and other Italian estates. Alberto's older son, Guelf IV, is the ancestor of the noble houses of Hanover and Brunswick. The younger son, Folco II (1060-1135), founded the Italian branch of the family. These Estes played an important role in Renaissance Italy. Many members were patrons of the arts. Beatrice d'Este (1475-97), Duchess of Milan, and Isabella d'Este (1474-1539), Marchioness of Mantua, were celebrated beauties. The family ended with the death of Ercole III Rinaldo in 1803.

Estournelles de Constant, Baron de (Paul Henri Benjamin Balluat). 1852-1924. French diplomat and politician. Devoted himself to furthering international peace. Received, with Auguste Beenaert, the Nobel peace prize in 1909.

Eugene, Prince of Savoy. 1663-1736. Austrian general. Some of his greatest exploits occurred during the War of the Spanish Succession (1701-13). With Marlborough he won the Battle of Blen-

heim (1704). He later expelled the French from Italy (1706).

Eugénie (*in full* **Eugénie Marie de Montijo de Guzman**). Countess of Teba. 1826-1920. Born in Granada. Empress of the French (1853-71). Daughter of a Spanish grandee and of Maria Manuela Fitzpatrick, whose father (William Fitzpatrick, a Scotchman by birth and an American by residence) had been the United States consul at Malaga. Educated in Paris, she married Napoleon III (Jan. 1853) soon after he became emperor. She was a leader in fashions in Europe. She influenced her husband in many matters. She was a staunch supporter of the Church. Upon the downfall of the empire, she fled to England where she was befriended by Queen Victoria.

European Coal and Steel Community. See Schuman Plan.

European Defense Community (EDC). To supply the land and air forces required by NATO (q.v.), an integrated military system, called European Defense Community, was created in May, 1952.

European Payments Union. This scheme, suggested by ECA Administrator (Marshall Plan, q.v.), Paul G. Hoffman, was adopted July 1, 1950. Seventeen European nations and the sterling bloc have subscribed to it. The initial working capital came from ECA grants and contributions from the participating countries. The funds are deposited in the Bank of International Settlement (Basel) (q.v.) and are managed by a committee of seven appointed by the OEEC (q.v.). The purpose of the Union is to provide credit for purchases of foreign goods.

Exarchate of Ravenna. 553-756. In 553, Justinian, the Emperor of the Eastern Roman Empire, conquered the Ostrogothic Empire. He organized his conquests into a province called the Exarchate of Ravenna. Its capital was the former Ostrogoth capital, Ravenna. This province was eventually conquered by the Lombards. It was then taken from them by the Franks under Pippin the Short. Since Pippin had no desire to hold lands in Italy, he gave the Exarchate to the Pope, thus beginning the temporal sovereignty of the Papacy. (See Donation of Pippin, q.v.)

Execution of Charles I. Jan. 30, 1649. Cromwell (q.v.) and other leaders of the English Parliamentarian army decided that King Charles I must die. On Jan. 6, 1649, the "Rump" Parliament (q.v.) passed an act creating a high court of justice of 135 persons to try the king. Only 59 of these men consented to serve. On Jan. 21, the trial began in Westminster Hall. The charge stated: "Charles Stuart, being admitted King of England with a limited power, out of wicked design to erect an unlimited power, had traitorously levied war against Parliament and people of England, thereby causing the death of many thousands, and had repeated and persevered in his offense." Sentence of death was pronounced Jan. 27. On Jan. 30, Charles was conducted to the scaffold erected outside the banqueting hall of the palace of Whitehall, and there beheaded in the presence of the soldiers and of the citizens of London. (See Regicides.)

Execution of Louis XVI. Jan. 21, 1793. The National Convention was faced with the problem of what to do with the king. When it was discovered that he had frequently bribed the National Assembly he was brought on trial. It was also suspected that he was in treasonable correspondence with foreign monarchs. The king was brought to trial before the Convention in December, 1792, and was condemned to death by a vote of 387 to 334. He was beheaded in the Place de la Révolution (now the Place de la Concorde). It was learned after his execution that he actually had written letters to foreign kings, urging their assistance and thus betraying his own country.

F

Fabian Society. This Second International Socialist organization was founded in England in 1883. It became well-known with the publication (1889) of the *Fabian Essays.* The Fabians have always held that revolutionary change should be achieved gradually through democratic action. Prominent Fabians were Sidney and Beatrice Webb (1859-1947; 1858-1943) and George Bernard Shaw (1856-1950).

Factory Act, English. 1833. Due to the efforts of Lord Ashley (later Earl of Shaftesbury) the labor of children under 9 was prohibited. Children between 9 and 13 were limited to 48 hours of work a week with a 9-hour day as the maximum. Young people between 13 and 18 were limited to 69 hours a week with a 12-hour day maximum. Even though these measures applied only to textile mills, they were forerunners of later remedial factory legislation.

Fairfax, Ferdinando, 2nd Baron. 1584-1648. He commanded the right wing of the Parliamentarian army at the battle of Marston Moor (July 2, 1644). His son, Thomas (1612-71), 3rd Baron, was the Parliamentary commander-in-chief (1645) who defeated the Royalists at Naseby (1645) and sat in judgment on the king (1649). He headed the commission (1660) which went to the Hague to recall Charles II.

Falk Laws. See Kulturkampf.

Faraday, Michael. 1791-1867. English chemist and natural philosopher. He discovered the principle of electromagnetic induction. This is the basis of the dynamo. The great work of his life is *Experimental Researches in Electricity.*

Farmers-general. Pre-Revolutionary French tax collectors. It was the custom to "farm-out" indirect taxes. In return for the payment of a lump sum of money, the government granted to companies of speculators the right to collect what taxes they could.

Farnese. An Italian family founded as the ducal family of Parma (1545-1731) by Alessandro, who became Pope Paul III. Alessandro, Duke of Parma, (1545-1592) was brought up in Spain. He fought at Lepanto and served Philip II of Spain in the Netherlands (1577-86). He led the Spanish armies in the Netherlands (1586-92). He was considered to be the ablest soldier of his day. Elizabeth Farnese (1692-1766) was queen of Spain and second consort of Philip V. Soon after marriage she gained a strong influence over her weak husband and virtually ruled Spain. Her ambition to re-coup Spanish losses at the Peace of Utrecht (q.v.) plunged Spain into sev-eral wars.

Fascist Party, Italian, Origin of. As early as October, 1914, numerous *fasci d'azione* were organized in Italy by young "men of action" who were eager to have Italy join the war on the side of the Allies. In 1919, hundreds of these organ-izations were formed, mainly by ex-service men who wished to solve Italy's problems. Mussolini led the Milan fascio and his *Il Popolo d'Italia* became the Fascist literary organ. Under Mussolini's guidance, these local groups consolidated into the *fascio di combattimento*. They later adopted the black shirt which had been worn by D'Annunzio's (q.v.) fol-lowers in the capture of Fiume (1919). The Fascists gained strength during 1920 and 1921. In October, 1922, after the "March on Rome," Mussolini and his fol-lowers secured power when King Victor Emmanuel III requested Premier Facta to resign and then asked Mussolini to form a cabinet.

Fascist Youth (Italy). Believing that the country's greatness lay in the hands of the youth of the land, Mussolini or-dered that all young people should be organized and disciplined. To accom-plish this purpose, various organizations were set up. They were: *Figli della Lupo* (Sons of the Wolf) for boys from 6 to 8; *Ballila,* for those from 8 to 14; *Avan-guardia* (Advance Guard), for those from 14 to 18; *Giovani Fascisti* (Young Fas-cists), for those from 18 to 21. Similar organizations were set up for girls. In 1939 there were about 5 million boys enrolled in the various organizations. They were given physical and military training and indoctrination in Fascist ideals.

Fashoda Incident. 1898-1899. A French expedition, headed by Capt. Marchand,

moved eastward from the French Congo with the express intention of linking the French African territories with the Red Sea. The expedition entered the Upper Nile valley and raised the French flag at Fashoda on the Nile. A British-Egyptian force at once left Khartoum in the Sudan to drive out the French. War seemed in-evitable. However, in 1899 the English and French signed an agreement where-by the French renounced all interest in the Anglo-Egyptian Sudan in return for undisputed right to occupy the kingdom of Wadai in the central Sudan. This was the beginning of cordial relations be-tween the English and French which cul-minated in the formation of the Entente Cordiale (q.v.).

Febronianism. A German attack on ul-tramontanism (q.v.) similar to Gallican-ism (q.v.). See Hontheim.

February Revolution. See Revolutions of 1848.

Ferdinand I. 1503-1564. Holy Roman Emperor (1558-64); king of Bohemia (1526-62), and of Hungary (1526-63). Younger brother of Emperor Charles V (q.v.). In 1521, Charles gave Ferdinand the Austrian duchies of the Hapsburgs. In the same year Ferdinand married Anna, sister of Louis II of Bohemia and Hungary. When Louis was killed in the Battle of Mohacs (1526) (q.v.), Ferdi-nand claimed the thrones of Bohemia and Hungary. This involved him in a struggle with John Zápolya, who laid claim to Hungary and who was supported by the Turks. Ferdinand at last bought off the Turks and secured both Bohemia and Hungary. He attempted to reconcile his Protestant and Catholic subjects, and urged, though in vain, the reformation of abuses on the Council of Trent (q.v.).

Ferdinand I. 1793-1875. Emperor of Austria (1835-48) and king of Hungary (1830-48). A weak ruler who left most of the work of government to Metternich. After Metternich was overthrown (1848), he abdicated in favor of his nephew Francis Joseph.

Ferdinand I. 1861-1948. King of Bulgaria (1887-1918). Son of Prince Augustus of Saxe-Coburg, he was offered the crown of Bulgaria in 1887. In 1908 he proclaimed Bulgaria independent and took the title of czar. His country lost heavily in the Second Balkan War (1913). To recoup losses, Ferdinand joined the Central Powers in World War I. Upon the collapse of the Central Powers, Ferdinand abdicated (Oct. 4, 1918) and was succeeded by his son Boris III (1894-1943).

Ferdinand II. 1578-1637. Cousin of Emperor Matthias and grandson of Holy Roman Emperor Ferdinand I. King of Bohemia (1617-19) and of Hungary (1621-25). Holy Roman Emperor (1619-37). He was educated by Jesuits who taught him to hate Protestants. His entire reign was occupied with war against the Protestants. He deposed Elector Frederick V of Palatinate. He drove Protestantism out of Bohemia. He issued the Edict of Restitution (q.v.) (1629) which nullified the Peace of Augsburg (1555) (q.v.). At first he was completely victorious. His ultimate success was thwarted by Gustavus Adolphus and Richelieu.

Ferdinand III. 1608-57. King of Hungary (1625-55) and Holy Roman Emperor (1637-57). Son of Ferdinand II. He continued the struggle against the Protestants, but finally had to agree to the Peace of Westphalia (q.v.) (1648). He was a scholar and a skilful composer of music.

Ferdinand V of Castile or Ferdinand II of Aragon (called the Catholic). 1452-1516. King of Aragon (1479-1516) and joint sovereign of Castile with his wife Isabella (1474-1504). He united the Kingdoms of Aragon and Castile, organized the Santa Hermandad (1476) and the Holy Inquisition (1480), conquered Granada from the Moors (1492), and expelled the Jews (1492). At first he supported Columbus, but later turned against him. He was king of Naples as Ferdinand III (1504-16).

Ferdinand VII. 1784-1833. King of Spain (1808 and 1814-33). He was proclaimed king after the forced abdication of his father Charles IV. He was invited by Napoleon to a conference at Bayonne, where he was imprisoned. Reinstated by Napoleon (1814). He abrogated all acts which had been promulgated by the French, abolished the constitution of 1812, reinstated the Inquisition, and abolished the Salic Law, causing the Carlist insurrection (q.v.). His reign was disastrous to Spain, which lost all colonies in North and South America except Cuba and Puerto Rico.

Ferdinand. 1865-1927. King of Romania (1914-27). Although related to the German imperial family, he entered (1916) the First World War on the side of the Allies. In 1922 he was crowned king of greater Romania, established by the peace treaties. During his reign agrarian reforms were enacted and universal suffrage was introduced.

Fermi, Enrico. 1901-. Italian physicist who has become a naturalized American. He investigated atomic structure and obtained element No. 93 by bombarding uranium with neutrons. He was awarded the Nobel Prize in Physics in 1938.

Ferry Laws. These laws were sponsored in the early 1880's by Jules Ferry (1832-93), the French minister of education. Compulsory attendance at some schools was ordered for all children. But it was left to parents to decide whether their children should attend public or Church schools. Only public schools were to receive financial support from the state. In public schools only laymen should teach and there was to be no religious instruction.

Feudal justice. The lord was the sole judge over his tenants. He held court three times a year. For every offense there was a fixed fine. On a large estate the income from fines each year might be quite large.

Feudal rents. Vassals were required to pay various types of rent in kind. Rent for the land, house, chimney, and even for each head of livestock was charged. A share was due of everything produced on the soil. There was a charge for pasturing livestock, for cutting firewood, for fishing in the lord's streams. Vassals were forced to use the lord's mill, oven, and wine-press for a fee. The tenant was required to labor for the lord without charge several days of the year (in France, called *corvée*) (q.v.).

Feudal society. Feudal society was divided into three classes: the tillers of the soil, the citizens or bourgeoisie, and the nobility. Tillers of the soil were of two classes: peasants (*rustici, villeins*) and serfs. The former were free men who paid so much a year for the use of their lands, which were hereditary. Being independent of their lords, they were free to dispose of their possessions and might amass considerable property. The serfs were slaves who were attached to the soil. They were allowed to marry and each received a bit of land to cultivate. Each paid a head-tax to his lord. A serf could neither leave his land nor be removed from it. If he ran away, he was returned if caught, unless he had entered the service of the clergy. Serfs might buy their freedom. Sometimes they were set free by the lord.

Citizens were inhabitants of cities. Since many cities arose after the establishment of feudalism, citizens were under the control of some lord. They resented this greatly. As cities grew large and rich, they resisted feudalism and ultimately contributed to its downfall.

Nobles were of two classes: secular and ecclesiastical. The only occupation of the former was the profession of arms. At first only those who could afford to equip themselves with arms could become nobles. By the 13th century, nobility had become hereditary. Wealth was no longer the passport to the noble rank. Marriage between nobles and commoners was forbidden, or else regarded as a mésalliance. In Germany and France, all children of a noble family inherited the title. In England only the eldest son received the family title and wealth. Only he was required to marry within the noble class.

Ecclesiastical nobles were the great cardinals, archbishops, bishops, and abbots. Since many people gave liberally to the Church, the Church soon acquired great properties. The income from these properties was considerable. It early became the custom to put the younger sons of nobles into the best Church positions.

Feudal terms. The following are terms which were used in feudal practices:

1. Fief, feud, benefice—the land, office, or right or privilege which was granted.
2. Lord, liege, suzerain—one who granted a fief.
3. Vassal, liegeman—receiver of a fief.
4. Subinfeudation—regranting a fief by a vassal to a third person, who thus became the vassal of a vassal.
5. Homage—the ceremony of becoming a vassal. The vassal-to-be knelt uncovered, with hands folded and sword ungirt, before his prospective lord and vowed to become the lord's "man" (homo). The lord then raised him, received his oath of fealty, and by a symbolic act (presentation of a sword, ring, bit of earth, etc.) invested him with the fief. One great duty of the lord to his

vassal was to protect him. The vassal, on his part, owed his lord various kinds of service and feudal dues.

6. Feudal dues—"Aids" (payment of money when the lord's eldest son was knighted, when his eldest daughter was married). "Relief"—paid by an heir when he entered his inheritance upon the death of his father. "First-fruits"—paid by a newly-appointed bishop, income for his first year in office. "Escheat"—when a vassal died without heirs, the property reverted to the lord. "Fodrum"—maintenance of the lord himself and his retinue when passing through a district. "Wardship and marriage"—in England the king claimed the right to act as guardian for minor children of deceased vassals; the king would have to be paid before he consented to the marriage of his wards.

Feudalism. This term applied to the economic, social, and political relations existing in Europe from the 10th to the 13th centuries.

1. Economic. These relations are best expressed by the phrase "feudal tenure of land." The theory was that the tenant had only the use of the land and that he must pay dues, or rent, to a lord (suzerain). Ownership of land was not absolute, but of a beneficiary nature. In theory the land belonged to God, who let it to the king, who, in turn, sublet it to his great vassals, and these parcelled it out to their subjects.

2. Social. The word expressing social relations is "vassalage," which indicated the personal relationship between the man who held the land and the man from whom he received it. It conveyed on the part of the vassal social inferiority.

3. Political. Political relations are expressed in the term "immunity." The holder of an estate was, in matter of government, free from all interference on the part of his lord. With the use of the land he received from the lord the right, within his own territory, to perform the

judicial, executive, and certain legislative functions of government.

Feudalism was not a "system." It varied from country to country and from place to place.

Feudalism originated when Charles Martel was preparing an army to resist the invasion of the Mohammedans (732). Being short of horses, he seized some church lands and granted the use of them to vassals in return for horses. Feudalism in Europe continued in modified form until the days of the French Revolution (1789) and Napoleon (1799-1815). However, it was at its height from the 10th to the 13th centuries. Following the break-up of Charlemagne's empire (814), conditions were so confused that men turned to feudalism for some sort of stability. From the 13th century on, the use of gunpowder diminished the power of feudal nobles and thus the effectiveness of feudalism.

Feuillants. A party which controlled about 150 members of the French Legislative Assembly (1791-92). They were conservatives and strict constitutionalists. They strove to strengthen the royal power.

Fianna Fail. A Republican party organized in Ireland by De Valera in opposition to the treaty of 1921 which created the Irish Free State and accepted a compromise position regarding North Ireland.

Field of Cloth and Gold. June 7, 1520. A meeting between Francis I of France and Henry VIII of England for the purpose of forming an alliance against Emperor Charles V. For three weeks these monarchs and their wives met in a valley near Calais for a series of interviews, feasts, and jousts. No substantial result was achieved.

Fielding, Henry. 1707-54. English novelist. He gained early fame with his novel *Joseph Andrews* (1742), a parody of

Pamela. Other works are *Tom Jones* and *Amelia.*

Fifth Monarchy Men. 17th century. A religious group in England at the time of the Puritan Revolution. They believed that Jesus was about to return to earth to rule. His monarchy was to be the fifth. The first four were the Assyrian, Persian, Greek, and Roman empires. This group originally supported Cromwell (q.v.), but later turned against him and tried unsuccessfully to assassinate him. After the Restoration (1660), one of the sect's preachers led a group through London, proclaiming the advent of the Fifth Monarchy. He and many of his followers were hanged for treason. The movement then collapsed.

"Filioque" controversy. A doctrinal dispute which arose in the 9th century and which led to the separation of the Greek Church from the Latin Church. The Greeks charged that the Latins added the word "filioque" ("and from the Son") to the clause in the Nicene Creed which declares that the Holy Ghost "proceedeth from the Father." Thus was altered the fundamental concept of the Trinitarian Godhead. The Latin Church insisted upon retaining this new usage. The Greeks denounced it as a "heresy" and to this day insist that this addition to the Creed makes union between the two churches impossible.

Fire of London, The Great. Sept. 2-7, 1666. During this five-day interval it is estimated that two-thirds of the inhabitants of London were unroofed. In rebuilding the city, the streets were made broader and straighter, and houses with overhanging upper stories disappeared. The newer London was less picturesque than the old, but more healthful and spacious. (See Wren, Christopher, q.v.)

First Empire of France. 1804-14. Bonaparte was proclaimed Napoleon I,

Emperor of the French, by the Senate and Tribunate on May 18, 1804. He was consecrated on Dec. 2, 1804, by Pope Pius VII. Napoleon placed the crown on his own head and later crowned Josephine as Empress. His elevation was ratified by a plebiscite (3,572,329 in favor; 2569 opposed). The imperial office was made hereditary in the male line. Napoleon had the right to adopt the children of his brothers. In default of such children, the crown was to pass to his brothers, Joseph and Louis. In 1805, Napoleon also made himself king of Italy. His stepson, Eugène Beauharnais, became the viceroy of Italy. The empire expanded, until in 1810 it attained its greatest extent. Collapse followed the Russian campaign (1812). Napoleon abdicated on April 11, 1814.

First International. 1864-76. Originating in an informal gathering of organizations of English, French, and Belgian workers (1862), the International Working Men's Association assumed permanent form in 1864 when it also adopted Karl Marx's teachings *in toto.* For several years it held annual conferences. However, its members were few and poor. Thus, the organization lacked proper financial support. The Franco-Prussian War (1870-71) (q.v.), the failure of the Paris Commune of 1871 (q.v.), and quarrels between the disciples of Marx and Bakunin led to the dissolution of the organization.

First Republic of France. 1792-1804. The First French Republic went through three phases: (1) The period of the National Convention (1792-95); the Directory (1795-99); and the Consulate (1799-1804). The Republic ended when Napoleon I created the First Empire (1804).

Fitch, Ralph. d. 1606. An English merchant who in 1583-91 traveled via the Euphrates to and from Bengal, Burma, and Siam. His account of this trip stimulated an interest in Far Eastern trade.

Five Mile Act. 1665. An English law which forbade a Non-Conformist minister to teach in any school or to come within five miles of a city or corporate town unless he had taken an oath that it was unlawful to bear arms against the king, and had pledged that he would never try to change the government of the church and state.

Five-Power Naval Disarmament Treaty. See Washington Conference.

Five Year Plans. Gigantic blueprints to increase Soviet productive capacity. Factories were to be located with reference to natural resources. The Urals and western Siberia were to be exploited. Arms production was to be stepped up drastically. The first Plan (Oct. 31, 1928–Dec. 31, 1932) nearly doubled Soviet heavy industry. The aim of the second Plan was to improve the quality of workmanship. The third Plan, interrupted by the war, was designed to improve the quality and quantity of consumers' goods. A fourth Plan was begun in 1946 and completed in 1951. Its purpose was to repair wartime damage and consolidate the new West Siberia industry. A fifth Plan was announced early in 1953.

Flaubert, Gustave. 1821-80. French novelist. He studied medicine, but abandoned it to devote himself to writing. He is regarded as a leader in the naturalist school. He is the author of *Madame Bovary, Salammbo, Herodias,* etc.

Fleming, Sir Alexander. 1881-. Scottish bacteriologist. Discoverer of penicillin. In 1945 he shared the Nobel Prize in Physiology and Medicine with Ernst B. Chain and Sir Howard W. Florey for work on penicillin.

Fleury, André Hercule de (1653-1743). French cardinal and statesman. Almoner to Queen Marie Thérèse (1679-83). Bishop of Fréjus (1698). Tutor of young Louis XV (1715). He exerted great influence during the early part of Louis XV's reign (1715-43). Member of the Council of State (1723). Virtual prime minister (1726-43). Cardinal (1726). His administration was peaceful and marked by economic growth.

Flodden, Battle of. Sept. 9, 1513. Taking advantage of the fact that Henry VIII and his army were in France, James IV of Scotland invaded England. Queen Catherine raised an army, which was placed under command of the Earl of Surrey. The Scotch army was annihilated at Flodden and King James killed.

Florence, Treaty of. March 18, 1801. Between France and Naples. All harbors were to be closed to British and Turkish vessels. Naples ceded to France its possessions in central Italy and the Island of Elba. French garrisons were to be installed in several Italian towns.

Flying shuttle. See Kay, John.

Fontenoy, Battle of. 1745. In this battle during the War of the Austrian Succession (q.v.), the French decisively defeated an allied army of British, Austrians, Dutch, and Hanoverians. In this battle, for the first time in three centuries, the French forced British troops to break and run from a battle field.

Food and Agricultural Organization (FAO). The FAO came into existence in 1943 to plan for post-war food production. It can only advise the various nations of the world. It encourages agricultural research, supplies information about proper nutrition, seeks to stimulate more production of food, furnishes technical advice on farming methods, and promotes the more efficient distribution of food from surplus to deficit areas.

Four - Power International Military Tribunal. See Nuremberg Trials.

Four-Power Treaty. See Washington Conference.

Four-Year Plan, Nazi. At the National Socialist Party Congress, held in Sept. 1936 in Nuremberg, Hitler announced that within four years Germany must be independent of foreign countries with respect to all those materials which could in any way be produced through "German capability, through German chemistry, or by our machine and mining industries." The execution of the plan was entrusted to Göring. When Göring and Schacht differed as to methods, the latter resigned and was replaced as minister of economics and head of the Reichsbank by Dr. Walther Funk. When Austria entered the Reich (1938), the Four-Year Plan was speedily introduced there. Chief emphasis was on development of synthetic fuel, rubber, and fabrics; and better use of old mines.

Fourier, François Marie Charles. 1772-1837. French social scientist and reformer. Born in Besançon. He devoted himself to a study of society and economic conditions. In *Théorie des Quatre Mouvements et des Destinées Générales* (1808) he advocated organizing society into cooperative phalansteries of 1800 people each. Earnings should be divided so that labor would receive 5/12; capital, 4/12; talent, 3/12. Fourierism appealed to many thoughtful people. Numerous attempts (cf. Brook Farm, Mass.) were made to organize model communities according to Fourier's principles.

Fourteen Points, The. Jan. 8, 1918. In an address to Congress, President Wilson outlined the Allied war aims. This speech paralleled an address by Lloyd George to the Trade Union Congress (Jan. 5, 1918). The Fourteen Points are as follows:

(1) Open covenants of peace, openly arrived at and the abolition of secret diplomacy.

(2) Freedom of the seas.

(3) Removal, as far as possible, of all economic barriers.

(4) Adequate guarantees, so that national armaments will be reduced to the lowest point consistent with safety.

(5) Impartial adjustment of colonial claims with proper consideration of the interests of the populations concerned.

(6) Evacuation of Russian territory and the free determination of its own political and national policy.

(7) Evacuation and restoration of Belgium.

(8) Evacuation and restoration of France and the return of Alsace-Lorraine.

(9) Readjustment of the frontiers of Italy along clearly recognizable lines of nationality.

(10) The freest opportunity of autonomous development for the peoples of Austria-Hungary.

(11) Evacuation and restoration of Romania, Serbia, and Montenegro and free access to the sea for Serbia.

(12) Autonomous development for non-Turkish possessions of the sultan and internationalization of the Dardanelles.

(13) An independent Poland with access to the sea.

(14) An association of nations to afford mutual guarantees of political independence and territorial integrity to great and small states alike.

Fox, Charles James. 1740-1806. English statesman and orator. Lord of the admiralty (1770-72) and of the treasury (1772-74). He favored the cause of the American Revolutionists and the French Revolution. He had much to do with investigating the East India Co. and the impeachment of Warren Hastings. He opposed slavery and urged emancipation of Roman Catholics.

Fox, George. 1624-90. English religious reformer. He founded the Society of Friends, or Quakers.

France, Anatole (pseudonym of Jacques Anatole François Thibault). 1844-1924. French novelist and playwright. He is regarded as an outstanding satirist and humorist. Among his writings are *Le Crime de Sylvestre Bonnard, Thaïs, La Révolte des Anges, Les Dieux ont Soif, La Vie en Fleur.* He was awarded the Nobel Prize in Literature in 1921.

Francis of Assisi, St. (name Giovanni Francesco Bernadore). 1182-1226. Italian monk, founder of the Franciscan Order. Son of a wealthy family, he consecrated himself (from 1206) to a life of poverty and religion. He attracted followers slowly. By 1210 his brotherhood increased to eleven members. Francis then drew up a rule to govern the group, which was approved by Pope Innocent III. Like other forms of monastic life, the Franciscan system was founded on the vows of chastity, poverty, and obedience. The second was stressed as being most important. Now followers flocked to the order. In 1216 the order was solemnly approved by Innocent III. Francis went to Egypt (1223), where he made a personal appeal to the sultan for more indulgent treatment of Christian captives. In 1224 (according to legend) he experienced the miracle of the stigmata (the marks of the wounds of the crucified Christ). He was canonized in 1228 by Pope Gregory IX.

Francis I. 1494-1547. King of France (1515-47). To gain control of Italy he continued war against the Holy League. He was victorious in northern Italy (1515) and gained possession of Lombardy. He was defeated for election to the position of Holy Roman Emperor (1519). He entertained Henry VIII of England at the Field of Cloth and Gold (1520) (q.v.). He undertook a series of wars with the Holy Roman Empire. (1) (1521-25) He was defeated by Charles V (q.v.) at Pavia and was taken prisoner (1525). He was released by the Treaty of Madrid (1526) after surrendering Burgundy and making concessions. He broke his word and (2) made a second war (1527-29) in which he lost his Italian possessions. (3) (1536-38) Third war. (4) (1542-44) Fourth War. He loved letters and the fine arts. During his reign the Renaissance came to France.

Francis II. 1544-60. King of France (1559-60). Eldest son of Henry II and Catherine de Médicis. Married Mary Queen of Scots (1558). Sickly and irresolute, he was the tool of his uncles, the Duke of Guise and the Cardinal of Lorraine.

Francis II. 1768-1835. Last Holy Roman Emperor (1792-1806). Emperor of Austria as Francis I (1804-35). He joined all coalitions against Napoleon and was defeated in all the Napoleonic wars except the last. He acquired much territory from the Congress of Vienna (1814-15). During his last years he was dominated by Metternich. His daughter Maria Louisa was the second wife of Napoleon.

Francis Ferdinand. 1863-1914. Archduke of Austria. Nephew of Emperor Francis Joseph. He became heir-apparent to the throne of Austria-Hungary following the deaths of Crown Prince Rudolf (1889) and his own father (1896). Upon his marriage to Countess Sophie Chotek (1900), he renounced the rights of succession to any children. He and his wife were murdered on June 28, 1914, in Sarajevo, Bosnia. This murder touched off a string of events which led to World War I.

Francis Joseph I. 1830-1916. Emperor of Austria (1848-1916); king of Hungary (1867-1916). He succeeded his uncle Ferdinand I when the latter abdicated

(1848). He pacified Italy and subdued Hungary (1849). Defeated in the Italian War of Liberation (1859), he lost Lombardy. Defeated by Prussia in the Seven Weeks' War (1866), he lost Venetia to Italy and was expelled from the German Confederation. He effected a Compromise (*Ausgleich*) with the Hungarians (1867) and became their king. He was a member of the *Dreikaiserbund* (1872-90). Concluded the Triple Alliance with Germany and Italy (1883). He saw Austria involved in the First World War when his nephew and heir, Archduke Francis Ferdinand, was assassinated at Sarajevo (June 28, 1914).

Franco, Francisco. 1892-. Dictator of Spain. Born at El Ferrol, he entered the army and rapidly rose to the position of general. He commanded the Spanish Foreign Legion in Morocco. In 1935 he became chief of staff. Because he was considered to be "politically dangerous," he was sent (1936) to govern the Canary Islands. He flew to Morocco and started the revolution there (July, 1936). When General Sanjurjo, the designated head of the rebellion, was killed in an airplane crash, Franco assumed leadership of the rebellion (1936-39). With the aid of Nazi and Italian troops he overthrew the socialist government and made himself head (Caudillo) of an authoritarian state.

Franco-Prussian War. 1870-71. In the years following the Austro-Prussian War (1866), a conflict between France and Prussia came to be regarded as "inevitable" by both countries. The war started because of a quarrel regarding the throne of Spain. In 1869, Spanish liberals expelled Queen Isabella II and invited Prince Leopold of Hohenzollern-Sigmaringen, a Roman Catholic cousin of King William of Prussia, to be their constitutional sovereign. Although Leopold at first demurred, on July 2 he accepted the throne at Bismarck's request. Napoleon III considered this acceptance a

19th century effort to revive the 16th century empire of Charles V, and informed William that France would consider the ascent of a Hohenzollern to the throne of Spain an act of war. On July 12, it was announced in Madrid that Prince Leopold, of his own accord, had changed his mind and would not accept the crown of Spain. Here the matter might have rested had not the Empress and the immediate advisers of Napoleon insisted that France must take some more positive action. Napoleon now instructed his ambassador to demand that William pledge himself never to permit a Hohenzollern prince to become king of Spain. This demand was made when William was taking the cure at Ems. William refused to make this pledge, and, when the ambassador asked for a future interview, refused to see him. King William informed Bismarck of these happenings by telegraph. Bismarck published this Ems telegram in the newspapers after first altering the language sufficiently to make Germans believe that their king had been insulted by the French ambassador and the French that their ambassador had been insulted by King William.

The news of the Ems interview reached Paris on July 14, 1870, Bastille Day. Immediately, France was thrown into an uproar. The same night, Napoleon and his cabinet decided on war. The next day the French Parliament voted almost unanimously for war.

To the great chagrin of the French, the South German states—the kingdoms of Bavaria and Württemberg and the grand duchies of Baden and Hesse-Darmstadt—joined with the North German Confederation. In their opinion, the Fatherland was again being attacked by Napoleon.

In the first phases of the war, the Germans were victorious everywhere. At Gravelotte (Aug. 18) the French armies in Alsace were defeated and immobilized in the fortress of Metz, where they were treacherously surrendered in October by Marshal Bazaine (q.v.). On Sept. 2, the

First French Army Corps was routed at Sedan. The Emperor himself was captured on this field of battle. On Sept. 4, Napoleon III's government collapsed. A "Government of National Defense," which had the inspiring Leon Gambetta as minister of war, now rallied France to a surprising degree. Paris was besieged from Sept. 15 to Jan. 28, when it surrendered. Hostilities were concluded by the Treaty of Frankfurt (May 10, 1871) (q.v.).

Franconian (or Salian) dynasty. Name of a dynasty of German emperors, founded by Conrad II, duke of Franconia (1024-39). His successors were:

Henry III   (1039-56)
Henry IV   (1056-1106)
Henry V   (1106-25), who died without an heir.

Agnes, sister of Henry V, was married to Frederick of Swabia. They were the founders of the Hohenstaufen dynasty (q.v.).

Frankfurt Assembly. See Revolutions of 1848.

Frankfurt, Treaty of. May 10, 1871. This treaty ended the Franco-Prussian War. France ceded to Germany the whole of Alsace, except Belfort, and eastern Lorraine, together with the great fortresses of Metz and Strassburg. France agreed to pay an indemnity of one billion dollars in gold. France was to be occupied by German troops until the indemnity was paid off.

Franks. A Teutonic tribe which settled originally along the Rhine from Cologne to the North Sea. In the 5th century they began to extend their territory. Under Clovis (466?-511) they extended their dominions first to the Loire and then to the Pyrenees. Under successors to Clovis, the Frankish dominions embraced nearly all that today is included in France, Belgium, Holland, and West Germany.

Frederick I (*called* **Frederick Barbarossa**). 1123?-1190. Holy Roman Emperor (1152-90). King of Germany (1152-90) and of Italy (1155-90). He endeavored to achieve a unified empire. With this in mind, he made six expeditions into Italy to bring that country completely under imperial control. Successful at first, he was defeated by the Lombard League at Legnano (1176). He was forced by the Peace of Constance (1183) to grant independence to the Italian cities. He overcame the Welfs (q.v.) and deposed their leader, Henry the Lion (1180). He led an army on the Third Crusade (1189) and was drowned (1190) in Asia Minor. Under his rule the empire was enlarged. He advanced learning. He encouraged the building of towns and cities. He is regarded by many as one of the greatest German rulers.

Frederick II (**Stupor Mundi i.e.- "Wonder of the World"**). 1194-1250. King of Sicily as Frederick I (1198-1212). Holy Roman Emperor (1215-50). Son of Henry II. He came (1198) under the guardianship of the pope. After the Battle of Bouvines (1214) (q.v.), he was the King of Germany (1215). He attempted to bring about a union of Germany and Italy but was opposed by the pope and the Lombard League (q.v.). He led the Fifth Crusade (1228-29). He secured Jerusalem and made a 10-year truce with the sultan of Egypt. Crowned king of Jerusalem (1229). His third wife (m. 1235) was Isabella, the daughter of John of England. He was a great patron of literature and science. He instituted a form of government in Sicily which was much like a modern system of government. He neglected Germany.

Frederick V (*called* **Winter King**). 1596-1632. Elector of the Palatinate (1610-23). Chosen king of Bohemia (1619). Completely defeated at the battle of White Mountain (1620) (q.v.). Deprived of his electorate (1623), he remained in exile until his death. These struggles were the first campaigns of the Thirty Years' War (q.v.). He married (1613) Elizabeth, daughter of James I of England. Their daughter Sophia married Ernest Augustus, elector of Hanover. The son of Ernest Augustus and Sophia became George I of England.

Frederick I. 1657-1713. Son of Frederick William, the "Great Elector." Elector of Brandenburg (1688-1701) as Frederick III. He became King of Prussia in 1701. King of Prussia (1701-1713). Patron of scholars, particularly Leibnitz. Founded the Order of the Black Eagle (1701) and the University of Halle (1694).

Frederick II (*called* **the Great**). 1712-1786. King of Prussia (1740-86). He tried to escape from the control of his father (1730); but was arrested, tried as a deserter, and later pardoned. Six months after he became king, Emperor Charles VI died, leaving his Austrian possessions to his daughter, Maria Theresa. Believing that Maria Theresa would not be able to keep her inheritance, Frederick seized Silesia, thus starting the War of the Austrian Succession (1740-48) (q.v.). By the Peace of Dresden (1745), he secured possession of Silesia. He built the palace of Sans Souci (1745-47) near Potsdam as his royal residence. He formed a new alliance (1756) with England against Maria Theresa, France, Russia, Sweden, and Saxony. The Seven Years' War (1756-63) (q.v.) followed this alliance. During the war, Frederick displayed great military genius against odds. He won many battles, but was badly defeated in some. By the Peace of Hubertsburg (1763) he established complete claim to Silesia. He was a great patron of literature. He was an "enlightened despot" and introduced many reforms into his country. He participated in the first partition of Poland (1772). A voluminous writer, his complete works fill 30 volumes.

Frederick III. 1831-1888. Son of William I of Prussia and Germany. Born in Potsdam. King and emperor of Germany (March 9-June 15, 1888). He married Victoria (1850), eldest daughter of Queen Victoria of England. Father of William II. Patron of literature and science. He died of cancer of the throat. He was nicknamed *Unser Fritz.*

Frederick William. 1620-1688. Elector of Brandenburg (1640-88). Called the "Great Elector." Finding his dominions greatly ravaged by the Thirty Years' War, he reorganized the finances, restored towns and cities, and built up the army. He was granted territory in the Peace of Westphalia (1648). He made war on Poland (1656) and secured control over the duchy of Prussia. He spent his last years in improving education, building up the army, and improving finances. He built roads, constructed canals, drained marshes, and improved agriculture. He received many Huguenot refugees who had been driven from France by the Revocation of the Edict of Nantes (1685). He laid a firm foundation for a great country.

Frederick William I. 1688-1740. King of Prussia (1713-40). Father of Frederick the Great. He spent most of his reign in improving the internal affairs of his kingdom. He devoted much energy to inspecting minute details of administration. Very economical. He left Prussia a strong country with a powerful army. Frederick William was rough, uncouth, and unfriendly to culture.

Frederick William II. 1744-97. King of Prussia (1786-97). His policies caused Prussia to decline in power. He joined Austria against France (1792-95). By losing this war he was compelled at Basel (1795) to surrender to France all Prussian territories west of the Rhine. He took part in the second and third partitions of Poland (1793, 1795).

Frederick William III. 1770-1840. King of Prussia (1797-1840). Born at Potsdam. After the subjection of his kingdom by Napoleon following the defeat at Jena (1806) and the dismemberment of it by the Treaty of Tilsit (1807) (q.v.), he initiated a nationalist revival which was led by Stein, Hardenberg, and others. Victory at Leipzig (1813) liberated Prussia. After Waterloo (1815) (q.v.), he disappointed Germans by joining the Holy Alliance and following the policies of Metternich. He established the Zollverein (q.v.) (1834).

Frederick William IV. 1795-1861. King of Prussia (1840-61). He failed to carry out the promises of liberal reforms. He was forced by the Revolution of 1848 to grant a constitution (1850). He refused the imperial crown which was offered by the Frankfurt Assembly (1849). Soon after he became insane and the country was ruled by his brother William (afterwards William I) as regent.

Frederick I (of Hesse-Cassel). King of Sweden. See Great Northern War.

Frederick Henry. 1584-1647. Prince of Orange-Nassau and stadholder of the Dutch Republic (1625-87). Son of William the Silent. He succeeded his brother Maurice. He took many cities from the Spanish, and negotiated a favorable treaty with Spain (1647).

Free French. See De Gaulle, Charles.

French Committee of National Liberation. Formed June 4, 1943 for the purpose of liberating France from the Nazis. It included both General de Gaulle and General Giraud.

French in Mexico. 1861-67. Upon the suspension of payment on the foreign debts by the Mexican government (May 29, 1861), France, Great Britain, and Spain by the Treaty of London (Oct. 31)

undertook a joint intervention to protect their interests. Napoleon III desired to create in Mexico a Catholic empire under the aegis of France, which would provide markets and raw materials and check the expansion of the United States. French designs became clear after the occupation of Vera Cruz (Dec. 17), and Spain and Great Britain withdrew (April 8, 1862). French troops entered Mexico City (June 7, 1863) and Archduke Maximilian of Austria (q.v.) was made emperor (April 10, 1864). After the close of the United States Civil War (1865), the United States was finally in a position to invoke the Monroe Doctrine against France. As a consequence, Napoleon recalled his troops (March 12, 1867). Maximilian was captured by Mexican republicans and executed by them at Querétaro (June 19, 1867).

French National Convention, Social reforms of the. 1792-95. Among the fundamental social laws that were passed by the National Convention were the following:

(1) Law of equal inheritance. All children of the deceased must share equally in the inheritance of property. This law abolished primogeniture. It is still the law of France.

(2) Abolition of imprisonment for debt.

(3) Abolition of Negro slavery.

(4) Protection of woman's claim on property in common with man's.

(5) Separation of Church and state.

The Convention also prepared an elaborate scheme of state education, which the philosopher Condorcet (q.v.) designed. It began the project, which was later completed by Napoleon, of preparing a single comprehensive code of law for the country.

French Republic, Second. 1848-52. This government was set up in France following the abdication of Louis Philippe in 1848. Its first and only president was Louis Napoleon. He overthrew it through a *coup* and replaced it with the Second Empire.

French Revolution, The. One of the major revolutions of history, which began in France in 1789. Its causes were complex. Among the most potent were the following:

1. The spirit of the 18th century. This was a spirit of questioning skepticism which sprang from the scientific method of Descartes (q.v.) and Newton (q.v.). Voltaire (q.v.), Diderot (q.v.), and Montesquieu (q.v.) subjected existing society to devastating criticism. Rousseau (q.v.) stressed the virtue of the natural man.

2. Agrarian conditions. Although French peasantry was almost wholly free and in many regions owned land, it was subject to certain annoying feudal dues and was taxed heavily, especially with the *taille*, a land-tax from which nobles and clergy were exempt.

3. Rise of a middle class. The middle class was generally excluded from politics (access to the royal bureaucracy was open to able bourgeoisie). The middle class had become more numerous and richer with the expansion of French trade and resented its inferior social and political position.

4. The government was inefficient. The French government was not so much tyrannical as unwieldy and unsuited to the needs of a large commercial and agricultural state. Taxation was inequitable. There was no true representative assembly. Justice was by no means arbitrary. Judges were usually competent and conscientious. The notorious *lettres de cachet* (q.v.) were made important in antigovernment propaganda, but were much less important in fact.

5. An ever-growing deficit. The government could not cope with this deficit. When the Estates-General (q.v.) were called to remedy this situation (1789), they proceeded to attempt to reform the state. France in 1789 was a prosperous society with a bankrupt government.

It is a mistake to call the French Revolution a revolt against feudalism. One of the main characteristics of 18th century France was absolute monarchy, a nonfeudal institution. The characteristic institutions of feudalism had been changed or destroyed. Though many medieval institutions remained (*corvée, gabelle,* etc., q.v.), the country had progressed a long way from feudalism.

In May, 1789, King Louis XVI (q.v.) was forced to convoke the Estates-General to deal with the financial situation. A debate in the Estates-General as to whether voting should be by order (giving the First and Second Estates dominant power) or by head (to the advantage of the Third Estate) became violent. When the king tried to adjourn the Estates-General by force (June 20), the Third Estate withdrew to a nearby tennis court and swore to remain together until they had prepared a constitution for France. On June 27, the king yielded and legalized the Third Estate as the National Assembly with Mirabeau (q.v.) as its head. The king now began to concentrate troops near Paris. It was rumored that these were to be used to dissolve the National Assembly. When the popular Necker (q.v.) was dismissed from the ministry (July 11), the Paris mob, led by Desmoulins (q.v.), revolted and on July 14 destroyed the Bastille. Louis XVI now recalled Necker and sanctioned the creation of a commune to govern Paris. A National Guard was formed under the command of Lafayette (q.v.) to preserve order. The attack upon the Bastille was a signal for a wave of violence to spread over France. Peasants burned the castles of the nobles in many places, while the government stood by powerless. At a night meeting (Aug. 4-5) the National Assembly voted to abolish feudalism. Meanwhile, radical clubs were gaining strength in Paris. Rumors of counterrevolutionary plots were circulated in Paris. On Oct. 5, 1789, a Parisian mob marched on Versailles. Lafayette was barely able to save the lives of the king and the queen, who were forcibly taken to Paris by the mob and placed as virtual prisoners in the Tuileries palace. The National Assembly (now known as the Constituent Assembly), under the leadership of Mirabeau, prepared a constitution (1791) calling for a limited monarchy, and also drew up the Declaration of the Rights of Man (1791) (q.v.). To solve the financial problems the Assembly issued the assignats (q.v.). The Assembly attempted to solve the religious question by nationalizing the Church lands (1789), suppressing religious orders (1790), and requiring the clergy to take an oath to support the Civil Constitution for Clergy (1790) (q.v.). Few obeyed. Those that refused were known as Non-Juring Clergy. Many nobles fled from France (Emigrés). Louis XVI decided to join them. He and the queen fled from Paris (June 20-21, 1791), but they were arrested at Varennes and returned to Paris (q.v.). On Oct. 1, 1791, the Legislative Assembly (the law-making body created by the Constitution of 1791) convened. Its right wing was made up of Feuillants (q.v.). Its left wing was composed of Girondists (q.v.), Cordeliers (q.v.), and Jacobins (q.v.).

War broke out on April 20, 1792. Emigrés incited the courts of Austria and Prussia to intervene in France. Many in France welcomed the war. Royalists believed that war would lead to a restoration of the old regime. Republicans hoped to spread their doctrines throughout Europe with the sword. Early reverses for France persuaded many that the king was in treasonable correspondence with the enemy. On Aug. 10, 1792, a mob invaded the Tuileries to seize the king. He saved himself by seeking protection from the Assembly. The Assembly now suspended royalty and ordered the election of a National Convention. Meanwhile, the Paris commune, led by Danton (q.v.) and Marat (q.v.), assumed control of the police. Mass arrests of royalist sympathizers were followed (Sept. 2-3) by the "September Massacres," in which mobs invaded the prisons and killed hundreds of prisoners. On Sept. 21, 1792, the National Convention convened, abolished monarchy, and proclaimed a republic. It tried and executed the king and queen, thus provoking a royalist insurrection in La Vendée (q.v.) and causing England to declare war on France. The Convention was torn by disputes between the Girondists and the Jacobins. The latter, led by Marat and Robespierre (q.v.), triumphed. The Convention governed France through a Committee of Public Safety (q.v.) and numerous agencies such as the Revolutionary Tribunal (q.v.). Now began the Reign of Terror (q.v.). First, thousands of royalist suspects were executed. Robespierre then began to strike at his own ranks. Jacobin leaders like Philippe Égalité (q.v.) and Danton were guillotined. The Terror had its economic aspects. Maximum prices and wages were fixed. The Terror ended when Robespierre was arrested during the *coup* of 9 Thermidor (July 27, 1794) and executed the next day. A new constitution creating the Directory (q.v.) went into effect Oct. 1795. (See also French National Convention, Social Reforms of; Calender, French Revolutionary; National Convention.)

The Directory was marked by corruption, bankruptcy, and constant intrigues. It was ended by the *coup* of Bonaparte on 18 Brumaire (Nov. 19, 1799) and the subsequent formation of the Consulate (q.v.).

The French Revolution put the French capitalist class and bourgeoisie firmly in control of the country. It ended the last vestiges of feudalism. It provided for social justice through the Code Napoleon (q.v.). The Revolutionary and Napoleonic Wars tore down the old regime in Europe and fostered nationalism.

Frescobaldi, Girolamo. 1583-1643. Organist at St. Peter's, Rome. He made instrumental music free from the influence of vocal music, developing a distinct instrumental style, and using the toccata, a composition for keyboard instruments.

Freud, Sigmund. 1856-1939. Austrian physician and psychologist. He is the founder of psychoanalysis. His work in the field of psychology worked a revolution in psychopathology.

Friars. St. Francis of Assisi founded the first order of friars (called Franciscans, *fratres minores*, friars, Minorites). He believed that holy men should not live isolated from the world, as the monks did. Rather, a holy man should call the world his home and minister to others when the occasion offered. His order became established between 1209 and 1223, when his rule was confirmed by the Pope. Saint Dominic, a Spaniard (1170-1221) also established an order of friars, the Preaching Brothers (*Fratres Praedicatores*, 1215), to resist the spread of heresy in the Church. Later, both orders became large, rich, and powerful. Both gave great attention to learning. During the Middle Ages, both orders furnished many of the great scholars of Europe.

Friedland, Battle of. June 14, 1807. In this battle, Napoleon defeated the Russian army. After the battle, the Russians retreated, and the French occupied Koenigsberg and all the country up to the Niemen River. Several weeks after this battle, Napoleon met the Czar of Russia at Tilsit (q.v.) and negotiated several very important treaties with him.

Frobisher, Sir Walter. 1535-94. Elizabethan seaman who is distinguished for his voyages of exploration to Labrador and his warfare against the Spanish.

Fronde (sling). The discontented nobles and officials of France undertook to exalt the powers of the Parlement of Paris and thus to undo the reforms which had been made by Richelieu and, more recently, by Mazarin. This was the last attempt prior to the French Revolution to cast off royal absolutism in France. This opposition was known as the Fronde, since contemporary opponents likened its members to mischievous boys who threw stones with slings. From 1648 to 1654 there were numerous wars between the Fronde and the supporters of the king. The Fronde was defeated completely. The result of these wars was a greater strengthening of the royal power. It is interesting to note that at almost the same time, the king of England was defeated and executed by Parliament for daring to usurp too much power.

Fugger. Name of a family of financiers and merchants descended from the weaver Johannes Fugger (1348-1409) of Graben, near Augsburg. His sons were Andreas (d. 1457), founder of the Fugger vom Reh branch, and Jakob I (d. 1469), founder of the main branch of the family and the Fugger firm. Jakob's sons (all ennobled) Ulrich (1441-1510), Georg (1453-1506), and Jakob II (1459-1525) carried on and extended the business. They were art patrons as well as money lenders. Descendants of the family are represented in the German princely houses of Kirchberg and Babenhausen.

G

Gabelle. Salt tax in pre-Revolutionary France. It was an indirect tax—as were taxes on alcohol, metal-ware, cards, paper, and starch. The *gabelle* was most unpopular. Each person above the age of seven was supposed to buy from the government salt-works each year seven pounds of salt at about ten times its real value.

Gainsborough, Thomas. 1727-88. English painter. Excelled in portraits and landscapes. *The Blue Boy, Mrs. Siddons, The Shepherd's Boy, Garrick, The Harvest Waggon* are some of his notable works.

Galilei, Galileo. 1564-1642. Italian astronomer and physicist. Born in Pisa. He discovered the isochronism of the pendulum. He demonstrated from the leaning tower of Pisa that bodies of different weights fall with the same velocity. He demonstrated that the path of a projectile is a parabola. Professor of mathematics at Padua (1592-1610). He invented a simple open-air thermometer (1593). He constructed a telescope that magnified the diameter of objects eight times (1610). With this he discovered the mountains on the moon, the moons of Jupiter, sun spots, and that the Milky Way is made up of many stars. He was appointed professor for life at the University of Florence and mathematician extraordinary to the duke of Tuscany. He was denounced by the Church for defending the Copernican system (1613). When he published *Dialogo dei due Massimi Sistemi del Mondo* (1632), he was summoned to Rome and tried by the Inquisition. He was forced to abjure his belief that the earth and planets revolve around the sun. He was allowed to retire for the rest of his life in his villa near Florence. He was blind after 1637.

Gallican Liberties. 1682. In 1516 Pope Leo X had agreed that French kings might appoint all bishops in France. In 1673 Louis XIV announced by edict that the king of France could appoint minor clergymen as well. This decree was resisted by two French bishops with the support of the pope. In 1681, Louis called an assembly of French bishops, which prepared (1682) the Declaration of Liberties of the Gallican Church. It stated that whereas the pope possesses spiritual authority, but does not hold temporal or civil authority, the king is not subject to any ecclesiastical authority and cannot be deposed by the head of the church. This declaration was approved by Louis and became law. The pope rejected it. For a time it seemed that the French church might separate from the Roman Catholic Church. But in 1693 the pope and Louis reached an agreement. The pope agreed that Louis might appoint the minor clergymen. In return, Louis agreed that the French bishops might sign a statement rejecting the Declaration of 1682. While this agreement seemed to be a victory for the pope, it really was a triumph for the king. Louis got his way about appointing all clergymen. Although the bishops rejected the Declaration of 1682, the king did not. Most important of all, the bishops rejected the Declaration because the king ordered them to do so. From this time on, the power of the pope over the French Church was small.

Gallipoli Campaign. April 25-Dec. 20, 1915. An attempt to capture Constantinople by way of the Gallipoli Peninsula. The attacking forces consisted of British, French, and Anzac (Australian and New Zealand Army Corps) troops. After months of futile fighting, in which the Allied armies suffered heavily from heat and disease, the campaign was abandoned. During the campaign the British warships *Goliath*, *Triumph*, and *Majestic* were sunk by one German submarine. This campaign was sponsored by Sir Winston Churchill (q.v.), who at that time was First Lord of the Admiralty. After the Gallipoli fiasco, Churchill was forced to resign.

Galsworthy, John. 1867-1933. English novelist and playwright. He wrote a series of novels entitled *The Forsyte Saga*, which give a vivid picture of English middle-class life in the early 20th century. His plays include *Strife, Justice,* and *Loyalties.*

Gama, Vasco da. 1469-1524. Portuguese navigator. He sailed from Portugal around the Cape of Good Hope, reaching Calicut, India, May 19, 1498, the first voyage of a western European around Africa to the Orient. Viceroy of Portuguese Asia (1524). His first voyage is the subject of Camöens' *Lusiad.*

Gambetta, Léon. 1838-82. French lawyer and statesman. Republican. One of the leaders of the opposition to Napoleon III. Member of the Government of National Defense (1870). He made a spectacular flight from Paris by balloon (Oct. 8, 1870) to organize the defense of France. President of the Chamber of Deputies (1879-81). Premier of France (1881-82).

Garcilasco de Vega. 1503-36. Spanish soldier and poet. Often called "The Spanish Petrarch." His works include sonnets, elegies, and three eclogues.

Garibaldi, Giuseppe. 1807-82. Italian patriot and soldier of fortune. Born in Nice. A life-long republican, he fought for ten years in various South American countries that were struggling for independence. During the Revolutions of 1848, he returned to Italy and vainly tried to defend Mazzini's Roman Republic. After he failed, he migrated to the United States where, first as a candlemaker and afterwards as a trading skipper, he amassed a small fortune. In 1854 he returned to Italy, purchased the small island of Caprera, and settled down. In 1860 he led the "Thousand Red Shirts" against the Kingdom of the Two Sicilies. After conquering this kingdom, he turned north and, on the outskirts of Rome, gave up his conquered territory to Victor Emmanuel II.

Garrick, David. 1717-79. English actor. He made an early reputation in Shakespearean plays. He became comanager of Drury Lane Theatre (1747). He was successful in a large repertory, amassed a large fortune, and retired to Hampton (1776). He enjoyed a long friendship with Dr. Samuel Johnson, whose pupil he had been at the Lichfield grammar school.

Gascoigne, William. 1612?-1644. English astronomer. Inventor of the micrometer. He invented methods of grinding glasses.

Gauguin, Eugène Paul. 1848-1903. French painter. Post-impressionist painter who lived in Tahiti and produced many brilliant pictures of the people and life of the island.

General Assembly of the UN. This body is the principal organ of discussion in the UN. All member nations are represented, and each delegation (five or less) has one vote. Important questions require a two-third majority; other questions are decided by a simple majority. The General Assembly meets once a year, although it may be called into special session.

The General Assembly does not make laws. It only *recommends* actions to the member nations, the Security Council, or other UN agencies. It admits new members, suspends or expels present members, elects the Secretary-General, elects the non-permanent members of the other agencies, draws up the budget, creates new agencies, and elects judges of the World Court.

General Strike, The British. May 3-12, 1926. This strike was called in sympathy with the coal miners. It involved about 2½ million of the 6 million trade-union members in Britain. Volunteers maintained essential services. The Trade Union Council called off the strike May 12 on the promise that wage negotiations would be resumed. However, the coal mines continued to strike until Nov. 19, when they gave up unconditionally. The original difficulty began with the curtailment in use of coal and consequent retrenchment in employment and wage cuts.

Geneva Conference on Naval Disarmament. June 20-Aug. 4, 1927. Great Britain, Japan, and the United States attempted to reach an agreement on limiting cruisers, destroyers, and submarines. The conferees failed to reach an agreement.

Geneva Convention. 1864. The Great Powers signed an agreement designed to regularize the treatment of wounded soldiers and prisoners of war. It was agreed that not only wounded soldiers but also the official staff of ambulances and their equipment were rendered neutral. To implement the Convention, an International Red Cross Society was organized with headquarters at Geneva and branches throughout the world. An international flag—the Swiss flag with the colors reversed—was adopted. In 1882 the United States, largely through the efforts of Clara Barton, became a party to the Convention.

Geneva Protocol, The. Oct. 2, 1924. This was the product of efforts to strengthen international machinery and to overcome the weakness in the League due to the absence of the United States, Germany, and the Soviet Union. It was a treaty of mutual assistance in which an aggressor was defined and schemes were proposed to contain and punish all acts of aggression. It provided for compulsory arbitration of all disputes and outlined a course of action for all signatory nations in case of warfare. Although many small nations were enthusiastic for the Protocol, the agreement was never adopted. The greatest opposition came from the British dominions.

Genghis Khan. 1155-1227. Mongolian conqueror. Born of Mongolian noble parents, he first organized an army and invaded China, capturing Peking in 1215. In China he secured the services of an able Chinese, Ye-liu Chu-Tsai, who became his administrator. Turning westward, Genghis Khan destroyed the Khorzem (Moslem) Kingdom consisting of Turkestan, Afghanistan, and Persia (1220). This force continued westward until it was repulsed by combined armies of Cumans and Russians (1224). After his death, his domain was divided among his three sons. His empire lasted until 1368.

Genocide, Outlawing of. On Dec. 9, 1948, the UN General Assembly unanimously adopted a convention branding as an international crime the mass murder of religious, national, and racial groups.

George I. 1660-1727. King of Britain and Ireland (1714-27), succeeding Anne. First of the Hanoverian dynasty. Elector of Hanover (1698-1727). Regarding the Tory Party as Jacobite, he favored the Whigs, leading to the ministries of Townshend and Walpole. George took little interest in England and spent much of his time in Hanover. Accordingly, the cabinet system became intrenched in British political life.

George II. 1683-1760. King of Great Britain and Ireland (1727-60). Elector of Hanover during the same period. His reign was marked by the War of the Austrian Succession (1740-48) (q.v.) and witnessed the outset of the Seven Years' War (1756-63) (q.v.).

George III. 1738-1820. King of Great Britain and Ireland (1760-1820). Also Elector (1760-1815) and then king (1815-20) of Hanover. His reign witnessed the successful revolt of 13 American colonies against England and the Napoleonic Wars. During the latter part of his reign he became mentally deranged and blind. During this period of incapacity, his son George (later George IV) acted as regent.

George IV. 1762-1830. King of Great Britain and Ireland (1820-30). Son of George III. He gained the ill will of his father by his dissolute habits and his open association with Fox and Sheridan. Regent (1811-20) when his father became mentally deranged. He refused to allow

Queen Caroline, from whom he had long been estranged, to attend his coronation. He tried to divorce Caroline, but had to drop the suit. Very conservative as king. The Catholic Emancipation Act was passed (1829) during his reign.

George V. 1865-1936. King of Great Britain and Northern Ireland; Emperor of India (1910-36). Second son of Edward VII. He became heir apparent (1892) when his brother, the duke of Clarence, died. Chief events of his reign were World War I (1914-18), the agreement with the Irish Free State (1921), the Great Depression of the 1930's, and the Commonwealth (Westminster) Conference (q.v.).

George VI. 1895-1952. King of Great Britain and Emperor of the British Empire. (1936-52). Second son of George V, he became king when his elder brother abdicated in December, 1936. Because of great devotion to duty during the second World War and post-war years, his health was undermined.

George I. 1845-1913. King of Greece (1863-1913). The second son of King Christian IX of Denmark, he was elected King of Greece in 1863. He was assassinated in 1913.

George II. 1890-1947. Succeeded in 1922 when his father, Constantine I, was deposed for the second time. George was deposed in 1923, but was restored in 1935. He was in exile in England during the German occupation of his country (1941-44).

German Constitution. 1871. The German Empire was created by the union between the four south German states and the North German Confederation (1871). The constitution for the Empire was identical in many respects with the constitution of the North German Confederation. Supreme direction of military and political affairs was vested in the King of Prussia, who, in this capacity, was called German Emperor (*Deutscher Kaiser*). He commanded the army and navy, appointed the imperial chancellor, could declare defensive war, make treaties, receive and appoint ambassadors. In the case of treaties relating to matters regulated by imperial legislation and in the case of declaring offensive war, the Emperor had to secure the consent of the Bundesrat (q.v.) and the Reichstag (q.v.). These two bodies made imperial laws. The Emperor had no direct veto over legislation.

The Bundesrat was made up of representatives of the 26 states of the empire. Representation was distributed according to the size of the states (from Prussia's 17 to 1 for the Duchy of Anhalt). The Reichstag was elected by adult males 25 years of age or older.

The central government had certain broad, delegated powers, although many powers were left to the states. Several states, notably Bavaria, were granted special privileges—such as the right to manage its own railways and post-offices. Execution of imperial laws was entrusted to the states themselves.

German Democratic Republic (East Germany). This region, which is under Soviet control, is the home of about 18 million people. It contains some of the best farm land of prewar Germany, as well as Berlin, the historic capital of the country. The government of East Germany was set up by the Soviets in October, 1949, to rival the newly-created Bonn Republic.

German Empire. 1871-1919. The German Empire was formed by the union of the North German Confederation with four South German states. It rapidly became one of the great countries of the world. Its industry developed rapidly, until Germany was one of the world's largest producers of steel, textiles, and

chemicals. It acquired colonies in Africa and Asia. Its army was the most powerful in the world. Its navy and merchant marine grew rapidly. Germany was a pioneer in the field of social legislation. However, the Empire became involved in a great world war and, through defeat, was liquidated. In the decade following the break-up of the Empire, the international position of Germany was substantially lessened.

German Empire, Proclamation of. Jan. 18, 1871. Joint action against the French during the Franco-Prussian War created a sense of patriotic unity between North and South Germans. By Nov. 1870, treaties of union had been concluded between Bismarck, representing the North German Confederation, and the four South German states. On Jan. 18, 1871, King William of Prussia was proclaimed German Emperor in the Palace of Versailles, exactly 170 years after the Hohenzollerns had assumed the title of King of Prussia.

German Federal Republic (West Germany). This region, which was originally occupied by Britain, France, and the United States, after the Second World War, contains 75% of the normal population of Germany, 70% of the minerals, 80% of the coal, and 85% of the steel industry. It contains also the great seaports on the North Sea. However, it contains relatively little agriculture. By the Occupation Statute of 1948, terms were set by which a constitution could be prepared for this region. By this statute, it was decided that West Germany should have a federal republic, composed of Länder (states). The Allied Military Government was to be replaced by three civilian High Commissioners from the United States, Great Britain, and France, who should have veto powers in the fields of reparations and security. German representatives met at Bonn in Sept., 1948, and prepared a constitution, which was adopted in April, 1949. The constitution contains features drawn from the political practices of the United States, Great Britain, France, and the Weimar Republic.

Ghiberti, Lorenzo. 1378-1455. Florentine sculptor. Trained as a goldsmith, he later became a sculptor. His master-work is the two bronze doors in the Baptistry in Florence. Michelangelo pronounced the second door to be worthy to serve as the gate of Paradise.

Ghirlandajo (*real name,* **Domenico Curradi; called Ghirlandajo, "garland-maker," from his father's calling**). 1449-94. Florentine artist who painted famous frescoes. Originally a goldsmith, he took up painting when 31 years old. Among his subjects are *Adoration of the Shepherds* in Florence and *Christ Calling Peter and Andrew* in the Sistine Chapel in Rome.

Gibbon, Edward. 1737-94. English historian. His monumental work is the *Decline and Fall of the Roman Empire.* This eight volume masterpiece was published between 1776 and 1788.

Gibraltar, Capture of. 1704. Sir George Rooke, heading home for England after an unsuccessful cruise in the Mediterranean, fell in with a fleet commanded by Sir Cloudesley Shovel. Finding the fortress of Gibraltar all but undefended by the Spaniards, they sent a force ashore and captured the fortress easily on Aug. 4, 1704. England has held Gibraltar ever since.

Gilbert, Sir Humphrey. 1539-83. English navigator and soldier. He abandoned law for the profession of arms, at which he was a great success. Becoming interested in the possibility of planting a colony in America, he attempted to colonize Newfoundland. Forced to abandon his project when the largest of his ships sank

off Cape Breton, he sailed for home. The ship on which he was sailing sank with all on board.

Gilbert, William. 1540-1603. Physician to Queen Elizabeth I of England. In his treatise on the magnet (1600), he conjectured that terrestrial magnetism and electricity were two allied manifestations of the same force. He was the first to use the terms "electricity," "electric force," and "electric attraction."

Gilchrist, Percy. See Thomas, S.G.

Giotto (Giotto di Bondone). 1267-1337. Painter and architect born near Florence. The first great Renaissance painter. He arrived at the highest pictorial expression of medieval Christianity. His most noted frescoes were at Assisi, Padua, and Florence.

Giraud, Henri Honoré. 1879-1949. French general. He served with distinction during World War I and the Riff campaign (1925-26). Captured by the Germans in World War II, he made a dramatic escape (April, 1942). It was the Anglo-American wish that he should command the French forces in Africa after the Allies landed there. Following the assassination of Darlan (Dec. 1942), he was made high commissioner of French North and West Africa. Despite strong backing by the United States, he never succeeded in securing a strong popular following. He was forced into retirement (April 14, 1944).

Girondists. A section of the Jacobin society, which flourished during the French Revolution. Their name came from the province of Gironde, which was the home of their most conspicuous leaders. They were moderate Republicans, and were mostly young, enthusiastic, and filled with noble, but impractical, ideals. They wished to recreate in Revolutionary France the best policies of the ancient

Greek and Roman Republics. Among their leaders were Brissot, Vergniaud, Condorcet, and Dumouriez. They frequently met in the home of Madame Roland. She exerted a great influence upon them. The Girondists were eventually overthrown by the more radical "Mountain" faction. Many of the Girondist leaders were guillotined.

Gladstone, William Ewart. 1809-98. The "Grand Old Man" (GOM) of British politics. Born in Liverpool. Educated at Oxford. M.P. (1832-95, with a break of only 1½ years). President of the Board of Trade in the Peel cabinet (1843-45); secretary of state for colonies (1845-46). Chancellor of exchequer in Aberdeen's cabinet (1852-55), and again in Palmerston's cabinet and at the request of the queen in Russell's cabinet (1859-66). His free-trade budgets were his greatest work. Leader of the Liberal Party (1867 ff.). Prime minister (1868-74; 1880-85; 1892-94). Among his important measures are the Irish Land Act (1870) and the Reform Bill of 1884. Author of *The State in Its Relations to the Church* (1838), *Juventus Mundi* (1869), etc.

Glinka, Mikhail Ivanovich. 1803-57. Real founder of Russian national music. He studied in Berlin and later developed a Russian symphonic and operatic style entirely on his own conception. He composed numerous works, among which are the operas *A Life for the Czar* and *Ruslan and Ludmila.*

"Glorious Revolution." 1688. When on June 10, 1688, a son was born to James II (a Roman Catholic), many leaders in England feared that there would be an endless succession of Roman Catholic sovereigns. On June 30, 1688, a letter signed by seven of the political leaders was sent to William of Orange, husband of the Protestant English Princess Mary (daughter of James II by his first wife), inviting him to come to England and

assuring him of the support of nineteen-twentieths of the people. On Nov. 5, 1688, William landed at Torbay. On Dec. 11, 1688, James II fled, but was captured. William arrived in London Dec. 18, 1688. James escaped and fled from England Dec. 23. On Jan. 22, 1689, a convention acknowledged William and Mary to be joint sovereigns with the administration in the hands of William.

Gluck, Christoph Willibald. 1714-87. German composer. Born in Erasbach in Bavaria. Court Kapellmeister (1754). Settled in Vienna (1756). He took up operatic composition and revolutionized operatic music by the dramatic quality of his music. He composed *Orfeo ed Euridice* (1762), *Alceste* (1767), *Paride ed Elena* (1769), etc.

Gneisenau, Count August Neithardt von. 1760-1831. Prussian field marshal. He served in the British mercenary force in America (1782-83). Fought in various wars against Napoleon. He was a leader in the movement to reorganize the Prussian army.

Godoy, Manuel de. 1767-1851. Spanish statesman. He gained the favor of Charles IV and Queen Maria Louisa. Made minister (1792-97). He negotiated the Treaty of Basel (1795) and was rewarded by being given the title of "Prince of Peace." He was compelled by the French to attack Portugal. He became unpopular for his arbitrary acts and the defeat at Trafalgar (q.v.) (1805). He was imprisoned by the king, but later aided and released by Napoleon (1808). He lived in Rome, Paris, and Madrid (1808-51).

Godunov, Boris. 1551?-1605. Czar of Russia (1598-1605). Chief member of the regency during the reign of his brother-in-law, the young Czar Fedor Ivanovich (1584-98). He is said to have caused the death of the Czarevitch Dmitri (1591). He defeated the Crimean Tatars, recovered territory from Sweden, and re-colonized Siberia. On the death of Fedor (1598) he was elected to the throne (1598). He died during a struggle with the boyars and the false Dmitri. His career is the subject of an opera by Moussorgsky.

Godwin, William. 1756-1836. English philosopher and novelist. Dissenting clergyman (1777-82). He then became an atheist and devoted himself to writing. Married (1797) Mary Wollstonecraft (1759-97), a pioneer in the feminist movement, who died the same year upon the birth of a daughter (this child became the second wife of the poet Shelley). Later, he was converted to theism by Coleridge. His greatest work is *Enquiry Concerning Political Justice* (1793).

Goebbels, Paul Joseph. 1897-1945. Nazi politician. A brilliant student of history, philosophy, and psychology, he took a leading part in organizing the Nazi Party. He became Hitler's famous propaganda chief (1929) and minister (1933). In the last days of Nazidom, he committed suicide, along with his wife and seven children.

Goethe, Johann Wolfgang. 1749-1832. German poet. Born at Frankfurt-am-Main. In 1772 he published *Götz von Berlichingen,* a tragedy which inaugurated a German literary movement known as "Sturm und Drang." In 1774 he published a romantic love story, *Die Leiden des Jungen Werthers.* In 1775 Goethe settled in Weimar, then the intellectual and literary center of Germany. He became a leader in the life in Weimar. He was ennobled, created privy Councilor, and was appointed to various administrative posts in which he acquitted himself with credit. Among his other writings are *Faust, Egmont, Hermann und Dorothea.*

Gogol, Nikolai Vasilievich. 1809-1852. Russian author. Of Ukrainian origin, in his stories he introduced many incidents of the life of the southern Russians. He was a realist. Although his works are humorous, behind the comedy is a profound sense of grief for the imperfection of human society. *The Government Inspector* and *Dead Souls* are representative works.

Golden Bull. 1356. So called from the golden capsule containing the imperial seal (bulla) which was attached to important documents. Emperor Charles IV (1347-78) issued this decree which reduced the functions of the king, the king's relations to princes, and the princes' sovereign rights to inflexible forms. Thus he created the fundamental law of the Holy Roman Empire. The emperor was to be chosen by seven electors—the archbishops of Mainz, Cologne, and Trier, the king of Bohemia, the duke of Saxony, the margrave of Brandenburg, and the count Palatine (possessed of royal prerogatives) of the Rhine. By custom the seven were assigned the following high offices: The three spiritual princes were chancellors of Germany, Italy, and Burgundy, respectively. The king of Bohemia was cupbearer; the count palatine, seneschal; the duke of Saxony, the marshal; the margrave of Brandenburg, the chamberlain.

"Golden Horde." Although the Mongolian Empire nominally was united under Kublai Khan (ruled from 1257 to 1298), it actually fell apart into *Ulus* or principalities. A leader, Djuchi, formed a Ulus on the Don and Volga which became known as "The Golden Horde," connoting wealth and power. The principal interest of the rulers of this Ulus was protecting trade. They practiced complete religious toleration. They secured complete submission from the Russian princes until in 1480 Ivan III of Moscow won freedom for his people.

Goldsmith, Oliver. 1728-74. English poet, playwright, and novelist. After failing in the practice of medicine, he tried his hand at literary hack work. He became acquainted with Dr. Johnson (1761) and joined Johnson's literary club. Among his works are: *The Vicar of Wakefield* (novel; 1776), *The Deserted Village* (poem; 1770), *She Stoops to Conquer* (comedy; 1773), and *A History of England* (1771).

Gonzalo de Córdoba. 1453-1515. Known as "El Gran Capitán." Spanish soldier. He negotiated the surrender of Granada (1492). Sent to assist Ferdinand II of Naples against the French (1495) he won many victories in southern Italy and conquered the Kingdom of Naples (1503-04).

Gordon Riots. 1780. Influenced by a bill (1778) which granted some measure of freedom to Roman Catholics in England, Lord George Gordon, a Scottish nobleman, organized a Protestant Association. He presented a monster petition to Parliament urging repeal of the bill of 1778. When Parliament refused, Gordon's followers rioted until they were vigorously suppressed by troops led by George III in person.

Göring, Hermann Wilhelm. 1893-1946. German aviator and statesman. Born in Rosenheim in Bavaria, he became a famous aviator during World War I. Upon the death of Richthofen, Göring became commander of the former's "Flying Circus." He became a Nazi and took part in the "Beer-Hall Putsch" in 1923 (q.v.). When Hitler came into power (1933), Göring became one of his chief collaborators. He was creator and marshal of the Luftwaffe, and from 1936 was economic dictator of Germany. In 1939 he was named Hitler's successor. In the last days of the regime he disappeared, but was captured by the Americans. Condemned to death at the Nuremberg Trials (q.v.), he escaped execution by suicide.

Gorki, Maxim (*pseudonym* Maksimovich Peshkov).** Russian writer. Born in Nizhn (renamed Gorki in his honor Orphaned at an early age, he formal education. He wrote sketch (1892) for a Tiflis new using the name Gorki ("the bitter He wrote many realistic stories (1900) portraying the life of a tra Active revolutionary. Chief of the So propaganda bureau (1918). Wro *Mother* (1907), *The Lower Depth* (1903), *Reminiscences of My Youth* (1924), etc.

Gosplan. 1921. USSR state planning commission.

Gotha Program. This was the program of action adopted by the German Social Democratic Party (q.v.) at its inception in 1875.

Gothic architecture. A type of architecture which truly reflects the religious aspirations of the Middle Ages. The best structures of this style are lofty and airy. Every line seems to lead upward. No effect of massiveness contradicts the vertical movement. The common features of this style are the flying buttress and the pointed arch. Other characteristics are rows of tall windows, elaborate doorways, ribbed vaults, and graceful ornamentation.

The term "Gothic" (synonymous with "barbarian") was coined during the Renaissance period, when men found disgusting everything that had been done during the Middle Ages. Actually, Gothic is a French style, which originated in the heart of France and spread all over the country and to neighboring lands. Between 1125 and 1500 it was the prevailing style of architecture for churches and many public buildings.

Gottfried von Strassburg. d. about 1220. Medieval German epic poet. Author of *Tristan and Isolde*. This poem furnished Wagner with the title for his opera.

Gounod, Charles. 1818-93. French composer. Organist in Paris. Conductor of the Orphéon in Paris. He composed six operas. Only the first, *Faust,* is in the repertoire of modern opera companies. He also composed much church music.

Government of Ireland Act. Dec. 23, 1920. A law passed by the British Parliament which provided for home rule for Ireland, but which separated Ireland into North Ireland (Ulster) and South Ireland. This law originally was unacceptable to the Sinn Feiners. But on Dec. 6, 1921, Irish representatives signed a treaty with the British which granted the Irish Free State dominion status. North Ireland had the option of keeping the original arrangement and did so.

Government-Ownership Socialism. This type of socialism arose in France in the 1840's and stems directly from Louis Blanc and his "national workshops." Government ownership of railroads, telegraph and telephone lines, forests, and the like, and city ownership of public utilities, libraries, markets, etc., are examples of this type of Socialism.

Gower, John. 1325-1408. English poet. Contemporary of Chaucer. Among his works are *Speculum Meditantis* and *Confessio Amatis.*

Goya y Lucientes, Francisco José de. 1764-1828. Spanish painter, etcher, and lithographer. He is considered the foremost painter of Spanish customs. He realistically portrayed battle, bullfighting, and torture scenes.

Grand Remonstrance. Nov. 22, 1641. The Remonstrance was presented by Parliament to Charles I. It was also printed and circulated throughout the country. It contained a preamble and 204 articles. It presented an indictment of the king for misgovernment. It outlined governmental and ecclesiastical reforms. It suggested methods of safeguarding the country from Roman Catholics, securing better administration of justice, and choosing ministers. The Grand Remonstrance engendered much passion. During the factional fights which followed it, the names "Cavaliers" and "Roundheads" were used for the first time.

Granvelle, Cardinal de (Antoine Perrenot). 1517-86. Roman Catholic prelate and statesman. Secretary of state under Charles V (1550). Prime minister to Margaret of Parma, regent of the Netherlands. Appointed by Philip II of Spain as president of the council for Italian affairs (1575).

Gray, Thomas. 1716-71. English clergyman and poet. His *Elegy Written in a Country Churchyard* is considered one of the most perfect poems in the English language.

Graziani, Rodolfo. 1882-. Italian marshal. After serving in colonial wars and World War I, he won fame in Libya (1921-29) by his pacification of numerous warlike tribes. He led Italy to victory in the Ethiopian War (1935) (q.v.). Viceroy of Ethiopia (1936-37). Chief of staff of the Italian army (1939). Governor of Libya (1940). His African army was routed by the British (1940-41) and Graziani resigned his command. He was tried for high treason (1948), but the trial was suspended (1949).

Great Council of England. See Magnum Concilium.

Great Elector. See Frederick William.

Great Interregnum. 1254-1273. During this period there was no Holy Roman Emperor. The Great Interregnum marks the end of the medieval Holy Roman Empire and the failure of the Emperor to establish German unity. From the Interregnum down until the middle of the 19th century, most German states felt free to promote their own individual interests without regard for the whole of Germany.

The death of Conrad IV marked the end of the Hohenstaufen dynasty. For the next 20 years there was no emperor of the Holy Roman Empire. William of Holland, Richard, duke of Cornwall (brother of Henry III, king of England), and Alfonso X of Castile each was proclaimed emperor by a small party. But none really ruled. When Rudolf I of Hapsburg was named emperor in 1273, the interregnum came to an end.

Great Northern Expedition. See Bering.

Great Northern War. 1700-21. This war was caused by the opposition of Russia, Poland, and Denmark to the Swedish supremacy in the Baltic. An alliance was formed between Peter the Great, Augustus II of Poland, and the king of Denmark (1699). The war began in 1700. The Swedes under Charles XII unexpectedly invaded Denmark and caused it to sue for peace (Treaty of Travendal, Aug. 18, 1700). Next, the Swedes defeated the Russians on the Narva (Nov. 30, 1700). During the next six years the Swedes fought against the Poles and Saxons. Augustus II was defeated and dethroned (Sept. 24, 1706) and replaced as king of Poland by Stanislaus Leszczynski. After this, Charles invaded Russia and eventually was completely defeated at Poltava (q.v.) (July 8, 1709). Charles escaped to Turkey. Augustus drove Stanislaus from Poland. Russia seized Livonia, Estonia, Ingermanland, Carelia, and Finland. Charles returned to Sweden (1714) but was killed in action in 1718. His sister, Ulrika Eleanora, assumed the throne of Sweden (1718-20), but was super-

seded by her husband Frederick (of Hesse-Cassel) (1720-51). The war ended with the treaties of Stockholm (q.v.) and Nystadt (q.v.). Sweden lost its dominant position in the Baltic. Russia emerged from the war as a great European power.

Great Plague of England. 1665-66. This epidemic carried off 70,000 people from London alone in the summer and autumn of 1665. During the following spring it spread through the southern and eastern counties. It was the first visitation of plague conditions for over 30 years and proved to be the last. Many think that the Great Fire of London (1666) caused the end of the plague.

Greek Independence, War of. 1821-29. Though long deprived by the Turks of their independence as a nation, the Greeks had never been obliterated as a people. A secret society—*Hetairia Philike*—was founded in 1815 and dedicated to the restoration of Greece as a country. The Greek revolt aroused the sympathy of many Europeans. Great Britain, France and Russia agreed at London (1827) to demand an armistice between the Turks and the Greeks. When this was refused, the combined allied fleets defeated a Turco-Egyptian fleet at Navarino (1827). Greek independence was acknowledged in 1829 and in 1832 Prince Otto of Bavaria became the first constitutional king of Greece.

"Greens" and "Blues." Rival factions in Constantinople during the reign of Justinian (527-65). They took their name from the colors of charioteers in the races. The Blues were orthodox Christians who believed in the single nature of Christ and who were devoted to the house of Justinian. The Greens were heterodox, believing in the dual nature of Christ. They were attached to a would-be usurper to the throne. The two factions rioted (532). The Greens got the upper hand and all but deposed Justinian. He was saved by the courage of the Empress and the devotion of Belisarius and the imperial guard.

Gregory I, Saint (*called* **Gregory the Great**). 540?-604. Pope (590-604). Born in Rome of a noble family. He enforced discipline among the monks and encouraged celibacy among the clergy. He sent Augustine as a missionary to England (597). He established the papal system into the form that it kept throughout the Middle Ages. He was a patron of music and is credited with arranging the Gregorian chant.

Gregory II, Saint. d. 731. Pope (715-31). He opposed the iconoclastic edict of Leo the Isaurian (726-31) (q.v.). He sent Boniface as missionary to the Germans (719).

Gregory VII, Saint (*name* **Hildebrand**). 1020?-1085. Pope (1073-85). Born near Siena, Tuscany. Benedictine monk. He exerted strong influence on the popes (1050-1073). As pope he aimed to establish the supremacy of the pope over the church and over the state. His decree regarding lay investiture (1075) aroused Emperor Henry IV to anger. Gregory summoned Henry to Rome to answer charges. On Henry's refusal, Gregory excommunicated him (1076). He received Henry's penance at Canossa (q.v.) (1077) and granted him absolution. Gregory again excommunicated Henry (1080). Henry drove him from Rome and replaced him with another pope (1084). Gregory retired to Salerno under the protection of Robert Guiscard, the Norman ruler of Sicily (q.v.).

Gregory of Tours, Saint (*name* **Georgius Florentius**). 538?-593. Frankish churchman and historian. Bishop of Tours (573). His principal work, *Historica Francorum,* is our main source of knowledge of the Merovingian kings to 591.

Grenville, George. 1712-70. English statesman. Prime minister (1763-65). Under his leadership the Stamp Act (1765) was enforced. This policy was a contributing factor in causing the American Revolution.

Gresham, Sir Thomas. 1519-79. English merchant and financier. Founder of the Royal Exchange. Appointed by Queen Elizabeth I to replace debased currency with sound money. Author of the famous principle, called *Gresham's Law,* that cheap money drives out good money.

Grévy, François Paul Jules. 1807-91. Third president of the Third French Republic. Born in Mont-sous-Vaudrez. Lawyer. Held prominent place in the Republican Party (1871-73). President of the Chamber of Deputies (1876-79). President of France (1879-87). His popularity was destroyed in his second term (1885-87) by scandals affecting his son-in-law. He was forced to resign.

Grey, Charles, 2nd Earl. 1764-1845. British statesman. Born in Fallodon. M.P. (1786 ff.). His outstanding work occurred when he was prime minister (1830-34). During this period, as the leading Whig statesman of England, he forced through Parliament the Reform Bill of 1832.

Grey, Sir Edward. Viscount Grey of Fallodon. 1862-1933. British statesman. Born in Northumberland. Educated at Oxford. For many years a prominent figure in the British Foreign Office. As secretary of state for foreign affairs (1905-16) he negotiated the Triple Entente (q.v.), took an active part in Balkan affairs, and steered the course of Britain in the early days of World War I. He resigned (1916) because of poor health and failing eyesight. Chancellor of Oxford (1928). Author of *Twenty-five Years, 1892-1916* (1925).

Grey, Lady Jane. 1537-54. Lady Jane Grey was the granddaughter of Mary, the sister of Henry VIII. On July 9, 1553, three days after the death of Edward VI, she was informed by the Royal Council that Edward had named her as his successor. On July 19, 1553 she was made a prisoner by Queen Mary and beheaded, along with her husband, Feb. 12, 1554. Lady Jane was rigorously brought up by her parents and made exceptional progress in learning, particularly in languages.

Grieg, Edvard. 1843-1907. Norwegian composer. He developed the school of national Norwegian music. He composed much for the theatre. Among these compositions is the famous music for *Peer Gynt*. He composed much piano music and many songs.

Groot Privilegie, *or* **Great Privilege.** The Magna Carta of Holland, secured from Mary of Burgundy in 1477.

Grotius, Hugo. (*Latinized form of Huig de Groot.*) 1583-1645. Dutch jurist and statesman. As a leader of the Remonstrants (q.v.) he was condemned to life imprisonment. He escaped to France (1621). There he completed and published *De Jure Belli et Pacis* (1625), regarded as the foundation of all international law. He entered the Swedish service and served as ambassador to France (1643-45).

Guelfs and Ghibellines. Two factions in Italy which engaged in a long struggle during the Middle Ages. The former were supporters of the popes; the latter, of the Emperors. "Guelf" is an Italian form of the word *Welf*, a German princely family whose head was usually the duke of Saxony and/or Bavaria. "Ghibelline" is the Italian form of the German word *Waiblingen*, a surname of Conrad III of Germany, derived from an estate which belonged to the Hohenstaufen family of Swabia. The original quarrel was initiated by the Hohenstaufen and Welf families in the 12th century. It was later taken up by rival factions in Italy. Guelf-Ghibelline warfare embroiled Italian cities in ruinous civil war for many generations. At no time did either faction clearly represent a political doctrine or a social class.

Guericke, Otto von. 1602-86. German physicist. Invented the air pump (1650). He invented the Magdeburg hemispheres to illustrate the pressure of the air. He is credited with inventing the first electrical generating machine.

Guild (gild). A corporation or association of persons engaged in similar pursuits for mutual protection, aid, or cooperation. Known in England from the 7th century. Guilds became quite popular and numerous in Europe during the revival of trade which accompanied the Crusades. Guilds fell into two classes: merchant and craft.

(1) Merchant guilds. In each town there was a guild of merchants who were bound together by oath. Each guild had its own meeting place, the guild-hall. Here meetings were held periodically to discuss matters of policy. Merchant guild members were subject to restrictions. They were permitted to sell their goods only at stipulated places and for fixed prices. They were forbidden to sell adulterated goods. Forestalling, regrating, engrossing, short weight, and selling goods above the fixed price were forbidden. Guild members helped one another in case of misfortune. Sick members were visited. The guilds provided for the burial of deceased members.

(2) Craft guilds. The functions of a craft guild were to regulate wages, fix prices and conditions of sale, determine hours and conditions of labor, and inspect the workmanship and quality of materials. Craft guilds also supervised the training of prospective guild members. A young man was bound to work for a mas-

ter as an apprentice. During this period (7 to 12 years) he worked for the master for no wages, or for small wages toward the end of the term. The master fed, clothed, and housed the apprentice and taught him the trade.

After the term of service, the apprentice became a journeyman—that is, he was a free man and could work for daily wages. If he passed an entrance examination, he could become a master workman and open a shop of his own. Towards the end of the Middle Ages, the social distinction between a master and a journeyman became quite sharp. The opportunities for a journeyman to become a master also became much less.

Craft guilds performed many social functions for their members. They played an active part in public feasts, ceremonials, and processions. Guilds frequently conducted schools for the young, and promoted civic projects such as hospitals, street-paving, and the like. Each guild had its patron saint and frequently had special chapels and its own religious festivals.

Guiscard, Robert. 1015?-1085. Norman adventurer. Founder of the Norman state of the Two Sicilies. Made duke of Apulia (1059). Strong supporter of the pope. Conquered part of Sicily from the Saracens (1077). Defeated Eastern Emperor Alexius Comnenius at Durazzo (1081). Captured Rome (1084) and delivered Pope Gregory VII from Emperor Henry IV.

Guizot, François Pierre Guillaume. 1787-1874. French historian and statesman. Born in Nièmes. As Minister of Public Instruction (1832-37), he established a system of primary schools throughout France. Premier of France (1840-48). He relapsed into reactionary methods of government, resisted the demands for parliamentary reform, and used bribery to secure political support. He was ousted at the time of the Revolution of 1848 (q.v.). Among his many works are *Histoire de la Civilisation en Europe* (1828) and *en France* (1830).

Gunpowder Plot. Nov. 5, 1605. Some of the Catholics of England, resenting the policy of James I towards them, planned to blow up Parliament, together with James and his eldest son when Parliament convened in November, 1605. Robert Catesby was the leading figure in the plot. Its execution was entrusted to Guy Fawkes. The plot was discovered, and the leaders were executed. More stringent laws against Catholics were then passed.

Gustavus I (also known as Gustavus Vasa or Gustavus Eriksson). 1496-1560. Founder of the Swedish royal house of Vasa. He procured the independence of Sweden (1523). King of Sweden (1523-60). He entered the service of the Regent Sture and fought against Christian II of Denmark. Held as hostage in Denmark (1518-19). Escaped. Sought by Christian (1520), who beheaded many nobles, among them Gustavus' father and brother-in-law. Led a successful revolt against the Danes. He was proclaimed king (1523). He nurtured the growth of the Lutheran religion, favored the peasants, and labored to build up his country.

Gustavus II Adolphus ("The Lion of the North"; "The Snow King"). 1594-1632. King of Sweden (1611-32). Soon after becoming king he was forced to engage in wars with Russia, Poland, and Denmark. He was victorious in all these wars. He entered the Thirty Years' War in 1630 as the champion of Protestantism. He secured the aid of France against the Holy Roman Empire (1630). He defeated Tilly at Leipzig (1631) and on the Lech (1632), occupied Munich, and found the road to Vienna open. He was confronted by the imperial army at Lützen (1632). He won the battle, but was

mortally wounded. He saved Protestantism in Germany.

Gustavus III. 1746-92. King of Sweden
(1771-92). He became king when the
royal power was at low ebb. He arrested
the council in a body and, through a
coup, regained absolute power (1772).
He tried to be an enlightened despot. He
abolished torture, improved the poor
laws, proclaimed religious toleration and
liberty of the press, and encouraged
trade. He was murdered by a Swedish
aristocrat.

H

Habeas Corpus Act. 1679. An English law which required that any prisoner held for a criminal charge must, on the issuance of the writ, be brought before the judge within a specified time to decide whether he should be discharged, released on bail, or held for trial.

Hague Peace Conferences. 1899, 1907. In August, 1898, Czar Nicholas II of Russia sent a memorandum to all independent states of Europe and Asia and to the United States and Mexico inviting them, with the permission of the Queen of Holland, to attend an international conference at the Hague, Holland, in the next year to promote the cause of peace. In January, 1899, the Czar's government defined as the major item on the agenda of the conference the subject of limitation of arms. The conference met from May 18 to July 29, 1899, and was attended by 26 states—20 European, 4 Asiatic, and 2 American. The conference at once dispelled the prevailing idea that *all* governments favored limitation of armaments. Some delegates, notably German, blocked every attempt to limit armed forces. The conference created the Hague Tribunal, a court of arbitration, where international disputes might be referred for adjudication. It modified the Geneva Convention (q.v.) of 1864 to the newer possibilities of warfare. Some of the nations—not all

—agreed to outlaw the use of poisonous gases and poisonous and "dum-dum" bullets.

The Second Hague Conference, called at the suggestion of President Theodore Roosevelt and the invitation of Czar Nicholas II, was attended by representatives of 44 states—19 American. Again no agreement about disarmament was reached. There were agreements regarding the more humane conduct of war. An international prize court was provided for. Conventions were adopted making mandatory a declaration of war prior to actual hostilities. Also restrictions were imposed on the use of force for the recovery of foreign debt.

Haklyt, Richard. 1552-1616. English author whose *Principal Navigations, Voyages, and Discoveries of the English Nation* is the best collection of the exploits of the Elizabethan seamen and explorers.

Halifax, Edward Frederick Lindley Wood, First Earl of. 1881-. British statesman. He entered Parliament as a Conservative (1910). President of the Board of Education (1924) and of the Board of Agriculture (1924-25). Viceroy of India (as Baron Irwin) (1926-31). Foreign Secretary (1938-40). Ambassador to the United States (1941-46).

Hals, Frans. 1580?-1666. Dutch portrait and genre painter. Born in Malines or Antwerp. He is ranked with Rubens and Rembrandt among the great Netherlands painters. Among his famous pictures are *Laughing Cavalier, Portrait of a Lady, Jolly Trio, Herring Vendor*, etc.

	Born	Ruled
George I	1660	1714-1727
George II	1683	1727-1760
George III	1738	1760-1820
George IV	1762	1820-1830
William IV	1765	1830-1837
Victoria	1819	1837-1901

Hampton Court Conference. 1604. James I called a conference to reconcile the Puritan and Anglican points of view. The conference produced a few minor changes in liturgy and the decision to translate the Bible into English (from this decision came the King James Version of the Bible in 1611). The threat of the king to "harry non-conformists out of the land" led to the migration of some irreconcilables to the Low Countries, whence they migrated to the Plymouth Colony.

Hampton, John. 1594-1643. See Ship Money.

Handel, George Frederick. 1685-1759. Composer. Born in Halle, Germany, he migrated to England and was naturalized a British subject (1726). At first he was a very successful composer of operas. Later, he turned to religious music and is best known today for his oratorios, among which are *Saul* (1739), *The Messiah* (1742), and *Judas Maccabaeus* (1746).

Hanover, House of. An electoral house of Germany and a royal family of England. The younger branch of this family succeeded to the electoral throne of Hanover in 1692. This elector, Ernest Augustus, had a son George. George became the second elector of Hanover and king of England, establishing the royal line there (1714-1901). The kings of England were electors of Hanover until the accession of Victoria (1837). No woman could inherit the title in Hanover. The following members of this house ruled in England.

Hanseatic League. Hanse is a word of Low German origin (*hansa*, a confederacy) by which was designated an alliance of German merchants resident abroad. The Hanseatic League was a union of medieval cities for the purpose of securing protection, which the weak central government could not give. In the period of the League's greatest vigor (1350-1500) it included 85 cities, stretching all the way from Novgorod to London. Its highway was the Baltic Sea. The Scandinavian countries became the economic vassals of the League. The League territory was divided into four spheres, with Lübeck, Cologne, Brunswick, and Danzig the center of each sphere respectively. The League controlled the money, provided for the security of the highways, and waged war in its region. The beginning of the Reformation and the discovery of America caused the League to decay.

Hapsburg. A German royal family which derived its name from the Castle of Habichtsburg (hawk's castle) or Hapsburg on the banks of the Aar River in Switzerland. One of the first Hapsburgs was Werner I, who assumed the title of count in 1096. Hapsburgs were Holy Roman Emperors, kings of Germany, Austria, Hungary, Bohemia, and Spain. Many rulers of numerous smaller states in Europe also were Hapsburgs.

Hardenberg, Prince Karl August von. 1750-1822. Prussian statesman. He was a member of the Prussian cabinet of Frederick William III (1798-1804). He worked for the reorganization of the state (1807-14). Chancellor of Prussia (1810-

17). Made prince for his part in the War of Liberation (1813-14) (q.v.). Took an active part in the Congress of Vienna (1814-15) (q.v.). Active in the Holy Alliance (q.v.).

Hardie, Keir. 1856-1915. Socialist and labor leader. Born in Scotland. He worked as a miner (1866-78). He became active in labor union matters. He was the chairman of the Scottish labor party when it was organized in 1888. He founded and edited the *Labour Leader* (1889). M.P. (1892-95; 1900-15). He was the first leader of the Labor Party in Parliament (1906-07).

Hardy, Thomas. 1840-1928. English novelist and poet. Among his many novels are *Tess of the d'Urbervilles, Far from the Madding Crowd, The Return of the Native.* Among his poetic works are *Wessex Poems, Poems of the Past and Present,* and the poetic drama *The Dynasts.*

Hargreaves, James. d. 1778. English inventor, weaver, and mechanic. He invented the spinning jenny (1764), the first major invention of the Industrial Revolution. It spun eight threads simultaneously.

Harold II. 1022-1066. King of England (1066). He served as chief minister for Edward the Confessor, his brother-in-law (1053-66). Upon the death of Edward, he was elected king (Jan. 6, 1066) by the Great Council. His brother, Tostig, led a revolt against him. Harold defeated the armies of Tostig and the king of Norway at Stamford Bridge (Sept. 25, 1066). He then hurried south to meet the invasion of the Normans under Duke William (the Conqueror). Harold was killed and his army was routed at the battle of Hastings (Oct. 14, 1066) (q.v.).

Harvey, Sir William. 1578-1657. English surgeon who discovered the circulation of the blood.

Hastings, Battle of (*or* Senlac). Oct. 14, 1066. In this battle the invading army of Normans, commanded by Duke William (the Conqueror), defeated the Anglo-Saxon army under command of Harold. Harold was killed during the battle. Following this battle, William seized control of London and was crowned king of England.

Hastings, Warren. 1732-1818. English statesman and administrator in India. He went to Calcutta to work for the East India Co. (1750). He became governor of Bengal (1772) and governor general of India (1773). He returned to England (1785) and was impeached for corruption and cruelty in his administration of India. He was acquitted (1795) after a famous trial in which Burke and Sheridan were among the opposition council. He is credited with establishing the British political and judicial organizations of India.

Hatto II, Archbishop of Mainz. d. about 970. According to legend he was eaten alive by mice for burning down a barn full of people caught stealing grain during a famine, whose dying shrieks he compared to the piping of mice. He is represented as building the Mouse Tower on the Rhine in a futile attempt to escape the mice.

Haussmann, Baron Georges Eugène. 1809-91. Under commission from Napoleon III, he carried through huge municipal improvements in Paris, including a new water supply and sewage systems. He planned the great boulevards of Paris, designed and landscaped the Bois de Boulogne, and created the park of Vincennes.

Hawkins, Sir John. 1532-95. An Elizabethan "sea dog." He was the first Englishman to traffic in Negro slaves (1562). He became navy treasurer (1573) and was knighted for his services against the Armada (1588). In 1595, with his kinsman Drake, he commanded an expedition against the Spanish Main, but died at Puerto Rico.

Haydn, Joseph. 1732-1809. Austrian composer. Sang in cathedral choir of St. Stephen's, Vienna (1740-49). Kapellmeister in the service of the Esterhazy family (1760-90). During this time he wrote masses, operas, an oratorio, overtures, symphonies, piano sonatas, etc. In England (1791-92) he wrote and conducted six symphonies. He returned to England (1794-95) and produced six more symphonies. He resided near Vienna (from 1795), where he wrote eight masses, chamber music, the Austrian national anthem, and the oratorios *The Creation* and *The Seasons.*

Heads of Proposals. 1647. This document was formulated by General Ireton, Cromwell's son-in-law. The army chiefs agreed to restore King Charles I of England to his throne and to accept Episcopacy if the king granted religious toleration. The plan was not accepted since it was too democratic and too tolerant for Royalists and too conservative and balanced for extremists.

Hebert, Jacques René. 1755-94. Often called "Père Duchesne" from the radical newspaper, *Le Père Duchesne,* which he edited (1790). Member of the Commune of Paris. He was popular, but was feared for the violence of his ideas. He instituted the worship of the Goddess of Reason. He was arrested and guillotined with many of his followers (March 24, 1794).

Heemskerk, Jan van. 1567-1607. Dutch navigator. He headed expeditions (1595-97) to discover a northeast passage to China. He was killed in action against the Spanish fleet (1607).

Hegel, Georg Wilhelm Friedrich. 1770-1831. German philosopher. Born at

Stuttgart. Educated at Tübingen. Lecturer at Jena (1801) and professor there (1807). Rector of a gymnasium at Nuremberg (1808-16). Professor at Heidelberg (1816-18) and at Berlin (1818-31). His system of philosophy is known as *Hegelianism,* and is a philosophy of the Absolute. It was the leading system of metaphysics during the second quarter of the 19th century.

Hegira (or hejira). June, 622. It is by this name that Mohammedans describe the flight of Mohammed from Mecca to Medina. The hegira is taken to be the first day of the Mohammedan calendar. In this calendar, all years before the hegira are designated by the abbreviation A. H.

Heimwehr (Austrian). A militant organization formed in Austria in the 1920's. It was composed of agrarians who were bitterly opposed to the Socialist program of the Vienna proletariat. The original program of the organization called for the overthrow of the Socialists in Vienna and union with Germany. Steidle, Pfriemer, and Rüdiger von Starhemberg were the leaders. By 1931 the Heimwehr included 60,000 armed men. (By the Treaty of St. Germain, the Austrian army was limited to 30,000.)

Heine, Heinrich. 1797-1856. German poet. His volumes of verses are *Gedichte, Buch der Lieder, Neue Gedichte,* and *Romanzero.* They contain some beloved German lyrics such as *Die Lorelei, Du Bist Wie eine Blume, Nach Frankreich Zogen Zwei Grenadier.*

Helmont, Jan Baptiste van. 1577?-1644. Flemish physician and chemist. Born in Brussels. First to use the word *gas.* First to distinguish that gases are distinct from air. He believed that digestion was due to the action of ferments which change food into body tissue.

Helvetic Republic. 1798. Switzerland was given this name when it was invaded and reorganized by the armies of the French Revolution.

Henderson, Arthur. 1863-1935. British statesman. Born in Glasgow. Secretary and Chairman of the Labor Party (1908-10, 1914-17, 1931-32). He was in the coalition cabinet (1915-17), Home Secretary in the Labor government (1924), Foreign Secretary (1929-31). He was president of the World Disarmament Conference (1932).

Henry I. 1068-1135. King of England (1100-38). Youngest son of William the Conqueror. A man of scholarly tastes, he was called *Beauclerk*. He developed an orderly system of justice and financial administration. When his only son and heir was drowned (1120), he made his barons swear to accept as ruler his daughter Matilda, wife of Geoffrey Plantagenet, Count of Anjou.

Henry II. King of England (1154-89). Son of Matilda, daughter of Henry I, and her second husband, Geoffrey Plantagenet. At 18 he was invested with the duchy of Normandy, his mother's inheritance, and within a year, following the death of his father, he became count of Anjou. By his marriage (1152) with Eleanor of Aquitaine, divorced wife of Louis VII of France, he acquired Poitou and Guienne. In 1153 he landed in England and by treaty became successor to Stephen. As king he confirmed his grandfather's laws, re-established the exchequer, banished foreign mercenaries, and recovered the royal estates. To aid in rebuilding the power of the church, he made Becket (q.v.) Archbishop of Canterbury. He compelled Becket to accept the Constitutions of Clarendon (q.v.). When Becket resisted, he was murdered at Henry's suggestion. By permission of the English pope, Adrian IV, Henry

(1155) invaded Ireland. Henry's later years were clouded by rebellions against him led by his sons Richard and John. Henry was an able general, a clear-headed politician, and his reign was marked by many legal reforms.

Henry III. King of England (1216-72). He was beset with favorites; his misrule and extortion roused all classes. In 1258, parliament, headed by his brother-in-law, Simon de Montfort, Earl of Leicester, forced him to transfer his power to a commission of barons (Provisions of Oxford) (q.v.). Henry later repudiated this oath. After a brief war (1263), the matter was referred to Louis IX of France, who annulled the Provisions. De Montfort and his followers defeated the king and forced him (1264) to sign the Mise of Lewes (q.v.). De Montfort summoned the first parliament (1265) in which the boroughs were represented. Within a year, the Earl of Gloucester deserted de Montfort and with Prince Edward, defeated and slew de Montfort at Evesham (1265).

Henry IV. King of England (1399-1413). First king of the house of Lancaster. Son of John of Gaunt. Named Bolingbroke from his birthplace. In 1398 he was banished and his estates were confiscated. He returned to England in 1399 and forced Richard II to abdicate. Parliament then chose Henry to be king. During his reign, rebellion and lawlessness were common. Under Owen Glendower, the Welsh maintained their independence. The Scots under Douglas, the Welsh, and Harry Percy (Hotspur) leagued against Henry, but were defeated at Shrewsbury (July 21, 1403). In this battle, Hotspur was killed and Douglas captured. In 1406, Prince James of Scotland (later James I of Scotland) was captured while enroute to France, and was detained and educated in England. In his later years, Henry was a miserable invalid, afflicted by epileptic fits.

Henry V. 1387-1422. King of England (1413-22). His greatest efforts were aimed at reconquering France. In 1414 he made claims upon the throne of France. In 1415 he sailed with a great army to France and on October 25, 1415, he gained a great victory at Agincourt. In 1420, he concluded a "perpetual peace" at Troyes under which he was recognized as regent and heir of France. He married the king's daughter, Catherine of Valois. He died before he could consolidate his successes.

Henry VI. 1421-71. King of England (1422-61 and 1470-71). He succeeded to the throne in his infancy under the protection of his uncles, John, Duke of Bedford, and Humphrey, Duke of Gloucester. He married Margaret of Anjou (1445). Crowned King of France (Dec. 16, 1431). The military successes of Joan of Arc and Charles VII expelled all the English forces from France except Calais (by 1453). The latter part of his reign was marked by his mental illness (1454 ff.) and by economic distress which was culminated by Cade's Rebellion (1450) (q.v.). A struggle for power between the houses of York and Lancaster, known as the War of the Roses (1455-85), began. After a Yorkist victory at St. Albans (1461), Henry was deposed, and the Duke of York was proclaimed King Edward IV. Henry was imprisoned (1465-70), but was rescued and restored by Warwick (1470). He was soon retaken and imprisoned in the Tower of London, where he is said to have been murdered.

Henry VII. 1457-1509. King of England (1485-1509). Founder of the Tudor dynasty. His father, Edmond Tudor, was the son of Owen Tudor, a Welshman, and of his wife, Queen Catherine, widow of Henry V. Edmond was made Earl of Richmond by his half-brother Henry VI. Henry's mother, Margaret Beaufort, was a descendant of the Lancastrians, claiming John of Gaunt as an ancestor. When the Lancastrians were defeated at Tewkesbury (1471), Henry found asylum in Brittany. He landed with an army at Milford Haven (1485) and defeated and slew Richard III at Bosworth. Upon ascending the throne, he married Elizabeth, daughter of Edward IV, a Yorkist. He improved the position of England by diplomatic marriages. Catherine of Aragon, daughter of Ferdinand and Isabella, became the wife of Henry's eldest son Arthur just before he died at the age of fifteen. She then married Henry's second son, Henry, who later became Henry VIII. His oldest daughter Margaret became the wife of James IV of Scotland. Through this marriage, the union of Scotland and England eventually came about. Henry was a lover of peace, a friend of the Church, a patron of scholarship, commerce, and adventure. Under him the trading class became powerful. When he died, he left to his heirs a large fortune.

Henry VIII. 1491-1547. King of England (1509-47). Married Catherine of Aragon, widow of his brother Arthur (June 11, 1509). He engaged in war on the continent, joining the Holy League against France (1511). He personally commanded the English troops in victory at the battle of the Spurs (Aug. 16, 1513). Meanwhile, in England his troops defeated and killed James IV of Scotland at Flodden (Sept. 9, 1513). He appointed Cardinal Wolsey lord chancellor (1515). He held a famous interview with Francis I of France at the Field of Cloth and Gold (1520). For his treatise *Assentio Septem Sacramentorum,* attacking Lutheranism, he was awarded by Pope Leo X (1521) the title, "Defender of the Faith." He became involved in a quarrel with the pope because of his desire to divorce Queen Catherine (the mother of Queen Mary). He dismissed Wolsey for failure to secure from the pope permission for divorce, appointing Sir Thomas More in his place (1529). On the advice of Cranmer, he secured opinions declaring his marriage with Catherine invalid (because she was his deceased brother's wife). He secretly married Anne Boleyn (Jan. 25, 1533) and by her became the father of Queen Elizabeth I. Because of continued conflict with the pope, he secured from Parliament the Act of Supremacy (q.v.), creating a national church with the king as its head. He executed Sir Thomas More (1535) for refusal to acknowledge royal supremacy in religion. He suppressed the monasteries in England and confiscated their property. He beheaded Anne Boleyn on the charge of adultery (May 19, 1536); married Jane Seymour (May 20, 1536; mother of Edward VI; died Oct. 24, 1537); married Anne of Cleves (Jan. 6, 1540; divorced, 1540); married Catherine Howard (1540; beheaded on charge of adultery, 1542); married Catherine Parr (July 12, 1543; survived him). From first to last he was popular with all ranks of his people as no other king of England has been before or since. Only a king of the most imperious will could have effected such a great ecclesiastical revolution.

Henry, Cardinal of York. Last of the male line of the Stuart kings of England. See Rising of 1745.

Henry I. 1008-1060. King of France (1031-60). He aided William, Duke of Normandy, in subduing rebellious nobles (1035-47). Later he became involved in war with William and was defeated.

Henry II. 1519-1559. King of France (1547-59). Second son of Francis I. Held hostage in Spain (1526-30). Married Catherine de Médicis (1533). Largely influenced by his mistress Diane de Poitiers. He seized the bishoprics of Toul, Metz, and Verdun from the emperor (1552). Captured Boulogne (1550) and Calais (1558) from the English. He was unsuccessful in his wars

(1556-59) in Italy and the Low Countries (see Cateau-Cambrésis, Treaty of). He died of wounds inflicted in a tournament. Three of his sons became kings of France.

Henry III. 1551-1589. Third son of Henry II and Catherine de Médicis. King of France (1574-89) and of Poland (1573-89). His reign was marked by a continuation of the wars between Catholics and Huguenots. After the death of his brother, the Duke of Alençon (1584), he was forced to take sides with the Huguenots. He fled from Paris on the Day of Barricades (1588). He arranged the murder of the Duke of Guise and the Cardinal of Lorraine (1588), prominent Catholic leaders. He was murdered by a monk. With his death the male Valois line became extinct.

Henry IV (Henry of Navarre). 1553-1610. King of Navarre (1572-89). King of France (1589-1610). Brought up as a Protestant, he took part in the religious wars (1568-70). Married Margaret Valois, sister of Charles IX (1577). Became heir presumptive on the death of the Duke of Alençon (1548). Concluded the War of the Three Henrys (1585-89) (q.v.) with the victory at Contras. Became king upon the death of Henry III (1589). Renounced Protestantism for Catholic faith (1593). Ended war with the Holy League (1596). Issued the Edict of Nantes (1598) (q.v.). Married Marie de Médicis (1600). His final years ushered in a period of peace. The finances of the country were reorganized and industry was encouraged. He was murdered by a religious fanatic. Much credit for the reorganization of finances and internal improvements of France should be given to Henry's great minister Sully (q.v.).

Henry I, the Fowler. 876?-936. Duke of Saxony (912-36). First of the Saxon line of kings of Germany (919-36) and considered as one of the Holy Roman Emperors, though never crowned. He fortified and strengthened many cities. Thus he laid the foundation for many famous medieval German cities which made Germany superior to other European countries in city life and progress. He defeated the Wends (929), the Hungarians (939), and the Danes (934).

Henry II (*called* **the Saint**). 973-1024. King of Germany and Holy Roman Emperor (1002-24). Last of the Saxon emperors. He engaged in a long struggle with Poland (1003-18). He was energetic in church reform. He founded many schools and monasteries.

Henry III (*called* **the Black**). 1017-56. Holy Roman Emperor (1039-56). Son of Conrad II. Subdued the Bohemians (1041) and the Hungarians (1045). He made an expedition to Rome and deposed three rival popes, appointing Clement II (1047). A patron of learning, he founded schools and built cathedrals. In the interests of peace, he tried unsuccessfully to put into effect the "Peace of God (q.v.)."

Henry IV. 1050-1106. King of Germany and Holy Roman Emperor (1056-1106). Son of Henry III. His reign was marked by a long struggle with Pope Gregory VII over the question of lay investiture. The Pope excommunicated Henry (1075) and forced him to do penance at Canossa (q.v.) (1077). Henry rallied, drove Gregory from the papal throne, and chose a pope of his own (1084). His last years were marked by rebellions of his sons.

Henry V. 1081-1125. King of Germany and Holy Roman Emperor (1106-25). Last of the Franconian dynasty. Son of Henry IV. Restored peace at home. Successful in wars against Flanders, Bohemia, Hungary, and Poland. Continued the controversy over lay investiture, but

finally accepted the Concordat of Worms (1122) (q.v.) which ended the controversy.

Henry VI. 1165-97. King of Germany and Holy Roman Emperor (1190-97). By his marriage with Constance of Sicily, he became king of Sicily (1194-97). He kept Richard I of England prisoner (1193-94) when the latter was returning from the Third Crusade. He died as he was about to set out on a crusade.

Henry the Lion. 1129-1195. Duke of Saxony and Bavaria (1156-80). He supported Frederick Barbarossa in Poland and Italy (1157-59). He quarreled with Emperor Frederick Barbarossa, lost his possessions, and was sent into exile. After 1190 he recovered his possessions. He colonized all northern Germany. His rule was beneficial.

Henry the Navigator. 1394-1460. Portuguese prince. Great patron of cosmography and discovery. Under his patronage, the Madeira Islands were discovered (1418), Cape Bojador was rounded (1433), Dias discovered Cape Verde (1445), Alvise da Cadmosto explored the Senegal River and discovered Cape Verde Islands (1455).

Heptarchy. Seven kingdoms of England which were set up following the Teutonic invasions of the 5th and 6th centuries. The number of kingdoms varied from time to time, and the name has little actual significance. There were three kingdoms of Angles—Northumbrians, East Angles, and Mercians; three kingdoms of Saxons—East, South, and West; and Kent, the kingdom of the Jutes.

Herriot, Édouard. 1872-. French statesman. Born in Troyes. Mayor of Lyons (1905-24). Premier (1924-25, 1926, 1932). President of the Chamber of Deputies in the Vichy government (1942-45). Freed after liberation, he resumed leadership of the Radical Socialist Party. In 1947, he became president of the National Assembly. Author of *The United States of Europe* (1930) and a biography of Beethoven (Eng. tr. 1935).

Herschel, Sir William. 1738-1822. Astronomer. Born in Hanover, Germany, the son of a bandsman. He visited England (1755) as an oboist in the Hanoverian Guards band. In 1766 he became organist and teacher of music in Bath. He took up astronomy in 1773. In 1781 he made a reflecting telescope with which he discovered the planet Uranus. In 1782 he was appointed private astronomer to George III. Knighted in 1816. He added to our knowledge of the solar system, the Milky Way, the nebulae, Saturn, and made a famous catalogue of double stars.

Hertz, Heinrich. 1857-1894. German physicist. He investigated the connection between light and electricity. He was the first man to produce the long electromagnetic waves now used in radio communication.

Herzen, Alexander. 1812-70. Russian Socialist whose publication, *Kolokol* (the Bell), paved the way to many 19th century reforms in Russia.

Hess, Walther Richard Rudolf. 1894-. Nazi leader. Born in Alexandria, Egypt. He took part in the Munich "Beer-Hall Putsch" of 1923 (q.v.) and was imprisoned with Hitler. While in prison he helped Hitler prepare *Mein Kampf*. In 1934 he was designated as deputy leader of the Nazi Party. In 1939 he was named third in order of succession after Hitler and Göring. In 1941, on the eve of the German invasion of Russia, he flew solo to Scotland, where he pleaded ineffectively for a negotiated peace between England and Germany. He was held as a prisoner of war in England. In 1946 he was condemned to life imprisonment by the Nuremberg Tribunal.

Hildebrand. See Gregory VII.

Himmler, Heinrich. 1900-45. Nazi police chief. Born in Munich. Flag-bearer in the "Beer-Hall Putsch" (1923) (q.v.). He organized the SS (1929) and soon made it a powerful force. In 1936 he became police chief. With his notorious secret police force (Gestapo) he unleashed an unmatched political and anti-Semitic reign of terror—first in Germany, then in war-occupied countries. In 1943 he was made Minister of Interior and was charged with crushing defeatism. In 1944 he became commander of the home army. In 1945 he made the offer of unconditional surrender to the British and Americans, but not the Russians. When the offer was rejected, he disappeared, but fell into British hands. After surrender of Germany, he committed suicide (1945).

Hindenburg, Paul von (*in full* Paul Ludwig Hans Anton von Beneckendorff und von Hindenburg). 1847-1934. German general. President of the Weimar Republic. Born in Posen. Fought in the Austro-Prussian and Franco-Prussian Wars. Member of the general staff (1877). Major general (1896). Lieutenant general (1900). Commanding general of the 4th corps (1903). Retired in 1911. Because of his knowledge of the defensive potentials of East Prussia, he was given command in the east in 1914. He won a complete victory over the Russians at Tannenberg (1914) (q.v.). Rewarded by being made field marshal. He waged a successful campaign in Poland (1915). Chief of staff (1916). With Ludendorff he directed all German strategy (1917-18). Retired (1919). Elected president (1925-32). Reelected (1932-34). Appointed Hitler chancellor (1933).

Hitler, Adolf. 1889-1945. German statesman. Born at Braunau, Upper Austria, the son of a customs official, he was originally named Schicklgruber. Orphaned early in life, he lived a life of hardship in Vienna. He held various jobs and read extensively in economics, history, etc. Becoming a draftsman, he migrated to Munich in 1912. He served honorably in the First World War, in which he was promoted to lance-corporal and decorated. In the post-war period, he attained, largely through persuasive oratory, leadership of the German National Socialist Party. Raising a semi-military organization, he attempted to seize control of the government through a *coup* (the "Beer-Hall Putsch," q.v.), 1923, but failed and was imprisoned for nine months, during which time he wrote *Mein Kampf.* After winning support of the large industrialists, he reorganized his party, now emphasizing anti-Semitism, anti-Marxism, and extreme nationalism. His party now attracted wide membership. Although Hitler unsuccessfully opposed Hindenburg for the presidency in 1932, he was appointed chancellor early in 1933. By exploiting the Reichstag fire (q.v.) (Feb. 1933), he gained absolute control of the state. In June 1934 he "purged" the most notorious opposition within his party (see Blood Purge, q.v.). Upon the death of Hindenburg (Aug. 1934), he assumed the title of Reichsführer. He rearmed Germany (1935) and sent troops into the Rhineland. He formed the Rome-Berlin Axis with Mussolini (1936) and annexed Austria (1938). He secured the Sudeten-lands of Czechoslovakia (1938) and Bohemia and Moravia (1939). In 1939 he seized Memel from Lithuania. Upon Poland's refusal to surrender Danzig, he attacked Poland, thus beginning the Second World War. His armies rolled over Poland, Denmark, Norway, Holland, Belgium, France, Romania, Yugoslavia, and Greece. His armies penetrated deep into European Russia and across north Africa. Then the tide of victory turned at El Alamein (Oct. 1942) and Stalingrad (Nov. 1942). As the invading armies closed in on Berlin, Hitler is alleged to have taken his own life (May 1, 1945).

Hobbes, Thomas. 1588-1679. English philosopher. His chief works are *De Cive* (1642), *Human Nature* (1650), and *Leviathan* (1651). The last contains the author's famous social contract theory. Hobbes ranks as one of the great English philosophers, an original thinker in psychology, ethics, and politics. His ethical theory, based upon pure selfishness, determined negatively ethical speculation in England for one hundred years, as the great moralists often devoted their entire efforts to prove that Hobbes was wrong. His most famous theory was his advocacy of political absolutism. The state of nature, according to him, is a state of war and insecurity. To attain some measure of protection and security, human beings enter into a species of contract by which they surrender their individual rights, and constitute a state under an absolute sovereign, monarchial or other.

Hogarth, William. 1697-1764. English pictorial and satirical artist. Among his best-known works are the *Rake's Progress* and *Marriage à la Mode.*

Hohenlohe-Schillingsfürst, Prince Chlodwig. 1819-1901. German statesman. A Liberal and a Catholic. Member of the Bavarian parliament (1846-1866). Prime minister of Bavaria (1866-70). German ambassador to Paris (1873-85). Governor of Alsace-Lorraine (1885-94). Chancellor (1894-1900). As chancellor he favored nationalism and imperialism. During his incumbency as chancellor Germany became definitely a world power.

Hohenstaufen. A German family which furnished kings for Germany between 1138 and 1208 and again between 1215 and 1254. It also provided kings for Sicily (1194-1268). It derived its name from the castle at Staufen in Swabia. It originated with Conrad III (1138-52), the King of Germany, who was the son of Frederick Hohenstaufen and Agnes, daughter of Emperor Henry IV. It included the following Holy Roman Emperors:

Frederick I	(1152-1190)
Henry VI (a)	(1190-1197)
Otto IV	(1198-1215)
Frederick II (b)	(1215-1250)
Kings of Germany:	
Philip of Swabia	(1198-1208)
Conrad IV (c)	(1250-1254)
Kings of Sicily:	
Henry VI (a)	(1194-1197)
Frederick II (b)	(1197-1250)
Conrad IV (c)	(1250-1254)
Manfred	(1254-1266)
Conradino	(1266-1268)

(*Letters in parenthesis indicate the same man.*)

Hohenzollern. A German royal family which derived its name from the Castle of Zollern in Swabia. Counts of Hohenzollern date back to the 11th century. The Swabian branch of the family furnished the electors of Brandenburg (after 1417). In 1701, the elector of Brandenburg assumed the title of King of Prussia. In 1871, the kings of Prussia became the hereditary emperors of Germany (1871-1918).

Holbein, Hans (the Elder). 1465?-1524. German painter. Born in Augsburg. He executed many altarpieces. His best is the Altar of St. Sebastian. Hans Holbein (the Younger) (1497?-1543), his son, was a portrait painter and wood engraver. He was the court painter to Henry VIII of England (1536). Among his portraits are those of Erasmus, Sir Thomas More, Anne of Cleves, and Henry VIII. He made a series of famous woodcuts entitled *The Dance of Death.*

Holland, Kingdom of. It dates from Sept. 27, 1815 when the Prince of Orange was crowned King of the Netherlands. At that time, Holland and Belgium were united. Belgium revolted and gained its independence Aug. 25, 1830. Prince Leopold of Saxe-Coburg was crowned king of Belgium July 21, 1831.

Holy Alliance, The. While loyally supporting the Quadruple Alliance (q.v.) as a means of maintaining the treaties of Vienna by physical force, Czar Alexander I of Russia believed that an expression by the sovereigns of Europe of the great Christian principles of peace, forbearance, and goodwill would supply the underlying spiritual motives for preserving modern society. On Sept. 26, 1815, he, along with the king of Prussia and the Emperor of Austria, signed the Holy Alliance. This was a declaration that justice, Christian charity, and peace should guide all the deliberations of princes in the future. All the rulers of Europe, except the sultan, the pope, and the prince-regent of England, eventually signed this agreement. To 19th century liberals, the Holy Alliance became a conspiracy to stamp out justice and democracy. This opinion was entirely mistaken; for, in the popular mind, the Holy Alliance was confused with the Quadruple Alliance. The Holy Alliance failed because few of its signatories tried to live up to it.

Holy League, The. 1511-14. Formed by Pope Julius II to drive the French out of Italy. The league was at first composed of the Papacy, Venice, and Ferdinand of Spain. Later it was joined by Henry VIII of England and Emperor Maximilian. The league was used by Ferdinand to further his interests in Navarre. When the English under Henry VIII defeated the French at the Battle of the Spurs, the alliance came to an end. The league accomplished very little during its existence.

Holy War. 1684-99. Fought against the Turks by the Holy League—Poland, Venice, and Austria. The League was joined later by Russia. The Turks were soundly beaten and at the Treaty of Carlowitz

(1699) (q.v.) gave up much territory. The Holy War marks the high tide of Turkish influence in Europe. During this war, a shell from a Venetian warship exploded a magazine which was situated within the Parthenon in Athens and fatally ruined the famous building. After this war, the power of the Turks waned in Europe.

Home Rule, Irish. 1914. Home rule for Ireland was promoted twice by Gladstone (1886 and 1893) without success. In the years 1895 to 1905 when the Conservative Union forces were in power, an attempt was made to "kill Home Rule by kindness." When the Liberal Party returned to power in 1906, they were so much absorbed in social reform that they paid little attention to Ireland. In 1912, an Irish Home Rule Bill was introduced which, while retaining 42 Irish representatives in the House of Commons, granted to Ireland the right to limited self-government. A bicameral Irish parliament was to meet in Dublin. A lord lieutenant would govern through a ministry which was responsible to the Dublin Parliament.

The bill met with great opposition in Ulster. The House of Lords twice defeated the measure. It was passed by Commons a third time (Sept. 18, 1914) and thus became the law. Since the first World War had broken out, the operation of the law was postponed until the end of the war. (See also Government of Ireland Act, q.v.)

Hontheim, Johann Nikolaus von. 1701-1790. German Roman Catholic prelate. Opponent of ultramontanism (q.v.). He is best known for his *De Statu Ecclesiae et Legitima Potestate Romani Pontificos* (concerning the Organization of the Church and the Lawful Power of the Pope) which he published in 1763 under the pseudonym of Justinius Febronius. This work was an attempt to revive the conciliar movement. It attracted much attention in Germany and Austria and in-

fluenced the attempted religious reforms of Joseph II of Austria.

Hooker, Richard. 1554-1600. English theologian. His book, *Ecclesiastical Polity*, did much to soften the strife between Anglicans and Puritans.

Hoover Moratorium. See Reparations.

Horn, Count Philip. 1518-68. Flemish statesman and soldier. He was executed, along with Count Egmont (q.v.), by order of Philip II of Spain. The execution of these two leaders precipitated the revolt of the Dutch against Spain.

Horthy de Nagybanya, Nikolaus. 1868-. Regent of Hungary (1920-44). Naval aide-de-camp to Emperor Francis Joseph, he commanded the Austro-Hungarian fleet in 1918. He was captured by Americans in 1945. He was then released. He lives in retirement in a country home near Munich.

House of Lords Bill, English. 1911. Throughout the 19th century the feeling increased in England that the House of Lords must be "mended or ended." The attitude of the House of Lords towards the "War Budget" of 1909 led to the famous Parliament Act of Aug. 18, 1911. It stated: (1) Money bills passed by Commons automatically become law one month after passage; (2) other bills would become the law, despite rejection by the House of Lords, if passed by the House of Commons in three successive sessions, provided that at least two years elapse between the first consideration of the bill and its final enactment. In 1948, the time was reduced to two sessions and one year.

Housing and Town Planning Act, English. 1909. By this law local authorities were given the power to close up damp cellars and tear down airless tenements. When necessary, these authorities had the power to erect sanitary dwellings for the poor.

Housman, Alfred Edward. 1859-1936. English classical scholar and poet. For many years he was a classical professor in University College, London (1892), and Cambridge (1911). He established his name as a lyric poet by *A Shropshire Lad, Last Poems,* and *More Poems.*

Howard, John. 1726-90. English prison reformer. On a voyage to Portugal he was captured by a French privateer and carried to a Brest prison. His experience there launched him on his life work. As a result of his work, laws were passed (1774) fixing salaries to jailors and enforcing cleanliness in prisons. He visited many prisons and published his findings in a series of books called *State of Prisons.*

Hubertsburg, Treaty of. 1763. This was a treaty between Prussia and Austria at the conclusion of the Seven Years' War. By this treaty, Prussia retained Silesia which it had taken from Austria in 1740.

Hugo, Victor. 1802-85. French poet, playwright, and novelist. He has won fame for such novels as *Les Misérables* and *Notre Dame de Paris.* Critics are divided about his relative greatness; but he was an outstanding figure in 19th-century French literature.

Huguenots. The name of French Protestants. The origin of the name is much disputed, although there is some reason to believe that it was derived from *Genossen* (brethren). A species of Protestantism had been in existence in France prior to Luther. Immediately following Luther's revolt, Protestantism in France made much progress, being given powerful support by Margaret, queen of Navarre, the sister of Francis I. By 1558 there were about 2000 Protestant churches in France, and the Huguenots organized into a powerful party. At first the French Protestants followed the teachings of Luther. Later, Calvinism took a firm hold, so that Huguenots should be thought of as Calvinists. Although Protestantism did not appeal to the majority of Frenchmen, it became firmly entrenched in the northern, southern, and western regions of the country. What the Huguenots lacked in numbers they made up in influence. Many of the Huguenot converts were from the powerful bourgeoisie class. During the 16th and 17th centuries there were many bitter wars between the French Catholics and Huguenots. In 1598 the Huguenots secured religious freedom by the Edict of Nantes (q.v.). They now became an important element in French life. In 1621, Cardinal Richelieu (q.v.) decided to break their power, since by that date the Huguenots constituted a foreign country within France. He did so. After the fall of La Rochelle (1628), the Huguenots lost all political power, but continued to enjoy religious freedom. This was taken from them by Louis XIV by the Revocation of Nantes (q.v.) (1685). Many Huguenots now emigrated from France; others gave up their religion. In 1787, Louis XVI granted Huguenots religious freedom, which they have enjoyed ever since.

Humanism. A system of thinking in which man, his interests, and development, are made dominant. Humanism was an aspect of the Renaissance. The first humanist was Petrarch (1304-74). Humanists studied the literature of the classic Greek and Latin authors not merely to derive scientific or theological information from it, but primarily for its literary and human interest. The humanists were impressed not only by the subject matter of these ancients but also by their elegant style of writing. They engaged upon a diligent search for old manuscripts. These they collected and published. The greatest of all humanists was Erasmus (1469?-1536).

Humbert I (*Italian,* **Umberto**). 1844-1900. Son of Victor Emmanuel II. Born in Turin. King of Italy (1878-1900). His reign was tranquil. He formed the Triple Alliance with Germany and Austria-Hungary (1882). He was killed by an anarchist.

Humboldt, Baron Alexander von. 1769-1859. Brother of Baron Wilhelm von Humboldt. German naturalist, traveler, and statesman. Born in Berlin. Superintendent of mines in the Frankish principalities (1792). He accompanied the French botanist, Aimé Bonpland, on a scientific journey to South America, Cuba, and Mexico (1790-1804). Settled in Paris (1804). Resided in Berlin (after 1827). Popularized the use of Peruvian guano. Made use of isothermal lines to study the climate of various regions. Studied the decrease of temperature with the increase of elevation. Studied volcanoes, and demonstrated the origin of igneous rock. Chief work: *Kosmos* (1845).

Humboldt, Baron Karl Wilhelm von. 1767-1835. Brother of Baron Alexander von Humboldt. German philologist and diplomat. He was one of the founders of the University of Berlin. Prussian minister to Rome (1801-08), Vienna (1810), London (1817). His great work, *On the Differences in the Construction of Language,* (1836-40, 3 vols.), has had great influence in developing the science of comparative philology.

Hume, David. 1711-76. Scotch philosopher and historian. Among his philosophical writings are *Treatise on Human Nature* (1739) and *Political Discourses* (1752). His *History of the Stuarts* appeared in 1754. While in France in the 1760's, he was on intimate terms with D'Alembert, Diderot, Buffon, and Rousseau. While his attacks on the prevailing systems of metaphysics and natural religion and his attempted reduction of all reasoning to a product of experience were destructive or sceptical, he prepared the way for constructive work in many fields. He even anticipated Kant (q.v.) in some of his metaphysical views.

Humiliation of Olmütz. See Erfurt Union.

"Hundred Days." After his abdication (April 11, 1814), Napoleon was exiled to the Island of Elba. He returned from there March 1, 1815, and once again became ruler of France. Following his defeat at Waterloo (June 18, 1815), Napoleon again abdicated (June 22, 1815). This brief period when he was in power is known as the "Hundred Days."

Hundred Years' War, The First. 1337-1453. A struggle between France and England which had far-reaching effects. Socially, it brought the middle and lower classes to the front, for it demonstrated the superiority of the archer over the knight on horseback. It produced poverty and discontent, which led to peasant uprisings. Politically, it led to concessions from the king to Parliament, since the king was continually in need of money. Because the papacy temporarily fell under the control of the kings of France, a conflict with Rome was begun that led to the Reformation (see Babylonian Captivity, q.v.). The war created a spirit of nationalism in both France and England.

When Charles IV of France died without male heir, Edward III of England claimed the throne of France, since his mother was the sister of Charles. The claim was groundless, since the Salic Law forbade women to inherit estates or to transmit them to their sons. At first, the English were victorious, and at Crecy (1346) and Poitiers (1356) crushed the French armies. The king of France was taken prisoner, but was released by the Treaty of Bretigny (1360) in which Edward III gave up claim to the throne of France, but received Calais, Ponthieu, and all of Aquitaine. By maladministration the English lost control of Aquitaine and by 1371 the English lost all of their French possessions except Calais, Cherbourg, Brest, Bayonne, and Bordeaux.

The war was renewed in 1414 by Henry V. He defeated the French severely at Agincourt (1415). Taking advantage of struggles between the rival factions of Orléans and Burgundy, Henry V at the Treaty of Troyes (1420) got himself proclaimed regent of France until the death of Charles VI, when he was to succeed him as king of France. Henry V died in 1422 and was succeeded by his infant son Henry VI. Charles VI died in the same year. Henry VI was recognized as king in many parts of France and John, duke of Bedford, the brother of Henry V, took over the government. However, the Dauphin (later Charles VII) claimed the throne. He captured Orléans with the aid of Joan of Arc (1429) and was crowned in Reims (1429). Now the power of France came into the ascendency. By 1453 the English had been driven from all of France except Calais.

Hundred Years' War, Second. From 1689 to 1815, there were seven wars between England and France. These wars lasted 64 years, or more than half the period. Five of them began and ended with France. Though the third began with Spain and the fifth with the American colonies, France became involved in both before the close. The seven wars are as follows:

1. King William's War   1689-1697
2. War of the Spanish
   Succession   1702-1713
3. War of the Austrian
   Succession   1739-1748
4. Seven Years' War   1756-1763
5. War of the American
   Revolution   1775-1783
6. War with France   1793-1802
7. War with France   1803-1815

England emerged from these wars as the dominant Atlantic Seaboard power.

Hungarian Republic, The. This was established in March, 1848, when the Hungarians revolted against the Austrians. The leader was Louis Kossuth. The republic collapsed when it was invaded by Austrian, Slavic, and Russian troops (1849).

Hus, John. 1369?-1415. Czech religious reformer. Born in Husinetz, near Budweis. Educated in Prague. Lecturer in the University of Prague (1398); rector (1402-03). Ordained a priest (1401). Influenced by the writings of Wycliffe. Popular preacher. Excommunicated (1410) for teaching Wycliffe's doctrines. A papal interdict was issued against him (1412). He attended the Council of Constance (1414) (q.v.) under the protection of King Wenceslaus and Emperor Sigismund. He was tried for heresy (1415), condemned, and burned at the stake (1415). His death aroused great popular indignation and led to the Hussite Wars (1419-34) (q.v.).

Huskisson, William. 1770-1830. English financier and statesman. M.P. (1796-1802; 1804-30); secretary to the treasury (1804-05; 1807-09); treasurer of the navy and president of the Board of Trade (1823-27); colonial secretary and leader of the House of Commons (1827-28). He was an active pioneer of free trade.

Hussite Wars. 1419-1434. Religious wars which originated in Bohemia following the burning at the stake of John Hus (July 6, 1415). Under their leader Ziska, the Bohemians repeatedly defeated imperial armies of the Emperor Sigismund. At length the Bohemians became divided among themselves on doctrinal matters and became easy prey to the machinations of the emperor. The rebellion was crushed in 1434.

Hutten, Ulrich von. 1488-1523. German nobleman. Friend and supporter of Martin Luther. Educated at the Benedictine monastery in Fulda and various universities in Germany and Italy. He joined the imperial army (1513) and took part in many campaigns. He became (1519) a strong supporter of Luther and by his writings appealed to the sympathies and patriotism of the nobles. He is best known as a satirist, being the author of a large part of the second half of *Letters of Obscure Men.*

Huxley, Thomas. 1825-95. English biologist. Born in Ealing, near London. Studied medicine. He entered the Royal Navy medical service (1846). Professor, Royal College of Surgeons (1863-69). Professor, Royal Institutions (1863-67). President, Royal Society (1883-85). He was the foremost advocate in England of Darwin's theories. Among his writings are *Man's Place in Nature* (1863) and *Evolution and Ethics* (1893).

Huygens, Christiaan. 1629-93. Dutch physicist. Born at the Hague, he was educated at Leyden and Breda. His mathematical *Theoremata* was published in 1651. In 1656 he invented the pendulum clock. In 1655 he discovered the ring and fourth satellite of Saturn. He announced the law governing the impact of elastic bodies (1669) and developed the wave theory of light (1678). He investigated the polarization of light and the micrometer. Fellow of the Royal Society of England (1663). Author of *Horologium Oscillatorium* (1673), *Traité de la Lumière* (1678), etc.

Hyde, Edward, 1st Earl of Clarendon. 1609-74. English statesman and historian. Although he was very active in securing political reform during the first session of the Long Parliament, he opposed the Grand Remonstrance and wrote the king's reply. He composed the king's manifestos and won half the nation to the support of Charles. He followed the royal family into exile (1646) and there wrote his *History of the Great Rebellion.* After the Restoration he became Lord Chancellor (1660). But he fell from favor and was banished (1667). He was the grandfather of Queen Mary, wife of William III, and Queen Anne through the secret marriage of his daughter Anne to James II when duke of York.

I

Ibsen, Henrik. 1828-1906. Norwegian dramatist. A force in the modern theatre. He is a passionate advocate of individual liberty. He strives to awaken men to a real comprehension of themselves. He is an uncompromising social reformer. Among his plays are *Peer Gynt, Pillars of Society, A Doll's House, Hedda Gabler,* and *The Master Builder.*

Icon. A religious picture expressing some of the customs of the Orthodox Church of Russia. The Orthodox believer places the icon in a prominent place in his home. It is a symbol or reminder of the spiritual world to the believers, and its purpose is to raise corresponding emotions in the soul.

Iconoclasm (Image-breaking). The worship of holy relics and especially holy pictures and holy images had reached a point in the Eastern Church where it could well be called a scandalous superstition and idolatry. In 725, Byzantine Emperor Leo the Isaurian ordered the removal of all holy images from Constantinople. The pious multitude, incited by monks, broke out in rioting. Part of the navy was affected. But the army remained loyal to Leo and the decree was enforced. In Italy, where imperial power was not strong, the popes defied the officers of the emperor as being heretics and defied the "Iconoclastic" edict. This controversy was one of the issues which led to the schism between the Greek and Latin churches.

Ignatius of Loyola (*name* Inigo de Onez y Loyola). 1491-1556. Spanish soldier and ecclesiastic. Founder of the Society of Jesus (1540). Wounded during the siege of Pamplona (1521). During his convalescence, he read religious books and dedicated his life to the Church. While in Paris (1534), he planned a new religious order, which was dedicated to the conversion of infidels. Canonized in 1622.

Imperial Catechism. To secure loyalty to himself and his dynasty, Napoleon adopted an old catechism which Bishop Bossuet had prepared during the reign of Louis XIV. All French children were to receive instruction from this catechism. It taught that whosoever disobeys "Napoleon I our Emperor" and refuses him "conscription and the United Duties" lays himself open to "eternal damnation."

Imperial Chancellor, German. According to the constitution of the German Empire (1871-1918), the chancellor enjoyed a commanding position, so long as he retained the confidence of the Emperor. He was the active agent of the

Emperor. By custom he was the head of the ministry of Prussia as well as chancellor. He presided over the Bundesrat and cast Prussia's 17 votes in that body. He might address the Reichstag whenever he wished. He proposed most of the laws for the empire and for Prussia. He appointed and supervised the heads of the imperial departments. He executed all imperial laws.

Imperial Conference. 1926. A meeting of representatives of Britain and the dominions. This conference (among other things) adopted the Balfour Report which declared: "They (Great Britain and the dominions) are autonomous communities within the British Empire, equal in status, in no way subordinate one to another in any aspect of their domestic or external affairs, though united by a common allegiance to the Crown, and freely associated as members of the British Commonwealth of Nations." This declaration became law in Dec. 1931, when Parliament passed the Statute of Westminster.

Independents. See Non-Conformists.

Index. From the earliest times it had been the custom of governments to prohibit the publication of books which they did not favor. Freedom of press developed nowhere before the end of the 17th century. In 1546 the University of Louvain published an index of books which were considered dangerous. The Council of Trent (1545-63) decided to systematize this idea as a method of counteracting the Protestant Reformation. It appointed a committee to draw up an index, or catalogue, of all books. There were two such lists. The *Index Librorum Prohibitorum* (list of forbidden books) contained a catalogue of books which were not to be read at all. The *Index Expurgatorius* (list of books to be expurgated) was a catalogue of books that might be read after certain passages were deleted.

Indulgences, Sale of. During the Middle Ages, the pope, as vicar of Christ on Earth, had claimed the power of remitting obligation, such, for example, as abstaining from meat on fast days. He also claimed the power of remitting from a penitent sinner the penance due for his error. To secure forgiveness, a sinner must regret the sin and resolve to do it no more. For the sin committed he must do pains or penance. One of the most usual penances was payment to the church. This money was to be used for some spiritual purpose. The theory was also developed that while many men and women had done fewer good works than they should have, others—the saints, for example—had done much more than was necessary for their salvation. There was, therefore, a "treasury" of surplus good deeds from which the pope, as administrator, might draw. The pope, thus, could transfer from this "treasury" a necessary quantity of good deeds to the "account" of a penitent sinner.

Whatever the theory was, some churchmen abused it. Indulgences were sold with little care about the sinner's repentance. Indeed, some men bought indulgences for sins which they planned to commit at some future date. The revenue from the sale of indulgences was great. It was to protest the sale of indulgences that Martin Luther posted his 95 theses on the door of the Wittenberg Cathedral on Oct. 31, 1517 and thus began the Reformation.

Industrial Revolution. A revolutionary change in manufacturing methods which began in England about 1750 and which spread to other countries. The revolution is characterized by the introduction of labor-saving machinery into manufacturing, the appearance of modern capitalism, and the formation of labor organizations. Beginning with a series of inventions in the textile industry, the transformation culminated in the application of the steam engine as a motive power about 1785. One invention paved the way for others. Thus was begun a far-reaching transformation of life and realignment of values which has radically affected every aspect of life among "Western" nations.

Innocent III (*name* Giovanni Lotario de Conti). 1161-1216. Pope (1198-1216). Born in Anagni, Italy. Son of a Roman noble, he was educated as a lawyer. As pope, he tried to make the papacy supreme over the state. Under his direction the papacy achieved its highest power. He initiated the Fourth Crusade (1202-04), which resulted in the capture of Constantinople and formation of the Latin Empire. He initiated a crusade against the Albigensians (1208). He became involved in a controversy with John of England over Stephen Langton (1206). He placed England under an interdict (1208), deposed John (1212), and compelled his submission (1213). He compelled Philip of France to restore his estranged wife Ingeborg to her lawful position. He received tribute from Sancho of Portugal. Peter of Aragon made his country a fief of the papacy (1204). He supported Philip of Swabia against Otto IV of Germany. After Otto was crowned emperor, Innocent excommunicated him (1210). He deposed Otto IV and crowned Frederick II of Sicily as emperor (1215). He presided at the fourth Lateran Council (1215).

Inquisition, Spanish. The Holy Inquisition originated during the papacy of Innocent III (1198-1216) at the time of the Albigensian heresies. Pope Sixtus IV authorized Spanish Catholic sovereigns to appoint inquisitors with all the powers of judges of ecclesiastical courts (1478). Thus the Inquisition became part of a scheme to subject the Church to the sovereign and to foster Spanish nationalism. The first *auto-da-fé* (q.v.) was held in Se-

ville (1481). The Dominican friar, Fray Thomas de Torquemada (1420-98), became Chief Inquisitor in 1483. Under him the Holy Office covered the land, and no one was so highly placed and so hardy as not to tremble at its name. The Inquisition continued in Spain until the first quarter of the 19th century.

Instrument of Government. Dec. 1653. Upon the overthrow of the Nominated Parliament (q.v.), the English army officers prepared an Instrument of Government vesting supreme power in a single person, to be known as the Lord Protector, assisted, and to some extent controlled, by a Council and a Parliament. The instrument was the first written constitution for governing a nation in modern times and the only one England has ever had in actual operation. Under the Instrument, there was virtual religious toleration. Jews, who had been expelled under Edward I, began to reappear in England. On Dec. 16, 1653, Cromwell was made Lord Protector for life.

Insurrection (French) of August 9-10, 1792. In anger against the Proclamation of the duke of Brunswick (q.v.), the people of Paris rose against the king. Led by Danton, they invaded the royal palace, massacred the Swiss Guard, and obliged the king and his family to flee to the Assembly for protection. On August 10, the Assembly voted to suspend monarchy in France, and authorized an election by universal manhood suffrage of a National Convention, which would have the duty of preparing a new constitution for France.

Intendants. 1637-1790. Governors of the provinces of France. The position was created by Richelieu (q.v.) and lasted until the days of the Revolution. The intendants, 34 in number, were called the "Thirty Tyrants of France" because of their great power. The intendant decided what share of the tax each

village and each taxpayer should pay.
He supervised the police, maintained
order, secured recruits for the army. He
relieved the poor. He gave sanction for
the erection and repair of churches and
public buildings. He ordered roads built
and repaired, and called out the peasants
to perform these tasks.

Inter-Allied Debts. Eighteen days after
the United States joined the belligerents
in World War I, Congress passed an act
which authorized the lending of 3 billion
dollars to the Allies at 5% interest. Other
loans were made during the war and in
the immediate post-war period. Approximately $10,338,000,000 was loaned to 20
nations. Of this sum, $7,077,000,000 was
loaned during the war and $3,261,000,-
000, or 31%, after the armistice. Britain
received 41% of the total; France, 33%;
Italy, 16%. During the 1920's various
debtor countries made funding arrange-
ments with the United States. There was
close correlation between what the debtor
countries paid and what they received
from Germany in the form of reparations,
despite the vigorous attempts of the
United States to divorce reparations from
debt payment. When Germany stopped
payment of reparations, all debtor countries, except Finland, stopped payments.
In 1934, the United States passed a law
forbidding defaulting nations to float
loans in the United States. All told the
borrowers repaid $2,628,000,000.

**International Bank for Reconstruc-
tion and Development.** 1945. A financial institution affiliated with the UN,
with headquarters in Washington, D.C.
The function of this bank is to make
long-term loans to nations which need
such funds for economic reconstruction or
expansion. It secures its capital from its
member nations or from sale of securities
on the market. Its purpose is not to replace private banks and investors but
rather to furnish funds when private capital is not available.

**International Court of Justice of the
UN.** The International Court of Justice is
similar to the Permanent Court of International Justice of the League of Nations.
In fact, its Constitution is the same as its
predecessor's. The principal difference is
that UN members adhere to the court
automatically, whereas in the League,
membership was optional. The permanent
seat of the Court is at the Hague, but it
may hold its hearings elsewhere.

International Labor Organization.
This body was created in 1919 by the
Treaty of Versailles. Its purpose was to
lay down equitable conditions for labor
and to induce governments to take steps
to incorporate these principles into their
national legislation. The Organization
works through an International Labor
Office located in Geneva. General conferences were convened whenever there was
a sufficient number of subjects for consideration. Sovereign states might be represented in these conferences by six delegates, one of whom should represent capital and one labor. States were at liberty
to accept or reject the recommendations
of these conferences. The International
Labor Organization was in effect part of
the League of Nations. Yet, it was independent from it. Non-League members
(the United States, for example) might
belong.
When the UN was organized, the International Labor Organization became
part of it. The ILO is now affiliated with
the Economic and Social Council of the
UN. Its headquarters are in Geneva,
Switzerland.

International Monetary Fund (IMF).
1945-. The purpose of this organization is
to stimulate world trade by maintaining
stable exchange rates for various national
currencies. The IMF first sets par value
for each national currency, and then by
using its financial power tries to prevent
excessive shifts in value above or below
par. The IMF has a working capital of 8

billion dollars, subscribed by the member states. It has set par values for the currencies of about 40 nations. The IMF also may make loans to countries. Its headquarters are in Washington, D.C.

Internationals, First, Second, and Third. An organization of socialists and labor leaders which grew out of the International Workingmen's Association formed in 1864. Its aim was to urge workers in all countries to unite to take over control of the means of production. The first congress met at Geneva in 1866. Karl Marx (q.v.) and Friedrich Engels (q.v.) were active members. Bakunin (q.v.) and a group of anarchists joined in 1869 and caused internal dissension, which finally led to the disruption of the movement. The last convention met in Philadelphia in 1874. The Second International (Socialist International) was formed in Paris in 1889. Since one of the cardinal aims of this body was pacifism, the First World War dealt it a mortal blow. The Third International (Comintern) was founded by Lenin (q.v.) in Switzerland in 1917. It supported the Marxian theory that capitalism would be overthrown by force because of its resistance to fundamental social changes. The Comintern was abolished by Stalin (1943) in the interest of wartime harmony among the United Nations. It was revived in the form of the Cominform (q.v.) in 1947.

Interregnum. See Great Interregnum.

Intolerable Acts. 1774. These laws were enacted by the British Parliament to punish Massachusetts, and especially Boston, for the Boston Tea Party. They included: (1) The port of Boston was to be closed and all its business transferred to Salem until the loss to the East India Co. was made good. (2) The charter of Massachusetts was amended, transferring more power to the governor and the king; all town meetings were suppressed. (3) All persons charged with a capital offense in Massachusetts were to be taken to Nova Scotia or England for trial. (4) A new Quartering Act was enacted.

Invasion of Spain by Napoleon. March, 1808. Spain was invaded by an army of 100,000 French troops under the excuse of guarding the coasts against the English. King Charles IV, his son Ferdinand, and Manuel Godoy were enticed by Napoleon to Bayonne. There the Spanish rulers were forced to abdicate. Napoleon's brother Joseph was made King of Spain. Napoleon's brother-in-law Murat succeeded Joseph as King of Naples.

Irish Church, Disestablishment of. 1869. Although Roman Catholics of Ireland had received political rights and virtual freedom of worship by the Catholic Emancipation Act of 1829 (q.v.), they were still compelled to pay tithes to the Protestant "Church of Ireland" for support of Protestant clergymen, many of whom lived in England. In 1869, the Church of Ireland was disestablished, which meant that the Protestant Episcopal Church was no longer the state church of Ireland and could no longer collect tithes.

Irish Free State. See Government of Ireland Act.

Irish Parliament, Independence of. 1782. Because of the poverty-stricken condition of Ireland and the prevalent unrest, and because of being embroiled in war with North American colonies and France and Spain, England relaxed many of the oppressive measures against Ireland. Legislative independence was granted May, 1782. (See Irish Union.)

Irish Union. Aug. 1, 1800. The grant of legislative independence to Ireland in 1782 (see Irish Parliament) had done little to relieve the situation there. Roman Catholics, Protestant Dissenters, Episcopalians, native Irish, Anglo-Irish, English, landowners, and peasants all had conflicting and intermingling interests. Conflicting religious views and exorbitant rents exacerbated the situation. Some Irish, headed by Wolfe Tone, turned to the French Revolutionists for help and (1791) formed the Society of United Irishmen. Faced by an armed revolution in 1798, the English government resorted to force, conciliation, and bribery to restore order. At last, the Irish Parliament was induced to vote for union with England. By terms of the agreement, four Irish spiritual peers, sitting in rotation in successive sessions, and twenty-eight temporal peers elected for life were to represent Ireland in the House of Lords. One hundred Irish members were to sit in the House of Commons. There was to be free trade between Ireland and England. The United Church of England and Ireland was to be preserved.

Iron Guard. A fascist pro-German organization of Romania. Under the leadership of General Antonescu, they forced King Carol to abdicate (1940). Thereupon, the Iron Guard set up a dictatorship for Romania which lasted until 1944, when it was overthrown by the conquering armies of the Soviet Union.

Ironsides. Cromwell's famous cavalry regiment during the English Civil War (1642-46).

Isabella I. 1451-1504. Wife of Ferdinand of Aragon. See Ferdinand V.

Isabella II. 1830-1904. Queen of Spain (1833-68). She became queen (1833) with her mother, Maria Cristina, as regent. Civil war waged by her uncle, Don Carlos (1833-39) (q.v.), resulted in court triumph. The Queen-regent resigned (1840) in favor of General Espartero, who was overthrown by a revolution (1843). Isabella was declared of age by the Cortes in 1843. The last 25 years of her reign were marked by continuous strife, intrigues, and changes of ministers. Overthrown by a revolution (1868) which endeavored to set up a republic, she abdicated in favor of her son Alfonso XII, who did not become king until 1875. In the interim, the Cortes chose the Duke of Aosta to be King Amadeo I (1871-73). Amadeo abdicated (1873) because he felt that the Spanish people did not want him as their ruler. Following Amadeo's abdication, Spain was a republic (1873-75).

Isidore of Seville. See Visigothic Kingdom of Spain.

Italia Irredenta. After the completion of unification (1870), the Italians claimed that there still were "unredeemed" territories. These were regions outside Italy which were inhabited overwhelmingly by Italians. These "irredentas" included Trentino, Trieste, Fiume, and the Istrian Peninsula.

Italian Cities, Medieval. In the days of the Roman Empire, Italy had been a country of excellent cities. Following the decay of the Empire and the coming of the Lombards, these cities went into decline. However, something of the old character of the Roman administration must have remained, for feudalism never got a firm grip upon Italy and was thrown off by that country first and with ease. In the 9th century, Italian cities surrounded themselves with walls for defense. Their government was in the hands of bishops. In the 11th century, the cities threw off the rule of the bishops and constituted themselves as *communes*, headed by elective *consuls* (consuls first appeared in Asti in 1095). Consuls, varying in number from 2 to 20, were the executives. An elected *council* (Credenza) was an advisory body. The *parliament* (parlamentum, concio) was a gathering of all the citizens—really a mob. Although this organization looks modern and democratic, it was weakened through the persistence of local, class feuds. Every town had its noble class, its bourgeois proprietor class, and its proletariat.

Emperor Frederick Barbarossa tried to break up the Italian communes, but was defeated by them at Legnano (1176) and was compelled to grant them independence at Constance (1183) (q.v.).

To reduce local feuds, cities (after 1200) appointed an official called *podestà* (from potestas, power). The *Podestàs* were chief magistrates with very wide powers. To secure some representation for themselves, the guilds now formed organizations which were called *commune del popolo* (people's commune), headed by the *capitano del popolo* (captain of the people). Whereupon civil war usually broke out within the cities. The party of the *podestà* sought support from the Emperor and called itself Ghibelline. The popular party clung to the Pope and called itself Guelf (q.v.).

Civil wars lasted until 1300, when most cities had lost their liberties and were ruled by tyrants.

Ivan III Vasilievich (*called* the Great). 1440-1505. Grand duke of Moscow (1462-1505). He conquered Novgorod (1471-78) and threw off the yoke of the Tatars (1480). He married (1472) Sophia (Zoë), niece of the last Byzantine emperor, and thus established the claim that Russia is the protector of Orthodox Christianity. He twice invaded Lithuania and acquired part of it through treaty. He added the two-headed eagle of the Byzantine empire to the Moscow coat of arms.

Ivan IV Vasilievich (*called* the Terrible). 1530-84. First ruler of Russia (1533-84) to use the title of czar. He annihilated the Kingdom of Khazan and annexed it to Moscow (1552). He subjugated Astrakhan (1556). Siberia paid homage to him (from 1555). Siberia was conquered for him by an army led by the Cossack chieftain Yermak (1584).

J

Jacobin Club. A radical club which was organized in Paris in the early days of the Revolution. It took its name from the confiscated monastery building where the club meetings usually were held. It was organized as a "society of the friends of the Constitution." Among its early members were Mirabeau, Sieyès, and Lafayette. Eventually the club came under the leadership of Robespierre and became quite as radical as the Cordeliers (q.v.). The Jacobins supplied most of the leaders of France during the period of the Reign of Terror.

Jacobite. An English supporter of the cause of the exiled Stuart kings. Jacobite is from the Latin form of the name James, who was the last Stuart king of England (1688). This word should not be confused with Jacobin, a radical party in revolutionary France.

Jacquerie. 1358. A violent peasant revolt in France against war taxes, the heavy ransom for captives taken at Poitiers (1358) (q.v.), and pillaging mercenary soldiers. This revolt was put down in merciless fashion by the nobles.

Jagellon. Name of a Polish dynasty (1386-1572). Jagello, the Grand Duke of Lithuania, married Jadwiga, the daughter of Louis I of Hungary and grand-daughter of Casimir III of Poland. Through this marriage he became king of Poland, taking the name of Ladislaus II. He and his descendants are known as the Jagellon kings.

Jahn, Friedrich Ludwig ("Papa Jahn"; "Father Jahn"). 1778-1852. German patriot. High school teacher. Identified with the movement to free Germany from Napoleon and the French. He organized a gymnastic association called *Turnverein*. This association was famous as a center of nationalism. Later, Jahn affiliated with the *Burschenschaften* (q.v.). The nationalist movement in Germany, even including Nazism, retained many features of Jahn's training.

James I and VI. 1566-1625. King of England (as James I) (1603-25) and of Scotland (as James VI) (1567-1625). He was the only son of Mary Queen of Scots and Lord Darnley. Upon the abdication of his mother (1567) he was proclaimed king of Scotland. Until 1578, when he became king in fact, Scotland was in a turmoil because of a succession of ambitious regents. As king of Scotland, James pursued a policy against Presbyterians and Catholics, and succeeded in introducing a system of bishops. Upon the death of Elizabeth I (1603), he became king of England. This union of crowns eventually led to the union of England and Scotland. His reign in England was marked by his partiality towards favorites, the sale of titles, and attempts to assert royal authority. He was characterized by Sully as "the wisest fool in Christendom." He was a witty, well-read scholar, but timorous and foolish in executive action.

James II. 1633-1701. King of England, Scotland, and Ireland (1685-88). Son of Charles I, he succeeded his brother Charles II. As duke of York, he received the grant of New Netherlands (1664). He accepted the Roman Catholic faith and thus aroused a conflict over the succession to Charles. Out of this conflict emerged the Whig and Tory Parties. When he became king, his open partiality to the Catholic religion aroused the fears of the English. James was deposed in favor of his son-in-law, William of Orange (see Glorious Revolution).

Janissaries (Janizaries). An élite corps of the Ottoman army, recruited from forced levies of Christian youths. The corps originated during the 14th century. The corps gained great power in the Ottoman Empire and made and unmade sultans. By the 16th century, Moslems began to enter the corps. In the 17th century, membership in it became hereditary. In 1826, the Janissaries were "liquidated" by Mahmud II; he had them all murdered in their barracks.

Jansen, Cornelis. 1585-1638. Dutch Roman Catholic theologian. Head of the Dutch theological college of St. Pulcherin, Louvain (1617). Professor at Louvain (1630). Bishop of Ypres (1636). Author of *Augustinus* (published in 1640). In this work he maintained that the teachings of St. Augustine on grace, free will, and predestination were opposed to the teachings of the Jesuit schools. In the controversies that followed, his followers, called Jansenists,

were championed by Pascal and the Port-Royalists (q.v.). They were opposed by the Jesuits and Pope Urban VIII. The bull, *Unigenitus Dei,* written in 1713 by Pope Clement XI, condemned Jansenist doctrines as heretical. However, the Jesuits lost much influence because of these controversies.

Jaurès, Jean Léon. 1859-1914. French Socialist. Born at Castres. He became interested in socialism and was elected a deputy (1893-98; 1902-14). With Briand (1904) he founded *L'Humanité* (editor 1904-14). Opposed militaristic legislation on the eve of the first World War and was assassinated (July 31).

Jeffreys, Judge George. 1648-89. English jurist. See Bloody Assize.

Jellachich, Joseph (Count Josip Jelacic od Buzima). 1801-59. Croatian general and governor. Ban (viceroy) of Croatia (1848). He helped to crush the Hungarian rebellion (1849). He returned to Zagreb as governor of Croatia and Slavonia.

Jena, Battle of. Oct. 14, 1806. Frederick William III of Prussia had been bribed by the gift of the Kingdom of Hanover to join the French and to close his ports to English ships. Unable to endure the humiliations which Napoleon forced upon him after this "alliance," he declared war upon the French. His armies were crushed by Napoleon at the twin battles of Jena and Auerstädt. After these defeats, the French occupied Berlin and reduced Prussia to the status of a third-rate power.

Jenkins' Ear, War of. 1739-41. A war between England and Spain which grew out of commercial rivalry between the two countries. The incident which touched off the war was the story of a shipmaster, Robert Jenkins. He claimed that his ship had been boarded by some Spanish coast-guards on April 9, 1731.

The Spanish captain was alleged to have cut off one of Jenkins' ears. This tale stirred up so much resentment that Prime Minister Walpole was forced to declare war on Spain against his will. This war soon became part of the larger War of the Austrian Succession (1740-48) (q.v.).

Jenner, Edward. 1749-1823. English physician. He developed the modern method of vaccination and used it to prevent smallpox.

Jesuits. See Society of Jesus.

Jiménez. See Ximenes.

Joan of Arc. 1412-31. Born at Domremy. At the age of 13, she saw a light and heard a voice from heaven urging her to help the Dauphin, then kept off the throne by the English. She made her way to the Dauphin (Feb. 1429), and convinced him of her sincerity. Putting on male dress and mounting a horse, she led a group of 4,000 soldiers against the English in relief of Orléans, and rescued the city (May 8, 1429). She urged the Dauphin to his coronation, and stood beside him at the ceremony in Reims. Joan continued to lead armies against the English. In May, 1430, she was captured by the Burgundians, and sold to the English. She was tried at Rouen by the Bishop of Beauvais. After being found guilty of sacrilege, she was imprisoned and later (May 30, 1431) burned at the stake. In 1894 she was beatified. In 1920 she was canonized.

John II (the Good). 1319-64. King of France (1350-64), succeeding his father Philip VI. His first years as king were tyrannical. He was defeated and captured at Poitiers (1356) by the English. He was detained as a captive in England (1356-60). During his absence his son Charles V ruled. He made the Treaty of Brétigny with the English (1360), whereby he was to be released upon payment

of a large ransom. He secured the duchy of Burgundy for his son Philip (1363). Failing to raise all of his ransom, he returned to England (1364), where he died.

John II Casimir. 1609-1672. King of Poland (1648-68). A Jesuit and cardinal (1640). He was absolved of his monastic vows by the pope upon becoming king (1648). During his reign occurred invasions by Tatars and Cossacks and a disastrous 13-year war with Russia (1654-67) which concluded with the treaty of Andrusovo (q.v.). He waged an unsuccessful war with Sweden (1655-60) and was forced to take refuge in Silesia. He resigned as king (1668) and went to France, where he became the abbé of St. Germaine.

John III Sobieski. 1624-96. King of Poland (1674-96). A soldier, he fought against the Tatars and Cossacks (1651-52), and helped Sweden (1654-55). Commander of the Polish army (1665). He plotted against Poland (1669-72), but redeemed himself by defeating the Turks at Hotin (1673). He was elected king in 1674. The height of his career was the relief of Vienna (1683) when it was besieged by the Turks. His later years were a failure because of bad internal political conditions. He was a patron of science and literature.

John (*called* Lackland). 1167-1216. King of England (1199-1216). Youngest and favorite son of Henry II. He attempted to seize the throne when his brother Richard was held captive in Austria, but was pardoned and named heir by Richard. In wars with France, he lost most of his territory there (see Angevin Empire), retaining only a portion of Aquitaine. When (1207) Pope Innocent III appointed Stephen Langton Archbishop of Canterbury, John declined to receive him. As a consequence, in 1208, England was placed under an interdict.

In 1209, John was excommunicated. In 1212, the pope issued a bull deposing John. Philip of France was given the task of enforcing the bull. Finding that his position was untenable, John submitted to the pope and (1213) agreed to hold his kingdom as a fief of the pope and to pay 1,000 marks yearly as tribute. On June 15, 1215, the barons of England forced John to sign the Magna Carta at Runnymede (q.v.).

John of Gaunt, Duke of Lancaster, fourth son of Edward III of England. 1340-99. For a time he assumed the title of king of Castile. He was the virtual king of England during the last years of his father's reign. He opposed the clergy and protected Wycliffe (q.v.). He is the ancestor of Henry VII.

Johnson, Samuel. 1709-84. English lexicographer, critic, and conversationalist. He gained early fame with a poem, *London* (1737), and *The Life of Savage* (1744). When he published a dictionary (1755), he achieved fame and an Oxford degree. He was a frequent contributor to the *Gentleman's Magazine* and the *Literary Magazine*. He edited the *Rambler* (1750-52) and wrote the *Idler* papers (1758-60). His *Lives of the Poets* (1779-81) is one of his best works. His literary club, among whose members were Reynolds, Garrick, Goldsmith, Boswell, and Burke, had a pronounced effect upon English literature.

Jones, Inigo. 1573-1652. English architect. He was influenced by Italian Palladio and was noted for his composite adaptation of ancient Doric, Ionic, and Corinthian styles.

Jonson, Ben. 1573-1637. English playwright and poet. His plays include *Everyman in His Humor, The Poetaster, Sejanus, Volpone,* and *The Alchemist.* Among his poems is the famous *Drink to Me Only with Thine Eyes.* He is generally regarded as the first poet laureate, although William Davenant (1606-88) was the first to receive the official title.

Joseph II. 1741-90. Holy Roman Emperor (1765-90). Son of Maria Theresa. He ruled Austria jointly with his mother (1765-80). A benevolent despot. He prohibited publication of any new papal bulls, suppressed convents, and reduced the powers of the clergy. He published the Edict of Toleration (1781). He abolished serfdom (1781) and torture in judicial questioning. The death penalty was to be used in only a few extreme cases. Many of his reforms were too advanced for his country and were later rescinded. Afterwards he was remembered as a visionary, rather than as a statesman.

Joyce, James. 1882-1941. Irish novelist. A major figure of modern world literature. He experimented with new literary techniques. He is the author of *Ulysses* and *Finnegan's Wake.*

Juan, Don of Austria (the Elder). 1547-78. Natural son of Emperor Charles V. He commanded the fleet of the Holy League and defeated the Turks at Lepanto (1571). Took Tunis from the Turks (1573). Appointed governor of the Netherlands (1576). Compelled to issue the "Perpetual Edict" (1577) (q.v.). Forced to remove Spanish troops from the Netherlands. Deposed by the Estates-General. Failed in the campaign against the Dutch because of lack of support by Philip II. Died suddenly in camp at Namur.

Juan, Don of Austria (the Younger). 1629-79. Spanish general. Natural son of Philip IV and Maria Calderón, an actress. Viceroy of Sicily (1647-51). He terminated the revolt in Catalonia (1651-53). He was removed from power by the queen regent (1665-69). Led a successful revolution (1677). Prime minister (1677-79).

Juana (*called* the Mad). 1479-1555. Daughter of Ferdinand and Isabella. Married Philip the Handsome (q.v.). Mother of Emperor Charles V.

Julius II (*name* Giuliano della Rovere). 1443-1513. Pope (1503-13). Born in Albissola, Italy. Administered the papacy in the manner of a temporal sovereign. Formed the League of Cambrai (1508) against Venice. He formed the Holy League against France (1511). He began to rebuild St. Peter's. He was the patron of Raphael, Michelangelo, Bramante, and other artists.

"July Monarchy." This is one of the names of the constitutional monarchy set up in France after the Revolution of 1830.

July Revolution. 1830. On July 26, five "July Ordinances" were enacted, establishing rigid government control of the press, dissolving the Chamber of Deputies, and changing the electoral system to disenfranchise the wealthy liberals of the middle class. Liberals, bourgeoisie, Napoleonic veterans, and workmen combined to oppose the would-be divine right monarchy of Charles X in France. Charles X, after a feeble struggle, abdicated in favor of his ten-year-old grandson, the Count of Chambord, and fled to England. Although the workmen, headed by Cavaignac, wanted a republic, the Liberal bourgeoisie, headed by the journalist Thiers and the banker Lafitte, succeeded in securing as the next government of France a constitutional monarchy headed by Louis Philippe, the duke of Orléans, a son of that Philippe Égalité (q.v.) who had voted for the death of Louis XIV. The success of the July Revolution had immediate consequences in Europe. In Belgium, Germany, Italy, Poland, and Switzerland revolutionary action followed immediately. As a consequence, Metternich had to abandon all thought of uniting Europe and forcing "legitimacy" upon France.

Junius, Letters of. See Letters of Junius.

Junker. Class of German aristocracy. They were conservative, nationalistic, and militaristic. Their sons formed the backbone of the Prussian army officer caste.

Junto. 1694-97. The Junto was the first party cabinet of England.

Jury System of England. The system of securing indictments by grand juries and verdicts from petit juries was inaugurated by Henry II of England in the latter part of the 12th century. This system, frequently spoken of as Anglo-Saxon in origin, was introduced into England from Norman France. It superseded ordeals and compurgations as a method of determining innocence or guilt of the accused.

Justinian I (*called* Justinian the Great). 483-565. Emperor (527-565). Born in Illyricum, probably of Slavonic parentage. Married (523) Theodora. His reign was brilliant. He is remembered for his conquests, his building, and his lawgiving.

His army under the brilliant leadership of Belisarius and Narses conquered the Vandal kingdom of north Africa (534) and the Ostrogothic empire of Italy (553). His wars against the Persians (530-32; 540-45) were less conclusive.

He built many churches and public buildings throughout the empire. The church of Santa Sophia in Constantinople, which he built (532-62), is considered to be the finest example of Byzantine art.

He preserved Roman law for future generations by appointing a commission, headed by Tribonian, to codify all imperial statutes. (See Codex of Justinian.) This work, the *Corpus Juris Civilis,* is the foundation of law in most European countries today.

K

Kalmar, Union of. 1397. Denmark, Norway, and Sweden united under the headship of Denmark. Each country was to retain its own customs and laws. They were to act together for common defense. The sovereign was to be elected by the three kingdoms. The son of the previous king was always to be preferred as successor. In 1439, Norway and Sweden broke away. The union was dissolved in 1448. The three countries were brought together again in 1457 under Christian I of Denmark. The final break occurred in 1523 when all of Sweden established its independence under the house of Vasa. (See Gustavus I.)

Kant, Immanuel. 1724-1804. German philosopher. Born in Koenigsberg, where he spent most of his life. Educated as a Pietist (until 1740) (q.v.). He studied science, mathematics, and philosophy in the University of Koenigsberg (1740-46) and under private tutors (1747-54). Professor of logic and metaphysics at Koenigsberg (from 1770). In 1781 he published the *Kritik der Reiner Vernunft* (Critical Judgment concerning Pure Reason). In this work he endeavored to ascertain the nature of general or transcendental ideas. By this and other writings he was the founder of critical philosophy.

Kapp Putsch. March 13-17, 1920. An attempt by a group of German monarchists, headed by Wolfgang Kapp, to secure control of the nation through a *coup d'état*. The Kapp forces seized the government buildings in Berlin, while the government fled to Stuttgart. The movement collapsed as a result of a general strike by trade unionists.

Karageorge (Black George). 1766-1817. Serbian leader in the struggle for independence from the Turks. Founder of the Serbian dynasty of Karageorgevich.

Karelian-Finnish Republic. See Russo-Finnish War, First.

Karl Marx Hof. Municipal houses built for workmen in Vienna by the Socialist government. Completed in 1930, the project was the largest dwelling house in Europe, being more than three-fifths of a mile long and containing almost 1400 apartments. Converted into a fort by the Schutzbund, a semi-military workers' organization, it was besieged (Feb. 11-15, 1934) when the government under Dollfuss (q.v.) crushed the Socialist Party. Many units of the Hof were ruined by artillery fire. Since the end of World War II, the Hof has been rebuilt.

Kay, John. ?-1764. English inventor of the flying shuttle (patented in 1733), a device to simplify weaving.

Keats, John. 1795-1821. English poet. He studied medicine but never practiced. His first published poem appeared in the *Examiner* in 1816. It was followed by *On First Looking into Chapman's Homer, Endymion, The Eve of St. Agnes, La Belle Dame sans Merci.* Keats contracted a lung ailment and went to live in Italy, where he died after a short illness.

Kellogg-Briand Pact, The. Also known as the Pact of Paris. Aug. 27, 1928. An agreement signed by the United States, France, Belgium, Czechoslovakia, Great Britain, Germany, Italy, Japan, and Poland by which these countries agreed to renounce aggressive war as an instrument of national policy. They agreed that, in the future, settlement of all disputes between them should be sought by pacific means. The wording of the treaty was identical with the draft of a Franco-American treaty proposed by Briand in June, 1927. Because this pact was signed in Paris, it is often called the Paris Pact. By the end of 1928, 46 other states, including the USSR, had signed the pact.

Kepler, Johannes. 1571-1630. German astronomer. Born at Weil, in Württemberg. Educated at Tübingen. Assistant to Tycho Brahe (1600) in Prague. Succeeded Brahe as imperial mathematician and court astronomer (1601) to Emperor Rudolph II. Resided at Linz (1612), Ulm (1626), and Sagan (1628). He discovered three important laws of planetary motion (Kepler's laws). He wrote on optics and did pioneer work that led to the invention of the calculus.

Kerensky, Alexander. 1881-. Russian revolutionary leader. He joined the Labor Party, although he really was a Social Democrat. He was made minister of justice in the Provisional Government (1917) which was set up after the abdication of the czar. Later (July 1917), he succeeded Prince Lvov as premier. He was overthrown by the Bolshevik revolution (Nov. 1917). He has since resided in the United States.

Khaki Elections. British elections held in December, 1918. In these elections, Lloyd George appealed to the people to support the wartime coalition on its record. He promised that William II of Germany would be tried as a war criminal and that Germany would be assessed large indemnities. He promised to protect "essential" industries and to take measures to prevent the dumping of foreign goods. He also promised to care for the veterans, settle the Irish Question, and reform the House of Lords. During the campaign the coalition was deserted by some Liberals and Conservatives and all Laborites. Nevertheless the coalition captured two-thirds of the seats in Commons.

Khlysty (flagellants). Russian mystics who repudiated the official church and its organization. They denied marriage. They organized secret meetings in which they attempted to call forth the Holy Spirit by means of ecstatic dances. Gregory Rasputin (q.v.) was associated with the Khlysty.

"King of the green umbrella." Louis Philippe, king of France from 1830 to 1848.

"King's Friends." Supporters of George III of England. Their "friendship" was secured by pensions and grants of money from the king.

Kipling, Rudyard. 1865-1936. English poet, short-story writer, and novelist. Born in Bombay. Many of his poems glorified British imperialism. He is one of the ablest short-story writers in the English language. He was awarded the Nobel Prize in Literature in 1907. He was a very prolific writer. Among his many works are *Plain Tales from the Hills, The Jungle Book, The Light That Failed, The Man Who Would Be King, Kim, Barrack-Room Ballads.*

"Kirke's Lambs." These were members of a notorious regiment headed by Col. Kirke. Following the unsuccessful attempt of the duke of Monmouth to overthrow James II of England (July 5, 1685), this regiment butchered scores of rebels without mercy.

Knights of St. John. See Military-monastic Orders.

Knights Templars. See Military-monastic Orders.

Knox, John. 1513-72. Scotch reformer, writer, and theologian who, early in life, came under the influence of the teachings of John Calvin. Through his efforts, the Presbyterian Church became the established church of Scotland. He wrote the *History of the Reformation of Religion within the Realme of Scotland.*

Koch, Robert. 1843-1910. German bacteriologist. He originally did research on wounds and septicaemia. Later he discovered the germs that cause tuberculosis and cholera. He worked in South Africa for seven years to discover the germs that cause the rinderpest and other cattle diseases.

Komsomol. The Communist Youth Movement. It is a training organization for future Communist Party members. It contains the elite of the Russian nation.

Königgrätz. See Austro-Prussian War.

Kosciusko, Thaddeus. 1746-1817. Polish patriot. He studied engineering and artillery in France. He joined the American Revolutionary army (1776) as colonel of engineers. He fortified West Point. Took part in many of the major campaigns. Brigadier general (1783). One of the founders of the Order of Cincinnati (1783). He returned to Poland (1784). Major general in the Polish army

(1789). He led a rebellion (1794) against the partitions of Poland (q.v.) and became the dictator of Poland (1794-96) but was captured and imprisoned in Russia. Returned to America (1797-98). Resident in France (from 1798).

Kossuth, Louis. 1802-94. Hungarian patriot, born in Monok. Editor of the *Pest Journal* (1840-44), a reform publication. Member of the Hungarian Diet (1847-49). Headed the Hungarian insurrection (1848-49) against Austrian rule. After the rebellion was crushed he fled to Turkey (imprisoned there, 1849-51), the United States (1851-52), and England. During the Austro-Sardinian War (1859) he organized a Hungarian Legion in Italy. Thereafter he resided in Turin.

Kotzebue, August von. 1761-1819. German writer and dramatist. Born in Weimar. A Russian spy for most of his life. Killed by a university student, K. L. Sand, for ridiculing the *Burschenschaft* movement. This murder set off a wave of repressive legislation in central Europe and Russia. A facile writer, he was the author of over 200 dramatic works. His son Otto (1787-1846) was a famous explorer who accompanied Krusenstein around the world (1803-06) and afterwards made two voyages of exploration to the Pacific.

Krupp, Alfred. 1812-87. German steel magnate. Born at Essen. He succeeded his father Friedrich Krupp (1787-1826), who had founded a small forge there in 1810. He established the first Bessemer steel works and the first forging-hammer erected in Germany. He acquired mines, collieries, docks, and greatly expanded his works. He was succeeded by his son, Friedrich Alfred (1854-1902), and he by his daughter, Frau Bertha Krupp von Bohlen und Halbach (b. 1886), and she by her son Alfred Krupp von Bohlen und Halbach (b. 1907).

Kultur. Kultur was a term used by pre-1914 Germans to describe the progress which they had achieved since unification in 1871. During that time they had successfully harmonized the conflicting interests of farmers and businessmen, of capitalists and workingmen. They had cherished literature, the arts, and the sciences. They had achieved a high measure of efficiency. Achievements of this nature were designated as Kultur.

Kulturkampf (struggle for civilization). 1872-1879. This was a struggle between the German Empire and the Catholic Church. The struggle grew out of a conflict between the Catholic hierarchy and the German state governments over the doctrine of papal infallibility, which was proclaimed by the Vatican Council (1869-70) (q.v.). In 1872, Bismarck expelled all Jesuits and broke off diplomatic relations with the Vatican. In 1874, the "May Laws" (or Falk Laws) (q.v.) specified that no one should be appointed to any Roman Catholic office in Germany unless he was a German who had studied in a German gymnasium and university and had passed examinations in philosophy, history, German literature and classics. All ecclesiastical seminaries were placed under the control of the state. Other laws strictly regulated the conduct of Roman Catholic clergy.

Roman Catholic laity flocked to support their clergy. They joined the Center Party in great numbers. Fearing a coalition between the Center Party and the Socialists, Bismarck withdrew the anti-Catholic laws. The Center Party, however, remained permanently solidified.

Kun, Bela. 1886-?. Hungarian communist. Born in Transylvania, he was a journalist and soldier. Captured by the Russians in 1915, he embraced communism and returned to Hungary (March, 1919) to set up a communistic republic. This collapsed in August, 1919. Kun then returned to Russia, where he may still be living. Rumor has it that he perished in the purges of the 1930's.

L

Labor Exchange Act, English. 1909. By this act the English government set up a system of government employment-bureaus to inform unemployed workmen where work was to be had and, if necessary, to pay the workman's transportation to the place where work was offered.

Labor Front, German. To replace labor unions, which had been abolished in 1933, and employers' associations, which were dissolved in 1934, a German Labor Front was set up by the Nazis. Headed by Dr. Robert Ley, this body was designed to coordinate all German workers and employers, both intellectual and manual. (In 1939 the Front had 30 million members.) It served as an apparatus for indoctrination of Nazi principles. It had some power to arbitrate labor disputes. Affiliated with it was a recreational organization, "Strength through Joy," which arranged cheap vacations for workers and their families.

Labor Party, British. When Joseph Chamberlain left the Liberal Party (1886), the labor vote was left completely stranded. In 1899, a general trade-union congress, held in London, formed a Labor Representation Committee, which sought to secure representation in Parliament. Angered by the Taff Vale Decision (1901) (q.v.), the Labor Representation Committee joined with the Fabian Socialists (q.v.), the Social Democratic Federation, and the Independent Labor Party (1906) to form the Labor Party. The Labor Party has had three ministries: 1924 (Ramsay MacDonald); 1929-31 (Ramsay MacDonald); and 1945-51 (Clement Attlee).

Lafayette, Marquis de (Marie Joseph Paul Yves Roch Gilbert du Motier). 1757-1834. French statesman and officer. He entered French military service (1771). Withdrew (1776) to enter American service in the Revolutionary War (1777). Commissioned a major general in the Continental Army by Congress (July 31, 1777). Became a close associate of George Washington. Went to France (1778-80) to promote the cause of the Americans. Served in Virginia (1781). Returned to France (1781). Visited the United States (1784; 1824-5). He was a member of the French National Assembly (1789). He organized the National Guard and secured the adoption of the tricolor flag. He commanded an army in the war with Austria. He opposed the Jacobins and was declared a traitor. He fled to Flanders and was imprisoned by the Austrians (1792-97). He returned to France (1799) but lived quietly, as he was against the policies of Napoleon. He became a member of the Chamber of Deputies (1815, 1818-24). He commanded the National Guard during the Revolution of 1830.

La Fontaine, Jean de. 1621-95. French author. Born in Château-Thierry. Author of fables. His reputation rivals that of Aesop, the Greek.

Laibach, Congress of. 1821. This was a meeting of the Quadruple Alliance (q.v.), called by Metternich, to deal with the uprising in Naples (1820). Ferdinand, King of the Two Sicilies, invited an Austrian army to invade Naples "to restore order." The Laibach Conference authorized this invasion. When the Austrian army approached Naples, the uprising collapsed. Ferdinand, with Austrian support, inaugurated an era of persecution. A similar revolt in Turin was put down (1821) by the Quadruple Alliance.

Lamartine, Alphonse Marie Louis de Prat de. 1790-1869. French poet. Best known for his *Méditations Poétiques* (1820), which strongly influenced the French romantic movement. Also known as an orator. Minister of foreign affairs in the provisional government (1848).

Lamb, Charles. 1775-1834. English essayist. A clerk in the India House (1792-1825). He devoted his life (from 1796) to the care of his sister Mary (1764-1847), who, in a fit of temporary insanity, attacked their father and stabbed and killed their mother. Brother and sister collaborated in *Tales from Shakespeare* and *The Adventures of Ulysses*. Lamb wrote many essays under the name of *Elia*. These have been collected under the title of *Essays of Elia*.

Lamb, William. 2nd Viscount Melbourne. 1779-1848. English statesman. Whig M.P. (1806). Irish secretary (1827-28). Home secretary (1830-34). Prime minister (1835-41). While he was prime minister he was the very tactful adviser of Queen Victoria.

Lancaster, House of. A line of kings who ruled England.

	Born	Ruled
Henry IV Bolingbroke	1366	1399-1413
Henry V	1387	1413-1422
Henry VI	1421	1422-1461;
		1470-71

Lancaster, Sir James (1550?-1618). English navigator who pioneered the East Indian trade. He sailed with the earliest English expedition to the Far East in 1591. He commanded the first fleet of the East India Company.

Land Purchase Act, Irish. 1891. By this act, a tenant could, if he wished, buy his holding from the landlord by borrowing from the government a sum equal to the full purchase price. This loan could be paid back in 49 annual installments.

Landsgemeinden. Swiss "town meetings." In the rural cantons, all male citizens of full age assemble in the open air at stated intervals to make the laws and elect their administrators. These assemblies are one of the few modern examples of "pure democracy."

Langland, William. 1332?-1400. Supposed name of an English poet who wrote the allegorical poem *The Vision of Piers the Plowman*.

Langton, Stephen. d. 1228. English theologian, historian, and poet. He studied in Paris and lived there 25 years after completing his training. He composed Biblical commentaries, divided the Old Testament books of the Vulgate into chapters, and wrote *Questions*, a discussion upon the limits of episcopal power. He was named Archbishop of Canterbury in 1207, but was kept out of office by King John until 1213. This act of John's precipitated the famous quarrel between him and the pope (see Innocent III). Langton sided with the barons against John and was largely instrumental in having the Magna Carta signed (q.v.). It was Langton who produced a document from the days of Henry I which strengthened the cause of the barons. All copies of this document were allegedly lost. Langton made the Church in England a truly national Church.

Langue d'oc. Language of southern France. In this dialect the word for "yes" was *"oc."* The destruction of the Albigensians (q.v.) (from 1209 on) put an end to this southern civilization and imposed the law and language of northern France (*langue d'oil*) upon the whole of France.

Langue d'oil. A French dialect which was used in northern France. In this dialect, the word for "yes" was *"oil."* This dialect became the universal language of France.

Lansdowne, Marquis of. See Shelburne.

Laplace, Marquis Pierre Simon de. 1749-1827. French astronomer and mathematician. Born in Normandy, the son of a farmer. He went to Paris (1767), and, by demonstrating his ability in mathematics to D'Alembert, secured a professorship in the École Militaire. He held various positions under Bonaparte. In *Mécanique Céleste* (1773) he announced the discovery of the invariability of the planetary mean motions (a discovery of importance in establishing the stability of the solar system). In *Exposition du Système du Monde* (1796), he set forth the nebular hypothesis. He investigated tides, capillary action, electricity, and worked on a theory of probabilities.

La Rochefoucauld, Duke François de. 1613-80. French writer. His literary fame rests upon his *Réflexions ou Sentences et Maxims Morales* (1665).

Lassalle, Ferdinand. 1825-64. German socialist. Born in Breslau. Disciple of Karl Marx. Champion of the working classes (from 1862). He formulated the so-called "iron law of wages." He is regarded as the founder of the German Social Democratic Party (q.v.).

Lateran Accord, The. Feb. 11, 1929. An agreement between the papacy and the Italian government, ending the "Roman Question" (q.v.). It contained the following:

1. The pope was recognized as an independent sovereign. A state, called Vatican City, was created in which the pope was the sole sovereign.

2. In the future, Roman Catholicism was to be the sole religion of the state. Bishops were to be selected by the Church, but all nominees for bishoprics must first be cleared by the state. Bishops were required to swear loyalty to the king and state. All clerical salaries were to be paid by the state. The state would assist in enforcing canon law. Marriage was recognized as a sacrament and a religious ceremony was to be sufficient. Religious instruction was made compulsory in both elementary and secondary schools.

3. Italy consented to pay an immediate cash indemnity of $39,375,000 and $52,-500,000 in 5% bonds. This money was to indemnify the papacy for the events of 1870.

Lateran Council. 1215. A great gathering called in Rome by Pope Innocent III. Four hundred bishops and eight hundred abbots and priors were present, as well as representatives from all the courts of Europe and even from the East. The Council established the Inquisition, and declared that heresy was a crime punishable by death. The doctrine of auricular confession was promulgated. A Christian was ordered to confess his sins to a priest at least once a year, and might receive the sacrament of the eucharist after so doing. If he did not confess, the Church was closed to him and he was denied Christian burial. The doctrine of transubstantiation, which up to that time had not been the universal belief of the Church, was adopted. It was decreed that none but an ordained priest could administer the sacrament.

Lateran Synod. 1179. This body decreed that whoever should receive two-thirds of the votes of the College of Cardinals was to be regarded as the duly elected pope. Nothing was said about the right of the emperor or the city of Rome to confirm the election. From this time on the whole matter of electing popes was in the hands of the cardinals.

Latitudinarians. These were European theologians who endeavored to reach a "golden mean." Originating in Holland in the 17th century, the movement made much progress in England. The Latitudinarians aimed to emphasize the essentials of faith and to minimize minor differences of dogma and church policy. The Latitudinarian tradition was continued (in the latter half of the 17th century) by the "Cambridge Platonists," who opposed excessive Puritanism on the one hand and materialism on the other.

Laud, William. 1573-1645. English prelate. Appointed Archbishop of Canterbury (1633) by Charles I, he became virtual first minister of the country and acted with Charles and Stafford to secure absolutism in church and state. His policy against English Puritans and Scotch Presbyterians led to heavy emigration. He was impeached of high treason (1641), imprisoned, and beheaded (1645).

Lausanne, Treaty of. 1923. A settlement which revised the Treaty of Sèvres (q.v.). Turkey gave up claims to all non-Turkish territory. It received eastern Thrace and the Islands of Imbros and Tenedos. Greece surrendered Smyrna, but received all of the Aegean Islands except the two just mentioned. Italy retained the Dodecanese Islands and England Cyprus. The Straits were demilitarized. Turkey and Greece exchanged populations. In accordance with this last provision, about 350,000 Turks migrated from Greek territory; but over one million Greeks were expelled from Turkey.

Laval, Pierre. 1883-1945. French politician. Born at Châteldon. Lawyer, deputy (1914), senator (1926), premier (1931-32, 1935-36). Originally a socialist, he eventually became a rightist. He became Petain's deputy (1940) and prime minister of the Vichy government (1942-45). He was condemned to death as a collaborationist with the Nazis and executed in 1945.

Lavoisier, Antoine. 1743-94. French chemist. Often called "the Father of Modern Chemistry." He greatly improved gunpowder, successfully applied chemistry to agriculture, and discovered oxygen by correctly interpreting Priestley's experiments. To supply himself with money to conduct his experiments, he became a farmer-general of taxes. During the Reign of Terror he was guillotined because he had been a farmer-general.

Law, Andrew Bonar. 1858-1923. British statesman. Born in New Brunswick, Canada, he migrated to England while still a boy. He was a Member of Parliament from 1900 for the Conservatives. Secretary of state for colonies (1915-16); chancellor of exchequer (1916-18); lord of the privy seal (1919-21); prime minister (1922-23).

Law, John. 1671-1729. Scottish financier and speculator. Founded the *Banque Générale* (1716), the first French bank which issued paper money and prospered. Developed the Mississippi Scheme which collapsed in 1720. It is known as the "Mississippi Bubble" (q.v.).

Law of Suspects. See Reign of Terror.

Lawrence, Thomas Edward (*called* Lawrence of Arabia. Changed his name to Shaw in 1927). 1888-1935. British archaeologist, soldier, and writer. Born in Portmadoc, Wales. Educated in Oxford. He served (1910-14) with a British archaeological expedition in the Euphrates valley. During World War I, he became a British agent and successfully organized an Arab revolt against the Turks. He described this revolt in *The Seven Pillars of Wisdom* (1926) and *Revolt in the Desert* (1927). Lieutenant colonel (1918), attached to General Allenby's staff. Attended the Paris Peace Conference (1919). Adviser on Arab affairs in the Colonial Office (1921-22). He joined the Royal Air Force (1922) under the name of Ross. Translated the *Odyssey* (1932). Killed in a motorcycle accident (1935).

Lay investiture. See Concordat of Worms.

League of Augsburg, War of. 1688-97. The League of Augsburg was formed by William of Orange against Louis XIV. It included the emperor, Holland, the kings of Sweden and Spain, the Electors of Bavaria, Saxony, and the Palatinate. When William of Orange became king of England (1689), he involved England in the alliance. The war between France and the League began when France claimed most of the lands of the Elector of the Palatinate upon the extinction of the male line of the Electors Palatine. The war was an exhausting one in which the French had successes on land at first, but later were driven back. At sea, the French crushed the allied fleet at Beachy Head, but later were annihilated at La Hogue (1692). The French navy was ruined and France's finances were in utter confusion. The allies suffered similarly. Peace was concluded at Ryswick (1697) (q.v.).

League of Nations. 1919-46. An international organization created by the Treaty of Versailles (1919) (q.v.). The main function of the League was the preservation of peace. The original members of the League were named in the Covenant, or constitution, of the League. Any fully self-governing state was eligible for membership if approved by a 2/3 vote of the League Assembly. Both Germany and Russia were excluded from the original list; but both subsequently became members. Germany resigned in 1933 at the time that Japan resigned because of the Manchurian affair. Russia was expelled from the League following its attack on Finland in 1939. Sixty countries were members of the League at one time or another. At the outbreak of the second World War there were 46 members. The United States never joined.

The League was administered by three major bodies: the Assembly, the Council, and the Secretariat. The Assembly consisted of representatives of all member countries. Each country had one vote. The Assembly convened for the first time on Nov. 15, 1920. Its last session adjourned Dec. 14, 1939. The Assembly might consider any matter within the sphere of action of the League or affecting the peace of the world. The Assembly became an international forum.

The League Council became a quasi-executive body. It was composed of permanent and elective members. The Council varied in size from 8 to 16. The first meeting took place Jan. 16, 1920. The last (107th meeting) closed Dec. 14, 1939.

The Secretariat, or "civil service," of the League consisted of a Secretary-General and a staff of assistants. The Secretariat was divided into sections: mandates, health, minorities, etc. The Secretariat registered and published all treaties submitted to it.

The Permanent Court of International Justice (World Court) and the International Labor Organization were constituted under terms of the League Covenant.

On the threat of war, the League was to take action to safeguard the peace. After suitable investigation established the aggressor, the members of the League might impose an economic boycott against the offending member (see Sanctions). Should economic sanctions fail to halt the aggressor, military force might be used. This last step was never used. About 40 minor disputes were settled by the League, 20 of which might easily have led to war. However, the League failed signally to halt aggression committed by a major nation.

The League's principal successes lay in health and social work. It helped Russian, Greek, and Armenian refugees. It administered mandated colonies, and the Saar and Danzig.

The League formally came to an end Aug. 1, 1946, at which time its properties and other assets in Geneva, the seat of the League, were turned over to the United Nations. In Dec. 1946, the General Assembly of the United Nations accepted agreements whereby eight former League mandates would be transferred to the United Nations trusteeship system.

Lebrun, Charles François. Duke of Piacenza. 1739-1824. French author and statesman. He translated Tasso's *Gerusalemme Liberata* and Homer's *Iliad* into French. During the days of the Revolution, he played an active part in public life, being a member of the Estates-General, the National Assembly, the Council of the Five Hundred, Third Consul (1799), and archtreasurer of the empire (1804). His son, Anne Charles (1775-1859), was the aid-de-camp to Napoleon and organized the defense of Antwerp (1809).

Ledru-Rollin, Alexandre Auguste. 1807-74. French lawyer and politician. He was identified with various radical groups. He took an active part in the Revolution of 1848 and was an unsuccessful candidate for president (Dec. 1848). He was forced into exile (1849) for revolutionary tactics but later returned to France (1870). He campaigned vigorously for universal manhood suffrage and was largely responsible for the adoption of it in France.

Leewenhoek, Anton van. 1632-1723. Dutch naturalist. Born in Delft. He made simple microscopes with which he observed microorganisms. He was the first to describe the red corpuscles. He described spermatozoa, striated muscle fibers, the crystalline lens of the eye. He observed hydra, bacteria, and yeast plants.

Leges Barbarorum. Codes of laws which governed the barbarians who invaded the Roman empire in the 4th and 5th centuries. None of these tribes had written laws originally. In time, these codes were written in Latin and provide us with important sources of knowledge of the customs of the Germans. Two important codes are the *Lex Salica* and the *Edictum Theoderici*. Of all the German barbarians who settled on Roman soil, only the Anglo-Saxons wrote their laws in their mother tongue. All the others used Latin.

Legion of Honor, French. An order of merit which was founded by Napoleon on May 19, 1802.

"Legitimists." French Ultra-Royalists who wanted to restore the line of Charles X to the throne after the Revolution of 1830.

Legnano, Battle of. See Lombard League.

Leibnitz, Gottfried Wilhelm. 1646-1716. German philosopher and mathematician. Born and educated in Leipzig. In 1672 he was summoned to Paris to explain a plan for the invasion of Egypt, which is believed to have been the basis for Napoleon's invasion of Egypt in 1798. In London he became acquainted with Boyle and Newton. He invented a calculating machine and devised a novel method of the calculus—giving rise to the controversy of the priority of Newton's "Fluxions." In 1676 he entered the service of Hanover, and was appointed librarian. He improved the system of drainage and coinage. Among his writings are *Systema Theologicum* (1686), *De Principio Individui* (1663), and *Monadologie* (1714).

Leipzig, Battle of ("Battle of the Nations"). Oct. 16-19, 1813. A decisive battle in which Napoleon was defeated by three allied armies. The allied victory was assured when the Saxon and Württemberg corps deserted the French and went over to the allies. The city of Leipzig was taken by storm on Oct. 19. The King of Saxony, one of Napoleon's chief allies, was captured. Napoleon lost 30,000 men in these engagements and was compelled to retreat across the Rhine.

Lend-Lease Act. March 11, 1941. A law passed by the United States Congress to assist those countries that were fighting against Fascist aggression. The President was empowered to provide goods and services to those nations whose defense seemed vital to the security of the United States.

Lenin, Nikolai (*real name* Vladimir Ilich Ulyanov). 1870-1924. Russian revolutionary and statesman. First practiced law in Samara (1892). Moved to St. Petersburg in 1894 where he began Socialist propaganda work. Arrested (1895). Exiled (1897) to eastern Siberia where he wrote *The Development of Capitalism in Russia.* Moved to Switzerland in 1900 and founded *Iskra* (the Spark), a revolutionary journal. Encouraged revolution during the Russo-Japanese War. Advo-

cated "defeatism" at the start of World War I. Laid the foundations for the Third International in 1915. Came to Russia in April, 1917, and assumed leadership of the revolutionaries. Overthrew the government of Kerensky (Nov. 7, 1917). Became premier following the dissolution of the constituent assembly at his motion (Jan. 7, 1918). Established the dictatorship of the proletariat. Fought against counter-revolutionaries (1918-21). Established far-reaching reforms, later (1921) modified by the New Economic Policy. Died at Gorki (Jan. 21, 1924). His body has been embalmed and is on permanent exhibition in Moscow.

Leo III the Isaurian. 680?-741. Byzantine Emperor (717-741). He seized the imperial throne by force and defeated the Turks in their first efforts to capture Constantinople (717). He made many administrative reforms in the army, finances, and codes of law. In 725 he began the long iconoclast (q.v.) struggle which caused insurrections in Greece and Italy and led to his complete break with the pope of Rome (730).

Leo IX, Saint (*name* Bruno). 1002-1054. Pope (1049-54). Born in Alsace. He was responsible for the rule that clergymen must practice celibacy. Before his term of office, many clergymen were married and fathered families. In the last year of his term of office (1054) there occurred the final break between the Greek and Latin Churches. The final schism concerned the use of leavened or unleavened bread in making the holy wafer used in the sacrament. The Greek Church favored the former.

Leo X (*name* Giovanni di Medici). 1475-1521. Pope (1513-21). Born in Florence. Second son of Lorenzo the Magnificent. Created cardinal (1488) at the age of 13. Chosen pope at 37. An able administrator. He drove the French from Italy, but was later defeated by

Francis I (1515). He made an agreement with the French (1516). He was a great patron of the arts and is often called the "Renaissance Pope." He failed to appreciate the full significance of the Lutheran movement, although he did excommunicate Luther (1520).

Leo XIII (*name* **Gioacchino Vincenzo Pecci**). 1810-1903. Pope (1878-1903). Born near Anagni, Italy. He received excellent classical Jesuit education. Papal nuncio to Brussels (1843). Cardinal (1853). His pontificate is one of the most notable in recent church history. He wrote important encyclicals on many subjects: marriage, study of the Bible, education, socialism (*Rerum novarum*, 1891).

Leonardo da Vinci. 1452-1519. Painter, sculptor, architect, engineer. Born at Vinci, between Pisa and Florence. He went to Florence (1466) as a protege of Lorenzo the Magnificent. He served Lodovico Sforza in Milan from 1482 to 1499. In Florence (1500) he was the military engineer for Cesare Borgia. He competed with Michelangelo for the commission to paint the Palazzo Vecchio. As court painter for Louis XII of France, he lived in Milan (1506). In 1516, Francis I of France also made him court painter. He lived in France from 1516 to his death. He originated the science of hydraulics and made many contributions to meteorology, anatomy, and mathematics. He built the Martesana canal and many military fortifications. He was employed as an architect in the construction of the Milan cathedral. He constructed a huge bronze monument to Francesco Sforza in Milan. His paintings include *Mona Lisa, The Last Supper, Annunciation, Adoration of the Kings, St. Jerome, Virgin of the Grotto.*

Leopold II. 1747-92. Holy Roman Emperor (1790-92). Third son of Francis I and Maria Theresa. Brother of Joseph II. He formed an alliance with Prussia against France (1792) and died just before war was declared.

Lerma, Duke of. 1552-1625. Spanish statesman. Prime minister (1598-1618). He practically ruled Spain, having complete control over Philip III. He failed completely in foreign policy. He was compelled to make peace with England (1604) and truce with the Netherlands (1609). He drove out the Moriscos (q.v.) (1609-10), thus giving Spain a blow from which it never recovered.

Lermantov, Mikhail Yurievich. 1814-41. Russian poet and novelist. Strongly influenced by Byron. The source of his inspiration was the Caucasus, its natural beauty, the primitive customs of the mountaineers, its constant state of war. Author of *The Demon, The Circassian Boy,* etc.

Les Cagoulards ("the Hooded Ones"). A French armed secret society which tried (1937) unsuccessfully to overthrow the republic and re-establish a monarchy.

Lessing, Gotthold Ephraim. 1729-81. German dramatist and critic. Born in Kamentz, Saxony. He enrolled in the theological seminary in Leipzig, but abandoned a clerical career to become a playwright. He did literary hack work for a time. He associated with Moses Mendelssohn and Nicolai in producing a critical Berlin journal, in which he revolted from the dictatorship of French taste and extolled Shakespeare. In 1766 he wrote his famous *Laokoon*, a critical treatise defining the limits of poetry and the plastic arts. His first success on the stage was *Minna von Barnhelm* (1767), the first German comedy on a grand scale. His drama *Nathan der Weise* (1780), is important in the history of liberalism in religion.

Leszczynska, Maria. 1703-68. Daughter of Stanislaus Leszczynski, King of Poland.

She settled in Alsace with her father after his expulsion from Poland (1709). She married Louis XV of France (1725). She spent most of her married life in retirement.

Letters of Junius. These were a series of letters which appeared in the London *Public Advertiser* between Jan. 1769 and Jan. 1772. The author, who is unknown, saw clearly the weaknesses and vices of the men in power and exposed them with fiendish skill. It is usually assumed that these letters were the work of Sir Philip Francis.

Lettre de cachet (sealed letter). A French device for arresting an individual and keeping him in jail without trial. These orders were signed in blank by the king and were intended to be used by him alone to suppress the enemies of the state. However, in the decades preceding the Revolution, the king frequently sold or gave them to his favorites, so that they might have their enemies jailed.

Liberal Party, British. Although the British Whigs won a major victory by securing the passage of the Reform Bill of 1832, many of their leaders felt that the party needed a new name and a new direction if it was to survive. The old Whigs had been just as aristocratic as the Tories, being dominated by a group of wealthy peers. After 1832, many wealthy iron and cotton manufacturers entered the party. They wished to be thought of as a liberal, reforming element. In time, the Whig Party became known as the Liberal Party, since it espoused any "liberal" idea which was current among the bourgeoisie. The Liberal Party was a major force in England until 1920.

Liberum Veto. After 1466 the Polish diet (sejm) was composed of delegates who were chosen from the noble class. It made the laws, took some part in execu-

tive affairs, and elected the king. The diet could not accomplish much, since unanimous vote was required for all decisions. A single member by exercising his privilege of *liberum veto* (free negative) could block any action.

Liebknecht, Wilhelm. 1826-1900. German journalist and politician. In exile in Switzerland and England (1849-62). He worked with Karl Marx to found the German Social Democratic Labor Party (1869) (q.v.). Member of the Reichstag (1867-70; 1874 ff.). Editor of *Demokratisches Wochenblatt* and *Vorwärts*. His son Karl (1871-1919) was a lawyer and communist leader. Member of the Reichstag (1912). He violently opposed Germany's entrance into World War I. He organized anti-war demonstrations. Imprisoned (1916-18). On release from prison, he organized (with Rosa Luxemburg) the Spartacist insurrection (Jan. 1919) (q.v.). He was arrested and murdered (with Rosa Luxemburg) on the way to prison.

Ligurian Republic. 1797. Formerly the Republic of Genoa. When the armies of the French Revolution conquered this region, they reorganized and renamed it. It became part of France in 1805.

Limerick, Treaty of. Oct. 3, 1691. After the Battle of the Boyne (q.v.), the bulk of the defeated Irish army took refuge at Limerick, which surrendered to the English in 1691. By the terms of the Treaty of Limerick, all Irish officers who desired should be transported to France. So many took this opportunity that formidable insurrections in Ireland ceased for a century. The English promptly violated the civil clauses of the treaty and imposed a regime of tyranny and avarice upon Ireland.

Lindet, Jean Baptiste Robert. 1746-1825. French lawyer. Member of the Legislative Assembly and the National Convention. He prepared a report on the crimes imputed to Louis Capet. This report was the basis for the accusations against Louis XVI (Louis Capet). Minister of finance (1799), in which capacity he rendered his greatest services to his country.

Linnaeus, Carolus (Carl von Linne). 1707-78. Swedish botanist. His great work is in the *Systema Natura,* published in 1737. In his *Species Plantarum* he gives a full account of specific names. This book laid the foundation for the modern system of botanic classification.

Lionne, Hugues de. 1611-71. French diplomat. Associate of Mazarin in negotiating the Treaties of Westphalia (q.v.) and Pyrenees (q.v.). French ambassador at Rome (1654), Madrid (1656), Frankfurt (1657), and Turin (1658). Secretary of state for foreign affairs (1663). Adviser to Louis XIV.

Lippi, Fra Filippino. 1458-1504. Florentine artist. Son of Fra Filippo Lippi. Painted frescoes in Florence and in Rome. Easel pictures by him include *The Virgin and the Saints, The Adoration of the Magi,* and *The Vision of St. Francis.*

Lippi, Fra Filippo. 1406-69. Florentine painter. He dropped completely the traditional severity which formerly marked religious paintings and filled his pictures with smiling children and the innocent pleasures of life. Chief work: frescoes in the Prato.

Lisbon Earthquake. Nov. 1, 1755. This devastating earthquake was accompanied by fire and the flood of the River Tagus. Tens of thousands of people lost their lives. Lisbon was destroyed with many of its treasures.

Lister, Joseph. 1872-1912. English physician. In addition to important observations on the coagulation of the blood, inflammation, etc., his great work was the introduction (1860) of the antiseptic system, which revolutionized modern surgery.

Liszt, Franz. 1811-86. Hungarian pianist and composer. Among his many notable compositions are his symphonies, symphonic poems, oratorios, Hungarian rhapsodies, and piano pieces.

Lit de justice. See Parlement of Paris.

"Little Englander." A British statesman who is more concerned with the problems that beset life in England itself than with imperial questions (education, poor relief, factory legislation, relations with Ireland, etc.). Gladstone was a typical "Little Englander."

Little Entente, The. An agreement between Czechoslovakia, Romania, and Yugoslavia with the encouragement and support of France. This alliance was an attempt to forestall a resurgence of the former Austro-Hungarian Empire. A formal agreement was signed at Belgrade May 21, 1929, after bilateral treaties among the three powers had been in effect for nearly nine years. When Germany seized Czechoslovakia in 1939, the Little Entente came to an end.

Little Parliament. See Nominated Parliament.

Litvinov, Maxim. 1876-1951. Russian communist leader and statesman. After the Russian Revolution (1917) he represented the Russian government in London. He signed the Kellogg Pact for Russia (1928). He was the people's commissar for foreign affairs (1930-39). During his term in office, he strove for cooperation between the USSR and other countries. When he was superseded by Molotov (1939), the change marked a radical departure in Russian foreign policy from internationalism to nationalism. He was the Russian ambassador to the United States (1941-43).

Livery Company. 1330. A name used in England since the time of Edward III (1327-77) to designate certain craft guilds. They were permitted to wear a distinctive livery in public processions and were much concerned with the general welfare of their members. As time went on, the richer members of the companies became more powerful at the expense of the poorer members. At present there are still 12 important livery companies: Mercers, Grocers, Drapers, Fishmongers, Goldsmiths, Skinners, Merchant Taylors, Haberdashers, Salters, Ironmongers, Vintners, and Clothworkers. Although the lord mayor of London is still elected by the livery companies, their power has been much reduced since the 19th-century Reform Acts.

Lloyd George, David. 1863-1945. British statesman. Born in Manchester of Welsh parents. Studied law. Solicitor (1884). M.P. (1890). President of the Board of Trade (1905-08). Chancellor of the exchequer (1908-15). (See War Budget of 1909, q.v.). Minister of Munitions (1915-16). War Secretary (1916). Coalition Prime Minister and virtual dictator (1916-22). He carried England to victory in World War I. He played a large part in the peace settlements at the end of the war and negotiations which resulted in the creation of the Irish Free State.

Locarno Conference and Treaties. Oct. 5-16, 1925. Delegates from Germany, France, Britain, Belgium, Poland, and Czechoslovakia drew up several treaties to preserve the peace of Europe (signed Dec. 1).
(1) A treaty of mutual guarantee of the Franco-German and Belgo-German frontiers (signed by France, Germany, Belgium, Britain and Italy).
(2) Arbitration treaties between Germany and Poland and Germany and Czechoslovakia.
(3) Arbitration treaties between Germany and Belgium and Germany and France.
(4) Treaties between France and Poland and France and Czechoslovakia for mutual assistance in case of attack by Germany.

Should violation of these treaties occur, the League Council was responsible for settlement. The treaties were to go into effect when Germany entered the League of Nations, which it did in 1926.

Locke, John. 1632-1704. English philosopher. He drafted a constitution for the Carolinas, was an adviser of the government regarding coinage, practiced medicine, and is the author of *Toleration, Treatise on Civil Government,* and *An Essay on Human Understanding.* In his writings he attempted to justify the Revolution of 1688 by stressing the social contract theory and by pointing up the right of people to resist the state when rulers fail to observe their trust. Jefferson drew upon Locke in writing the Declaration of Independence. In psychology he upheld empiricism (as opposed to nativism) and anticipated the doctrine of the conditioned response.

Lombard League. 1167. A union of cities in northern Italy against Frederick Barbarossa, who had deprived them of their liberties. After a bitter struggle, they finally defeated Frederick at Legnano (1176) (q.v.). This battle was followed by the Treaty of Constance (1183) (q.v.) in which the Lombard cities won their freedom. They acknowledged the overlordship of Frederick; but his control over them was in name only.

Lombards. A Germanic barbarian tribe which overran the Po Valley in Italy in the 6th century. This region has been called Lombardy ever since. At first they were a savage and pagan race. In time they settled down and adopted the habits and religion of the people among whom they settled. Their kingdom lasted 200 years until it was conquered by Charlemagne (773).

London Naval Conference. Jan. 21-Apr. 22, 1930. Great Britain, the United States, France, Italy, and Japan met to consider the problems of extending the Washington Naval Disarmament Treaty (q.v.) and of limiting types of warcraft not included in the Washington Treaty. France and Italy did not sign the really vital parts of the pact, since France was determined to have the largest navy of any continental European nation, and Italy wished parity with France. Britain, Japan, and the United States settled the problems of cruisers and destroyers by compromise (10-6-10 ratio). The three powers were to have parity in submarines. No new capital ships were to be laid down until 1936. Aircraft-carrier figures remained the same as in the Washington Treaty: 135,000 tons each for Britain and the United States; 81,000 tons for Japan. An "escalator" clause permitted each signatory to increase tonnage in any category if, in its opinion, national security was endangered by new construction on the part of any nonsignatory.

London, Secret Treaty of. April 26, 1915. Between Italy, France, Russia, and Great Britain. Under the terms of this treaty, Italy agreed to join the Allies within a month in return for the following concessions:
Italy was to receive
(1) Trentino, Trieste, and all of south Tyrol.
(2) Gorizia, Gradisca, Istria, and the islands of the Gulf of Quarnero.
(3) Northern Dalmatia.
(4) A protectorate over Valona and its hinterland.
(5) The Dodecanese Islands.
(6) A sphere of influence in Asiatic Turkey.
(7) An extension of its African colonies, if France and England should annex the German African colonies.

(8) A war loan.
(9) A promise that the papacy would not be supported in any diplomatic action taken contrary to the wishes of the Italian government.

Long Parliament. Nov. 3, 1640–Mar. 16, 1660. Called together by Charles I because of financial difficulties, this Parliament defied the king, waged victorious war against the crown, deposed and executed the king, abolished the House of Lords and the established church, and proclaimed England a commonwealth.

Louis VI (the Fat). 1081-1137. King of France (1108-37). By continuous warfare, he subdued the robber barons who surrounded Paris. Made war against Emperor Henry V and Henry I of England (1116-20). He encouraged the communal movement among his vassals. He protected the Church. His counsellor was Suger, Abbot of St. Denis (q.v.).

Louis VII (the Younger). 1121?-1180. King of France (1137-80). Son of Louis VI. He married Eleanor of Aquitaine (1137), but divorced her (1152); whereupon she married Henry of Anjou, who became Henry II of England. Louis took part in the Second Crusade (1147-49). Louis engaged in a long struggle with Henry II (1157-80) without much actual fighting. During his reign, many parts of France were lost to the king of England.

Louis VIII (called the Lion). 1187-1226. King of France (1223-26). Son of Philip II. Married Blanche of Castile (1200). Before becoming king he established the reputation of being a warrior prince. He was offered the crown of England by the barons who opposed King John. He led an expedition to England (1216-17). He crusaded against the Albigensians (1215-19). As king he tried to drive the English out of southern France. He overpowered Avignon and received the submission of the Albigensians in 1226.

Louis IX (Saint Louis). 1214-70. Son of Louis VIII. King of France (1226-70). He went on a crusade (1248-54) against Egypt, but was captured (1250). He remained in Syria as a captive for four years. By the Treaty of Corbeil (1258) he gave up French claims to Rousillon and Barcelona. By the Treaty of Paris (1259) with England, Normandy, Anjou, Touraine, Maine, and Poitou became French territories while regions in the south went to England. He encouraged his brother, Charles of Anjou, to attack Naples (1265). He died in Tunis while on a crusade. He was canonized in 1279. Louis was first of all a Christian, and all his judgments were formed in accordance with Christian ideals. Few rulers have taken Christianity so seriously. His religious conscience was his absolute master. Accordingly, he acquired the reputation for dispensing perfect justice. He became the arbiter of all Europe. Although deeply religious, he was not an ascetic. He loved to hunt. He was lavish in expenditure and rich in dress.

Louis X (the Quarreler). 1289-1316. King of France (1314-16). Son of Philip IV.

Louis XI. 1423-83. King of France (1461-83). Married Margaret of Scotland (1436). He attempted to seize the throne from his father Charles VII (1446, 1456). As king he destroyed the power of the great nobles. He conducted a successful struggle against Charles the Bold of Burgundy (q.v.) (1467-77). He secured the Burgundian territories for the French crown as well as Anjou, Marne, and Provence. He laid the foundations for absolute monarchy in France.

Louis XII. 1462-1515. King of France (1498-1515). Known as "The Father of the People" for his just and kindly rule.

By marriage to Anne of Brittany, he insured the continuance of the union between Brittany and France. He overran Milan and helped the Spaniards conquer Naples. He humbled the Venetians (1509). The Holy League (q.v.) was formed against him. As a result, he was driven from Italy (1513) and defeated in the Battle of the Spurs (1513) (q.v.). He was succeeded by his son-in-law Francis I.

Louis XIII. 1601-43. King of France (1610-43). Married Anne of Austria (1615). During his minority (1610-17) his mother, Marie de Médicis, was regent. During most of his reign he was under the influence of Richelieu (q.v.), who entered the council of ministers in 1624 and soon became the chief minister. Under Richelieu's direction, France made war on the Huguenots (1622-28) and took a decisive part in the Thirty Years' War (1618-48). Louis XIII's eldest son succeeded him as Louis XIV. His second son, Philippe, Duke of Orléans, founded the great Orléans family.

Louis XIV (*called* the Great; Le Grand Monarque; Le Roi Soleil). 1638-1715. King of France (1643-1715). During his minority, his mother, Anne of Austria, acted as regent. The actual power was in the hands of the chief minister, Cardinal Mazarin (1643-61) (q.v.). On the death of Mazarin, Louis was aided chiefly by Colbert (q.v.), minister of finance, and Louvois (q.v.), minister of war. Under Louis, the aim of France was to extend its boundaries up to the mountains and the Rhine River. Other countries of Europe, fearing that such expansion would upset the balance of power in Europe, made numerous coalitions against France and prevented expansion to the lower Rhine. When Louis tried to seat his grandson on the throne of Spain, a great European war broke out in which France and Spain were defeated. Despite defeat, Louis did succeed in seating his grandson on the Spanish throne. By revoking the Edict of Nantes (1685) (q.v.), he drove thousands of Frenchmen into neighboring countries. His reign was the epitome of absolute monarchism. France reached its zenith during his reign. His court was the most magnificent in Europe. Letters, music, art, and architecture enjoyed a "golden age."

Louis XV. 1710-1774. King of France (1715-74). Great-grandson of Louis XIV. The Duke of Orléans, who was regent (1715-23), came under the influence of John Law, whose disastrous financial schemes brought about a great panic (1720) (see Mississippi Bubble) (q.v.). Married (1725) Maria Leszczynska (q.v). Cardinal Fleury became prime minister (1726-43). His administration restored France's finances. France took part in the War of the Polish Succession (1733-35) and secured possession of Lorraine. After Fleury's death (1743) Louis personally managed affairs. The administration of the country gradually became worse. Discontent and hatred of the king by the masses became steadily more bitter. Louis had several mistresses, particularly Mme. de Pompadour (1745-64), whose influence was harmful. It was due to her influence that France allied with Austria and engaged in the Seven Years' War with disastrous results. France lost both Canada and India as a result. Louis suppressed the Jesuits (1764) and abolished the Parlement of Paris (1771). Mme. du Barry had great influence with the king (1768-74). Gifts to her in five years amounted to 180 million livres. Louis died of smallpox during a game of blindman's buff in the grounds of Versailles.

Louis XVI. 1754-93. King of France (1774-92). Third son of the Dauphin Louis (only son of Louis XV). Born at Versailles. Married Marie Antoinette (1770). At first he was aided by able ministers and attempted to abolish evil laws and improve the serious financial

conditions of his country. This reform program was soon overruled by the extravagant queen and court. At last he was forced to summon the Estates-General (1789) to deal with the financial crisis. The next four years of his reign witnessed the first phases of the French Revolution. He sought to escape from France (June 20-21, 1791), but was captured at Varennes and brought back. He took the oath to be a constitutional king (Sept. 1791). He was deposed by the National Convention (Sept. 21, 1792), tried for treason (Dec. 1792), and guillotined (Jan. 21, 1793). He left two children: a son, who is known as Louis XVII, but was never crowned; a daughter, who became Duchess of Angoulême.

Louis XVIII (in full Louis Xavier Stanislas). 1755-1824. Grandson of Louis XV. Brother of Louis XVI and Charles X. Comte de Provence. Born in Versailles. King of France (1814-15 and 1815-24). He fled to Belgium at the same time that Louis XVI tried to escape (1791). Lived with emigrés in Germany. Took the title of regent when Louis XVI was executed (1793) and king when Louis XVII died (1795). Lived in Germany, Russia, Poland, and England during the Napoleonic period. As king his policy was prudent and conciliatory.

Louis Philippe (often called the Citizen King; Le Roi Citoyen). 1773-1850. Eldest son of Louis Philippe Joseph (Philippe-Égalité), duke of Orléans. Born in Paris. King of the French (1830-48). Like his father, he joined with the revolutionists (1789). He was a Jacobin (1790) and a colonel in the revolutionary army. During the Napoleonic regime (1796-1814) he traveled in Scandinavia and later resided in Philadelphia, England, and Sicily. After the Napoleonic period he lived in France (1817-30), administering his large estates and great wealth. As king, he was at first democratic, but later became a typical Bourbon. He was deposed by a revolution (Feb. 1848) (q.v.).

Louvois, Marquis de (François Michel Le Tellier). 1641-91. French minister of war under Louis XIV (1668-72). After the death of Colbert (1683), he became the chief adviser of the king, but later lost his influence. He was a great military organizer. His reform measures—efficient provisioning system, the flintlock musket and bayonette, etc.—made the French army the most powerful in Europe at the time.

Lübeck, Treaty of. May 22, 1629. An agreement between Emperor Ferdinand II and Christian IV of Denmark, following the defeat of the latter in the Thirty Years' War. Christian was to receive back his lands upon promising not to interfere in German affairs. The Dukes of Mecklenburg were put under the ban. Wallenstein (q.v.) was invested with their lands.

Lublin Committee. 1944. This was a Soviet-sponsored government which was set up in Lublin in disregard of the Polish Government-in-Exile in London. It was recognized at the Yalta Conference (q.v.) and became the government of Poland (1945).

Luddite Riots. 1811-16. The use of machinery in England had thrown many hand-laborers out of work. With the end of the Napoleonic Wars (1815) came a severe curtailment of English exports. As a result, many workers were unemployed. The poorest classes, believing machines to be the cause of their distress, began burning factories and smashing machines. The riots reached their climax in 1816. The name, Luddite, came from one Ned Ludd, a feeble-minded resident of Leicestershire. Irritated one day by tormentors, he pursued one into a house. Not finding his tormentor, he broke several stocking frames which were on the premises.

Ludendorff, Erich Friedrich Wilhelm. 1865-1937. German general. At the outbreak of World War I, he was made quartermaster-general. He worked with Hindenburg to defeat Russia. He engineered the collapse of Serbia and Romania. He planned the campaign which led to the defeat of the Italians at Caporetto. His plan of attack in 1918 nearly defeated the Allies. He fled to Sweden at the end of the war and then (1919) took up residence in Munich. He worked with Hitler in the early days of the Nazi movement. He later broke with Hitler and became an ardent pacifist.

Ludwig (also called Louis) the Pious. 778-840. Son of Charlemagne. Holy Roman Emperor (814-40). A weak ruler who could not prevent internal disorder nor repel recurring Norse raids.

Ludwig II (also called Louis), the German. 804-876. King of Germany (843-876). By the Treaty of Verdun, he became king of all Germany east of the Rhine. Usually regarded as the founder of the German kingdom.

Lully, Jean Baptiste. 1633-1687. French composer. Born in Florence, Italy. Called the founder of the national opera of France. He was among the musicians attached to the court of Louis XIV. He won the favor of the king, and was made court composer (1653) and superintendent of court music. One of his duties was to compose masques and ballets for court functions. He headed the Académie Royale de Musique (1672-87). Among his operas are *Alceste* (1674), *Proserpine* (1680), *Persée* (1682).

Lunéville, Treaty of. Feb. 9, 1801. This treaty between Napoleon and the Austrians virtually ended the Holy Roman Empire. It ratified the conditions of the Treaty of Campo Formio (q.v.). It called for the cession of Tuscany to Parma. The emperor consented to the cession of the left bank of the Rhine to France, with the middle of the river as the boundary. The rulers who thus lost territory were to receive compensations in other German territory. The Batavian, Helvetic, Cisalpine, and Ligurian Republics were recognized. Germany lost 25,180 square miles and 3½ million inhabitants by this treaty. The negotiations for indemnifications lasted more than two years (see Reichsdeputationshauptschluss).

Lusitania, Sinking of. May 7, 1915. The Lusitania, a British Cunard Liner, was torpedoed seven miles off the southeastern coast of Ireland by a German submarine. Almost 1200 lives were lost, including those of more than 100 Americans. Before this act, public opinion in the United States had been largely neutral or anti-British. Now it became strongly anti-German. The sinking of the Lusitania was the most important single event which caused the United States to declare war on the Central Powers.

Luther, Martin. 1483-1546. Religious reformer. Born in Eisleben, Germany. He became an Augustinian friar and was ordained a priest (1507). He went on a mission to Rome (1510-11), where he was unfavorably impressed by the conditions of the Church. Professor of Biblical exegesis in Wittenberg University (1511-46). He attacked the sale of indulgences by nailing 95 theses to the door of the church in Wittenberg (Oct. 31, 1517). He publicly defended his act before a chapter of his own order (May, 1518) and appeared before Cardinal Legate Cajetanus (Oct. 1518). He publicly debated the issue with Johann Eck (July, 1519) in Leipzig, and went further than the indulgence issue by denying the supremacy of the pope. He defended his position by writing pamphlets, among which was *An Address to the Christian*

Nobility of the German Nation. His basic doctrine was justification by faith, which makes the priestly offices of the Roman Catholic Church an unnecessary intermediary between the individual and God. He was excommunicated (June 15, 1520) by Pope Leo X, but publicly burned the bull of excommunication. He appeared before Emperor Charles V at the Diet of Worms (April 17 and 18, 1521). The Diet passed the Edict of Worms, placing Luther under ban. Frederick the Wise of Saxony concealed Luther in the Castle of Wartburg (1521-22), where he translated the New Testament into German. He returned to Wittenberg (1522) and devoted his life to organizing his church, writing, and translating the Old Testament into German. In 1525 he married Katherine von Bora, a former nun. He lost much popularity by opposing the Peasants' War (1524-25) (q.v.). After 1530, the control of the Lutheran Church passed into the hands of the Protestant princes, and Luther devoted most of his time to matters of faith and worship.

Luxemburg, Rosa. 1870-1919. German socialist agitator. Associated with Karl Liebknecht (q.v.) in the Spartacist movement. She was involved with him in the Spartacist insurrection (1919). She was arrested with him and killed by police while being taken to prison.

Lyell, Sir Charles. 1797-1875. British geologist. Born in Forfarshire, Scotland. He made geological expeditions to many parts of Europe. In his *Principles of Geology* (3 vols., 1830-33) he refuted the catastrophic theory for great geological changes. *The Geological Evidences of the Antiquity of Man* (1863) presents a general summary of the arguments for man's very early appearance on earth. He is considered the father of modern geology.

M

Macaulay, Thomas, Lord. 1800-59. English writer and statesman. Called to the bar (1826). M.P. (1830-34; 1839-47; 1852-56). Raised to the peerage (1857). Member of the Supreme Council of India (1834-38). Secretary of war (1839-41). Paymaster of the forces (1846-47). He is the author of a *History of England,* covering the reigns of James II and William III. Author of the *Lays of Ancient Rome* and numerous essays which appeared in the *Edinburgh Review.*

MacDonald, James Ramsay. 1866-1937. British statesman. Born at Lossiemouth, Scotland. Joined the Labor Party (1894). Its secretary (1900-12) and treasurer (1912-24). M.P. (1906-18). Prime minister of the first Labor Ministry in Britain (Jan.-Oct. 1924). Prime minister (1929-31). Broke with the Labor Party to become coalition prime minister (1931-35). Lord president of council in the Baldwin cabinet (1935-37).

Machiavelli, Niccolò. 1469-1527. Italian statesman, political philosopher, and historian. Born in Florence. He carried out several diplomatic missions for Florence (1498-1512). He was removed from office (1512) and imprisoned for a time. He retired to devote his time to writing. Author of *The Prince, Discourses, History of Florence, The Art of War,* etc.

The Prince contains a number of maxims regarding practical statecraft, which have since been known as *Machiavellian.* The broad scheme of the book is that for the establishment and maintenance of authority all means may be used, and that the worst and most treacherous acts of a ruler are justified by the wickedness and treachery of the governed.

Mackensen, August von. 1849-1945. German field marshal. He commanded the invasion of Poland (1914-15) and Romania (1916).

MacMahon, Comte Marie Edme Patrice Maurice de. 1808-93. Marshal of France and second president of the Third Republic. Born in Sully of Irish ancestry. He fought in Crimea (1855) and Algeria (1857-58). He distinguished himself at Solferino (1859). Governor of Algeria (1864-70). Commanded first army corps in the Franco-Prussian War, but was defeated badly at Sedan (1870). Suppressed the Commune of Paris (1871). President of France (1873-79).

"Mad Parliament." See Provisions of Oxford.

Madrid, Treaty of. 1526. Francis I of France was defeated and taken captive at the battle of Pavia (1525) by the army of Charles V. Francis was taken to Spain and held captive until he signed the Treaty of Madrid. By this treaty Francis surrendered Burgundy, many of his eastern territories, and all his claims to Italian lands. Francis broke his word upon his release and renewed the war. However, the French definitely lost Milan and Naples.

Magellan, Ferdinand. 1480-1521. Portuguese navigator who was employed by the Spanish crown to find a strait to the Moluccas. He rounded South America through the strait which now bears his name. He renamed the South Seas "*Mare Pacificum.*" He was killed in a skirmish in the Philippines. One of his ships under the command of Sebastian del Cano continued westward and reached Spain, thus circumnavigating the globe, the first time the feat had been accomplished.

Maginot Line. A series of forts built by France along the Franco-German frontier to prevent Germany from invading France. Since the western end of the line ended at the Belgian frontier, it was fairly simple for the Germans to outflank the line by attacking France through Belgium. Although the Maginot Line was said to be impregnable, events proved otherwise. The Germans broke through it in 1940. In 1944, when it was in the possession of the Germans, the Americans broke through it.

Magna Carta. 1215. Signed by King John of England at Runnymede, June 15, 1215, at the insistence of the barons of England. The charter specifies:
(1) That the Church is to be free and to hold its rights entire, particularly in the elevation of bishops.
(2) The barons are promised many concessions—renunciation of feudal abuses; no scutage except as imposed by the Common Council, etc.
(3) Ancient liberties of London and other towns are to be preserved; mer-

chants are to come in and go out of the kingdom freely; all goods seized for the king's use are to be paid for.
(4) No freeman shall be arrested and imprisoned unless by lawful judgment of his peers and by the law of the land.

Magnum Concilium. 1070. The Great Council (Magnum Concilium) or King's Court (Curia Regis) was an institution founded by William the Conqueror of England. Meeting thrice annually, it dealt largely with judicial matters and tendered advice to the king on legislation and taxation. It was composed mainly of Norman nobles and bishops.

Maintenon, Marquise de (Françoise d'Aubigné). 1635-1719. Mistress and second wife of Louis XIV. Born on the Island of Martinique. Married the poet Scarron (1652). Left in poverty at his death (1660). Favored by Mme. de Montespan. Entrusted with the education of her children (1669). She became a favorite of Louis XIV. After the death of Queen Marie Thérèse (1683), Louis married her (1685). She exerted a strong religious influence over Louis. She favored the revocation of the Edict of Nantes (q.v.). On the death of Louis (1715), she retired to a convent.

Maistre, Comte Joseph Marie de. 1753-1821. French philosopher, statesman, and man of letters. He emigrated from France at the time of the Revolution. He was opposed to the Revolution and all its works. He was a staunch defender of the authority of the pope.

Majestätsbrief (Letter of Majesty). 1609. Emperor Rudolf II granted religious liberty to Bohemia with this decree.

"Major Domus." The head official of the Frankish kings. Sometimes called "Mayor of the Palace." He performed duties which one associates with a modern prime minister. It was from this position that Pippin the Short (q.v.) promoted himself to be king of the Franks.

Malthus, Thomas Robert. 1766-1834. English clergyman and economist. He aroused controversy by his argument in *An Essay on the Principles of Population* (1798) that population tends to increase unchecked in geometric ratio while means of subsistence increase in an arithmetical ratio. Hence, population must be held in check by overcrowding, disease, vice, war, famine. In a second essay (1803) he disregarded the mathematical ratios and recognized the existence of moral restraint as a positive check. He remained pessimistic concerning the future potentialities of mankind.

Manchester Massacre. See Peterloo Massacre.

Mandate system. Begun in 1919. A system set up by Article 22 of the Covenant of the League of Nations for the administration of the former German colonies and the non-Turkish portions of the Ottoman Empire. These territories were divided among the Allied powers at the end of World War I. By this system, the Allied powers shared sovereignty over the mandates with the League of Nations. The mandates fell into three classes. Class A consisted of Iraq, Syria, Palestine, the Lebanon, and Transjordan. It was believed that these countries could soon achieve independence. Today, they are all independent. Class B mandates included the Cameroons, Tanganyika, and Ruanda. It was thought that considerable time would elapse before these countries could be self-governing. Class C consisted of Southwest Africa, German Samoa, New Guinea, and many islands in the Pacific. In these mandates, self-government is more remote than in the Class B group.

With the creation of the UN, the mandates became Trust Colonies, and are administered by the Trusteeship Council of the UN. Mandates formerly under Japan are now administered by the United States.

Manin, Daniele. 1804-57. Italian patriot. Active as liberal leader in Venice (1831 ff.). President of the Venetian Republic of St. Mark (1848-49). One of the heroes of the Risorgimento (q.v.).

Maniu, Iuliu. 1873-. Romanian politician, head of the Peasant Party. Premier (1928-30, 1932-33), he endeavored to introduce liberal reform. He opposed both King Carol and the Iron Guard dictatorship (q.v.). When the communists came into power (1946) he was denounced as a reactionary, tried for treason, and (1947) imprisoned for life.

Mann, Thomas. 1875-. German novelist. He moved to the United States in the 1930's to escape Hitlerism. He is a naturalized United States citizen. Winner of the Nobel Prize in Literature in 1929. Author of *The Magic Mountain, Buddenbrooks, Joseph in Egypt,* etc.

Mannerheim, Baron Carl Gustav Emil. 1867-1951. Finnish field marshal. He rose to the rank of general in the Russian army. From January to May, 1918, he led the victorious anti-revolutionary Finnish armies. In 1919 he was regent of Finland. He emerged from retirement in 1931 to head Finland's defense council. He commanded Finland's troops in the war against Russia (1939-40; 1941-44). In 1944 he became president of Finland, but resigned in 1946. The Mannerheim Line, a line of defenses against Russia, was planned by him. It was captured and destroyed (1940) by the Russians.

Manorial system. The method of organizing rural society which was in vogue in western Europe during the Middle Ages. Although the word "manor" comes from the French *manoir,* which, in turn, is derived from the Latin *manere* (to live), we are by no means sure where or how the manorial system originated. Some claim that the manor was the descendant of the ancient German mark, which was a community of free people who held land in common. With the passing of time, these marks gradually became subject to a master or "lord," and the free village sank to the status of a quasi-servile community. Others think that the manor was evolved from the *villa* of the Roman Empire. Whatever its origin, the manor performed vital economic, political, and social functions during the Middle Ages, particularly during those years when cities were in eclipse.

(1) Economic. The manor was an almost completely self-sufficient economic unit. On the typical manor there were seven different divisions of the land: (1) The lord's demesne (domain), which was cultivated by special serfs and villagers; (2) the lord's close, which was rented to free peasants; (3) the shares of the villagers, which were scattered in strips through several tillable fields; (4) grazing land; (5) communal wood-lot; (6) waste land; (7) land of the village priest. This division was supplemented by a further two-fold division: (1) Land of the lord which was held in "villeinage" by peasants; (2) land cultivated for the sole use of the lord.

Cultivation of manorial land was surrounded by all sorts of local customs and observances. In general, it was customary to cultivate 2/3 of the land in any given year and to allow the other third to lie fallow.

(2) Political. The lord of the manor usually was the judge and law-enforcement officer of the manor. He also had the responsibility of organizing the defense of the manor from all marauders.

(3) Social. Residents of a manor, except for the lord and his family, rarely traveled beyond its bounds. The entire social life of the community had to be organized around the village church and various local festivals. This routine was interrupted only when traveling players or minstrels visited the manor, or when a fair was held in a nearby community.

Manors persisted in England until the 14th century. The Black Death in England (1348-49) was a great blow to the manorial system. It led to the Peasants' Revolt (q.v.) (1381) (also called Wat Tyler's Rebellion, q.v.). By the end of the 15th century, English manors were no longer farmed by quasi-servile men but by hired laborers, freeholders, leaseholders, and copyholders. On the continent, the manorial system died more slowly. It took the French Revolution (1789) to bring it to an end.

Mansard (or Mansart), François. 1598-1666. French architect. His works include several churches and public buildings in Paris and several châteaux. He is usually credited with inventing the mansard roof. His grandnephew, Jules Hardouin-Mansard (1646-1708), was the building superintendent and architect for Louis XIV. He was ordered by the king to complete the Palace at Versailles, begun by Le Vau. His other works include the Grand Trianon, the dome of the Hôtel des Invalides, and the Place Vendôme.

Mantegna, Andrea. 1430-1506. Italian Renaissance painter. Born in Vicenza. He settled (1460) in Mantua and resided there for most of the remainder of his life. His nine tempera pictures, *Triumph of Caesar*, were produced in Mantua. He also was an engraver, sculptor, architect, and poet. He did not aim at grace and beauty in his pictures. His technical excellence greatly influenced Italian art.

Manutius, Aldus (*Latin form of* Aldo Teobaldo Manucci). 1450-1515. Italian printer and classical scholar. Founder of the Aldine press. He was the first to use italic type.

Marat, Jean Paul. 1743-93. Born in Switzerland, he became an active French revolutionary. A doctor of medicine, he was honored with an honorary degree by St. Andrew's University, Scotland. He edited the revolutionary newspaper, *L'Ami du Peuple* (1789). Member of the National Convention (1792). He was attacked by the Girondists and arrested, but was acquitted (April 24, 1793). He joined the Jacobins in overthrowing the Girondists (q.v.). He was murdered by Charlotte Corday (July 13, 1793) (q.v.).

"March on Rome." 1922. At the Fascist National Congress in Naples in Oct. 1922, Mussolini delivered a threatening speech in which he specifically invoked force as a justifiable method of getting control of the government of Italy. Following this speech he entrained for Milan. His followers began to concentrate on Rome. Although the army might have scattered them, King Victor Emmanuel refused to invoke martial law. Instead he asked Premier Facta to resign. On Oct. 29, the king asked Mussolini to form a cabinet. On Oct. 30, the new cabinet took office. Of the 15 portfolios, only 4 were held by Fascists. But no Socialists were appointed to the ministry. Mussolini consolidated his position *after* he was appointed to the premiership.

Marconi, Guglielmo, Marchese. 1874-1937. Italian engineer. The inventor of a system of wireless telegraphy. Winner of the Nobel Prize (1909). Senator of Italy (1914). President of the Italian Royal Academy (1930).

Marengo, Battle of. June 14, 1800. A great victory (but by a narrow margin) of Napoleon over the Austrians in north Italy. Because of this success and the successes of General Moreau in Bavaria, the way was opened for the Treaty of Luneville (q.v.).

Margaret of Parma. 1522-86. Natural daughter of Charles V. Regent of the Netherlands (1559-67). She secured the recall of the unpopular Cardinal Granvelle (q.v.), head of the council of state. She favored the national party of the Netherlands; but after the outbreak of violence, she turned against the leaders (Egmont, q.v.; Horn, q.v.; William the Silent, q.v.). When in 1567 the Duke of Alva (q.v.) arrived at Brussels to suppress the rebellion by force, she resigned as regent. She possessed great ability and firmness. Her departure from the Netherlands was generally regretted.

Maria Theresa. 1717-80. Archduchess of Austria; queen of Hungary and Bohemia. Married (1736) Francis Stephen, Duke of Lorraine (later Francis I, Holy Roman Emperor). Since her father, Charles VI, had no male heir, he induced his nobles to sign the Pragmatic Sanction (q.v.) (1740) by which she succeeded to the Hapsburg dominions. She was attacked by France, Spain, and Prussia in the War of the Austrian Succession (1740-48). She negotiated an alliance with France, which brought on the Seven Years' War (1756-63). After the death of her husband (1765), she shared the imperial throne with her son, Joseph II. She joined Prussia and Russia in dividing up Poland.

Marie Antoinette (*called in contempt* "The Austrian Woman" *and* "Madame Deficit"). 1755-93. Daughter of Emperor Francis I and Maria Theresa of Austria. Born in Vienna. Married (1770) the future Louis XVI of France. Queen of France (1774-92). Because of her love of luxury and extravagance and her indifference to the conditions in France, she did much to precipitate the Revolution. Consigned with the king and the royal children to the Tuileries as prisoners (1793), she was later tried by the Revolutionary Tribunal, found guilty of treason, and guillotined (Oct. 16, 1793).

Marlborough, John Churchill, 1st Duke of. 1650-1722. Great English military commander. His greatest exploits occurred in the Low Countries during the War of the Spanish Succession (1701-13) (q.v.). Because his wife, the former Sarah Jennings (1660-1744), was intimate with Queen Anne, he was virtual ruler of England during most of Anne's reign (1702-1714).

Marlowe, Christopher. 1564-93. English dramatist. Marlowe was the greatest of Shakespeare's predecessors in the English drama. Among his works are *Tamburlaine the Great*, *The Tragical History of Dr. Faustus*, and *The Jew of Malta*.

Marne, First Battle of. Sept. 6-10, 1914. One of the major battles of the First World War. In this great engagement the French, under Marshal Joseph Joffre, stopped the German advance into France and converted the war from a war of movement to trench warfare. The French were reinforced by troops released from duty on the southern frontier following Italy's declaration of neutrality and by a few thousand soldiers who were sent from Paris to the front in commandeered taxicabs. The Germans were weakened by the dispatch of troops from the Marne to East Prussia, which was being overrun by the Russians. These troops, incidentally, were not needed on the Eastern Front, and did not arrive in time to be of any assistance. This error on the part of the German General Staff, plus its departure from the Schlieffen Plan (see World War I), contributed much to the success of the French.

Marranos (or Conversos). Spanish Jews who were converted to Christianity during the 15th and 16th centuries.

Marseillaise. A song composed by Rouget de Lisle at Strassburg for the French soldiers. It was first heard in Paris when a detail of 400 volunteers from Marseilles arrived in Paris at the outset of war in 1792 and sang the song as they marched through the city. The Marseillaise became the Revolutionary anthem of France, and eventually became the French national anthem.

Marshall Plan, The. In an address delivered at Harvard University in June, 1947, General Marshall (at that time Secretary of State) proposed a plan of economic aid for Europe. At a conference held in Paris the following July, 22 nations, including the USSR, discussed Marshall's proposals. Despite the active opposition of the Soviets, the conference accepted Marshall's proposals and appointed a Committee on European Economic Cooperation (CEEC). This Committee prepared a balance sheet, estimating Europe's needs for the next four years. Congress created an Economic Cooperation Administration (ECA) to administer the program. The nations participating formed an Organization for European Economic Cooperation (OEEC). During more than four years of existence, the Marshall Plan countries received about 11 billion dollars in aid from the United States. Great Britain, France, Belgium, Luxemburg, Holland, Italy, and Western Germany were the largest beneficiaries. The plan succeeded in promoting economic recovery. In 1952 the overall industrial index was 40% higher than in 1938 and the agricultural index 9% higher.

Marston Moor, Battle of. July 2, 1644. The bloodiest battle of the English Civil War. It was a decisive victory for the Parliamentary army and enhanced the reputation of Cromwell.

Martel, Charles. See Charles Martel.

Martin, Pierre Emile. 1824-1915. French engineer. Inventor of an open-hearth process of making steel.

Marx, Karl. 1818-83. German political philosopher. Born in Treves, Prussia. Educated at Bonn and Berlin. Much influenced by Hegel. Editor of the *Rheinische Zeitung* at Cologne (1842) which was suppressed (1843). He lived in exile in Paris and Brussels. Returned to Cologne (1848), but was expelled (1849). He settled in London and devoted himself to the philosophical development of the theory of socialism and to agitation for the spread of socialism. He proposed a plan for an International Workingmen's Association (London, Sept. 28, 1864). He helped Liebknecht found the Social Democratic Party in Germany (1869). His great work is *Das Kapital* (3 vols. 1867, 1885, 1895). He collaborated with Friedrich Engels in publishing the *Communist Manifesto* (1848). He is the founder of modern socialism. He was one of the world's great economic theoreticians. He was one of the great figures of the 19th century and a world force. To this very day the recognized principles of socialism, those that inspire fear in its opponents and hope in its adherents, are Marxian.

Mary I. 1516-58. Queen of England (1553-58). Daughter of Henry VIII and his first wife, Catherine of Aragon. She was well educated, a good linguist, and very devout. Upon the divorce of her mother, her troubles began. Henry forced her to sign a declaration that her mother's marriage had been unlawful. Upon the death of her half-brother, Edward VI (1553), she became queen, following the suppression of the short usurpation of Lady Jane Grey (q.v.). Her reign was marked by severe religious persecutions, for she was determined to restore the Catholic religion. Hence, she was called "Bloody Mary." Ridley, Latimer, and Cranmer were some of her prominent victims. She married her cousin, Philip of Spain. This marriage brought her sorrow, since Philip was unfaithful. She bore him no son. He involved England in a European war in which England lost

Calais (see Cateau-Cambrésis, Treaty of), its last possession on the continent.

Mary II. 1662-94. Queen of England, Scotland, and Ireland (1689-94). The eldest child of James II and Anne Hyde, she married William of Nassau, stadholder of Holland. She and her husband were invited by English nobles to replace her father, James II, in 1688. Following the "Glorious Revolution" (1688) (q.v.), she and her husband were crowned rulers of England, Scotland, and Ireland.

Mary, Queen of Scots. 1542-87. Only surviving child of James V of Scotland. Daughter by his second wife, Mary of Guise. Next heir to the English throne (through her grandmother, Margaret Tudor, James IV's queen) after the children of Henry VIII. Became queen of Scotland when she was six days old. She was brought up in France and (1558) married Francis (crowned Francis II of France in 1559. He died in 1560). She returned to Scotland (1561) where she was distrusted for her Catholic religion and her seeming frivolity. She married (1565) her cousin Henry Stewart, Lord Darnley, a Catholic, and gave him the title of king. She bore him a son (1566), who later became James VI of Scotland and James I of England. She connived in the murder of Darnley and then married the Earl of Bothwell. This marriage provoked the Scottish nobles to rebellion, and, defeated by the Earl of Moray at Langside (1568), she abdicated, fled to England, and threw herself on the mercy of Elizabeth I. In England she was held prisoner the rest of her life. Because she was implicated in several Catholic plots against Elizabeth, she was beheaded.

Masaccio (*real name* **Tommaso Guidi**). 1402-29. Florentine painter who broke with the past and has been called the "Father of Modern Art." All that remains of his work are the frescoes in the Brancacci chapel in Florence.

Masaryk, Thomas Garrigue. 1850-1937. Czech statesman. Born in Hodonin, Moravia. While in exile during World War I, he organized the Czechoslovak Independence movement. He was president of Czechoslovakia (1918-35). His son Jan (1886-1948) was a diplomat. He returned from exile after World War II and became Foreign Minister. He committed suicide (or was murdered) after the communist coup.

Matisse, Henri. 1869-. French post-impressionist painter. Among his paintings which are in American collections are *Interior with Violin Case, Girl in Green,* and *Three Sisters.*

Matteotti, Giacomo. 1885-1924. Italian socialist politician. Member of the Italian legislature. His murder (June 10, 1924) by the Fascisti nearly led to the fall of Mussolini. However, by clever manipulation, Mussolini managed affairs to emerge stronger than ever.

Matthias. 1557-1619. Holy Roman Emperor (1612-19). Younger son of Maximilian II. Governor of Austria (1593). Declared head of the House of Hapsburg after a revolt of Hungarian Protestants (1606). Chosen emperor to succeed his brother Rudolf (1612). Failed in his efforts to reconcile his Protestant and Catholic subjects. An uprising against him in Prague (1618) began the Thirty Years' War.

Maurice (*known* as Maurice of Nassau). 1567-1625. Son of William the Silent. Stadholder of the Dutch Republic (1587-1625). Great military leader. He worked with John Barneveldt until 1609. Thereafter, Barneveldt was Maurice's enemy because of a religious quarrel. (See Remonstrants.) Maurice ordered Barneveldt executed in 1619.

Maurois, André (*original name* Émile Herzog). 1885-. French biographer and novelist. His first great success was *Ariel,* a biography of Shelley. He followed this with biographies of Byron, Disraeli, Chateaubriand, Washington, and others. He is the author of *Proust: Portrait of a Genius.*

Maximilian (*in full* Ferdinand Maximilian Joseph). 1832-1867. Arch-duke of Austria. Brother of Emperor Francis Joseph (q.v.). Emperor of Mexico (1864-67). Viceroy of Lombardo-Venetia (1857-59). After the French had conquered Mexico (q.v.), he accepted the throne of the country (Apr. 10, 1864). The United States refused to recognize him and demanded (Feb. 12, 1866) that France withdraw its army from Mexico. When France complied, the Mexicans, led by Juárez, forced Maximilian to surrender (May 15, 1867). He was condemned by a court-martial and shot (June 19, 1867).

Maximilian the Great. 1573-1651. Duke of Bavaria (1597-1651). Elector of Bavaria (1623-51). Educated by Jesuits, he was an active opponent of Protestants. He organized and headed the Catholic League (1609) (q.v.). He fought throughout the Thirty Years' War (q.v.) on the imperial side as an ally of emperors Ferdinand II and Ferdinand III.

May Laws. See Kulturkampf.

Mayfield. A gathering or diet of the great nobles of medieval Germany to confer with their king upon matters of policy.

Mayor of the Palace. See Major Domus.

Mazarin, Jules (*born* Giulio Mazarini). 1602-61. French cardinal and statesman. Born at Pescina in Abruzzi. Educated by Jesuits at Rome and at Alcalá, Spain. He executed several diplomatic missions for Pope Urban VIII (1629-34). Nuncio to France (1634-36).

He entered the service of Richelieu and became a naturalized Frenchman (1639). Cardinal (1641). Succeeded Richelieu as prime minister (1642). Retained by the Regent, Anne of Austria (1643-61), until Louis XIV was of age (1661). He followed Richelieu's foreign policy regarding the Thirty Years' War. Crushed the Fronde (1648-53), thus destroying the power of the feudal nobles. He greatly strengthened the position of France in Europe and paved the way for the greatness of Louis XIV. He amassed a fortune. He founded a great library, the Bibliothèque Mazarin.

Mazepa, Ivan Stepanovich. 1640?-1709. Cossack leader. He was brought up in the Polish court. Discovered intriguing with a lady of the court, he was, at the command of the lady's husband, tied to the back of a wild Ukrainian horse, which galloped off to its native haunts, where Mazepa was rescued. This incident is the subject of a poem *Mazeppa* by Byron. Elected hetman (1687). He sought independence for the Ukraine. He allied with Charles XII of Sweden. They were defeated by the Russians at Poltava (q.v.) (1709). Mazepa fled to Turkey, where he died.

Mazzini, Giuseppe. 1805-72. Italian patriot. Born in Genoa. Associated with the democratic movement in Italy. Joined the Carbonari (1830). Organized the secret revolutionary society *Young Italy* (1832). During the revolution of 1848, he organized a republic in Rome (1849). He went into exile when the republic was overthrown. Aided Garibaldi (1860; 1862; 1867). Refused to accept the monarchical government of Italy. Remained a republican until his death. His magic voice aroused Italian youth as nothing else had ever done before. His real contribution was in awakening the Italian people to patriotic enthusiasm without which Italian unification could never have been accomplished.

McAdam, John. 1756-1836. British engineer. Born in Ayr, Scotland. General surveyor of roads in England (1827). He introduced improved roads built of crushed stone, known as "macadamized" roads.

Medici. Italian family, famous and powerful in Florence and Tuscany, especially from the 14th to the 16th centuries. The founder was Giovanni di Medici (1360-1429), a Florentine banker who was a strong supporter of the smaller guilds and the common people. He was the virtual ruler of Florence (1421-29). His two sons, Cosimo and Lorenzo, founded the two great branches of the family.

(1) *Elder Branch.* Cosimo (1389-1464), banker, patron of the arts, ruler of Florence. He welcomed to his palace Greek refugee scholars who were driven from Constantinople when it was captured by the Turks (1453). His son, Piero (1414-69), ruled Florence from 1464 to 1469. Lorenzo (1449-92), known as *Lorenzo the Magnificent,* eldest son of Piero, was a statesman and patron of the arts and letters. He ruled Florence jointly with his brother Giuliano (from 1469). After the murder of Giuliano (1478), he ruled alone (1478-92). Lorenzo's sons: Pietro (1471-1503), ruled Florence two years. He was driven out (1494) by Savonarola (q.v.). Giovanni (1475-1521) became Pope Leo X (q.v.).

The last of this line was Alessandro (1510-37). He was the first duke of Florence (1531-37) under Emperor Charles V.

(2) *Younger Branch.* Lorenzo ("the Elder"). 1395-1440. He confined himself to banking. Cosimo I (1519-74) ("Cosimo the Great"), duke of Florence (1537-74). The last of the Medici, Giovan Gastone (1671-1737) was driven out of Tuscany when it was annexed by Austria in 1737.

Médicis, Catherine de. 1519-89. Daughter of Lorenzo di Medici of Florence. Married (1533) Henry, the future Henry II of France. Three of her four sons became kings of France—Francis II, Charles IX, and Henry III. She exerted a profound influence over her sons. She stirred up the wars between Catholics and Huguenots and planned the Massacre of St. Bartholomew's Day (1572).

Meistersingers. Guilds of musicians which were organized in medieval Germany. They attempted to continue the traditions of the minnesingers (q.v.).

Melanchthon (Philipp Schwarzert). 1497-1560. German religious reformer. He collaborated with Luther in the Protestant Reformation. Professor of Greek at Wittenberg (1518) and of theology (1526). He drafted the Augsburg Confession (1530), thus making an important contribution to the Protestant Reformation.

Melbourne. See Lamb, William.

Mendel, Gregor Johann. 1822-84. Austrian botanist. An Augustinian monk; later abbot at Brünn (1843). In his experiments in breeding peas in the monastery gardens he observed certain laws of inheritance which have since been called *Mendel's Laws.*

Mendeleyeff, Dmitri. 1834-1907. Russian chemist. Professor of chemistry at St. Petersburg from 1866. He worked out a periodic table of the elements. A chart of this periodic table hangs today in every chemistry classroom in the world. During his tenure as chemistry professor, he trained a whole generation of chemists, many of whom became outstanding.

Mendelssohn, Felix. 1809-47. German composer. He toured as a pianist and conductor in England and on the Continent. He became musical director in Düsseldorf in 1833. He became director of the famous Gewandhaus concerts in Leipzig in 1835. He was the cofounder and director of the Leipzig Conservatory. His compositions include five symphonies, overtures, compositions for the piano, dramatic works, oratorios, chamber music, etc.

Mendelssohn, Moses. 1729-1786. German Jewish philosopher. Often called "the German Socrates." Grandfather of Felix Mendelssohn (q.v.). His friendship with Lessing (q.v.) inspired the latter's *Nathan der Weise.* Helped found and contributed to Nicolai's *Bibliotek.* Author of *Philosophische Gespräche* (1755), *Phädon* (in support of the immortality of the soul, 1767), etc.

Mendoza, Cardinal Pedro Gonzales de. 1428-95. Spanish prelate, statesman, soldier. Made cardinal (1473). Aided Isabella to secure the Spanish throne. Occupied Granada in the name of Ferdinand and Isabella (Jan. 2, 1492).

Merchant Adventurers. An English association engaged in trade, particularly with the Far East. Granted a patent by Henry VII, the association was incorporated in 1564. There was no common pool of actual capital. But the ships of the members were sent out together.

Merovingian kings. A dynasty of kings of the Franks from Clodion (428-448) to Childeric III, who was dethroned in 751 by Pippin, the first of the Carolingian rulers. The family was descended from Merovens, a traditional chief of the Salian Franks. After the death of Clovis (511), the first Merovingian of importance, the family often ruled two or more kingdoms at the same time. The scattered possessions were united under Clotaire (584-628) and Dagobert I (628-639). After 639, the power of the Merovingian kings declined, the real ruler being the mayor of the palace. Hence these kings were called "Do Nothing Kings" (Rois Fainéants).

Mersen, Treaty of. 870. Ludwig the German and Charles the Bald divided the kingdom of Lotharingia between them in this treaty (see Verdun, Treaty of). Ludwig received all the territory east of the Meuse, containing Utrecht, Nijmegen, Aachen, Cologne, Trier, and Strassburg. Charles received all territory west of the Meuse and all of Burgundy.

Mesta. A great Spanish sheep-herding combine which, in the days of Philip II (1556-98), won the support of the crown at the expense of other kinds of agriculture. The activities of the *Mesta* contributed heavily to the economic decline of Spain.

Metaxas, John. 1871-1941. Greek general and statesman. Chief of staff (1915-17), but exiled as pro-German when Greece joined the Allies. He returned from exile (1920), led a counter-revolution, and was again exiled (1923-24). He was a royalist. After the king was restored (1935), he became premier (1936). He was later (1936) named dictator and (1938) dictator for life. He was directing Greek resistance to the Italian invasion when he died.

Métayer system. A method of share-cropping. Under this system the peasant paid rent with a share of the crop. This system became common in southern Europe upon the disintegration of the manorial system (after the 14th century).

Metchnikoff, Ilya. 1845-1916. Russian bacteriologist. He discovered the function of the white cells in the blood.

Methuen, Treaty of. Dec. 27, 1703. An agreement between England and Portugal, negotiated by Lord Methuen, British ambassador to Portugal. By the agreement, English textiles were to be admitted freely into Portugal. Portuguese wines were to be admitted into England at one-third of the duty charged to French wines. The treaty resulted in a rapid domination of Portuguese trade by the British. It made Portugal virtually a vassal of England. Portugal constituted for England a great naval base, and could be used for a flank attack upon countries to the east.

Metric System. Inaugurated in France by the National Convention (1792-95), this system of uniform weights and measures, based on decimal calculation, has become standard in many countries of the world.

Metternich, Prince Klemens Wenzel Neponink Lothar von. 1773-1859. Austrian statesman and diplomat. Born at Coblenz where his father was an Austrian diplomat. In his youth he witnessed certain acts of the French revolutionaries, and thus developed a life-long aversion to reform. Austrian envoy to Saxony (1801-03); ambassador to Berlin (1803-05); ambassador to Paris (1806-09); Austrian minister of foreign affairs (1809-48). His influence brought about the marriage of Napoleon and Marie Louise (1810). By diplomacy and deceit he kept Austria out of the war between France and Russia (1812). He joined with Russia against France (1813). Made an hereditary prince of the Austrian Empire (1813). He was at the height of his power at the Congress of Vienna (1814-15). His policies restored stability in Europe and crushed liberal movements (1815-30). Although the revolution of 1830 weakened his position somewhat, he did not resign until forced to do so by a Vienna mob (1848). He lived in retirement in England, Belgium, and Vienna.

Metternich System. A system of repression, planned by Prince Metternich, to stamp out liberal movements. It featured secret police, informers, censorship of the press and stage, and control of education. It set the tone for all of Europe in the period 1815-30. It inspired conservative measures such as the Carlsbad Decrees of Germany (1819), the Six Acts of England (1819), and the July Ordinances of France (1830).

Michelangelo (*full name* **Michelangelo Buonarroti**). 1475-1564. Famous Italian sculptor, painter, and architect. Apprenticed to the painter Ghirlandajo, he soon caught the eye of Lorenzo the Magnificent (Medici). Lorenzo took the boy to live in his palace, gave him a seat at his own table, and set him to studying the antiques which he had collected. From this time on, Michelangelo was self-taught. In 1496, Michelangelo journeyed to Rome. Until his death, he lived partly in Rome, partly in Florence. His best-known pieces of sculpture are: *David, Pieta,* a number of *Madonnas* in relief, *Moses, The Bound Slaves,* the *Medici Tombs.* His frescoes adorn the ceiling of the Sistine Chapel. On the back wall of the same chapel is his fresco of *The Last Judgment.* He was the architect of St. Peter's.

Middle Ages. The millennium between 500 and 1500 A.D. By common consent, 476 is accepted as the end of Ancient Times and the beginning of the Middle Ages. Probably few contemporaries saw an end of the Roman Empire in the West when Romulus Augustulus gave up his imperial crown (476). Yet that act and its subsequent consequences marks the end of a great epoch in history.

The end of the Middle Ages cannot be associated with one comparable event. In 1469, Giovanni Andrea of Aleria spoke of writings of the "middle period." In 1518 the Swiss scholar Vadian used the phrase "middle ages" (*medias aetas*). In 1604 the German historian Goldast used a similar expression. To a Russian, the Middle Ages ended in 1462, when Ivan III (the Great) became Czar. He is regarded as the first national sovereign of Russia. Many date the end of the Middle Ages in 1453, when the Ottoman Turks captured Constantinople. Others have a preference for 1492, the year of the discovery of America. Still others make a good case for 1517, the year when the Protestant Reformation began. Certainly, between 1450 and 1550 a fundamental change in living took place, which marks the end of one epoch and the beginning of a new one.

Milan Decree. Dec. 17, 1807. This decree reinforced the Berlin Decree (q.v.) against British trade. Napoleon now closed the entire European coastline to the British.

Military-monastic Orders. During the Crusades, the Knights of St. John were organized (1099) to care for the sick and wounded. In 1119 the Knights Templars were organized in imitation of the Knights of St. John. Both were composed of men who took the vows of monks, but spent all of their time in fighting. They were monks and soldiers. Both orders became wealthy and degenerated rapidly. They soon quarreled with each other. Between 1307 and 1314, Philip IV of France abolished the Knights Templars. The Knights of St. John remained in the eastern Mediterranean. They held many of the islands, including Rhodes and Malta, and did good service in checking the aggression of the Turks. In 1190, during the siege of Ptolemais, a hospital was established for Germans by some of the merchants of Lübeck and Bremen. The members of this hospital formed an order called *Equites Teutonici Hospitalis Sanctae Mariae Virginis.* They could not get a foothold in the East and in 1226 went to Prussia, upon invitation, to fight the heathen there. In 1202 the Bishop of Riga founded the Sword Brothers (*Fratres Militiae Christi sive Gladiferi*). The two Teutonic orders united in 1237 and vigorously worked to expand Germanism and Christianity east of the Vistula until they declined rapidly in the 15th century.

Military Service, Compulsory. Compulsory military service for all able-bodied male citizens was first introduced in Prussia in 1862 at the behest of King William I. This policy proved to be such a huge success in effecting the political unification of Germany that other countries felt bound to imitate it. Austria-Hungary adopted universal military service in 1868; France, in 1872; Japan, in 1873; Russia, in 1874; Italy, in 1875.

Millenary Petition, The. 1603. A petition handed to James I of England by Puritan clergymen. Said to have been signed by 1,000 clergymen, it was actually assented to by only 800. It petitioned the king to "purify" the Anglican Church and to abolish certain abuses, such as pluralities (holding of many church offices in one hand).

Millerand, Alexandre. 1859 - 1943. French statesman. Born in Paris. He studied law, edited socialist papers, and was Minister of Commerce (1899-1902), of Public Works (1909-10), of War (1912-13, 1914-15), Commissioner General of Alsace-Lorraine (1919), Premier (1920), President of the Republic (1920-24).

Milton, John. 1608-74. English poet. He published *L'Allegro, Il Penseroso, Comus,* and *Lycidas* between 1632 and 1637. He took an active part as a propagandist for the Roundhead cause during the Civil War (1642-46). *Areopagitica,* a prose work, belongs to this period. He was an official of the government during the Commonwealth. Before the Restoration (1660), he had become blind. Between 1660 and his death he wrote his most sublime poetry: *Paradise Lost, Paradise Regained,* and *Samson Agonistes.*

Mindszenty, Joseph. 1892-. Hungarian prelate. As bishop of Veszprem during World War II, he maintained such a strong anti-German attitude that he was imprisoned. In 1945 he was made archbishop of Eszterzom and prelate of Hun-

gary. He was made cardinal in 1946. In 1948 he was arrested on the charge of treason by the Communist government, which he strongly opposed. After a sensational trial, during which he pleaded guilty to most of the charges, he was sentenced to life imprisonment.

Mines Act, English. 1842. This law prohibited the underground labor of children under 10 years of age and of women.

Ministry of Public Education in Czarist Russia. Created in 1802, it divided the country into six educational districts. The program was completed by 1825, when Russia had 6 universities, 46 gymnasiums, and 337 schools. There were 5,000 students in the gymnasiums and 30,000 in the schools. The interest of the authorities was in secondary, not primary, education.

Minnesingers. Medieval German troubadours. The themes of their songs were usually service to one's lady, to one's liege lord, and to God.

Mirabeau, Honoré Gabriel Victor Riqueti, Comte de. 1749-91. French orator and revolutionary leader. Born near Nemours. He joined a cavalry regiment (1767) and was imprisoned several times for intrigues and wild conduct (1774-80). He lived in England and Germany most of the time between 1784 and 1788. He was elected by the Third Estate to represent Aix and Marseilles in the Estates-General (1789). Here he assumed a position of leadership. Until his death he had great influence in the National Assembly and with Louis XVI. He was a strong believer in constitutional monarchy.

Mise of Lewes. 1264. In the civil war between Henry III of England (q.v.) and Simon de Montfort (q.v.), the royal forces were defeated at Lewes. The king was forced to sign the Mise (agreement) in which he promised to uphold the Magna Carta (q.v.) and the Provisions of Oxford (q.v.).

Missi Dominici. Royal messengers sent out by Charlemagne (q.v.) to inspect his dominions. They were sent in pairs, one clergyman and one layman. They examined the conduct of officials and clergy and heard appeals. They inspected the army, the collection of taxes, the condition of churches and schools, the morals of the clergy, and the administration of justice.

Missions, Foreign. The desire to convert heathen people to Christianity has been a striking characteristic of the Christian Church in all ages. St. Paul carried the gospel to Asia Minor and Greece in the 1st century. St. Patrick Christianized Ireland in the 4th century. St. Boniface worked with the Germans in the 8th century and St. Methodius was a pioneer missionary among the Slavs in the 9th century. Franciscan friars entered China in the 13th century. St. Francis Xavier converted thousands in India and Japan in the 16th century. Missionary motives were partly responsible for the Commercial Revolution. The Congregation of the Propagation, organized by Pope Gregory XV in 1622, sent many missionaries to the New World.

Until the 19th century, Protestant sects took only a small part in carrying the gospel to the heathen. The Society for the Propagation of the Gospel in New England (1649), the Society for the Propagation of the Gospel in Foreign Parts (1701), and the work of the Moravians (1731-32) foreshadowed an era of Protestant missions.

Just at the close of the 18th century, a new interest in foreign missions gripped European Protestant churches. William Carey organized the Baptist Society for Propagating the Gospel among the Heathen (1792). The London Missionary Society was organized by Presbyterians and Congregationalists (1795). The Anglican Church Missionary Society was founded in 1799. Thereafter, many missionary societies were organized. This movement was most important in fostering an interest in imperialism. For many devout Christians, who might otherwise have frowned upon foreign conquests, became enthusiastic when they considered that the annexation of a part of Africa or the Far East or the South Seas might result in the propagation of the faith.

Mississippi Bubble. 1718-20. A plan to relieve the financial distress of France. Its proponent was a Scotch financier, John Law. A company to develop Louisiana was organized. Speculation in the stock of this company led to a rise in the value of the stock, inflation (made worse by paper money), and a sudden collapse. This boom, like many other examples of speculative mania, left behind it some positive achievements: increased shipping, some colonization of Louisiana, and private fortunes for those who sold out in time. Law's scheme and the contemporary South Sea Bubble of England mark the beginning of modern speculative finance.

Model Parliament. 1295. Called by Edward I of England. It represented all classes of men. In 1332, the clergy, together with the temporal peers, united into the House of Lords, while the knights of the shire and the representatives of the cities and boroughs united to form the House of Commons.

Mohacs, Battle of. Aug. 29-30, 1526. In this battle the Turks defeated King Louis of Hungary and his 20,000 ill-disciplined knights and peasants. Louis was killed on the field of battle. A greater part of Hungary now fell under the control of the Turks. At a second battle of Mohacs (Aug. 12, 1687) the Turks were defeated by Charles of Lorraine and driven permanently from Hungary.

Mohammed II. "The Conqueror." 1430-81. Sultan of Turkey (1451-81). He captured Constantinople (1453). He subdued Serbia (1456-58), conquered Trebizond, Greece, Crimea, and Albania. He waged a great war with Venice (1463-79) and unsuccessfully besieged Rhodes.

Mohammedans, Impact of on Europe. The impact of Mohammedans upon Europe is divided into four phases:

1. 632-1096. During this period the Mohammedans made great conquests. They threatened Europe repeatedly, but were repulsed at Constantinople (711) and Tours (732). In Italy the Normans broke their power. The struggle between Mohammedans and Christians was principally commercial and political. Religious interests were in the background. Christian pilgrims, travelers, and merchants were rarely disturbed.

2. 1096-1270. This is the period of the great Crusades. Christians were motivated by a religious zeal to secure the holy places. As the Crusades continued, many of the Christian leaders were influenced more by the desire to secure lands than by religious zeal.

3. 1270-1683. Once again the Mohammedans were on the march. Although they lost ground in Spain, they captured the Byzantine Empire and pushed up the Danube valley to the walls of Vienna.

4. 1683-. The power of the Mohammedans in Europe gradually waned. The past hundred years has seen it diminish to almost nothing.

Molasses Act. 1763. By this law, the English Parliament levied heavy taxes on rum, molasses, and sugar imported from the French, Dutch, and Spanish West Indies into the English colonies in North America. The enforcement of this act would have ruined colonial trade. Fortunately it remained a dead letter until 1763.

Moldavian Republic. See Bessarabia, Annexation of.

Molière (real name Jean Baptiste Poquelin). 1622-1673. French actor and playwright. Born in Paris. He formed his own company and performed in Paris and the provinces (from 1643). He gained the patronage of Louis XIV (1658) and his company became known as the King's Comedians. Author of *Les Précieuses Ridicules* (1659), *École des Maris* (1661), *Le Misanthrope* (1666), *Le Médecin Malgré Lui* (1666), *Tartufe* (1669), etc.

Molotov, Vyacheslav Mikhailovich. 1890-. Russian statesman. A communist from his early youth, he changed his name from Skriabin to Molotov to escape the imperial police. After the Bolshevist Revolution, he rose rapidly in the ranks of the party. He was Chairman of the Council of the Peoples' Commissars (that is, premier of the USSR) from 1930 to 1941, when the position was taken over by Stalin. Molotov then became vice chairman. In May, 1939, he succeeded Litvinov as commissar of foreign affairs (later changed to foreign minister), a post which he held until 1949. During this period he had charge of some of the most fateful negotiations in recent Russian history: the non-aggression pact with Nazi Germany (1939), creation of the UN (1945), the various war-time conferences, etc. Since the death of Stalin (1953), he has been one of the major forces in Russia.

Moltke, Count Helmuth von. 1800-91. Prussian soldier. Chief of staff (1858-88). Directed the strategy in wars against Denmark (1864), Austria (1866), and France (1870-71). Created field marshal (1871). One of the great military heroes of Germany. Considered the father of the German army.

Monasticism. Living a life of religious seclusion. The philosophical basis of monasticism is neither Jewish nor Christian. According to Jewish belief, God created man for society, and therefore there is nothing contaminating in it. Jesus himself was no ascetic. Nor did He hesitate to mingle with people, even with the outcasts of society. He taught that sin is in nothing that is external to man, but has its seat in the heart. He made no fixed rules of conduct.

Monasticism probably began during the 3rd century. When the Church was made popular by the action of Constantine, many who really were not Christians, but were pagans at heart, entered the Church. With the advent of these new Christians, many of the really religious sought to escape from the Church to avoid contamination.

The earliest monks were hermits, who lived alone. The hermit movement began in Egypt and spread to Syria. This form of asceticism was never popular in western Europe because the climate was too cold during many months of the year.

Soon communities of hermits began to appear. From these communities of cenobites there evolved the monastic organization. The first monastery of western Europe was organized in the 4th century on the Isle of Lérins, near Cannes. When St. Benedict organized the famous monastery at Monte Cassino near Naples in 528, the monastic movement became a definite part of the life of Europe.

The Cluniac reforms (q.v.) of the 10th century greatly stimulated the movement, leading to the formation of such orders as the Carthusians (1084), Cistercians (1098), Premonstrants (1120), and the Carmelites (1156).

Monasticism furnished the missionaries who Christianized western and northern Europe. Monasteries were centers of learning. Monks cleared and cultivated lands and taught by example the dignity of labor in an age which exalted the warrior. They preserved and transmitted the civilization of Rome to the Barbarians. They copied and wrote books. Monas-

teries were the hotels of the Middle Ages. Monks cared for the poor and sick. They were the greatest builders of the Middle Ages.

Unfortunately, monasticism has its dark side also. There are many periods of decadence in its history. The principles of monasticism are opposed to the dignity of the family and to the proper position of women in society. During the Middle Ages, the best human talent was frequently drawn into the monastery and thus lost to the state.

Monet, Claude. 1840-1926. French painter. A landscape artist. One of the greatest impressionists.

Mongol *or* Tartar invasion of Russia. It began in 1223. The Mongols were led by Generals Djebe and Subutai. After defeating the Prince of Kiev, the Mongols turned back and did not reappear for 15 years, when they conquered great areas of European Russia.

Mongolian influence upon Russia. The Mongolian state was based upon the principle of unquestioning submission of the individual to a group; first the clan, then the state. The power of the ruler was absolute and autocratic; submission to it was unqualified. The prince was the sole owner of the land, and all other persons had tenure and use of it temporarily. Russians borrowed these concepts as well as methods of taxation, census, postal system, and organization of the army.

Montagu, Charles. See National Debt of England and Bank of England.

Montagu, Lady Mary Wortley. 1689-1762. During her early married life she lived in London and was an intimate friend of Addison, Pope, and others. Between 1716 and 1718 her husband was the British ambassador at Constantinople. From there Lady Mary wrote her famous

Letters. She learned in Constantinople a method of inoculation for smallpox. She introduced this method into England.

Montaigne, Michel Eyquem de. 1533-92. French essayist. Born at the Château de Montaigne in Perigord. A courtier (1561-63) at the court of Charles IX. In 1571, his two elder brothers being dead, Montaigne retired to his estate, where he resided until his death. His fame rests upon his *Essais,* which reflect the spirit of skepticism and which were inspired by his study of Latin (he spoke no other language until he was six). Both in style and thought, the Essays exerted an important influence upon French and English literature.

Montespan, Marquise de (Françoise Rochechouart). 1641-1707. Mistress of Louis XIV (1667-1685). She was replaced in the king's affections by Mme. de Maintenon.

Monteverdi, Claudio. 1567-1643. Italian composer. Born in Cremona. From 1613 he was *maestro di capella* at St. Mark's, Venice. He composed operas, sacred music, etc. He substituted the harmonic for the polyphonic style of composition.

Montfort, Simon de, Earl of Leicester. 1208-65. Brother-in-law of Henry III, king of England. He led a successful movement in opposition to the king and set up a parliament (1265) in which the boroughs were represented. When he was deserted by some of his followers, he was defeated and killed in battle.

Montgomery, Bernard Law, 1st Viscount Montgomery of Alamein. 1887-. British field marshal. He entered the army in 1908 and rose in rank through long service. In the Second World War he commanded the 3rd Division in France until the evacuation at Dunkirk.

In 1942 he was sent to Egypt, where at El Alamein he decisively defeated the Germans under Rommel, one of the turning points of the war. He led his victorious 8th Army across northern Africa in pursuit of the Germans. He led the Anglo-American invasion of Sicily and Italy. In the Allied invasion of Normandy (1944) he was commander of all ground forces until August, when he was made commander of the 21st Army Group. He headed the British occupation of Germany (1945-46). He was made field marshal (1944) and viscount (1946). He was chief of the imperial general staff (1946-49) when he was made commander-in-chief of the permanent defense of Britain, France, Belgium, Holland, and Luxemburg.

Montreux Straits Convention. July, 1936. The Turkish government appealed to the signatories of the Lausanne Treaty for permission to fortify the Straits (Bosporus and/or Dardanelles). The Montreux Convention (Italy not signing) permitted the refortification of the Straits. In time of peace the Straits were to be open to all commercial ships and to a limited tonnage of war vessels. In war, Turkey might close the Straits to belligerents unless these were acting under League authority.

Montrose, James Graham, 1st Marquis and 5th Earl of. 1612-50. Often called "The Great Marquis." He played an active part on the side of Charles I during the English Civil War (1642-46). At one time he was complete master of Scotland. When he endeavored to avenge the death of the king, he was defeated, captured, and executed by order of Parliament.

More, Sir Thomas. 1478-1535. English statesman and author. In 1516 he wrote *Utopia,* a satire which exposes the evils of contemporary England. After the fall of Wolsey (1529), he was made lord chancellor of England, the first layman to hold the office. He refused to take the oath renouncing the jurisdiction of anyone but the king over the Church. For this refusal he was beheaded.

Moreau, Jean Victor. 1763-1813. "Jacobin general" of France. He commanded the army of the Rhine and Moselle (1796) and drove the Austrians back to the Danube. Again he commanded the army of the Rhine (1800) and won a brilliant victory at Hohenlinden. He headed a conspiracy against Napoleon, but was exposed and exiled. He lived in Trenton, N. J. (1805-13). He entered the Russian service and was mortally wounded at the battle of Dresden (1813).

Morgarten, Battle of. 1315. In this engagement the Swiss Confederates soundly defeated the forces of Louis of Hapsburg. From this time onward modern Switzerland began to emerge as an independent country.

Moriscos, Expulsion of from Spain. 1609-10. The Moriscos were Christianized Moors in Spain. Alarmed at the great increase in the number of Moriscos (they married early, did not become monks, did not emigrate to America), the Duke of Lerma, prime minister of Spain for Philip III, ordered them to leave the country lest they aid a foreign invader. As they controlled the commerce, agriculture, and mechanical arts of southern Spain, their expulsion resulted in a severe economic loss.

Morton's Fork. 1487. So called after its inventor, Thomas Morton, chancellor under Henry VII. It was a form of royal extortion upon the wealthy. Persons who lived magnificently were compelled to pay huge sums on the grounds of their manifest wealth. Those who lived plainly were subject to similar extortions on the ground of their supposed savings.

Moscicki, Ignacz. 1867-1946. President of Poland (1926-39). Chemist in Switzerland (1897 ff.), teacher in a technical high school in Lvov (1912-26).

Mountain, The. Radical faction of the Jacobin Club of the French Revolution. They were given the name "Mountain" because they occupied seats high in the gallery of the Convention. They advocated direct and radical reform measures by direct and immediate popular action.

Mountbatten, Louis Francis Albert Victor Nicholas, 1st Earl Mountbatten of Burma. 1900-. British admiral and statesman. His mother was the granddaughter of Queen Victoria. He served as a midshipman during the First World War. In the Second World War he was in the destroyer service, director (1942-43) of combined operations, head of the Southeast Asia Command (1943-45). He was the last viceroy of India (1947). As governor-general of the dominion of India (1947-48) he relinquished British power to native rule (June, 1948).

Moussorgsky, Modest. 1835-81. Russian composer. His most notable work was the opera *Boris Godunov*, based on Pushkin's play of the same name. He also composed orchestral works and songs. His incomplete *Khovanshchina* was finished by Rimsky-Korsakov.

Mozart, Wolfgang Amadeus (real name Johannes Chrysostomus Wolfgangus Theophilus). 1756-1791. Composer. Perhaps the most gifted all-around composer who has ever lived. Born in Salzburg, where his father, Leopold (1719-87), was *Kapellmeister* to the archbishop. A child prodigy, he was taken on tour with his sister Maria Anna (Nannerl) (1751-1829), also a gifted musician, at the age of six. In 1781 he made his home in Vienna. He married (1782) Constance Weber (1763-1842), a soprano. In Vienna Mozart lived in poverty, despite the fact that he was "*Kammer-Musicus*" to Emperor Joseph II. This position carried only a small salary, and Mozart and his wife were extravagant. He died in 1791, shortly after completing a *Requiem* Mass. Mozart wrote 624 compositions. Operas: *Marriage of Figaro* (1786), *Don Giovanni* (1787), *Cosi Fan Tutti* (1790), *The Magic Flute* (1791), and several others. Symphonies: of the 41 symphonies, three hold eminence—C major, G minor, and E flat. In addition to these works, Mozart composed music for most instruments and for many different combinations of instruments. His complete works were indexed (1862-64) by Ludwig Köchel (1800-77).

Mudros, Armistice of. Oct. 30, 1918. This agreement between Turkey and the Allies took Turkey out of World War I. The Turks were forced to open the Straits, repatriate Allied prisoners, demobilize their armies, sever relations with the Central Powers, and permit Allied troops to cross Turkish territory.

Mun, Thomas. 1571-1641. English writer on economics. He wrote on the theory of balance of trade. He defended the export of gold and silver. He attacked the mercantile theory. Author of *England's Treasure by Forraign Trade.*

Münchengrätz Agreement. See Nicholas I.

Munich Conference and Agreement. (The Munich Pact.) Sept. 29, 1938. A critical state of affairs between Germany and Czechoslovakia developed during 1938. After the annexation of Austria, the situation of Czechoslovakia became precarious. Konrad Henlein and his Sudeten Germans kept up continual agitation. On Sept. 12, at Nuremberg, Hitler demanded that the Sudeten Germans be given the right of self-determination. This address was a signal for wide-spread dis-

orders in the Sudeten Land. On Sept. 15, Neville Chamberlain flew to Berchtesgaden to confer with Hitler, who bluntly stated his demand for annexation of the German areas on the basis of self-determination. Hitler threatened war if this demand were denied. England and France now persuaded Czechoslovakia to agree to the demand. Chamberlain now visited Hitler in Godesberg (Sept. 22-23), where Hitler increased his demands, calling for the surrender of predominantly German lands at once. There followed (Sept. 24-29) a period of acute international crisis. Hitler finally agreed to one more conference, after being strongly urged to do so by Mussolini and President F. D. Roosevelt. At Munich (Sept. 29), Hitler, Ribbentrop, Mussolini, Ciano, Chamberlain, and Daladier (Premier of France), arrived at the following decisions: Evacuation of all areas of Czechoslovakia which were German between Oct. 1 and Oct. 10. England and France undertook to guarantee the new frontiers of Czechoslovakia against aggression. When the Polish and Hungarian minority questions were solved, Germany and Italy would give a like guarantee. On Sept. 30, the Czech government signed the agreement.

Municipal Government Act, British. 1835. An English law which abolished the oligarchic town corporations and which allowed all rate-payers to vote for aldermen and the mayor. This bill was forced through Parliament over the stubborn opposition of the House of Lords.

Münster, Treaty of. Jan. 30, 1648. In this treaty Spain renounced all claim to the United Provinces of Holland and acknowledged their sovereignty. This treaty was part of the negotiations which concluded the Thirty Years' War (see Westphalia, Peace of).

Murillo, Bartolomé Esteban. 1617-82. Spanish painter of the Andalusian school.

Known especially as a colorist, particularly as a master of color contrast.

Mussolini, Benito. 1883-1945. Italian statesman. Born near Forli. After self-imposed exile in Switzerland, he returned to Italy and became editor of the socialist paper *Avanti*. During World War I he broke with Socialism and advocated entering the war on the side of the Allies. After serving in the war, he founded *Il Popolo d'Italia* and organized the Fascist Party. In 1922, his black-shirted followers marched on Rome, and Mussolini was made Premier of Italy. He quickly consolidated his position to that of dictator (Il Duce). He formed a concordat with the Vatican (1929). (See Lateran Accord.) Later he joined with Hitler to create the Axis. He helped Franco in Spain (1936-39). He conquered and annexed Ethiopia (1936) and Albania (1939). He entered the Second World War on the side of Germany at a favorable moment (1940). But in 1943, he was compelled to resign. He was arrested, but was rescued by German paratroopers.

On Aug. 28, 1945, he was captured by Italian partisans at Dongo on Lake Como, and, after a drum-head court trial, was shot. His corpse, hanging head down, was exposed to ridicule in Milan.

Mustafa Kemal Atatürk. 1880-1938. Turkish general and statesman. Born in Salonika. General in the First World War. He was the chief founder and director of the Turkish Republic, and was its first president (1923-35). He set up a program of "Westernization." Within 15 years his rule changed Turkey profoundly, even in the minutest aspects of its life.

Mutual Security Program. The Mutual Security Program is a plan devised by the United States to assist friendly nations and to strengthen the defenses of the free world. It is divided into three channels: military aid, economic aid, and Point Four. There is a Director for Mutual Security who coordinates the entire program. Military aid is administered by the Department of Defense. Point Four is administered by the State Department.

N

Nantes, Edict of. See Edict of Nantes.

Napier, John. 1550-1617. Scotch mathematician who invented logarithms.

Napoleon I. Napoleon Bonaparte (*known as* **Napoleone Buonaparte** *until* **1796**). 1769-1821. For parentage and immediate family: see Bonaparte. He attended military schools in Brienne (1779-84) and Paris (1784-5). Second lieutenant of artillery (1785-91). He took some part in French revolutionary action in Paris, Corsica, and Marseilles in 1792. His name is first mentioned in connection with a successful artillery action that led to the capture of Toulon (1793). General of brigade (1793). A Jacobin (1793). Imprisoned briefly after the downfall of Robespierre (1794). Placed in defense of the Tuileries, he treated the mob to a "whiff of grapeshot" (1795). Commander of the Army of the Interior (1795). Married Josephine de Beauharnais (1796). He fought the very successful Italian campaign (1796-7) and secured the favorable treaty of Campo Formio (1797) from Austria. He conducted a campaign in Egypt and Syria (1798). His success was made impossible by Nelson's victory in the battle of the Nile (Aug. 1-2, 1798) in which the French fleet was destroyed. Napoleon abandoned his army and hastened to Paris where, helped by Sieyès and his brother Lucien, he overthrew the Directory (Nov. 9, 1799) and set up the Consulate with himself as first consul. He defeated the continental powers of the Second Coalition and made peace with them at Lunéville (1801) (q.v.). This was followed by peace with England at Amiens (1802) (q.v.). He now turned his attention to internal affairs in France, constructing many public works, codifying the laws, stabilizing finances, reconstructing the educational system, and making peace with the papacy (see Concordat between France and the papacy). He attempted several colonial ventures by securing Louisiana from Spain and conquering Haiti. When he failed in the latter attempt, he sold Louisiana to the United States (1803). He was crowned emperor (Dec. 2, 1804) and assumed the title of king of Italy (1805).

Empire (1805-09). A third coalition was formed against him. He contemplated the invasion of England, but gave up the project after Nelson defeated and destroyed the French and Spanish fleets at Trafalgar (Oct. 21, 1805). Instead, he turned against Austria, and at Austerlitz (Dec. 2, 1805) crushed the armies of Austria and Russia. By the treaty of Pressburg he forced the coalition to dissolve. On Aug. 6, 1806, he dissolved the Holy Roman Empire. He made his brothers Joseph and Louis the kings of Naples and Holland respectively. A fourth coalition (England, Sweden, Prussia, and Russia) was now formed to oppose him. He crushed the Prussians at Jena and Auerstädt (1806) and occupied Berlin. He defeated the Russians at Friedland (1807) and concluded the Treaty of Tilsit with the Czar and the King of Prussia (1807), ending the coalition. He began a commercial war against England (Continental System) (q.v.) with the Berlin Decree (1806). To enforce the Continental System his armies invaded Portugal and Spain. The royal family of Portugal fled to Brazil. The king of Spain was deposed (1808) and his brother Joseph was made king (brother-in-law Murat succeeded Joseph as king of Naples). However, the Spaniards resisted this move vigorously, thus starting the Peninsular War (1808-14). A fifth coalition (England and Austria) was formed (1809). Napoleon defeated the Austrians under Archduke Charles Louis at Wagram (1809) and forced upon Austria the humiliating Treaty of Schönbrunn (q.v.). He created the Kingdom of Westphalia for his brother Jerome. He enlarged France by annexing Holland, the Papal States, etc. He divorced Josephine (1809).

Empire (1810-14). He married Archduchess Maria Louisa of Austria (1810). They had one son, Napoleon II (1811-32). Napoleon invaded Russia (1812) with a great army. He entered Moscow (Sept. 14). But the city caught fire and Napoleon was forced to retreat. In retreat his army suffered terribly. A sixth coalition attacked him in 1813 and, after defeating him at Leipzig (q.v.), forced him to retreat to France. After a brilliant but futile defensive campaign, he was forced to abdicate (April 11, 1814). He was exiled to Elba.

Career (1815-21). He returned from Elba and entered Paris (March 20, 1815). Now began a period known as the Hundred Days. This ended with the defeat of Napoleon at Waterloo (June 18). Napoleon abdicated a second time (June 22) and surrendered to the British on board the *Bellerophon* (July 15). He was taken to St. Helena (Oct. 16, 1815) as a prisoner until his death (May 5, 1821). His remains were removed (1840) to the Hôtel des Invalides in Paris.

Napoleon II (L'Aiglon). 1811-32. Son of Napoleon I and Maria Louisa, Napoleon's second wife. Given the title of King of Rome while he was still in his cradle, he was reared at the Austrian Court after his father was exiled. He was treated as an Austrian prince and was given the title of Duke of Reichstadt.

Napoleon III (*known as* Louis Napoleon. *Full name* Charles Louis Napoleon Bonaparte). 1808-73. Son of Louis Bonaparte, King of Holland, and Hortense de Beauharnais (Josephine's daughter). Nephew of Napoleon I. Born in Paris. Emperor of the French (1852-71). Lived in exile in Germany and Switzerland (1815-30). Acquired "liberal" ideas. Upon the death of Napoleon II (1832), he assumed leadership of the Bonaparte family. Twice plotted unsuccessfully (1836 and 1840) to seize control of France. Elected president of the Second Republic (Dec. 10, 1848), he staged a *coup d'état* (Dec. 2, 1851) and made himself dictator. He proclaimed himself emperor (Dec. 2, 1852). Married (Jan. 29, 1853) Eugénie de Montijo, a Spanish countess (q.v.). He was very successful in promoting prosperity at home. But his foreign wars (Austro-Sardinian, 1859 [q.v.]; invasion of Mexico, 1862-67; Franco-Prussian, 1870-71 [q.v.]) proved disastrous. Captured by the Germans at Sedan (Sept. 2, 1870), he was held as a prisoner near Kassel until the end of the war. He was deposed by the National Assembly (March 1, 1871). He died in England in exile. His only son, Eugène Louis Jean Joseph Napoleon (1856-79), joined an English expedition against the Zulus in South Africa and was killed in ambush (June 1, 1879).

Narses. 478?-573. General under Justinian I. A eunuch. In command in Italy (548-52) after the recall of Belisarius. He defeated the last of the Ostrogoths (553). He brought Italy again under Justinian's control by subduing the Franks and the Alemanni (555). Exarch of Italy (554-67).

Narva, Battle of. 1700. The Russians under Peter the Great were defeated here by the Swedes under Charles XII. As a result of this victory, Charles was able to overrun Poland and depose the king, Augustus II. (See also Great Northern War.)

Naseby, Battle of. June 14, 1645. This was the culminating defeat of the Cavalier army in the English Civil War. King Charles I managed to escape from the field of battle. Although he eluded capture for more than a year, his cause was doomed.

National Assembly of France. The present law-making body of the Fourth Republic. There have been many National Assemblies in French history. For the famous National Assembly of the Revolution, see French Revolution.

National Convention (France). 1792-95. The National Convention remained in continuous session for three years. Its work constituted the second phase of the French Revolution. In the main, it dealt with six major problems: (1) What to do with the deposed and imprisoned king? It solved this problem by executing Louis XVI and constituting a republican form of government, based on democratic principles. (2) It organized national defense by creating a citizen-army. With this army it turned back foreign invasion. (3) It suppressed insurrection in France. (4) It provided a strong government for France. (5) It completed and consolidated the reforms of the earlier phase of the Revolution. (6) It framed a new constitution to establish a republican form of government.

National Debt of England, Beginnings of. 1693. Under the guidance of Charles Montagu (1665-1715), created Baron and later Earl of Halifax, the English government for the first time borrowed one million pounds from its subjects. The purpose of the measure was to secure for the use of the government some of the surplus capital that was being wasted in futile speculations.

National Guard of France. See French Revolution.

National Insurance Act, English. 1911. This bill contained two main provisions. (1) Each worker should pay 2½ d. per week, to which the employer and the government would add, as insurance against unemployment. In the event of unemployment, the worker would receive 6 s. or 7 s. a week. This provision applied only to the engineering and building trades. (2) Workers were compelled to insure against sickness. Each wage-earner had to pay from 1 d. to 4 d. each week. The employer added 3 d. and the state 2 d. to this fund. In return, workmen were to receive free medical attention, free treatment in hospitals, and weekly sick allowances. These laws were greatly expanded by the Labor Ministry after 1945.

"National Ministry" of Britain. 1931-1945. Organized on Aug. 24, 1931, it contained members of the three major parties of Britain. Its purpose was to solve the economic distress of the country and later the critical international situation which followed it immediately on a coalition, rather than on a partisan, basis. Shortly after the formation of this ministry, the Labor Party expelled MacDonald, Snowden, and Thomas for "desertion."

The National Ministry was headed by MacDonald (1931-35), Baldwin (1935-37), Neville Chamberlain (1937-40), and Churchill (1940-45). It was supplanted in 1945 by the Labor Ministry.

National Socialist German Workers' Party (Nazi). A German party which Hitler joined in 1919 and which he later led. This party envisioned a "Third Reich," a Greater Germany wherein all should be united because of their pure German blood. The party called for the repudiation of the Treaties of Versailles and St. Germain, refutation of war guilt, revision of all reparations, reacquisition of colonies, expulsion of all persons not of German blood, governmental assurance of employment, abolition of unearned income and high interest, nationalization of trusts and department stores, and parity with other great powers in armaments. Although this program was later much modified, the catchwords of the movement remained anti-Semitism and anti-Bolshevism. The chief pillar of the Hitler movement was the white-collar section of the middle class. Army officers, anti-Semites, professionals, small business men, farmers, and college students also gave the party much support. Many large industrialists, notably Fritz Thyssen, were Hitlerites. Labor and some of the strong Catholic districts gave Hitler small support. The party eventually secured control of the government (1933) and destroyed the Weimar Republic.

Navigation Act. Oct. 1651. This law was the first in a series aimed by the English against the Dutch maritime supremacy. It provided that no goods could be imported into England from Asia, Africa or America except in English or colonial ships, or from any European country except in English ships or those of the country that produced the goods.

Nazi. See National Socialist Workers' Party.

Nazi-Soviet Pact. Aug. 23, 1939. Acting through Foreign Ministers von Ribbentrop and Molotov, Germany and the Soviet Union signed a non-aggression pact. This agreement, effective at once and for 10 years, provided that neither state would wage war upon the other. Neither would support a third power in case it attacked either signatory. They would consult each other in the future on all matters of common interest. They would refrain from associating with any grouping of powers aimed at the other. By a secret agreement (first made public in 1948), they divided eastern Europe into German and Soviet spheres. This pact freed Hitler to attack western Europe. It was a monumental reversal of Hitler's anti-Russian policy.

Necker, Jacques. 1732-1804. French financier and statesman. Born in Geneva. Apprenticed to a Paris banking house (1747-62). Set up his own banking house (1762) and gained a fortune during the Seven Years' War (1756-63) (q.v.). Became minister of finance (1776-81) and introduced some reforms. He prepared the *Compte Rendu* (1781) (q.v.). Dismissed for his Protestantism and insistence on financial retrenchment. Recalled (1788). He now became the virtual premier of France. His second dismissal (not effective) precipitated the storming of the Bastille (July 14, 1789). Resigned (Sept. 1790) and retired to Geneva. His wife Suzanne (*nee* Curchod) (1739-94) was a talented author and famous hostess. Their daughter was Madame de Staël.

Nelson, Horatio. Viscount Nelson. 1758-1805. British naval hero. He saw his first active service in the West Indies (1780). He served under Hood in the taking of Bastia and Calvi (where he lost the sight of his right eye). He met (1793) Emma Hamilton, wife of the British ambassador at the Court of Naples. He fell in love with her. The two formed a liaison which only death severed. Appointed commodore (1796). Joined with Jarvis in the great victory over the Spanish at Cape St. Vincent (1797). Rear admiral (1797). In the futile attempt to take Santa Cruz de Tenerife (1797), he lost his right arm. Defeated the French fleet at Aboukir Bay (Battle of the Nile) (1798). Vice-admiral (1801). Second in command in the attack on Copenhagen (1801). Created viscount (1801). In command of the Mediterranean (1803) where he blockaded Toulon for two years. In the battle of Trafalgar (1805) he was killed. Trafalgar was his greatest victory. It established English seapower as supreme for the next 125 years. Nelson is Britain's greatest naval hero.

NEP (New Economic Policy). Soviet Union—1921-27. A strategic retreat from socialism towards capitalism made necessary by the chaotic conditions following the inception of the Revolution and the Civil War. It substituted taxation for levy in kind. It permitted peasants to sell surplus food directly to consumers and permitted small-scale industry. Limited foreign investment was allowed. Forced labor was abolished.

Nepotism. Favoritism toward nephews or other relatives. The practice of nepotism by the higher clergy of the Catholic Church was one of the causes of the Protestant Reformation and the Catholic Counter-Reformation.

Nesselrode, Count Karl Robert. 1780-1862. Russian statesman. He took part in the Congress of Vienna (1814-15) (q.v.). Russian minister of foreign affairs (1816); vice-chancellor (1829); chancellor (1844); concluded the treaty which ended the Crimean War (1856) (q.v.).

Neuilly, Treaty of. Nov. 27, 1919. An agreement between Bulgaria and the Allies at the end of World War I. Bulgaria was deprived of its only outlet on the Aegean Sea. Bulgaria recognized the in-

dependence of Yugoslavia. It agreed to pay reparations of 445 million dollars. Its army was reduced to 20,000 men.

Neustria. Medieval kingdom of the Franks during the reign of the Merovingians (q.v.). It corresponded in area to modern France.

Nevsky, Alexander. d. 1263. A prince of Moscow who opposed the rule of the Mongolians and stopped the advance of the Swedes, Germans, and Lithuanians into the northwest territories of the Russians. He was canonized by the Russian Church.

New Model. An army created by Parliament during the English Civil War (1642-46). It was to be regularly paid by taxes assessed upon those parts of the country which suffered least from the war.

Newcomen, Thomas. 1663-1729. An English blacksmith who invented the atmospheric steam engine (1705). In connection with Thomas Savery (1698), he invented a steam engine which was used to pump water from coal mines.

Newman, John Henry, Cardinal. 1801-90. English theologian. Leader in the Oxford movement (q.v.) and later Roman Catholic cardinal. Upon graduation from Oxford he was elected a fellow (1822) and tutor (1826-32). He was vicar of the university church (1828-43). He wrote *Lead, Kindly Light* (1833). He contributed to *Tracts for the Times* (from 1833). He became a Roman Catholic (1845) and was ordained priest in Rome (1846). Rector of Dublin Catholic University (1854-58). Created cardinal (1879). Among his many writings are *The Idea of a University Defined* (1873) and *Apologia pro Vita Sua* (1864).

Newspapers, Origin of. It was the custom in the Roman Empire to post official bulletins of news, known as *acta diurna* (daily events). Copies of these bulletins were made and distributed. In 16th century Venice, official bulletins, *gazetti* (from the Greek, *gaza*—treasury, that is, of news) were posted. News letters, written by hand, were often passed from hand to hand. In Italy such a letter was called a *coranto;* in France, a *courant.* After the invention of printing, pamphlets were often circulated. During the English Puritan Revolution, as many as 40,000 pamphlets were published. Perhaps the earliest newspapers were the *Frankfurter Journal* in 1615, the Antwerp *Niewe Tijdinghen* (New Tidings) in 1616, the London *Weekly News* (1622). In Sweden, the Stockholm *Ordinarie Post-Tidene* (Ordinary Post News) started publication in 1643. In 1702 began the St. Petersburg *Viedomosti* (Gazette). The *Diario di Roma* appeared in 1716. The first Spanish newspaper was the *Gaceta de Madrid* (1726). These papers were all small in size and contained little recent news. They all contained poems and essays and many advertisements of remedies and nostrums.

Newton, Sir Isaac. 1641-1727. Great English scientist and mathematician who discovered the law of gravitation, the theory of fluxions or differential calculus, and the compound nature of white light. His abiding masterpiece is the *Principia,* published in 1687.

Nibelungenlied. Medieval German epic poems which have been immortalized in the operas of Richard Wagner. First put in writing during the 12th century, these epics tell of the tragic relations of Siegfried and Brünnhilde, characters from early German mythology. The setting of the plot is in the days of the invasions of the Huns. It is constructed around the destruction of the kingdom of Burgundy (q.v.) by the Huns in 437 and the death of Attila in 453.

Nicholas I, Saint (*sometimes called* **Nicholas the Great). 800?-867.** Pope (858-867). A strong pope. He attempted to overrule the patriarch of Constantinople in his quarrel with the Byzantine emperor. This interference, plus the "filioque" controversy (q.v.), widened the chasm between the Greek and the Latin Churches. He upheld the right of bishops to appeal to Rome. He supported the pseudo-Isidorian decretals (q.v.) (865).

Nicholas II (*name* **Gerard of Burgundy). 980?-1061.** Pope (1059-61). He was much under the influence of Hildebrand (see Gregory VII). He established regulations for electing popes by the college of cardinals, regulations which are still followed.

Nicholas I. 1796-1855. Czar of Russia (1825-55), succeeding his brother Alexander I. He was much more primitive by nature than his elder brother, with more limited interests and not the slightest shade of liberalism. His political wisdom consisted in imposing strict discipline in military and civil matters.

Domestic policies: Nicholas ordered the first codification of Russian laws. This work was done by Speransky, who had been exiled to Siberia by Alexander I in 1812, but was returned to favor 13 years later. The work, *The Complete Collection of Russian Laws,* was published in 1832. Nicholas took severe measures to limit serfdom. He stabilized the currency. He suppressed liberalism by censoring the press, controlling the universities, and organizing the "Third Division" of the Imperial chancellory to suppress political unrest.

Foreign policies: Nicholas supported the Greek War for independence, thus involving Russia in the Russo-Turkish War of 1828-29, which concluded with the Treaty of Adrianople by which Russia secured control of the mouth of the Danube. This moderate treaty paved the way for the treaty of Unkiar-Skelessi (July 10,

1833), which placed Russia in the position of protector of Turkey and closed the Dardanelles to vessels of all countries except Russia and Turkey. The effect of this treaty was diminished by the Münchengrätz agreement with Austria in 1833 in which the Czar promised to preserve the unity of Turkey and agreed to the dismemberment of it only with the consent of Austria. When Poland revolted, following the French Revolution of 1830, the rebellion was suppressed, the Polish Constitution was abolished, and most of Poland was annexed to Russia. In 1848, when the Austrian Empire tottered because of a revolution, Russian troops quelled the Hungarian uprising and saved Austria. Following a quarrel between Russia and Turkey in 1853 regarding the rights of the Orthodox Church in Jerusalem, war broke out. This developed into the Crimean War (1854-56) (q.v.) in which French, English, Sardinian, and Turkish troops attacked Russia. The Treaty of Paris (1856) restored Sevastopol to Russia in exchange for Kars, forbade Russia to maintain a fleet on the Black Sea, closed the Dardanelles to warships of all nations, took from Russia southern Bessarabia, which was annexed to Moldavia to deprive Russia of access to the Danube, and deprived Russia exclusive protection of Orthodox pilgrims to the Holy Land.

Nicholas II. 1868-1918. Czar of Russia (1894-1917). Initiated the Hague Peace Conferences (1899, 1907). Completed the Trans-Siberian railway. Waged a losing war against Japan (1904-05). Compelled to grant a constitution (1905). Joined the Allies in World War I (1914). Compelled to abdicate (Mar. 15, 1917) because of failure of his domestic and foreign policies. Executed with his whole family by the Bolsheviks at Ekaterinburg (July, 1918).

Nihilism. 1861. A Russian philosophy fathered by Pisarev, who began writing

in 1861. It was practically the same thing as the 18th-century Enlightenment (see Age of Reason). Nihilists were proponents of westernization. They exalted reason, science, and materialism; they abhorred orthodoxy, faith, mysticism, and custom. They were said to believe in nothing (*nihil*), that is, nothing dear to the hearts of conservative Russians. Turgenev (q.v.) popularized the concept of nihilism in *Fathers and Sons*.

Nijmegen, Treaties of. 1678-79. Treaties which concluded the Dutch War (q.v.). (1) Holland received back its whole territory on condition of remaining neutral. (2) Spain ceded to France: Franche-Comté and Valenciennes, Cambray, Aire, Poperinger, St. Omer, Ypres, Condé, Bouchain, Mauberge, and several other towns. France ceded to Spain: Charleroi, Binche, Oudenarde, Ath, Courtray, Limburg, Ghent, Waes, and Puycerda. (3) The emperor ceded to France: Friedburg. The Duke of Lorraine was to be restored to his duchy, but on such terms that he refused to accept them.

Nika riots. See Greens and Blues.

Nile, Battle of. Aug. 1, 1798. In 1798, Napoleon invaded Egypt with the intention of founding a French empire in the East. On Aug. 1, the English Mediterranean fleet, commanded by Lord Nelson, destroyed the French fleet, which had convoyed Napoleon's army and was guarding it, at Aboukir Bay. Without a fleet to support him, Napoleon was forced to abandon his dream of an Oriental empire.

Nine-Power Treaty. See Washington Conference.

Ninety-five Theses of Martin Luther. Oct. 31, 1517. In 1517 a Dominican monk, Johann Tetzel, undertook to raise money for the elector of Mainz by selling indulgences. He drove a thriving trade, and eventually came to Wittenberg, a Saxon village on the Elbe River near Magdeburg. Martin Luther, a monk who was a professor in the University of Wittenberg, vehemently denounced the sale of indulgences. On Oct. 31, 1517, he nailed to the door of the castle church in Wittenberg ninety-five theses, which, according to medieval university custom, he was prepared to defend. In these theses Luther declared that an indulgence could remit only a penalty imposed by the Church. No indulgence could remit the guilt of a sin. Nor could it affect a soul in purgatory. A Christian who truly repented received forgiveness from God, and needed no indulgence.

The theses were written in Latin. They were soon copied, translated into German, and circulated over a wide area. This act of Luther's is considered as the beginning of the Reformation.

NKVD (People's Commissariat of Internal Affairs).
A secret police organization of the Soviet Union which, on July 10, 1934, replaced the OGPU (United Department of Political Police).

Nobel, Alfred Bernhard. 1833-1896.
Swedish manufacturer, inventor, and philanthropist. Born in Stockholm. Educated in St. Petersburg and the United States. He invented dynamite (1866); one of the first smokeless powders (1888); and over 100 patented items. He acquired wealth by manufacturing explosives in various parts of the world and through his interests in the Baku oil fields in Russia. He bequeathed a fund of $9,200,000 for the establishment of the Nobel Prizes, which were first awarded in 1901.

Nobel Prizes.
Upon his death (1896), Alfred Nobel (q.v.) left a fund from the interest of which annual prizes were to be awarded for the best work in the fields of physics, chemistry, physiology and medicine, and literature and towards the promotion of international peace. The judges are the Swedish Academy of Science, the Caroline Medico-Surgical Institute, the Swedish Academy, and five members elected by the Norwegian Storting (parliament). (At the time of Nobel's death, Norway and Sweden were united. The Norwegians have the duty of selecting the winners of the peace prize.) The awards are made in Stockholm on Dec. 10, the anniversary of Nobel's death. The first awards were made in 1901.

Nobili popolani.
A medieval Italian term used to describe a class of people who had noble aspirations because of their wealth. (The "fat people," as they were often called.) In Florence there were 21 guilds. Seven of these—notaries, cloth-makers, money-changers, wool-weavers, silk-weavers, physicians, and furriers—were classified as *nobili popolani*.

Nominated Parliament.
July-December, 1653. After the dissolution of the Rump Parliament, Cromwell wrote to the Congregational ministers of each county, asking them to nominate suitable persons to be members of Parliament. Thus was assembled the Nominated (also called Little, or Barebones) Parliament. It was made up of zealous reformers whose excellent ideas were too far in advance of the times. It was expelled from the Parliament buildings by soldiers under orders from Cromwell.

Non-Conformists.
The completion of the establishment of the Church of England materialized in 1563 with the adoption of the 39 Articles in place of the 42 Articles of Cranmer (q.v.). To these Articles there were numerous dissenters or non-conformists, chief of which were the following: (1) Puritans—a broad, inexact term applied to those who wished to "purify" the church; to revert to the simple, early-Christian ritual; to make the Church more Protestant. (2) Separatists—Puritans who left the Church completely to form a

church of their own. (3) Presbyterians—
Puritans who wished to substitute the organization of elders and synods for the
organization of bishops within the Church
of England. (4) Brownists—extreme leftist Puritans religiously, the nucleus of the
later Congregationalists or Independents.
Brownists and Roman Catholics could not
be brought under Elizabeth's policy of
toleration. They were persecuted along
with Unitarians (those who denied the
doctrine of the Trinity).

Non-Juring Clergy. See Civil Constitution for Clergy.

Norman Kingdom of Sicily. The Normans, led by the Guiscard brothers, captured Sicily from the Saracens (1071).
They set up a kingdom there which lasted
until Henry VI, Hohenstafen Holy Roman
Emperor, married Constance of Sicily
(1186), the heir to the kingdom. Henry
assumed the title of King of Sicily in
1194. His son, Frederick II (q.v.), made
Palermo the cultural capital of Europe.

Normandy, House of. A dynasty of
kings of England which was founded by
William the Conqueror. It contained the
following:

	Born	Ruled
William I		
the Conqueror	1027	1066-1087
William II the Rufus	1056	1087-1100
Henry I Beauclerc	1068	1100-1135
Stephen of Blois	1100	1135-1154

Normandy, Origin of. France had been
subject to raids by the Northmen (Normans) for half a century. In 911, the
French king, Charles the Simple, offered
a Norman leader, Rolf (Rollo), the lower
valley of the Seine and his daughter in
marriage if he would settle there, become
a Christian, and leave the rest of the
country in peace. Rolf agreed. He was
baptized and given the name Robert. His
domain was called Normandy. Under

Robert's leadership the raids of other
Northmen were beaten off.

Normans (Northmen). Scandinavians
who were forced by population pressure
to begin a series of raids upon other countries in the 8th century. They went to
England, Ireland, Spain, southern Italy,
Sicily, Novgorod, and Kiev. Their most
important settlement was in northeast
France, where they founded the Duchy
of Normandy. They seized this area in
the latter part of the 9th century. Their
occupancy was legalized by a treaty between Charles the Simple and the Norse
leader Rolf (Rollo) in 911.

North Atlantic Pact, The. In June,
1948, the United States Senate adopted
the Vandenberg Resolution, favoring
membership of the United States in a
regional scheme for defense, as allowed
under the UN Charter. Conversations
were then conducted with Canada, the
states which signed the Brussels Pact
(q.v.), Portugal, Italy, Iceland, Norway,
and Denmark. Sweden was invited to
participate in the discussions but refused,
because of its proximity to the Soviet
Union. After discussions, these countries
signed a mutual-defense agreement in
Washington (April 4, 1949). The treaty
was ratified by the Senate in July, 1949.
(See: NATO.)

**North Atlantic Treaty Organization
(NATO).** As a result of conferences
among the leaders of the Atlantic Community (U. S., Canada, Iceland, Norway,
Denmark, Holland, Great Britain, Belgium, Luxemburg, France, Portugal, and
Italy), a permanent North Atlantic Treaty
Organization was prepared, following the
Lisbon Conference (Feb. 1952). The
original membership was later increased
to 14 by the admission of Greece and
Turkey. West Germany is an associate
member. NATO consists of two divisions
—civilian and military. The civilian branch
consists of a Council of Foreign Minis-

ters, who meet frequently to determine policy. It is under the charge of a Secretary-General. The military branch is under the command of the Supreme Allied Commander in Europe (SACEUR). The first Secretary-General was Lord Ismay; the first SACEUR was General Eisenhower.

North Briton Review. See John Wilkes.

North, Frederick Lord. 1732-92. English statesman. As prime minister (1770-82) he was completely dominated by George III. His ruinous policy led to the revolt and loss of 13 American colonies.

North German Confederation. 1867. Following its triumph in the Austro-Prussian War (1866) (q.v.), Prussia invited the 21 German states north of the Main River to join with it in a confederation. This union was ruled by the king of Prussia as hereditary president, a federal chancellor, and a legislature consisting of a Bundesrat (federal council of representatives of the princes of the several states) and a Reichstag (a diet elected by universal manhood suffrage). The conduct of foreign affairs, the control of the army, and the declaration of defensive war were entrusted to the president. This confederation later became the political basis of the German Empire (1871).

Nuremberg Laws. See Anti-Semitism, Nazi.

Nuremberg, Religious Peace of. 1532. A treaty between Emperor Charles V and the Protestant League of Schmalkalden (q.v.). Lutherans were not to be harmed because of religion, nor were they required to restore confiscated church property. These terms did not apply to the

followers of Zwingli (q.v.) or to Anabaptists (q.v.). In return, the League was to furnish Charles with men and money. The peace, which lasted 14 years, permitted Protestantism to become solidly established.

Nuremberg Trials. According to agreements reached at Yalta (1945) and Potsdam (1945), various Nazi leaders were tried before a Four-Power International Military Tribunal. This court convened in Nuremberg in November, 1945. Twenty-two top Nazis were brought before this court. They were charged with being war criminals because (1) they had participated in a conspiracy to commit crimes against the peace and against humanity; (2) they had planned and executed a war of aggression; (3) they had violated the rules of warfare by mistreatment of civilians and prisoners of war; (4) they had murdered and enslaved people because of race, religion, or political belief. On Oct. 1946, the court condemned 12 to death by hanging; seven were sent to prison for terms of 10 years to life; and three were set free. Separate trials of lesser Nazis were held from time to time. All told, 1539 Nazis were convicted of various crimes; of these, 444 were sentenced to death.

Nystadt, Treaty of. Aug. 30, 1721. Between Sweden and Russia, ending the Great Northern War (q.v.). Sweden ceded to Russia: Livonia, Estonia, Ingermanland, part of Carelia, and a number of islands. Russia restored Finland to Sweden and paid 2 million rix dollars. This treaty ended a war in the Baltic area which produced these results: Sweden ceased to be a potent force in Baltic affairs. Russia emerged as a great European power.

O

Oates, Titus. See Popish Plot.

Obrenovich. Name of a Serbian dynasty founded by Prince Milos (1817). It ruled Serbia from 1817 to 1903, being interrupted (1842-58) by the rival Karageorgevich dynasty.

Occupation Statute. See German Federal Republic.

O'Connell, Daniel. 1775-1847. Irish national leader. Known as "The Liberator." Born in Cahirciveen, County Kerry. He united the Irish Catholics. Originated the Catholic Association (1823). Elected M.P. (1828); took his seat after the enactment of the Catholic Emancipation Act (1829). Lord mayor of Dublin (1841). Arrested for seditious conspiracy (1843) but released on writ of error by the House of Lords (1844). His power in Ireland was broken by dissensions, the Young Irish movement, and the distress from the potato famine (1845).

Odo, or Eudes. Count of Paris. King of France (888-898).

Oglethorpe, James Edward. 1696-1785. English reformer and philanthropist who, after investigating prison conditions (1729), projected a colony in America for debtors from English jails.

George II gave him a grant of land in America, which Oglethorpe named Georgia. The colony was founded in 1732.

OGPU (United Department of Political Police). Created in the Soviet Union in 1922 to replace the Cheka. Its original purpose was to supervise voting and administration of the country. It became a potent secret police force. It was replaced in 1934 by the NKVD (q.v.).

Ohm, Georg. 1787-1854. German physicist. He studied the nature of electric circuits and worked out the basic relationship now known as Ohm's Law, which states that the intensity of current in any circuit is equal to the electromotive force divided by the resistance of the circuit. From 1849 he was a professor at Munich.

Old Age Pensions, English. 1908. For years attempts had been made to abolish the unsavory workhouses for the aged which had been created by the New Poor Law of 1834 (q.v.). In 1908 the Liberal Parliament began the system of old-age pensions. Every person over 70 years of age whose annual income did not exceed $105 was granted a weekly pension of $1.25.

Old Poor Law, English. 1601. An English statute which provided that contributions for the poor were to be compulsory; habitations were to be furnished for the impotent and the aged; children of paupers were to be apprenticed; stocks of hemp and wool were to be provided for the employment of "sturdy idlers."

Old Regime. A social system that flourished in Europe prior to the French Revolution. Under it society was divided into classes—the court, the nobles, the clergy, the bourgeoisie, the artisans, the peasants. These classes bore relations to one another as sanctioned by ancient custom and precedent. Every individual was born into his class, or, to use the popular expression, to "a station to which God had called him." To question this arrangement was stupid, if not blasphemous.

Old Ritualists. A religious faction in Russia which opposed the changes advocated in 1652 by Patriarch Nikon. These changes consisted in correcting certain ungrammatical expressions in the worship service of the church and a new method to be used by people in crossing themselves. This new method followed the Greek practice and destroyed the concept of the "Third Rome" (Rome, Constantinople, Moscow). The Old Ritualists protested that Moscow could not be the center of religious life if it followed the model of the Greeks. Nikon fell from favor and was exiled to a monastery. The schism in the church continued many years. It evoked the most intense religious emotions. At one time, many Old Ritualists, believing that the end of the world was near and that Antichrist was due to appear, burned themselves to death.

Oliva, Treaty of. May 3, 1660. Concluding the First Northern War between Sweden and Poland. By this treaty Poland lost to Sweden its last Baltic territories.

Olmütz, Humiliation of. See Erfurt Union.

Omayyad Dynasty of Cordova. 756-1031. This dynasty ruled Spain during the best years of Moslem domination. It was founded by Abder-Rahman I (731-778), grandson of the Omayyad caliph of Damascus, who made Spain independent from Africa and took the title of emir. Christians were not persecuted in return for paying a heavy poll tax. Jews were well treated. In 929 the emir took the title of caliph. In the 10th century, Cordova became the greatest seat of learning in Europe.

Oran, Battle of. July 3; 1940. In the terms of the armistice with France, the Nazis promised not to make use of the French navy. The British feared that this promise would be disregarded once the ships fell into German hands. The British Cabinet unanimously voted to forestall this eventuality. On July 3, the French commandant at Mers-el-Kebir, a naval base near Oran where numerous units of the French navy were at anchor, received an ultimatum from the British Vice-Admiral Somerville demanding that the French fleet give itself up to be interned or risk sinking within six hours. The French chose the latter alternative. They were attacked and most of the ships were put out of commission, although several managed to escape to Toulon. This "battle" greatly intensified the anti-British feeling of the French.

Ordeals. Ordeals were methods used by medieval German courts to determine the innocence or guilt of an accused person. There were ordeals by fire, water, and combat. After a solemn prayer, the accused was required to plunge his bare arm into a pot of boiling water or to carry a heated iron bar in his bare hand for a specified number of paces. If after three days the hand or arm gave no sign of infection, he was pronounced free. The water ordeal might be by cold water. In that case, the accused was cast, bound, into a stream or lake. If he floated, he was declared guilty, since the water spurned him. If he sank, he was declared to be innocent, since the water received him to its bosom. In an ordeal by combat, the accused and accuser fought what was called a judicial combat. The victor was declared to be vindicated. Either contestant might secure the services of a champion to fight in his stead.

Orders in Council, British. Jan. 7, 1807. The English government forbade neutrals, under the threat of the seizure of ships and cargoes, to trade between the ports of France and her allies, or between the ports of countries that obeyed the Berlin Decree. This was England's answer to Napoleon's Continental System.

Ordinamenti della Giustizia. (Ordinances of Justice). A constitution adopted in Florence in 1293 by which nobles were excluded from office altogether. A *gonfaloniere della giustizia* (banner-bearer of justice), appointed on purpose to watch over the decree against the nobility, together with eight priors of the greater arts, elected for two months, formed the executive. Two councils assisted in the deliberations. In spite of modifications and interruptions, this system continued 200 years.

Organization for European Economic Cooperation. See Marshall Plan.

Organizzazione Volontaria per la Repressione dell'Antifascismo (OVRA). 1925. A secret-police force which was organized in Fascist Italy and made directly responsible to Mussolini. Its function was to hunt out all those who plotted against the existing government.

Orlando, Vittorio Emanuele. 1860-1952. Italian statesman. Prime minister (1917-19). He led the Italian delegation at the Paris Peace Conference (1919). He retired from political activity at the advent of Fascism. After the fall of Mus-

solini (1943) he briefly reentered political life.

Ormonde, James Butler, 1st Earl and 1st Duke of. 1610-82. He pacified Ireland as lord lieutenant for Charles I. He retired to France during the Cromwellian period. He became lord lieutenant of Ireland again following the restoration of the Stuarts (1660). His son, James (1665-1745), the second duke, supported William III, commanded a regiment at the Battle of the Boyne (1690). He succeeded Marlborough as captain-general (1711-14). He was impeached for Jacobitism and settled in Spain.

Orsini. A Roman family of noble birth. It furnished 2 popes (Nicholas III and Benedict XIII), and many other distinguished leaders.

Ostrogoths, or Eastern Goths. A branch of the Goths who invaded the Roman Empire in the 4th century. Under their leader, Theodoric, they invaded Italy in 488. Theodoric formed an empire which included Italy, Sicily, Dalmatia, and some German lands. This empire was conquered by Justinian, the Roman emperor of the East, in 553.

Otto I (*called* **the Great**). 912-973. King of Germany and Holy Roman Emperor (936-73; crowned 962). He spent the early years of his reign subduing revolts of his nobles. He defeated the Hungarians in the great battle on the Lechfeld (955). His coronation revived the empire of Charlemagne.

Otto II. 955-983. Holy Roman Emperor (973-983). Son of Otto I. He drove the French out of Lorraine. He claimed southern Italy, but was badly beaten by the Saracens and the Greeks (982). He married Theofano (955?-991), the daughter of the Byzantine emperor, Romanus II. She had great influence at his court and introduced many of the refinements of Constantinople. After his death, she ruled (983-991) for her son Otto III.

Otto III. 980-1002. Holy Roman Emperor (983-1002). Son of Otto II and Theofano. He lived in Rome (998-1002) and sought to make it the capital of a new Roman empire. He established Sylvester II as pope (999) which marks the beginning of the purification of the papacy, which had become very secular.

Otto of Freising. 1114?-1158. German bishop and historian. He wrote one of the most remarkable medieval histories, *De Duabus Civitatibus,* a philosophical work in 8 books. He also began to record the chronicles of the reign of Frederick Barbarossa (1152-1190).

Ottoman Turks. See Turks.

OVRA. See Organizzazione Volontaria per La Repressione dell' Antifascismo.

Owen, Robert. 1771-1858. Welsh socialist. Pioneer of cooperation in industry. Philanthropist. Born in Newton, Wales. Part owner of New Lanark mills in Scotland. He initiated a program to improve working conditions for laborers; stopped the employment of children; established sickness and old-age pensions; opened educational and recreational facilities. He founded several "Owenite" communities (at Orbiston, Scotland; New Harmony, Indiana; Ralahine, Ireland; and Tytherly, England). All of these met with discouraging failure.

Oxenstierna, Count Axel Gustafson. 1583-1654. Swedish statesman. Appointed chancellor (1612) by Gustavus Adolphus. Successfully designed victorious wars against Russia, Poland, and Denmark. Held supreme control in the Rhine region in the Thirty Years' War (from 1631). Directed Swedish policy in Germany after 1632. Became guardian of Queen Christina (1636). He remained the virtual director of Swedish foreign and domestic policy after her ascension to the throne (1644).

Oxford Movement. A 19th century school of thought among members of the Anglican Church. A few young clergymen —John Keble (1792-1866), John Henry Newman (1801-1882) (q.v.), Edward Pusey (1800-1882)—initiated the movement. Because it centered in Oxford University, it was known as the Oxford Movement. Its promoters urged their views in *Tracts for the Times.* Hence, they were nicknamed *Tractarians.* The Oxford Movement held that the Anglican Church was not Protestant, but was a real part of the Holy Catholic Church. Its disciples inculcated the medieval doctrine of the seven sacraments, including what was practically the same as the dogma of transubstantiation. Newman was received into the Catholic Church in 1845 and created a cardinal in 1879.

Ozanam, Antoine Frédéric. 1813-53. French historian. A leader in the Catholic movement. A founder of the Society of Saint Vincent de Paul (1833).

P

Pacification of Ghent. Nov. 8, 1576. In the universal horror and indignation which followed the sack of Antwerp by Spanish soldiers, the southern Catholic provinces of the Netherlands joined the northern Protestant provinces in an agreement to drive the Spaniards out of the Netherlands completely. Protestantism was privately permitted in 15 Catholic provinces and recognized as the creed of Holland and Zeeland. The Inquisition was abolished. Confiscated property was restored.

Pacifism, International. During the 19th century there was a remarkable growth in the movement for international peace. In 1816 an English Peace Society was founded. In 1828 a Peace Society was organized at Geneva; a second was organized at Paris in 1841. Thereafter many more were founded. By 1914 there were 160 similar societies with large membership. International Peace Congresses met at intervals from 1843 to 1891. In the latter year, a permanent headquarters was set up in Bern. Prominent men—Alfred Nobel, Baron D'Estournelles de Constant, Count Tolstoy, for example—gave their money, time, and talents to promote world peace. During the 1920's and 1930's the peace movement reappeared with great vigor. Peace conferences, the pledge of the Students'

Union of Oxford University, the peace strikes staged by American college students, and Gandhi's doctrine of non-resistance are examples of it. At the conclusion of the Second World War, the peace movement again revived.

Paderewski, Ignace. 1860-1941. Polish pianist and statesman. Born in Podolia. He studied in Warsaw and in Vienna under Leschetizky. He made his professional debut in Vienna in 1887. He soon established himself as a pianist of international renown, particularly as an interpreter of Chopin, Liszt, Rubinstein, and Schumann. He composed many pieces for the piano, concertos, a symphony, and an opera. During the First World War he devoted himself to the cause of Polish independence. After the war he went to Warsaw and organized a government in which he was premier and minister of foreign affairs (Jan. 17, 1919 —Nov. 27, 1919).

Palace School (Scola Palatina) of Charlemagne. c. 800. This famous school was founded by Charlemagne in the royal palace at Aachen. He formed his whole court into a school. All members assumed either classical or biblical names. Charlemagne himself was called David. Sessions were held in the winter because in the summer there usually were wars.

Learned men lectured, and there were many discussions on serious subjects. This school was part of Charlemagne's "revival of learning." Among the famous scholars who visited the school were Alcuin (q.v.), Einhard (q.v.), Paul the Deacon (q.v.), and Peter of Pisa, the grammarian.

Palaeologus. The name of a Byzantine family which furnished the last eight emperors of the Eastern Roman Empire (1259-1453).

Pale, The. That part of Ireland under English control.

Palestrina, Giovanni. 1526?-1594. Italian composer of church music. Born at Palestrina, near Rome. In 1551 he was made *maestro di capella* by Pope Julius III, a post to which he was restored in 1571, after having been from 1555 choirmaster at the Lateran and at St. Maria Maggiore. The Council of Trent (q.v.) entrusted to Palestrina the reform of church music. His compositions include masses, hymns, litanies, etc.

Palladio, Andrea. 1518-80. Italian architect. Born and died at Vicenza. He founded modern Italian architecture, as distinguished from the earlier Italian Renaissance. The Palladian style is modelled on the ancient Roman.

Palmerston, 3rd Viscount. Henry John Temple. 1784-1865. English statesman. Tory M.P. (1807). Secretary for war (1809-28). He associated himself with the Whig Party (1830). Foreign secretary under Grey (1830). Effected the independence of Belgium (1830-31). Annexed Hong Kong (1840). Foreign secretary under Lord John Russell (1846) until dismissed (1851). Home secretary (1855-65, except for short intervals). He is conceded to have been the outstanding English statesman since Pitt the Elder.

Pan-Slav Congress. 1848. In June, 1848, Czechs, Poles, Russians, and Serbs met in Prague as brother Slavs to initiate a Liberal movement of all the Slavic peoples of Europe. The Congress was dispersed by Austrian soldiers without accomplishing anything. However, the Congress was an important step in initiating the Pan-Slav movement.

Papal Guarantees, Law of. 1871. Shortly after the Italian government occupied Rome (Sept. 20, 1870), the Italian government enacted the Law of Papal Guarantees which stated: (1) The Pope was to be accorded sovereign rights on a par with those of the king of Italy; (2) he was to have full sovereign rights over the Vatican and Lateran buildings and the villa of Castel Gandolfo; (3) he was to have free use of Italian telegraph, railway, and postal systems; (4) he was to have an annual subsidy of 3¼ million *lire*. Pope Pius IX denounced the law and remained a "prisoner" in the Vatican. His example was followed by subsequent popes until the agreement of 1929.

Papal Infallibility, Dogma of. 1870. Pope Pius IX convened the Vatican Council (1869-70), a convention of nearly 800 prelates. This Council proclaimed the dogma of Papal Infallibility, which was defined as a "dogma divinely revealed, that the Roman pontiff, when he speaks *ex cathedra,*—that is, when in discharge of the office of pastor and doctor of all Christians, by virtue of his supreme apostolic authority, he defines a doctrine regarding faith or morals to be held by the universal church,—by the divine assistance promised him in Blessed Peter, is possessed of that infallibility with which the divine Redeemer willed that His Church should be endowed for defining faith or morals; and that therefore such definitions of the Roman pontiff are *per se* immutable and independent of the consent of the Church. But if anyone— which God avert!—presume to contradict this our definition: let him be anathema."

Papen, Franz von. 1879-. German politician. As German military attaché in Washington during World War I, he was largely responsible for directing sabotage against munitions factories, etc. After being deported from the United States (1915), he became chief of staff of the Turkish army. He entered politics in Germany as a member of the Center Party. He was chancellor (1932) and Hitler's vice-chancellor (1933-34). In the latter capacity he signed a concordat with Rome. Ambassador to Austria (1936-38) and to Turkey (1939-44). Captured in 1945, he was acquitted by the Nuremberg Court. Sentenced to eight years' imprisonment by a German "denazification" court, he was released (1949) by an appeals court.

Paris Commune. See Commune of Paris.

Paris, Congress of. (1856). This body made peace at the end of the Crimean War. The treaty included the following points:

(1) The Black Sea was neutralized.

(2) The Danube River was open to free navigation by the ships of all countries.

(3) The provinces of Moldavia and Wallachia were declared autonomous, but were bound to recognize the "suzerainty" of the sultan of Turkey.

(4) The Ottoman Empire was admitted to the Concert of Europe. (See also Nicholas I.)

Paris, Peace of (1763). See Seven Years' War.

Paris Peace Pact. See Kellogg-Briand Pact.

Paris, Treaty of. Sept. 3, 1783. By this treaty (1) England acknowledged the independence of the United States and defined the boundaries of the new country. (2) The United States was to have the right to fish off the Banks of Newfoundland and in the Gulf of St. Lawrence. (3) Navigation of the Mississippi was to be open to both countries. (4) Congress was to recommend to the several states that the confiscated estates of loyalists were to be restored.

Paris, Treaty of. May 30, 1814. By this treaty, signed by Louis XVIII, the new king of France, and the allies—Great Britain, Austria, Prussia, and Russia—the boundaries of France were reduced to those of 1792 and the independence of the various states which were conquered by Napoleon was recognized. To readjust the disturbed situation in Europe, a congress was called to meet in Vienna in Sept. 1814.

Parlement of Paris. The supreme court of Paris (pre-Revolutionary), which had among its duties the task of registering royal decrees. If it disapproved of a decree, it might refuse to register it. The decree would then not become operative unless the king summoned a *lit de justice* (bed of justice), that is, formally summoned the Parlement and in person commanded it to register the decree.

Parnell, Charles Stewart. 1846-91. Irish nationalist. M.P. (1875). He initiated a policy of obstruction, always standing with the party of opposition, in order to secure concessions for Ireland. A Protestant, an opportunist who was also a fierce lover of justice, he was able to unite all types of Irish patriots—land reformers, advocates of Home Rule, moderates, extremists — into a common cause. He reached the apex of his career when Gladstone became Prime minister in 1886.

Pascal, Blaise. 1623-1662. French scientist and philosopher. Born in Clermont. A mathematical prodigy, he completed an original treatise on conic sections at the age of sixteen. He contributed to the development of differential calculus. He originated, with Fermat, the mathematical theory of probability. He experimented with the equilibrium of fluids and with the difference of atmospheric pressure at various altitudes. His important literary work began with his association with the Port-Royalists (q.v.) (1655). He was a champion of Jansenism (q.v.). His *Provinciales* (1656) and *Pensées* (published after his death) are regarded as classics because of their literary style.

Passau, Peace of (1552). See Schmalkaldic War.

Pasteur, Louis. 1822-95. French chemist. Born in Dôle, Jura. Educated at Besançon and École Normale, Paris. Professor of physics at Dijon (1848) and Strassburg (1849). Dean and professor of chemistry at Lille (1854-57). Director of École Normale at the Sorbonne (1857-63). Professor of chemistry at the Sorbonne (1867-89). Director of the Institute Pasteur, Paris. He investigated diseases of wine and beer. Demonstrated that alcoholic fermentation is caused by bacteria. Discovered that bacilli caused diseases of silk-worms and found methods of checking these diseases. Discovered the causes of anthrax and chicken cholera. Discovered curative and preventative treatment for hydrophobia.

Pataria. An 11th century party formed in Milan. Its members were composed of the masses. Hence the party was opposed to the higher and wealthy classes. The Pataria accepted certain philosophical ideas regarding the nature of matter. From these they concluded that marriage was an unholy state. Thus, they favored celibacy of the clergy.

Patrick, Saint. 389?-?461. Apostle and patron saint of Ireland. Born near Severn, Britain. Son of Calpurnius, a decurion of Celto-Roman family of high rank. Captured at the age of sixteen by Irish marauders. Sold as a slave in Antrim. Escaped after six years into Gaul. Returned to his parents in Britain. He heeded the call which came to him in a dream to return and preach in Ireland. He spent 14 years at Auxerre, France, in preparation. Entrusted by Pope Celestine I with the conversion of the Irish. He was consecrated bishop (432) and landed in Wicklow. Founded churches and consecrated the faith. He founded the church and monastery at Armaugh.

Paul I. 1754-1801. Czar of Russia (1796-1801). He succeeded his mother Catherine the Great. He was a tyrannical and mentally unbalanced ruler. He tried to put limits upon serfdom by limiting the work of serfs to three days a week. He was assassinated in the course of a palace revolution and succeeded by his son Alexander I.

Paulus Diaconus (Paul the Deacon). d. 787. Lombard Benedictine monk and historian. His chief writings are *History of the Lombards* (from 568 to 747 in 6 books) and *History of Rome* (364-553).

Pavia, Battle of. 1525. The French army of Francis I was completely defeated by the imperial army of Charles V under the Marquis of Pescara. Francis was taken captive. It was the greatest disaster to French arms since Agincourt. Francis was taken to Spain and held captive until he signed the Treaty of Madrid (q.v.) (1526).

Pavlov, Ivan. 1849-1936. Russian physiologist. After teaching in Germany, he returned to Russia to head the Institute of Experimental Medicine (1913) in St. Petersburg. He worked at the physiology of the circulation and the digestion, but is best known for his work with the conditioned reflex.

Peace Moves during World War I. Long before the end of the war, various attempts were made to conclude the struggle.

(1) In January and February of 1916, President Wilson's intimate adviser, Col. House, visited Europe and conferred with various leaders. This visit resulted in the House Memorandum (Feb. 22, 1916), which stated that the president was ready to propose a peace conference. The terms on which the United States would mediate included the restoration of Belgium and Serbia, the cession of Alsace-Lorraine to France, the cession of Constantinople to Russia, the independence of Poland, the transfer of the Italian-speaking parts of Austria to Italy. As the Allied leaders were then optimistic of victory, this offer came to nought.

(2) Dec. 12, 1916. The Central Powers notified the United States to inform the Allies that Germany and its allies were ready to negotiate peace. No specific terms were mentioned. As the Central Powers were then at the summit of their success, the Allied governments rejected this advance.

(3) Dec. 18, 1916. President Wilson submitted peace suggestions to the belligerents. He called for "peace without victory."

(4) Feb. 1917. When Charles became emperor of Austria following the death of Francis Joseph (1916), he tried twice to end the war. He asked his brother-in-law, Prince Sixtus of Bourbon-Parma, who had served in the Belgian army, to inform President Poincaré of France of Charles' willingness to acknowledge France's just claims to Alsace-Lorraine and to agree to the complete restoration of Belgium and Serbia. In December, Foreign Minister Czernin reiterated the offer.

(5) May 10, 1917. Delegates from the Socialist parties of Russia, Germany, Austria-Hungary, Bulgaria, and several neutral states convened in Stockholm to discuss methods by which workers might end the war. Since the move was interpreted in Britain, France, Italy, and the United States as German propaganda, the governments of these four countries refused to issue passports to any of their own nationals. In September the conference broke up in failure.

(6) Aug. 1, 1917. Pope Benedict XV issued a plea for a "just" and "durable" peace. He called for a restoration of all occupied territories, no indemnities, freedom of the seas, international arbitration, decrease in armaments, plebiscites to decide rival territorial claims. President Wilson, as spokesman for the Allies, rejected the idea of negotiation with the Imperial German Government. Only when the German people repudiated their "irresponsible" government would the Allies discuss peace.

(7) Shortly after the Bolsheviks seized power in Russia, they tried to bring about peace by publishing the texts of the Secret Treaties to which Russia had been a party.

(8) Jan. 8, 1918. In an address to Congress, President Wilson enunciated his "Fourteen Points." (q.v.)

Peace of God. A device attempted by the Church (10th century and ff.) to abolish warfare by forbidding men to fight one another on the grounds that they were Christians. Those who persisted in fighting were threatened with excommunication. It was impossible to enforce the Peace of God. The times were too wild.

Peace Treaties at the end of World War II. For treaty with Germany, see Contractual Agreement. For treaties with Italy, Hungary, Finland, Bulgaria, and Romania, see Axis Satellites, Fate of. Also see Council of Foreign Ministers.

Peasant Revolt, England. Also known as Wat Tyler's Rebellion (q.v.). 1381. Infuriated at attempts since the Black Death to revive old villein services, the peasants of Essex and Kent marched on London. Choosing Wat Tyler as their leader, they advanced (June 12) to Mile End, near London, where John Ball preached a fiery sermon. On June 14, youthful King Richard II and his counsellors arrived for a conference with them. Tyler was murdered, and the revolters dispersed. While it is notable as the first great revolt of labor against capital, the revolt of 1381 led to no startling changes.

Peasants' War (Germany). 1525. The inception of the Protestant Reformation aroused great hopes in many hearts, particularly in those of the depressed peasantry of central Europe. Revolution in spiritual affairs was soon transformed by the peasantry into a social and economic uprising. In 1525 there began in Bavaria a huge, unorganized, disorderly revolt of the peasants. This revolt soon spread through south Germany. The revolt was suppressed with great violence, but only after fearful excesses had been practiced against the rural nobles. So thoroughly were the peasants suppressed that they never revolted again and remained in serfdom until they were liberated by Napoleon. Luther was horror-stricken by the revolt, and urged the nobles to suppress the peasants. Many people, however, ascribed the revolt to the teachings of Luther and withdrew their support from the Reformation.

Peel, Sir Robert. 1788-1850. English statesman. Born near Bury in Lancashire. Tory M.P. (1809). Under-secretary for war and colonies (1810-12). Chief secretary for Ireland (1812-18). Instituted the Irish constabulary (Peelers). M.P. (1817). He built a reputation as a financial expert by carrying the resolutions embodying the recommendations of Huskisson, Ricardo, and others for the resumption of cash payments (1819). House secretary (1821-27). First lord of the treasury, chancellor of the exchequer, and prime minister (1834-35). He built up the Conservative Party. Reorganized the

Bank of England (1841). Carried the measure to repeal the Corn Laws (1846). Organized the first uniformed London police force (Bobbies).

Peninsular Campaign. 1808-1814. The English landed an army in Portugal in the hope of gaining a foothold in Europe against Napoleon. The English army was commanded by the Duke of Wellington. By 1814 the English had driven the French completely out of Spain and had invaded France as far as Toulouse. The abdication of Napoleon (April 11, 1814) ended this campaign.

Penny Postage in England. 1839-40. In the year 1839, the adhesive stamp for letters was introduced. In 1840, it was ruled that any letter which weighed one-half ounce or less would be delivered anywhere in the United Kingdom for one penny. These two factors revolutionized communications in England.

People's Budget. See War Budget.

People's Charter. See Chartist Movement.

Pepys, Samuel. 1633-1703. Famous English official in the navy office and diarist.

Permanent Court of International Justice. This court was created by international agreement on Dec. 16, 1920. The court sat at the Hague and consisted of 15 justices, 9 of which had to be present at each meeting. The judges were elected by the Council and Assembly of the League of Nations. No two judges might be of the same nationality. States, not individuals, could be parties to cases before the court. Under the "Optional Clause" states were free to make decisions of the court compulsory.

The new International Court of Justice, which is one of the major divisions of the UN, follows in many of its provisions and in much of its phraseology the statute of the Permanent Court of International Justice set up by the League of Nations.

Perpetual Edict. Feb. 12, 1577. A document drawn up by 15 Netherlands provinces which guaranteed the national rights of the Netherlands, and called for the departure of foreign troops, the maintenance of the Pacification of Ghent (q.v.) and of the King's authority, and the acceptance of the governor-general, Don Juan of Austria.

Peter I (*called* the Great). 1672-1725. Czar of Russia (1628-1725). The reign of Peter opened a new period in Russian history. Russia became a typical state according to the European pattern. The government, courts, army, and social classes were organized along Western lines. Industry and trade developed rapidly and a great improvement in technical training and science took place. Europeanization of Russia brought new political, religious, and social ideas which were absorbed by the upper classes only, thus creating a split between the intellectuals and the people. The chief psychological basis of the old Russian state, formed in the Orthodox Church, was shaken. The national assembly, Zemsky Sobor, ceased to function after 1682 and local self-government ceased in 1708. To carry out his Europeanizing program, Peter was forced to act harshly. Thus, absolutism became habitual and traditional. Peter secured many of his Western ideas through a trip to Brandenburg, Holland, England, and Vienna.

Peter II of Yugoslavia. See Alexander I.

Peter the Hermit. Born in the diocese of Amiens, he became a monk or hermit. He attempted to go on a pilgrimage to Palestine, but was turned back by the Turks. After the Council of Clermont (q.v.), where Pope Urban II called for a crusade, Peter went about through central and northern France calling for volunteers. In short order he enlisted an "army" of 15,000, containing few soldiers and many women and children. En route to Palestine, this band was joined by another under Walter the Penniless. They reached Constantinople July 30, 1096, and invaded Asia Minor a week later. Here they were deserted by Peter. They were attacked by the Turks (October) and massacred. Their bones were found by another group of crusaders who passed by one year later. Peter joined the army of the First Crusade at Constantinople and completed the journey to Jerusalem with it. He seems to have been a leader of the hangers-on of the camp and was called the "Beggar King." He is the hero of the "Song of Antioch."

Peterloo Massacre. Aug. 1819. In the post-Napoleonic War years, English industry stagnated. The year 1819 was the worst of these depression years. In the industrial cities of the north and center, great meetings were held to demand parliamentary reform. One of these, held on St. Peter's Field, Manchester, was charged by royal troops with drawn swords and broken up after six bystanders were killed. This has since been known as the "Peterloo Massacre" from a popular poem describing the event. The poet altered the name *St. Peter's* to *Peterloo* to find a rhyme for *Waterloo*. This event and its consequences constitute one of the milestones in English labor relations.

Petition of Right. 1628. Before granting Charles I the five subsidies which he demanded, Parliament demanded that he sign the Petition of Right. This document states: (1) No man hereafter shall be compelled to make or yield any gift, loan, benevolence, or tax without common consent by act of Parliament. (2) No freeman shall be imprisoned or detained without cause shown. (3) Soldiers shall not be billeted in private homes. (4)

Commissions to punish by martial law shall be revoked and no more issued. This Petition has always been ranked with the Magna Carta (q.v.) and the Bill of Rights (q.v.) as a great landmark in the progress of the English toward liberty.

Petrarch (Francesco Petrarca). 1304-74. Italian poet and humanist. Born in Arezzo. Educated in Avignon. He assumed ecclesiastical orders (1326) in order to devote himself to the study of the classics (1326 ff.). In Avignon he met Laura, the subject of many of his celebrated *Canzoniere*. He traveled widely. He collected many ancient manuscripts and is considered to be the first humanist.

Petrograd Soviet of Workers' and Soldiers' Deputies. This Soviet played an important part in the Russian Revolution of 1917. Activities of this body precipitated events which led to the abdication of Czar Nicholas II of Russia (March 15, 1917). It issued (March 14) the famous "Order Number 1" to the army which led to the destruction of the army, since it transferred command from the officers to soviets to be chosen by each army unit.

Petty, Sir William. 1623-87. An English pioneer in the field of economics. He advocated the use of statistics in economic studies. He contributed much toward exposing the fallacies of mercantilism.

Philip I. 1052-1108. King of France (1060-1108). Son of Henry I. His kingdom was at low ebb because of powerful feudal lords. He increased the royal domain and the power of the king by arms and diplomacy.

Philip II Augustus. 1165-1223. King of France (1180-1223). Son of Louis VII. One of the great kings of France. He engaged in various wars (1181-85) which increased the size of his kingdom. He set out on the Third Crusade (1190)

but quarreled with Richard I of England and returned (1191). He conspired with Richard's brother John to seize English lands in France. He later attacked John and captured from him Normandy, Maine, and other provinces, which were annexed to France (1202-04). He defeated the allies (the forces of the Emperor and the Count of Flanders) at the Battle of Bouvines (1214), a defeat which enabled Frederick II to become emperor. He gave the first charter to the University of Paris (1200). He married three times. His second marriage to Ingeborg (1193), whom he repudiated, brought him into violent conflict with the papacy. By seizing so many dependencies from England and adding them to the royal domain, he made the king the largest land-holder in France.

Philip III (the Bold). 1245-85. King of France (1270-85). Son of Louis IX. A weak ruler, pious but uneducated. Much influenced by his favorites, his wife, and his mother. During his reign the royal territory was augmented by the acquisition of Toulouse. By the marriage of Philip's second son (who afterwards succeeded him) to the heiress-apparent of Navarre, a claim to that kingdom was established which later led to the annexation of that territory by Henry IV.

Philip IV (the Fair). 1268-1314. King of France (1285-1314). Son of Philip III. He engaged in a long controversy with the papacy. The papal bulls, *Clericis Laicos* (1296) and *Unam Sanctam* (1302), were directed against him. He summoned the first Estates-General (1302) to seek popular support in this controversy. He is responsible for moving the papacy to Avignon (1309). His reign is significant in that he strengthened the monarchy and restricted feudal usages. He persecuted the Jews (1306) and suppressed the Knights Templars (1313), largely to confiscate the property of both. Under Philip, Roman law became the established law of the land. To combat England, Philip made an alliance with Scotland, an alliance which lasted 300 years to the detriment of England.

Philip V (the Tall). 1294-1322. King of France (1316-22). Son of Philip IV. He was appointed regent on the death of his brother Louis X (1316), for the latter's infant son John. When John died, Philip became king by the application of the Salic Law. Philip tried to unify the coinage, weights, and measures.

Philip VI. 1293-1350. King of France (1328-50). First of the Valois line of kings. Disputes between him and Edward III of England led to the outbreak of the Hundred Years' War (1337). He lost naval control of the Channel to the English at the battle of Sluis (1340). The English then invaded Normandy and routed the French at Crecy (1346). The English captured Calais (1347). Philip annexed Dauphiné to France in 1349 by purchase.

Philip I (*called* the Handsome). 1478-1506. Son of Hapsburg Emperor Maximilian I and Mary of Burgundy. Married Juana (the Mad), daughter of Ferdinand and Isabella. When Isabella died (1504), Philip and Juana became joint sovereigns of Castile (1504-06), although Ferdinand actually ruled because of their absence in Flanders. Philip founded the Hapsburg dynasty in Spain. His sons became emperors Charles V and Ferdinand I of the Holy Roman Empire.

Philip II. 1527-98. King of Spain (1556-98). Only son of Charles V and Isabella of Portugal. Married four times: Maria of Portugal (1543), Mary I of England (1554), Elizabeth of Valois, daughter of Henry II of France (1560), and Anna, daughter of Emperor Maximilian II. He was given the government of Milan (1540), of Naples and Sicily (1554), of Netherlands (1555), and of Spain

(1556). He inherited vast possessions in the New World. He was determined to crush out all opposition to Roman Catholicism. With that end in view, he developed the Inquisition in Spain, tried unsuccessfully to subdue the Netherlands, and sent the Armada to its defeat against England. He conquered Portugal (1580) and helped to subdue the Turks in the Mediterranean by sending his half-brother, Don Juan, with a fleet to assist the Genoese in crushing them at Lepanto (1571). Philip was bigoted and morose. His policies in commerce and industry started Spain upon its decline. Because he insisted on personally inspecting and approving every state paper, he very seriously delayed the execution of government business.

Philip III. 1578-1621. King of Spain (1598-1621). Son of Philip II. He took no interest in the government, but left all direction of it to his favorite, the Duke of Lerma (q.v.). Agriculture and trade declined. The grandees gathered huge estates into their hands. The Church prospered, opening some 9,000 new monasteries and nunneries. Culturally, Spain enjoyed a "golden age." Cervantes (q.v.), Lope de Vega (q.v.), and El Greco (q.v.) were some of the bright ornaments of the period.

Philip IV. 1605-65. King of Spain (1621-65). Son of Philip III of Spain. He left the administration of the country to Olivares (1623-43). Spain's industry and commerce continued to decline. The country was impoverished by disastrous foreign wars, particularly with France, Germany, and Holland. Portugal regained independence in 1640.

Philip V. 1683-1746. King of Spain (1700-24 and 1724-46). Founder of the Bourbon dynasty of Spain. His accession caused the War of the Spanish Succession (1701-14) (q.v.). He married Maria Louisa of Savoy (1701) and (1714)

Elizabeth Farnese of Parma, both of whom strongly influenced his foreign policy. Both queens introduced many French ideas, such as the Royal Academy of Madrid (1711) and the Academy of History (1738). Philip abdicated Jan. 1724, in favor of his son Louis; but when Louis died (Aug.), Philip resumed the throne.

Philippe Égalité (Louis Philippe Joseph, Duke of Orléans). 1747-93. Descended from Philippe I, Duke of Orléans, the son of Louis XIII and brother of Louis XIV. Duke of Montpensier, Chartres, and Orléans. Liberal in views. He supported the cause of the American Revolution. He opposed Louis XVI, was sent abroad, but returned (1790) to work with Mirabeau and Danton. He renounced his title and took the name of Philippe Égalité. He was forsaken by the Jacobins (1793). His estates were confiscated by the Jacobins (1793). He was arrested on the charge of aspiring to the crown. He was imprisoned in Marseilles and later guillotined in Paris. His son Louis Philippe became King of France (1830-48).

"Phony War." Oct. 1939—April, 1940. A period in World War II between the conquest of Poland and the invasion of Norway. Because no military operations were undertaken by either side, the period was called the "Phony War" or the "Sitzkrieg."

Physiocrats. French school of economics, based on the theories of François Quesnay. The physiocrat theory stated: (1) society should be governed by a natural order inherent in itself; (2) land and unmanufactured products are the only true wealth; (3) precious metals are a false standard of wealth; (4) the proper source of revenue is direct taxation of land; (5) natural rights include freedom of trade, person, opinion, and property.

Picasso, Pablo. 1881-. Spanish painter. Along with Braque he invented cubism (c. 1910). He has made many etchings, illustrations, drawings, and stage sets.

Pietists. Representatives of Pietism, a religious awakening in the Lutheran Church of Europe in the latter decades of the 17th century. Pietists laid stress on practical piety, zeal in spiritual work, study of the Bible, and charity towards heretics (see Kant, Immanuel).

Pilgrimage of Grace. 1536-37. A Catholic protest against the Reformation in England. Led by a lawyer, Robert Aske, the movement was strongest in Yorkshire, where, at one time, 40,000 men were in arms. The rising was put down severely, and all the leaders were beheaded and quartered.

Pillnitz, Declaration of. August, 1791. A joint declaration issued by Emperor Leopold I of Austria and Frederick William II of Prussia to the effect that the two rulers considered the restoration of order and of monarchy in France an object of "common interest to all the sovereigns of Europe." This declaration could not be implemented by the two powers, since their armies were not ready for war. It aroused great resentment in France among those Frenchmen who were patriotic, as well as among the revolutionaries.

Pilsudski, Josef. 1867-1935. Polish general and statesman. Born in the province of Wilno. In his youth he joined the Young Poles. He served five years in Siberia (1887-1892) for complicity in a plot on the life of Czar Alexander III. He continued his agitation for a free Poland until 1914. He then organized an army of 10,000 which fought with Austria against the Russians. He resigned (1916) and worked independently for Polish independence. He was imprisoned by the Germans (1917-18). After the collapse of the Central Powers, he returned to Warsaw. He was elected chief of state, head of the Polish army, and marshal (1920). He directed the war against Lithuanians, Ukrainians, and Bolsheviks (1919-20). He was dictator of Poland until a constitution was ratified (1921). From 1926 to his death he was virtual dictator of his country. He was premier (1926-28, 1930) and minister of war (1926-35).

Pippin, or Pepin. The name of three Frankish mayors of the palace, the ancestors of the Carolingian kings.

Pippin the Elder. d. 640? Mayor of the palace (628-39) for Dagobert I. With Arnulf, the bishop of Metz, he controlled the policy of state.

Pippin II. d. 714. Son of Pippin the Elder. Mayor of the palace and ruler of all the Franks (687-714).

Pippin the Short. 714?-768. Son of Charles Martel. Mayor of the palace (741-51). He deposed the last of the Merovingian kings (751) and founded the Carolingian dynasty. He aided Pope Stephen II against the Lombards (754-55). He conquered them and made the pope ruler of the Exarchate of Ravenna (Donation of Pippin). He was the father of Charlemagne.

Pisano, Niccolo. d. 1278. A native of Pisa, he was the first great sculptor of Italy. He broke sharply with the old grotesque forms and returned to a study of nature and antiquity. His best work is the pulpit of Siena.

Pitt, William. Earl of Chatham. 1708-1778. Called "Pitt the Elder" and later "The Great Commoner." English statesman. Great orator. He became secretary of state and virtual prime minister (1756). He was the great war minister of England during the Seven Years' War, but was forced from office in 1761 shortly after George III came to the throne (1760). He collapsed in the House of Lords protesting the disruption of the empire and the duke of Richmond's motion for withdrawing forces from America.

Pitt, William (Pitt the Younger). 1759-1806. Second son of the Earl of Chatham (Pitt the Elder), he was born at Hayes near Bromley. From his youth he was schooled for a career in politics. He entered the House of Commons (1781). Following the resignation of the Prime Minister, Lord North (1782), a coalition ministry was formed. Following a death and a resignation in it, Pitt was made Chancellor of Exchequer (1782). As the result of Parliamentary conflict over a bill to modify the East India Co.'s charter, Pitt opposed the Fox-North coalition and won. In Dec. 1783, he took office as Chancellor of Exchequer, 1st lord of the treasury, and prime minister. He undertook measures to finance and reduce the public debt, established a new constitution for the East India Co., and was the first statesman to apply the principles of Adam Smith to government problems. He formed (1793) the First Coalition against France with Russia, Sardinia, Spain, Naples, Prussia, Austria, and Portugal. In 1798 he formed the Second Coalition with Portugal, Naples, Russia, Turkey, and Austria. He resigned (1801) while the Treaty of Amiens was being negotiated. He resumed office (1804) and formed a Third Coalition with Russia, Austria, and Sweden. His health was broken by news of Napoleon's victory at Ulm (Oct. 1805). Napoleon's defeat of Austria and Russia at Austerlitz (Dec. 1805) caused his death. By many he is thought to have been England's greatest prime minister.

Pius II. See Renaissance Popes.

Pius IX (name Giovanni Maria Mastai-Ferretti). 1792-1878. Pope (1846-78). Born in Senigallia. Upon becoming pope, he instituted wide reforms in the

Papal States. After the insurrection in Rome (1848) he was forced to flee to Gaeta. He was restored by the French in 1850. Now he became extremely conservative. He proclaimed the dogma of the Immaculate Conception (1854). He lost most of the Papal States in the Italian War (1859-60). He issued the *Syllabus of Errors* (1864). He convened the Vatican Council (1869-70) which promulgated the doctrine of papal infallibility. He lost all his temporal powers (1870) to the Italian government. He became the first "prisoner of the Vatican." His pontificate was the longest in the history of the church.

Pius X (*name* Giuseppe Melchiore Sarto). 1835-1914. Pope (1903-1914). Born in Riese, near Venice. Bishop of Mantua (1884). Cardinal (1893). Much interested in social questions, principally improving the conditions of the poor. As pope he was much opposed to Modernism, which he condemned in an Encyclical *Pascendi* (1907).

Pius XI (*name* Achille Ambrogio Damiano Ratti). 1857-1939. Pope (1922-39). Born at Desio, Italy. Prefect of the Ambrosian Library, Milan (1888-1910), subprefect and prefect of the Vatican Library (1911-18), sent to Poland as nuncio (1919-20), cardinal and archbishop of Milan (1921). His outstanding achievement as pope was the concordat with the Italian government, ending the historic feud between the Church and state in Italy. This quarrel was concluded by the Lateran Treaty (Feb. 11, 1929) (q.v.).

Pius XII (*name* Eugenio Pacelli). 1876-. Pope (1939-). Nuncio to Bavaria and Germany (1917-20), cardinal (1929), sent on important papal missions (1934-38), papal secretary of state (1930-39). His pontificate has been characterized by unremitting opposition to communism, the enunciation of the doctrine of the mystical body of Christ, biblical studies, a new doctrine of the Immaculate Conception, and a report accepting the geological conception of the great antiquity of the earth. Like his predecessors, Pius XII opposed laissez-faire capitalism and preached social reform.

Place, Francis. 1771-1854. English reformer. A tailor who prospered greatly in his occupation. Champion of radicalism and the right of combination (i.e. labor unions). Campaigned successfully for the Reform Bill of 1832. Drafter of the People's Charter. A pioneer of birth-control study.

Plain, The. The majority of the French National Convention (1792-95). This group had no real policies or convictions of its own, but usually followed the policy of expediency. Both the Girondists and the Mountain strove to win the votes of the Plain. At first, the Plain tended to follow the Girondists. As time went on, the Parisian populace demonstrated vigorously against anyone who opposed their champions, the Mountain. Hence the Plain gradually was completely captured by the Mountain.

Plantagenet, House of. A dynasty of kings which ruled England. These kings also held feudal possessions in France (see Angevin Empire). The name Plantagenet comes from the sprig of broom (*planta genista*) worn by Geoffrey of Anjou, the founder of the line.

	Born	Ruled
Henry II	1133	1154-1189
Richard I		
Coeur de Lion	1157	1189-1199
John Lackland	1167	1199-1216
Henry III	1207	1216-1272
Edward I Longshanks	1239	1272-1307
Edward II	1284	1307-1327
Edward III	1312	1327-1377
Richard II	1367	1377-1399

Plateresque style of architecture. From (Sp.) *plateros,* meaning silversmith. It is a blend of later Gothic and Italian Renaissance. Decoration is laid on, in the manner of the decorations made by silversmiths. The style is characteristically Spanish.

Plehve, Viatscheslav von. 1846-1904. Russian lawyer and administrator. Appointed head of the secret police (1881), he first hunted out and punished the assassins of Alexander II. He pursued Nihilists, Socialists, and Terrorists with so much vigor that the reign of Alexander III experienced a lull in revolutionary activity. He was killed by a bomb (July 28, 1904).

Pletho (Giorgios Gemistos). 1355?-?1450. Byzantine student of Plato. He is one of the pioneers in the revival of learning in the West. Because he stimulated interest in Plato, he shook the secure position of Aristotle in the minds of Europeans. He began the cult of Neo-Platonism.

Pobêdonostsev, Konstantine. 1827-1907. Russian philosopher. A professor of civil law in the University of Moscow, he tutored the sons of Czar Alexander II in the theory of jurisprudence and administration. Appointed (1880) the secular head of the governing body of the Russian Orthodox Church ("Procurator of the Holy Synod"), he exerted tremendous influence upon Russia and on Czar Alexander III. He was a complete reactionary. He believed that "Western ideas" were especially bad for Russia. He opposed parliaments, free press, secular education, limited monarchy, and trial by jury.

Podestà. See Italian cities.

Poggio Bracciolini. 1380-1459. Italian humanist. Papal secretary (1404 ff.). Chancellor of Florence (1453 ff.). He is remembered chiefly as the finder, in various monasteries of Germany, Switzerland, and France, of lost Latin classics. The list includes eight orations of Cicero, Lucretius' *De Rerum Natura,* Quintilian's *Instituto Oratoria,* and Tacitus' *Dialogus* and *Germania.*

Poincaré, Raymond. 1860-1934. French statesman. Born at Bar-le-Duc. Deputy (1887), senator (1903), Minister of Public Instruction (1893, 1895), Minister of Finance (1894, 1906), Premier (1911-13, 1922-24, 1926-29), President of the Republic (1913-20). He adopted an inflexible policy of opposition to a strong, prosperous Germany. He occupied the Ruhr (1923). His National Union ministry averted ruin in 1926. He is a controversial figure. Some regard him as a prophet who foresaw a powerful, militant Germany. Others maintain that his intransigent nationalism drove the German people into Hitler's arms.

Poitiers, Battle of (*sometimes called Battle of Tours*). 732. In this battle the Franks under Charles Martel (q.v.) defeated the Moors who were attempting to invade France from Spain. After this defeat, the Moors withdrew south of the Pyrenees and never again tried to invade France. For this reason it is called one of the decisive battles of the world.

Poitiers, Battle of. 1356. A decisive battle of the Hundred Years' War. The English, under the Black Prince, crushed the French and captured King John.

Poland, Fourth Partition of. See Vienna, Congress of.

Poland, Fifth Partition of. Sept. 28, 1939. Two weeks after the Nazi invasion of Poland, Russian troops poured into east Poland. President Moscicki, Foreign Minister Beck, and Marshal Smigly-Rydz then fled to Romania, where they were interned. On Sept. 28, von Ribbentrop and Molotov signed a new German-Soviet treaty by which Poland was partitioned between the two conquerors. The boundary line ran through old Poland from the southwest tip of Lithuania to northeast Hungary. The USSR acquired about half the territory, but only 14 million people. This land was incorporated into White Russia and the Ukraine. Vilnius was ceded to Lithuania. After the Nazi invasion of Russia, the USSR signed a treaty with the Polish Government-in-Exile (July 30, 1941) which declared that the German-Soviet partition of Poland was void. About 36,000 square miles of the German portion were incorporated into Germany. Teschen was ceded to Slovakia. The remaining 36,000 square miles of western Poland was called a "Gouvernement-General." Its capital was Cracow. The eventual intentions of the Germans towards this last area are not clear. Temporarily it became a depository for Poles, Jews, and 1½ million "Germans" whom the Nazis assembled from the Tyrol, the Baltic States, and eastern Poland.

Poland, Partitions of. 1772, 1793, 1795. In the first partition of Poland (1772), Prussia, Russia, and Austria took advantage of the internal weakness of Poland to seize parts of its territory under the guise of strengthening Poland's government. In 1793, Prussia and Russia seized additional parts of Poland. In 1795, Prussia, Russia, and Austria each took parts of the remaining Polish territory. Poland disappeared from the map as a country until 1919. During the time of Napoleon, there appeared for a time the Grand Duchy of Warsaw. This was divided by the Congress of Vienna (fourth partition). A fifth partition occurred in 1939 (see Fifth Partition of Poland).

Polish Revolution. 1830. Inspired by the French, the Poles revolted against the Russians. This revolt began with a mutiny in Warsaw (Nov. 1830), the murder of a number of Russian officials, and the expulsion of the viceroy, Grand Duke Constantine. The revolt lasted until Sept. 1831. The Poles were defeated and severely punished. The Polish constitution of 1815 was abrogated and Poland was incorporated into Russia. Hundreds of Poles were executed and thousands exiled. The Czar tried in every way to wipe out Polish nationality. Only the tiny republic of Cracow remained as a center of Polish nationalism until it was annexed by Austria in 1846.

Polish Revolution. 1863-64. Attempts by the Russians to win the support of the Poles by a mild and liberal policy failed. After considerable disorder, the czarist government decided to draft the malcontent Poles into the army. This decision provoked an insurrection, which soon spread into Lithuania and White Russia as well. Diplomatic protests by England, France, and Austria against the methods employed by the Russians to quell the revolt only stiffened the Russian nationalistic attitude. Throughout the revolt the Russians had the complete support of the Prussian government. The revolt was finally quelled with great severity. Polish autonomy was abolished and the use of the Russian language was made obligatory in Poland.

Polish Succession, War of. 1733-35. The Poles, supported by France, elected as their king Stanislaus Leszczynski, who was the father-in-law of Louis XV. The Russians and Austrians insisted on the election of Augustus III of Saxony. A huge Russian army invaded Poland and drove out Stanislaus, who fled to Danzig. After the capitulation of Danzig (June 2, 1734), Stanislaus fled to Prussia, and Augustus became King Augustus III of Poland. Meanwhile, France, supported by Spain and Sardinia, declared war on the empire. Much of the fighting took place in northern Italy. The war ended with the Treaty of Vienna (q.v.) (Oct. 5, 1735—ratified 1738) which made great changes in Italy and assured the victory of the Austro-Russian policy in Poland. As a result of this war, France acquired Lorraine (1733).

Poltava, Battle of. 1709. The Swedish army under Charles XII was completely crushed by the Russians under Peter the Great. This battle has often been counted as one of the decisive battles of European history. The military power of Sweden, already on the wane, was utterly broken. Charles fled to Turkey after defeat. Some years later he returned to Sweden and was killed during the siege of a town in Norway (1718).

Pompadour, Marquise de (Jeanne Antoinette Poisson). 1721-64. Mistress of Louis XV of France. Educated by the wealthy financier, Lenormand de Tournehem. Married his nephew Lenormand d'Étoiles. First met the king in 1744. She was established at Versailles (1745) and presented with the estate of Pompadour. Duchess (1752). She completely controlled Louis XV and the political situation. In foreign affairs, she changed Richelieu's policy of weakening Austria to alliance with Austria. This alliance brought on the Seven Years' War, which was disastrous to France.

Poor Law of England, New. 1834. Before 1834, justices of the peace and church wardens had the authority to impose taxes on the parish to provide a dole for the aged, infirm, or those able-bodied folk whose earnings were below a fixed standard. The first Parliament which was elected after the passage of the Reform Bill of 1832 contained many industrialists who believed that the old law encouraged idleness, increased the number of illegitimate children, and wasted money. The New Poor Law (1) abolished home relief, except for the sick and aged; (2) put able-bodied unemployed folk to work in workhouses (there were separate houses for men, women, and

children); (3) permitted several parishes to form a union with one board of guardians and a single poor tax. The workhouses which were created under this act acquired great odium (cf. Dickens' *Bleak House*).

Pope, Alexander. 1688-1744. English poet. His poetry is written in the form of heroic couplets. He gave this particular poetic form an exquisite finish that has never been surpassed. Among his works are: *Essays on Criticism* (1711), *The Rape of the Lock* (1712), *Dunciad* (1728), *Essay on Man* (1730), translations of the *Iliad* (1715-20) and the *Odyssey* (1725-26). Often called "The Wasp of Twickenham."

"Popish Plot." 1678. This was a false story about a plot to establish Roman Catholicism in England, spread by a notorious informer, Titus Oates. His motives were either to obtain employment as an agent in Catholic intrigues in England or to sell Catholic secrets to the English Protestant party. Many Englishmen suspected that the king, Charles II, was secretly Catholic and feared the succession of his brother, James, who was an avowed Catholic. Many suspects were tried and executed before the popular fury against the "Plot" ebbed.

Popular Front, French. 1936-7. A French coalition, made up mainly of Radical Socialists, Socialists, and Communists. Headed by Léon Blum (q.v.), they denounced Fascism, urged the nationalization of industries, and denounced the "two hundred families" who allegedly ran France. Upon coming to power, the Popular Front enacted laws calling for the 40-hour week, collective bargaining, the closed shop, paid vacations, wage increases, and a form of compulsory arbitration in labor disputes. It reorganized the Bank of France and the coal industry and created a national wheat office to control the price of bread. The Popular

Front disintegrated because of increasing conservative pressure and because its measures did not restore economic stability and prosperity to France.

Port-Royalists. French Jansenists established themselves as a company in connection with the Cistercian abbey for nuns, Port-Royal, in Paris. They were strongly attacked by the Jesuits. The latter, having influence with Louis XIV, succeeded in having the Port-Royal suppressed in 1709. (See also Jansen, Cornelis; Pascal, Blaise.)

Porte, Sublime (*or* Grande). A term used in western Europe to describe the head of the government of the Ottoman Turks. In the minds of the Turks the administration of the state was conceived as one of the tents of their nomad forefathers, with various doors (in French, *portes*) where the different kinds of business were done. The palace of the grand vizier was the principal "door" of Turkish administration, and was called by Europeans the *Sublime Porte*.

Portugal annexed to Spain. 1580-1640. In 1580 the Spaniards annexed Portugal. In 1594 Lisbon was closed to the enemies of Spain—France, England, and Holland. As this was the period of the Dutch War of Independence and Holland's principal strength was on the sea, the Dutch now attacked Portuguese ships, as well as Spanish ships. When the Dutch were barred from Lisbon, they retaliated by seizing some of the Portuguese overseas trade and the possessions of Portugal from which the goods came. They seized the following Portuguese colonies: Cape Colony in Africa (1651), various places in India, the Moluccas (1607), Java (1610), Sumatra (1649), Ceylon (1658), Celebes (1660), and a vast extent of Brazil (1624). When Portugal regained its independence, the Dutch retained most of these colonies.

Portuguese Republic. Following an insurrection in Lisbon (Oct. 3-5, 1910), the king was forced to flee to England. A republican government was established. Portugal has been a republic in name ever since. It is perhaps more accurate to describe it as a dictatorship.

Potsdam Conference. July 17-Aug. 2, 1945. A meeting between Truman, Stalin, and Churchill (after July 28 Churchill withdrew in favor of Attlee, the Churchill government having been replaced by the Attlee Ministry) to decide the fate of Germany. The decisions reached at Potsdam were as follows:

1. Disarmament and demilitarization.
2. Abolition of all Nazi institutions.
3. Trial of war criminals.
4. Restoration of local self-government and civil liberties.
5. Prohibition of manufacture of war materials.
6. Controlled production of metals, chemicals, etc., that might be used for war.
7. Decartelization of industry.
8. Control of imports, exports, and scientific research.

A Council of Foreign Ministers was empowered to prepare treaties for the Nazi satellite countries (q.v.).

Pound sterling. The standard coin of England. During the days of the Hanseatic League, the position of the Hanse merchants was so important in the commercial life of London that the money of these Easterlings, or eastern merchants, became the standard coin of England. Sterling is derived from Easterling.

Poynings' Law. 1495. To keep Ireland in order, Henry VII dispatched Sir Edward Poynings and a group of English officials. The new Lord Deputy secured the passage of a law which provided that no Irish Parliament should meet and pass a law without the consent of the King in Council, and that all English statutes should be in force in Ireland. This law is also known as the Statute of Drogheda.

Praemunire, Statute of. 1353. An English law which forbade anyone from carrying suits to foreign courts. The law was aimed at the church and church courts.

Pragmatic Sanction. 1740. With the death of Emperor Charles VI, the male line of the Hapsburg dynasty of Austria came to an end. Charles wished that all the Austrian dominions should go undivided to his daughter, Maria Theresa. By much negotiation, Charles had secured the adherence of the European powers to an agreement guaranteeing this arrangement. According to the diplomatic language of the day, this agreement was known as the Pragmatic Sanction (*pragmata,* affairs of state; *sanction,* agreement). The emperor had not, however, provided a strong military force to uphold this agreement. Upon his death, Austria was at once attacked by Prussia, France, and Spain (War of the Austrian Succession).

Prague, Treaty of. May 30, 1635. An agreement between the emperor and the Elector of Saxony. By this treaty, many of the provisions of the Edict of Restitution (1629) (q.v.) were annulled. Amnesty was proclaimed for all except those who had caused disturbances in Bohemia and the Palatinate. Lutherans alone were accorded freedom of worship. Brandenburg and the majority of the other Protestant states accepted this peace.

Prague, Treaty of (1866). See Austro-Prussian War.

Pre-Mongolian Russia, Political organization of. Every prince had his own council. There was a popular gathering called *Vieche* consisting of all adult males. The prince was served by two elected aids—the *Posadnik* (mayor) and the *Tysiatsky* (chief of the Thousand).

The aristocratic element was represented by a council of *Boyars.* Ancient Russian society was divided between freemen and slaves with a class—*Zapuky,* half slave, half free—between. Among the freemen there were four classes which were very flexible: churchmen, boyars, townsmen, peasants.

Presbyterians. See Non-Conformists.

Pressburg, Treaty of. Dec. 26, 1805. Between Austria and France, following the French victory of Austerlitz. Austria recognized Napoleon as king of Italy and ceded to Italy all the Venetian territory which it had secured in the Treaty of Campo Formio, as well as Istria and Dalmatia. Austria also ceded extensive territories to Bavaria, Württemberg, and Baden. Austria was indemnified by being given Salzburg, Berchtesgaden, and the estates of the Teutonic Order, which were secularized.

Pride's Purge. Dec. 6, 1648. Colonel Pride was sent with a body of troops into the House of Commons to arrest those members who were known to oppose the army and who opposed executing King Charles I. After Pride removed the opposition party from Commons, the remaining members constituted what was known as the "Rump" Parliament (q.v.).

Priestley, Joseph. 1733-1804. English scientist and non-conformist clergyman. Although he was held in high repute as a scientist (he was elected to the French Academy of Sciences in 1772 and the St. Petersburg Academy in 1790), his house in Birmingham was attacked by a mob (1791) and its contents destroyed because of his radical religious views and his opinions about the French Revolution. In 1794 he removed to the United States and lived at Northumberland, Pa., until his death. He is one of the discoverers of oxygen. His *Essay on the First Principles of Government* (1768) suggested to Jeremy Bentham the criterion of "the greatest happiness for the greatest number."

Privileged Classes, Old Regime. In the days of the Old Regime, the highest place in society was reserved for the clergy and nobility, the First and Second Estates, respectively. These were comparatively small groups. Of the 25 million inhabitants of pre-Revolutionary France, for example, there were 130,000 clergymen and 150,000 nobles. In countries where the wealth of the Church had not been confiscated by Protestants, a "prince of the church" (bishop, abbot, etc.) enjoyed during his lifetime great possessions. Castles, cathedrals, valuable pictures, rentals from rich lands belonged to the clergy. Clergymen were exempt from taxation. In France, the Church made annual gifts to the king, but less than one per cent of its income. Frequently dissolute young nobles were nominated bishops or abbots. While many of the lesser clergy subsisted on meagre funds and did excellent work, the church received a bad name from its "princes."

Nobles were assumed to be inherently better than other men. Hence, they refused to marry into the lower classes. Because of "gentle" birth, they were admitted to the court or to preferred positions in the Church or army. The nobles considered payment of direct taxes a disgrace to their gentle birth and frequently evaded indirect taxation through trickery.

Procopius. c. 499-562? Byzantine historian. Private secretary to Belisarius (527). Accompanied him on his campaigns. Procopius' *Histories* are records of the wars during the reign of Justinian I (527-65). He is the reputed author of the *Anecdota* (Secret History), a gossipy account of the private lives of Justinian and Theodora, Belisarius and his wife Antonina.

Prokofiev, Sergei. 1891-1953. Russian composer. His work is an interesting compromise between classical and modern forms. Among his compositions are *Love of Three Oranges, Peter and the Wolf, Lieutenant Kije,* and the oratorio which was composed to be sung with the film *Alexander Nevsky.*

Protective Tariff Law of Britain. Feb. 29, 1932. Because of economic problems which had beset Britain since the end of the first World War, the government abandoned the policy of free trade, which had been in existence since 1850. Included in the tariff law was a new "corn law," which guaranteed to British farmers about $1 a bushel for a specified quantity of home-grown wheat.

Protestant, Origin of the term. See Speier, Second Diet of.

Protestant Union. 1608. Protestant rulers of Germany feared the growing tide of Catholic reaction. In 1608 some of them formed a 10-year defensive alliance. Calvinistic communities made up the majority of this union. Its leader was the Palatinate, the leading Calvinistic state of the empire. The ruler of the Palatinate was Elector Frederick V, who had married Elizabeth, the daughter of James I of England. Frederick persuaded the Dutch Netherlands to join the Union. Some Lutheran states joined it as well; but as the opposition between Calvinists and Lutherans was strong, many Lutheran states refused to join. The formation of the Union was a decisive step towards starting the Thirty Years' War. Resistance to the Protestant Union came from the Catholic League (q.v.) under the leadership of Maximilian of Bavaria (q.v.).

Proudhon, Pierre Joseph. 1809-65. French journalist and politician, regarded as the father of anarchism. Founded and edited radical journals *Le Peuple* (1848-49), *La Voix du Peuple* (1849-50), and *Le Peuple de 1850* (1850). He wrote *Qu'est-ce que la Propriété?* (1840) and many other books which influenced the French syndicalist movement.

Proust, Marcel. 1871-1922. French novelist. Author of a series of novels under the general title, *Remembrance of Things Past.* He introduced detailed psychological analysis as an element of fiction.

Provisional Government of Russia. 1917. Organized after the abdication of Czar Nicholas II (March 15, 1917), it attempted to run the country until it was overthrown by the Bolshevik Revolution of Nov. 6, 1917. It was headed by Prince George Lvov as chairman. Paul Milyukov was head of the Foreign Office. Alexander Kerensky was Minister of Justice.

Provisions of Oxford. 1258. A Great Council demanded (April 28, 1258) that Henry III of England should dismiss all aliens and appoint a committee of 24 to draw up a scheme of reform. The following June there met in Oxford the so-called "Mad Parliament" which drew up a plan whereby all authority was to be transferred to a committee of 15 barons. Other committees were to undertake financial and Church reforms. All officials, including the king and his son, took an oath of loyalty to the Provisions.

Prussia, Origin of. Prussia was formed from the North Mark, a frontier state founded by Henry the Fowler from country along the Elbe, which he conquered from the Wends (918). Albert, called the Bear, thoroughly subdued the Wends (1134), spread Christianity among them, and took the town of Brandenburg. He assumed the title of Margrave of Brandenburg. This territory was gradually expanded. In 1417, a Hohenzollern became the Margrave of Brandenburg. In 1609, Cleves was added to Brandenburg. In 1525, the Teutonic Order of Knights dissolved. They made Albert of Hohenzollern, their late grand master, the owner and first duke of their former possessions in East Prussia.

During the Thirty Years' War, Brandenburg was severely ravaged, so that the ruler, George William, removed to East Prussia and governed from his residence in Koenigsberg. Frederick William (1640-88), the Great Elector, greatly expanded the power and influence of Brandenburg-Prussia. His son, Frederick III (1688-1713), assumed the title of Frederick I, King of Prussia, in 1701.

Prussian Constitution of 1850. See Revolutions of 1848.

Pseudo-Isidorean Decretals. Documents which appeared in the 9th century. Besides authentic material, they contained 60 spurious decrees of the Bishops of Rome. Their purport was to exalt clergy above laymen, subject to no earthly tribunal; also, to set as highest authority over clergymen the Bishop of Rome, who was called Universal Bishop.

Puccini, Giacomo. 1858-1924. Italian composer. Fifth in a family of distinguished composers. His particular field was operatic music. His operas include *Madame Butterfly, Girl of the Golden West, Tosca, La Bohème.*

Purcell, Henry. 1658-95. One of England's first musical geniuses. He composed much church music and the first opera ever to be written to an English poem, *Dido and Eneas* (1675).

Purge, Soviet. 1935-6; 1937-8. A liquidation of "rightist" groups and Trotskyites in the Soviet Union set off by the assassination of S. M. Kirov (Dec. 1, 1934). Included in the purge were prominent leaders like Kamenev, Zinoviev, Piatakov, Radek, Bukharin, Rykov, and Yadoga.

Puritans. See Non-Conformists.

Pushkin, Aleksander Sergeevich. 1799-1837. "The Sun of Russian Poetry." The greatest genius of Russian literature. He wrote chiefly in verse. In his youth he was a liberal and a "Decembrist" (q.v.). He was always a humanitarian and unhappy in the world of politics and intrigues. He was killed in a duel defending the honor of his wife. Among his works are *Ruslan and Ludmila, Boris Godunov, Eugeni Onegin, Pique Dame,* and *The Captain's Daughter.*

Pym, John. 1584-1643. English Parliamentary statesman. He played a decisive part in the struggle between Charles I and Parliament. According to his theory of government, Parliament was the chief element in the constitutional life of the nation; the House of Commons was superior to the House of Lords; the rights of the people were preeminent.

Pyrenees, Treaty of. 1659. (1) France received from Spain a part of Roussillon, Conflans, Cerdagne, and several towns in Artois, Flanders, Hainault, and Luxemburg. (2) Partial reinstatement of the Duke of Lorraine, an ally of Spain. (3) Marriage between Louis XIV and the Infanta Maria Theresa of Spain. Upon marriage, Maria Theresa renounced her claims upon the throne of Spain for herself and her descendants. In lieu of this claim, Spain contracted to pay France a dowry of 500,000 crowns. This dowry was never paid. (See War of Devolution.)

Q

Quadragesimo Anno. May 25, 1931. An encyclical issued by Pope Pius XI on the fortieth anniversary of *Rerum Novarum* of Leo XIII. It deplored the fact that economic life had become hard and cruel. It advocated a "just" wage and urged that workers be given some share in the profits of industry. Unemployment was called a "dreadful scourge." It was blamed, in part, on "extreme freedom of competition." Communism was denounced and socialism and Catholicism were called incompatible.

Quadrilateral, The. Four strong Austrian fortresses (Mantua, Peschiera, Legnano, Verona) between Lombardy and Venetia in northern Italy (in the 1850's).

Quadruple Alliance. Aug. 2, 1718. England, France, Holland, and Austria combined to counteract Spanish attempts on Italy. The English fleet landed an Austrian army in Sicily. The French invaded the Basque country and Catalonia. The war ended with the Treaty of the Hague (Feb. 17, 1720) by which the Spanish gave up claims on Italy in return for the succession in Parma and Tuscany of the eldest son of the king of Spain. The emperor gave up his claims on Spain. Savoy was given Sardinia in place of Sicily, which was turned over to Austria. (See also Alberoni, Giulio.)

Quadruple Alliance, The. By the treaty of Paris (Nov. 20, 1815), Austria, Prussia, Russia, and Great Britain were bound to call subsequent conferences to preserve peace and to maintain the status quo in Europe. Between 1815 and 1822, four great conferences were convoked: Aix-la-Chapelle (1818); Troppau (1820); Laibach (1821); Verona (1822). France was admitted to all these conferences. Strictly speaking, it was a Quintuple Alliance.

Quanta cura. 1864. An encyclical issued by Pope Pius IX in which he condemned the widely accepted notions that a secular state had supreme power over all affairs within its territories and that every state had a moral obligation to accord religious liberty. The pope strongly upheld the older idea of the Catholic state based on the complete independence of the ecclesiastical power and on the compulsory unity of faith.

Quebec Act. 1774. This measure was designed to deal with problems which arose after England annexed French Canada in 1763. The boundaries of Canada were extended to the Ohio and Mississippi Rivers. Roman Catholics were given freedom of worship. French law was to be used in civil cases, but English law applied to criminal cases.

Quebec Conference. Aug. 11-24, 1943. Prime Minister Churchill and President F. D. Roosevelt met with large staffs of advisers to plan for a second front in Europe. The French Committee of National Liberation was recognized by the United States, Great Britain, Canada, and the Soviet Union as the administrative government for French overseas territories.

Quercia, Jacopo della. 1374-1438. Italian sculptor. Born in Siena. Chief master of early Renaissance Sienese sculpture. His masterwork is the portal of the church of San Petronio in Bologna. The *Gay Fountain* in Siena, the tomb of Ilaria del Carreto in the cathedral of Lucca, and the bronze relief, *Zacharias in the Temple,* in the baptistry at Siena are good examples of his work.

Quesnay, François. 1694-1774. French physician and economist. Physician to the Duke of Villeroi and later to the king of France. Wrote articles on economics for the Encyclopedia (q.v.) on the basis of the theory of the physiocrats (q.v.). Author of *Tableau Économique* (1758) and *Physiocratie* (1768).

Quietist. An advocate of quietism, a doctrine that spiritual exaltation is attained by self-abnegation and withdrawing the soul from outward activities, fixing it upon passive religious contemplation. It was cultivated by certain devotees of the 17th century, notably the Spaniard, Miguel Molinos, and the French woman, Jeanne de la Motte-Guyon.

Quisling, Vidkun. 1887-1945. Norwegian Fascist leader. Army major, League of Nations official, he had charge of British interests in the USSR (1927-29). Defense minister of Norway (1931-33). He founded the Norwegian Nazi party in 1933. He was Hitler's puppet ruler in Norway from 1940 to 1945. In 1945 he gave himself up, was tried, and executed. His name is synonymous with traitor.

R

Rabelais, François. 1494?-?1553. French humorist and satirist. Born in a farmhouse near Chinon. He became a monk (1509-24). He studied medicine at Montpellier (1530) and practiced in Lyons (1532). He traveled widely in France and Italy. In Italy he amused himself by collecting plants. To him France owes the melon, the artichoke, and the carnation. He took the parish of Meudon (1550-52). His fame rests on two novels, *Pantagruel* (1533) and *Gargantua* (1535). These were published under the name of Alcofribas Nasier, an anagram of François Rabelais.

Racine, Jean Baptiste. 1639-99. French dramatist. Born in La Ferté-Milon. At court (from 1663), he was a member of a group that included La Fontaine, Boileau, and Molière. Author of *Alexandre* (1665), *Andromaque* (1667), *Phèdre* (1677), etc.

Radetsky, Count Joseph Wenzel. 1766-1858. Austrian soldier who first served against Napoleon. He commanded the Austrian army which defeated the Sardinians at Custozza (1848) and Novara (1849) and captured Venice (1849). He was the governor-general of Lombardy-Venetia (1849-57).

Radic, Stefan. 1871-1928. Croatian politician. He organized the Croatian Peasant Party (1903). Before 1914 he struggled for freedom from Hungary. In 1918 he opposed the union of Croatia with Yugoslavia and led a Croatian separatist movement. Minister of Education (1925-27). He died of wounds inflicted by an assassin in the Yugoslav parliament.

Radical Socialists. French political party. They claim to be the spiritual heirs of the Jacobins. Nevertheless, the membership of the party is made up of petit bourgeoisie. It is a "bourgeois party with a popular soul." Radical Socialists are anti-clerical and favor strict government regulation or ownership of the means of transportation and communication, mines, forests, oil-fields, etc. Briand, Millerand, Herriot, and Viviani have been outstanding French Radical Socialists.

"Radicals," English. About the time (1830's) that the Liberal and Conservative Parties were formed in England, there sat in Parliament 25 or more Radicals who believed that neither major party was sufficiently progressive. These men were followers of the principles of Jeremy Bentham (q.v.). The Radicals suggested many reforms, but did little to accomplish them. After 1837, Radicalism died out.

Raeder, Erich. 1876-. German admiral. Chief of staff to Admiral Hipper in the battles of Dogger Bank (1915) and Jutland (1916). Appointed commander of the German navy (1935), he secretly rebuilt the navy in defiance of the Treaty of Versailles. In 1943 he was succeeded by Admiral Doenitz. Captured in 1945, he was sentenced to life imprisonment as a war criminal.

Raleigh (or Ralegh), Sir Walter. 1552-1618. English courtier, navigator, historian, and poet. After gaining a good reputation as a soldier, he was introduced to the court of Queen Elizabeth by Leicester. Gaining the favor of the queen, he was given estates, a license for exporting woolen goods, and a monopoly on wine. Granted a patent to lands in America, he named them "Virginia" and tried unsuccessfully to settle colonists there. One attempt was the settlement of Roanoke Island (1585). He introduced potatoes and tobacco into England and Ireland, where he had estates. He became the friend and supporter of the poet Spenser. He took part in the expedition against Cadiz (1596) and the attack on the Azores (1597). On the death of Elizabeth (1603) he was sent to the Tower of London on the charge of conspiring against James I. He lived there with his wife and son until 1616. During his captivity he composed his *History of the World.* He was released to head an expedition to seek gold on the Orinoco in Venezuela. The expedition was a failure. On his return to England, he was beheaded on the demand of the Spanish ambassador.

Rameau, Jean Philippe. 1683-1764. French organist and composer, especially of operas and ballets.

Rapallo, Treaty of. Nov. 12, 1920. An agreement between Italy and Yugoslavia which stated that Fiume was to be an independent state. Italy renounced claims to Dalmatia, except Zara. Istria was to be divided between the two countries.

Rapallo, Treaty of. April 16, 1922. An agreement between the German Republic and the Soviet Union. Reciprocal consular and trade relations were reestablished, and all pre-war debts and claims were mutually cancelled. This treaty is considered to be a step forward in the restoration of normal diplomatic relations between the new Soviet Union and the remainder of Europe.

Raphael (Raffaello Santi *or* Sanzio). 1483-1520. Italian painter. Born in Urbino. He studied under his father and later resided in Florence (1504) and Rome (after 1508). He was employed by Pope Julius II and later became the protege of Pope Leo X. Chief architect of St. Peter's (1514). Chief conservator of excavations in Rome (1520). His works include *St. Michael, St. George and the Dragon, Coronation of the Virgin, La Belle Jardinière, Holy Family, Madonna of the Chair,* and *Sistine Madonna.* He is especially famous for the frescoes that adorn the walls of the Vatican and for cartoons for tapestries in the Sistine Chapel. He is the architect for the Palazzo Pandolfi and the Villa Madama (both in Florence).

Rasputin, Grigori. 1871-1916. Russian monk and court favorite. He gained ascendancy over the Czarina and was suspected of using his influence to betray Russia to the Germans. He was assassinated (Dec. 31, 1916) by a group of Russian nobles as a patriotic measure.

Ravel, Maurice. 1875-1937. French composer. Leader of the anti-Wagner, impressionist movement. He was the master of the piano and excelled at orchestrations as well. Among his popular compositions are *Pavane pour une infante defunte, Ma Mère L'Oye, Daphnis et Chlöe,* and *La Valse.*

Raznochisti. They were 19th century Russians of no definite class: children of peasants and merchants having received secondary or higher education; children of clergymen who did not desire to enter the church; children of impoverished nobles. These "intelligentsia" formed the nucleus of the movement for Russian socialism.

Recognition of the Soviet Union. For a number of years after the Bolshevik Revolution no European country which fought among the Allies recognized the Soviet Union. The first one to do so was England (Feb. 1, 1924), when the Labor government was in power. Within two months, Italy, Norway, Austria, Greece, and Sweden also recognized the USSR. France extended de jure recognition Oct. 28, 1924. The United States recognized the USSR on Nov. 17, 1933.

Recusants. Those who persisted in refusing to conform to the Church of England. The term frequently applies to a Roman Catholic.

Red Army *or* Workers' and Peasants' Army. It was organized in the Soviet Union by Trotsky on Feb. 23, 1918.

Redi, Francesco. 1626?-?1698. Italian naturalist, poet, and court physician to the dukes of Tuscany. Through controlled experiments he helped to establish the principle that living things arise from other living things. He demonstrated that maggots in rotting meat did not arise spontaneously, as had been previously believed. He is also known as a philologist and poet.

Reform Bill of 1832, English. From the Glorious Revolution of 1688 to 1832,

England was essentially aristocratic rather than democratic. Parliament was unrepresentative in character and the franchise was too narrow. The Industrial Revolution had greatly increased the number, wealth, and prestige of the middle class. These bourgeoisie now demanded a voice in Parliament. Upon hearing of the successful bourgeoisie French Revolution of 1830, the controversy in England reached an acute stage, leading to the fall of the Wellington ministry. In 1831, a Whig ministry, headed by Earl Grey, prepared a reform bill, which was passed three times by Commons and rejected as many times by the House of Lords. King William IV refused to appoint new peers to outvote the House of Lords. The Whig ministry resigned and Wellington again became prime minister. Huge demonstrations then took place in Birmingham and London. It seemed as if civil war were about to break out. Since Wellington could not form a cabinet, the king had to invite Earl Grey to head a new government. The king now promised to create enough new peers to assure passage of the bill. The bill passed both houses and became law on June 7, 1832. King William was not forced to make good his threat to create new peers.

The bill (1) redistributed seats in the House of Commons. Boroughs containing less than 2,000 inhabitants were completely disfranchised. Boroughs with from 2,000 to 4,000 inhabitants lost one of their two seats. Of the 143 seats thus released, 65 were given to the larger English counties, 8 to Scotland, 5 to Ireland, and 65 to large towns. Some of these—Manchester, Birmingham, Sheffield, Leeds—had never been represented. (2) *Reform of franchise.* In the counties, copyholders and leaseholders of lands worth £10 a year, and tenants-at-will of lands worth £50 a year were given the vote. In boroughs, all those owning or renting houses worth £10 a year received the vote. County electors were increased from 247,000 to 370,000 and borough electors from 188,000 to 286,000. But the proportion of the electors to the population was only 1 to 22; before it had been 1 to 32. City workmen and farm laborers were still without votes. (3) Voting had previously occupied a period of 15 days. Polling was now limited to 2 days.

Reform Act of 1867, English. This bill was sponsored by the Conservative Party under the leadership of Disraeli, who described it as "taking a leap in the dark." It provided the following: (1) Fifty-eight seats in the House of Commons were transferred from smaller boroughs to more populous boroughs. (2) In the counties, the vote was given to tenants-at-will of property worth £12 a year (formerly £50), and to lease- or copyholders of land worth £5 a year (formerly £10). (3) In boroughs, before 1867 one could vote only if his residence was worth £10 or more a year. Now, an occupant of a separate dwelling, no matter what its value, could vote. Lodgers in tenement-houses, who rented unfurnished rooms for one year at £10 rent, were given the vote. Suffrage was still a minority right, as there were only 2½ million qualified voters out of a population of 32 million. However, this act was a turning point in British constitutional history, since it doubled the electorate by creating one million new voters, most of whom were drawn from the city working class.

Reform Bills of 1884 and 1885, English. These two bills, sponsored by Gladstone, gave Great Britain universal manhood suffrage. The Representation of the People Act of 1884 made the rural franchise identical with the borough franchise (see Reform Act of 1867), and gave the vote to 2 million rural workers, thus increasing the electorate 40%. The Redistribution of Seats Bill of 1885 divided the country into constituencies so that each member of Commons represented approximately 50,000 people.

Reformation, The Protestant. An open secession from the Roman Catholic Church which ran its course between 1517 and 1648. This movement has been called both the Protestant Reformation and the Protestant Revolution. Catholic writers prefer the second term because "Reformation" suggests that Protestant Reformers actually improved the Catholic religious system of the Middle Ages, something which Catholics are unwilling to admit. The movement started as a reformation within the Church and ended in a revolution and secession from the Church.

The reformation was due to a sequence of complex causes. The Babylonian Captivity and the Great Schism had greatly weakened the prestige of Rome (q.v.). Corruption and worldliness of the Church during the period of the Renaissance had disgusted many. Out of these causes had come the idea that the priestly offices of the Catholic Church were an unnecessary intermediary between the individual and God; that the Catholic Church was not the sole instrument of salvation.

Coupled with these spiritual factors were several potent non-spiritual aspects: (1) For years there had grown up a critical attitude towards the tremendous material wealth of the Church and the economic advantages it enjoyed. (2) The new national states opposed the international concept of the Church. (3) Certain German princes wished to destroy the authority of the clergy within their domains. (4) Many bourgeoisie desired to do away with the Church supervision of business life.

Although many Protestant sects came into being during the Reformation, the dominant sects were the following: (1) The Lutheran Church, which became firmly established in north Germany and Scandinavia; (2) the Zwinglian religion, the established faith in many Swiss cantons; (3) the Calvinist religion, the recognized faith of Holland, Scotland, Geneva, and of some of the German states;

(4) the Anglican Church, the established church of England.

Regicides. The name given to the judges and court officials responsible for the trial and execution of Charles I of England (see Execution of Charles I). After the Restoration (q.v.) in Oct. 1660, a court of commissioners condemned 10 regicides to death and 25 to life imprisonment. Three others were arrested in the Netherlands and executed in London in 1662. Some, however, escaped.

Regular clergy. A term applied to monks who lived by a rule (*regula*) or a constitution.

Reichsdeputationshauptschluss. Feb. 1803. According to the terms of the Treaty of Lunéville (q.v.), France was to hold all territory along the left bank of the Rhine. Many German rulers lost territory because of this provision. However, they were to be indemnified for their losses with German territory on the right bank of the Rhine. After two years of haggling, this "Enactment of the delegates of the Empire" was concluded, announcing all the indemnifications. Ecclesiastical estates and imperial cities were transferred to various rulers. Of the ecclesiastical estates, only the former Elector of Mainz (now Electoral Archchancellor) was left. Of the 48 free imperial cities, only 6 were left (3 Hanseatic cities: Lübeck, Hamburg, and Bremen; and Frankfurt, Augsburg, and Nuremberg). Tuscany, Modena, Bavaria, Baden, Württemberg, Prussia, Oldenburg, Hanover, Hesse, Nassau, and Orange-Nassau all were indemnified. As a rule, all those who were indemnified gained considerably in territory and subjects.

Reichstadt, Duke of. See Napoleon II.

Reichstag. German legislative body. Under the Empire it had no real authority. Under the Weimar Republic and the German Federal Republic (West Germany; Bonn Republic) it corresponds to the British House of Commons.

Reichstag Fire. Feb. 27, 1933. Following a fire which partly destroyed the Reichstag building and which the Nazis blamed on the Communists, President von Hindenburg issued emergency decrees which suspended free speech and press, as well as other liberties. The Reichstag elections which followed soon after (March 5) gave the Nazis 44% of the vote and their National allies 8%. On March 23, with only small dissenting vote, both the Reichstag and the Reichsrat passed an Enabling Act, which gave the government dictatorial powers until April 1, 1937, thus firmly establishing the Nazi dictatorship.

Reign of Terror. 1793-94. Faced with enemies at home and the invasion of their country by Austria and Prussia, the French Committee of Public Safety created a Committee of General Security and a Revolutionary Tribunal to deal with the danger. The former was given police power so that it could maintain order throughout France. The latter was a special court, with special rules of procedure, to try those accused of sabotaging the regime. The National Convention passed the Law of Suspects, whereby anyone was liable to arbitrary arrest who was of noble birth, or who had held public office before the Revolution, or who had any relations with an *emigré*, or who could not produce a signed certificate of citizenship. It is estimated that 2500 were executed in Paris during the Terror. In the provinces, many more were executed, particularly in Lyons and Nantes. Altogether, 10,000 persons may have been executed in the whole of France. Some of the prominent people who were guillotined during the terror were: Marie Antoinette, Madame Roland, Danton, Brissot, Robespierre, and St. Just.

Religious Wars in France. 1562-1589. During this period there were eight different wars between Catholics and Huguenots. The wars ended after Henry IV became king (1589). In 1598 he issued the Edict of Nantes (q.v.), which granted religious liberty to Huguenots, thus saving Protestantism in France for the time being.

Rembrandt (Rembrandt Harmenz van Rijn). 1606-1669. Dutch painter and etcher. Born in Leyden. The leading representative of the Dutch school. Master of the use of light and shadow. Settled in Amsterdam (1631) as a portrait painter and teacher. At first he enjoyed a great vogue, but later his work became unfashionable and he suffered financial reverses and was declared bankrupt (1656). His art became unfashionable, but he continued to paint until his death. His existing works consist of over 650 oil paintings, 2,000 drawings and studies, and 300 etchings. Among his paintings are *The Anatomy Lesson, The Night Watch, The Syndics, Descent from the Cross, Christ Healing the Sick,* etc.

Remonstrants. Followers of a Dutch theologian, Arminius (1560-1609). The conflict between them and their opponents, Contra-Remonstrants, followers of a rival theologian, Gomarus, led to severe religious dissensions in Holland in the early 17th century. Among the chief victims of the conflict was John Barneveldt (q.v.).

Renaissance. A "rebirth" of learning which began in 13th century Italy and spread to other European countries. The Renaissance was at its height during the 14th and 15th centuries. In its broadest significance, the Renaissance was a new civilization which gradually displaced, in the minds of men, the medieval conceptions of the state, society, art, and philosophy. Whereas the civilization of the Middle Ages was clerical and feudal, the Renaissance was secular and expansive. While the Renaissance succeeded in uprooting the world of medieval thought, in the end it adopted the better possessions of its predecessor.

The revolt against medieval institutions began in Italy about 1250 with the rise of cities. Feudalism had never taken deep root in Italy and was easily cast off. Italians, living under the shadow of the ruins of the ancient Roman civilization and equipped linguistically to read the ancient classics, were the pioneers in the Renaissance movement.

The Renaissance is usually thought to have begun with Petrarch (1304-74). It consisted of three interrelated spheres of activity:

(1) Humanism—Humanists were men who were passionately interested in collecting ancient Greek and Latin manuscripts. From reading these classics they developed a system of thinking in which man, his interests and development, are made dominant.

(2) Rebirth of art—architecture, painting, sculpture.

(3) Revival of interest in geography, exploration, and natural science.

Renaissance Popes. These popes were greatly interested in the Renaissance movement and devoted much of their time and energy to collecting manuscripts, writing, etc. Among them the following should be noted:

Nicholas V (*name* Tommaso Parentulecci) (1397?-1455) Pope (1447-55). He was an enthusiastic builder and a collector of manuscripts.

Calixtus III (*name* Alfonso Borgia) (1378-1458). Pope (1455-58). Born in Spain. Uncle of Pope Alexander VI. Founded the fortunes of the Borgia family.

Pius II (*name* Aeneas Silvius Piccolomini). (1405-64). Pope (1458-64). Born near Siena, Italy. He was a great scholar and writer. His works include a novel, poems, letters and dialogues, a history of the times, and a geography which is said to have influenced Columbus.

Renan, Joseph Ernest. 1823-90. French philologist and historian. Among his most famous works are a series entitled *Histoire des Origines de Christianisme*, including *La Vie de Jésus* (1863), *Les Apôtres* (1866), and *L'Eglise Chrétienne* (1879). From his critical studies he reached the conclusion that the Scriptures and Christian theology were an evolution of primitive fable and myth.

Renner, Karl. 1870-1950. Austrian statesman. A Socialist deputy since 1907, he became head of the provisional government after the abdication of Emperor Charles I (Nov. 1918). After elections were held, he became the first chancellor of the Austrian Republic. He signed the Treaty of St. Germain for Austria. Out of the political spotlight after 1920, he became (April, 1945) premier and minister of foreign affairs of the provisional Austrian government and in Dec. 1945, he was elected president.

Renoir, Pierre. 1841 - 1919. French painter. A leader of the impressionist school of painting. His paintings of women and children are among the finest products of this school of painting.

Reparations. Reparations were charged the Central Powers by the Allies at the conclusion of World War I. These payments were to compensate the civilian populations of the Allied Powers for war damage. A Reparations Commission was created to determine the amount of reparations. It was soon evident that only Germany could pay reparations and that some of these payments would have to be in goods. At the Spa Conference (July, 1920) the Commission determined that payments should be distributed as follows: France, 52%; British Empire, 22%; Italy, 10%; Belgium, 8%; Japan and

Portugal, 1½%; the other Allies, 6½%. It also decided to charge 56 billion dollars. This amount was reduced (April 28, 1921) to 32 billion dollars (plus interest). Germany paid the first installment (250 million dollars) promptly. Then, German currency became so highly inflated that further payments could not be made. Accordingly, in January, 1923, French, Belgian, and Italian troops occupied the Ruhr district as far east as Dortmund, a move which the British opposed vigorously. The inhabitants of the Ruhr countered this act with passive resistance. Conditions in the Ruhr and elsewhere in Germany worsened rapidly. In September, 1923, Berlin announced the end of passive resistance.

In 1924, the Dawes Commission (q.v.) prepared a plan which solved the reparations problem for the next five years. In 1929, the Young Commission (q.v.) prepared a 58½-year plan for the payment of reparations.

Because of the financial difficulties caused by the depression, Germany was in no position to make reparations payments in 1931. President Hoover then proposed a Moratorium. Under this proposal all payments on Inter-Allied debts and German reparations were to be postponed from July 1, 1931 to June 30, 1932.

On June 16, 1932, representatives of Germany, Belgium, France, Great Britain, Italy, and Japan met at Lausanne and agreed to set aside German reparations in consideration for payment of $714,600,000 by Germany for the general reconstruction of Europe. To meet this debt the German government was to deposit with the Bank of International Settlement 5% bonds for the whole amount. It was soon learned that this agreement was contingent upon having the United States remit the remainder of the Inter-Allied debts. This the United States refused to do. The plan of the Lausanne Conference accordingly came to naught. It is estimated that Germany paid the various Allies 5½ billion dollars in reparations.

In World War II, the principle of payment of reparations by Germany was determined at the Yalta Conference (Feb. 1945). At the Potsdam Conference (July-August, 1945) it was decided that half the German reparations were to be paid to the USSR, which agreed to pay Poland 15% of that half. The remainder was to be distributed among the United Nations by the United States and Britain. Russian reparations were paid by removing machinery and equipment from the Soviet Zone of Germany (see Dismantling). The Paris Peace Conference of 1946 imposed reparations payments on Bulgaria ($125,-000,000), Finland ($300,000,000), Hungary ($300,000,000), Italy ($360,000,-000), and Romania ($300,000,000). The United States, Britain, and France claimed no reparations from these five countries.

Reparations, German, Second World War. See Bonn Protocol.

Republic of St. Mark. This was a republic which was set up in Venice during the Revolution of 1848. It lasted until Aug., 1849. (See Revolutions of 1848.)

Republic, Proclamation of the First French. The National Convention proclaimed a republican form of government for France Sept. 22, 1792. This date was also proclaimed as the first day of the Year I.

Rerum Novarum. 1891. In this encyclical, Pope Leo XIII strove to apply Christian principles to the relations between capital and labor. Against Socialism, the encyclical stated that holding private property was an abstract human right older than any state. It combatted the notion of class warfare, contending that the Church draws rich and poor together by reminding each of the obligations which it owes the other. Religion teaches employers that their workers are not slaves. Every man must respect the dignity and worth of every other man. The encyclical approved factory regulation, regulation of hours of employment, particularly of women and children, the creation of labor unions, and the increase of small landowners. It stated that employment is the right of each person.

Restoration, The. May 25, 1660. Following the death of Oliver Cromwell (Sept. 3, 1658), his son Richard became Lord Protector of England. He did not desire the office and could not control the army. George Monck, a general who commanded all the troops in Scotland, now suddenly announced himself as the champion of the authority of Parliament. Marching south, he swept aside all opposition, was made commander of all the English armies, and compelled the Long Parliament to adjourn. He entered into correspondence with Charles II, who was in Breda, and arranged for his return. Charles II landed in Dover on May 25, 1660.

Retz, Cardinal de (Jean François Paul de Gondi). 1614-79. French clergyman and politician. Of Florentine descent. Led a riotous life and fought many duels when young. Took prominent part in the war of the Fronde (q.v.) (1648-9). Created cardinal (1651). Imprisoned (1652), but escaped. Archbishop of Paris (1654-62). Resigned and lived in retirement where he wrote his *Memoirs,* which are valuable as a source of information about court life and intrigue.

Reunion of the French People. See De Gaulle, Charles.

"Revisionists," Socialist. By 1890 many Socialists concluded that some of Marx's doctrines needed revision, since his prophecies regarding the concentration of wealth and the coming of the social revolution apparently were incorrect. Under the leadership of Edward Bernstein, the German Socialists drew up the Erfurt Program (1891) (q.v.). It outlined the following objectives:

(1) *General measures*: (a) Universal suffrage for all men and women twenty years of age or over; (b) direct control of legislation through the initiative and referendum; (c) military training for all citizens and abolition of standing armies; (d) complete freedom of press, religion, and assembly; (e) graduated income taxes; (f) compulsory universal free education; (g) free legal advice; (h) free medical service and free burial for the poor.

(2) *Special measures*: (a) Eight-hour work day; (b) one day of rest per week; (c) non-employment of children under 14; (d) prohibition of night work, with certain exceptions; (e) right to form unions which could bargain collectively; (f) workmen's compensation; (g) official inspection of factories to secure the rights of labor.

Revolutionary Tribunal. See Reign of Terror.

Revolutions of 1830 in Germany and Italy. In the year 1830, many European countries experienced revolts similar to the one in France (see July Revolution). Among the members of the Germanic Confederation, neither Austria nor Prussia was affected by the revolutionary movement. Hanover, Brunswick, Saxony, and Hesse-Cassel, however, secured liberal constitutions. In Italy, there was no revolution in Piedmont or Naples. In the Papal States, Parma, and Modena there were uprisings (1831) against the pope and the Hapsburgs. (The red, white, and green flag, eventually the flag of Italy, was first used at this time.) Austrian troops soon quelled the uprisings. The French occupied the papal town of Ancona in feeble protest against Austrian

intervention (this garrison was maintained until 1838).

Revolutions of 1848. The year 1848 was marked by revolutions in most of the countries of Europe. These uprisings were part of the struggle to democratize the governments of the various countries and as protests against the Metternich system. In Germany and Italy the revolutions were part of the movement for national unification. As in 1830, the revolutions were touched off by France.

France. Many factions in France had become dissatisfied with the regime of Louis Philippe. The democrats disliked the fact that only 200,000 men could qualify as voters. The Royalists wanted to see a descendant of Charles X upon the throne. The Catholics were scandalized by the corrupt practices of Guizot, the Huguenot premier. The underpaid workmen wished to improve their lot and, in general, looked to the Socialist, Louis Blanc, for guidance. On Feb. 23, 1848, royal troops fired on a crowd of demonstrators, killing 23. The following day, barricades appeared in many Paris streets. Louis Philippe at once abdicated in favor of his grandson, the Count of Paris, and fled to England. This phase of the revolution is known as the February Revolution.

A provisional government was then set up. To placate the followers of Louis Blanc, "national workshops," or cooperative industrial associations, were established. By May, over 100,000 workers were employed in these workshops. Unfortunately, the workshops were poorly managed and soon acquired a bad reputation for supporting men in idleness. On April 23, an election for a Constituent Assembly was held. In this election, moderate and conservative Republicans won an overwhelming majority. The Assembly promptly abolished the national workshops. Whereupon, the the workers rioted. Then occurred the "Terrible June Days" (June 24-26, 1848) when the Army, headed by Cavaignac, suppressed the riots with much bloodshed. Some leaders of the rioters were shot; 4000 were exiled to the colonies. The Constituent Assembly then drew up a constitution for France very much like the constitution of the United States. Thus began the Second Republic of France. In the elections which were held Dec. 10, 1848, the Socialist Ledru-Rollin, the Catholic Lamartine, and the bourgeoisie Republican Cavaignac, defeated one another. Louis Napoleon Bonaparte, nephew of the great Napoleon, was elected to the office of president in a landslide.

Italy. News of the downfall of Metternich (March 14) was received with joy in Milan. An uprising forced the Austrian garrison to withdraw from the city. Venice proclaimed a republic (Republic of St. Mark). Detachments of troops from all over the country hastened north to drive the Austrians from Italy. But on April 29 the pope repudiated the War of Liberation. In May, the king of the Two Sicilies abrogated constitutional government and withdrew his armies. At Custozza (July 24) the Austrian army crushed the Sardinian army and restored the *status quo*. In Feb. 1849, Mazzini's "Young Italy" party seized Rome and proclaimed a republic. By the end of June it had been crushed by French troops, ordered there by President Louis Napoleon. On March 23, 1849, Charles Albert of Sardinia was defeated by the Austrians, abandoned his throne to his son Victor Emmanuel II, and went into exile. However, the constitution which he had granted, the *Statuto*, remained in force. In August, 1849, the republic of Venice surrendered to the Austrians. Except for the liberal monarchial constitution of Sardinia, restoration in Italy was complete.

Austria. Hard upon the heels of the February Revolution of France, reform swept over Europe. News of these liberal movements caused riots in Vienna. On March 14, 1848, Metternich resigned.

The revolutionary movement now spread to all parts of the Empire. It looked as if Austria was to become five separate nations. However, the revolutions failed largely because of conflicting nationalist interests of the revolutionaries and because the Austrian army under Windischgrätz and Radetsky remained loyal to the throne. At one point, a Russian army, sent by Czar Nicholas I, helped to crush the uprisings. At the height of the revolution, Dec. 2, 1848, Emperor Ferdinand I abdicated in favor of his nephew Francis Joseph. The new emperor, aided by his chancellor, Prince Felix Schwarzenberg, put down the revolutionary uprisings in various parts of the empire until by August, 1849, when the imperial troops entered Budapest and crushed the infant Hungarian Republic, the revolution was at an end. Except that servile dues had been abolished, there was virtually nothing accomplished in this revolution.

Switzerland. During the revolutions of 1848, the Swiss cantons adopted a Federal Constitution which gave the country a strong federal government and, at the same time, granted the people of the various cantons democratic-republican governments.

Germany. Almost all the states of Germany experienced disturbances during March, 1848. During the remainder of 1848 and part of 1849, various attempts were made to liberalize and unify Germany. But the sum total of these efforts was small due to the following factors: (1) Inability of the revolutionists to agree upon the form of government (some were republicans—some were limited monarchists). (2) The unwillingness of Frederick William IV of Prussia to assume leadership of the movement. On March 31, 1848, a *Vorparlament* (preliminary parliament) met in Frankfurt and exerted so profound an influence upon the German Diet that the latter called a Constitutional Convention, the famous Frankfurt Assembly, composed of one deputy for every 50,000 inhabitants of the Germanic Confederation. This Assembly convened May 13, 1848. On Dec. 27, 1848, the Assembly announced equality before the law, freedom of persons, of press, of petition, of meeting to be the rights of Germans. But it failed to provide a national government, appointing Prince John of Austria *Reichsverweser* (Vicar of the Empire). This last step gave offense to many, particularly to republicans. In May, 1849, there were many republican uprisings, especially in the Palatinate, Saxony, and Baden.

When the Prussian government suppressed these uprisings (June-July, 1849), many German republicans migrated to the United States. In April, 1849, the Frankfurt Assembly offered the crown of hereditary German Emperor to Frederick William IV. But he refused to accept a "crown of shame" from a revolutionary assembly of social inferiors (April, 1849). The Frankfurt Assembly then slowly disintegrated.

Two plans to unify Germany were now proposed—one by the Prussian Radowitz; the other by the Austrian Schwarzenberg. Both plans were eventually discarded, and the old Frankfurt Diet reconvened. It promptly repealed the "fundamental rights" of Germans and undid all the work of the revolution.

Frederick William IV did grant a constitution to Prussia (1850). It asserted the "divine right" of the king and made the king head of the army, the church, and the civil service. The cabinet was responsible only to the king. The members of the upper house (Herrenhaus) were appointed by the king; the members of the lower house (Abgeordnetenhaus) were chosen by a three-class system of indirect elections which favored the rich and the landowners.

The revolutionary movement apparently accomplished little. Switzerland, Holland, Denmark, Prussia, Sardinia, and a few other states secured constitutional governments. Servile dues were abolished

in Austria. Nationalism, by its conflicting claims, had defeated the revolution. However, within half a century, most of the aims of the revolutionaries had been accomplished.

Reynaud, Paul. 1878-. French lawyer and politician. He held cabinet posts in 1930, '31, and '32. In 1938, as finance minister in the cabinet of Daladier (q.v.), he followed an inflationary policy. He succeeded Daladier as premier (Mar. 1940), but resigned (May 18) in favor of Petain. He was arrested (1940) and held prisoner by the Germans until 1945. He re-entered politics as an advocate of free enterprise.

Reynolds, Sir Joshua. 1723-92. English portrait painter. Suggested founding the Literary Club (1764), of which Dr. Johnson, Garrick, Goldsmith, Burke, Boswell, and Sheridan were members. Reynolds is admired for his studies of women and children, including *Master Bunbury, The Strawberry Girl, Penelope Boothby,* and *The Age of Innocence.*

Ribbentrop, Joachim von. 1893-1946. Nazi statesman. A wine-merchant who became Hitler's adviser in foreign affairs. Ambassador to Great Britain (1936-38), foreign minister (1938-45). He was condemned to death as a war criminal by the Nuremberg Tribunal and executed. (See Nazi - Soviet Pact, his greatest achievement.)

Ribera, José (La Spagnoletto). 1588-1652. Spanish painter and etcher. One of the leading painters of the Neapolitan school. Lived most of his life in Naples.

Richard I (Coeur de Lion). 1157-99. Third son of Henry II and king of England (1189-99). Although born in Oxford, he was taken to Aquitaine when an infant and while still a child invested with the duchy. It is doubtful whether he ever spent one complete year in England. It is also doubtful whether he could speak English. In 1190 he set out on the Third Crusade. After much inconclusive warfare in Palestine, he made a three-year truce with Saladin, and set out for home. He was shipwrecked in the Adriatic, and in disguise made his way through the territory of his bitter enemy, Leopold, Duke of Austria, was recognized and seized. He was handed over to Emperor Henry VI (1193), who demanded a heavy ransom. Richard's loyal subjects raised the money, and Richard returned to England (1194). He spent most of his remaining years in France, and was killed while besieging the Castle of Chaluz.

Richard II. 1367-1400. King of England (1377-99). Son of the Black Prince, he succeeded his grandfather, Edward III. During his minority, the government was entrusted to a council of twelve. But John of Gaunt gained control of it. War, hard times, and the poll tax led to a popular uprising of the men of Essex and Kent. When the popular leader, Wat Tyler, was killed, Richard rode among the rebels and said that he would be their leader. He granted them the concessions which they demanded. In 1389, Richard declared himself of age, and for eight years ruled as a constitutional monarch. He was under the good influence of his wife, Anne of Bohemia (1366-94). After her death he married Isabella, daughter of Charles VI of France. He adopted many French manners, and became an absolute ruler. A rising against him, headed by Henry of Lancaster, son of John of Gaunt, succeeded, and he was deposed (1399) by Parliament, which chose Henry as his successor. Richard seems to have been murdered early in 1400.

Richard III. 1452-85. King of England (1483-85). Youngest brother of Edward IV, he was a brave soldier and an able administrator. As Duke of Gloucester, he was a powerful supporter of his brother, particularly in the north of Eng-

land. Upon the death of his brother, he was made king, after confining the two young sons of his brother in the Tower. These two young princes perished mysteriously. Popular belief is that they were murdered at Richard's order. Richard lost his kingdom and his life at the battle of Bosworth (Aug. 22, 1485). He was overthrown by Henry Tudor, the Earl of Richmond, a Lancastrian, who became Henry VII. Had Richard been born a lawful heir to the throne and succeeded to it peacefully, he probably would have been a great king. Despite his short reign, he has left an indelible impression upon history. He was short of stature and slight of build, with one shoulder slightly higher than the other; whence his nickname "Crook-back."

Richelieu, Duc de (Armand Jean du Plessis. *Often known as* **the "Red Eminence.").** 1585-1642. French statesman and cardinal. Bishop of Luçon (1606-14). Member of the Estates-General (1614). He was a favorite of the queen-mother Marie de Médicis. He was made cardinal (1622). As chief minister of Louis XIII (1624-42), he completely dominated the government. At home he strove to achieve unity for France by diminishing the political powers of the Huguenots and the powers of the nobles. After the capture of LaRochelle (1628), the Huguenots were shorn of all political power. By suppressing the plots of Gaston d'Orléans (1626) and the Duke of Montmorency (1632), he greatly diminished the power of the nobles. In foreign affairs, his aim was to reduce the power of the Hapsburgs. This he did by supporting the Protestants in the Thirty Years' War—first by grants of money, and later by military intervention. The Peace of Westphalia which ended the war (1648) followed ideas and principles which Richelieu originated.

Rienzi, Cola di (*real name* Niccolo Gabrini). 1313-1354. Italian revolutionary leader. Often called "the last of the Romans." He led a revolution in Rome (1347) which overthrew the aristocratic government. He took the title of tribune. He alienated people by his luxury, arrogance, and pride. He was exiled (1348), but was recalled (Aug. 1354). His tyranny now led to a riot in which he was massacred (Oct. 1354).

Rimsky-Korsakov, Nicolai. 1844-1908. Russian composer. He prepared himself for a naval career when a young man. As his talents in music matured, he determined to devote his life to music. He retired from the navy in 1873. Among his compositions are *Sadko, The Snow Maiden, Le Coq d'Or,* and *Scheherazade.*

Riom Trials. 1942. Instigated by the Nazis, the Vichy government of France brought many of the former leaders—for example, Daladier, Blum, Gamelin, Reynaud, Mandel—to trial. The Nazis wanted these men pronounced guilty of having *caused* the war. Actually, they were accused of having failed to *prepare* France for war. When it became evident that the trials were coming close to proving what neither Berlin nor Vichy wanted, they were indefinitely suspended. The accused remained under arrest. In 1943 they were transferred to German soil lest they be freed and assist in a United Nations' invasion attempt.

Rising of 1745. Prince Charles Stuart, the "Young Pretender" to the throne of England, sought to regain the throne. Unsupported by any European power, he landed in west Scotland July 25, 1745, and began to form an army. After some initial success, his army was routed at Culloden (April 16, 1746). Charles fled to Europe, and finally took refuge in Rome. With the death of his brother, Henry, Cardinal of York, in 1807, the male line of the Stuarts became extinct.

Risorgimento (resurrection). A 19th century nationalist movement in Italy aimed at unifying the country. The name was popularized from a newspaper of the same name, founded in 1847 by Cavour and Balbo. The movement was largely the work of highly educated young men, whose earnest, glowing enthusiasm and self-sacrifice aroused the admiration of the world. During the Napoleonic regime, Italy was united politically for the first time since the 5th century. Italians were bitterly disappointed when their country was split up by the Congress of Vienna (q.v.). The Carbonari (q.v.) was formed to combat post-Congress-of-Vienna tyranny. During the 1830's there appeared *Young Italy,* a radical, republican, anticlerical party founded by Mazzini (q.v.). It did much to prepare the minds of Italians for unification. Bourgeoisie hoped to achieve unity by supporting the King of Sardinia in his nationalistic efforts. In 1848 (see Revolutions of 1848) efforts to unite Italy failed. Unification came in the 1860's (see Unification of Italy).

Riurik (in Frankish annals, Roric). ?-873. A Norse adventurer and pirate who in 856 (according to tradition, 862) entered Russia upon invitation, restored order, established himself in Novgorod. This is the traditional "Beginning of Russian History."

Rivet Laws. 1871. On Aug. 31, 1871, the French National Assembly passed the Rivet Laws whereby it took to itself full power not only to make the laws of France but also to draw up a constitution. It conferred on Thiers the title of "President of the French Republic." The National Assembly did not dissolve until 1875.

Robbia, Luca della. 1400-82. Florentine sculptor and ceramics worker. He is known for his work in the cathedral of Florence. This work consists of a bas-relief around the balustrade, showing choirs and bands of children. He brought into vogue the so-called della Robbia ware (blue and white glazed terra-cotta). Luca's nephew, Andrea, and Andrea's five sons contributed to the ceramic work. With the passing of time, the quality of workmanship deteriorated rapidly. Perhaps it is just as well that these later della Robbias allowed the secret of the glaze to perish with them.

Robert II (the Pious). 970?-1031. King of France (996-1031). Son of Hugh Capet. Born in Orléans.

Robespierre, Maximilien François Marie Isidore de. 1758-94. French Revolutionary. Called the "Incorruptible." Lawyer at Arras (1781-89). Member of the Estates-General (1789). Radical member of the Constituent Assembly (1789-91). Leader in the Jacobin Club (1791-92). Ardent disciple of the teachings of Rousseau. Member of the National Convention (1792). Demanded the death of Louis XVI (1793). Chosen as a member of the Committee of Public Safety (1793). Virtual dictator of France (1793-94). Sent Danton and Desmoulins to the guillotine. Began the worship of the Supreme Being (1794). Overthrown (July 27, 1794). Guillotined the next day. His death ended the Reign of Terror. He fell from public favor because as head of the Committee of Public Safety he signed the decrees which conscripted men for the army and rationed food.

Rocroi, Battle of. 1643. When a Spanish army crossed the frontier between France and the Spanish Netherlands, it was met and completely defeated by a French army, led by the great Condé. This battle marked the beginning of French military supremacy in Europe, as it marked the end of Spain's greatness in war. In the century-and-one-half prior to this battle, Spanish troops had been all but invincible in Europe.

Roebuck, John. 1718-91. English inventor. He invented the lead-chamber process of producing sulphuric acid at Prestopans (1749). He owned a great iron works at Carron (c. 1760).

Roentgen, Wilhelm Konrad von. 1845-1923. German physicist. He discovered X-rays, which are usually called after him.

Roger I of Sicily (Roger Guiscard). 1031-1101. Norman conqueror in Sicily. He aided his brother Robert Guiscard in capturing Messina (1061), Palermo (1071), etc. He assumed the title of count of Sicily (1071). His son, Roger II (1095-1154), succeeded him and assumed the title of grand count of Sicily (1101-30) and king of Sicily (1130-54). He waged successful wars against the Byzantine emperor Manuel Comnenus.

Roland de La Platière, Jean Marie. 1734-93. French revolutionary statesman. A leader of the Girondists (1791) (q.v.), by whom he was called "Cato." Minister of the interior (1792-3). Attacked by Robespierre as being a royalist at heart, he fled from Paris to Normandy and committed suicide (Nov. 15, 1793) upon learning of the execution of his wife, Jeanne Manon, *nee Phlipon* (1754-93). Commonly known as Madame Roland, her salon in Paris was the meeting place for Girondist leaders. She exercised great influence upon them. Upon the fall of the Girondists, she was arrested and guillotined (Nov. 8, 1793).

Roman Question. 1870-1929. During the Franco-Prussian War (q.v.), the French garrison in Rome was withdrawn. King Victor Emmanuel now invited Pope Pius IX to make terms with the Italian government. When the pope refused, Italian troops occupied Rome (Sept. 1870). The royal government then conducted a plebiscite among the Romans in which the vote was an overwhelming majority in favor of joining the kingdom of Italy. The Italian government tried to reconcile the pope to this situation by enacting the Law of Papal Guarantees (q.v.). The pope condemned this law and refused to accept the money offered by the royal government as indemnity. He regarded himself as a prisoner and forbade Italian Catholics to vote or hold office in the royal government. This "Roman Question" was finally settled by the Concordat with Mussolini (1929) (q.v.).

Romanesque. A style of architecture that prevailed from 800 to 1150. Church builders during these years used the Roman basilica (law court) as a model. The most striking feature of the Romanesque style is the round arch.

Romania, Origin of. Romania traces its history to 101 A.D., when the Romans under Emperor Trajan defeated the king of the Dacians and colonized the province. In 271 the Emperor Aurelian withdrew all Roman troops from the Dacian colony. Following the withdrawal of Roman soldiers, Romania, like Britain, became a battle ground for invading armies (until the 7th century). Many Slavs settled in Romania. To distinguish them from the Romans, Byzantine writers called the Slavs "Vlachs" (from this word comes modern Wallachia). In the 11th century, the Romanians were Christianized by the Greek Orthodox Church.

In 1003 the Hungarians subjugated Transylvania and kept it in subjection (except when both were vassals of the Turks) until 1919.

Moldavia and Wallachia, which together form the nucleus of the present Romanian nation, were conquered by the Turks—the former in the 15th century and the latter in 1393. Toward the end of the 16th century, Michael the Brave (1593-1601) almost succeeded in uniting and freeing Romania.

In 1774, Turkey regained Moldavia and Wallachia after losing them first to

Austria and then to Russia. In 1821, Russia forced Turkey to restore Romanian princes to their principalities. At the Congress of Paris (1858), Moldavia and Wallachia were united. Col. Alexander Cuza became prince of the united principalities, but was forced to abdicate (1866). Charles of Hohenzollern-Sigmaringen then became ruler as Carol I. He declared his country independent May 19, 1877.

Romanov, Michael. 1596-1645. Czar of Russia (1613-45). A young boyar, grandnephew of Ivan IV (1533-84), who was elected czar in 1613 by the Zemsky Sobor (popular assembly) at the conclusion of the "Time of Troubles" (1610-13) (q.v.). He was descended from a family that migrated originally from Prussia to the principality of Moscow. Michael founded the Romanov dynasty which furnished all the czars of Russia until the 1917 revolution.

Rome, Treaty of. (1924). An agreement between Italy and Yugoslavia, repudiating the Treaty of Rapallo (1920) (q.v.). Italy was to receive Fiume, while Yugoslavia received Port Baros and a 50-year lease of part of the Fiume harbor.

Rommel, Erwin. 1891-1944. German field marshal. An early member of the Nazi Party, he served as Hitler's bodyguard and rose high in the SS. He was made a general in the army after the Polish campaign (1939). His tank corps headed the break-through into France (1940). He trained a special body of tank troops, the Afrika Korps, for desert warfare. He had great success in North Africa and was created marshal. Defeated by Montgomery at El Alamein, he was driven into Tunisia and recalled to Germany. He was in command of N Forces in France at the time of the Allied invasion of Normandy. The manner of his death is not clear. It seems that he was ordered to take poison for complicity in the plot to assassinate Hitler in July, 1944.

Romney, George. 1734-1802. English historical and portrait painter. Among his works are *Death of General Wolfe, Milton and His Daughters,* and *Newton Making Experiments with a Prism.*

Roncaglian Diet. 1154. In 1154 Frederick Barbarossa led his army across the Alps and pitched camp on the Roncaglian plain. He announced a diet and called upon all Lombard cities to send their consuls to meet him. Virtually all complied, and Frederick proceeded to make himself master of northern Italy. A second diet was held in 1158 in the same place in which Frederick asserted his authority over all Italian cities. Milan resisted, was captured (1162) after a three-year siege, and was destroyed. See also Lombard League and Treaty of Constance.

Roncesvalles. 778. In 777, Charlemagne invaded Spain. This invasion was checked by the heroic defense of Saragossa. Charlemagne's rearguard was annihilated at Roncesvalles (778). Although this was a minor military operation, it gave rise to the famous poem *The Song of Roland.*

Ronsard, Pierre de. 1524-85. French poet. In his youth he was a court page. Becoming deaf (1542) he gave up court life and devoted himself to poetry. His *Odes* (1550), *Amours de Cassandre* (1552), etc., made him a great favorite of Charles IX. He was attached to the court until the death of Charles (1574). He is regarded as the father of French lyric poetry.

Roon, Count Albrecht Theodor Emil von. 1803-79. Prussian soldier and statesman. Member of the general staff (from 1836). Prussian minister of war (1859-73). Famous for his effective organization of the Prussian army which made

possible its speedy mobilization leading to decisive victories over Austria (1866) and France (1870-71).

Rossini, Gioacchino. 1792-1868. Italian composer. A very prolific composer of operatic music. Among his 39 operas are *William Tell, The Barber of Seville,* and *Moses in Egypt.*

Rousseau, Jean Jacques. 1712-78. French philosopher and writer. Born in Geneva. He ran away to Italy and Savoy. He lived in Annecy and Chambéry from 1731 to 1741. After 1741 he lived chiefly in Paris except for the period 1766-70 when he lived in England. He wrote articles on music and economics for the *Encyclopedia.* His fame as a writer was established by *Discours sur les Arts et Sciences* (1750), which developed the idea that savage society is superior to civilized society. Other great works are: *Julie, ou la Nouvelle Héloïse* (1761), *Le Contrat Social* (1762), and *Émile, ou Traité de l'Éducation* (1762). Rousseau's influence on posterity has been equalled by few men, and it is still potent. He affected most strongly politics, literature, and education. In politics he popularized the idea of the "social contract" that exists among men who attain civic liberty. In literature he was the father of the whole school of romantic sensibility. He influenced greatly the German and English romantic schools. He popularized the belief that schools should teach men to live. He also made it fashionable for mothers to breast-feed their babies, and propagated the idea that fresh air and hygiene are essential to the proper upbringing of children.

Royal Charter of France of 1814. Under Louis XVIII, France was to have a constitutional government like that of England. There was a parliament of two chambers: a chamber of peers, nominated by the king; a lower house elected by men who paid a heavy direct tax. Although the parliament could not initiate legislation, no measure could be promulgated without its consent. There was to be freedom of worship and the press. Land sales made during the Revolution were inviolable. The Legion of Honor, Bank of France, University of France, and the Concordat were retained.

Royal Council of France (pre-Revolutionary). Composed of 6 chief ministers and about 30 councilors who helped their chiefs to supervise the affairs of the kingdom. They issued decrees, conferred on foreign policy, levied taxes, and acted upon reports from local officials.

Rubens, Peter Paul. 1577-1640. Flemish painter. He painted landscapes, portraits, historical, and sacred subjects. He is renowned for the excellence of his coloring. He consorted with nobility and was frequently sent as an envoy. Among his most noted works are *The Descent from the Cross, The Fall of the Damned,* and *The Rape of the Sabines.*

Rudolf I of Hapsburg. 1218-91. Landgrave of Alsace (1239-91). Elected king of Germany (1273) and Holy Roman Emperor (1273-91). To secure recognition by the papacy, he renounced imperial claims to Rome and Sicily. He consolidated the imperial power in Austria. He defeated and killed Ottokar, king of Bohemia, at Marchfield (1278). His accession to power in 1273 ended the Great Interregnum (q.v.). He made his sons rulers over Austria and Styria, thus laying the foundation for Hapsburg control of Austria.

Rudolf II. 1552-1612. Holy Roman Emperor (1576-1612). Educated at the court of Spain by Jesuits. As emperor he determined to stamp out Protestantism in his domains. Successful revolts in Hungary forced him (1608) to make his brother Matthias king of Hungary and

governor of Austria and Moravia. In 1609 he gave the Bohemians religious liberty. In 1611 he transferred Bohemia to Matthias.

Rule of St. Benedict. The constitution prepared by St. Benedict (520) to govern the monastery at Monte Cassino. To enter a monastery, a candidate had first to pass through a novitiate. He had to vow conversion of life and obedience. He had to swear to obey the abbot and to remain within the monastery walls unless he had special permission to leave. He had to agree to live a life of poverty and chastity.

A monk's day was divided between eight regular services, which occupied four or five hours, and manual labor. Some monks were given the duty of cultivating the monastery fields. Others were given the duty of cooking and serving the food. Still others labored at skilled crafts or clerical tasks. Some taught the younger monks, looked after guests, or cared for the destitute who applied at the monastery for relief. The Rule became the almost universal model for all monastic orders.

Rumiastsev, Chancellor Count Nikolai Petrovich. 1754-1826. Russian statesman. At the beginning of the 19th century, his interest in history and geography induced him at his own expense to collect and publish ancient Russian documents. He gave money for geographical expeditions and historical research. His collections were housed in the Rumiastsev Museum in Moscow, now called the Lenin Library.

"Rump" Parliament. Following Pride's Purge (Dec. 6, 1648) (q.v.), a group of members of the House of Commons continued in session until dissolved by Cromwell (April 20, 1653). This group was known as the "Rump Parliament." The Rump voted to execute King Charles I; it created the Commonwealth; it abolished the House of Lords and the Established Church.

Rupert, Prince. Count Palatine of the Rhine and Duke of Bavaria. 1619-82. Rupert was the nephew of Charles I, king of England. He commanded the Royalist armies during the English Civil War (1642-46). After the Restoration (1660) he held high offices in England, such as admiral of the fleet (1673) and first lord of the admiralty (1673-79). He improved the process of mezzotint, experimented with gunpowder and boring of guns, and invented a brasslike alloy, Prince's metal.

Russell, Lord John. 1st Earl Russell of Kingston Russell. 1792-1878. British statesman. Born in London. Whig M.P. (1813). Active leader for Parliament reform. One of the four framers of the Reform Act of 1832. Leader of the Whigs in the House of Commons (1834). Home secretary (1834). Colonial secretary (1835). Prime minister and first lord of the treasury (1846-52). President of the council (1854-55). Foreign secretary (1859-65). Prime minister (1865-66).

Russian Campaign. 1812.
Causes: The Continental System (q.v.) was never popular in Russia. Napoleon's marriage with a Hapsburg princess was interpreted by the Russians as an alliance between France and Austria against Russia. It also seemed to the Russians that Napoleon was bent on restoring the Kingdom of Poland.
Preparations: Napoleon made an alliance with Austria and Prussia. Russia made peace with Turkey. Russia, Sweden, and England formed an alliance. Sweden was to be indemnified with Norway for the loss of Finland to Russia (1809).
Napoleon invaded Russia with an army of perhaps 500,000 men. In June, 1812, this army crossed the Niemen River. After the destruction of Smolensk by the French (Aug. 17-18), the Russian commander, Barclay de Tolly, was replaced by General Kutusov. He fell back, destroying all food and buildings until Sept. 7, when he fought the French at Borodino. Both sides suffered severe losses in this battle. Although the result was inconclusive, the Russians retreated, and the French occupied Moscow on Sept. 14. On Sept. 15-19, Moscow burned. It could not be used for winter quarters. On Oct. 19 the French began a retreat, harassed by the Russians and Cossacks, and very much beset by cold and hunger. On Nov. 26-28 occurred the crossing of the Beresina. Ney and Oudinot forced the passage of the river in one of the most horrible episodes of the retreat. From this point, the Grand Army disintegrated. Napoleon abandoned the army and hurried to Paris. Only 100,000 men remained of the host which had invaded Russia.

Russian Expansionism. The USSR seized the initiative immediately after the end of World War II and proceeded to bring the Baltic and Slavic nations of Europe under its control. Latvia, Lithuania, and Estonia were annexed outright. Native communistic groups, strongly supported by Moscow, gained control of Yugoslavia, Czechoslovakia, Romania, Poland, Bulgaria, Hungary, and Albania. The Soviets occupied eastern Germany and eastern Austria. Around these regions the USSR erected an "iron curtain." Only Yugoslavia rebelled and escaped from Russian domination. In Greece, the Communists made a strong bid for control but failed. To checkmate Soviet expansion, a policy of containment (q.v.) has been designed by western Europe and the United States.

Russian Political Parties. The first Russian political party was the Workers' Social Democratic Party, organized in 1898, on the model of the German Social Democratic Party, which followed the teachings of Karl Marx. The party attempted to get in touch with the workers through party "cells," a form of political organization peculiar to Russia, in which a secretly organized group of trusty party members attempted to control a large group of non-party members. In 1903, the Social Democratic Party split into two groups. The radical group, the Bolsheviks, or majority, sought to realize a social revolution through violent means. The Mensheviks, or minority, contended that before the social revolution could be effective, a bourgeoisie or democratic regime had to develop. The Bolshevik leader was Vladimir Ulianov, whose pseudonym was Lenin. The Menshevik leader was Plekhanov, a theoretical Marxist.

The Social Revolutionary Party undertook to defend the interests of the peasants. They tried to organize "cells" among the peasants. Whereas the Social Democrats advocated a mass movement to achieve their goal, the Social Revolutionaries contented themselves with terrorist acts against the government. They derived their theory not from Marx but from French socialism of the Utopian school. Both socialistic groups recruited many followers from university students. They also attracted many teachers, doctors, and lawyers.

In 1903 the Constitutional Democratic Party (Cadets) was formed to organize the middle classes into political action. Their program was based on the teachings of constitutional groups of Western Europe and America.

Russian Serfdom, Origin of. Under Ivan the Terrible (1530-84) the power of the boyars was greatly reduced by the creation of the *Oprichina*, a "separate" or "private" household or court. The new courtiers, known as *Oprichniks*, waged relentless war against the boyars. This struggle is comparable to the war waged by the communists against the bourgeoisie. Land seized from the boyars was given to a new land-owning class, called

Pomiestchicks, that is, those who served the czar. On these new holdings were peasants who at first were freemen and had the right of migration. Later, migration was prohibited and the peasants were fixed to the ground, but not to the proprietor. The peasant was not the property of the landowner and retained his civil rights; he could sue in court and own both land and slaves. Following the death of Ivan, a census was taken. Peasants were registered as being fixed to the land which they occupied, and were thenceforth regarded as serfs.

Russian Serfs, Freeing of. According to the law of March 3, 1861, during the reign of Alexander II household serfs were to be freed within two years without redemption, but were to receive nothing on gaining their freedom. Peasant serfs were to receive not only their freedom but also certain allotments of land. The land which the serfs received did not become their private property but was held for their benefit as the actual property of the landowner. If the former serf desired actual ownership, the land was bought from the landowner by the government and paid for by the serf on a long-term plan. Eighty-five percent of the peasants' land was bought in this fashion. However, the peasants did not secure complete ownership of the land. Each peasant village (mir) received the whole area of land in communal ownership under collective responsibility for the redemption payments of all the members of the commune. The principles of communal ownership and collective responsibility became features of the Russian social and political system.

Russo-Finnish War, First. Nov. 1939– Mar. 1940. In Oct. 1939, the Soviet government demanded from Finland (1) a number of islands in the Gulf of Finland; (2) surrender of part of the Karelian Isthmus; (3) an outlet at Petsamo in the north; (4) demilitarization of the Russo-

Finnish frontier; (5) a 30-year lease of the port of Hangö. In return, Finland was to receive 2134 square miles of Russian territory. When the Finns refused, war broke out. For this aggression Russia was expelled by the League of Nations (Dec. 14, 1939). England and France wanted to help Finland, but were prevented from doing so because Norway and Sweden forbade the passage of foreign troops. After heroic defense, Finland gave in and surrendered to Russia (1) all the Karelian Isthmus; (2) the city of Viipuri; (3) all the territory around Lake Ladoga; (4) most of the islands in the Gulf of Finland; (5) enough of the Rybacki Peninsula to give the USSR dominance of the port of Petsamo and the nearby nickel mines. The USSR organized these new territories into the Karelian-Finnish Republic, which became part of the Soviet Union.

Russo-Japanese War. 1904-05. The war began without declaration on Feb. 9, 1904, when the Japanese naval vessels attacked Russian ships in the outer harbor of Port Arthur. The Russians suffered from supply difficulties, since the eastern army depended upon the Trans-Siberian railway, which was not yet completed. There was no line around Lake Baikal. The war was unpopular with the Russian people. The Russian army was led by inferior commanders. The Baltic Fleet under Admiral Rozhdestuensky was sent to the Far East, only to be destroyed by the Japanese in the Battle of Tsushima Straits. The defeats led to internal disorders in Russia. The Russian peace delegation, headed by Witte, concluded peace with the Japanese at Portsmouth, N. H., under the aegis of Pres. Theodore Roosevelt on Sept. 5, 1905. Russia ceded to Japan the southern half of the Island of Sakhalin and its lease to the Liaotung Peninsula, but retained control of the railroads in northern Manchuria and paid no indemnity.

Russo-Turkish War. 1828-29. During the Greek war for independence, Russia attacked Turkey and fought nearly to Constantinople. By the Treaty of Adrianople, Turkey acknowledged the independence of Greece, granted autonomy to Serbia and the principalities of Moldavia and Wallachia (Romania). It also surrendered claims on Georgia in the Caucasus and recognized jurisdiction of Russian consuls over Russian traders in Turkey.

Russo-Turkish War. 1877-78. Assuming the rôle of the champion of Christendom, Russia (aided by Romania) attacked Turkey with the avowed aim of assisting the Christians in the Balkan Peninsula. Although the Turks put up a fierce resistance, in March, 1878, the Russians were at the gates of Constantinople and the Turks sued for peace. By the Treaty of San Stefano (1878), the independence of Montenegro was reaffirmed and Serbia and Romania were declared to be independent principalities (not kingdoms). An autonomous Bulgaria, under the suzerainty of the sultan, was created. Russia was to secure territory in Transcaucasia. Austria-Hungary demanded that the terms of this treaty be submitted to a European congress for approval. Accordingly, the Congress of Berlin (q.v.) was convened.

Ruthenia (Carpatho-Ukraine). A province of Czechoslovakia lying between Hungary, Romania, and Poland. Originally part of Poland, it became part of Austria in the Polish partitions in the 18th century. It was awarded to Czechoslovakia in 1919, so that Czechoslovakia might have a common frontier with Romania and thus hem in Hungary. After Munich (1938), the Hungarians seized Ruthenia. It was intended that Ruthenia be returned to Czechoslovakia in 1945. Instead, the USSR annexed it, adding it to the Ukrainian Republic.

Ruyter, Michel Adriaanszoon de. 1607-76. Dutch admiral and naval hero. He defeated the English fleet under Monck in a four day battle off Dunkirk (1666). He sailed up the Thames in defiance of England. He commanded against the combined English and French fleets at Southwold Bay (1672). He commanded the Dutch-Spanish squadron against the French and Sicilians (1676) and was mortally wounded in a battle off the coast of Sicily.

Ryswick, Treaty of. Sept. 30, 1697. Between France, England, and Holland ending the War of the League of Augsburg (q.v.). Restoration of conquests between France and England and Holland. William of Orange was acknowledged king of England with Anne as his successor. The chief fortresses in the Spanish Netherlands were to be garrisoned with Dutch troops as a barrier between Holland and France. France restored to Spain all places which had been "reunited" since the Treaty of Nijmegen (q.v.) with the exception of 82 places, and all conquests. Holland restored Pondicherry in India to France, but received commercial privileges in return. France ceded to the emperor all "reunions" except Alsace, which was thus lost forever to the empire. France received Strassburg. Lorraine was restored to Duke Leopold. The Rhine was made free.

S

Sack of Rome by the Normans (1084). Henry IV besieged Rome, hoping to capture Pope Gregory VII who had shut himself up in the Castle of St. Angelo. This was the final act in the duel between these two men (q.v.). Gregory appealed for help to Robert Guiscard, the leader of the Normans in Italy. Robert arrived with an army and drove off Henry's forces. Then the Normans sacked Rome so thoroughly that Gregory was afraid to remain in Rome. He traveled south with the Normans and died (1085) in Salerno.

Sadowa. See Austro-Prussian War.

St. Bartholomew's Day, Massacre of. Aug. 23-24, 1572. Massacre of Huguenots in France during the Religious Wars (q.v.). The massacre was instigated by the queen-mother, Catherine de Médicis, and the Duke of Guise and his brother, the Cardinal of Lorraine. Admiral Coligny, the ablest Huguenot leader, was among the slain. In Paris the massacre continued two days and nights. The example of Paris was followed in rural areas. Murdering of Huguenots continued until mid-October. At the time it was thought that 100,000 had been slain. Perhaps as many as 7,000 did perish. The news of the massacre was received in other countries with various emotions. Philip II of Spain laughed. The pope had a commemorative medal struck off. Many Catholic princes mourned the deed. Elizabeth of England ordered her court into mourning.

St. Germain, Treaty of. Sept. 10, 1919. An agreement between Austria and the Allies at the end of World War I. This treaty recorded the break-up of the Hapsburg dominions. Austria recognized the independence of Czechoslovakia, Yugoslavia, Hungary, and Poland. Eastern Galicia, Trentino, south Tyrol, Trieste, and Istria were ceded to various countries. The Austrian army was limited to 30,000 men. Austria was required to pay reparations for 30 years. A union (Anschluss, q.v.) between Austria and Germany was forbidden, except with permission from the League of Nations.

St. James of Campostella. The miraculous discovery of the bones of St. James the Greater (one of the Twelve Disciples) at Campostella in Spain (899) led to the founding of one of the most influential shrines in Europe. St. James (Diego) is the patron saint of Spain.

St. Just, Louis Antoine Léon de. 1767-94. French revolutionary leader. Member of the National Convention (1792). Member of the Committee of Public Safety (1793). Active in overcoming the

Girondists and bringing on the Reign of Terror. Intimate of Robespierre. Arrested and guillotined with Robespierre (July 28, 1794).

Saint-Saëns, Camille. 1835-1921. French pianist, organist, composer. Composer of operas, symphonies, symphonic poems, chamber music, and much piano and church music. The opera *Samson et Dalila*, the symphonic poem *La Danse Macabre*, the humorous suite *Le Carnaval des Animaux*, the symphonies in A minor and C minor, and a G minor piano concerto are some of his notable compositions.

Saint-Simon, Comte de, Claude Henri. 1760-1825. French philosopher and social scientist. Born in Paris. He served (1777-83) as a volunteer in the French troops fighting with the Americans in the American Revolution. He returned to France (1783) and amassed a fortune in land speculation. He then lost all of his money in various experiments. Among his writings are *Système Industrial* (1820-23) and *Nouveau Christianisme* (1825). His disciples developed a moral-religious cult, which, though split and disintegrated by 1833, exerted much influence upon later socialistic thought. Thus, Saint-Simon is regarded as the father of French socialism.

Saint Sophia (Santa Sophia). A church in the Byzantine style which was built in Constantinople by the Emperor Justinian (527-65). It later became a Mohammedan mosque. It is a classic example of Byzantine art.

Saladin. 1138-1193. Sultan of Egypt and Syria. Proclaimed sultan (1174). Conquered most of Syria. Campaigned to drive Christians from Palestine. Captured Acre, Jerusalem, and Ascalon. Fought against the crusaders in the Third Crusade (1189-92) (q.v.). Although he lost some territory to them, he was in the main victorious and signed a favorable three-year truce. Introduced to Europe by Sir Walter Scott as a character in *The Talisman.*

Saladin Tithe. 1188. This is the first example of taxes imposed upon property and income in England. It called for 1/10 of the revenues and goods of all subjects to assist in the recovery of Jerusalem, which had been conquered by Saladin in the preceding year.

Salic Law. A code of law for the Salian Franks published by Clovis in the latter part of the 5th century. Like other records of the continental Germans of the time, it was published in Latin. It contained many provisions to regulate the administration of justice. The only provision of this code that has come down to modern times is the principle that no woman shall succeed to the throne of a country.

Salisbury Plain, Oath of. 1086. In this oath, all vassals and landowners of England swore loyalty to the king, as against all other lords. It was a device used by William the Conqueror to modify the power of the great barons.

Salonika, Armistice of. Sept. 30, 1918. An agreement between Bulgaria and the Allies which took Bulgaria out of World War I. The Bulgarian army was demobilized and Bulgarian territory was made available for Allied operations. Following this armistice (Oct. 4), Czar Ferdinand abdicated and was succeeded by his son Boris.

San Francisco Conference. April 25, 1945. This conference drafted the Charter for the United Nations. It was attended by delegates from fifty nations (forty-six original members and four newly admitted). The conference was in session nine weeks. The Charter was unanimously approved by the delegates.

The United States Senate ratified it in July 28, 1945, by a vote of 89 to 2. By Oct. 24, 1945, enough nations had ratified the Charter for the document to go into effect.

San Ildefonso, Second Treaty of. Oct. 1, 1800. France secured Louisiana from Spain in return for the promise to enlarge Parma.

San Stefano, Treaty of. See Alexander II.

Sanctions. This term has come to mean an economic boycott of a country that resorts to war contrary to its obligations to the League of Nations. Economic sanctions were authorized under Article 16 of the Covenant. The League imposed sanctions only once: against Italy when it invaded Ethiopia (Oct. 1935). Export of arms and ammunition to Italy was forbidden. However, petroleum, iron and steel, coal and coke, all essential to Italy in the conduct of the war, were not placed on the list. Imposition of sanctions against Italy was of such little effect that sanctions were abandoned by April, 1936.

Sans-culotte. Literally, "without knee-breeches." During the Reign of Terror it became fashionable to wear long trousers, which, in the days of the Old Regime, were the garb of workingmen. A true revolutionary was said to be a man without knee-breeches, that is, he was not affiliated with the old nobility.

Santa Hermandad (Brotherhood). An organization formed in medieval Castile for the mutual protection against outlaws, criminals, etc. It was revived (1476) and strengthened by Ferdinand and Isabella.

Saracen conquest of Sicily. In 827, at the invitation of some Christian rebels, a native Berber dynasty of North Africa invaded Sicily. Palermo was taken in 831 and became the Moslem capital. Most of the island was subjugated by 850. From time to time the Saracens conquered parts of southern Italy. Here they remained until they were finally driven out by the Normans (1077).

Sardinia and France, Alliance between. 1858. Napoleon III and Cavour "accidentally" met at Plombières and reached the following agreement: France was to assist Sardinia in driving the Austrians from Lombardy and Venetia and to allow the formation of a single Italian state in the north. France was to receive Savoy and Nice. Prince Napoleon (Plon-Plon), Napoleon's cousin, was to marry the daughter of Victor Emmanuel II of Sardinia. This alliance was of paramount importance in the unification of Italy for the war did come about as planned.

Savonarola, Girolamo. 1452-1498. Italian reformer. Born in Ferrara of noble parentage. He joined the Dominican Order (1475). He went to Florence in 1482 and became prior of St. Mark's in 1491. He preached violent sermons, denouncing luxury, the corruption of the clergy, and the licentiousness of the nobles. Leader of the democratic party, he drove the Medicis from power (1494) and became the virtual dictator of Florence. He instituted a regime which was severely Puritan in nature. He fell from power and was excommunicated (1497). He was imprisoned and demanded a trial by ordeal of fire. This public trial failed to come off, and Savonarola fell from public favor. He was tortured and hanged, with two other Dominicans, and burned (May 23, 1498).

Savory, Thomas. See Newcomen, Thomas.

Scarlatti, Alessandro. 1659-1725. Italian composer. Born at Trapani. At the court of Queen Christina of Sweden at Rome he produced his first opera (1680). He was musical director of the court of Naples (1694-1703), conducted the conservatory there, and founded the Neapolitan school of composition. He wrote nearly 120 operas, 200 masses, 10 oratorios, 500 cantatas, and many madrigals and motets. His son, Domenico (1685-1757), was a composer of sonatas for the piano.

Schacht, Hjalmar Horace Greeley 1877-. German financier. President of the Reichsbank (1923-30, 1933-39). Minister in Hitler's cabinet (1933-37). He instituted a complicated system of currency controls and barter trade with foreign countries which enabled Germany to secure raw materials for its rearmament program and extended German economic influence in Central Europe, the Balkans, and South America. Being accused of taking part in a plot against Hitler (1944), he was arrested and placed in a concentration camp. He was acquitted (1946) by the Allied Court for War Criminals at Nuremberg and (1948) by a German "denazification" court.

Scharnhorst, Gerhard Johan David von. 1755-1813. Prussian general. Born in Hanover. He began to reorganize the Prussian army in 1807. He originated the General Staff of the German army.

Scheidemann, Philipp. 1865-1939. German Socialist. Minister of finance and colonies in the provisional government (1918). First chancellor of the Weimar Republic (1919).

Schiller, Friedrich. 1759-1805. German poet and playwright. He is regarded as second only to Goethe in the field of German literature and as first among the German dramatists. Among his plays are *Wilhelm Tell, Maria Stuart, Die Jungfrau von Orleans, Die Braut von Messina.* He translated into German *Macbeth* and *Phèdre.* His histories include *Geschichte des Abfalls der Vereinigten Niederlande* and *Geschichte des Dreissigjährigen Krieges.*

Schism, The Great. 1378-1417. Pope Gregory XI moved the Papacy back to Rome from Avignon in 1377, but died the next year. (See Babylonian Captivity.) Now there appeared two rival papal lines, one in Rome and one in Avignon. Germany, England, Denmark, Sweden, and Poland acknowledged the Roman Pope. France, Naples, Savoy, Scotland, Lorraine, Castile, and Aragon supported the Avignon Pope. The Council of Constance (q.v.) (1414) deposed the rival popes and elected Martin V (1417), thus ending the schism. The spectacle of two rival popes, each calling the other a heretic, shook the foundations of the doctrine of Petrine supremacy and paved the way for the Protestant Reformation.

Schmalkalden, League of. In 1530-1 the Protestant communities of Germany formed the League of Schmalkalden to defend themselves from attack. Francis I of France made an alliance with the League.

Schmalkaldic War. 1546-47. Emperor Charles V made war upon the Schmalkaldic League, a union of Protestant German nobles, for the purpose of crushing Protestantism in Germany. He was greatly aided when Maurice, Duke of Saxony, suddenly deserted the League and went over to the emperor. The confederates were soundly defeated by Charles at Mühlberg (1547). Maurice became Elector of Saxony. Charles tried to make a compromise which would settle religious problems in Germany. He prepared the Augsburg Interim (q.v.), designed to maintain a truce until some settlement might be reached by a church council. In 1552, Maurice of Saxony suddenly attacked Charles, forced him to flee, and completed his overthrow. In this attack, Maurice was joined by Henry II of France. Charles was forced to sign the Peace of Passau (1552), which provided that an imperial diet should be summoned to settle religious questions, that

Lutherans and Catholics should not molest one another, and that Lutherans and Catholics both should be admitted to the supreme court of the empire. In 1555 a diet assembled at Augsburg concluded the Religious Peace of Augsburg (q.v.). This agreement settled that any state in the empire might permit Catholic and Lutheran worship, or permit one and exclude the other. No other sect was included in the arrangement. The doctrine of *cuius regio eius religio* (of whom the region of him the religion) was put into practice. Thus, the government of a state would prescribe the religion of the subjects. This principle created religious liberty for princes, but not for subjects. The Peace of Augsburg created a period of truce before the greater struggle of the Thirty Years' War (1618-48).

Scholasticism. An intellectual system which developed during the 11th century and continued to be in vogue in schools until the days of the Reformation. It was an effort to explain by reason the dicta of faith. Scholastics had secured from the Arabs some of the rules of Aristotle's logic. These principles were applied, not as a method of acquiring knowledge, but only for arranging it. The syllogism was highly valued as a tool of reason. As it was used, the syllogism had value only to discipline the mind. Scholasticism was created by churchmen. It accomplished little or nothing for lay society.

Schönbrunn, Treaty of. Oct. 14, 1809. After the defeat at Wagram, the Austrians were forced to sign this treaty with Napoleon. Austria lost 32,000 square miles and 3½ million inhabitants. To Bavaria Austria ceded Salzburg, Berchtesgaden, the Innviertel, and half of Hansrückviertel. To the Grand Duchy of Warsaw, West Galicia. To Russia, the Tarnopol section of East Galicia. To France, all the lands beyond the Save River. Austria agreed to join the Continental System and to break off all connections with England.

"School of Navigation." Later, Naval Academy. Founded in Russia in 1700 by Peter the Great with a Scotchman, Henry Fargwarson, as head. The pupils of this school later became teachers of mathematics throughout Russia.

Schubert, Franz Peter. 1797-1828. Austrian composer. Born in Vienna. He began writing songs at the age of 14. During his short life he composed about 600 songs. Among his other compositions are a symphony in C major, one in B minor (unfinished), 16 sonatas, and chamber music.

Schuman Plan. In May, 1950, Foreign Minister Robert Schuman of France proposed that the coal and steel industries of France and Germany be pooled and placed under a single international agency. After a series of conferences, Belgium, the Netherlands, Luxemburg, and Italy joined with France and West Germany in a treaty which was ratified in June, 1952. Thus was created the European Coal and Steel Community. It is managed by a nine-man High Authority which has taxing power and the right to direct and finance the modernizing of plants; to set prices, wages, and working conditions; and to control production. There is a six-member Council of Ministers, which represents labor and the producing interests of the participating nations. The political interests of the six nations are represented by a 78-member Common Assembly, chosen by the national parliaments.

Schuschnigg, Kurt von. 1879-. Austrian statesman, born in Riva, South Tyrol. A lawyer, he became minister of justice and education under Dollfuss (1932-34). Upon the death of Dollfuss, he became chancellor (1934-38). After the *Anschluss* (q.v.), he was a prisoner of the Germans until 1945. In 1947 he settled in the United States.

Schutzbund (Austrian). A semi-military organization formed in Austria in the 1920's among the workers to protect the socialistic gains which they had achieved. In 1931 the Schutzbund numbered 90,000 trained armed men. (By the Treaty of St. Germain, the Austrian army was limited to 30,000.)

Schutzstaffeln (SS). See Elite Guards.

Schwarzenberg, Prince Felix. 1800-52. Austrian diplomat. Prime minister of Austria (1848-52). He suppressed the insurrections in Hungary and Italy. He restored (1850) the old federal diet and caused Emperor Francis Joseph I to suspend entirely the new constitution (Dec. 31, 1851).

Schweitzer, Albert. 1875-. Alsatian philosopher, theologian, physician, and musician. Mission doctor in Lambaréné, French Equatorial Africa, since 1913. He is one of the world's greatest organists and an authority on the building of pipe organs. His theological books include *The Quest of the Historical Jesus* and *The Mysticism of Paul the Apostle.* His philosophy is developed in *The Philosophy of Civilization.* He is an authority on J. S. Bach (q.v.) and Goethe (q.v.). He won the Nobel Peace Prize in 1952.

Scientific Socialism. This type of Socialism was originated by Karl Marx. Marx made four significant contributions: (1) He systematized existing socialistic theories. (2) He emphasized the political, as well as the economic, character of Socialism. (3) He conferred on Socialism a philosophy and a claim to be considered a science. This philosophy, often called economic determinism, contains three formulas: (a) the course of history has always been determined by economic factors; (b) present society has been evolved out of class struggles of the past; (c) present capitalistic society will inevitably change into another type of social organ-

ization. (4) He appealed, not to theorists or philanthropists, but directly to workmen themselves.

Scott, Sir Walter. 1771-1832. English poet and novelist. In his early years he was a popular poet whose *The Lady of the Lake, Marmion,* and *The Lay of the Last Minstrel* enjoyed wide popularity. He next turned to writing novels. Here he also had great popular success. His novels are grouped under the general title "Waverley Novels."

Scutage. A tax on each knight's fee which the king might impose in lieu of military service. Originating in England under Henry I, it was greatly increased by Henry II. The money secured from this source was used to hire foreign mercenaries.

Secretariat of the UN. The Secretariat is a kind of international civil service. It is made up of a staff of permanent members, drawn from all parts of the world, who carry on the day-to-day activities and the "housekeeping" of the UN. At the head is the Secretary-General. He is elected for a term of 5 years by the General Assembly on nomination by the Security Council. He is eligible for re-election. The Secretary-General has the power to ask the Security Council to act on a matter which he believes threatens international peace, and he may appear personally before the Council or take individual action to preserve the peace.

Secular clergy. A term applied to those who are properly ordained as bishops, priests, deacons, and others to serve the Church in the world (*saecula*).

Security Council of the UN. The primary responsibility of the Security Council is to safeguard peace. To accomplish this aim, the Security Council is in continuous session at UN Headquarters in New York City. The Council is composed of five permanent members (the United States, the Soviet Union, Great Britain, France, and China) and six non-permanent members, rotated among the smaller nations (2-year terms). The Security Council may try to settle a dispute peacefully by negotiation, mediation, conciliation, arbitration, judicial settlement, and the like. It may act on its own initiative or may have its attention called to the matter by the Secretary-General, the General Assembly, a member state, or a non-member state. Unlike the League of Nations, the Security Council does not have to wait for the actual outbreak of war, but may act upon a threat to peace.

The UN Charter does not define aggression. The Security Council has broad discretion in deciding what constitutes aggressive action. The Security Council may punish offenders by severing diplomatic relations; by cutting off all communications; by boycott. It was originally intended that the Security Council should have a military force of its own to use to halt aggression, but this goal has not yet been achieved.

Each permanent member of the Council can block action by its negative vote.

The General Assembly has delegated to the Security Council the problems of controlling atomic energy and reduction of armaments.

Sejm. The Polish Diet (see also Liberum Veto).

Seljuk Turks. See Turks.

Selim. Name of three Turkish sultans.
Selim I (1467-1520). Sultan (1512-1520). Conquered sections of Persia (1514), and annexed Syria (1516) and Egypt (1517).
Selim II (1524-74). Sultan (1566-74). Conquered Cyprus (1570) and lost the naval battle of Lepanto (1571).
Selim III (1761-1808). Sultan (1789-1807). Tried to reorganize his army on western European models. Thus he pro-voked a revolt of the Janizary corps. He was deposed and strangled in prison.

Sempach, Battle of. 1386. A critical battle which was won by the Swiss Confederates over the Austrians. It marks a milestone in Swiss liberty. In this battle, Arnold of Winkelried is said to have made a breach in the ranks of the enemy by gathering in his breast as many spears as he could grasp.

Senlac, Battle of. See Hastings, Battle of.

Separation Law. 1905. This law repealed the Concordat of 1801 between France and the Catholic Church. Adherents of all creeds were placed on an equal footing. The state was relieved of paying the salaries of clergymen. All buildings actually used for public worship and as dwellings in that connection were to be made over to the associations for public worship. The Church was henceforth free to manage its internal affairs without state interference. This law is a landmark in the history of France.

Separation of Church and State, France. Sept. 1794. The National Convention (1792-95) formally separated Church and State in Sept. 1794, established liberty of worship, and restored the churches to Christian worship on condition that the clergymen submitted to the laws of the state. At the same time, Jews were made French citizens upon affirmation that they belonged to a religious community and considered themselves bound by the laws of France, rather than by their own laws.

September Massacres. Sept. 2-5, 1792. In the period from August 10, when the king was suspended from office, to September 21, when the National Convention assembled, France was in a state of anarchy. Supreme control fell into the hands of the revolutionary commune of

Paris. Danton was virtual dictator. When the news of the capture of Verdun by the Austrians and Prussians reached Paris on September 2, the people rose up and began to massacre royalists in Paris. For five days, royalists were dragged from prisons and executed after a farcical trial by a self-constituted court. From 2,000 to 10,000 folk were killed during these September massacres.

Serbia, Origin of. The cradle of the Slavic race was the north slopes of the Carpathians, where the Slavs were an agricultural people. When the Roman Empire was in the process of disintegration in central and southern Europe, the Slavs migrated south and west during the 6th and 7th centuries, following the Teutonic tribes. At the end of this period, the Slavs were in possession of all of southeastern and central Europe. The invasion of the Magyars and expansion of Teutonic tribes from the west compressed the territories held by the Slavs and separated the Northern from the Southern Slavs. The Serbs were in possession of the Balkan Peninsula by 650. Some of them extended as far west as Carniola and Carinthia. The Slovenes were conquered by the Franks in the 9th century and were thenceforth part of the German Empire. The Croats were conquered by the Franks, regained their independence, and were again subdued. Gradually the Serbs built up a powerful kingdom. Under Stephen Dushan (1334-1356) they even threatened to conquer the Byzantine Empire. In 1389 they were defeated by the Turks at the Battle of Kossovo. They became subject to the Turks and were made part of the Turkish Empire (1458). They remained under Turkey until 1878.

Two small portions of Serbia were never conquered by the Turks. One was the mountain country Montenegro, which finally became part of Yugoslavia (1919). The other was the Republic of Dubrovnik (Ragusa), which became rich by trade and was a center of Slavic art and literature. It was captured by Napoleon's Marshal Marmont in 1804.

Serbian War of Independence. 1804-17. Under the successive leadership of Karageorge and Obrenovich, the Serbs fought until they won autonomy. This autonomy was placed on an international basis by the treaty of Adrianople (1829).

Seven Weeks' War. See Austro-Prussian War.

Seven Years' War, The. 1756-63. Known in the United States as the French and Indian War, this world-wide struggle decided (1) whether France or England was to rule India; (2) whether French manners, language, and institutions or the English were to dominate North America; (3) whether Germany was to exist as a nation; (4) whether Spain should monopolize the tropics; (5) what nation was to dominate the ocean; (6) what country was to secure key positions in world commerce. Beginning with struggles between the French and English in the Carnatic and Deccan areas of India and the Ohio Valley of North America, the war soon spread to Europe where there was a pronounced regrouping of old allies. Maria Theresa, in her anxiety to recover Silesia, combined Austria with France against Prussia. They were joined by Russia, Poland, Saxony, and Sweden. Spain joined this alliance in 1761. England was Prussia's principal ally.

After a blundering start, England found a great war leader in William Pitt the Elder (q.v.). George II died in 1760 and the new English king, George III, refused to pay Prussia the annual subsidy which was so necessary to keep the Prussians equipped for fighting. On Jan. 5, 1762, the Russian Czarina Elizabeth died. It was because of her personal enmity to Frederick II of Prussia that Russia had entered the war. The new Russian ruler, Peter III, was a great admirer of Prussia and wanted to join in the war on the side of Frederick II. But Peter was murdered (July, 1762) and the Czarina Catherine II (the Great) withdrew from the war completely. Thus, the cause of England and Prussia triumphed finally on the continent.

In the colonial areas, English arms achieved great triumphs in North America, the West Indies, the Philippine Islands, and India.

The war was ended by the Peace of Paris (Feb. 10, 1763). France withdrew its troops from Germany. It restored Minorca to the British. It ceded to England Canada, Nova Scotia, Cape Breton Island, and all territory of North America east of the Mississippi River except New Orleans. England received St. Vincent, Tobago, and Grenada in the West Indies and part of Senegal. In India there was mutual restoration of conquests, though the French were forbidden to have troops in Bengal. Spain ceded Florida to Britain. In return, England gave back to Spain Havana and Manila which had been captured, but reserved the right to cut logwood in Honduras. France ceded Louisiana and New Orleans to Spain as compensation for the loss of Florida. Prussia retained Silesia (see Treaty of Hubertsburg).

Sévigné, Marquise de. 1626-96. French writer and lady of fashion. She is famed for the letters which she wrote to her daughter, who lived in Provence where her husband was lieutenant governor.

Sèvres, Treaty of. Aug. 20, 1920. An agreement between the Sultan of Turkey and the Allies at the end of World War I. The Kingdom of Hejaz was made independent. Syria was to become a mandate of France. Mesopotamia and Palestine were to be mandates of England. Smyrna and its hinterland were to be administered by Greece for five years, after which a plebiscite was to be held. The Dodecanese Islands and Rhodes were to be ceded to Italy. Thrace and the remaining Aegean Islands were to be ceded to Greece. Armenia was recognized as an independent country. The Straits were to be internationalized and demilitarized. Turkey retained Constantinople and Anatolia.

This treaty was not recognized by the Turkish nationalist government, headed by Mustafa Kemal. The Treaty of Sèvres was later replaced by the Treaty of Lausanne (q.v.).

Seyss-Inquart, Arthur. 1892-1946. Austrian Nazi. In Feb. 1938, Chancellor Schuschnigg was forced by Germany to make Seyss-Inquart minister of interior and security. On March 11, Schuschnigg resigned and Seyss-Inquart became chancellor. He invited Germany to send troops into Austria to maintain order. Thus the *Anschluss* (q.v.) was brought about. On March 13, Seyss-Inquart proclaimed the union of Germany and Austria. He now became governor of the Ostmark, as the Germans called Austria. In 1940 he was made Nazi governor of Holland, which he ruled ruthlessly. Captured in 1945, he was tried at Nuremberg, convicted, and hanged.

Sforza. The name of an Italian family that ruled Milan (1450-1535). The founder of the family was a peasant of Romagna whose family name was Attendolo. He became a leader of condottieri and took the name of Sforza (force). The duchy of Milan eventually passed to Emperor Charles V.

Sforza, Count Carlo. 1872-1952. Italian statesman. After holding high government posts, he became foreign minister (1920-21). After heading the opposition to Mussolini for several years, he went into exile (1927). In 1942 he returned to Italy, where he took an active part in politics. He was again foreign minister (1947-48).

Shaftesbury, Anthony Ashley Cooper. 1st Baron Ashley and 1st Earl of Shaftesbury. 1621-83. English statesman. He took an active part as a Roundhead leader during the English Civil War (1642-46). Leader under Charles II. Member of the "Cabal" (q.v.). He secured the passage of the Habeas Corpus Act (1679) (q.v.). One of the organizers of the Whig Party. He encouraged anti-Catholic persecutions at the time of the "Popish Plot" (q.v.).

Shaftesbury, Anthony Ashley Cooper, 7th Earl of (*called* Lord Ashley, 1811-51). 1801-85. English philanthropist. Chairman of the lunacy commission (1828-85). Urged 10-hour day for factory workers (1833-34; became the law in 1847). Obtained abolition of women and children work in coal mines (1842). Brought about the erection of model tenements.

Shakespeare, William. 1564-1616. English dramatist and playwright. Established in London as a player-actor (1592); member of the chamberlain's players (1594). He prospered financially and became part owner of a theatre. He purchased the largest house in Stratford-on-Avon, where he was born, and other property. He lived in London until 1610, when he sold his interest in the theatre and retired to Stratford. Individual plays were first published in quarto form (19 of them, some reprinted, appearing from 1594 to 1622). The first folio edition of his collected works appeared in 1623. For twenty years, from about 1591, when he wrote *Love's Labour's Lost,* until 1611, when he completed *The Tempest,* he was actively writing. He wrote about 40 plays, 154 sonnets, and the poems *Venus and Adonis* and *Lucrece.* On the contemporary stage and in contemporary criticism, Shakespeare has continued to hold his place as the greatest poet and dramatist in all literature.

Shaw, George Bernard. 1856-1950. British playwright, novelist, and critic. Born in Dublin. He went to London to devote himself to writing (1876). He was art, music, and dramatic critic on London journals. He was prominent as a Fabian Socialist. His first success as a playwright was *John Bull's Other Island* (1904). *Caesar and Cleopatra* (1900), *Man and Superman* (1903), *The Doctor's Dilemma* (1906), *Heartbreak House* (1917), *Saint Joan* (1923) are some of his plays. He was awarded the Nobel Prize for literature (1925).

Shelburne, 2nd Earl of (1st Marquis of Lansdowne. Sir William Petty). 1737-1805. English statesman. Secretary of state under Pitt (1766-68). First lord of the treasury and prime minister (1782-83). He conceded the independence of America and made peace with France and Spain (1783).

Shelekhov, Gregory. 1747-95. The "Russian Columbus." He migrated to Siberia at the age of 28. In 1777 he chartered his first ship to the Kuril Islands, then made voyages to the Aleutian Islands. In 1784 he formed a trading company with the Golikov brothers and occupied Kodiak in Alaska, expanding further on North America and trading in seal and bear furs.

Shelley, Percy Bysshe. 1792-1822. English revolutionary poet. Throughout his life he was a revolutionary against the conventions of society. His poetry reflects some of this attitude. He is the author of *Prometheus Unbound, The Cenci, Ode to the West Wind, To a Skylark,* etc.

Sheridan, Richard Brindsley. 1751-1816. Irish dramatist and parliamentary orator. Born in Dublin, he settled in London in 1773. He wrote three great comedies: *The Rivals* (1775), *The School for Scandal* (1777), and *The Critic* (1779). He bought Garrick's share in the Drury Lane Theatre. After 1780 he entered Parliament and there made celebrated speeches in the impeachment of Warren

Hastings, in reply to Mornington's attack against the French Republic, and in opposition to Irish union.

Ship Money. It was an ancient English custom to call upon port towns and maritime counties for ships for defense against pirates. Frequently, money was called for in lieu of ships. In 1634, Charles I called for money from port towns for the purpose of building up the royal navy. In 1635, a similar levy was made on inland towns as well. When a third and fourth levy followed in 1636 and 1637, it was widely believed that the king was trying to assess an illegal tax without the consent of Parliament. In 1635, John Hampden (1594-1643), a wealthy landowner, refused to pay his tax of 20 shillings. He was tried in November, 1637. In June, 1638, the court declared that he must pay. Since it appeared that the courts would not protect the liberties of the people, the way was opened for the English Revolution.

Shostakovitch, Dmitri. 1906-. Russian composer. One of the best-known modern composers. He has composed nine symphonies, music for various instruments, ballets, an opera, and much music for films.

Sibelius, Jean. 1865-. Finnish composer. He is considered to be one of the greatest living composers. His many compositions include tone poems, symphonies, vocal music, selections for the piano, violin, and other instruments. His tone poem *Finlandia* is the Finnish national anthem.

Sic et Non. A method of teaching employed by Abelard (q.v.). He made a compilation of contradictory statements from the Church fathers, called *Sic et Non,* and taught his students to draw upon it for support when maintaining one or other side in any doctrinal discussion. This method was regarded by Abelard's contemporaries as revolutionary, since it threatened unquestioned submission of the intellect. For this reason, Abelard was often brought to trial, eventually condemned, and compelled to recant.

Sicilian Vespers. 1282. Charles of Anjou, King of the Two Sicilies (1266-85), established a stern and cruel rule. He was regarded as a foreigner, for he had secured Sicily by conquest. In 1282, the Sicilians rose in rebellion and killed all the French on the island (Sicilian Vespers). The next year they invited Peter of Aragon (Spain) to become their king. After a long war (1302), the House of Aragon secured Sicily, but Naples remained under the House of Anjou.

Sidney, Sir Philip. 1554-86. Elizabethan courtier, soldier, and author. His best known work is *Arcadia.*

Siemens. Family of German electrical engineers and industrialists. Werner von (1816-92) was the first to use gutta-percha for insulating electrical conductors. With J. G. Halske he founded (1847) the Berlin firm of Siemens and Halske for manufacturing telegraphic equipment. This firm built the first telegraph line in Germany. His brother Wilhelm (*later* Sir William Siemens) (1823-83), went to England in 1844. He was naturalized in 1859. He invented the open-hearth steel furnace. He designed the ship, *Faraday,* which laid the Atlantic cable (1874). He built one of the first electric street car systems in Great Britain (1883) at Portrush, Ireland.

Sieyès, Emmanuel Joseph, Comte (Abbé Sieyès). 1748-1836. French statesman. Born at Fréjus. Educated for the clergy, he became chancellor and vicar-general of Chartres. In 1788-89 he wrote three famous pamphlets, the most famous of which was *Qu'est-ce que le Tiers-État?* He had much to do with forming the National Assembly (1789).

He had much to do with drawing up the Declaration of the Rights of Man. He was the one who was entrusted with dividing France into departments. He voted for the death of the king. But as the Revolution progressed, he sank into "philosophic silence." He plotted with Bonaparte to overthrow the Directory (Nov. 9, 1799). Under the Consulate, which followed the Directory, he and Ducos were Consuls with Bonaparte. Finding himself fooled by Bonaparte, he resigned his consulship, received the title of count, a pension, and an estate. Exiled at the Restoration, he lived for 15 years in Belgium, but returned to France in 1830.

Sigismund. Name of three kings of Poland. Sigismund I (1467-1548). Grand duke of Lithuania (1505-1548) and king of Poland (1505-48). He waged war with success against the Russians. Aided Hungary against the Turks at Mohacs (1526) and the siege of Vienna (1529). During his reign, Lutheranism was introduced into Poland.

Sigismund II (1520-72). King of Poland (1548-72). During his reign the Reformation was extended. Lithuania and the Ukraine were added to Poland (1569). He was the last of the Jagellons.

Sigismund III (Vasa) (1566-1632). Son of John III of Sweden. King of Poland (1587-1632) and of Sweden (1592-1604). He lost the crown of Sweden to his uncle Charles IX (1604). He involved Sweden and Poland in a conflict which was ruinous to both countries.

Simon, Viscount John. 1873-1954. British statesman. A lawyer, he entered politics and became an M.P. in 1906. He was knighted in 1910 and became a viscount in 1940. Solicitor-general (1910-13), Attorney-general (1913-15), Home Secretary (1915-16), Foreign Secretary (1931-35), Home Secretary (1935-37), Chancellor of the Exchequer (1937-40), and Lord Chancellor (1940-45). He will be remembered for his attempt to solve the Indian question and his determined stand against appeasement.

Simon de Montfort's Parliament. 1265. This parliament, called by Simon de Montfort, is often called the first English parliament, because it was the first body in which both knights of the shire and representatives of the towns sat with the Great Council.

Simony. The practice of selling church offices to the highest bidder. Under Conrad II (1024-39) the practice was widespread.

Sinn Fein ("We Ourselves"). An Irish society which had been organized originally to bring about industrial betterment among the masses and to develop Irish national sentiment. In 1914 the society entered the political field and during World War I became identified with the republican movement.

Sitzkrieg. See Phony War.

Six Acts. 1819. Following the Peterloo Massacre (Aug. 1819) (q.v.), the English Parliament passed (Nov. 1819) six reactionary laws designed to stamp out liberalism. (1) Unauthorized persons were forbidden from practising military exercises. (2) Offenders were to be tried speedily. (3) Magistrates were granted the power to issue warrants to search private homes for arms. (4) Writers of seditious or blasphemous articles could be banished on the second offense. (5) Public meetings were severely regulated and restricted. (6) All publications below a certain size were subjected to heavy stamp duties. Except for the third and fifth, these acts were designed as permanent measures.

Six Articles. 1539. An English statute of Henry VIII's reign defining heresy. Denial of any of the following constituted heresy: (1) transubstantiation, (2) communion in one kind for laymen, (3) celibacy of the priesthood, (4) inviolability of vows of chastity, (5) necessity of private masses, (6) necessity of auricular confession.

Sixtus IV (*name* Francesco della Rovere). 1414-84. Pope (1471-84). Born at Celle Ligure, Italy. He became deeply involved in Italian politics. He took part in a conspiracy against the Medici and thus became involved in a war with Florence. He built the Sistine Chapel (1473) and the Sistine Bridge across the Tiber. He became unpopular because of heavy taxation and nepotism.

Sixtus V (*name* Felice Peretti). 1521-1590. Pope (1585-90). He revised the regulations governing the College of Cardinals, built the Lateran Palace and the Vatican Library. He was a patron of the arts. He published a new edition of the Vulgate (1590). He sanctioned the Spanish Armada against the English (1588).

Slavery, Abolition of in English colonies. 1833. In 1807, England abolished slave trade. On Aug. 31, 1833, Parliament passed a law which abolished slavery in English overseas possessions. Under it, all children under six years of age and all born subsequently were to be free. Others were to serve as apprentices to their former masters for seven years, devoting at least ¾ of their time to their masters. Slave owners were paid £20 million to compensate them for their slaves. After four years of trial, the apprentice system was abolished as being unworkable. William Wilberforce was a leader of the movement to emancipate the slaves.

Smeaton, John. 1724-92. English civil engineer. He invented the air-blast furnace for smelting iron. He built the great Eddystone lighthouse (the third), Ramsgate Harbor facilities, and the Forth and Clyde Canal.

Smith, Adam. 1723-90. Scotch economist. His great work is the *Inquiry into the Nature and Causes of the Wealth of Nations* (1776). In this book Smith advocates a system of natural liberty as opposed to the scheme of artificial regulators that then checked trade and commerce. Smith argues that the individual should be left free to pursue gain in his own way; that the greater the sum total of individuals who prosper, the greater is the national wealth.

Smollett, Tobias. 1721-71. English picaresque novelist. *Roderick Random, Peregrine Pickle,* and *Humphrey Clinker* are his best-known works.

Snowden, Philip, Viscount. 1864-1937. British statesman. He left the civil service for journalism and politics, and became a Socialist M.P. in 1906. He was chancellor of the Exchequer in the Labor and Nationalist governments (1924, 1929-31), Lord of the Privy Seal (1931-32). As a freetrader, he broke with the government in 1932. Created viscount in 1931.

Social Democratic Party, Germany. In 1863, Ferdinand Lassalle wrote the *Open Letter* in which he advocated Louis Blanc's ideas of universal suffrage and national workshops (q.v.). Because of the interest which the *Open Letter* evoked, a German political party, called *Social Democrat,* was founded. Side by side with this party was the German "section" of the First International, headed by Liebknecht (q.v.) and Bebel. Both groups fused in 1875 to form the single Social Democratic Party, which was essentially Marxist in theory. It served as a model for similar groups in other countries: in Belgium, the Socialist Party (1885); in Austria, the Social Democratic Party (1888); in France, the United Socialist Party (1905); in Great Britain, the Labor Party (1906). By 1914 every civilized country had a Socialist party whose gospel was the teachings of Karl Marx.

Social Legislation, French. The following important social legislation was enacted by the Third French Republic prior to 1914:

(1) 1884—law granting full protection for labor unions.

(2) 1892—law regulating the employment of women; forbidding employment of children under 13; fixing the maximum working day at 10 hours; prohibiting manual labor on Sunday except in certain industries whose workers were to have a substitute day of rest; strictly regulating work in mines.

(3) 1892—law providing for conciliation in labor disputes.

(4) 1893—law providing for the hygiene and safety of workers.

(5) 1898—law providing for workmen's compensation.

(6) 1900—law requiring shopkeepers to provide seats for all women and children employed by them.

(7) 1905—law limiting the working day for miners to 9 hours; amended 1907 to 8 hours.

(8) 1911—a system of old-age pensions for all workers except railroad workers, sailors, and miners for whom special provisions had already been made. Premiums were to be paid by the workers, employers, and the state.

Social Legislation, German. 1881-1890. In 1875 the German followers of Karl Marx united with those of Lassalle to form the Social Democratic Party. Its principles were absolute political democracy, direct taxation, social legislation, and anti-militarism. Within two years the party polled half a million votes and secured 12 seats in the Reichstag. Taking advantage of public indignation which was aroused by two unsuccessful attempts to assassinate the Emperor by alleged Socialists, Bismarck tried to crush Socialism by repressive legislation (1878-90). When the Social Democratic Party increased in size despite this move, Bismarck adopted a new policy to counteract its influence —protective tariff, imperialism, and social legislation. In the field of social legislation, Bismarck was a pioneer. In advocating it he was supported by the new school of economics, by the old Prussian tradition of benevolent paternalism, and by the Catholic Center Party. The program was as follows:

1883—a law insuring workmen against sickness.

1884—employers were required to insure workmen against accidents.

1887—laws limiting child and female labor, establishing a maximum number of hours of work and a Sunday day of rest.

1889—compulsory insurance of workmen against old age and incapacity.

National insurance, together with enlightened factory regulations, an excellent system of labor exchanges, and the growth of trade-unionism all contributed greatly toward making Germany one of the most efficient industrial nations of the world.

Social Legislation, Italian. From the unification of Italy to World War I, numerous social laws were passed comparable to those of other European countries. Among them were the following:

1886—regulating the labor of women and children. No child under 13 was to be employed. Women and children were forbidden to work underground or at night.

1898—Workmen's compensation.

1908—a weekly day of rest for laborers.

1912—life insurance was nationalized.

1912—universal manhood suffrage.

Society of Jesus (*Societas Jesu*). 1540. A religious order of the Roman Catholic Church founded by Ignatius of Loyola (q.v.). Members of the order are commonly called *Jesuits* in English-speaking countries from the original Spanish name, *Compañia de Jesús*. It is the largest single religious order of the Church. The chief labors of the order have been the education of boys and foreign missions, although Jesuits have always been ready to undertake any mission. No other order has presented over four centuries such a spectacle of purity and zeal. The order has been in frequent difficulties and has been suppressed in many countries. In 1773 the entire order was dissolved by Pope Clement XIV. In 1814 Pope Pius VII reestablished the order, which has now spread all over the world. In culture and learning there have been many distinguished Jesuits. This has been notably true in the natural sciences, in astronomy, geology, and physics.

Society of Saint Vincent de Paul. A French organization for the relief of the poor. It was founded in 1833 by Antoine Frédéric Ozanam.

Socinians. In the 16th century, the Italian theologians, Fausto (1539-1604) and Lelio (1525-1562) Sozzini, founded this sect. They taught that Christ was a man, but divinely endowed. They denied the Trinity and the existence of a personal devil, of the natural depravity of man, of vicarious atonement, and of eternal punishment. Socianism is sometimes called Old Unitarianism.

Somme, Battle of. July 1-Nov. 18, 1916. This was a major offensive staged by the British on the Western Front during World War I. Its objectives were to try to break the German lines and to take some pressure off the French at Verdun. During this campaign the British used tanks for the first time. The Allies conquered 125 sq. mi. of territory. The furthest advance was 7 miles. The British lost 400,000 and the French 200,000. The German losses were between 400,000 and 500,000.

Sorel, Agnès. c. 1422-1450. Mistress of Charles VII (q.v.) of France. The first mistress of a French king to be recognized officially. She had considerable in-

fluence with the king. She was closely connected with Jacques Coeur (q.v.).

Sorel, Georges. 1847-1922. French journalist. A leader in proclaiming the doctrine of syndicalism (q.v.). Author of *L'Avenir Socialiste des Syndicats* (1898), *Réflexions sur la Violence* (1908), etc.

South Sea Bubble. A scheme of speculative finance in England which was a counterpart of the contemporary Mississippi Bubble (q.v.) in France. When the Bubble burst (Jan. 1720), a disastrous financial panic ensued.

Spain, Christian Conquest of. Early in the 8th century the Visigothic Kingdom of Spain was overthrown by the Moors. Only in the mountain districts were the Spanish Christians unsubdued. In time their power revived and gradually they conquered the country to the south. In the course of this struggle, various Christian states were formed: Asturias (718), Leon (914), Castile (1003), Aragon (1035). In the northeast the county of Barcelona (Charlemagne's Spanish March) was attached to the kingdom of France. In 1002 the Caliphate of Cordova fell into decline and broke into a number of emirates. This gave the Christians an opportunity for conquest. Under Ferdinand I and Alfonso VI of Castile (1035-1108) the Douro Valley was conquered and Portugal began its history as a subject province of Castile (1095). The western part of the plateau was conquered as far as Toledo (1085). The advance was halted by the Almoravides, a Berber tribe from Africa, who defeated Alfonso VI at Zallaca (1086). During the 12th century the reconquest was carried on by Portugal, Castile, and Aragon. It was checked by a new body of African Moslems, the Almohades, whose victory at Alarcos (1185) stopped the advance for a generation. In 1212 the united Christian forces won a great victory at Las Navas de Tolosa. James I of Aragon

(1213-76) and Saint Ferdinand of Castile (1214-52) completed the work. By 1257 the Moors were penned into the Emirate of Granada from which they were finally expelled in 1492.

Spain, Moslem Conquest of. 711-718. In 711 a force of Arabs and Berbers led by Tarik (from whose name comes Gibraltar—Gebel-al-Tarik) invaded Spain and defeated and killed the last Visigothic king, Roderick. Tarik was soon followed by his overlord Musa, who conquered Cordova, Toledo, Seville, and Merida, reaching the Pyrenees by the end of 718. Spain was annexed to North Africa.

Spanish Civil War. 1936-39. The conflict began with a revolt in the army in Melillo, Spanish Morocco. The Insurgent leaders were General Francisco Franco, General Emilio Mola (subsequently killed in an airplane crash), and General José Sanjurjo (killed in an airplane crash at the very outset). On July 30, the Insurgents set up a Junta of National Defense at Burgos. The war was fought viciously on both sides. Foreigners participated on both sides. Both Germany and Italy supported the Insurgents, recognizing the government of Gen. Franco on Nov. 18, 1936. (Franco had been appointed Chief of State on Oct. 1.) The Loyalists were supported by an International Brigade of foreign volunteers and the Soviet Union. The war ended with victory for the Franco forces when Madrid and Valencia surrendered (Mar. 28, 1939). The United States recognized the new regime April 1, 1939. On April 7, Spain announced adhesion to the German-Italian-Japanese anticomintern pact.

Spanish Concordat with the Vatican. 1754. By this agreement the Spanish Church became practically independent of Rome and was placed under the control of the Spanish government.

"Spanish Fury." Sack and pillage of the city of Antwerp (Nov. 3, 1576) by Spanish soldiers during the War of Dutch Independence.

Spanish Interregnum and First Republic. 1868-74. After Queen Isabella was forced to abdicate (Sept. 29, 1868), a provisional government under Serrano and Prim was set up. A Cortes (Feb. 1869) called for a constitutional monarchy. The Duke of Aosta, son of Victor Emmanuel II of Italy, was made king (Amadeo I, 1871-73). Being regarded as a foreigner, he never commanded the loyalty of the Spaniards. Realizing that he could never command the loyalty of the Spaniards, he abdicated. The First Spanish Republic was then proclaimed (Feb. 12, 1873). On Dec. 29, 1873, a group of generals overthrew the republic and proclaimed Alfonso XII, son of Isabella, king.

Spanish Netherlands. Eight provinces of the Netherlands which chose to remain with Spain during the Dutch War of Liberation (1568-1609). By the Peace of Utrecht (q.v.) they became the Austrian Netherlands. Today, this region is Belgium.

Spanish Republic, Second. 1931-36. Under the presidency of Alcalá Zamora, an elective legislature and a responsible ministry were created. Separation of church and state was proclaimed, as was secular education. The new government soon experienced grave difficulties, of which the revolt in Catalonia was one of the greatest. Catalonia was granted autonomy (Sept. 25, 1932). Political factions crystallized into a rightist faction, representing conservative Republicans, Monarchists, and Clericals, and a leftist faction, the Popular Front (Socialists, Syndicalists, Communists). The latter decisively won the election of Feb. 16, 1936. Following this election, the Civil War broke out (July 18, 1936).

Spanish Succession, War of. 1701-13. When Charles II of Spain died without direct heir, the House of Bourbon, headed by Louis XIV of France, and the House of Hapsburg, headed by Emperor Leopold I, both tried to seat one of their family upon the Spanish throne. A third claim was made for Joseph Ferdinand, the infant son of the Elector of Bavaria. Charles II willed his throne to Philip of Anjou. Louis XIV stated that if his grandson, Philip of Anjou, mounted the throne of Spain, he would not thereby renounce his claim to the throne of France. To forestall a possible union of France and Spain, on Sept. 7, 1701, Austria, England, and Holland signed the Grand Alliance, which stated also that in the event of war against Spain and France, Austria was to get the Spanish possessions in the Netherlands and Italy, and England and Holland were to have any conquests which they might make in the western world.

There were four main theatres of the war: the Dutch border, the valley of the Danube, the Po valley, and Spain. The allies succeeded in driving the French out of Germany (1704); out of Italy (1706); and out of the Netherlands (1706-08). They were successful in all theatres except Spain, largely due to the brilliant generalship of Marlborough and the Imperial commander, Prince Eugene.

The war ended with the Peace of Utrecht (1713). Louis XIV agreed to abide by the Act of Settlement (1701) (q.v.) and exiled the son of James II of England from France. He further accepted the renunciation of his rights to the throne of France which Philip V had made (Nov. 5, 1712). He ceded to England Hudson Bay settlement, Acadia, and Newfoundland, retaining fishing rights and the islands of St. Pierre and Miquelon off Newfoundland. Spain ceded to England Gibraltar and Minorca. By the *Asiento*, she gave to England a thirty-year monopoly of importing Negro slaves to Spanish America. English merchants secured the right to send one ship a year to trade in Spanish-American ports. The Spanish Netherlands were given to Holland to be transferred to Austria. Austria secured various Spanish possessions in Italy.

Spartacist movement. In 1916, Liebknecht (q.v.) began to publish over the signature "Spartacus" letters which denounced the German war effort. Hence, his followers came to be known as Spartacists. In November, 1918, after the abdication of William II, the Spartacists began an insurrection against the social-democratic republic which had been set up. Through their newspaper, *Die Rote Fahne* (The Red Flag), and by acts of terrorism they strove to prevent the calling of a constitutional convention. In January, 1919, the "insurrection" came to a head. Had the Spartacists been resolutely led, they might have taken over the government. The movement collapsed when on Jan. 15 both Liebknecht and Rosa Luxemburg (q.v.) were arrested and killed on the way to jail.

Specialized Agencies of the UN. See ILO, International Bank for Reconstruction and Development, IMF, UNESCO, WHO, FAO.

Speier, Second Diet of. 1529. An imperial Diet called by Charles V to consider what was to be done to suppress the growth of Lutheranism. The Diet decided to settle religious matters in the near future by means of a council or assembly. In the meantime, the Edict of Worms should be strictly enforced, that nowhere should change be permitted, and that there should be no interference with the celebration of the mass. On April 19, 1529, the Lutheran princes of Germany published a protest against the work of the Diet. From this act, they and their followers were subsequently called "Protestants."

Spencer, Herbert. 1820-1903. English philosopher. Born at Derby. As subeditor of the *Economist* (1848-53) he made the acquaintance of Huxley, George Eliot, and John Stuart Mill and developed those ethical and social views which were incorporated into *Social Statistics* (1851), in which he advocated extreme individualism. He began to apply the doctrine of evolution in *Principles of Psychology* (1855). Following Darwin's *Origin of the Species* (1859), he announced a *System of Synthetic Philosophy* (1860) in which the doctrine of evolution would be carried into the realms of philosophy, psychology, sociology, and ethics. His work (10 volumes) required 36 years to complete. Spencer first used the phrase "survival of the fittest."

Spenser, Edmund. 1552-94. Elizabethan poet. Among his works are *Shepheard's Calendar, The Faerie Queene,* and *The Prothalamion.*

Spinning jenny. See Hargreaves, James.

Spinning mule. See Crompton, Samuel.

Spinola, Ambrogio di. 1569-1630. Italian general in the service of Spain. He led an army in the Netherlands against Maurice of Nassau (1602-09). Captured Ostend (1604). Dissolved the Protestant Union (1621). Captured Breda (1625). Later he commanded Spanish armies in Italy.

Spinoza, Baruch *or* Benedict. 1632-77. Dutch philosopher. Born in Amsterdam of Portuguese-Jewish parentage. Excommunicated from the synagogue (1656), he supported himself by grinding lenses. He devoted himself to the study of philosophy, especially the system of Descartes. He is now regarded as the most eminent expounder of pantheism. Among his works are *Tractus Theologico-Politicus* (1670) and *Ethica Ordine Geometrico Demonstrata* (finished 1674, but published after his death).

Spurs, Battle of. Aug. 17, 1513. This was a defeat of the French by the English under the personal leadership of Henry VIII at Guinegate. The battle is so named because of the hasty flight of the French.

Stakhanovism. A system of piece wages, speed-up, and competition, begun in the Soviet Union in 1935 by a coal miner, Alexei Stakhanov.

Stalin, Joseph (*real name* Joseph Vissarionovich Dzhugashvili). 1879-1953. Russian communist leader. Born near Tiflis, Georgia. There is not much accurate information available about his pre-1917 days. He was for a time a student in a theological seminary. He joined the Bolsheviks (1903) and was repeatedly exiled to Siberia, but always managed to escape. After the Russian Revolution of 1917 he became a close associate of Lenin. Peoples' commissar for nationalities (1921-23). General secretary of the Central Committee of the Communist Party (1922 ff.). After the death of Lenin (1924) he became the dominant person in the USSR. He initiated the Five Year Plans, the collectivization of farms, and the purge of the 1930's. During the Second World War he was made marshal and premier of the Soviet Union. At the Yalta, Teheran, and Potsdam Conferences he showed that he was a consummate diplomat. After the end of the war, his public appearances became less frequent than usual. His remoteness stimulated public worship that was bestowed on him. On the occasion of his 70th birthday in 1949 the praise and adulation of him reached a climax. Stalin was the author of many books, some of which have been translated into English, such as *Leninism, Problems of Leninism,* etc.

Stalingrad, Battle of. Aug. 22, 1942-Feb. 2, 1943. One of the major turning-points of World War II. Up to this point the Nazi offensive against the Soviet

Union was successful. Following Stalingrad, the Nazis were continually on the defensive on the eastern front. The city was strategically important as a communications center on the Volga River. The battle was waged with extreme bitterness. On Sept. 1, the Russians counterattacked northeast of Stalingrad. A gigantic Russian pincers movement developed, cutting off 22 German divisions. When the entrapped Germans finally surrendered, they had been reduced to 80,000 men.

Stamp Act. 1765. This law was designed to raise money in the English North American colonies to support a North American army. It was argued that since the East India Co. and Ireland each supported its own army, the North American colonists should do likewise. The Act taxed newspapers, bills, policies of insurance, and legal documents. The Act stirred up a storm of resistance in North America. A Stamp Act Congress representing nine colonies met in New York (Nov. 7, 1765) to petition the king and Parliament to withdraw the Act. Finding that business could not be transacted under the confused conditions, colonial governors were authorized to issue orders permitting non-compliance with the Act. The Act was repealed in 1766.

Stanislas. 1030-1079. Polish Roman Catholic prelate. Bishop of Cracow (1071). He denounced the practices of King Boleslav II and finally excommunicated him. He was murdered at the order of the king. He was canonized in 1253 and is known as the patron saint of Poland.

Stanislas II Poniatowski. 1732-1798. Last independent king of Poland (1764-95). Elected to the Diet (1752). Polish representative to the court of Russia (1755) where he gained the favor of the future Catherine the Great. Through her influence he was elected king of Poland (1764). Under his reign the condition of Poland rapidly deteriorated. Poland was thrice (1772, 1793, 1795) divided among Russia, Prussia, and Austria. After the third partition, when Poland ceased to exist, he resigned as king.

Staple Towns. By the close of the 13th century, England had come to be a great wool-producing country. Its best customers were the weavers of Flanders. Various attempts were made to fix the towns or "staples" where English wool was to be sold. Sometimes these towns were located in England; sometimes, in the Low Countries. In 1362 the staple was removed to Calais, where it remained, except for short intervals, until the town passed back to the French in 1558.

Star Chamber, Court of. 1487. Henry VII created a court composed of certain officers from the Privy Council plus two judges to have special jurisdiction over misconduct of sheriffs, riots, and unlawful assemblies. Later, more and more members were added to this court until it came to be a judicial session of the whole Privy Council plus two judges. The court was subsequently used as a device for oppression, both political and ecclesiastical. It was abolished in 1641. It was called the Court of the Star Chamber because it usually met in a chamber of Westminster palace whose ceiling was decorated with stars. The name is now synonymous with any unjust or secret court.

Statute of Mortmain *or* **de Religiosis.** 1279. The church had secured ownership of 1/3 of the land of England. Many nobles, to escape military obligations and other services, such as wardships, marriages, and reliefs, granted their lands to the church on condition of enjoying part of the income. Edward I, by this statute, put an end to this practice.

Statute of Wales (or Rhuddlan). 1284. By this statute Wales was formally annexed to England by Edward I. In

1301, the title of Prince of Wales was bestowed on Edward's oldest surviving son, born at Carnavon in 1284. Since that time it usually has been the custom for the heir of the British throne to be called the Prince of Wales.

Statutes of Westminster. 1275, 1285. These statutes, prepared during the reign of Edward I, reaffirmed the Magna Carta and the Provisions of Winchester (q.v.). In addition, the second statute established entailed estates.

Statute of Westminster (1931). See Imperial Conference, 1926.

Statute of Winchester. 1283. By this statute Edward I of England sought to revise and reorganize the old institutions of national police and defense.

Statuto. This was a constitution granted to the Kingdom of Sardinia by Charles Albert (March 4, 1848). It eventually became the constitution of the Kingdom of Italy and remained in force until the Fascist revolution of the 1920's.

Steele, Sir Richard. 1672-1729. English essayist and dramatist. Best known for *The Spectator Papers* which he wrote in collaboration with Joseph Addison.

Steelyard. A portion of the harbor of London which formerly belonged to the Hanseatic League.

Stein, Baron Heinrich Friedrich Karl von und zum. 1757-1831. Prussian statesman. Born in Nassau. Prussian minister of foreign affairs (1807-08). He accomplished many reforms in the civil service and administration and abolished serfdom. Napoleon forced his resignation (1808). He fled to Austria and lived there (1809-12). In the service of the Czar (1812-13). He was frustrated at the Congress of Vienna (1814-15) in his plans for a united Germany. He spent his latter years in retirement (1815-31), promoting German art and science.

Stem-Duchies of Germany. Great tribal duchies from which came modern Germany. They were the Duchies of Saxony, Franconia, Thuringia, Swabia (formerly Alemannia), and Bavaria.

Stephen. 1105-54. King of England (1135-54). Son of Stephen, Count of Blois, and Adela, daughter of William the Conqueror. Upon the death of Henry I, Stephen was accepted as king of England rather than Matilda, Henry's daughter. During his reign he had to fight a continuous war against the supporters of Matilda until she retired from England (1148). Her son Henry (later Henry II of England) forced Stephen to acknowledge him as successor.

Stephen Dushan. 1308?-1355. King of Serbia (1335-46). Crowned emperor of the Serbs, Greeks, Bulgars, and Albanians (1346). He drew up a legal code known as the Code of Dushan (1349-54). He was a great conqueror and might have overcome the Byzantine Empire had not death intervened.

Stephen I (Saint Stephen). 975?-1038. First king of the Arpad dynasty of Hungary (997-1038). Crowned king (1001) with a crown sent by the pope. He was given the title of the "Apostolic King," a title which was held thereafter by the kings of Hungary until 1918. He encouraged the spread of Christianity, agriculture, and trade. Canonized in 1087. The patron saint of Hungary.

Sterne, Laurence. 1713-68. English novelist. His best-known works are *Tristram Shandy* and *A Sentimental Journey through France and Italy*.

Stinnes, Hugo. 1870-1924. German industrialist. Son of a Westphalian mine owner, he founded his own company in 1892. He rapidly expanded his interests until he controlled a "vertical" trust. He was responsible for the gigantic Siemens-Rhein-Elbe-Schuckert Union. At the time of his death he was reputed to have an interest in more than 1300 firms.

Stockholm, Treaties of. 1720-21. At the conclusion of the Great Northern War (q.v.). *Status quo* restored between Sweden, Saxony, and Poland. Hanover retained Verden and paid Sweden one million thalers. Prussia received Stettin, part of western Pomerania, and several islands and paid Sweden two million thalers. Denmark restored all conquests; in return for which Sweden paid 600,000 rix dollars.

Stolypin, Peter Arkadevich. 1863-1911. Russian lawyer and statesman. Governor of Grodno (1902) and Saratov (1903). Minister of Interior (1906). Premier of Russia (1906-1911). He attempted to put liberal ideas into operation. His ministry ended when he was assassinated.

Storm Troops (Sturmabteilungen; SA). Organized originally by Capt. Röhm, this semi-military organization of "Brown Shirts" was assigned to such duties as the protection of Nazi meetings and the breaking-up of radical gatherings. The SA was disbanded by the government in April, 1932, but was recreated several months later.

Strafford, Thomas Wentworth, Earl of. 1593-1641. English statesman. One of the advisers of Charles I. He became the king's chief adviser in 1639. He urged Charles to resort to various despotic actions. As lord-deputy of Ireland, he coerced the country into order and obedience. He was impeached by Commons, imprisoned, and beheaded.

Strassburg Oaths. 842. Ludwig and Charles (sons of Charlemagne) were rulers of Germany and France respectively. Fearing an attack by a mutual foe, they met at Strassburg and swore to support one another. Ludwig took the oath in the language of Charles' people; Charles repeated it in the language of Ludwig's followers. These oaths have been preserved. They are among the earliest specimens of French and German. For that reason they are of interest to modern men.

Strauss, David Frederick. 1808-74. German theologian and philosopher. In his *Life of Jesus* (1835), he assailed the inspiration of the New Testament and the supernatural attributes of Christ. Later he accepted Darwinism. With his associates he founded the Tübingen School of "higher critics" of the Bible.

Strauss, Richard. 1864-1949. German composer. He is regarded as a leader of the New Romantic school. He composed ballets, symphonies, chamber music, and songs. His operas include *Salome* and *Der Rosenkavalier*.

Stravinsky, Igor. 1882-. Russian composer. He is regarded as a leader in the futurist group in modern music. Among his works are *Le Sacre du printemps, The Fire Bird, Petrouchka, Le Rossignol, Le Baiser de la fée*.

Streltzy. Troops of the Moscow garrison, organized by Ivan the Terrible (1533-84). In their free time they were allowed to engage in trade and crafts, giving them close contact with the people of the town, but making it difficult to enforce discipline among them.

Strength through Joy. See Labor Front, German.

Stresemann, Gustav. 1878-1929. German statesman. Chancellor (1923). Foreign secretary (1923-29). He followed a post-war policy of conciliation with France. He engineered the Locarno Pact and brought Germany into the League of Nations. He advocated adoption of the

Dawes and Young Plans. He shared the Nobel Peace Prize with Aristide Briand (1926). He was the outstanding statesman of the Weimar Republic.

Stuart, House of. A family supplying rulers to Scotland from 1371 to 1603 and to England from 1603 to 1714.

	Born	Ruled
James I	1566	1603-25

(he ruled Scotland as James VI from 1567 to 1603)

Charles I	1600	1625-1649

Period of the Commonwealth (1649-1660)

Charles II	1630	1660-1685
James II	1633	1685-1689
Mary II	1662	1689-1694

(joint ruler with her husband, William III of the House of Orange-Nassau)

Anne	1665	1702-1714

Sturmabteilungen (SA). See Storm Troops.

Suevi. A Germanic tribe which migrated into northwest Spain and established a kingdom there which lasted from 419 to 585. We know little about them except the names of their kings.

Suger. 1081?-1151. French churchman and statesman. Abbot of St. Denis (1122). Counsellor to king Louis VI and minister for Louis VII (1137-51). Regent of France while Louis VII was absent on the Second Crusade (1147-49).

Suleiman (or Solyman) I (or II) "The Magnificent." 1496-1566. Sultan of Turkey (1520-66). Annexed by conquest Belgrade, Budapest, Rhodes, Tabriz, Baghdad, Aden, and Algiers. He reformed the administration of his country. Encouraged the arts and sciences. He was the contemporary of Emperor Charles V. Under Suleiman the Ottoman power reached its zenith.

Sully, Duke of (Maximilien de Bethune; Baron de Rosny). 1560-1641. French statesman. Brought up a Protestant, he early attached himself to Henry of Navarre. After Henry became king of France (Henry IV), Sully became finance minister (1597) and held many other high offices. He reorganized French finances. He promoted agriculture, constructed roads, bridges, and canals. After the death of Henry, he was forced into retirement.

Sussex Pledge. In March, 1916, the unarmed channel steamer Sussex was attacked by a German submarine, and several Americans were injured. The United States protested to Germany in a note, which contained the threat of severance of diplomatic relations, should submarine attacks against passenger vessels continue. The Germans replied with a pledge to confine wartime acts to the fighting forces of the belligerents. The outcome of the Sussex affair was regarded as a diplomatic triumph for President Wilson. On the strength of this pledge, he campaigned in 1916 as one who had kept the United States out of war.

Swein Forkbeard. d. 1014. Son of Harold Bluetooth and father of Canute the Great. King of Denmark (985-1014). In his early years he was a Viking. He led a large fleet against England, which did great damage (994). He fought Olaf Tryggvesson of Norway (1000), defeated and killed him. He led annual expeditions against England (1003-14) for plunder and tribute.

Swift, Jonathan. 1667-1745. English satirist. Among his works are A Tale of a Tub, The Conduct of Allies, Gulliver's Travels, and A Modest Proposal.

Switzerland, Constitution of 1848. Following a brief civil war, the Swiss people overwhelmingly voted for a written constitution which made provision for a fairly strong federal government.

The constitution of 1848, modeled after the Constitution of the United States, made the Swiss Confederation what it is today. There was to be a bicameral federal legislature—one house representing the cantons; the other, the people. The chief executive was to be a president. He with a seven-member Federal Council was to execute the laws. Since 1848, the rights of the cantons have been whittled away gradually. The country has experimented with a number of novel forms of political democracy, such as the initiative and the referendum.

Switzerland, Origin of. Switzerland dates from 1291, when the three forest cantons—Schwyz, Uri, and Unterwalden —formed a union. This original "Everlasting Compact" was reinforced by the Priests' Ordinance (1370), the Ordinance of Sempach (1393), and the Compact of Stanz (1481). By alliance, the country gradually expanded as follows: Luzern (1330), Zürich (1351), Glarus (1352), Bern (1353), Freiburg (1481), Solothurn (1481), Basel (1501), Schaffhausen (1501), Appenzell (1513). In addition, there were communities which allied to certain confederates, like Geneva, which allied with Freiburg (1518) and with Basel (1526). There were also allied districts, confederates, and "protected" districts. Switzerland was granted recognition by the Treaty of Westphalia (1648). During the 15th century, Swiss mercenary soldiers were among the best in Europe. Their services were much in demand. They were well paid. Mercenaries brought back to Switzerland great sums of money. During this period, war was the leading Swiss industry. At Marignano (1515), a large Swiss army was defeated by the French under Francis I. Thereafter, the Swiss took little part in foreign wars. During the 16th century, the country was hurt internally by religious wars. During the 17th and 18th centuries the Swiss took no part in the wars and ambitions of neighboring states.

Syllabus of Errors (1864). In this document Pope Pius IX condemned the "principal errors of our times." He condemned the following: freethinkers; agnostics; indifferent people who would take away the official privileges of the church and reduce it to a private, voluntary organization; those who would establish lay marriages and state schools; advocates of secular authority; and opponents of the temporal power of the church.

Sylvester II (*name* **Gerbert**). 940?-1003. Pope (999-1003). Born near Aurillac, Auvergne, France. A celebrated scholar, particularly in mathematics and natural sciences. As archbishop of Ravenna (998), he took a lively interest in the affairs of Central Europe. He is said to have sent a golden crown to St. Stephen, King of Hungary. He wrote textbooks and fostered the study of music and science.

Syndicalism. Syndicalism is a type of French trade-unionism. Syndicalists organized workers by whole industries, rather than by trades or crafts. Syndicalists tried to bring direct pressure upon the employers by "direct action"—the general strike or sabotage. They were opposed to political action or the betterment of conditions through legislative action. Thus, Syndicalists are closely akin to revolutionary Anarchists.

Synod of Whitby. 664. A religious gathering called at Whitby by King Oswy, where Wilfrid, a young Northumbrian noble just returned from a pilgrimage to Rome, presented the claims of the Roman Church. The main point of discussion was the date of Easter. The synod voted to follow the leadership of Rome, thus bringing England into closer cultural contact with the continent. It also led to the founding of a school for boys at Canterbury.

T

Taff Vale Decision. 1901. In the Taff Vale Railway vs. the Amalgamated Society of Railway Servants the House of Lords ruled that trade unions were liable to suits for damages whenever their actions (as in a strike) caused loss to other persons. Angered by this decision, trade unionists worked for the establishment of a Labor Party and, in the election of 1906, secured 29 representatives in the House of Commons.

Taille. A direct tax in France during the days of the Old Regime. It was a land tax which was paid almost entirely by peasants. The amount to be raised was apportioned among the intendants by the Royal Council. Each intendant then fixed the tax for each taxpayer of his *généralité* (district) according to his ability to pay. Each villager, accordingly, tried to appear as poor as possible to avoid paying a larger tax.

Talleyrand-Perigord, Charles Maurice de. Prince de Benevent. 1754-1838. French statesman. Born in Paris. Took holy orders (1775). Made bishop of Autun (1789). Member of the Estates-General (1789) and of the National Assembly (1789). Proposed confiscating church property. Excommunicated by the pope (1791). Envoy to England (1792). Minister of foreign affairs (1797-1807). Made Prince de Benevent (1806). Quarreled with Napoleon over Spanish and French policies. After the fall of Napoleon, he was largely instrumental in securing the restoration of the Bourbons. He took part in the Congress of Vienna (1814-15). Ambassador to Great Britain (1830-34).

Tannenberg, Battle of. Aug. 31, 1914. A German army under Hindenburg and Ludendorff annihilated a Russian army and completely changed the course of World War I. On this same spot in 1410, Polish, Lithuanian, and Russian troops defeated the German Knights in a decisive battle.

Tasso, Torquato. 1544-95. Italian poet. Born at Sorrento. Known especially for his *Jerusalem Delivered* (1575), an epic poem dealing with the capture of Jerusalem during the First Crusade.

Teheran Conference. Dec. 2-7, 1943. F. D. Roosevelt, Churchill, and Stalin met here to plan wartime strategy. After a series of talks, they agreed to continue full cooperation in the war and in peace and to undertake unified military action against Germany from the east, west, and south.

Telford, Thomas. 1757-1834. Scottish civil engineer. His numerous works include the Ellesmere Canal (1793), the Caledonian Canal, the Gotha Canal in Sweden (1808-10), and 920 miles of road and 20 bridges in Scotland. He developed the idea of the "crowned" road to facilitate drainage.

Tenant-Right League, Irish. 1850. This organization demanded "three F's"—fair rent, fixity of tenure (a peasant could hold his land as long as he paid rent), and free sale (the right of a peasant to sell his tenancy). The Land Act of 1870 forbade landlords to raise rents at will or evict peasants arbitrarily without paying for improvements which they had made. The Second Land Act (1881) conceded all the points of the "3 F" program.

Tennyson, Alfred Lord. 1st Baron Tennyson. 1809-92. English poet. He was first coolly received. His fame was established in 1842 with the publication of *Poems* (2 vols.), which included such works as *Morte d'Arthur, Ulysses, Locksley Hall, Godiva.* He was appointed poet laureate on the death of Wordsworth (1850). He was a very prolific poet. Among his other works are *In Memoriam, Idylls of the King,* and *Charge of the Light Brigade.*

Tercios. Spanish infantry of the 16th and 17th centuries. From the days of Gonzalo de Córdoba (q.v.) to the Battle of Rocroi (q.v.), this infantry was regarded as the best in Europe.

"Terrible June Days." See Revolutions of 1848.

Test Act. 1673. As a reply to Charles II's Declaration of Indulgences (q.v.), Parliament passed the Test Act, which provided that all holders of civil and military office must receive the sacrament according to the Church of England and take an oath declaring disbelief in transubstantiation. This act excluded Roman Catholics and conscientious Non-Conformists from office for over 150 years.

Test and Corporation Acts, Repeal of. 1828. These acts of the British Parliament, which excluded all but Church of England men from municipal corporations and which prevented Roman Catholics from holding office in the government either in the civil service, in the army, or in the navy, were repealed in 1828.

Teutonic Knights. See Military-monastic Orders.

Thackeray, William Makepeace. 1811-63. English novelist. His novels present an accurate picture of English life in the mid-19th century. *Vanity Fair* and *Pendennis* are representative examples of this type of novel. *Henry Esmond* is one of the finest historical novels ever written.

Theodora. 508?-548. An actress noted for her beauty, she married Justinian I (523) (q.v.) and for 20 years exerted a great influence over him and over religious and political events.

Theodoric. Often called Theodoric the Great. (*German,* Dietrich). 454?-526. King of the Ostrogoths and founder of the Ostrogothic kingdom of Italy. Born in Pannonia. He became chief in 474. Aided Emperor Zeno (474-487). Invaded Italy (488). He defeated and killed Odoacer, the barbarian leader who had deposed the last Roman emperor. Issued the Edict of Theodoric (506). Made Ravenna his capital. Consolidated his empire to include Sicily, Dalmatia, and some German lands.

Theresa, Saint. 1515-1582. Spanish saint. Carmelite nun from 1534. She tried zealously to restore discipline among the religious orders of her time. She founded the reformed order of Carmelites (1562).

Famous for her mystical visions. Author of *El Camino de la Perfección*.

Thermidorian Reaction. July, 1794. In the period following the guillotining of Robespierre (q.v.), a reaction against the more extreme features of the French Revolution set in. During this period, called Thermidor from the month of July, there nearly was a restoration of monarchy.

Thiers, Louis Adolphe. 1797-1877. French statesman and historian. He first opposed the Polignac ministry (1829-30) and helped depose Charles X. Under Louis Philippe he held various cabinet posts (1832-36). Foreign minister (1836; 1840). He spent the years 1840-45 in travel and writing. After the Revolution of 1848 he was the leader of the right-wing liberals and bitterly opposed to the Socialists. He was opposed to the *coup d'état* of Louis Napoleon. For this he was banished from France (1851-52). He led the opposition to Napoleon III (1863-70). After the Franco-Prussian War he led in the rehabilitation of France. He was elected the first president of the Third Republic (1871-73). His economic policies enabled France to pay off the German reparations in an astonishingly quick time. He is the author of *Histoire de la Révolution Française* (1823-27; 10 vols.) and *Histoire du Consulat et de l'Empire* (1845-62; 19 vols.).

Third Republic, French. 1870-1940. The Third French Republic was proclaimed Sept. 4, 1870. It lasted for 70 years; no other regime since 1789 lasted for more than 18 years. Weakened seriously by losses during World War I and the economic depression of the 1930's, France was an easy victim of the onrushing Nazis during the early days of World War II. An armistice with Germany was signed June 22, 1940. The Third Republic was voted out of existence July 10, 1940 by the National Assembly at Vichy.

Third Rome. Moscow. According to the Russian point of view, Rome was the first center of the Christian Church. After the barbarian invasions (5th century), the center of Christianity shifted to Constantinople. After that city was captured by the Turks (1453), the center of Christianity shifted to Moscow.

Thirty Years' War. 1618-1648. A series of religious wars which wrought havoc to Germany. The war went through various phases:

(1) The Bohemian Period. 1618-20. Emperor Rudolf II (1576-1612) set his heart upon restoring the Roman Catholic Church. His successor, Matthias (1612-19), continued Rudolf's policies. These acts met with great opposition in Bohemia, where the population was overwhelmingly Protestant. In 1618 the Bohemians rose in revolt, invaded the royal palace in Prague, and threw out of a window the two representatives of the emperor. After this act, the Bohemians called upon the Protestant Union (q.v.) for help.

After the death of Matthias, Ferdinand II (1619-37) became the emperor. He moved promptly to crush the rebellion. Meanwhile, the Bohemians offered the crown to Frederick, Elector of the Palatinate. He accepted and was crowned King of Bohemia on Nov. 4, 1619. The army of the Catholic League, headed by Maximilian of Bavaria and Tilly, attacked and defeated the Bohemians at the Battle of the White Mountain (Nov. 8, 1620). Frederick was compelled to abdicate (he is known as the *Winter King*). Bohemia was overrun by the Catholic armies. The estates of the nobles who had revolted were confiscated, and the people were gradually forced back into Catholicism.

(2) Palatine Period. 1621-23. Urged by his advisers, the emperor now carried the war into the Palatinate. By 1623 the

imperial army had completely conquered that state. Frederick went into exile. Maximilian of Bavaria was made Elector in place of Frederick.

(3) The Danish Period. 1625-29. James I of England sought in vain for an ally to take up the cause of his son-in-law Frederick (the *Winter King*). At last, Christian IV of Denmark espoused the Protestant cause. He was confronted by two armies: the army of the Catholic League, commanded by Tilly; and the imperial army, commanded by Wallenstein. The latter army supported itself by living off the country, a practice soon followed by all armies in this war. It was this practice which completely ruined Germany. Christian was completely defeated and forced to take refuge in the Danish islands. In 1629 he signed the Peace of Lübeck in which he promised not to meddle in German affairs, provided he got back his Danish territories.

The end of the Danish period marks the zenith of the fortunes of the Catholic powers. In March, 1629, Ferdinand published the Edict of Restitution, by which the Protestants were deprived of all church territories seized by them since the Peace of Augsburg (1555). In 1630 a Diet held in Regensburg compelled the emperor to dismiss Wallenstein.

(4) The Swedish Period. 1630-35. The Protestant cause now received a great lift when Sweden entered the war under the leadership of its king, Gustavus Adolphus. Before entering the war, Gustavus came to an understanding with Richelieu (q.v.). The Germans at first regarded the Swedes with coolness. But after the sack of Magdeburg by an imperial army under Tilly (May, 1631), they flocked to Gustavus' support. Gustavus defeated Tilly's army repeatedly. In the battle of the Lech, Tilly was killed. Gustavus entered Munich in triumph (1632). Wallenstein was now called out of retirement. He engaged the Protestants at Lützen (Nov. 16, 1632). Although the Protestant army won the battle, Gustavus Adolphus was killed on the field of battle. Wallenstein was murdered in Eger in Feb. 1634 by a cabal of officers who thought he was disloyal to the emperor.

The war dragged on under the direction of Swedish Chancellor Oxenstierna. At Prague, in May, 1635, a treaty was signed between the contesting parties which withdrew the Edict of Restitution (q.v.).

(5) The French Period. 1635-48. The French, directed by Richelieu, now entered the war, hoping to secure some advantage from the exhausted contestants. The French armies, commanded by Condé and Turenne, achieved some notable victories. At length, Emperor Ferdinand III (1637-57) sued for peace. It was agreed (1644) that the French should confer with the Emperor at Münster, and the Emperor and the Swedes should meet at Osnabrück—both of which towns lie in Westphalia.

The Treaty of Westphalia (1648) (q.v.) ended the war. The sufferings of Germany almost defy description. Thousands of villages were wiped out. Augsburg was reduced from 80,000 to 16,000 inhabitants. Some areas had only one-third as many inhabitants as at the start of the war. Many German cities did not regain their pre-1618 size until 1900. Until the year 1800, Germany remained too poor to make any considerable contribution to Europe. The treaty also marks the final acceptance of the religious division of Germany.

Thirty-nine Articles of Religion, Adoption of. 1563. In 1551, Cranmer (q.v.) published Forty-two Articles of Religion. These were essentially the basis of Anglican Protestantism. In 1563, thirty-nine Articles, in place of the forty-two, were adopted by Parliament. Thus was established the Church of England. It was a compromise Church, largely Protestant in dogma but with an organization and liturgy very much like the Roman Catholic Church.

Thomas, Sidney Gilchrist. 1850-85. English metallurgist who invented a process (1875) of eliminating phosphorus from iron in the Bessemer converter. His cousin, Percy Gilchrist (1851-1935), applied this process, now called the Thomas-Gilchrist process, to the open-hearth furnace, inventing the so-called basic open-hearth furnace.

Thomas a Kempis. 1380-1471. German churchman and author. Member and later abbot of the Augustinian monastery located near Zwolle. Author of the *Imitation of Christ*.

Thorn, Peace of. 1411. It followed the defeat of the Teutonic Knights at Tannenberg (1410) by the Poles under Jagello. Poland restored most of the land which it had conquered, but the power of the Teutonic Knights was permanently broken.

Thorn, Treaty of. 1466. An agreement between Poland and the Teutonic Order of Knights. The Order was compelled to cede one-half of its dominions (West Prussia) outright to Poland. After having given up East Prussia outright, the Order received it back from the Polish crown as a fief. This treaty marks the end of the Power of the Teutonic Knights.

Three Emperor League. See Dreikaiserbund.

Tilly, Count of (Johan Tserclaes). 1559-1632. Flemish soldier who was appointed (1610) by Maximilian, Duke of Bavaria, to reorganize his armies. At the beginning of the Thirty Years' War, Tilly was made commander of the army of the Catholic League. He crushed the Bohemian Protestants at White Mountain (1620). He campaigned successfully in the Palatinate (1621-23). He defeated the Danes at Lutter (1626). Succeeded Wallenstein as imperial commander (1630). Sacked Magdeburg (1631).

Routed by the Swedes under Gustavus Adolphus at Breitenfeld (1631) and at the Lech (1632). He was fatally wounded during the battle on the Lech.

Tilsit, Treaties of. July 7-9, 1807. Napoleon, Czar Alexander I, and Frederick William III of Prussia, met on a raft in the middle of the Niemen River and there concluded two treaties.

Between France and Russia: Russia recognized the Grand Duchy of Warsaw, which was created out of the parts of Poland which Prussia had secured in the Polish partitions. The Grand Duchy was to be under the King of Saxony. Danzig was restored as a free city. A part of East Prussia was ceded to Russia. Russia recognized Joseph Bonaparte as King of Naples, Louis Bonaparte as King of Holland, Jerome Bonaparte as King of Westphalia (not yet created). Russia also recognized the Confederation of the Rhine. Secretly, Alexander allied himself with Napoleon against England.

Between France and Prussia: Prussia ceded to France all lands between the Rhine and the Elbe. To Saxony went the circle of Cottbus. All lands taken from Poland were ceded to the new Grand Duchy of Warsaw. Danzig became a free city. Napoleon's brothers were recognized as kings. All ports were closed to British goods and ships. Prussia's standing army was reduced to 42,000 men. By this treaty Prussia was reduced in size from 89,120 square miles to 46,032 square miles. At Tilsit Napoleon and Alexander I divided Europe between them. Tilsit marks the apogee of Napoleon and the complete humiliation of Prussia. Following Tilsit, Napoleon's power declined, while Prussia experienced a rebirth.

"Time of Troubles." Russia. 1598-1613. Following the death of childless Czar Fedor, son of Ivan the Terrible, Boris Godunov was elected Czar by the National Council (1598). Following his death (1605), there were a series of revolts, one a radical movement of peasants and slaves much like the Communist revolt of 1917. Russia was invaded by Poles and Swedes. Under the leadership of Prince Pozharsky the Poles were defeated in 1612. In 1613, Michael Romanov was elected Czar, ending the period of confusion.

"Tinder Box of Europe." The Balkan Peninsula in the days just before World War I. Here were a group of relatively young countries with little experience in self-government and little stability. They all hated one another intensely because of the Balkan Wars (1912-13). Great Britain, France, Italy, Austria-Hungary, and Russia all had strong interests in the Balkans. An outbreak of war there—a highly probable possibility—could easily involve the great powers. Hence, any little event that occurred in the Balkans was viewed with alarm by all the European chancelleries.

Titian (Tiziano Vecelli). 1477-1576. Italian painter. Chief exponent of the Venetian school. Born in Pieve di Cadore. Succeeded Giovanni Bellini as state painter in Venice. Protege of Alfonso d'Este, Duke of Ferrara, and Emperor Charles V. Court painter for Charles V (1532 ff.). Among his works are *Holy Family, Assumption of the Virgin, Ecce Homo, Medea and Venus, Bacchus and Ariadne, Danaë, Venus and Cupid, Rape of Europa.*

Tito, Josip Broz. 1892-. Yugoslav leader, marshal of Yugoslavia. Son of a Croatian blacksmith, he fought in the Austro-Hungarian army against the Russians in World War I. He was captured by (or surrendered to) the Russians. He fought with the Red Army during the civil war (1918-20). He returned to Croatia as a Comintern agent. From 1929 to 1934 he was jailed as a political agitator. His movements from 1934 to 1941 are obscure. Then he emerged as a guerilla

leader. Despite the opposition of the Yugoslav government-in-exile and Mikhailovitch, he secured the backing of the United States and Great Britain, as well as Russia. In March, 1945, he organized a federated Yugoslav government. He deposed the government of King Peter II. He suppressed internal opposition by jailing Archbishop Stepinac and executing Mikhailovitch. He proceeded to organize his country upon communist principles, although he did not attempt to collectivize the land. In June, 1948, he broke with the Cominform when the latter accused him of partiality to Western "imperialism." Tito has kept his position despite hostility to the USSR and all his neighbors. He has likewise refused to give up any part of his internal communist program.

Toleration Act. 1689. An English law which granted wide toleration to Non-Conformist religious groups. While it did not repeal existing penal laws, it suspended their operation against those who did not attend the services of the Established Church. However, Papists and those who did not believe in the Trinity (Jews and Socinians—forerunners of the Unitarians) were expressly excluded from the act.

Tolstoy, Count Leo Nikolaevich. 1828-1910. Russian novelist, social and moral philosopher, religious mystic. Born in the province of Tula. He entered the army and served in the Crimean War (1854-56). He retired from the army and thereafter devoted his time to writing. Emancipated his serfs according to the Act of 1861. Underwent a spiritual transformation (1876) which led him to renounce the Russian Orthodox Church and evolve a new Christianity whose central creed was nonresistance to evil. Tolstoyism became organized into a sect. Author of *Childhood* (1852), *War and Peace* (1866), *Anna Karenina* (1875), *Resurrection* (1899), etc.

Tone, Theobald Wolfe. 1763-98. Born in Dublin. An Irish lawyer who helped to organize the United Irishmen. He sought to induce the French Republicans to invade Ireland so as to drive out the English. He was captured (1798) in a naval engagement between the French and the British. He was taken to Dublin, tried as a traitor, and sentenced to be hanged. He cut his throat in prison.

Torgau, League of. 1526. Lutheran leaders in Germany formed this organization for their mutual protection against Emperor Ferdinand and his Catholic Bavarian allies.

Torquemada. See Inquisition.

Torricelli, Evangelista. 1608-1647. Italian mathematician and physicist. Served as amanuensis for Galileo after the latter became blind (1641). After Galileo's death, Torricelli became mathematician to the grand duke of Tuscany and professor at the Florentine academy. He made many improvements in the telescope. He discovered the principle of the barometer and constructed one (1643). He constructed a simple microscope.

Tory Party. This great English party originated in 1678 at the time of the Popish Plot (q.v.). The name was first applied by Titus Oates to those who disbelieved in the Plot. It passed from them to those men who opposed excluding James, the Duke of York, from succeeding his brother Charles II. Originally the Tories favored landowners, wished to restrict the privileges of Non-Anglicans, and opposed foreign entanglements. The party reached its maximum power under Queen Anne (1702-1714). Upon the accession of George I (1714), the party fell from power for half a century. Under George III (1760-1820) it resumed control of the government. Upon the impact of the French Revolution it became very strongly intrenched in the government.

The Reform Bill of 1832 (q.v.) so demoralized the party that it soon died out.

Tours, Battle of. See Poitiers, Battle of.

Townshend Acts. 1767. Charles Townshend, the Chancellor of the Exchequer in the Pitt Ministry, carried laws through Parliament to impose import duties on the North American colonies on glass, lead, painters' colors, paper, and tea. The colonists replied with a boycott against English goods that so crippled trade that in 1770 all the measures except the tax on tea were rescinded.

Townshend, Charles, Viscount. 1674-1738. He held many government posts for most of his adult years. In 1730 he retired to private life. He became interested in scientific agriculture. He encouraged turnip-growing, and greatly improved the rotation of crops. Hence, his nickname, "Turnip Townshend."

Trade Boards Act, English. 1909. This law adopted the principle that the government has the right to set minimum wages. The law was aimed primarily at "sweated" trades (tailoring, blouse-making, etc.) in which the workers worked in their own homes for very low wages.

Trade Disputes Act. 1906. This law granted to trade unions the right to picket and to use peaceful persuasion in their efforts to induce fellow-workmen to go on strike. The act also safeguarded union funds from suits for damages. This last provision came as the result of the Taff Vale (q.v.) Decision.

Trade Unions, British, Recognition of. By the law of 1800, combinations of workmen were forbidden. This law was repealed in 1824 to the extent of allowing unions to make wage agreements with their employers. An outbreak of violent strikes in 1825 caused Parliament to withdraw most of the concessions of the law of 1824. In 1859, Parliament gave partial recognition of unions by permitting a person peaceably to persuade others to abstain from work. However, the criminal law still regarded strikes as conspiracies. In 1871, the combination laws were repealed and unions were put on a legal basis.

Trafalgar, Battle of. See Nelson, Horatio.

Treitschke, Heinrich von. 1834-96. German historian. Born in Dresden. Professor of history in Kiel (1866), Heidelberg (1867), and Berlin (1874). Strong advocate of German nationalism, colonialism, and anti-British policy.

Trent, Council of. 1545-63. A council called at the instance of Emperor Charles V to heal the break between Lutherans and Roman Catholics. The council convened at long intervals during 18 years. An attempt was made to reconcile the Lutheran doctrine of *consubstantiation* with the Catholic doctrine of *transubstantiation*. Urged by the Jesuit leaders, the Lutheran doctrine was completely rejected. A rigid definition of transubstantiation was drawn up. The council reaffirmed the seven sacraments: baptism, confirmation, the eucharist, matrimony, penance, extreme unction, and holy orders of the clergy. Church tradition and authority as well as the Bible were declared the basis of Christian faith. Belief in purgatory, in indulgences, in prayers to saints, in reverencing images and relics were all upheld. Protestant doctrines were rejected and condemned. The Council played a major part in revitalizing the Church and launching the Counter-Reformation (q.v.).

Trianon, Treaty of. June 4, 1920. An agreement between Hungary and the Allies at the end of World War I. Following the collapse of the Hapsburg rule,

a republic, headed by Count Karolyi, was established. It was overthrown (March 22, 1919) by a communist government, headed by Bela Kun. This government became involved with Hungary's neighbors. The Romanians invaded and captured Budapest (Aug. 4) after the communists had been overthrown (Aug. 1). A monarchial government, with Admiral Horthy at its head, gained control (Feb. 1920). The Romanians withdrew under Allied pressure (Dec. 10, 1919). The Horthy government accepted the Treaty of Trianon by which Hungary lost 3/4 of its territory and 2/3 of its inhabitants. Slovakia was ceded to Czechoslovakia. Austria received western Hungary. Yugoslavia received Croatia-Slavonia and part of the Banat of Temesvar. Romania received the rest of the Banat, Transylvania, and part of the Hungarian plain. Hungary agreed to pay reparations and to limit its army to 35,000 men.

Tribonian. d.?545. Roman jurist. Born in Pamphyllia. He headed the commission which was formed by Justinian to codify Roman law.

Triennial Act. 1694. By this act the length of a session of an English Parliament was limited to three years.

Triennial Bill. Feb. 16, 1641. By this bill the king of England was forced to convene a Parliament at least once in three years. The bill was designed to prevent long inter-parliamentary intervals such as had occurred under James I and Charles I. A companion measure provided that Parliament should not be dissolved without its own consent.

Trieste, Free Territory of. By the peace treaty with Italy (Feb. 1947), Trieste was separated from that nation and established as a Free Territory under the control of the UN Security Council. It was demilitarized, neutralized, and internationalized. It was divided into two zones: Zone A (86 square miles) was placed under Anglo-American control; Zone B (200 square miles) came under Yugoslav supervision.

Triple Alliance. 1882. A defensive alliance among Germany, Austria-Hungary, and Italy. The agreement bound each party to come to the aid of the others should they be attacked. The alliance was directed primarily against France and Russia and was for a specified number of years. It was renewed in 1887, 1902, and 1912, and lasted until May, 1915, when Italy denounced its agreement with Austria-Hungary, although still preserving an agreement with Germany. Italy was an uneasy partner in the Triple Alliance, since Italy claimed Trent, Trieste, and the Istrian Peninsula, all held by Austria-Hungary. However, Italian rage at the French annexation of Tunis (1881), coupled with the need of an alliance, persuaded Italy to become a member of the Triple Alliance.

Triple Entente. 1907. France had agreements with both Great Britain and Russia. It seemed unlikely that Britain and Russia could become allies because of rivalry in the Near and Far East. Following the defeat of Russia in the Russo-Japanese War (1904-05), her influence in the Far East was much reduced. In 1907, Britain and Russia reached agreements regarding spheres of influence in Iran and Afghanistan. The way was now clear for an agreement between France, Great Britain, and Russia, which was signed in 1907. Japan entered into friendly agreement with the Entente powers by a renewal (1911) of her treaty with England and an understanding with Russia (1910) regarding Manchuria. The Triple Entente was formed to checkmate the Power of the Triple Alliance.

Tromp, Maarten Harpertszoon. 1597-1653. Famous Dutch admiral. He won significant victories over the Spanish and

English. His son, Cornelius (1629-91), was also an admiral. His greatest triumph was over the English at Southwold Bay (1665).

Troppau, Protocol of. 1820. The Quadruple Alliance declared at the international conference of Troppau that it was the duty of the Great Powers to stamp out revolution, even to the extent of armed intervention in the domestic concerns of a friendly state. Until the revolutions of 1830, this principle was the cornerstone of European international policy.

Trotsky, Leon (*real name* Lev Davydovich Bronstein). 1877-1940. Russian communist leader. Born near Elisavetgrad. He took an active part in revolutionary activities before 1914 and was exiled and imprisoned several times. After the Russian Revolution of March, 1917, he returned to Russia and became Peoples' Commissar for foreign affairs. He negotiated the Treaty of Brest-Litovsk (q.v.) with the Germans. He became War Commissar (1918) and organized the Red Army. In 1920 he organized labor battalions to save Russian economic life. After Lenin's death he was relegated to a minor post and later banished from Russia (1929). He was hounded from country to country until (1937) he found refuge in Mexico. Here he was murdered (Aug. 21, 1940). Author of *History of the Russian Revolution*.

Troyes, Peace of. See Henry V.

"Truce of God." A device tried by the Church (1030-50) to diminish warfare by calling for a cessation of fighting from Wednesday evening to Monday morning.

Truman Doctrine. In its policy of containing Russia, Great Britain adopted a protective attitude towards Greece and Turkey throughout the 19th century and the first half of the 20th century. Early in 1947 the British announced that they were financially unable to continue their traditional role of "keeping order" in the eastern Mediterranean. President Truman then urged Congress to provide aid to help Greece and Turkey maintain their independence. As the result of this request, the United States today is the protector of Greece and Turkey and has assumed the responsibility for the defense of the eastern Mediterranean. The Truman Doctrine is part of the policy of containment (q.v.) and is aimed directly at Communistic expansion in the Mediterranean.

Trusteeship Council of the UN. The UN is concerned with the welfare of 750 million colonial people living throughout the world. To prepare them for eventual self-government, there has been set up the trusteeship system. Under this system there are three types of territories: (1) territories held under League of Nations mandates granted after World War I; (2) colonial territories taken from the Axis during and after World War II; (3) territories voluntarily placed under the trusteeship system by the states responsible for their administration. The Trusteeship Council is made up of eleven members. The Big Five (United States, France, Great Britain, USSR, China) are guaranteed membership. Other members are chosen by the General Assembly. Each member has one vote, and decisions are made by a simple majority.

The Council makes periodic inspections of the trust regions. It may make specific recommendations for reforms.

There is a special class of trusteeships called *strategic areas*. These are supervised, not by the Trusteeship Council, but by the Security Council.

Tschaikovsky, Peter. 1840-93. Russian composer. One of the outstanding composers of the world. He wrote six symphonies, ballet music (*The Nutcracker, Swan Lake*), chamber music, and concertos for the violin and piano.

Tübingen School. See Strauss, D. F.

Tudor, House of. An English royal line (1485-1603) descended from Sir Owen Tudor of Wales.

	Born	Ruled
Henry VII	1457	1485-1509
Henry VIII	1491	1509-1547
Edward VI	1537	1547-1553
Jane (Lady Jane Grey)	1537	1553-1553

(nominal queen for nine days; not counted by some authorities)

Mary I ("Bloody Mary")	1516	1553-1558
Elizabeth I	1533	1558-1603

Tugenbund (League of Virtue). A widespread secret society which was formed in Prussia during the time of Napoleon for the purpose of inculcating patriotism. It was one of the manifestations of the desire of the Germans to free themselves from French domination. Some of the great men of the time belonged to it. Others made use of it without joining. Others held entirely aloof from it. Stein condemned it as a sort of modern Vehmgericht (q.v.).

Tull, Jethro. 1674-1741. English agronomist and inventor. He perfected a mechanical drill for sowing seed. He introduced new farm methods to his native country. He demonstrated the value of turnips and clover as a substitute for fallow.

Turenne, Vicomte de. Henri de la Tour d'Auvergne. 1611-75. One of France's greatest soldiers. Brought up a Protestant, he was induced by Louis XIV to become a Catholic (1668). Served in the Dutch Wars of Independence (1625-30). Entered the French Army (1630). Served with distinction in the Thirty Years' War (1635-48). Joined the Fronde (1649), but was reconciled with the court (1651). Commanded the armies that invaded the Spanish Netherlands (1667). Commanded armies in the wars (1672-

75) in Holland, the Palatinate, and Alsace against the Empire. Killed in action near Offenburg.

Turgenev, Ivan. 1818-83. Russian novelist. Author of *Fathers and Sons* and *Annals of a Sportsman,* books which portray the conflicts in Russian society in the latter part of the 19th century. He introduced and defined the term *nihilist* (q.v.). He was a great admirer of the American novelist William Dean Howells.

Turgot, Anne Robert Jacques. Baron de l'Aulne. 1727-81. French statesman and economist. Intendant of Limoges (1761-74). Minister of marine (1774). Finance minister (1774-76). He was removed from office because Marie Antoinette opposed his reforms. He retired from public life to devote himself to scientific and literary studies. A strong believer in the physiocrat theories of economics, he is considered to be one of the founders of the science of political economy. Author of *Réflexions sur la Formation et la Distribution des Richesses* (1766).

Turin, Treaty of. March, 1860. Sardinia ceded Savoy and Nice to France in return for help during the Austro-Sardinian War (1859) (q.v.). In return, France recognized the annexation to Sardinia of Modena, Parma, Tuscany, and Romagna (see Unification of Italy).

Turks. An Asiatic people, distantly related to the Mongols, Tatars, Hungarians, and Finns. Originally they were nomadic tribes that roamed the highlands of central Asia. Europeans knew of them in the 6th century. They formed a considerable empire and eventually seized the Caliphate of Baghdad. In the 11th century, a section of them, the Seljuk Turks, overran most of the Asiatic possessions of the Byzantine Empire and threatened Constantinople. By the end of the 11th century, the Seljuk possessions included Asia minor, Persia, Syria, and Mesopotamia. This empire was broken up through civil wars. The large Sultanate of Iconium (Roum) in Anatolia was attacked by the Crusaders and, in time, broken up into 30 emirates. By 1300, a branch of the Turks, the Ottomans, began to construct a strong state. Presently they crossed into Europe and conquered the Slavic peoples one by one. In 1361 they captured Adrianople in Thrace. In 1453 they took Constantinople. By 1450 they were the strongest government in Europe. For the next 2½ centuries they constituted one of the most powerful states in Europe. After 1700 their power declined (see Treaty of Carlowitz).

Turner, Joseph. 1775-1851. English painter. He painted landscapes, chiefly in water colors. Among his great works are *The Fighting Téméraire; Rain, Steam, and Speed; The Approach to Venice,* and *The Sun of Venice.*

Tyler, Wat. d. 1381. Leader of the unsuccessful peasant revolt in England in 1381. After some initial success, the rebels met in conference with Richard II at Smithfield. Blows were exchanged. William Walworth, mayor of London, wounded Tyler, and later had him beheaded. After Tyler's death his followers scattered and did not resume the rebellion.

Tyndale, William. 1484-1536. English reformer. He spent many years of his life on the continent. He translated the New Testament into English. A copy of it was printed in England (1536), the first volume of the Holy Scripture printed in England.

U

Ulrika, Eleanora, Queen of Sweden.
See Great Northern War.

Ulster, Plantation of. 1611. Due to an uprising in the north of Ireland over religious affairs, James I allotted the most fertile tracts of Ulster to English and Scottish settlers. The economic results of this act were excellent. But the act created new political bitterness which led to a bloody rebellion thirty years later. Ulster and the problems attached to its existence have been major factors in Irish history ever since.

Ulster Rebellion. 1641. Freed from the iron grip of Strafford (q.v.), and smarting under generations of grievances, the peasantry of Ulster rose in rebellion and massacred upwards of 5000 people. Twice as many more died of exposure and starvation. This Irish problem hastened the British Parliament to pass the Grand Remonstrance (q.v.).

Ultramontanism. Jesuits and many other Roman Catholics supported the pope in all respects. By themselves and their opponents they were conceived as looking beyond the mountains (*ultra montes*) that guard Italy's frontier to the pope in Rome for guidance in all things that con-

cerned religion. Ultramontanes wanted to see absolute authority in all religious matters vested in the Pope. The term, ultramontanism, was used principally in France before the French Revolution. It was revived in Germany in the 19th century. The Council of the Vatican (1869-70) accepted ultramontanist doctrines completely.

Umberto. See Humbert I.

Unam Sanctam. 1302. A bull issued by Pope Boniface VIII in which he asserted that the pope was entrusted with both temporal and spiritual power, and that whoever resisted him was resisting the ordinance of God. Submission in temporal matters to the pope was declared to be necessary for salvation.

Unification of Germany. 1862-71. The successful movement for the unification of Germany began when Bismarck was made chancellor of Prussia. Bismarck believed that to achieve unity, Germany must expel Austria from German affairs and must forge some bond of union upon the field of battle in which Germans strove to repel a common foe. He accomplished these goals by three wars: (1) The Danish War (1864); (2) The

Austro-Prussian War (1866); (3) The Franco-Prussian War (1870-71) (q.v.). The first war provided the cause for the second. In the second war, Austria was soundly thrashed and expelled from the German union. In the third war, all Germans united to repel the attack by the French. The German Empire was proclaimed Jan. 18, 1871, in the Palace of Versailles in France. King William of Prussia was named German Emperor.

Unification of Italy. 1859-61. The unification of Italy was accomplished largely through the work of Victor Emmanuel II (king of Sardinia), Cavour, Mazzini, and Garibaldi (q.v.). In 1859, Sardinia, assisted by the French, drove the Austrians from Lombardy and annexed it. Early in the following year, the duchies of Parma, Modena, and Tuscany and the Papal State Romagna joined with Sardinia. In May, 1860, Garibaldi and his "Redshirts" invaded Sicily, which he conquered within three months. In September he captured Naples. In November he turned over all of his conquests to Victor Emmanuel. Together they turned north and conquered all of the Papal States except Rome, which was garrisoned by the French. On March 17, 1861, Victor Emmanuel was crowned King of Italy. As Prussia's ally in the Austro-Prussian War (1866), Italy secured Venetia. When the French soldiers were withdrawn from Rome during the Franco-Prussian War, the Italians secured the city (Sept. 20, 1870). In July, 1871, Rome was proclaimed the capital of Italy.

Union of Scotland and England, Act of. 1707. The Act of Union provided that the two kingdoms were to be united under the name of Great Britain and to have one Parliament. There was to be complete freedom of trade between the two countries at home and abroad. Scottish laws and legal procedure were to be preserved. Forty-five Scotch members

were to sit in the House of Commons, while for each session the Scotch peers were to elect sixteen of their number to to represent them in the House of Lords.

Unionist Party of England. 1895-c. 1914. When Gladstone took up Irish Home Rule, Joseph Chamberlain openly rebelled, and John Bright followed him with the rest of the radical Liberals. Chamberlain formed the Liberal Unionists, a group which was determined not to dissolve the legislative union of Ireland and Great Britain. In 1895, Chamberlain allied his group with the Conservative Party, and the coalition ruled the country for the next ten years. The party made a great appeal to patriotic ardor. Nobility, clergy, gentry, lawyers, university graduates, merchants, manufacturers, financiers, as well as clerks, tradesmen, shopkeepers, and many of the lower classes were Unionists. The party was dissolved during the First World War for the sake of harmony.

United Nations Charter. The Charter of the UN is a document of 111 articles covering all phases of international organization. In addition to the main Charter, there are the charters of the many specialized agencies through which the UN accomplishes its purposes. The aims of the UN, as stated in the Charter, are (1) to maintain international peace and security by collective action; (2) to develop friendly relations among the nations; (3) to achieve international cooperation in solving economic, social, cultural, or humanitarian problems and in promoting respect for human rights and fundamental freedoms; (4) to serve as a center for harmonizing the actions of nations in the attainment of these common ends.

The principal organs of the UN are the General Assembly, the Security Council, the Economic and Social Council, the

Trusteeship Council, the International Court of Justice, and the Secretariat.

(See separate listing for discussion of each organ. See also Specialized Agencies of the UN.)

United Nations Educational, Scientific, and Cultural Organization (UNESCO). The object of UNESCO is to insure peace through international understanding. It has undertaken many projects to restore schools that were destroyed during the war; to stimulate the free interchange of ideas through travel, films, broadcasts, and publications; to reduce illiteracy; to sponsor international cultural exchanges through music, the theatre, art, and literature; and to encourage the interchange of scientists, educators, and students.

United Nations Relief and Rehabilitation Administration (UNRRA). An organization founded Nov. 9, 1943 to give aid to those regions which had been liberated from the Axis. Altogether, 52 countries participated. Of the 4 billion dollars which was spent, half was contributed by the United States. The three directors—Fiorello La Guardia, Herbert Lehman, and Gen. Lowell Rooks—were Americans. China, Czechoslovakia, Greece, Italy, Poland, the Ukraine, and Yugoslavia were the chief recipients of aid. The organization returned 7 million displaced persons to their homelands and maintained camps for one million more. The European operations ended July 30, 1947; those in China, March 31, 1949. Much of the work formerly done by UNRRA was taken over by UN organizations, such as the FAO and the IRO.

Universities, Origin of, Medieval. The word "university" comes from *universitas*, which was a term applied during the Middle Ages to any form of association. The workmen of a guild formed a *universitas*, as did the citizens of a commune. Perhaps the oldest university is the University of Paris, which took form about 1100, although it was not officially called a university until 1207. It was founded from a gathering of teachers and pupils who were attached to the Cathedral of Notre Dame. These schools first met on the Île de la Cité, but later moved to the left bank of the Seine to a spot which is still called the Latin Quarter. Bologna claims to house the oldest university, dating from 1088. Paris specialized in theology; Bologna, in law. Salerno (probably founded by the Saracens) specialized in medicine, as did Montpelier (1300). Oxford and Cambridge are contemporary with Paris. Valencia (1221) and Salamanca (1243) are the oldest Spanish universities. Prague was founded in 1348; Vienna, 1365; Heidelberg, 1386; Cologne, 1388; Leipzig, 1409; Rostock, 1419. By the end of the Middle Ages there were some 80 universities in Europe.

The chief groundwork of general culture was considered to be a course of study which embraced the *trivium* (grammar, rhetoric, logic) and the *quadrivium* (arithmetic, music, astronomy, and geometry), which together were termed the liberal arts. These basic subjects were complemented by courses in more advanced fields, such as Theology, Law, Medicine, and Philosophy. Since books were few, most instruction consisted of lectures. Memorizing of authorities was the usual educational method. Much stress was placed upon Aristotle. Upon completion of a course, a student was granted a degree by a particular faculty or guild of the university. Doctor, professor, and magistrate were the kinds of degrees offered. All of them meant "teacher."

Since universities were offshoots of cathedral schools, teachers and pupils felt that they could not be tried by secular courts. Therefore, there was a certain amount of friction between "town" and "gown." Students who attended universities organized themselves into "nations" or other unions. Thus at Paris there were four nations: English, Normans, Picards, and "French."

University of France. May 1, 1802. This body was incorporated by law to supervise the instruction of all students in France. It set up state examinations for teachers who were to serve in the institutions of higher learning. The *Institute National* was reorganized and divided into four (later five) academies: Académie Française (founded in 1635); Académie des Inscriptions et Belles-Lettres (1663, 1701); Académie des Sciences (1666); Académie des Beaux Arts (1648); Académie des Sciences Morales et Politiques (1832). It will be noted that this reorganization of education concerned only secondary education. It was designed to affect the education of the well-to-do classes and to mould the minds of those who were to be leaders in the state and army. On March 7, 1808, by imperial decree, all public education was entrusted to the University. Since the state had not created schools for all children, it could not monopolize all education. However, such free schools as remained were forced to model their teaching and organization upon the lycées and collèges of the state. The French system of education and particularly the French concept of secondary education have influenced the school systems of many countries. Early in the 20th century, many in France felt that their school system should experience some basic changes. Following World War I the following reforms were put into effect: A common primary foundation school was adopted; fees were abolished; and the number of scholarships in secondary schools was increased. These reforms were temporarily set back during the Vichy regime (1940-45). Since 1945 the reforms have been reinstated.

University of Moscow. The first Russian university. Founded in 1755. The first teachers were Germans. It had two preparatory "gymnasiums"—one for the children of nobles; one for the children of other classes.

Unkiar-Skelessi, Treaty of. See Nicholas I.

Urban II (*name Odo*). 1042?-1099. Pope (1088-99). Born in Châtillon-sur-Marne, France. Benedictine monk. He continued the policy of Gregory VII in opposing Emperor Henry IV. He excommunicated Henry IV and Philip I of France. He called the Council of Clermont (1095) (q.v.). During the Council he preached the sermon which launched the First Crusade.

Usher, James. 1581-1656. Protestant bishop of Meath, Ireland, and subsequently archbishop of Armaugh. In his *Annales veteris et novi testamenti* (1650-54), he calculated the chronology of man's existence on earth. He estimated that the first man, Adam, had been created on a Friday in the month of October in 4004 B.C.

Utopian Socialism. This type of Socialism is exemplified by such men as Fourier, Saint-Simon, and Robert Owen (q.v.). Today many would call them philanthropists rather than Socialists. They urged men to live in common in "model" communities and to share on equal terms the labor and the profits. Profit-sharing in industry and cooperative producers' and consumers' organizations stem from Utopian Socialism.

Utraquist. 15th and 16th centuries. The moderate wing of the Bohemian followers of Hus (q.v.). They insisted upon communion in both kinds (Latin *sub utraque specie*), whence their name. The sect played a part in the religious wars in Bohemia in the 15th century. Eventually the group split into two sections: one returned to the Catholic fold through an agreement (*Compactata*); the other was absorbed into the Lutheran Church and was granted official status through the *Majestätsbrief* (1609) (q.v.).

Utrecht, Union of. Jan. 29, 1519. Holland, Zealand, Gelderland, Zutphen, Utrecht, and the Frisian provinces pledged union against all enemies. Civil and religious liberties were guaranteed. Although the document says nothing about throwing off the yoke of Spain, it actually was the beginning of modern Holland.

Utrecht, Union of. 1579. When the Spanish governor of the Netherlands, Alexander of Parma, broke up the union of the seventeen Netherland provinces, by guile, the ten southern provinces, being predominantly Catholic, fell back to Spain. The seven northern provinces, by the Union of Utrecht (1579), combined under William of Orange and, after an heroic struggle, finally achieved independence (1648).

V

V-1 and V-2. *Vergeltungswaffe,* or "vengeance weapons." These German weapons were first launched against England on June 15, 1944. V-attacks continued until the forces of the United Nations captured all the launching fields in Europe. The V-1 was a pilotless, jet-propelled bomb. About 2300 of them got through to London, where they killed or wounded 20,000 people. In Sept. 1944, the attacks of V-1's ceased. Then began the V-2 attacks. These weapons were rockets which shot through the stratosphere at supersonic speed. The Germans continued to send them against England until the spring of 1945.

Valla, Lorenzo (*Latin,* Laurentius). 1406-57. Italian humanist. Papal secretary (1455 ff.). Authority on Latin. He made Latin translations of Homer, Herodotus, and Thucydides. He exposed the fraud known as the Donation of Constantine.

Valmy, Battle of. Sept. 20, 1792. The first military success of the French Revolutionary armies. Danton infused new spirit in the French armies. Dumouriez replaced Lafayette as commander. The news of the victory reached Paris Sept. 21, the day that the National Convention met for the first time. On the flush of this victory, the Convention proclaimed a republic on Sept. 22. This battle was a pivotal point in the fortunes of the French Revolution.

Valois. A royal house of France which first came to the throne upon the death (1328) of Charles IV, the last Capetian king. The first Valois king was Philip VI (1328-50), nephew of Philip IV. The house consists of three branches, as follows:

Capetian (1328-1498)	*Born*	*Ruled*
Philip VI	1293	1328-1350
John II (the Good)	1319	1350-1364
Charles V (the Wise)	1337	1364-1380
Charles VI (the Well-Beloved)	1368	1380-1422
Charles VII	1403	1422-1461
Louis XI	1423	1461-1483
Charles VIII	1470	1483-1498

Orléans (1498-1515)		
Louis XII (the Father of the People)	1462	1498-1515

Angoulême (1515-1589)		
Francis I	1494	1515-1547
Henry II	1519	1547-1559
Francis II	1544	1559-1560
Charles IX	1550	1560-1574
Henry III	1551	1574-1589

Henry III was succeeded by Henry IV, the first of the Bourbon kings.

Vandals. A central European tribe which migrated across France and Spain and settled in Carthage in Africa in 429. Here they ruled until they were conquered (533) by Belisarius, a general of the Emperor Justinian. Because of their manner of sacking Rome (455), their name has come to stand for wanton destruction.

Vane, Sir Harry. 1613-62. An English Puritan statesman. He settled in Boston (1635) and became governor of Massachusetts (1636). He lost popularity by taking the side of Anne Hutchinson in a theological dispute, and was defeated for re-election (1637), whereupon he returned to England. He took an active part in the Civil War on the side of Parliament. He was imprisoned by Cromwell (1656). He was arrested after the Restoration (1660) and executed for treason (1662).

Van Gogh, Vincent. 1853-1890. Dutch post-impressionist painter. Noted for brilliantly-colored, dynamic pictures. Some of his best known works are *L'Arlésienne, Sunflowers,* and *A Starry Night.*

Varennes, Flight to. June, 1791. Louis XVI of France and Marie Antoinette fled from Paris in disguise to avoid the spying vigilance of the Parisians. They made straight for the eastern frontier, ostensibly to join the emigrés. At Varennes, near the frontier, they were recognized and returned to Paris under heavy guard. In the future they were treated like captives. They were eventually tried and executed. The flight of the king and queen marks the end of whatever hope France might have had for a stable constitutional government.

Vasari, Giorgio. 1511-74. Born in Arezzo. Studied under Michelangelo. His fame rests on his book, *The Lives of the Painters.*

V-E Day. May 8, 1945. On this day, President Truman for the United States

and Prime Minister Churchill for Great Britain proclaimed the end of the Second World War in Europe. On the following day, Marshal Stalin announced the end of the war to the Russian people. German army chiefs completed the surrender formalities in Berlin.

Vega, Lope de. 1562-1635. Spanish dramatic poet and founder of the Spanish national drama. Born in Madrid. Served in the Spanish Armada (1588). Ordained as a priest (1614) after the death of his second wife. Doctor of theology (1627). He is the reputed author of 1800 plays.

Vehmic court (Vehm, Fehm, Vehmgericht). An institution peculiar to Germany, especially Westphalia, from about 1150 to 1568, consisting of irregular tribunals. During the latter part of this period, civil authority was weak or lacking. These courts were very popular, as they provided the only way for many to secure some form of justice. Although the Vehms tried civil cases publicly, they tried serious cases (heresy, witchcraft, murder) by night in secret session. The sentence of these courts always was death and was executed by one who had taken part in the secret trial. Thus, Vehmic courts were extra-legal institutions which resembled lynching or vigilante committees. The institution was favorably received during the 14th and 15th centuries. Only when the secret nature of the organization bred abuses did complaints against it lead to its suppression.

Velasquez, Diego Rodriguez de Silva y. 1599-1660. Spanish painter. Born in Seville. Leading painter of the Spanish school. Appointed court painter (1623). Quartermaster-general of the king's household (1652 ff.). Considered the leading representative of naturalism in painting. His works include *Surrender of Breda, Royal Household of Philip IV, Adoration of the Magi.*

Vendée, La. Department of west France in Poitou on the Atlantic coast. The department gave its name to a counter-revolutionary uprising against the French Revolution (1793-95). Peasants and nobles united and raised a formidable army. The uprising was put down with terrible violence. After the death of Robespierre (q.v.), the department again revolted. This second revolt was put down by General Hoche, whose moderate policy led to the pacification of the region in 1796. (See French Revolution.)

Venice, Republic of. Situated on half-flooded islands, Venice was poorly settled in Roman times by fishermen and traders. The invasion of the Huns (452) and the Lombards (568) drove thither many people for refuge, and the real life of the city began. Neither the Lombards nor the Franks could conquer Venice. It remained nominally subject to the Byzantine Emperor. In 697 the communities of several islands met and elected a duke, called *doge*. By this act, Venice became independent. Its power and wealth increased. By the year 1100, Venice had secured control of the Dalmatian coast. Venice took part in the Crusades because of commercial, rather than religious, motives. The Fourth Crusade gave Venice control of the Peloponnesus (Morea), Crete, and the Greek Archipelago. Genoa's threat to Venice was defeated by the battle of Chioggia (q.v.) (1380).

The doge, although at first an absolute ruler, was stripped (after 1200) of much of his power. The authority was vested in the *Great Council* of 480 members. In 1311, the *Council of Ten* was created. This group had unlimited powers of arrest and punishment.

In the 15th century, Venice expanded its power on the mainland, acquiring control of Treviso, Padua, and Vicenza. By 1484, Venice secured frontiers on the mainland which remained unchanged to the days of Napoleon.

In the 16th century, Venice began to lose some of its overseas possessions to the Turks. After 1718, Venice lost all overseas territories except the Ionian Islands and the Dalmatian coast. Politically Venice stagnated, while artistically it remained one of the most active centers in Europe.

In May, 1797, Napoleon conquered the Venetian Republic. By the Treaty of Campo Formio (Oct. 17, 1797) he transferred it to Austria.

Venizelos, Eleutherios. 1864-1936. Greek statesman. Born on the Island of Crete. He organized the first Balkan League (1912). Because he championed the cause of the Allies in World War I, he was ousted by the pro-German king (1915). After King Constantine abdicated (1917), Venizelos returned to Greece and sided with the Allies. At the Peace Conference of Versailles, he was on the committee which wrote the Covenant of the League of Nations. Premier (1919-20; 1924). He advocated the formation of a republic (1924). Again premier (1928-32; 1933). Forced into exile (1935). Pardoned by King George II upon the resumption of the monarchy (Nov. 1935).

Verdi, Giuseppe. 1813-1901. Italian composer. He is the greatest master of the Italian opera of the 19th century. Among his operas are *Rigoletto, Aida, Il Trovatore, La Traviata, The Masked Ball, Falstaff,* and *Otello.* In addition he composed the *Hymn of the Nations,* a *Requiem,* and some church music.

Verdun, Battle of. Feb. 21-July 11, 1916. The Germans tried to break through the French front in World War I by striking "at the heart of France." The German troops were led by Crown Prince William. The French defense was organized by General (later Marshal) Pétain, who coined the famous phrase "They shall not pass." Later, Pétain was replaced by General Nivelle. At the end of the campaign the opposing lines were at virtually the same locations as they had been at the beginning. It is estimated that between them the French and Germans lost 700,000 men in this campaign.

Verdun, Treaty of. 843. By this treaty the empire of Charlemagne was divided among his grandsons. Lothar retained the imperial crown. He had two capitals—Rome and Aachen. He received Italy and a strip of land extending from Italy to the North Sea. Charles (the Bald) received all the land west of this strip. Ludwig received all the land east of this strip along with the dioceses of Mainz, Worms, and Speier. The kingdom of Lothar was called after him, Lorraine (*Lotharingia*). Charles was called king of the Franks. Ludwig was known as the king of the Germans. Thus the history of France and Germany as separate nations began in 843. Lothar's kingdom eventually went to pieces, since it was broken in two by the Alps. The narrow strip along the Rhine was fought over for centuries by the French and the Germans.

Vergniaud, Pierre Victurnien. 1753-93. French lawyer and revolutionary. President of the Legislative Assembly (1791). Member of the National Convention (1792). Member of the Girondist Party. Famous orator. Guillotined (Oct. 31, 1793).

Verocchio, Andrea del. 1435-88. Florentine goldsmith, painter, and sculptor. Like many other Florentine artists, he began life as a goldsmith. He next took up painting, at which he did not achieve great success. When he turned to sculpture he achieved lasting greatness. His *David* and *Doubting Thomas* are among the world's treasures. His equestrian statue of *Bartolomeo Colleoni* (in Venice) is perhaps the finest representation in the world of a warrior and a war-horse.

Verona, Congress of. 1822. In 1820, a revolt broke out in Spain against the re-

actionary rule of Louis VII. Czar Alexander I of Russia offered to lead a great army across Europe to restore absolutism in Spain. But the French demurred at this offer. After protracted international negotiations, the Quadruple Alliance met at Verona and proposed that a French army, acting upon a general European mandate, should intervene in Spain. Great Britain insisted that the independence of Spain must not be destroyed, that France must not take any Spanish colonies, and that the occupation must not be permanent. Under these stipulations, a French army entered Spain (April, 1823) and suppressed the revolution within a year.

Versailles, Peace Conference of. This conference convened in Paris on Jan. 18, 1919 for the purpose of concluding peace with Germany, following the end of World War I. Seventy delegates, representing 27 of the victorious nations, gathered in Paris. Full sessions of the conference were of little importance. From the beginning, decisions were made by the Supreme Council (Big Ten), composed of Wilson, Lansing, Lloyd George, Balfour, Clemenceau, Pichon, Orlando, Sonnino, Saionji, and Makino. On March 25, the Big Ten was replaced by the Big Four (Wilson, Lloyd George, Clemenceau, and Orlando). The Japanese withdrew from deliberations of the Supreme Council after their ambitions in the Pacific were fully satisfied. The Big Four in reality became the Big Three when Orlando and Wilson disagreed over the Fiume question. On April 28 the Covenant of the League of Nations was presented in its final form. The authors of the covenant were Wilson, House, Cecil, Smuts, Bourgeois, and Venizelos.

The conference was marked by violent controversies. Clemenceau insisted upon the cession by Germany of the left bank of the Rhine and the annexation by France of the Saar Basin. Wilson and Lloyd George opposed these demands. England and France insisted that Germany must pay all the costs of the war. Wilson objected to this proposition. The Polish claims (supported by France), the Japanese intentions toward Shantung, and the Italian claims to the Dalmatian coast also were major matters of discord. (The Italian delegates left the conference on April 23 and did not return until May 6.) All these questions were finally settled by compromise.

The treaty was submitted to the German delegation on April 29. The Germans protested against the terms of the treaty as violating the armistice agreement. After an acute domestic crisis, the Germans agreed to sign. The signing of the treaty took place on June 28 (five years to the day after the assassination of Archduke Francis Ferdinand at Sarajevo) in the Hall of Mirrors in Versailles.

Versailles, Treaty of. Sept. 3, 1783. This treaty was between France and Spain and England. It was signed on the same day that England and the United States signed the Treaty of Paris which ended the American Revolutionary War. France received certain West Indian islands and restored to England some that it had conquered. France was to secure full sovereignty of St. Pierre and Miquelon. French commercial establishments in India were restored. Spain retained Minorca and West Florida, both of which it had captured from England recently. England gave East Florida back to Spain.

Versailles, Treaty of. June 28, 1919. An agreement between Germany and the Allies at the end of World War I. It contained the following provisions:

(1) *Territory.* Germany ceded Alsace-Lorraine to France; Moresnet, Eupen, and Malmedy to Belgium; a large part of Posen and West Prussia to Poland; Memel to the Allies; the colonies to the Allies, who were to organize them as mandates under the supervision of the League of Nations. The Saar was to be placed under the control of the League of Nations for 15 years, after which a plebiscite was to be held, France exploiting the coal mines meanwhile. Plebiscites were to be held in northern and central Schleswig and Upper Silesia. Danzig was to be an international city under League of Nations supervision.

(2) Germany accepted the sole responsibility for starting the war.

(3) *Disarmament.* The German army was limited to 100,000 volunteers. The navy was limited to 6 battleships and corresponding supporting vessels. There were to be no submarines nor military aircraft. The Allies were to occupy the Rhineland for 15 years or longer at German expense. A belt 30 miles wide on the right bank of the Rhine was to be demilitarized. The Kiel Canal and all German rivers were to be internationalized.

(4) The former German emperor and all other offenders were to be tried for war guilt.

(5) *Reparations.* The Germans were to pay for all civilian damage caused by the war, the amount to be fixed by May 1, 1921. In the meanwhile, Germany was to pay 5 billion dollars. Germany was to surrender all merchant ships of more than 1600 tons, half of those between 800 and 1600 tons, and one-fourth of the fishing fleet. Germany was to build 200,000 tons of shipping annually for the Allies for the next five years. Also Germany was to deliver large quantities of coal to France, Belgium, and Italy for 10 years.

(6) The treaty contained provisions for a League of Nations.

Germany ratified the treaty July 7, as did France (Oct. 13), Great Britain (Oct. 15), Italy (Oct. 15), and Japan (Oct. 30). The United States never ratified the treaty. Nor did it ratify a treaty of alliance with England and France (signed June 28) (q.v.), providing for assistance in case of attack by Germany.

Vesalius, Andreas. 1514-64. Belgian anatomist. Born in Brussels. One of the first to dissect the human body in the study of anatomy. Lectured at Padua, Basel, Pisa, and Bologna. Physician to Charles V and Philip II. He made a pilgrimage to the Holy Land (1564) to commute a death sentence which the Inquisition had imposed on him for dissecting the human body. Author of *De Humani Corporis Fabrica* (1542).

Vespucci, Amerigo. 1451-1512. Italian navigator. He took part in several voyages to the New World (1497, 1499, 1501, 1503). He made maps. His accounts of the New World were published by Martin Waldseemüller (1507), a German geographer, who suggested that the new lands be named "America."

Vichy Government of France. By the terms of the German-French armistice (June 21, 1940) in the Second World War, France was divided into two parts by a line which ran from the Swiss border near Geneva to a point 12 miles east of Tours. The line then ran to the southwest to St. Jean Pied de Port. The Germans occupied the northern portion, which included most of the industrial regions of France, Paris, and the entire Channel and Atlantic coast. Unoccupied France was ruled from Vichy, where Marshal Pétain ruled as "Chief of State." A National Assembly of two houses was entrusted with the task of preparing a constitution (July 10, 1940). Being dilatory in its duty, in August, 1942, Pétain abolished the National Assembly and ruled by decree. Pierre Laval was designated as Pétain's successor. In Dec. 1940, Laval was removed from office and was succeeded by Admiral Darlan. In April, 1942, the Nazis persuaded Pétain to restore Laval to authority as "chief of government." The Vichy government took as its motto "Labor, Family, Fatherland." It enacted anti-Semitic laws, forbade labor unions and strikes, revised the inheritance laws to perpetuate the peasant basis of agriculture, regulated every phase of

the nation's economic life, instituted strict censorship, instituted military training for the youth, and made the position of the Catholic Church more favorable. After the Allied invasion of North Africa, the Germans invaded and took over control of Unoccupied France (Nov. 11, 1942).

Victor Emmanuel II. 1820-78. King of Sardinia (1849-61). King of Italy (1861-78). Born at Turin. He became the King of Sardinia when his father, Charles Albert, abdicated (1849) following the defeat at Novara. Guided by Cavour, he took steps to strengthen his kingdom and to unite Italy. He became the first king of Italy (1861). Despite his personal limitations, he was highly regarded by his contemporary countrymen. He was the active symbol around whom the leaders in the movement for national unification rallied.

Victor Emmanuel III. 1869-1947. King of Italy from 1900 to 1946 (from 1944 in name only). Succeeded his father Humbert. The First World War added greatly to his kingdom. A tool of Mussolini from 1922. The Second World War stripped him of the empire of Ethiopia and the kingdom of Albania. He abdicated in 1946.

Victoria. 1819-1901. Queen of Great Britain and Ireland (1837-1901) and (from 1876) empress of India. Born in London. Only child of George III's fourth son, Edward, Duke of Kent. In her first years as queen she was guided by Lord Melbourne, Whig prime minister. She married Prince Albert of Saxe-Coburg-Gotha (Feb. 1840). She was much influenced by him and his adviser, Baron Stockmar. She achieved a measure of personal authority by requiring Lord Palmerston to inform her of every proposed course of action. Founded the Order of Victoria Cross (1857). Made her husband Prince Consort (1857). After the death of her husband (1861) she followed policies which she believed he would have endorsed. She accepted the title of Empress of India (1876). Celebrated her golden jubilee (1887) and her diamond jubilee (1897). At the time of her death she was recognized as symbolizing a new conception of British monarchy and a unified empire.

Vienna, Congress of. 1814-15. This was a conference among the leading statesmen of Europe to determine what was to be done with the former conquests of Napoleon and how to maintain the social stability of Europe. The Congress was dominated by Metternich, the foreign minister of Austria. Czar Alexander I of Russia, Castlereagh and Wellington of Great Britain, Hardenberg and von Humboldt of Prussia, Talleyrand of France, and Nesselrode and Stein of Russia were outstanding personalities in a throng of kings, princes, dukes, electors, and the like.

A guiding principle of the Congress was "legitimacy," meaning that families which reigned in various countries of Europe before the outbreak of the French Revolution were to be given back their thrones. The boundaries of these same countries were to be pre-Revolution, as far as practical. In the name of legitimacy, France was not compelled to pay heavily for the Hundred Days (q.v.). The Bourbon kings were restored, as were France's 1789 boundaries. The art treasures which Napoleon seized were to be restored. France was to pay an indemnity of 700 million francs within 5 years. The Bourbons were restored in Spain and the Two Sicilies; the House of Orange, in Holland; the House of Savoy, in Sardinia and Piedmont. The pope was given back his temporal possessions. Austria received the Tyrol and the Illyrian provinces. The Swiss Confederation was restored under a guarantee of neutrality. Poland was divided among Prussia, Russia, and Austria as in 1795 (called the Fourth Partition). The Czar was to grant

autonomy and a separate constitution to his portion of Poland.

The second guiding principle was "compensation." This meant that countries should be paid for loss of territory. During the Napoleonic Wars, Great Britain had captured Malta, Mauritius, Tobago, St. Lucia, Trinidad, part of Honduras, the important Dutch colonies of Ceylon, South Africa, and Guiana. As compensation for colonial losses, Holland was permitted to annex the former Austrian Netherlands (Belgium). As compensation for the loss of Belgium, Austria secured Lombardy and Venetia, and Hapsburgs were made rulers of Tuscany, Parma, and Modena. (Marie Louise, Napoleon's second wife, became Grand Duchess of Parma.) As compensation for the loss of Finland to Russia and Pomerania to Prussia, Sweden was given Norway, which was taken from Denmark. Prussia was given two-fifths of Saxony. The kingdom of Sardinia was allowed to annex the republic of Genoa.

Very little was done to satisfy the national aspirations of the Germans, due to the reluctance of the Prussian king, Frederick William III, to assume leadership. A loose confederation of 38 states, called the Germanic Confederation, was created. It sponsored a Diet, consisting of the delegates of the reigning princes. This Diet was to be presided over by Austria.

The Congress declared that slave trade should be abolished, each power being permitted to fix such a date as suited its convenience. There were also provisions respecting free navigation of international rivers and the rights of precedence among diplomats.

Vienna, Treaty of. Oct. 5, 1735—ratified 1738. The treaty which concluded the War of the Polish Succession (q.v.). It contained the following terms: (1) Stanislaus Leszczynski renounced the throne of Poland. As compensation, he received the duchies of Lorraine and Bar, which were to go to France at his death. He died in

1766. (2) The Duke of Lorraine, Francis Stephen, received the duchy of Tuscany. (3) Austria ceded Naples and Sicily, the Island of Elba and the Stati degli Presidi to Spain and received in return Parma and Piacenza. (4) France guaranteed the Pragmatic Sanction (q.v.). After this treaty, Bourbons ruled France, Spain, and southern Italy and Sicily. Thenceforth, the Bourbons were the most powerful dynastic group in Europe.

Villafranca, Armistice of. See Austro-Sardinian War.

Villon, François. b. 1431. French poet of humble birth. It is not definitely known what his real name was. He led an irregular life. He fatally stabbed a priest (1455). He was arrested for theft (1462) and for brawling (1462). He was sentenced to death. The sentence was commuted to banishment in Jan. 1463. Here Villon passes from our sight. It is clear from his works that he was a wreck, shattered by debauchery, prison-life, and torture. His works consist of the *Petit Testament* (1456) and the *Grand Testament* (1461) and some 40 short pieces, chiefly ballades.

Vincent de Paul, Saint. 1581?-1660. French priest, famous for his benevolence, zeal, and charitable organizations. He founded the Priests of the Mission (1625), the Sisters of Charity (1634), and hospitals for foundlings in Paris. Beatified (1729). Canonized (1737).

Vingtième. Direct tax in Old Regime France. It was one-twentieth of the incomes of individuals—5% on the salary of the judge, on the rents of nobles, on the earnings of the artisan, on the produce of the peasant. Only the clergy were entirely exempt from this tax.

Visconti. A powerful Lombard family of Milan, of the Ghibelline (q.v.) faction, which furnished the ruling dukes (1311-1447). After mastering Milan, the Visconti turned to territorial expansion. By 1350, Milan had conquered all the cities of Lombardy. Gian Galeazzo (1385-1402) brought Milan to the height of its power. In the north only Venice remained independent. South of the Apennines, Pisa, Lucca, and Siena were captured by force or fraud. Then the tide turned. By 1447, when Filippo Maria, the last of the Visconti died, some of the conquered cities had regained their freedom.

Vishinsky, Andrei Yanuarievich. 1885-. Russian jurist and diplomat. After studying law, he entered the Social Democratic Party. He fought in the Bolshevik ranks through the civil wars. He was appointed state prosecutor (1923) and professor of jurisprudence in the University of Moscow (1925). He was the prosecutor who conducted the purges of 1936-38 (see Purge, Soviet). After the start of the Second World War, he became a diplomat, representing his country on the Allied Mediterranean Commission and the Allied Advisory Council for Italy (1944-45) and in the Balkans, particularly in Romania. After the creation of the United Nations, he was one of the key figures there. In 1949 he replaced Molotov as foreign minister of the USSR. On the death of Stalin (1953), he was replaced by Molotov and appointed instead to be chief USSR delegate to the UN.

Visigothic Kingdom of Spain. At the time of King Euric (466-485), Visigothic rule extended from the Loire to Gibraltar. Clovis (q.v.) forced the Visigoths to withdraw south of the Pyrenees (q.v.). Their capital was Toledo. The Visigoths had little statesmanship; they added nothing to the arts of farming, mining, breeding sheep or cattle; they had no literature. They set an example of physical courage, personal independence, and self-respect. Roman tradition survived. Isidore of Seville (560-636), a bishop, historian, and man of letters, produced during this period the *Etymologiae*, a general reference work that served as a manual for 500 years. The Visigoths were conquered by the Moors in 711 (q.v.).

Visigoths, or Western Goths. The Goths were a barbarian Germanic tribe which probably originated in Scandinavia. About 150 the Goths departed from their homeland and eventually settled to the north and east of the Danube. Here they split into two groups—the Ostrogoths and the Visigoths. The latter successfully invaded the Roman Empire first and in 410, under Alaric, sacked Rome. Induced by the Roman emperor to invade Gaul, they did so. They also invaded Spain, securing control of all of it by 507 (see Visigothic Kingdom of Spain). Here they remained until they were conquered by the Moors in 711.

Vittorino da Feltre (*name* Vittorino Ramboldoni). 1378-1466. Italian educator. Known for his famous school which he founded in 1425. He admitted both noble and poor children. He is celebrated for the practical methods of instruction which he employed.

Vizier (Wazir). A high executive officer of various Moslem countries, especially the former Turkish empire.

Vladimir (the Saint). 956?-1015. Ruler of Russia (980-1015) who in 986 investigated the rival claims of Roman Catholicism, Orthodoxy, Judaism, and Mohammedanism. Choosing Orthodoxy, he ordered a general christening of his subjects in 989.

Volta, Alessandro. 1745-1827. Italian physicist. He discovered the electrical decomposition of water. He invented a new electric battery, the electrophorus, and an electroscope. He made investigations of heat and gases.

Voltaire (*assumed name of* François Marie Arouet). 1694-1778. French writer. Born in Paris. Educated by Jesuits. He began writing at an early age. Imprisoned in the Bastille (1717-18) for writing a satire. He wrote a tragedy *Oedipe* (1718) while in prison. Again in the Bastille (1726). Released on his promise to leave France. Resided in England (1726-29). Wrote *Letters on the English* (1734) which caused criticism and made it necessary for him to seek seclusion. He lived in the Château de Cirey in Lorraine with Mme. du Châtelet (1734-49). After her death he resided in the court of Frederick the Great of Prussia (1750-53). While there he published his great work of history, *Le Siècle de Louis XIV*. Quarreled with Frederick and left Prussia. Resided at Ferney, near Geneva (1758-78). Author of *Zadig* (1747), *Candide* (1759), *Essai sur Moeurs*, etc. For more than 50 years he preached freedom of thought and denounced cruelty and oppression in all its forms. He was the champion of reason and tolerance. By the end of his life he had completely conquered the realm of public opinion. Neither Church nor State dared to interfere with him. He did for France what the Renaissance did for Italy and what the Reformation did for Germany.

Vondel, Joost van den. 1587-1679. Dutch poet and dramatist. Author of lyric, patriotic, and religious poems. He made translations and adaptations from Ovid, Seneca, Sophocles, and Euripides. He translated the Psalms. He is the author of 30 dramas, mostly Biblical and historical. Many think that John Milton drew heavily from Vondel's writings.

W

Wagner, Richard. 1813-83. German composer. Originator of the music-drama type of opera. Many of his operas are based upon medieval German legends. *Tannhäuser, Lohengrin, Siegfried, Tristan und Isolde, Parsifal, Die Meistersinger* are some of his representative operas.

Wagram, Battle of. July 6, 1809. Austria once more engaged Napoleon in war but was decisively defeated at Wagram. Napoleon forced the Austrians to sign the Treaty of Vienna, which took Austria out of the war for the next four years. As the result of further negotiations, Napoleon secured a Hapsburg archduchess, Maria Louisa, for his wife.

Wallace, Alfred Russel. 1823-1913. English naturalist. Born in Monmouthshire. Trained as a surveyor and an architect, he devoted himself to natural history from 1845. He visited the Amazon Valley (1848-52) and the Malay Archipelago (1854-62). While on the latter expedition he arrived independently at the theory of natural selection. He investigated the geographical distribution of animals. Among his many writings are *Travels on the Amazon and Rio Negro* (1853), *Contributions to the Theory of Natural Selection* (1870), *The Geographical Distribution of Animals* (1876), and *Man's Place in the Universe* (1903).

Wallace, Sir William. 1274-1305. Scottish patriot who opposed Edward I of England (1297). After marked success against the English, all of Scotland submitted to him. When (1298) Edward invaded Scotland, Wallace was defeated at the battle of Falkirk (July 22). He was later betrayed by a Scot, captured, and executed in London (1305).

Wallenstein, Albrecht Eusebius Wenzel von. Duke of Friedland and Mecklenburg. Prince of Sagan. 1583-1634. Austrian general. He lost his estates when Bohemia became Protestant. Made duke (1625) and made commander of the imperial armies in the same year. He began the practice of supplying his army by foraging the countryside. This custom, later adopted by other commanders, led to frightful destruction in Germany. He was very successful against the Danes (1626-27). Because of jealousy, he was removed from command (1630). He was reinstated (1632) and was defeated by Gustavus Adolphus at Lützen. He was again removed from command and assassinated by some of his Irish and Scottish officers.

Wallingford, Treaty of. 1153. Henry of Anjou forced Stephen of England to sign this treaty. In it Stephen agreed that Henry should succeed him as king of England.

Walpole, Hugh, 4th Earl of Orford. 1717-97. Famous English collector, virtuoso in arts, author. His *Castle of Otranto* (1764) is a famous medieval romance.

Walpole, Sir Robert. 1st Earl of Orford. 1676-1745. English statesman. He favored the Hanoverian cause. Became prime minister (1721). He was the first to unify the cabinet in the person of the prime minister. He established sound finance at home and laid the foundations of modern colonial policy and free trade. Believing in peace, he kept his country out of war until 1739. He was forced to resign Jan. 1742.

Walsingham, Sir Francis. 1536-90. One of the principal secretaries of state of Elizabeth I of England. His administration of foreign affairs was founded on bribery, espionage, and intrigue.

Walter the Penniless. See Peter the Hermit.

Walther von der Vogelweide. 1170?-?1230. German lyric poet and minnesinger. He lived the life of a wandering singer (after 1198), chiefly in the courts of Philip of Swabia, Hermann of Thuringia, Otto IV, and Frederick II. His poems include love songs, political songs, and religious songs, in which he championed German independence and opposed the claims of the popes. He is considered one of the greatest poets of the medieval period.

War Budget of 1909, English. This budget was the work of Lloyd George (q.v.) "to make war on poverty." It contained a graduated income tax; an inheritance tax; taxes on the unearned income of land; on undeveloped land; on motor cars, motor cycles, gasoline; stamp-taxes, licenses, and excise taxes on beer, spirits, and tobacco. Besides providing ample revenue, this budget attacked landlords and shifted part of the tax burden upon the wealthy. Because the House of Lords tried to obstruct this bill, Parliament in 1911 greatly limited the power of the House of Lords (see House of Lords Bill, 1911).

War of Liberation (Prussia). After the disasters of 1805-06, Prussia took vigorous steps to reorganize. Under the leadership of Stein (q.v.), widespread political and social reforms were adopted. Serfdom was abolished. Industry was liberated from burdensome restrictions. Taxes were reformed. Universal military service was adopted. Fichte delivered his famous *Address to the German Nation* (q.v.). The patriotic society, *Tugenbund*, was founded (q.v.). As a result of these reforms, Prussia was able to play a decisive role in the ultimate defeat of Napoleon.

"War of Revenge." Following the Franco-Prussian War (1870-71), many Frenchmen advocated a war of revenge against Germany to recover Alsace-Lorraine.

War of the Roses. 1455-85. Conflict between the rival houses of York and Lancaster for the throne of England. The former assumed the white rose as its badge; the latter, the red rose. After twelve major battles, Henry Tudor, of the house of Lancaster, became king and married a Yorkist wife, ending the struggle. The conflict severely depleted the ranks of English nobility. It also arrested the progress of English freedom for more than a century.

War of the Three Henrys. 1585-89. One of the French Religious Wars (1562-89). Its name comes from Henry III of Valois, Henry of Navarre (later Henry IV), and Henry of Guise. The last of the Valois kings, Henry III, leaned to the Protestant side because he feared the growing power of Henry of Guise. The king was driven from Paris by the Catholic supporters of Guise (1588) on the Day of Barricades. Soon after, Guise was lured to Blois by the king and murdered by royal henchmen. The next year Henry III was murdered by a fanatical monk. Thus Henry of Navarre became king of France.

Wartburg Festival. Oct. 1817. During the period of Metternich reaction, liberalism flourished among German student secret societies called *Tugenbund* and *Burschenschaft*. When on Oct. 31, 1817, the three-hundredth anniversary of Martin Luther's launching the Protestant Reformation, some students at Wartburg burned some of the emblems of the Old Regime, the event was magnified by Metternich into a rebellion. When two years later a fanatical student murdered Kotzebue (q.v.), a dramatist who was a Russian spy, a meeting of German statesmen was called at Carlsbad where they drew up the notorious Carlsbad Decrees (q.v.).

Warwick, Richard Neville, Earl of. "The Kingmaker." 1428-71. A Yorkist leader in the War of the Roses (1455-85) (q.v.). Although defeated at St. Albans and Wakefield, he was able to seize London (1461) and proclaim Edward IV king. He captured Henry VI and confined him in the Tower of London. When a rupture developed between Edward IV and Warwick, the latter deposed Edward and placed Henry upon the throne. Edward returned to power (1471), and defeated and killed Warwick in battle (at Barnet). Warwick was the last of the great barons. He was a skilled diplomatist and politician. He was the greatest landowner in England, and dispensed lavish hospitality.

Washington Conference, The. Nov. 12, 1921-Feb. 6, 1922. This conference was part of a general movement to prevent wars by reducing armaments. Great Britain, France, Italy, Holland, Belgium, Japan, China, and Portugal met with the United States to consider naval disarmament and the Far Eastern problems. The following agreements were secured:

(1) A Nine-Power Treaty (Feb. 6) which guaranteed the territorial integrity of China and the principle of the "Open Door."

(2) A Four-Power Treaty (U. S., Britain, France, Japan. Signed Dec. 13) guaranteed the signers' rights to certain insular possessions in the Pacific.

(3) The Shantung Treaty (Feb. 4), by which Japan agreed to return Kiaochow to China.

(4) A Five-Power Treaty. The United States, Britain, Japan, France, and Italy agreed upon a 10-year "naval holiday" during which no new capital ships were to be built. A ratio for capital ships was established under which both the United States and Britain were each allowed 525,000 tons; Japan, 315,000 tons; and France and Italy, each 175,000 tons.

Water frame. See Arkwright, Sir Richard.

Waterloo, Battle of. June 18, 1815. In this battle, the military power of Napoleon was finally crushed. After his return from exile in Elba (March 1, 1815), Napoleon raised an army and marched for the Channel in the hope of separating the English from the Prussians and Austrians. At Waterloo he engaged the English under the Duke of Wellington until late afternoon. Then, the arrival of the Prussians under Blücher turned the tide against the French, who were driven in utter rout from the field. This battle ended the reign of Napoleon and ushered in a period of peace for Europe which lasted 40 years.

Watt, James. 1736-1819. Scottish mechanical engineer and inventor. In his capacity of instrument maker for the University of Edinburgh, he was given the task of repairing a Newcomen (q.v.)

steam engine. This led him to invent the modern steam engine (1769). This invention not only revolutionized technology, but also profoundly affected the social, political, and economic structure of the whole world. He formed a partnership with Matthew Boulton (1775) and manufactured steam engines in the Soho Engineering Works, Birmingham. He originated the term *horsepower*. The watt, a unit of power, is named for him.

Wavell, Archibald Percival, first Earl. 1883-1950. British field marshal and Viceroy of India. He saw service in South Africa and on the Western Front in World War I, where he lost an eye. Later he served under Allenby in Palestine and there learned much about the strategy of desert fighting. In World War II he was made Middle East Commander. He repulsed the Italian invasion of Egypt (1940-41), but was later driven back by Rommel when many of his troops were diverted to Crete. In 1942 he became Allied Supreme Commander in the Far East. He was Viceroy of India (1943-47), during which time he worked for Indian independence. Author of *The Palestine Campaigns* (1928), *Allenby* (1940), *The Good Soldier* (1947), etc.

Webb, Sidney James. 1st Baron Passfield. 1859-1947. English economist, socialist, and statesman. Born in London. One of the founders of the Fabian Society (q.v.). Author of *Socialism in England* (1890). Taught economics in the University of London (1912-27). Member of the royal commission on trade-union law (1903-06). With his wife Beatrice (*nee* Potter) (1858-1943) he wrote on economics and sociology. Founded the *New Statesman* (1913). M.P. (1922-29). Secretary for the colonies (1929-31) and dominions (1929-30). Created Baron Passfield (1929). With his wife he wrote *History of Trade Unionism* (1894), *Industrial Democracy* (1897), *Decay of Capitalist Civilization* (1921), etc.

Wedgewood, Josiah. 1730-95. Famous English potter. He patented (1763) and perfected (1769) a glazed, cream-colored earthenware, called queen's ware. He named his new factory "Etruria." He laid the foundations for the famous English potteries of the "Six Towns" of Staffordshire.

Weimar Constitution of the German Republic. Adopted July 31, 1919. The head of the state was to be a president, chosen for a 7-year term. The president was to appoint a chancellor, who, in turn, chose a cabinet which could command a majority in the Reichstag. The president had the power to suspend constitutional guarantees and the Reichstag in a case of emergency. The Reichsrat, composed of delegates from the 18 states (Länder), could delay but not prevent legislation. The members of the Reichstag were elected, not as individuals, but by party lists for all Germany. Elections were held according to the Baden method of proportional representation whereby each party secured one delegate for each 60,000 votes that it polled. There was to be separation of church and state and complete religious liberty. All education was placed under the control of the state and all teachers were state officials. Provision was made for state insurance against sickness, accident, old age, and unemployment. All private property was to be used "to serve the public good." Article 25 empowered the president to dismiss the Reichstag and to order a new election within 60 days. Article 48 permitted the president, acting with the chancellor, in times of emergency to suspend the constitutional guarantees and to issue decrees with the force of law. These two articles were used by the Nazis in 1933 to seize control of the government and destroy the Republic. This constitution continued in effect until March 22, 1933, when the Reichstag, by a vote of 441 to 94, passed an enabling act which suspended the constitution and gave Hitler dictatorial power.

Welf. A German princely family, taking its name from the original home in Altdorf, Swabia. Throughout the 12th and 13th centuries, the Welfs frequently were at war with the Hohenstaufens. The outstanding Welf of this period was Henry the Lion, Duke of Saxony and Bavaria, who defied Emperor Frederick Barbarossa and lost his possessions (1180). In Italy the supporters of the Welfs were called Guelphs. The British house of Windsor (formerly called Guelf) are descendants of the Welfs through the German houses of Hanover and Brunswick.

Wellington, 1st Duke of. Arthur Wellesley. "The Iron Duke." 1769-1852. One of Britain's greatest military heroes. Born in Ireland. Entered the army (1787). Irish M.P. (1790-95). Appointed by his brother (the governor-general of India) to supreme military command in the Deccan (to 1805) where he defeated the Maratha chiefs. Returned to England (1805). Irish secretary (1807-09). He was given command of the English forces in the Peninsular War (1808) (q.v.). He defeated the French and drove them from Spain (1814), pursuing as far as Toulouse. Made duke (1814). English representative at the Congress of Vienna (1814-15). Crushed Napoleon at Waterloo (1815). Prime minister (1828-30). Forced the Catholic Emancipation Act through Parliament (1829) (q.v.). Opposed the Reform Bill (1831-32). Foreign secretary under Peel (1834-35). Supported Peel's Corn Bill (q.v.). Organized protection for London during the Chartist uprisings (1848) (q.v.).

Wells, Herbert G. 1866-1946. English novelist and historian. He is the author of many novels which deal with contemporary problems, such as *Tono Bungay* and *Mr. Britling Sees It Through.* He may be considered as the pioneer of "science fiction" with such works as *The Time Machine* and *The Invisible Man.* He wrote the *Outline of History,* which had the virtue at least of having had many readers.

Wergeld. Among the medieval Germans, homicide, assault, theft, and the like were considered to be offenses against the individual and his kinsmen. If the injured parties were not bought off, they were lawfully entitled to seek revenge through a blood-feud. The compensation to the individual and his kinsmen was called *Wergeld.* The compensation was in proportion to the value of the part affected. Thus, stealing a calf was valued at 3 *s.* (*solidus,* a Frankish coin which was the ancestor of the shilling); housebreaking, 35 *s.*; slaying a Roman, 100 *s.*; slaying a free Frank, 200 *s.*

For over 500 years this form of justice superseded Roman law throughout most of the western world.

Wesley, John. 1703-91. English clergyman. He is the founder of the Methodist Church. When Anglican churches closed their pulpits to him, he took to preaching in the open air. He is said to have traveled 250,000 miles and preached 40,000 sermons during his lifetime. His converts were mainly working-class people—miners, weavers, artisans, day-laborers. In addition to his preaching, he found time to do a prodigious amount of writing, including English, French, Latin, Greek, and Hebrew grammars, histories, and religious books. His brother, Charles Wesley (1707-88) was his constant companion and a famous composer of hymns. He is said to have written 6500 hymns, among which are *Jesu, Lover of My Soul* and *O for a Thousand Tongues to Sing.*

Westminster Assembly. July 1, 1643. This was a gathering held during the English Civil War (1642-46) to work out an agreement between the Church of England and the Scotch Presbyterians so that they could present a united front against the Cavaliers. Although the work of the assembly eventually came to little, it did prepare the Westminster Confession, the form of belief held by the Presbyterian Church today.

Westminster Confession. See Westminster Assembly.

Westphalia, Kingdom of. 1807-13. A portion of western Germany which was organized into a kingdom by Napoleon for his brother Jérôme.

Westphalia, Peace of. 1648. These treaties concluded the Thirty Years' War. Negotiations were in progress for four years before the treaties were signed. The French and the emperor met at Münster; the Swedes and the emperor met at Osnabrück—both towns in Westphalia. Sweden received the western half of Pomerania and the Bishoprics of Bremen and Verden. Thus it gained control of the mouths of the Oder, Elbe, and Weser Rivers. France was confirmed in its possession of the Bishoprics of Toul, Metz, and Verdun, which had been acquired under Henry II (1552); also Alsace, but not the free city of Strassburg. With regard to Church property, whatever was in Protestant hands on Jan. 1, 1624, was to remain Protestant; what was in Catholic hands on the same date was to remain Catholic. However, no concessions were made about Bohemia, which remained in the emperor's hands. Calvinism was put on the same footing as Lutheranism. The Palatinate was restored in a mutilated condition. The son of the "Winter King" (q.v.) was made its ruler and the eighth elector. The dignity of the seventh elector, which had formerly been given to the ruler of the Palatinate, was transferred to the Duke of Bavaria. The princes of Germany were given a number of new sovereign rights, thus reducing the authority of the emperor. Brandenburg received eastern Pomerania and four

bishoprics, enabling it to replace Saxony as the dominant German state after Austria. Switzerland and the Dutch Netherlands were formally declared sovereign and free states.

Whig Party. This great English party, first known as the Country Party, was organized in the House of Lords by Shaftesbury (q.v.) and in the House of Commons by William Sacheverell to oppose Danby and the court party. The center of activity of the Whig Party was the Green Ribbon Club, founded in 1675. The party drew its strength from the landed gentry and the commercial classes. Many religious dissenters belonged to it. The Glorious Revolution of 1688 (q.v.) ushered in a long period of Whig dominance. Except for the reign of Queen Anne (1702-14), the party controlled the government until 1760. In the 1720's and 30's the leading Whig was Sir Robert Walpole (q.v.), who gave shape to modern British cabinet government. The party at this time advocated mercantilism and religious toleration. After the accession of George III (1760), the Whigs rarely controlled the government until 1830. By this time the party was middle-class in character and was identified with social and political reform. After enacting the Reform Bill of 1832 (q.v.), the Whig Party by choice discarded the name "Whig" for "Liberal."

White Mountain, Battle of. Nov. 8, 1620. A crushing defeat of the Bohemian Protestants by the imperial troops under Tilly. Following this defeat, Bohemia was overrun by the imperial army. Protestantism was ruthlessly crushed. Frederick, the "Winter King" (q.v.), was driven into exile and deprived of his electoral vote as Count Palatine.

White Terror. 1815. This was a period of rioting in France fomented by the Ultra-Royalists. Thirty-eight leaders during the Hundred Days (q.v.) were banished and a few, among them Marshal Ney, were shot. Protestants in Nimes were attacked for heresy and some were murdered.

Whitefield, George. 1714-70. English clergyman, one of the founders of the Methodist Church. Many of his most effective sermons were delivered out of doors. He spent most of his life in constant travel and incessant preaching, everywhere moving audiences by his eloquence and earnestness.

Wilberforce, William. 1759-1833. English philanthropist and anti-slavery crusader. Due to his efforts, England abolished slavery in the colonies in 1833.

Wilhelmina. 1880-. Queen of the Netherlands. She succeeded her father, William III, in 1890. Despite her great influence upon the government, she was always a strictly constitutional monarch. Her court was distinguished by its simplicity and high moral tone. She lived in exile (1940-45) in the United States, Canada, and England when the Nazis occupied her country. She abdicated in 1948, and was succeeded by her daughter Juliana.

Wilkes, John. 1727-97. English reformer. He founded the *North Briton* in 1762 and in it attacked Lord Bute and charged George III with falsehood. As a result he became involved in a libel suit during which he became the idol of the London mob. He championed parliamentary reform, abolition of rotten boroughs, and the colonial rights of the American colonies. He secured abolition of general warrants, freedom of the press in reporting debates in Parliament, and enfranchisement of artisans and the middle class.

Wilkinson, John. 1728-1808. English ironmaster. He invented the machine for accurate boxing of cylinders. He was one of the first to attack the problem of precision machinery in ironwork.

William I. "The Conqueror." 1027 or 8-1087. Bastard son of Robert III, Duke of Normandy, by Arletta, a tanner's daughter. In 1051 he visited his cousin, Edward the Confessor (q.v.), and received promise of the English succession. In 1064, Harold (q.v.) was at his court and swore to help him gain the crown of England. When Edward died in 1066, Harold became king. William appealed to the pope, who supported his claim. At the battle of Hastings, Oct. 14, 1066, Harold was defeated and slain. William was crowned king of England Dec. 25, 1066. His rule was stern and orderly. He died in Rouen Sept. 9, 1087, from an injury suffered when he fell from his horse. He left Normandy to his son Robert and England to his son William.

William II (called Rufus). 1066-1100. King of England (1087-1100). Son of William the Conqueror. He had considerable abilities as a soldier, but was cruel, capricious, and wasteful. He had to contend with rebellions and invasions by the Scots. He was shot with an arrow by Wat Tirel.

William III. 1650-1702. King of England, Scotland, and Ireland (1689-1702). Stadholder of Holland (1672-1702). Because of his marriage to Mary, daughter of the duke of York (later James II), he was invited to become king of England in 1688 when the English feared that they might have a long succession of Catholic sovereigns. He became joint sovereign of England with Mary in 1689 and sole sovereign after her death in 1694. He died without issue and the throne passed to Anne (q.v.), the last of the Stuarts.

William IV. Sometimes called "The Sailor-King." 1765-1837. King of Great Britain and Ireland and Hanover (1830-37). Third son of George III. He served in the navy during the Napoleonic Wars. He became heir to the throne and lord high admiral in 1827. During his reign the Reform Act of 1832 (q.v.) was passed. He was succeeded by his niece Victoria and on the Hanoverian throne by his brother Ernest Augustus.

William I (Wilhelm Friedrich Ludwig). 1797-1888. King of Prussia (1861-88). Emperor of Germany (1871-88). Born in Berlin. He fought against Napoleon (1814-15). Became prince of Prussia (1840) when his brother Frederick William became king. Regent (1858-61). Upon becoming king, he determined to strengthen the army. When his parliament resisted, he made Bismarck (q.v.) his chancellor. Now began a series of wars—the Danish War (1864) (q.v.), the Austro-Prussian War (1866) (q.v.), and the Franco-Prussian War (1870-71) (q.v.)—which led to the unification of Germany. As first Emperor of Germany and the symbol of German unity, William was very popular. But his reactionary policies caused the radicals to hate him and led to two attempts upon his life. His reign was crucial in German history, as it saw Germany rise to the position of one of the foremost nations of the world.

William II (*full German name* Friedrich Wilhelm Viktor Albert). 1859-1941. Emperor of Germany and king of Prussia (1888-1918). Born in Berlin. On accession to the throne (1888) he asserted the divine mission of the Hohenzollerns to rule. He dismissed Bismarck (1890). He maintained the Triple Alliance. He was interested in social questions, built up the German fleet, and unsuccessfully opposed the growth of Socialism. He played a prominent part in the Boxer Rebellion (1900-01), sided with Austria-Hungary against Serbia (1914) and thus precipitated the First World War. His prestige waned as the war progressed. He fled to Holland (Nov. 6, 1918) and abdicated (Nov. 28, 1918).

He resided at Doorn, near Utrecht. He married a second time (to Princess Hermione of Schönaich-Carolath; 1922) and was granted a payment (1926) by the Prussian government for confiscated property. He was living at Doorn when the Nazis invaded Holland (May, 1940).

William of Orange (*known as* William the Silent). 1533-84. Founder of the Dutch Republic and first stadholder (lieutenant). Prince of Orange and Count of Nassau. Page to Emperor Charles V. Commander of imperial armies (1555). He refused to attend the "Council of Blood" (1567) (q.v.). He led the revolt (1568-76) and the "War of Liberation" against the Duke of Alva and the Spanish armies. He united the seven northern provinces against Spain. By the Union of Utrecht (1579) (q.v.) they declared independence from Spain. Made stadholder in 1579. Assassinated at Delft by Balthasar Gerard.

Windisch-Grätz, Prince Alfred zu. 1787-1862. Austrian field marshal. Commander of Bohemia (1840-48). He suppressed the Czech uprising in Prague (1848), helped to elevate Francis Joseph I to the throne (1848), and assisted in the quelling of the uprising in Hungary (1849).

Windsor, Duke of. See Edward VIII.

Windsor, House of (until 1917 it was called the House of Saxe-Coburg). The present royal family of England.

	Born	Ruled
Edward VII	1841	1901-1910
George V	1865	1910-1936
Edward VIII	1894	1936-1936
(He abdicated. He has been known since as the Duke of Windsor.)		
George VI	1895	1936-1952
Elizabeth II	1926	1952-

Winter King, The. See Frederick V.

Witenagemot. The highest body in Anglo-Saxon England, composed of Ealdormen, bishops, and nobles who were close to the king. Its business was to advise the king, give consent to land grants, and to name the king—though their choice was limited to the ablest male next in descent of the royal family.

Witte, Count Sergei Yulievich. 1849-1915. Russian statesman. Born in Tiflis in the Caucasus where his father (of Dutch extraction) was an administrator. Minister of finance (1892-1903). Negotiated the Treaty of Portsmouth (1905) ending the Russo-Japanese War. First constitutional premier of Russia (Nov. 1905-May, 1906). Resigned (1906) and became a member of the council of the empire. He fostered railroad building, industry, colonial expansion, and established the gold standard for Russian money. He promoted social legislation and tried to lessen the evils of heavy drinking.

Wittelsbach. A German family that ruled in Bavaria (12th century—1918) and in the Rhenish Palatinate for part of that time. The duchy of Bavaria became an electorate in 1623 and Duke Maximilian (q.v.) was made elector. The electorate was made a kingdom by Napoleon (1806). Maximilian I (1806-25), Louis I (1825-48), Maximilian II Joseph (1848-64), Louis II (1864-86), Otto (1886-1913), and Louis III (1913-18; abdicated) were kings of Bavaria. Three kings of Germany have been Wittelsbachs: Louis IV of Bavaria (1287-1347; Holy Roman Emperor, 1314-47), Rupert of the Palatinate (1352-1410; king 1400-10), and Charles VII of Bavaria (1697-1745; Holy Roman Emperor, 1742-45).

Wolfram von Eschenbach. d. 1220. Medieval German epic poet. Author of *Parzival,* from which Wagner derived the libretto for Parsifal.

Wollstonecraft, Mary. 1759-97. See Godwin, William.

Wolsey, Thomas, Cardinal. 1475-1530. English clergyman and statesman. Educated for the church, he entered the royal service under Henry VIII and forged rapidly to the front. All kinds of honors were heaped on him. In 1514 he was made Archbishop of York; in 1515, cardinal and Lord Chancellor; in 1518, Papal Legate. In 1521, he was a candidate for the papacy. But Adrian of Utrecht was elected, due to the support of Emperor Charles V. Wolsey's foreign policy aimed at maintaining a balance between Francis I of France and Emperor Charles V. His domestic policy aimed at strengthening the power of the king. He founded the College of Ipswich and Christ Church College at Oxford. Because he could not secure papal consent for Henry's divorce from Queen Catherine, he fell from favor. He was indicted under the Act of Praemunire (q.v.) for securing bulls from Rome and was deprived of the Great Seal. Faced with a charge of treason, he died on the way to his trial. His arrogance offended all classes of people.

Women's suffrage, English. Agitation for women's suffrage gathered momentum in England in the second decade of the 20th century. A group of "militant" suffragettes attempted to focus public opinion on the justice of their claims by spectacular stunts, such as slashing pictures in art galleries, pouring acid in mail boxes, smashing windows, etc. With the advent of the war, the militant suffragette movement collapsed as its proponents devoted their energy to war efforts. In 1918, all English women over 30-years of age were enfranchised. In 1928, the so-called "Flapper Law" was passed, which gave the vote to all women citizens 21-years of age or older.

Wordsworth, William. 1770-1850. English poet. Pioneer of the romantic school of poetry. He was primarily a poet of nature. He wrote *The Prelude, Ode to Duty, Intimations of Immortality, The Solitary Reaper,* etc.

Workmen's Compensation Laws, English. 1897-1906. In 1897 the principle of compensation for accidental injury was recognized by law for a few trades. In 1900 the principle was extended to agricultural laborers. In 1906 the Liberal Parliament extended compensation to virtually all workers. In this connection, it is well to note that between 1884 and 1907, 20 other countries enacted workmen's compensation laws.

World Court. See Permanent Court of International Justice.

World Health Organization (WHO). 1948. The WHO is concerned with raising the standards of health throughout the world. It first concentrated upon eradicating malaria and tuberculosis. Through the FAO it is trying to promote better nutritional standards throughout the world.

World War I. 1914-18. The fundamental causes of this war were:

(1) Imperialism and its rivalry for markets, raw materials, etc. (See Drang nach Osten.)

(2) Militarism, which made Europe an armed camp.

(3) Nationalism with its irredentist movements.

(4) International anarchy—the absence of any established organization which might seek to settle differences between nations and work for peace.

(5) The system of alliances, which enabled each member to call for assistance from all other members whenever it was confronted with some difficulty. (See Triple Alliance. See Triple Entente.)

The immediate cause was the assassination of Archduke Francis Ferdinand of Austria-Hungary at Sarajevo by a Serbian nationalist.

The contestants were called the Central Powers (q.v.) and the Allies (q.v.).

1914. The German supreme commander, General Helmuth von Moltke, put into operation a revised version of the so-called Schlieffen Plan. This had been prepared by General Alfred von Schlieffen, who was chief of the general staff from 1891 to 1906. Schlieffen anticipated a war on two fronts. Believing that Germany could mobilize more rapidly than Russia, he called for a holding action on the eastern front by a relatively small number of troops, thus allowing the use of a crushing force against France. The German left wing was to pivot on the fortified area near Metz. The powerful right wing was to follow the Meuse River valley through Belgium, pass Paris on the west, and fall upon the main French army from the rear. Moltke modified this plan to some extent. It was expected to take six weeks to complete the campaign.

As the German armies smashed through Belgium, England entered the war. Despite the assistance of the British, the French fell back before the powerful drive of the German right wing. By Sept. 1, the Germans were 15 miles from Paris. The French government fled to Bordeaux. General Joffre, noting that the German right wing had lost contact with the rest of the army, launched the First Battle of the Marne (Sept. 6-10, 1914) (q.v.). The German drive was halted. The Germans retreated to the Aisne River, where they "dug in." After the Marne, there began a race between the Germans and the Allies to occupy the Channel Ports. The Germans captured most of these. But the British, in the First Battle of Ypres, kept control of a small part of southwest Flanders and the French ports of Calais, Dunkirk, and Boulogne. During the winter of 1914-15 the enemies consolidated their positions on the 600-mile front from Belgium to the Alps.

Meanwhile, on the eastern front the Russians made surprising progress. Their rapid advance came to an abrupt end when they were decisively beaten by the Germans under Ludendorff and Hindenburg at Tannenberg (Aug. 26-31, 1914). This was followed by the rout of the Russians at the Masurian Lakes (Sept. 5-15, 1914) and at Augustovo (Feb. 1915). The Russians lost 1½ million men in these campaigns. Against Austria-Hungary the Russians were very successful, capturing most of Galicia and driving the defenders back to the Carpathian Mountains.

1915. The Central Powers drove the Russians out of Galicia. Bulgaria joined the Central Powers and helped in the conquest of Serbia. Italy entered the war on the side of the Allies (see Treaty of London). A Franco-British attack upon Constantinople by way of the Gallipoli Peninsula failed. On the Western Front the Allies made some progress in Flanders, but were repulsed in the Second Battle of Ypres, where, on April 22, the Germans first used poison gas. An Allied drive in the summer also failed.

1916. This year was marked by two enormous campaigns: the German assault upon Verdun, from February to July; the Allied attack on the Somme, from June to November. Although the British used tanks in the Somme offensive, neither side possessed offensive weapons that were strong enough to effect a break-through. Both drives resulted in insignificant gains and tremendous casualty lists. The Austrians penetrated deep into north Italy, but had to withdraw when the Russians, under Brussilov, gained much ground in Galicia. The Russians were repulsed in a combined attack by the Central Powers, which also led to the conquest of Romania.

1917. Early in 1917 the position of the Germans seemed to be fairly strong. They held Serbia, Montenegro, Romania, Po-

land, most of Belgium, and northern France. Russia was beaten down. When the Czar abdicated in March, Russia all but withdrew from the war. One year later (March 3, 1918), Russia signed the Treaty of Brest-Litovsk (q.v.) with the Germans and withdrew from the war in fact. However, in April, 1917, the United States declared war on Germany.

On the Western Front the Germans retired to the Hindenburg Line. In April, the British attacked at Arras and the French at Laon, without much success. From July to November the British fought the Third Battle of Ypres, eventually taking Passchendaele Ridge. On Oct. 24, the Germans and Austrians launched a heavy attack on the Italian front, and hurled back the Italians with great losses.

1918. On March 21 the Germans began a great offensive on the Western Front. To cope with this menace, the Allies created a Supreme War Council and made General Foch commander-in-chief. The German drive was halted at Château-Thierry on July 18. Now the Allies began a counter-attack in which the United States Army played a major rôle and which resulted in bringing the war to an end with an armistice, which was signed Nov. 11.

Colonial and Naval Operations. Kiaochow in China was captured by the Japanese in 1914. In the same year, British, Japanese, Australian, and New Zealand ships captured all the German islands in the Pacific. Togoland in Africa was captured by the British and French in 1914 and the Cameroons in 1916. German Southwest Africa was captured in 1915 by the Union of South Africa. German East Africa was attacked by troops from South Africa, Belgian Congo, British East Africa, Rhodesia, India, and Portuguese East Africa. But it held out until Nov. 14, 1918.

Naval operations consisted mainly of blockading action by the British and attempts of the Germans to break the blockade by use of the submarine. There was only one large surface engagement —the Battle of Jutland (May 31-June 1, 1916). In it the British suffered heavier losses, but compelled the Germans to retire to their home ports for the duration of the war. (See also Peace Moves during World War I.)

World War II. 1939-1945. World War II was caused by the aggression of Japan, Italy, and Germany during the 1930's. This aggression was possible because of the failure of the League of Nations and because of the unwillingness of England, France, or the United States to resort to force to check it. When Germany and the USSR signed a non-aggression pact (Aug. 1939) (q.v.), the outbreak of war was inevitable.

The war began Sept. 1, 1939, with the invasion of Poland by Germany. The Germans had demanded from Poland the city of Danzig and a strip of land through Polish territory which would unite East and West Prussia. When Poland refused this demand with the support of England and France, Germany began the invasion. The active fighting ended within two weeks, as the Russians moved in from the east, thus crushing Poland in a pincers movement (see Poland, Fifth Partition of).

Now came a six-months period of inactivity known as the "phony-war" or "Sitzkrieg" (q.v.). During this period, Russia occupied the Baltic Republics of Estonia, Latvia, and Lithuania and engaged in a war with Finland (q.v.) to improve its boundaries. Active war resumed in April, 1940, when Germany invaded and crushed in rapid succession Denmark, Norway, Holland, Belgium, Luxemburg, and France. An English expeditionary force which had been serving in France was evacuated from Dunkirk in one of the most memorable operations of the war. France was partly occupied by the Germans. The remainder of the country was ruled from Vichy (q.v.).

On August 8, 1940, began the "Battle

of Britain." During the fall and winter of 1940 and the spring of 1941 the Luftwaffe (Nazi airforce) tried to bring about the surrender of Britain through repeated aerial bombings. Coordinated with the air attack was a vicious submarine attack on ships which carried goods to the British Isles. The air attack became more intense in the spring as the days became longer and the skies clearer. On May 10, 1941, there was one final huge assault upon London during which the Houses of Parliament and the British Museum were damaged. After this great assault, the air attacks, which had resulted in enormous losses of German airplanes, tapered off as the Germans prepared for their attack upon Russia.

Italy declared war against France and Great Britain on June 10, 1940. Italy launched two offensives: one against Greece and one against Egypt. Since neither attack succeeded, Germany was forced to come to Italy's assistance in both areas. Thus, Germany overran Yugoslavia and Greece in 1941 and launched General Rommel (q.v.) and his Afrika Korps on their spectacular career in North Africa.

On June 22, 1941, the Germans invaded Russia. Although the blitzkrieg rolled into Russia in high gear and large areas of the country fell into Nazi hands, the campaign did not come to an end during this year as the Germans had hoped.

On Dec. 7, 1941, the Japanese attacked the United States at Pearl Harbor. Thus the United States entered the war against the Axis.

By mid-1942, the fortunes of the Axis reached their peak. The Germans had overrun most of southern Russia in Europe and invaded the oil fields of the Caucasus. In North Africa the Germans were in Egypt only 70 miles from the Suez Canal. Japan had captured all of Southeast Asia, the Philippine Islands, and the Dutch East Indies and were poised for the invasion of India and Australia. Then the tide of battle swung against the Axis. The British under General Montgomery turned back the Germans in Africa at El Alamein (Oct. 23, 1942). On Nov. 7, 1942, an Anglo-American expedition landed in North Africa. Thus the Germans were caught in a giant pincers and crushed in Tunis (May 8-12, 1943). In July, 1943, the Allies landed in Sicily and Italy. Mussolini's government fell and the new Italian government joined the Allies as a "co-belligerent."

Meanwhile at Stalingrad (Aug. 22, 1942-Feb. 2, 1943) the attacking German army was encircled and forced to surrender. From that point on, the Nazis fought a defensive action on the Eastern Front.

On June 6, 1944 (D-Day), the Allied troops under General Eisenhower established a bridgehead in Normandy. From there they fought on until the Germans surrendered, May 7, 1945. As Eisenhower's troops attacked and invaded Germany from the west, the Russians invaded from the east. Thus Germany was crushed between the forces of the United Nations.

Starting with a landing on Guadalcanal in Aug. 1942, the Americans began the long "road-back" in the Pacific. War in the Pacific was largely a naval action with "island-hopping" from one strategic group of islands to another as the major feature of the plan of attack. In the final action of the war, the vital islands of Iwo Jima and Okinawa, both close to Japan, were captured. Atomic bombings on Hiroshima (Aug. 6, 1945) and Nagasaki brought the war to an end. Japan surrendered in Tokyo Bay, Sept. 2, 1945.

Worms, Diet of. In Oct. 1520, Charles V was crowned Holy Roman Emperor in Aachen. In Jan. 1521, he held his first Diet at Worms. Martin Luther was ordered to appear before this gathering.

He did so (April 17 and 18). He refused to retract his doctrines or any of his writings, unless they were contrary to the Bible. Although some now urged Charles to violate Luther's promised safe-conduct and to seize him as a heretic, Charles refused and permitted Luther to depart. On May 26, the Diet issued the Edict of Worms, which outlawed Luther. He was declared a heretic, as were those who sheltered him or printed or published his books. Luther would have been in mortal danger had not his friends spirited him away to the Castle of Wartburg, where he lived during 1520 and 21.

Worms, Edict of. See Worms, Diet of.

Wren, Christopher. 1632-1723. English architect. The great fire of London (1666) (q.v.) gave him the chance of rebuilding 50 or more churches. He rebuilt St. Paul's Cathedral and built the Royal Hospital at Greenwich.

Wycliffe, John (*also spelled* Wyclif, Wiclif, Wickliffe, etc.). 1320-84. An English clergyman who attacked the manifest abuses of the church. The election of an anti-pope (1378) shook the foundations of Christendom and enabled Wycliffe to secure a wide hearing. He denied the priestly power of absolution, and the whole system of enforced confession, penances, and indulgences. He also attacked transubstantiation. He organized a company of "poor priests," the Lollards. He began the translation of the Bible into English. He was protected by John of Gaunt (q.v.) and king Richard II (q.v.). Thus, he died a natural death. Thirty years after his death, some of his writings were declared heretical by the Council of Constance (q.v.). His bones were then exhumed, burned, and cast into the Swift River. John Hus (q.v.) was one of his disciples.

X

Ximenes de Cisneros, Cardinal Francisco. 1437-1517. Spanish statesman and prelate. Confessor to Isabella. Primate of Spain (1495). Cardinal (1507) and Inquisitor-General for Castile and Leon. Regent of Castile for Charles I (1516). He hated heresy and as Inquisitor-General caused the death of 2500 persons who were convicted heretics. He broke down the power of the nobles, much as Richelieu (q.v.) did in France. He was a patron of the arts, founded the University of Alcalá de Henares, and published the Polyglot Bible.

Y

Yalta Conference. Feb. 7-12, 1945. World War II Conference attended by F. D. Roosevelt, Churchill, and Stalin. *Concerning Germany*: Plans were made for the ultimate defeat of Germany. Zones of occupation were created. Plans were made to demilitarize the German military machine and German industries. A reparations commission was appointed to determine how much Germany was to pay and how the payments were to be made. *Concerning Japan*: Within three months after the surrender of Germany, Russia promised to enter the war against Japan on condition that: the *status quo* of Outer Mongolia was preserved; the southern half of Sakhalin Island and the Kurile Islands were restored to Russia; Dairen was internationalized; and the Chinese Eastern Railway and the South Manchurian Railway were operated by a joint Soviet-Chinese company. China was to have full sovereign rights to Manchuria.

Concerning Poland: It was decided to accept the Curzon Line (q.v.) as the Polish-Russian boundary. Poland was to be compensated at Germany's expense for war losses. The Lublin Committee (q.v.) was to be strengthened.

Concerning a world security league: A call was issued for the San Francisco Conference (April 25, 1945) (q.v.).

Yeats, William Butler. 1865-1939. Irish poet and playwright. After studying art for three years he settled in London (1888), and taking to literature, published a succession of volumes of poems, plays, and collections of Irish tales. He became a leader in the Neo-Celtic movement. His later work was influenced by French symbolism and Eastern mysticism. He was an Irish senator (1922-28). He won the Nobel prize for literature (1923). Among his numerous works are *Deirdre, Four Plays for Dancers, The Tower,* and *Last Poems.*

York, House of. An English family of kings.

	Born	Ruled
Edward IV	1442	1461-1483
(except for a few months in 1470-71).		
Edward V	1470	1483-1483
(he was one of the young princes who perished in the Tower of London).		
Richard III	1452	1483-1485

Young, Arthur. 1740-1820. English writer on agriculture. Although most of his own agricultural experiments were failures, his writings pioneered a movement to make agriculture a science. Among his works are *A Tour through the*

Southern Counties and *Travels in France during 1787-88-89-90.* The latter is a remarkable description of pre-Revolutionary France.

Young Italy. See Mazzini.

Young Plan. 1929. A plan for the payment of German reparations prepared by a committee headed by Owen D. Young. This committee held its first session in Paris on Feb. 11, 1929. The Young Plan contemplated the payment of $8,032,-500,000 to be made over a period of 58½ years; the average annuities for the first 37 years were to average $511,000,-000. The remaining 22 annuities were to average $390,000,000. To handle the details of the payments a Bank of International Settlement (q.v.) was set up in Basel.

Young Turks. 1908. A nationalist movement in Turkey designed to correct the abuses of the government of Abdul Hamid II. On July 23, 1908, the Young Turks staged a successful coup and compelled Abdul to reinstate the constitution of 1876. They later (1909) forced him to abdicate. Once in power, the Young Turks were more interested in nationalism than in constitutional reform. They attempted to "Ottomanize" all the nationalities in the Turkish Empire.

Z

Zemsky Sobor. A Russian popular assembly which was called together from time to time in the 17th century by the Czars. It exercised considerable influence until it was abolished in 1682. It deliberated on questions of war and peace, taxation and legislation. It contained two houses and was composed of representatives of all walks of life, who were chosen by the house-owning heads of families. The powers of this body were determined by custom, not by law.

Zemstvo. A unit of local self-government in Russia created by the law of 1864. By this law the Zemstvos were given the supervision of public education, public health, charity, care of roads, fire insurance, and all other questions relating to local life and economy. The Zemstvos first directed their attention to the development of public education and to matters of sanitation. By 1914 there were 50,000 Zemstvo schools with 80,000 teachers and 3 million school children. Besides their activity in public education and hygiene, the Zemstvos undertook to assist the public in agriculture and the development of roads and telephones.

Zimmerman Note. Jan. 19, 1917. German Foreign Secretary, Alfred Zimmerman, addressed a note to the German minister in Mexico, explaining that unrestricted submarine warfare was about to be resumed, but that efforts would be made to keep the United States neutral. Should these efforts fail, Germany was ready to propose an alliance with Mexico for a joint war against the United States. As a reward, Mexico was to regain some of the territory which it had lost to the United States. Japan was to be invited to join the alliance. The British intercepted this note and turned it over to the United States for publication. When it was made public, it strengthened the war fever in the United States, particularly in the Southwest.

Zinoviev Letter. Oct. 24, 1924. This letter was purported to have been written by Zinoviev, a Bolshevik leader, to British communists, urging the latter to prepare for revolution. It was published in England during a national election, and was directly responsible for the defeat of the first Labor Ministry. Later it appeared that the letter was a forgery.

Zola, Émile. 1840-1902. French novelist. Born in Paris. Achieved reputation as one of the leaders of naturalism in French literature. Figured in the Dreyfus Case (q.v.). Wrote the celebrated open letter *J'Accuse*. Awarded burial in the Pantheon. Author of *La Confessions de Claude*

(1865), *Nana* (1880), *La Débâcle* (1892), etc.

Zollverein, The. In 1818 Prussia established a uniform tariff for all parts of the kingdom, with 10% on manufactured goods and 20% on colonial produce. On Jan. 1, 1834, upon invitation, Saxony, Bavaria, and 14 other German states joined with Prussia in a Zollverein, or Customs Union, in which the above tariff regulations were adopted by all members. Later, Hanover, Baden, Nassau, Brunswick, Luxemburg, and Frankfurt-on-Main joined the union. Only Austria remained outside. German merchants now could trade as freely within the Zollverein as if Germany were a united nation; at the same time, German manufacturers were protected from British and French competitors. The Zollverein paved the way for ultimate political union. Its immediate effects were the construction of 400 miles of railroad (1835-40) which bound the nation together, and the rapid increase of industrialization.

Zürich, Treaty of. See Austro-Sardinian War.

Zwingli, Hulderich. 1484-1531. Swiss religious reformer. Pastor at Glarus (1506). Chaplain to Swiss troops who served in Italy (1513-15). Pastor at Einsiedeln (1516). Preacher attached to the cathedral of Zürich (1519). By his preaching he inaugurated the Reformation of Zürich (1523). He was killed in a religious war in the battle of Kappel (Oct. 11, 1531).